HOW TO REASON ABOUT THE LAW:

An Interdisciplinary Approach to the Foundations of Public Policy

By

David Crump
Newell H. Blakely Professor of Law
University of Houston Law Center

LexisNexis™

ISBN 0-8205-5369-7

Library of Congress Control Number: 2001098375

Editorial Offices
744 Broad Street, Newark, NJ 07102 (973) 820-2000
201 Mission Street, San Francisco, CA 94105-1831 (415) 908 3200
701 East Water Street, Charlottesville, VA 22902-7587 (804) 972-7600
www.lexis.com
(Pub.3159)

CHAPTER TABLE OF CONTENTS

Page

TABLE OF CONTENTS

Part I
LOGIC AND FALLACY IN THE LAW

Page

Part II
ECONOMICS, FINANCE, AND MARKETS

Page

Part III
ETHICAL AND POLITICAL REASONING

Page

Page

Page

CHAPTER 11. PSYCHOLOGY
**Psychological Disorders, Learning Theory, Intelligence,
and Social Psychology--and How They Affect Lawyers** 349

Page

Page

Page

Page

Preface
How to Reason about the Law

This book is a kind of "thinker's tool kit" for law students. It is a guide to clear legal reasoning.

The sources range from Plato to Pareto, from Kant to Clausewitz, from Rawls to Rousseau, from Freud to Friedman, and from Adam and Eve to Adam Smith. In these pages, you will be amused by the fallacy of Bertrand Russell's chicken, as well as game theorists' analyses of the game of chicken. You will see how air conditioning works, how the obsessive-compulsive personality disorder is diagnosed, and how General Norman Schwartzkopf started the invasion of Iraq in Desert Storm. And most importantly, you will apply every one of these ideas to interdisciplinary issues of law and justice.

If some of these names are unfamiliar to you, don't worry. They are unfamiliar to many well educated people. Clausewitz, for example, is the father of modern warfare, but even the broadest liberal arts curricula tend to neglect him. We'll study how his strategies apply in the law to civil and criminal litigation, which involves some of the same tactics.

Legal Reasoning Tools That Often Are Overlooked. In fact, the purpose of this book is to cover methods of thinking, like Clausewitz's study of military strategy, that are useful in legal reasoning but get left out of a lot of peoples' educations. And besides Clausewitz, you will meet many more interesting characters in these pages. Did you know, for example, that there is a form of deductive logic named Barbara? It got that name from a Latin acronym invented by medieval scholars. In Chapter 1, you will see how the Barbara syllogism works, in the same form in which Aristotle developed it. (And you will consider how you use it each time you write answers to a law school examination!)

You also will encounter the ontological proof of the existence of God, the Keynsian multiplier, the Coase Theorem, the trolley problem, and Arrow's Theorem of Public Choice, and you will apply each one of these ideas to issues of law and justice. You will see how physicists compute gravitational forces, as well as how psychologists think falsehoods can best be detected. You will be introduced to the concept of entropy, correlation coefficients, logical positivism, Festinger's theory of cognitive dissonance, Nash equilibria, and Shapley values.

What are these things? Well, Shapley values are a method used by game theorists to explain how coalitions form in multi-party competitions. In the law, Shapley values can help to model the behavior of corporate shareholders. All of these concepts are thinking tools. They can help you to analyze the arguments that other people make, as well as to develop your own. They can guide your thinking about issues of public policy, and they can sharpen your personal decisions. And every one of them will help you to become a more competent student of the law.

How Were the Contents of the Book Decided Upon? That's easy to answer. I used two questions to guide me in deciding what to include. First, is it an important aid to clear thinking about the law? And second, is it left out of the educations of many people who justly can claim to be well educated?

I included a big dose of economics, for example. The subject is vital for understanding public policy, and it also is important in personal decisions. There is a vast and influential literature about law and economics. Of course, many people already have studied economics, some of them intensively. But on the other hand, many educated people have not. If you fall into the latter group, the economics coverage is included for you. If you've already mastered the subject, then you'll have an easy time with that part.

I've also included some selected scientific principles, ranging from the inverse square relationship to the second law of thermodynamics. Again, some readers already understand these subjects. But lawyers frequently must contend with scientific issues, in lawsuits, in regulatory or legislative matters, and in real estate contracts, and it will be a serious disadvantage for your clients if your eyes glaze over anytime these issues arise.

There's also coverage of ethical philosophy, at a level that a few students already have mastered. The same is true of psychology, political theory, probabilities, statistics, regression analysis, accounting, finance and management. In each instance, if you already know the subject well, then you will find the material familiar.

But few people, even if well educated, have mastered all the subjects in this book. Even fewer have applied them all to the law, in an interdisciplinary way. And that is what the book is for.

Why Was the Book Written? That's easy to answer, too. I decided to write the book when I learned that many students at the law school where I teach had never been exposed to basic concepts in logic. It just hadn't been included in their educations.

For example, I discovered that a large percentage of my students did not know what a "syllogism" was.[1] And yet my students score in the highest percentages in the nation on standardized tests, and their educations are among the finest anywhere. So if you don't know what a syllogism is either, don't feel bad. It seems to be one of those things that a liberal education, today, lets slip through the cracks.

And it matters to you, in law school. Syllogistic logic is the backbone of formal legal reasoning. You use it regularly, whether you know it by that name or not. You can use it better if you understand it. And that's what this book is for.

You Didn't "Learn It All in Kindergarten," Either. Recently there was a best-seller called "Everything I Really Needed to Know I Learned in Kindergarten." The author was a successful businessman. He gave out advice such as, cookies and milk are good for you, and you should hold hands with others when you go out into the world.

Now, there's nothing wrong with nostalgia and romanticism. Those are good things. But shouldn't they take the place of formal analytical reasoning.

---

1   A "syllogism" is the basic method of deductive logic, covered here in Chapter 1.

Humans have a long tradition of romantic thinking. Just to give one example, there is Rousseau's noble savage: "Nature has made man happy and good-- society corrupts him and causes his misery." As Ernest van den Haag said, "This is as patently wrong as wishful thinking can ever be." The sales of the kindergarten book may be evidence of an excessive desire for simplicity in American thinking.

Meanwhile, America's divorce rate shows that kindergarten does not teach people how to avoid bad choices in impulsively getting married. The popularity of consumer bankruptcy shows how poorly kindergartners learn to handle money even after they become adults. Advice about cookies and milk hasn't improved the American diet. It hasn't prevented our collective ignorance of scientific thinking, and the American people's understanding of statistics makes us fall for the same kinds of fallacies over and over again. And the real point is, it's important for courts, regulators, and policymakers to avoid those kinds of fallacies.

People need romanticism and faith. They even need a dose of children's wisdom, like the kindergarten book. But they also need to be able to think. Lawyers, especially, need to reason dispassionately about complex subjects. And that's what this book is about.

How Is the Book Put Together? Each chapter relates the law to a single discipline. Some disciplines, such as logic and economics, are split into two chapters each. I've tried to keep every concept reasonable in size. In each instance, the book explores only selected topics, and then it applies them to the law. This isn't a treatise. The idea isn't to make you into a logician, social psychologist, political scientist or game theoretician, but rather to use ideas from these fields to sharpen your reasoning about the law.

After most of the explanations, I have included sections called "Examples and Problems." These sections put the ideas to work by applying them to the law. The Examples and Problems should be useful for students and teachers who use the book in structured courses. And for readers, they are designed to illustrate and reinforce the explanations of ideas.

Using Other Disciplines to Reason about the Law. The goal, throughout, is to understand the law better. And so as soon as a given concept has been developed, the book will give you illustrations from lawsuits, regulatory questions, constitutional issues, and many other subjects in the law.

In other words, the most important Examples and Problems involve court decisions, lawyering, public policy, or legislation. They ask you to analyze a bill considered in a legislature or to simulate the conditions faced by an attorney defending a lawsuit. But all of the Examples and Problems are written so that they will be understandable to the general reader. In many instances, this means starting outside the complexities of the law so that we can use the clearest possible illustrations. And so the problems actually range widely in subject, from baseball to business to salesmanship. In each instance, however, we shall tie the principles you have learned to the law or to public policy.

Does the Book Cover Technical Subjects and (Shudder) Does It Require Mathematics? To a degree, yes. You will learn five basic operators in symbolic logic. You will see how to compute p-values in statistics and how to use a payoff matrix in game theory. The point of reading the book, after all, is to learn something new.

But all the mathematics is at the seventh- or eighth-grade level. The only operations you need to know are addition, subtraction, multiplication, division, exponents, and conversion of fractions to decimals or percentages. Although mathematics is essential to a few of these reasoning tools, it is a very small part of the book. And it has been kept at a level that will be accessible to every reader who can follow the rest of the book.

The point is for you to understand how the underlying concepts, such as correlation coefficients and regression lines, apply to the law--not to do sophisticated calculations with them. In each instance, the book approaches technical subjects with the assumption that you have no prior understanding of them.

The Book Should Be Interesting, and It Should Be Fun. In these pages, you will analyze the logic of humor--the reasoning behind a joke. You will apply game theory to the Battle of the Bismarck Sea. You will find out about the psychology of persuasion, and you will apply symbolic logic to the definition of a strike from the official baseball rules. In other words, this book should be interesting. And fun, too.

But every time, this interdisciplinary approach will be tied to legal questions. The purpose is to make you a more complete lawyer.

I hope that you will grow from reading the book, as I did from writing it, and I hope you will enjoy it as much as I have.

--David Crump
Houston, Texas
Fall 2001

ACKNOWLEDGEMENTS

The following experts read and critiqued the indicated chapters, although it must be emphasized that deficiencies inevitably remain in a work of this kind and are solely the responsibility of the author:

Economics	Professor Ben Friedman, Economics, Harvard
Management	Caryn Crump, Vice President, Pennzoil Corporation
Ethics	Professor John Mixon, Law, University of Houston
Politics	Professor David DeNoon, Politics and Economics, NYU
Science	Professor Lawrence Pinsky, Physics, University of Houston, Professor Robert Palmer, History, University of Houston, and Professor Carl Hacker, Public Health, University of Texas
Jurisprudence	Professor John Mixon, Law, University of Houston
Psychology	Professor Richard Evans, Psychology, University of Houston and Professor William Winslade, Law, University of Houston
Statistics	Professor Richard Vitale, Statistics, University of Connecticut, and Professor Joseph Sanders, Law, University of Houston
Game Theory	Professor Seth Chandler, Law, University of Houston
Finance	Professor Arthur Warga, Business, University of Houston

In the Logic and Fallacy chapters, there is one short work in particular that has been an excellent resource: Dan Hunter, *No Wilderness of Single Instances: Inductive Inference in the Law*, 48 J. Legal Educ. 365 (1998).

ERRATA OR COMMENTS: AN INVITATION
TO READERS TO COMMUNICATE WITH THE AUTHOR

This book already has benefitted from suggestions submitted by many pre-publication readers. The author will appreciate the input of future readers who see improvements that can be made to the book in its current form. You may either tear out or reproduce this page, describe the issues that you have spotted and your suggestions for change in the lines below, and either mail the result to David Crump, 100 Law Center, University of Houston, Houston, Texas 77204-6060, or fax it to David Crump, (713) 743-2088.

_____

_____

_____

_____

_____

_____

_____

_____

_____

_____

_____

_____

_____

Chapter 1
Logic

Syllogisms, Deduction, Induction, and Logical Propositions in the Law: From the IRAC Method to the Commerce Power

> *"Cogito ergo sum (I reason; therefore I exist.)"--René Descartes, Meditationes de Prima Philosophia*

> *"You can observe a lot by watching."--Yogi Berra*

§ 1.01 What This Chapter Is About

FROM SYLLOGISMS TO SYMBOLIC LOGIC: THE TOOLS OF FORMAL LEGAL REASONING

(1) *Deductive Logic, Syllogistic Reasoning, Analogy, and Induction: The Logic of Inferences.* In this chapter, we consider "deductive" logic, which is the kind that produces conclusive results. The fundamental form of deductive logic is the "syllogism," which uses the format, "all trees are plants; all oaks are trees; therefore, all oaks are plants." This chapter analyzes syllogisms extensively, looking at their validity, their different types, their internal terms, and means of testing them. The chapter also shows how you routinely

use deductive argument in various fields, from public policy to sports rules. And it will help you to develop better legal reasoning, because you use syllogistic reasoning every time you answer a law school examination question. The backbone of the so-called "IRAC" method is a syllogism, as we shall see.

To use a more general example, consider the quotation above of René Descartes's famous "cogito" argument: "I think, therefore I am," or (better translated), "I reason, therefore I exist." This logic sounds good, but is it really? Descartes's argument is not a syllogism, and efforts to reconstruct it in syllogistic form tend, instead, to demonstrate the difficulty of relying on Descartes's proof. We shall consider this issue further in this chapter, and you will see how it helps to spot fallacious reasoning about the law.

The chapter also considers "inductive" logic, or the logic of generalizations, as well as reasoning by analogy. Perhaps Descartes's proof would seem more credible if considered as an induction, or a generalization from experience. It then would be equivalent to saying, "Everything I know of that reasons seems to exist, and therefore I can infer that I exist." But the question remains, is this inference reliable? And then, there is Yogi Berra's epigram that "you can observe a lot by watching." Is Yogi's logic deductive, inductive, or merely funny nonsense? This chapter explores these questions, and it also shows how logical reasoning forms (deduction, induction and analogy) can be used in fields ranging from mathematics to baseball and, of course, in the law.

(2) *Legal Reasoning and Law School Examination Strategy: Heavy Use of Syllogisms and Deduction; Also, Analogy and Generalization.* Why do some students do well on law school examinations while others, who seem equally bright and who studied as hard, don't do as well? There can be many reasons, but surely one reason is the structure of the students' logic. As we shall see in this chapter, deductive (syllogistic) logic is the backbone of sound answers to typical law school exam questions. And so, if you learn how to use a syllogism, you may see your grades improve. Analogy and generalization also must be a part of your legal reasoning. This chapter contains a section that shows you how.

(3) *Symbolic Logic and the Logic of Propositions.* The chapter also takes up what is called the "logic of propositions." Every inference depends upon chains of logical statements, and the logic of propositions is concerned with

the contents of these statements and with combining them, shortening them, and verifying them. Our coverage, here, also includes simple treatment of symbolic logic. You will see how this device helps to analyze legal rules.

(4) *Fallacy and the Limits of Logic.* This chapter also briefly previews how misuse of syllogistic structure or inductive reasoning can lead to fallacy. In-depth treatment of these subjects, however, is left to the next chapter, Chapter 2, in which we shall take up a large number of false argument styles and consider how to guard against them.

§ 1.02 The Logic of Inferences

[A]   Induction and Deduction: Syllogism, Analogy, and Generalization

THE FORMAT FOR DEDUCTIVE LOGIC: THE SYLLOGISM

(1) *Syllogism.* A syllogism is a logical statement that contains a first premise, a second premise, and a conclusion (in that order). "All emeralds are green; this object is an emerald; therefore, this object is green." See Figure 1 for another example. This is a type of "deductive" logic, meaning that its result is conclusively valid if the premises are true and syllogistic in form. Notice that the first premise in this type of syllogism must be absolute rather than probabilistic (for example, the logic would not be valid if the premise were "*some* emeralds are green," as opposed to "all"), and the premises must be true (the argument would be fallacious if it were inaccurate to state that all emeralds are green).

Figure 1	
The Syllogism: Deductive Logic	
"All trees are plants."	First premise
"All oaks are trees."	Second premise
"Therefore, all oaks are plants."	Conclusion

(2) *The Simplicity and Universality of the Syllogistic Concept.* The basic concept of the syllogism is so simple that people often assume it can't be that simple. But it is. "All owls are birds; all birds are animals; therefore, all owls are animals." Not that everything is that simple: It is possible to have

a long, complex major premise with multiple factors, connected by "ands" and "ors." In that case, each of the controlling factors also must be present in the minor premise, producing another long, complicated sentence. But the syllogistic method remains the same.

Furthermore, although Aristotle wrote the first noteworthy Western analysis, the syllogism is universal. Early logicians in India and China also developed the same basic structures. We use syllogistic logic every day in our thinking, although we usually omit the formal structure.

(3) *Syllogisms Are the Backbone of Formal Legal Reasoning.* "The governing statute says (1) that if A, B, and C are present, then certain defined consequences follow: the facts in this case are (2) that A, B, and C are present: therefore, (3) the consequences specified by the statute follow." This kind of syllogism is the essence of formal legal reasoning. Things are never quite so simple in real life, of course; the statute and the facts may be ambiguous. But formal legal reasoning usually begins with a syllogistic structure like this one (or more likely, a chain of syllogisms).

(4) *Other Syllogisms, Using "Some" or "No."* There are other syllogistic formats in addition to the one demonstrated above. For example, there is the no-all-no structure ("No sharks can fly; all hammerheads are sharks; therefore, no hammerheads can fly") and there is the some-all-some structure, also called the Aristotelian Syllogism ("Some trees are oaks; all trees are plants; therefore, some plants are oaks"). Later in this chapter, we shall look more systematically at the different varieties of syllogisms. For now, what is important is that you understand the first-premise-second-premise-conclusion format of the syllogism.

(5)   *Examples of the Widespread Use of Syllogistic Reasoning: Mathematics, Accounting and Law.* You have been using syllogisms since you first learned to think, whether you knew it or not. For example, when you apply a mathematical formula, you use syllogistic reasoning. "All circles have circumferences equal to $2\pi r$; this circle has a radius, r, of 3 feet; therefore, this circle has a circumference of $2\cdot\pi\cdot3$ feet, or 6π feet." This reasoning is syllogistic even though we usually omit the formal elements, and even though we may not think about its logical structure when we use it.

We use the same method whenever we apply established legal principles to new facts: when a securities lawyer fits a generally accepted accounting principle to an SEC filing, a syllogism is involved. "In all instances of inventory valuation, the general rule is to use market value if it is less than cost; market value in this case is less than cost; therefore, application of the general rule in this case requires inventory to be valued at market." (We shall see later what this inventory valuation principle means, in the chapter on Financial Reasoning.) And when a prosecutor or defense lawyer fits a criminal statute to a fact situation, the fitting is done by a syllogism. "All cases in which a person enters a building not then open to the public with intent to commit theft are burglaries; Sylvester entered a building not then open to the public with intent to commit theft; therefore, Sylvester committed a burglary."

In fact, whenever you apply a definition, rule or equation, you use it as the first premise in a syllogism. Can you see, now, why we have said that the IRAC method is fundamentally syllogistic?

(6) *Fallacy Arising from Defective Premises or Inaccurate Syllogism Form*. The syllogism is a powerful device because, unlike inductive logic, it always produces a correct conclusion if properly used. But syllogistic logic lends itself to possibilities of fallacy. For example, it is possible to introduce fallacy by manipulation of the syllogistic form: "All fish can swim; John can swim; therefore, John is a fish."

This last example has superficial resemblances to deductive logic, but it mixes unpersuasive analogy with a nonsyllogism. It is surprising how often arguments embodying this kind of fallacy can persuade people, and that is why it is important to understand the formal elements of syllogistic logic. The next chapter will look at fallacies resulting from manipulation of the form. Lawyers, obviously, are good at this; the legal system functions as well as it does only because judges and opposing lawyers are good at recognizing it.

ANALOGY: A TYPE OF INDUCTIVE REASONING

(1) *Inductive Reasoning as Contrasted with Deductive Logic*. As we have seen, "deductive" logic is a process in which the conclusion follows necessarily from the premises presented. A properly constructed syllogism, based on premises that are true, leads to an accurate conclusion. (We can imagine a dreamland or parallel universe in which syllogisms do not hold, but short of that assumption, the result of a syllogism is due absolute confidence.)

"Induction," on the other hand, refers to any form of reasoning in which the conclusion does not follow as a matter of necessity. Induction is reasoning about what is likely, not about what is absolute. For example, reasoning by analogy is a form of induction.

(2) *Analogy.* Analogy is a form of inductive reasoning in which one thing is inferred to be similar to another thing in a certain respect, on the basis of known similarities in other respects. If the controlling or most important aspect of the thing is the same, the inference is that the characterization is the same. Figure 2 contains an example of reasoning by analogy.

But whereas the syllogistic form produces uniformly valid deductive logic, analogy does not. It is "fuzzier." For example, an analogy is useful only if we pick out the correct aspects of the known subject on which to build the analogy. Thus, the argument that John is a fish, because he is like a fish in that he can swim, is a species of analogy, but not a persuasive one. On the other hand, analogy can be a powerful device: "A whale is more like a mammal than it is like a fish, because it is warm-blooded, breathes air and births its young live."

Figure 2
Analogy: A Type of Inductive Logic

A whale is like mammals because it is   Comparison
    warm-blooded, breathes air, and
    births its young live.

Therefore, a whale probably shares other   Conclusion
    characteristics with mammals.

---

(3) *Analogy in the Law.* "This case is controlled by the principle announced in the previous case of *Jones v. Smith*," one lawyer might argue. "No, it isn't," replies his opponent. "It's distinguishable." This kind of reasoning is pervasive in the law. It involves the use of analogy. The lawyers' disagreement results from their choices about which similarities and differences to emphasize.

(4) *The Shortcomings of Analogy.* The usefulness of reasoning by analogy is offset by the need to avoid confusing it with the universal validity of syllogistic logic. An analogy is easily manipulated by the selection of

characteristics on which to base the comparison. "John is a fish because he can swim" is an example. But we can't do everything with syllogisms, and in the law, analogy is a frequent and powerful alternative.

GENERALIZATION: ANOTHER TYPE OF INDUCTIVE REASONING

(1) *Inductive Generalizations.* The term "induction" also applies to the use of samples as evidence for a proposition about the whole class of things from which the sample is taken. "Every year that we know of, the average temperature here has been colder during December than in July. Therefore, inductive logic tells us that during this coming year, December again will be colder than July." Figure 3 contains another example.

(2) *Life Experiences, Rules of Thumb, and Lawyering Competencies: Inductive Reasoning.* Imagine that you are waiting to meet a friend at a cafe. As the appointed time approaches, you tell yourself, "I shouldn't have come early, because Bill is bound to be late." How do you know this? The same way you know most of what you know about your friends: by induction. From many past experiences with Bill, you have generalized that he "always" is late.

This method also forms the basis of some lawyering competencies and attributes of professionalism. "I always maintain a double-entry calendaring system for deadlines." Or, to a new law clerk: "What we usually do in this kind of case is to send a set of interrogatories to sort out the important documents and witnesses." These choices are informed by experience, which is to say they are inductive. Sometimes, too, an appellate court uses induction to announce a new legal rule based upon a string of similar cases that reach a common result through dissimilar reasoning. "In every appellate case in which the defendant's vehicle has collided with the plaintiff's from the rear, we easily have found sufficient evidence to sustain a finding of negligence; therefore, today we announce a rule that a collision from the rear gives rise to a presumption of negligence." In fact, the law of products liability coalesced in exactly this way. There was a mixture of cases recognizing claims about defective products, based on warranty, negligence, and other theories, and the inference of a strict liability principle resulted from a reformulation that generalized the results.

(3) *Is Analogy the Same as Induction?* Some people refer to analogy as a special case of induction, considering analogy and generalization to be fundamentally the same. At some level, this probably is correct, because both methods operate by non-deductive comparisons. But other people distinguish the two, and this also is correct, at least in the sense that analogy and generalization probably describe different mental processes. For example, our inductive generalization, that December will be colder than July, is probably not based on any conscious process of analogy, but instead it is based on the direct application of experience.

Figure 3
Generalization: A Type of Inductive Logic

The sun arose in the east on day one, and   Repeated Observations
  on day two, . . . and on day 1,000.

Therefore, the sun likely will arise in the   Conclusion
  east tomorrow, too.

---

(4) *Scientific Method as Inductive; Validity.* Sometimes inductive reasoning merits a high level of confidence. Our knowledge of the law of gravity, for example, is based on induction, but we are sure enough of it to know, with a strong level of certainty, what will happen if someone jumps off the Empire State Building. The scientific method is dependent on induction. In fact, some definitions of science rely on verification by experiment, which is to say, on proof by induction.

(5) *But Inductive Reasoning Can Mislead You: The Fallacy of Bertrand Russell's Chicken.* Induction is only generalization from experience, and it is vulnerable to fallacy. Your friend Bill, whom you expect to be late, arrives right on time, and he explains, "I've changed. My New Year's resolution is to be punctual." Improper sampling techniques, mischaracterization of evidentiary facts, and other errors can result in fallacious conclusions from induction.

Bertrand Russell

One famous illustration, attributed to Bertrand Russell, tells the sad story of a chicken who has been fed by a farmer every day of his life, and who confidently runs to greet the farmer with the expectation of food; but one day, instead, the farmer wrings the chicken's neck (which, after all, is the purpose of chickens). Russell's blunt conclusion: "It would have been better for the chicken if its inductive inferences had been less crude." Indeed, if the chicken had adopted a different sampling technique, it would have learned that a large percentage of its fellows had been killed by the farmers who fed them, giving rise to the inductive insight that confidence in one's human guardian is unjustified if you are a chicken. More broadly, Russell's example shows why it is hazardous to repose excessive confidence in any method of inductive logic.

EXAMPLES AND PROBLEMS

(1) *Which Are Syllogisms, Among the Following Examples?* To test your recognition of deductive logic, consider which of the following examples are in the form of proper syllogisms.

    (a) All ABX's are farfles; all farfles are Z3's; therefore, all ABX's are Z3's.

    (b) No Wookies have feathers; Chewbacca is a Wookie; therefore, Chewbacca does not have feathers.

    (c) Every third Thursday of every month, the firm's board of directors is scheduled to meet; today is the third Thursday of this month; therefore, the board is scheduled to meet today.

    (d) Every past Thursday, the stock market has closed with a gain; today is a Thursday; therefore, today the stock market will close with a gain.

    (e) I reason; therefore, I exist.

The answer is that (a), (b) and (c) are syllogisms. Notice that you don't need to know what an ABX or a farfle or a Wookie is, to be able to have absolute confidence in the conclusion. That's the beauty of syllogisms. (You do, however, need to be certain that the premises are true, either from your own reasoning or from an infallible source.)

On the other hand, (d) and (e) are not syllogisms. There is a superficial resemblance between the true syllogism in (c), about the third-Thursday board-of-directors meetings, and the non-syllogism in (d), about past-Thursday stock market gains. But the resemblance is misleading. The major premise in (c) is universal ("every" third Thursday), while in (d) it is not (every "past" Thursday).   The statement in (d) is only an induction, a generalization.   Fallacious reliance on such reasoning has seduced many stock market investors.

(2) *Legal Conclusions: Which Are Syllogisms?* Now, let's look at some examples of legal reasoning.   Which one(s) are syllogistic in form?

    (a) When Andrea Yates drowned all of her six children, she was insane, because she acted in a psychotic state. (NO. Why?) [This example is taken from a heartbreaking case that made worldwide news.]

    (b) The law of this jurisdiction is that a defendant is insane if she does not know the wrongfulness of her conduct; when Andrea Yates acted, she did not know the wrongfulness of her conduct; therefore, she was insane." (YES. Why?)

    (c) The law of this jurisdiction is that a defendant is insane if she does not know the wrongfulness of her conduct; when Andrea Yates acted, she *did* know the wrongfulness of her conduct; therefore, she was *not* insane." (NO. Why?) [Note: the premises do not fit together in the required way.   There might be another way to be insane.   We'll consider this aspect of syllogisms again in more detail, below.]

(3) *Descartes's "Cogito" Argument: A Syllogism Without the Right Structure?* "Cogito, ergo sum," said René Descartes.   "I reason, therefore I exist."   This profound proof of the reality of experience is one of the most famous statements in all of philosophy.   But is this "cogito" argument, as it is called, really persuasive? Notice that, although it purports to be deductive, it is not structured as a syllogism should be.   It lacks a first premise.

This kind of reasoning is pervasive in the law, but it easily leads to fallacy; and during a law school examination, it is a poor strategy.   "There is jurisdiction in this case, because there are sufficient minimum contacts," a test-taker might write.   The professor who reads this answer is likely to downgrade it.   The professor is thinking, "Where's the rule or principle of law?   Where are the facts?"   The thought, just as well, might be: "Where is the first premise?   Where is the second premise?"   The student thus receives a disappointing grade, and may never know why.

Let's return to Descartes.   Perhaps the first premise in the cogito argument is implicit.   It is there, but unspoken.   The trouble is, however, that almost any major premise that we might try to articulate will be debatable. Consider the following attempt: "Everything that reasons exists; I reason; therefore, I exist." The deduction now is properly structured as a syllogism, with the first premise being, "Everything that reasons exists."

But this premise is vulnerable. How can we really be sure that "everything that reasons exists?" For example, in Charles Dickens's story, "A Christmas Carol," Ebeneezer Scrooge experiences transforming encounters with three spirits, and his reasoning changes his life. Since Ebeneezer Scrooge thus "reasons," does it follow that he exists? Obviously not; Scrooge is a fictional character. Perhaps the example can be attacked as not pertinent, precisely because Scrooge is fictional, but the question remains: how can we really know that everything that reasons exists? Consider whether this critique of Descartes' cogito argument is valid.

Notice that a one-premise imitation of a syllogism can be seductively false. In ordinary life, we often use one-premise reasoning: "This politician is dishonest, and therefore I'm not going to vote for him." "This jacket is too expensive, so I'm not going to buy it." This is fine, so long as the omitted premise is obvious and noncontroversial. But whenever the issue is doubtful and important, it's worth analyzing the omitted premise. You may find that the tacit assumption of its truth is unwarranted and fallacious, although seductive.

(4) *How to Do Poorly on a Law School Examination: Adopt the Format of the Cogito Argument.* "There are minimum contacts," a law student might write on an examination. "And therefore, the court has jurisdiction." The professor probably will give this answer part credit, but it definitely is not an A answer in law school, and perhaps it is not even a B. Your professors want the answer structured in a syllogism. Perhaps somebody as famous and brilliant as René Descarte can do this sort of thing, but you shouldn't. The same criticism applies to an answer that begins, "The court has jurisdiction because . . . ." See whether you can adapt our critique of DeCartes's cogito argument to explain (a) why this "because" reasoning is not a syllogism and (b) why it matters that it is not.

(5) *Supporting Descartes' Cogito Argument With Induction.* Perhaps induction supplies proof of the major premise in Descartes' cogito argument. All of our experience points to the conclusion that every person who reasons exists independently. Does the induction solve the problem?

Not really. Descartes' effort was to discover a proof based on pure reason. He came as close as anyone ever has, but to use induction spoils the proof and makes it uncertain. Second, the use of induction about realms of existence that we do not fully understand is itself uncertain. Can you explain why?

(6) *The Wisdom of Yogi Berra: You Can Observe a Lot by Watching.* Perhaps the famous statement by Yogi Berra that "you can observe a lot by watching" is a syllogism. "'Watching' always means that you 'observe'; you are capable of watching; therefore, you can observe a lot by watching." Is this a reasonable explanation of this Yogi-ism (is it a syllogism)?

On the other hand, perhaps the statement is an induction. Yogi has noticed, from repeated experience, that by watching, he has observed a lot; therefore, he generalizes by saying that you can observe a lot by watching. Is this a better way to treat Yogi's wisdom?

Finally, there is the possibility that Yogi's saying is just a piece of nonsense intended to be funny. But it has to have a logical structure to be funny (as opposed to being gibberish); therefore, even if merely funny, it must be logical. Can you explain?

(7) *The Problem of Induction: The Affirmative Action Example.* A friend of yours has a case before a court that has decided many affirmative action cases. Your friend's side of the case is arguing that the affirmative action plan at issue is valid, and she is gloomy: "I'm going to lose because in every case this court has decided, it has held that the plan was unconstitutional." [Note: If you generally are opposed to affirmative action, just assume the opposing lawyer's position.] Your friend knows that this reasoning is not a syllogism but sees it as a generalization or induction. What advice would you give about this reasoning, and how could careful thinking enhance the likelihood of correct prediction by refining the induction? (In the next chapter, we shall consider this issue in depth; for now, you should recognize that proper sampling has a lot to do with successful induction. Remember Russell's chicken: There's always a first time.)

(8) *Mixing Inductive and Deductive Logic.* History has never disclosed an instance of two different individuals with identical fingerprints. As a matter of inductive logic, we therefore infer that all occurrences of an individual's fingerprint demonstrate the presence of that identified individual.

On the basis of this inductively created first premise, coupled with the second premise that the defendant's fingerprint was found on the murder weapon, we infer syllogistically, as a matter of deductive logic, that the defendant touched the murder weapon.

But this series of logical arguments, as in virtually all such complex chains, is vulnerable. What are the possible sources of error in the inductive inference of the first premise, that all fingerprints show the presence of the person to whom they belong? What possibilities of error inhere in the second premise, that this particular item of evidence is the defendant's fingerprint?

(9) *The Imperfection (Treachery?) of Language.* Sometimes language obscures the syllogistic form of a given proposition. And more insidiously, sometimes language camouflages the lack of validity in a proposition. For example, imagine that one lawyer tells another one, "Slip-and-fall negligence cases are no good unless you can prove the defendant knew about the slippery condition." If this statement expresses a rule or definition, it may qualify as the major premise of a syllogism: "All slip-falls without proof of knowledge fail to qualify for recovery in this state; this case is a slip-fall without proof of knowledge; therefore, it fails to qualify for recovery." If you are the plaintiff and the premises are true, you have no chance.

On the other hand, if the statement is not intended to express universal validity, or if the statement is hyperbole or metaphor (it means, in effect, "every slip-and-fall I've seen without proof of knowledge has ended in a judgment for defendant, and I'm starting to think my client doesn't have a chance"), then the plaintiff need not infer an absolute bar. Explain why this statement would not justify a syllogistic inference, whereas a rule of qualification, such as the statement that all slip-falls without knowledge fail to qualify as a matter of law, would justify a syllogistic inference of disqualification. What does this example show about the difficulty of using ordinary language in logic?

(10) *Chain Syllogisms.* A series of chain calculations by which a physicist fills the blackboard with squiggly symbols is, if one understands it, a chain of syllogisms. Likewise, a common-sense observation or rule of thumb may have several syllogistic sub-propositions. In the law, a chain of syllogisms may involve serial definitions, fact applications, and conclusions about negligence, proximate causation, and the ultimate viability of a claim with these elements combined.

**[B]   Visualizing Deductive Logic: From Venn Diagrams to a
          Syllogism Named "Barbara"**

EULER DIAGRAMS AND VENN DIAGRAMS

(1) *Euler Diagrams and Venn Diagrams: Devices for Visualizing
Deductions and Syllogisms.* In this section, we still are concerned with the
same concepts, particularly deductive logic, which is to say syllogisms.
Sometimes it can be helpful to show these concepts visually. That is the
purpose of the squiggles and circles in this section. Euler diagrams and Venn
diagrams are just methods of visualizing what you already have learned about
syllogisms.

(2) *Euler Diagrams: Visualizing Group Relationships, Including
Syllogisms.* Swiss mathematician Leonhard Euler ("OY-ler") popularized a
system of five diagrams to show the relationships between two groups of
things, the "a" group and the "b" group, as follows (Figure 4).

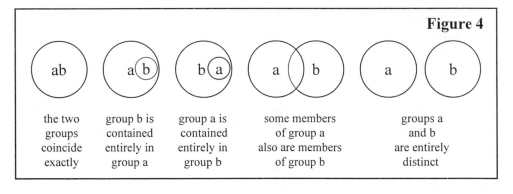

Figure 4

| the two groups coincide exactly | group b is contained entirely in group a | group a is contained entirely in group b | some members of group a also are members of group b | groups a and b are entirely distinct |

We can use these diagrams to demonstrate syllogisms by introducing a
third variable "m." (We call it "m" because it is the "middle" term; it appears
twice in the two premises, and it helps perform the linkage between the other
two terms.) In the next two figures, we diagram "all a are m; all m are b;
therefore, all a are b" (Figure 5), as well as "no a are m; all b are m; therefore,
no a are b" (Figure 6).

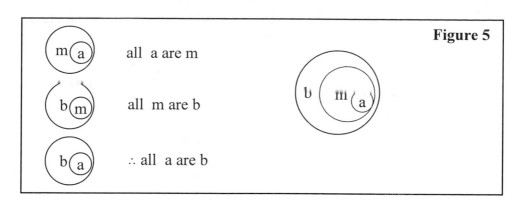

Figure 5

all a are m

all m are b

∴ all a are b

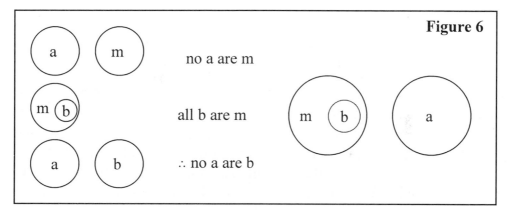

Figure 6

no a are m

all b are m

∴ no a are b

These two syllogisms are valid, and the Euler diagrams in Figures 2 and 3 help to visualize why. The diagrams add nothing new, really; they just provide another way of looking at things.

(3) *Venn Diagrams: Visualizing Syllogisms through Three Interlocking Circles.* British mathematician John Venn devised a diagram for checking syllogism validity that uses three interlocked circles, whose intersections reflect various combinations. Thus, Figure 7.

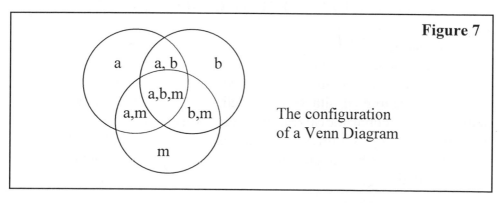

Figure 7

The configuration of a Venn Diagram

If we want to diagram a particular syllogism--all a are m; all m are b; therefore all a are b--we block out those parts of the diagram that cannot exist, as in Figure 8.

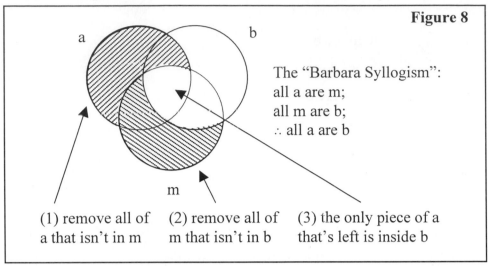

Figure 8

The "Barbara Syllogism":
all a are m;
all m are b;
∴ all a are b

(1) remove all of a that isn't in m

(2) remove all of m that isn't in b

(3) the only piece of a that's left is inside b

First, we remove all of the circle called "a" that isn't in the circle called "m" (because all a are m). Then, we block out all of the circle called "m" that isn't in the circle called "b" (because all m are b). Now, we observe that all of circle a that remains is inside circle b, and thus all a are b.

As Figure 8 shows, this syllogism is true, because drawing the two premises produces a diagram that demonstrates the third statement (conclusion). Similarly, Venn Diagrams can be used to demonstrate other valid kinds of syllogisms as well (the term "some" can be diagramed by lighter shading, by differently sloped cross hatches, or, as logicians often do, by an "x" placed in the appropriate intersections).

THE FOUR PREMISE FORMS
(A,E,I AND O) AND THE BARBARA SYLLOGISM

(1) *Different Kinds of Syllogisms: The A, E, I and O Forms of Premises.* This section continues to examine the syllogism. There are other premise forms besides the all-all-all format that we have seen to this point. In fact, premises can be formed with the words "all are," "none are," "some are," and "some are not." For historical reasons, these forms are assigned the letters A, E, I and O: "all are" is form A, "none are" is E, "some are" is I and "some are not" is O. There is nothing magic about the letters, and they actually come from the Middle Ages.

(2) *Latin Notation Using A, E, I, and O as Symbols.* During the Middle Ages, a series of logicians designated the "all x are y" premise as "A," from the first vowel in the Latin word "*A*ffirmo" (I affirm). They labeled the contradictory premise, "no x are y," as "E," from the first vowel in the Latin "n*E*go" (I negate). The letter "I" (the second vowel in Aff*I*rmo) symbolized "some x are y," while "O" (the second vowel in neg*O*) stood for "some x are not y." To recapitulate: "all are" is form A; "none are," E; "some are," I; and "some are not," O.

Figure 9		
The Four Syllogistic Premise Forms		
Form	**Designation**	**Latin Derivation**
"All ___ are ___"	A	*A*ffirmo (I affirm, absolute)
"No ___ are ___"	E	n*E*go (I deny, absolute)
"Some ___ are ___"	I	aff*I*rmo (I affirm, weak)
"Some ___ are not ___"	O	neg*O* (I deny, weak)

These Latin-speaking logicians then proceeded to catalogue all possible three-letter combinations of A, E, I and O to see which would produce valid syllogisms. They found more than a dozen valid forms, plus others that are not valid. The "AAE" format--"All oceans are wet, the Atlantic is an ocean, therefore the Atlantic is not wet"--is an example of the invalid ones they discovered. It does not follow that the Atlantic is "not" wet, from the fact that it "is" wet.

Thus, AAE--all are, all are, none are--is a possible arrangement of premises, but it does not make a syllogism. You could, if you desired, construct a Venn diagram that would show this.

(3) *The AAA or All-All-All Syllogism (Also Known as the "Barbara" Syllogism).* The first possible syllogism, using this Latin notation, is the AAA form: "All terriers are dogs; all dogs are mammals; therefore, all terriers are mammals." Here's what's fun about this: The logicians of the Middle Ages named this syllogism "Barbara," because the three vowels, AAA, appear in that order in the word "Barbara": B*A*rb*A*r*A*.

And so, we have--a syllogism named Barbara?? Yes, Barbara! Exactly! And Figure 8, above, happens to be a diagram of the Barbara syllogism.

EXAMPLES AND PROBLEMS

(1) *Using the Euler Diagrams: What if All a Are b and All b Are a?* Consider the three Euler diagrams in Figure 10.

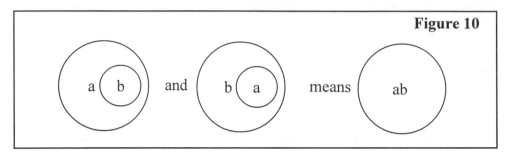

Figure 10

"All b are a," and "all a are b," taken together, mean that "a and b coincide exactly." Can you interpret how the three Euler diagrams, above, show this relationship?

(2) *A Venn Diagram of the "Barbara" Syllogism: Figure 8, Above.* Remember, "Barbara" designates a syllogism of the all-all-all variety. Figure 8 above, which diagrams "if all a are m and all m are b, then all a are b," is a Venn Diagram of Barbara. Can you see why?

The next valid form, in sequence, is called "Barbari," for AAI; this form also produces a valid syllogism (if all terriers are dogs and all dogs are mammals, it follows that "some" terriers are mammals, especially since we already know that "all" of them are). This is sometimes called a "weak" syllogism, because its conclusion is that "some" are, when we actually could conclude, more strongly, that "all" are. Nevertheless, Barbari is a true syllogism, because the conclusion is due absolute confidence.

But the form AAE (all are, all are, none are--"E" stands for negation) is not a valid syllogism. (From "all terriers are dogs and all dogs are mammals," it does not follow that "no terriers are mammals.") Can you interpret Figure 8 to demonstrate the falsity of AAE?

(3) *Another Example: The "Festino" Syllogism (in the EIO Format).* In the same way, these Latin-speaking logicians proceeded to catalogue all the

other possible three-premise formats, after the Barbara syllogism. One that they recorded was the EIO arrangement: "No a are m ('E'); some m are b ('I'); therefore, some b are not a ('O')." As a device for cataloguing and remembering this syllogism, the logicians looked for a then-common boy's or girl's name that contained the letters E-I-O, just as they had done for AAA with "Barbara." They came up with "Festino," which has the letters E, I and O in the proper order. (Although you may not know anyone by this name, Festino evidently was a popular moniker for boys back then. More to the point, it fits.)

Can you see why the Festino arrangement is a proper syllogism? "No birds are fish ('E'); some fish are edible ('I'); therefore, some edible things are not birds ('O')." This is a clumsy-sounding construct, but it follows the EIO arrangement, and no doubt there are some important rule applications or other deductions out there, in real life, that follow the format symbolized by the name Festino.

SO, HOW MANY SYLLOGISMS ARE THERE?

(1) *Twenty-four Valid Forms of Categorical Syllogisms.* Each syllogism has three lines, and there are four types for each (A, E, I and O). Therefore, there are four-to-the-third-power (4^3), or 64 "moods" (as they are called), of the syllogism. There also are four configurations that the subject, middle term, and predicate term can fit, so actually there are 4 x 64 = 256 separate formats. Most are invalid (for example, all forms of the AAE type mentioned above).

It turns out that exactly twenty-four of the 256 formats are valid.[1] Aristotle identified nineteen of them, and the five he didn't discover are all "weak" forms, like those that substitute "some" for "all" in the conclusion (the Barbari syllogism, above). Thus, Aristotle's logic was quite an achievement, for so many years B.C.!

---

1 This enumeration requires certain assumptions, such as that all premises are categorical formulas and that none of the subjects, predicates or middle terms refers to an empty set. But don't worry about these details; they're just included here for formal accuracy.

(2)   *Other   Syllogistic   Types:*
Disjunctive and Hypothetical Formats (as
Differentiated   from   Categorical   Ones).
Actually,   there   are   many   other   forms,
including those with disjunctives ("or") and
hypothetical terms ("if").   "If Troy Aikman
is a quarterback with either the Dallas
Cowboys or the Green Bay Packers, then
Aikman is a football player; Aikman is a
quarterback with the Dallas Cowboys but
not with the Green Bay Packers; therefore,
Aikman is a football player." This, too, is a
valid syllogism.   It has a disjunctive in its

Aristotle

premises (the word "or"), and the first premise is hypothetical ("if").
Therefore, it differs from the "categorical" syllogisms we have been dealing
with.   Nevertheless, such disjunctive and hypothetical constructs can be
proper syllogisms.

§ 1.03 Analyzing the Law with Formal Logic: Applying What You Have Learned

[A]   Deduction in Legal Reasoning: Rules, Crimes, Claims, and the "IRAC" Method

(1) *Using the Law as an Example for Types of Deductive, Analogic and*
Inductive Reasoning that Occur Also in Other Fields, from Medicine to
Accounting. In this section, we shall explore how deduction, analogy and
induction are used in legal analysis. (Actually, the particular field does not
matter.   Even the arts, from poetry to music to painting, have logical
structures, and it helps in those fields to know these reasoning types just as
it does in other fields, from medicine to accounting.)

(2) *Use of Syllogisms in Legal Reasoning: Applying a Rule or a Statute.*
A great deal of reasoning used in the law is syllogistic. For example, legal
principles, statutes, rules, and definitions of crimes or claims, typically are
used as first premises in legal reasoning.

Thus, in analyzing a possible criminal homicide under the Model Penal
Code, one might set forth (1) a major premise: "the elements of murder
under Code § 210 are present when a person 'causes the death of another

human being recklessly under circumstances manifesting extreme indifference to the value of human life'" [we get this from reading the statute]; (2) a minor premise: "This defendant is a person who caused the death of another human being by driving 100 miles per hour in a school zone and thus recklessly under circumstances manifesting extreme indifference to the value of human life" [we get this from the case evidence]; and (3) a conclusion: "The elements of murder under the Model Penal Code are present."

(3) *Fallacy in Legal Reasoning from Deduction.* This kind of logic lends itself to numerous possibilities of fallacy. For example, if the homicide described above were subject to the defense of insanity, it would not be a murder; the first premise really can be stated only as that "some" such incidents are murder. Further, the defendant can be convicted only if the minor premise is true. Here, the factual analysis omits such requirements as proof beyond a reasonable doubt and the use of properly admitted evidence. Nevertheless, this deductive system is a basic form of legal reasoning.

(4) *The So-Called "IRAC" Method (Issue, Rule, Analysis, Conclusion): Deductive Reasoning in the Law.* Law students often are taught the "IRAC" method as a means of answering law examination questions: (I), identify the "issue," (R), state the "rule," (A), "apply" the rule to the case facts, and (C), draw a "conclusion." The four steps are abbreviated as I-R-A-C.

This IRAC method is a deductive methodology, because the "rule" is the first premise in a syllogism, and its "application" to the case facts is the second premise, from which the conclusion follows. Deductive reasoning is essential to success in the law, just as it is in engineering (where every application of a mathematical model or formula is a syllogism), or in accounting, or any other field requiring reasoning.

Admittedly, this explanation oversimplifies the art of writing the "A" law school examination. One must first spot all of the right issues, and one must exhaustively state the correct rule--with all exceptions, refinements, and qualifications (remember the example of the murder that isn't a murder because of insanity, above?). Then, one must ferret out all relevant facts and apply the rule to them, again exhaustively. But if one follows these steps, the basic reasoning is deductive. The "guts" of formal legal reasoning, in other words, are syllogistic.

(5) *This Analysis, of Course, Is Simplistic and Idealized.* Rather than uniformly constructing premises and deducing results from them syllogistically, it seems likely that judges and juries sometimes decide "holistically." That is to say, they make a judgment based on the "story" of the case as a whole. Then, if a judge writes an opinion explaining the reasons, the result may be an after-the-fact justification. Some observers think that a holistic judgment, or judicial "hunch," may sometimes be better that deduction through chains of pigeonholed syllogisms. (We shall consider holistic reasoning, including story theory, in greater depth in the next chapter.)

But even so, the deductive method described by the "IRAC" label is important. It aids predictions of outcomes and therefore facilitates compliance with rules. The justifications constructed in an opinion, even if done after the fact, can be examined for coherence and presumably can be used in future cases. And even though not all judicial decisions are arrived at syllogistically, many surely are.

The deductive nature of the reasoning is easier to see if the court uses "formalism," or explicitly formal logic. In a later chapter on jurisprudence, we shall see that some legal analysts use a quite different approach called "instrumentalism" to interpret a legal rule or doctrine. Still, the deductive step remains important in the reasoning, although instrumentalism makes it more complex.

[B]   Analogy and Induction in the Law: Evolving New Rules or Fitting the Rules to Case Facts

(1) *Use of Analogy in Legal Reasoning.* Legal reasoning includes heavy use of analogy, just as it does of syllogism. "Newspapers are covered by the First Amendment's protection of the freedom of speech; radio is like newspapers in the relevant aspects; therefore, radio is protected by the First Amendment exactly as are newspapers."

This analogy might be valid for many propositions, such as the illegality of government censorship of truthful matters of public concern on the radio, *see CBS, Inc. v. Democratic Nat'l Comm.*, 412 U.S. 94 (1973), but it would falsely predict other propositions, such as the obligation to publish a reply to a personal attack, which exists in broadcast media but not print. *Compare Red Lion Broadcasting Co. v. FCC*, 395 U.S. 367 (1969) (broadcasters can be required to allow reply to personal attack) *with Miami Herald Pub. Co. v. Tornillo*, 418 U.S. 241 (1974) (newspaper may not be required to print such a reply). In fact, the entire process of applying and distinguishing case law is heavily reliant on analogy. This is the endeavor that consumes most of law school.

(2) *Induction in Legal Reasoning.* Induction in law is used in many ways. Sometimes it is applied to the evidence: We know from experience that the guilty sometimes flee, and so evidence of flight is often admitted before juries considering criminal cases. Sometimes induction helps a judge or lawyer reading a series of cases to infer a rule that is hidden in them. "In all reported cases in this state where the defendant's car has struck the plaintiff's from behind, the court has upheld a finding of negligence; therefore, perhaps the courts should recognize an inference of negligence when there is a collision from behind, as the general rule." Induction, like analogy, helps to create or recognize new rules of law. Thus, deduction, analogy, and induction all have their places in legal analysis.

§ 1.04 The Logic of Propositions and Symbolic Logic

[A]   The Logic of Propositions

THE LOGIC OF "PROPOSITIONS" (AS CONTRASTED TO THE LOGIC OF "INFERENCES")

(1) *The Logic of Inferences (Above).* The reasoning described above is called the "logic of inferences." It tells about the rules for inferring relationships among premises or propositions whose truth has been established. Now, in this section, we shall consider a different subject, called the logic of propositions.

(2) *The Logic of Propositions.* A separate branch of reasoning is called the "logic of propositions." This tells us the truth or falsity of a given proposition, derived from other propositions by the use of certain standard "axioms" (which are rules of validity) and "operators" (which are simply relational words like "and," "or," "is the same as," "is not," or "implies").

(3) *An Example of Inferences From Well-Formed Propositions: Is the Secretary-General of the U.N.: (1) Russian; (2) A Compulsive Horse Thief; and/or (3) Unfit for Office?* In this paragraph, we introduce the logic of

propositions by a series of related statements (some of which are strange and are used for illustrative purposes only). Consider the proposition, "The Secretary-General of the U.N. is Russian." This is what is called a "well-formed proposition" (it is declarative, definitive, and either true or not; for now, you should ignore the fact that it doesn't fit the existing universe).

From this well-formed formula about the Secretary-General, we can infer other propositions. For example, "It cannot be true both that the Secretary-General *is* Russian *and* that the Secretary-General *is not* Russian." Also, if we happened to have an honest Russian Secretary-General, it would be true that "The Secretary-General *is* Russian *and* the Secretary-General *is not* a horse thief"; whereupon, the following odd proposition also would be true: "*Either* the Secretary-General is Russian *or* the Secretary-General is a horse thief."

Further, assuming we would regard a kleptomaniac as a bad Secretary-General, we can say, "A Secretary-General's being a compulsive horse thief *does imply* that the Secretary-General is unfit for office"; but assuming there is no rule of ethnic fitness for the Secretary-General, we can say, "The Secretary-General's being Russian *does not imply* that the Secretary-General is unfit for the office." All of these statements are "well-formed formulas": declarative, and either true or not. (Admittedly, a Russian Secretary-General seems politically unlikely in the near future, but that is not our concern here.)

EXAMPLES AND PROBLEMS

(1) *A Longer Chain: "Being Russian and Not a Horse Thief Does Not Imply a Secretary-General's Unfitness."* From our system of relationships, as defined, this formula is true: "Being Russian and not a horse thief does not imply that the U.N. Secretary General is unfit." Can you derive this proposition from the definitions above? Also, consider the following (false) proposition: "Being either Russian or a compulsive horse thief implies that a Secretary-General is unfit." Can you demonstrate, from the reasoning above, why this statement is false?

Admittedly, this is a silly set of propositions. But the point is, once you master the material you will see in this section, you can use it to analyze an environmental regulation, a statute in the Internal Revenue Code, or SEC Rule 10b-5. In fact, we'll use it later to analyze the Supreme Court decisions about the negative Commerce Clause.

(2) *The Power of this System; The Use of Symbolic Logic (below).* This (relatively simple) system enables us to create infinitely long logical chains of propositions and to test their truth or falsity. It also allows us to translate other people's chains of reasoning into analytical steps. For example, we can use this analytical system to consider a mathematician's description of a rocket trajectory, a salesman's pitch about a product, or an opinion written by a Justice of the Supreme Court. We then have a better chance of detecting error. However, words make the system too clumsy for long chains, and we shall take this matter up again, in the next section, when we consider symbolic logic.

(3) *A Symbolic Logic Preview.* In symbolic logic, the letters "p, q, and r" stand for whole sentences. Let us let "p" mean "The Secretary-General is Russian"; "q" means "The Secretary-General is a compulsive horse thief"; and "r" means "The Secretary-General is fit for office." Also, we need certain standard "operators," or relational terms. The symbol $\lor$ means "or"; ~ means "not"; and $\supset$ means "implies."

We'll go over all of this again, below. This is just a preview, now.

Therefore, the last statement above translates into, "$(p \lor q) \supset {\sim} r$." (In other words, "Being either Russian or a thief implies that the SG is not fit.") But since, as we have seen, this formula is untrue, we can say, "${\sim}[(p \lor q) \supset {\sim} r]$." (This means, "It is not true that being Russian or a thief implies that the SG is not fit.") Can you see how these symbolic expressions are derived, and why they mean the same thing as their English translations? If you can't, don't worry; we shall take the subject up again, in simple form, in the section that follows.

[B]   Symbolic Logic: Making Complex Propositions Manageable

THE SYMBOLIC LOGIC OF PROPOSITIONS

(1) *A Comforting Thought for the Non-Mathematically Inclined: This Introduction Involves Elementary Symbols (Even if Unfamiliar), No More Complex Than the Various Kinds of Symbolic Logic You Have Used Since at Least the First Grade.* Early in school, you learned that the logical symbol "S" stood for the sibilant sound in words such as "see" or "snake." You

learned that the letters O-N-E spelled "one." When you studied math, you learned that the alternate logical symbol "1" also stood for one.

It would have been possible, back then, to write, "When a quantity of one is treated by an operator that cumulates it with another quantity of one, the resulting addend is two." But it was more practical to write, "1 + 1 = 2." Here's the point: The symbolic logic that follows may be unfamiliar, but it really is no more complex than the language and mathematical conventions you learned way back then, in elementary school. In fact, English sentences are merely another form of symbolic logic, and so are the numerals that we all learned years ago in studying addition and subtraction.

(2) *Three Kinds of Symbols: Propositions, Operators and Brackets.* For our simplified system of symbolic logic, here, we need three kinds of symbols. First, there are "propositions." We use p, q, and r and, if necessary, other letters to stand for these propositions. A proposition can be any well-formed declarative formula: "the moon is green cheese" can be p, and q can stand for "Socrates is dead," or for something else. Or, p can be the Model Penal Code definition of theft, and q can be the definition of robbery, etc.

Second, we need "operators." Here, we shall introduce five: ~, ·, ∨, ⊃, and ≡.[2] In English, these symbols translate roughly to "not," "and," "or," "implies," and "is equivalent to." Thus, "~p" stands for "not p," or "the converse of p"; if p is "the moon is green cheese," then ~p is "It is not true that the moon is green cheese." The combination ~p·q means "not-p and q," or "'It is not true that the moon is green cheese'; and 'it is true that Socrates is dead.'" Third, p∨q means "p or q but not both": "The moon is green cheese, or Socrates is dead." If either is true (but not both), then p∨q is valid (as it is here, because Socrates is dead and the moon isn't green cheese).

Next, p⊃q means "the truth of p implies the truth of q." "'Everyone who lived more than two thousand years ago is dead' implies that 'Socrates is

---

2 Some students may have used other symbols. But since all symbols are arbitrary, this set is as good as any other once you've learned it. Maybe it would have been better to use an ampersand (&) instead of a dot (·) for the conjunctive operator, but then, our effort to define highly specific meanings might get confused by the relationship between the ampersand and the English word "and," which has a more ambiguous meaning. Also, some past students of logic may be more familiar with the so-called "nonexclusive 'or'," roughly equivalent to "and/or," than with the "exclusive 'or'" we are using here (which means one or the other but not both). The nonexclusive or allows for useful axioms, including one called the "De Morgan Axiom," which our version of "or" (the exclusive or) does not allow; on the other hand, the exclusive or allows for other axioms that the nonexclusive would not. But if you don't understand this footnote, don't worry. It is included for completeness, to address a few of the concerns that experienced students of logic might raise.

dead.'"[3] The fifth operator, p≡q, means "the truth value of p is the same as the truth value of q." If p is true, so is q, and if p is false, so is q. "'Socrates once lived but is no longer living' has the same truth value as 'Socrates is dead.'"

Finally, our third type of symbol is very simple: parentheses and brackets. Sometimes the grouping of propositions and operators makes a difference, and we use parentheses or brackets to group them.

(3) *Restating These Operators in Chart Form: Figure 11.* The chart in Figure 11 may help you to keep these ideas in mind.

Figure 11: Symbols for Symbolic Logic		
Propositions	Operators	Meaning
	~p	not-p (or, p is not true)
p	p·q	p and q (both are true)
q	p∨q	p or q (either p or q is true but not both)
r	p⊃q	p implies q (if p is true, q must be too)
etc.	p≡q	p is the same as q (they have the same truth value)

(4) *Reducing "It Is Not True That Being Russian or a Thief Implies That a U.N. Secretary-General Is Not Fit" to Symbols: Generating Two Propositions.* In the previous section, we considered the proposition, "Being Russian or a thief implies that the U.N. Secretary-General is not fit for office." We saw that this proposition was false, because although a Russian Secretary-General is politically unlikely, such a Secretary-General would not be "unfit." Let p stand for "The Secretary-General is Russian" and r stand for "the Secretary-General is fit for office." Does p imply not-r? This would be written, "p⊃~r." But this combination is untrue, because it says, "The Secretary-General's being Russian implies that the Secretary-General is unfit." Therefore, the truthful proposition is "~(p⊃~r)," or "It is not true that being Russian implies that the SG is not fit."

---

3   This construct, p⊃q, is false if p is true and q is false, but it is to be taken as true in all other cases (including that in which p is false and q true, or that in which both are false). But this exact definition is more precise than we need, here.

Next, we consider the proposition, "The Secretary-General is a compulsive thief." Let us label this proposition as "q." Then, "q⊃~r," because being a compulsive thief makes the Secretary-General unfit.

(5) *Combining the Two Propositions into One.* Now, we have two propositions: "~(p⊃~r)" and "(q⊃~r)." "Russian doesn't imply unfitness"; "Being a thief does imply it." We can then further combine these two true propositions with a "·" or "and": "~(p⊃~r)·(q⊃~r)." This means, "It is *not* true that being Russian would make a U.N. Secretary-General unfit for office, and it *is* true that being a compulsive thief would make a Secretary-General unfit."

We also can say, as an additional statement, "It is not true that being Russian or being a thief would imply that a Secretary-General would be unfit for office." This proposition, too, is true, because although thiefdom implies unfitness, Russian nationality does not, and therefore "Russian *or* thief" does not imply it either.

(6) *Repeating this Russian-or-Thief Reasoning about the Secretary-General, in Chart Form.* We can now set out the same reasoning in shorter sequence in a chart, as in Figure 12.

Figure 12: Translating Some Logical Propositions	
Symbolic Proposition	Meaning or Translation
p	The Secretary-General is Russian
q	The SG is a compulsive thief
r	The SG is fit for office
~(p⊃~r)	The SG's being Russian does not imply the SG is not fit
(q⊃~r)	The SG's being a thief does imply the SG is not fit
~(p⊃~r)·(q⊃~r)	The SG's being Russian does not imply unfitness and the SG's being a thief does imply unfitness
~[(p∨q)⊃~r]	It is not true that being either Russian or a thief necessarily implies unfitness (because the SG may be Russian but not a thief)

(7) *Why Use These Odd, Squiggly Symbols When You Can Use the English Language Instead?* A good question! But there are several answers. First, language lacks the precision of these symbols. Words like "unless," "if," "maybe," and "probably" have multiple meanings, depending on the context. Second, we can construct and transform lengthy propositions in a reliable way with symbols. Anyone who has attempted to read Internal

Revenue regulations can appreciate how difficult it can be to follow long chains of propositions in English, especially when they require transformations (which are required whenever there are references to other rules).

But one need not look for a source so abstruse as the IRS to find a complex proposition. The rule of baseball known as the "infield fly rule" contains a long chain of terms that depend, in turn, on other rules. If you visit enough amateur baseball games, you will discover that most players do not fully understand the rule, although they vigorously argue subsidiary elements of it with umpires who sometimes do not understand it either. They sound just like lawyers. Symbolic logic helps us argue better about such complicated rules because it sharpens our reasoning and enables us to work with lengthier chains of propositions.

EXAMPLES AND PROBLEMS

(1) *In Baseball, What Is a "Strike"?* The rules of baseball are familiar to many people, and yet the definition of a strike is surprisingly complex, making it a useful example of the precision and economy of symbols. And for law students, the example is apt, because this rule and its application resemble legal thinking.

Let p mean, "The pitch crossed the plate within the strike zone but the batter did not swing"; q, "The batter hit a foul ball that was not a bunt"; r, "The batter bunted foul"; s, "The batter swung and cleanly missed"; u, "The batter hit a foul tip that the catcher caught directly in the mitt"; and t means "The batter already has two strikes." Let "x" stand for "The pitch is a strike."

Then, $p \lor (q \cdot {\sim} t) \lor r \lor s \lor u \supset x$.[4] Can you interpret this proposition to show how it fits the definition of a strike?

(2) *Translating the Supreme Court's Interpretation of the Commerce Clause into Symbolic Logic.* The Commerce Clause, in Article I, Section 8

---

4 We have not yet introduced the notion of an "or" ($\lor$) that operates on more than two propositions, and therefore this notation might seem ambiguous to a careful reader. Here, however, each of the alternatives is exclusive of the others, and so extending our definition of $\lor$ to mean "one but no more than one of the alternative propositions" will allow this composite proposition to stand. We also could use parentheses and brackets to do it, but that looks messy, and it requires the associative axiom, which we haven't yet introduced (see below). If the issue raised by this footnote did not occur to you, don't worry; it's only here for completeness and to satisfy students who otherwise might worry.

of the Constitution of the United States, grants to Congress the power "to regulate Commerce among the several States." The Supreme Court has interpreted the Commerce Clause as limiting the power of States to regulate in ways that affect interstate commerce.

The principle that the Supreme Court uses to apply the Commerce Clause is stated in the cases in various ways that are not completely consistent, but the following is an approximation: "A law passed by a State is unconstitutional (1) if it discriminates against interstate commerce and is not the least discriminatory alternative for achieving the State's legitimate purposes, or (2) if it is not discriminatory, but it imposes a burden on interstate commerce that is much greater than its local benefits."

Now, let us translate this proposition into symbols. Let "D" mean "the law is discriminatory"; "l" means that it is the "least discriminatory alternative"; and "[b>g]" means that "the burden on interstate commerce is much greater than any local gain." Finally, "The law is unconstitutional under the Commerce Clause" is symbolized by U.

Then, $[(D \cdot \sim l) \lor (\sim D \cdot [b>g])] \supset U$. Now, can you interpret this expression to show that it is equivalent to the longer English statement that precedes it?

Actually, law students often have trouble mastering the Commerce Clause rule in English. It has five propositions and seven operators. The symbols shorten the statement and make it more manageable, and (believe it or not) they actually seem to help some students to apply the rule better!

PROPOSITIONAL CALCULUS ("PC") FOR SYMBOLIC LOGIC

(1) *What Is a Propositional Calculus ("PC")?: A Set of Rules About Valid and Invalid Propositions and Relationships Among Them.* In this section, we consider various rules about combinations of propositions and operators. These rules, taken together, are called a "propositional calculus." You learned a propositional calculus for arithmetic in elementary school years ago. The rules here are analogous, and although they may be unfamiliar, they actually are no more difficult than the ones you mastered back then.

(2) *Invalid Propositions.* There are some kind of propositions that are invalid, or that cannot be true. For example, $p \cdot \sim p$ ("p is true and p is not

true") is invalid, because p must be a well-formed formula that is either true or not true but not both.

(3) *Some Simple PC Axioms: Identity, Double Negation, Excluded Middle, and Noncontradiction.* The "axiom of identity" is very simple. $p \equiv p$. (By substitution, if $p \equiv q$, then also, $q \equiv p$.) The "axiom of double negation" is $p \equiv \sim (\sim p)$. This means the negative of the negative of p is p, or "not-not-p" is p.

Then, there is the axiom, $p \lor \sim p$, meaning "p or not p." Either p or not-p must be true, but not both, if p is a well-formed formula. This axiom is called the "law of the excluded middle." To repeat, it's either p or not-p but not both, and $p \lor \sim p$ means that there is no middle ground. And, from the invalid proposition in (1) above, we derive the "axiom of noncontradiction": $\sim (p \cdot \sim p)$, or "not (p and not-p)": it cannot be true both that p is true and that p is not true.

(4) *Grouping Relationships: The Commutative, Associative and Distributive Axioms.* We now develop what are called the "commutative," associative," and "distributive" axioms. These rules apply in arithmetic, too, although you may not know them by their names. The "commutative axiom" in arithmetic is that (1+2) is the same as (2+1); similarly, in logic, $p \cdot q \equiv q \cdot p$ and $p \lor q \equiv q \lor p$. The "associative axiom" in arithmetic is that $[(1+2)+3] \equiv [1+(2+3)]$; likewise, in logic, $(p \cdot q) \cdot r \equiv p \cdot (q \cdot r)$ and $(p \lor q) \lor r \equiv p \lor (q \lor r)$.

The "distributive axiom" is that $[2 \times (3+1)] \equiv [(2 \times 3)+(2 \times 1)]$. Translation: If three propositions are in an "and" or an "or" relationship, it doesn't matter how you group them. In logic, $[p \cdot (q \lor r)] \equiv [p \cdot q) \lor (p \cdot r)]$. Again, the order of operations doesn't matter.

(5) *Axioms of Implication: Transposition and Syllogism.* The "axiom of transposition": $p \supset q \equiv \sim q \supset \sim p$. If p implies q, then not-q must imply not-p. And finally, $[(p \supset q) \cdot (q \supset r)] \supset (p \supset r)$: If p implies q, and q implies r, then p implies r. This is the "axiom of syllogism."

(6) *Using Symbolic Logic in the Law.* Below, in the Examples and Problems, we'll see how this propositional calculus can help us to understand, evaluate, and simplify chains of legal principles. Again, we shall use the negative commerce clause as our example. For now, though, let us consolidate and reinforce the propositional calculus.

(7)   *Putting It All into a Simple Chart.*   These axioms (and the substitution axiom below) can be expressed in a chart, as in Figure 13.

Figure 13: A Propositional Calculus ("PC")		
Proposition	Meaning	Axiom Name
p≡p	p is the same as p	Axiom of Identity
p≡~(~p)	p is the same as not-(not p)	Axiom of Double Negation
p∨~p	p or not-p	Axiom of the Excluded Middle
~(p·~p)	p and not-p cannot both be true	Axiom of Noncontradiction
p·q≡p·q p∨q≡q∨p	in an "and" or "or" grouping, the order of propositions doesn't matter	Commutative Axiom
(p·q)·r≡p·(q·r) (p∨q)∨r≡p ∨(q ∨ r)	in an "and" or "or" grouping, the order of operations doesn't matter	Associative Axiom
[p·(q∨r)]≡(p·q)∨(p·r)	an "and" operator may operate on two "or" propositions in a group or separately	Distributive Axiom
[(p⊃q)·(q⊃r)]⊃(p⊃r)	p implies q and q implies r means that p implies r	Axiom of Syllogism
If p≡q, we may substitute either for the other	equivalency allows substitution of any propositions with the same truth values	Axiom of Substitution
If p⊃q, we may substitute p for q (but not q for p)	we may replace what is necessarily implied by what implies it (but not vice versa)	Axiom of Implication

(8)   *The Axiom of Substitution of Equivalents: We Can Exchange Any Proposition for Any Other That Is Equivalent (or That Always Has the Same Truth Value), and We Can Substitute in a More Limited Way for Implied Propositions.*   The Axioms of Substitution add two more rules to our propositional calculus. The substitution of equivalents is a powerful axiom. It says, simply, that we can substitute any proposition p in place of any other proposition q that is equivalent, or has the same truth value. If p≡q, we can substitute q for p (or vice versa) in any true proposition, and the resulting proposition will be true, too. Thus, if p≡q, and if (p∨r)·(p·s), then (q∨r)·(q·s).

A more limited rule applies to implication under the symbol ⊃. If p⊃q, then q always will be true when p is true. Therefore, we can substitute p for

q. For instance, if we know that an event is both a homicide and a murder we can call it just a murder, and by that, we communicate that it is a homicide too, because murder implies homicide. But notice: It doesn't work the other way. Just because p⊃q does not mean that because q is true, p is also true. Just because an event is a homicide doesn't mean that it's a murder.

(9) *Why Go to the Trouble of Formulating All These Axioms? And Why Should Lawyers Study Them? The Answer: Because Reduction and Equivalence Are Useful!* This substitution axiom, together with the other axioms, is a powerful device: We can substitute a short expression for a longer one, and we can reduce long redundant chains into equivalent but more manageable ones. This device makes it easier both to use and to verify our logic. A lawyer who has this ability can do things other lawyers can't. What is more, the mental training that results from thinking about reduction and equivalency will make you more adept at reading the tax code, environmental statutes, or the Federal Rules of Civil Procedure, even if you don't remember the axioms. Now, let us look at examples, including legal reasoning.

EXAMPLES AND PROBLEMS

(1) *Reduction and Simplification.* Can you reduce the proposition $(p \equiv q) \cdot [(p \cdot q) \vee (p \cdot r)]$ to its shortest form? Here is a suggested answer. Step 1, $(p \equiv q) \cdot [p \cdot (q \vee r)]$ (distributive axiom). Step 2, $(p \equiv q) \cdot [p \cdot (p \vee r)]$ (substitution of equivalents, p for q). Step 3, $(p \equiv q) \cdot p \cdot \sim r$ (axiom of excluded middle). Now, can you explain these steps?

Actually, this reduction is more complicated than necessary. Can you find a simpler way, by eliminating the first step? (Note: since $p \equiv q$, you can eliminate the second q by substitution, giving $(p \equiv q) \cdot [(p \cdot (p \vee r)]$. This is what we got in Step 2 above.)

(2) *Reconsidering the Supreme Court's Formula for the Commerce Clause, in the Preceding Section.* In the preceding section, we saw a formula representing the Supreme Court's statement of the conditions under which a state law affecting interstate commerce is unconstitutional. Here it is again: $[D \cdot \sim l] \vee (\sim D \cdot [b > g])] \supset U$. This means, "A state law that discriminates against interstate commerce (D) and is not the least discriminatory alternative for achieving the state's purposes ($\sim l$), or a law that does not discriminate ($\sim D$)

but imposes a much greater burden on interstate commerce than any gain it produces (b>g), is unconstitutional (U)."

Notice how much shorter the symbolic expression is than the English sentence! But--could it be made even shorter? Perhaps!

(3) *Reducing the Commerce Clause Formula to a Statement That Is Shorter than the Supreme Court's, but Equivalent.* The first condition, "discriminatory and not the least discriminatory alternative," must really mean, simply, "not the least discriminatory alternative"--because if the law is not the least discriminatory alternative, then implicitly it contains some discrimination, or $\sim l \supset D$. We therefore can substitute $\sim l$ for D. This will allow us to shorten the Supreme Court's rule and make it simpler, while keeping its rigor.

Therefore, the first condition is really $(\sim l \cdot \sim l)$, and the entire expression becomes $(\sim l \cdot \sim l) \vee [\sim D \cdot (b>g)] \supset U$. Next, the axiom of identity allows us to remove one of the "$\sim l$'s" from the beginning: $\sim l \vee [\sim D \cdot (b>g)] \supset U$. In English, "If a state law is not the least discriminatory alternative, or if it is not discriminatory at all but the burden is much greater than the gain, it is unconstitutional." This statement is shorter, and maybe it is easier to absorb correctly.

(4) *Why Shorten the Statement? And How Does Symbolic Logic Help?* A shorter statement of the meaning of the Commerce Clause might mean less confusion and fewer possibilities for error. It might mean that trial courts and intermediate appeals courts would apply the principle more consistently. And perhaps lawyers could master and apply the principle more accurately to their arguments.

Does this mean that our propositional calculus is the only possible way to achieve this simplification? Certainly not. We can do it by wrestling with the longer English statement of the principle, because after all, English is merely another form of symbolic logic. But the propositional calculus facilitates it. PC almost invites us to make substitutions, transformations and equivalent reductions.

Chapter 2
Fallacy

False Reasoning, Inquiry, and the Limits of Logic

> *"The temptation to form premature theories on insufficient data is the bane of our profession."--Sherlock Holmes (in "The Valley of Fear," by Arthur Conan Doyle)*

> *"He's probably stuck in traffic*
> *"And he'll be here in a little while:*
> *"Just call me Cleopatra, everybody,*
> *"Cause I'm the queen of denial."*
> *--Pam Tillis, Queen of Denial*

§ 2.01 What This Chapter Is About

FALSEHOOD, HEURISTICS AND EPISTEMOLOGY

(1) *False Reasoning in the Law: Structural, Linguistic, Inductive, and Psychological Fallacies.* Here, we consider how manipulation of syllogistic formats, false premises, and mistaken inductions can produce defective reasoning. We shall illustrate each fallacy, give it a name, and examine how it works, in fields ranging from government to personal decisionmaking.

For example, Pam Tillis's impression of her boyfriend, quoted above, seems to be a manifestation of a psychological fallacy called "anchoring." The "premature" theories that Sherlock Holmes criticized are due to the fallacy of "inadequate sampling." The chapter considers each of these fallacies, and it shows how they affect legal reasoning.

(2) *Heuristics and the Limits of Logic.* "Heuristics" is a complex word to convey a simple idea: Inquiry or testing by rules of thumb, as opposed to the use of established logical forms. We shall see how heuristics can help us test our inductive generalizations. The chapter also explores such different heuristic methods as "dialectics" and "story theory," both of which are familiar to lawyers. Finally, we consider the problem of knowledge and the limits of logic, subjects that are part of a philosophical branch called "epistemology."

§ 2.02 Fallacy and Bias: Some Common Forms

[A]   Structural Fallacies: Deficiencies in the Syllogistic Form

FALLACIES RESULTING FROM MANIPULATION
OF THE SYLLOGISTIC STRUCTURE

(1) *What This Section Is About: Structure, Language, Induction, and Bias as Sources of Deficiencies in Legal Reasoning.* There are many ways for fallacy to creep into legal reasoning. In this section, we shall explore some of them. We shall give a name to each of the identified fallacies and explain how it works. By knowing its name, and understanding how it can mislead you, you may be able to avoid a given kind of fallacy.

(2) *The Structural Fallacy of Assuming the Conclusion, or Circular Reasoning: Chocolate Is Good because I Like It because It Is Good.* The term "circular reasoning" is well known, but to see how it works and where its fallacy lies, it is useful to compare it to syllogistic reasoning. "I like chocolate (because it is good), whatever I like is good, therefore chocolate is good." The form is that of a syllogism, but the first premise assumes the conclusion rather than depending on separate verification. Often the circularity is buried in language or is implicit: The speaker considers "I like" and "is good" to be equivalent, but without expressly saying so. Such is the "fallacy of circular reasoning."

(3) *The Structural Fallacy of Definition (A Type of Circular Reasoning):*
"Abortion Is Choice" or "Abortion Is Murder." The "fallacy of definition"
is a particular type of circular reasoning. This fallacy creates a purported first
premise merely by unjustified assertion of a definition, which actually is an
unprovable slogan instead. Both sides of the abortion debate use this device.
"Abortion is murder," says one side. "Abortion is a choice," the other retorts.
Both attempt implicitly to install the statement as the first premise in a
syllogism proving what they believe, and so the respective (circular)
conclusions are that abortion is murder or is a matter of choice.

But both of these syllogisms about abortion are fallacious, in that neither
assertion is demonstrated. More to the point, neither would be legitimately
persuasive to an audience of neutrals, because abortion has been
distinguished from murder even in societies that have disapproved it, and
likewise, abortion is not the same as idiosyncratic choices like the selection
of vanilla or strawberry. Thus, the fallacy of definition bypasses the need to
demonstrate the truth of the first premise.

(4) *The Structural Fallacy of Issue Transformation: Ridiculing the CIA*
by Replacing Its Objectives with Confusingly Similar but Different
Objectives. The "fallacy of issue transformation" substitutes a different
syllogism for the one at issue and then either establishes or refutes it.
Consider the following news item from *U.S. News and World Report*, April
12, 1999, at 5, concerning a public request to the CIA to declassify a formula
for invisible ink. "The CIA wants us to believe that a government that put a
man on the moon can't replace an 82-year-old recipe for invisible ink," the
magazine reported dramatically. "The [formula was created] in 1917 and
1918." But the issue isn't whether the CIA "can replace" a given method;
instead, it is whether substitutes would be inferior or, more accurately,
whether the CIA's insistence on continued secrecy is justifiable given all the
costs and risks. Furthermore, it would not be surprising if a modern
technology were built entirely from ideas more than eighty years old. The
U.S. News item simply substitutes a different syllogism with a different
conclusion ("can the current secret formula be replaced," rather than "should
the secret be disclosed").

In fact, the *U.S. News* item went on to demonstrate its own fallacy: "The
CIA says the product is still used by agents and that it's the basic formula in
more sophisticated secret spook inks." Furthermore, "making the documents

public would give terrorists a leg up" by showing them how to read confidential messages and use them themselves.

Perhaps the government is wrong (often it is), but if so, *U.S. News's* approach can never help us to know it. Thus, the fallacy of issue transformation enables the proponent to divert analysis into a syllogism that the proponent prefers but that does not address the question at hand.

Incidentally, your opponents in litigation often will use this fallacy. And, of course, they will accuse you of the same thing. "The most important thing about this case is that the defendant lied to you," a prosecutor tells the jury. This subtle change of emphasis succeeds by sidestepping the elements of the crime, some of which may be supported by marginal proof. Meanwhile, the defense attorney tells jurors that the defendant is "a decent, hard-working family man."

(5) *The Structural Fallacy of Authority: A Champion Golfer Sells Brokerage Services.* Invocation of an authoritative source sometimes justifies confidence in the premise. But not always: One large investment banking firm features golf legend Tiger Woods in advertisements about its prowess in helping people reach their financial goals, and former late-night television personality Ed McMahon pitches everything from magazine sweepstakes to insurance. The fallacy of authority works by avoiding the question, "Does this purported authority know what he's talking about, and if he does, will he tell it to me straight?" (This fallacy is closely related to the fallacy of issue transformation, above.)

For lawyers, citing a case that is not on point, or citing a United States Supreme Court decision to resolve an issue of state law, can be examples of the fallacy of authority.

(6) *The Fallacy of a Structure Without a Middle Term: Legal Arguments That Deceptively Mimic Syllogisms.* The two premises must contain a "middle term": a categorization that appropriately links the other categories in the premises. In the all-all-all form of the syllogism, the middle term must contain all of one of the other terms, and it must, in turn, be contained within the remaining term. Thus, we have the form, "All x are m; all m are y; therefore, all x are y." Here, all members of the class called "x" are contained in the class called "m," the middle term; and all members of the class called "m," the middle term, are contained in the class called "y." Thus, "All oaks

are trees, all trees are plants, and therefore, all oaks are plants," is a valid syllogism, with the middle term correctly linking the two other terms.

The tricky thing about this concept is that a structure without a middle term, a fallacious structure, can "look like" a syllogism. "All fish can swim, John can swim, and therefore, John is a fish." We already have noted this fallacious example. And consider the following one:

> All dogs have four legs.
> All cats have four legs.
> Therefore, a cat is a dog.

These examples are easy to spot because we know extrinsically that the conclusions are false. We know that a cat is not a dog. But this "obviousness" method of detecting fallacy breaks down when the conclusion "sounds" plausible, and indeed it may sound plausible if the deduction concerns a fact that is new and unfamiliar--or in other words, when we most need to rely on it. "All ABX's are farfles, all YPZ's are farfles, and therefore, all ABX's are YPZ's," is an example of this fallacy, but for those of us who do not know what an "ABX," a "YPZ," or a "farfle" is, the only way to detect the fallacy is to recognize that the construction lacks a middle term.

Again, this fallacy is a frequent tool in legal arguments. "The case of *Jones v. Smith* involved a store that didn't have a security guard, and the court upheld a finding of negligence; this case involves a store with no security guard; therefore, this defendant was negligent." The reasoning involves only an analogy, and a dubious one at that. But the attorney has attempted to dress it up in the form of a syllogism, which it is not.

(7) *The Structural Fallacy of Conflation: Leaving Out Essential Terms in a Legal Argument.* The "fallacy of conflation" results when a required element is left out of one of the premises. "Conflation" means reducing two or more independent elements into one. For example, imagine that we reason as follows: "A foul ball in baseball is a strike; this batter has just hit a foul ball; therefore, it's a strike. And since this is his third strike, he's out." The error is that a foul ball is a strike only if the batter does not already have two strikes. By leaving this required element out, the speaker has committed the fallacy of conflation.

Any law student is prone to commit this fallacy on a law school examination, if he or she gets into a hurry. "If the defendant was negligent, there is liability. The facts [recited] show that defendant was negligent. Therefore, there is liability." This reasoning conflates the legal principle by omitting duty, proximate causation, and damage, all of which must be present in addition to negligence.

(8) *Conflation of an Entire Statement: The Fallacy of Omitting an Entire Premise.* A special case of the fallacy of conflation occurs when a speaker omits a whole premise. Informally, we use this kind of reasoning often, by saying that one proposition is true "because of" another one. "The stock market went up because inflation is low." "She dislikes Clinton because Clinton is a Democrat." "There is federal jurisdiction in this case because the parties are of diverse citizenship and more than $75,000 is in controversy." This informal reasoning often is an acceptable shorthand, but it always should be viewed skeptically. If the issue is important, it's worth asking whether the omitted premise really is true. And on a law school examination, it usually is best to give the rule or principle rather than to use this "because" conflation.

[B]   Linguistic and Conceptual Fallacies: Symbols That Differ from Reality

SEMIOTICS AND METAPHYSICS: SYMBOLS, CONCEPTS, AND REALITY

(1) *A Practical Problem in This Symbolism We Call Language: The Example of Joseph Wambaugh's Experienced Police Officer.* In this section, we shall digress from the study of syllogisms to consider how words and concepts are related to the true nature of reality. A vignette from one of Joseph Wambaugh's wonderfully realistic police stories will provide a practical introduction. Wambaugh tells about an experienced police officer who apprehends a suspect wearing a brown shirt. His rookie partner asks him how he recognized the perpetrator, since the victim described a suspect in a red shirt. "It was a color that could be *called* red," the veteran answers.

(2) *Semiotics: The Study of Signs and Symbols as Devices for Communicating Truth.* Wambaugh's veteran officer was an excellent student of "semiotics," even if he didn't know it. Semiotics is the study of signs and symbols as devices for communicating truth. When we use the term "red,"

we may actually be describing something that another person would call magenta, orange, purple, brown, or even black (e.g., a heavy "red" wine in a thick bottle). The word is one thing; the reality may be quite another. A "semiotician" studies how symbols can be refined to convey truth better, how they create errors, and related topics.

(3) *A Deeper Problem: Concept, Reality, and Metaphysics.* But there is a deeper problem. How closely does the concept that underlies a symbol correspond to reality? What is the true nature of things? The Greek philosopher Plato, for example, postulated the existence of ideal "forms": Somewhere in the universe there floated the ideal concept of a flower, and real flowers could be understood only as approximating this ideal form. He generalized this idea to every concept: There was an ideal form of an apple, of a horse, and even of justice. This is a problem of "metaphysics," which studies how closely concepts resemble reality.

Plato's metaphysical forms may seem a crude idea today, but in fact they illuminate an important point. When we say the word "horse" to another person, we need to be aware of at least two problems. First, at one level, there is the issue of semiotics: the symbol may not mean the same thing to the listener as to the speaker. Second, at a deeper level, there is the issue of metaphysics: what is the true nature of a "horse"? Does it include a pony, a mule, or an equine animal with only three functional legs? Does it include the evolutionary ancestors of horses? More fundamentally, every horse that exists is different from every other one, and any concept of a "horse" that we might formulate will be different from them all in at least some details. In this sense, there is no such thing as a horse. There is only a continuum of unique specimens.

(4) *Application of This Reasoning to Abstract Concepts: Law, Justice, and Syllogisms.* This kind of dithering may seem silly when applied to commonly understood objects like horses. At the Kentucky Derby, for example, every observer will agree that each jockey is riding a "horse." Still, semiotic and metaphysical problems might arise in some cases, even with horses. Imagine a biological taxonomist who struggles to decide whether a variant animal should be classified as a horse or designated as a newly minted species.

And here is the real point: These problems of semiotics and metaphysics increase as we maneuver in the realms of more abstract ideas. For example, whether a day care center is a school for purposes of a state regulation may be highly debatable, both because the symbol, "school," is vague and because the true nature of a "school" is imprecisely knowable. At a higher level of abstraction, whether an act is a "murder," or "negligent," or "illegal," can be the subject of fundamental disagreement over both terminology and concept. And if we use words like "good" or "justice," we must realize that, apart from the semiotic question about our understanding one another, the underlying concepts do not correspond to any verifiable external reality, and they have meaning only to the extent that we imagine them to.

EXAMPLES AND PROBLEMS

(1) *The Rookie Police Officer's Mistake.* The mistake made by Wambaugh's rookie police officer, then, was to overlook these semiotic and metaphysical problems when he searched the vicinity of the crime for a red shirt. "The perpetrator will be wearing a red shirt," he reasoned. "This individual is not wearing a red shirt, and therefore this individual is not the perpetrator." Can you explain why the rookie's syllogism, although structurally sound, led to a false conclusion, for both linguistic and conceptual reasons? [What does the symbol "red" mean among different people, and is there really a solid reality that corresponds accurately to that concept?]

(2) *A Word as "The Skin of a Living Thought."* Oliver Wendell Holmes once wrote that, rather than embodying a static reality, a word resembles "the skin of a living thought." This metaphor captured both the semiotic problem (the word is only a "skin") and the metaphysical issue (under the skin, there is a "living" thought). Can you explain?

(3) *The Semiotics and Metaphysics of a Cherished Childhood Belief: Can We Construct a Teleological Proof of the Existence of Santa Claus?*[1] "Yes, Virginia, there is a Santa Claus." These words in a famous newspaper column answered a question posed in a little girl's letter. The columnist went on to explain the catch, mainly for the benefit of adult readers: Santa "exists"

---

1   "Teleology" is the doctrine that final causes exist, that they can be discerned in nature from evidences of design and purpose, and that natural phenomena are guided not merely by mechanical forces but by movement toward goals that are a part of their nature. This "Santa" proof is teleological, therefore, in the sense that it infers a purposive agent (namely Santa, or Christmas, or something) that causes nature (people) to behave as part of a grand design. We shall consider teleology again in later chapters on ethics and science.

in the Christmas spirit, and he can be observed in the hearts of people who spread holiday cheer.

But was this "teleological" proof of Santa's existence really valid? Consider what is meant by the semiotics of a child who speaks about Santa Also, consider the metaphysics of inferring a unifying force in the form of an omnipresent spirit in the hearts of people at Christmas (particularly if Virginia's family happened to be Jewish, or Muslim, or Agnostic, or Christian but opposed to Santa's commercialism). Can you analyze, then, the extent to which the columnist's reasoning was "true"? Virginia would have been disappointed by his meaning, wouldn't she?

(4) *How This Discussion Relates to Law and to Logic (Particularly Syllogistic Logic).* This discussion is important to logic because syllogistic reasoning depends on definitive premises. We can achieve this condition by using uniquely defined terms. But the result, then, like a hothouse orchid, may be reasoning that cannot be used in the real world. To make our reasoning meaningful, we must use symbols and concepts. And this step may introduce fallacy, particularly when we reason about such important topics as whether something is a "good investment," a "sensible strategy," a "sound foreign policy," or "proper parenting." In the law, when we use symbols and concepts such as "offer," "acceptance," "negligent," or "illegal search," we must watch for slippage in their meanings. In other words, problems of semiotics and metaphysics are inherent in our most important reasoning, and our logic may be simply an organized way of being wrong.

Now, let us return from this digression into semiotics and metaphysics to our study of syllogisms. In the next section, we shall consider linguistic and conceptual fallacies in deductive reasoning.

FALLACIES BASED ON IMPRECISION OF LANGUAGE OR CONCEPT

(1) *The Linguistic Fallacy of Substituted Meaning: When Is a Silverfish Not a Silverfish?* The "fallacy of substituted meaning" exploits the ambiguity of language. Often, a word means two different things, and fallacy results from use of both meanings in the same syllogism. For example, "silverfish" include certain varieties of shiny-scaled fish, such as tarpon. But "silverfish" also are lustrous gray wingless insects that eat books and wallpaper in people's homes. Imagine this attempted syllogism: "All fish have gills; all

silverfish are fish; therefore, all silverfish have gills."   A "fallacy of substituted meaning" results if we substitute the "insect" meaning of silverfish in the conclusion, when the rest of the syllogism is based on the "fish" meaning.

The fallacy in this silverfish example is deliberately obvious for illustrative purposes. But only slightly greater subtlety can lead to serious mistakes, and this is especially so if the conclusion is promulgated by one group of people as a rule or principle to be followed by a separate group of people who are not aware of the linguistic assumptions upon which the rule was constructed. In fact, this is one of the major reasons for misapplication of the law. And if we use a more abstract term in one of the propositions, such as "illegal" or "good," we increase the likelihood of the fallacy of substituted meaning.

(2)   *The Linguistic Fallacy of the Ambivalent Middle Term (A Subcategory of the Substituted-Meaning Fallacy).*   Often, the substituted meaning is in the middle term. This is the term that occurs twice in the premises. Therefore, we define this fallacy as "the fallacy of the ambivalent middle term." It is a species of the substituted-meaning fallacy, but it "looks" different from the predicate-conclusion substitution in the silverfish example above.

(3) *Legal Reasoning That Contains the Fallacy of the Ambivalent Middle Term: "Punishing the Illegal Search."* Consider the following attempted syllogism: "A court must redress illegal searches by suppression, to deter them in the future; this particular search has been determined by a 5-to-4 vote of the Supreme Court to have been illegal; therefore, the Court must redress this search by suppressing the evidence, to deter future illegal searches." In fact, this reasoning closely resembles the logic in some of the Supreme Court's actual search-and-seizure decisions. But it is deceptive logic.

The source of the fallacy is in the middle term, "illegal," which is ambivalent. Worse than that, "illegal" produces a blizzard of finely-differing interpretations that can change the reasoning: sometimes it means "criminal"; sometimes, "reckless but unintentional"; sometimes, "careless"; sometimes, "carefully done but unreasonable in light of after-the-event discoveries"; sometimes, "perfectly reasonable but mistaken"; and sometimes, "legally mandated but mistakenly ordered" (for example, an officer carries out a court order to conduct a search but later discovers that the court prepared the order on the wrong preprinted form, so that its literal language is too confused to supply a legally sufficient warrant even though everyone knows what it means).

In recent years, the Supreme Court has recognized the ambivalence of the word "illegal" by, for example, refusing to suppress the results of certain kinds of arguably illegal searches based on reasonable mistakes. The earlier failure to distinguish reasonable, good-faith searches from brazenly criminal ones is an example of a simple ambiguity in language that has major public policy results. Such is the fallacy of the ambivalent middle term.

(4) *The Linguistic Fallacy of Metaphor, or Confusion of Analogy with Syllogism: "My Love Is Like a Red, Red Rose."* The "fallacy of metaphor" uses an unexamined metaphor as the first premise or substitutes analogy for deductive logic, without recognizing that analogy carries all the dangers of induction.

A metaphor is nothing more than a species of analogy. "My love is like a red, red rose" conjures up romantic, intense, vivid beauty, but it tells nothing about the limits of the analogy: Roses grow best in acid soil, but it might be wrong to conclude that an acid environment will make love grow. In fact, fresh and powerful metaphors--those that are most artistic and seductive--usually contain internal contradictions that heighten their poetic effect, and they depend on rhetorical devices such as alliteration, repetition, meter and imagery.

The point is simple. Literature can be dangerous to the health of your reasoning. Many good things can be dangerous. Automobiles are good, but they are dangerous, and poets, too, are good but sometimes misleading. A writer can prove anything with a good story. You can prove that love causes death (Romeo and Juliet), that persistence leads to disaster (Moby Dick), or that solo practitioners are more moral than big-firm or government lawyers (any John Grisham novel chosen at random). This kind of proof uses no logic. It produces no evidence. And yet it can be more convincing than sound argumentation. The public, indeed, does seem to believe that solo practitioners are more moral than big-firm lawyers (and law students may, too). This belief usually is based on Grisham and Perry Mason, not on examined reasoning.

(5) *Seduction by Myth: The Power of Metaphorical Fallacies.* Could people be fooled by this metaphorical device? Yes, indeed. Myths are a powerful part of culture; in fact, simple sayings, metaphors or fairy tales are ways of inculcating shared perceptions in a society. Cinderella "married the handsome prince and lived happily ever after"; "strangers in the night" exchanged glances; and it all happened on one single "enchanted evening." And so, for similar reasons, many real people buy into the premise that love at first sight has a good chance of lasting, and they marry on theories of sudden-but-effortless romance, sometimes without getting to know their spouses.

Or, imagine a corporate executive impressed by Robert Frost, who chooses the "road less traveled by," and who leads his employees into the wilderness with a new, but unworkable, production decision that bankrupts the company. In 1996, the Clinton-Gore Presidential campaign successfully advocated a "Bridge to the Twenty-first Century," without any acknowledgment of the limits of this kitschy figure of speech. This linguistic fallacy works by concealing the imperfections of analogy in the appeal of metaphor and applying it directly in deduction. And it works in legal argument also, as we shall see, now.

(6) *Metaphorical Fallacies in the Law: The "Penumbra" Reasoning in Griswold v. Connecticut,* 381 U.S. 479 (1965). The Constitution does not provide for (or even mention) a generalized right of privacy. The privacy rights that have been inferred are exactly that--inferred--and the reasoning that supports them varies in persuasiveness from case to case. One of the most unusual derivations of privacy is in the *Griswold* case: Justice Douglas cited the First Amendment (speech and religion), then the Third (quartering of soldiers), the Fourth (unreasonable searches), as well as the Fifth, Ninth, and Fourteenth, all to infer a broad right to procreative freedom. The vehicle for this conclusion was a literary metaphor: the actual Amendments, Justice Douglas announced, created a "penumbra" (a penumbra is a vague shadow), and this "penumbra" illuminated a broad right of privacy.

To its credit, the Supreme Court has never again used this metaphor-based reasoning to justify its privacy decisions. Those decisions remain controversial, but they at least avoid the easy ridicule that critics understandably have used to attack *Griswold.*

EXAMPLES AND PROBLEMS

(1) *Examples in the Law of the Fallacies of Circular Reasoning and of Definition: Illegal Searches and the Death Penalty Debate.* The search-and-seizure example, above, may reflect more than one kind of fallacy. It may also include the fallacy of circular reasoning, *if* the minor premise really means something like, "This particular search is 'illegal' because the Supreme Court majority thinks it ought to be suppressed." Can you show why this reasoning is circular? (Remember, the major premise was, all illegal searches must be suppressed, and the conclusion was, this search must be suppressed.)

As another example, some arguments by death penalty proponents and opponents embody the kind of circular reasoning that we call the fallacy of definition. Can you give examples, using terms such as "barbarism" or "justice" (and can you offer other pro and con arguments about the death penalty that don't embody this fallacy)?

(2) *The Fallacy of Issue Transformation in Legal Reasoning: Is President Clinton a "Perjurer" if He "Gave False Testimony under Oath"?* Imagine that, some day, a hypothetical grand jury must consider whether William Jefferson Clinton is guilty of perjury in connection with his testimony about Monica Lewinsky. Imagine further that a newspaper columnist, outraged that there even is any question, editorializes, "Did Clinton give false testimony under oath? He testified that he never was alone with Ms. Lewinsky when in fact he was. And so, unequivocally, Clinton is a perjurer." This editorial contains the fallacy of issue transformation. Can you explain why? (The fallacy in this particular reasoning does not preclude alternate proofs of Presidential perjury, which many people might accept as valid; this reasoning fails, however, because "false testimony" is not the same thing as "perjury.")

(3) *The Fallacy of Conflation: False Testimony as "Perjury"?* This perjury example also could be viewed as containing the fallacy of conflation, since it defines perjury erroneously as false testimony, thus omitting the element of intent to make a false statement. Can you explain the error?

(4) *The Fallacy of Structure Without a Middle Term: Criticizing the Mayor by Comparison to Adolf Hitler Because of One Innocuous Shared Characteristic.* In a blast of negative campaigning, the challenger in the mayoral race criticizes the opponent by saying, "The mayor gives speeches

calling for law and order; Adolf Hitler gave speeches calling for law and order; therefore, the mayor is an Adolf Hitler clone." Explain why this structure lacks an appropriate middle term. (Also, can you explain why this "logic" really is a species of analogy, although not a very persuasive one, rather than a deduction?)

(5) *Linguistic Fallacy, or the Fallacy of the Ambivalent Middle Term: How Some Lawmakers Have Condemned the American Psychiatric Association's Diagnostic Treatment of Pedophiles.* The Diagnostic and Statistical Manual ("DSM") published by the American Psychiatric Association ("APA") is an extremely important guidebook, used by many kinds of mental health professionals as a uniform basis for diagnostic criteria. The fourth edition ("DSM-IV") contains the jarring statement that some pedophiles are diagnosable as "psychologically normal." Politicians have criticized this proposition, producing headlines like "[House Whip Tom] DeLay Blasts Writings on Pedophilia . . . [but] Experts Deny They Suggest Habit is Acceptable," Houston Chronicle, April 16, 1999, at 5A.

The politicians' criticisms all can be paraphrased in a purported syllogism such as: "The APA says some pedophiles are psychologically normal; normal implies acceptable; therefore, the APA is really saying some pedophiles' behavior is acceptable." Can you see how the middle term, "normal," may be ambivalent? (Perhaps some bank robbers, rapists, drunk drivers and serial killers would be diagnosed as "psychologically normal" too, but consider whether this diagnosis would imply anything about whether their conduct would be "acceptable.") An APA spokesperson responded that DeLay was "completely mistaken," that "sex with a child is a crime; it should be," and that DSM-IV is used only for mental disorder diagnoses, "not for making a legal decision."

(6) *A Federal Judge's Decision That a Prison Is Unconstitutional Because of the "Mental . . . Deprivation" That It Inflicts: A Fallacy of the Missing Middle Term?* In *Ruiz v. Estelle*, 37 F. Supp.2d 855, 914-15 (S.D. Tex. 1999), Judge William Wayne Justice reviewed numerous aspects of a state prison system in a case presenting Eighth Amendment issues of cruel and unusual punishment. The judge appeared to reach the striking conclusion that even physically humane incarceration would be illegal if it resulted in psychological isolation. He reasoned that because physical torture is unconstitutional, excessive "mental . . . deprivation" in prisons is equally unconstitutional:

It goes without question that an incarceration that inflicts daily, permanently damaging physical injury and pain is unconstitutional. . . . Given the relatively recent understanding of the primal necessity of psychological well-being the same standards that protect against physical torture [also] prohibit . . . the mental torture of excessive deprivation.

. . . Persons who, with psychiatric care, could fit well into society, are instead locked away, to become wards of the state's penal system. . . . [T]hey may be confined in conditions that nurture, rather than abate, their psychoses. The United States Constitution cannot abide such a perverse and unconscionable system of punishment. . . .

Opponents of this rhetoric argued that "mental deprivation" was one of the primary purposes of prisons, because they are supposed to deter crime. To what extent is the judge's reasoning syllogistic (as structurally it appears to be)? Is it really only a species of analogy?

(7) *A False Syllogism about the Erie Doctrine: Hanna v. Plumer*, 380 U.S. 460 (1965). In *Hanna v. Plumer*, the plaintiff served the suit papers on the defendant by a method allowed in Federal Rule 4. But the defendant claimed that even though the suit was in federal court, service of the papers was required to be done under state law. And since the statute of limitations had run, this reasoning would have resulted in an immediate victory for the defense. This logic created a Catch-22: the plaintiff had complied with the governing federal rules because those rules were the proper rules in a federal court, but by doing so (the defendant argued), the plaintiff had failed to comply with the state rules for service of process, which seemed inapplicable but actually were required by law to be followed, unbeknownst to plaintiff. The defendant argued that this odd application of state law was required under a previous decision, in which the Supreme Court had said that federal courts must follow state law whenever the rule of decision was outcome-determinative. In other words, the defendant's reasoning was syllogistic: "(1) whenever state law would change the outcome from that under federal law, the court must follow state law; (2) here, the papers weren't served in compliance with state law, and the statute of limitations has run under state law, even though the service was valid under the Federal Rules, and thus, the outcome will be different under state law; therefore, (3) the federal court must follow state law, resulting in a quick victory for the defendant."

The Court described the defendant's argument as a "syllogism" but rejected it as fallacious.

> Respondent, by placing primary reliance on [previous cases], suggests that the Erie doctrine acts as a check on the Federal Rules of Civil Procedure, that despite the clear command of Rule 4(d)(1), Erie and its progeny demand the application of the Massachusetts rule. Reduced to essentials, the argument is: (1) Erie, as refined in York, demands that federal courts apply state law whenever application of federal law in its stead will alter the outcome of the case. (2) In this case, a determination that the Massachusetts service requirements obtain will result in immediate victory for respondent. If, on the other hand, it should be held that Rule 4(d)(1) is applicable, the litigation will continue, with possible victory for petitioner. (3) Therefore, Erie demands application of the Massachusetts rule. The syllogism possesses an appealing simplicity, but is for several reasons invalid.

The Court reasoned, "[O]utcome determination was never intended to serve as a talisman." The previous decision, mandating use of state law whenever it was outcome-determinative, could not form a proper first premise in a syllogism in this particular case. Other factors, such as the plaintiff's compliance with a controlling Federal Rule and the purposes or policies supporting the *Erie* doctrine, also mattered. In summary, the defendant's concept of "outcome determination," as defining the immediate result in this case, was not the kind of "outcome determination" that the Court had meant in its prior cases. The Court had not intended to include mechanical, housekeeping rules governing federal service of process, or to subordinate them to state requirements.

Can you see why the defendant made the argument she made? And can you categorize the fallacy that it involved?

[C]   Inductive Fallacies: Structure and Bias

STRUCTURAL FALLACIES IN INDUCTION

(1) *The Inductive Fallacy of Causation, or "Post Hoc, Ergo Propter Hoc": "Everyone Who Has Died Has Drunk Water; Therefore, Water Causes Death."* Now, let us shift subjects. We have been talking about syllogisms,

and next, we shall begin to discuss a different problem: generalizations and analogies. What kinds of fallacies affect inductive reasoning?

First, there is the "fallacy of causation," which infers causation inductively from the coincidence of two factors. For example, in March 1999, the United States and European allies reacted to Serbian genocide by strategic bombing, but the Serbian leaders nevertheless continued and actually increased their atrocities. On the basis of this dubious evidence, critics charged that the bombing had "caused" the Serbs to commit atrocities. (Isn't it possible that the Serbian leaders possessed sufficient viciousness to come up with the idea themselves?)

This fallacy is venerable enough to wear a Latin label: "post hoc, ergo propter hoc," which translates as "[it happened] after this; therefore, [it happened] because of this." To give another example, it would not be accurate if we inductively concluded that drinking water "causes" death, simply by the observation that "everyone who has ever died drank water" during his or her lifetime. This is a classic, if obvious, example of the fallacy of causation. Or, sometimes the inference points to a "cause" that itself is a result: HIV antibodies are present in people who are HIV positive, but that does not mean that the antibodies "cause" the HIV-positive condition; both the condition and the antibodies are produced by a separate thing, the HIV virus.

The fallacy of causation draws its appeal from the usefulness of everyday inductions, such as that drunk drivers "cause" accidents and that boiling an egg "causes" it to harden. But scientists tend to avoid the word "cause," or else they use it with an awareness that it can be misleading. They prefer the term "correlation," which means the observed coincidence of two manifestations, without inference of which is the agent of the other. The fallacy of causation substitutes an inference of cause and effect for a mere correlation.

(2) *The Inductive Fallacy of Consistency, or Inferring a Fact from Evidence that Does Not Refute It (But Does Little to Establish It): "I Shot a Bear from behind a Tree, and There's the Tree."* The "fallacy of consistency" infers a fact from evidence that merely is consistent with it. "I shot a bear from behind a tree, and in case you don't believe me, there's the tree I stood behind when I shot him." The proponent of this argument is correct in one

respect: The tree is consistent with his story. Its existence does not refute the proposition. But it supplies little to justify a belief that he shot a bear.

We sometimes can be overly impressed with physical evidence, and we pay more attention to stories with specific details. The fallacy of consistency uses physical evidence, story enhancement, and neutral detail to "prove" a proposition whose likelihood it does not establish, merely from its failure to refute it.

In fact, every veteran trial lawyer has used this fallacy more than once. An amusing example involves a trial in which the defense lawyer argued that his client couldn't possibly have intended to shoplift when she walked out of the store with that compact disk in her purse; she just forgot to pay for it. He put an evidence tag on the defendant's shoes and introduced them before the jury with a fanfare. The devastating peroration was "Ladies and gentlemen, she obviously didn't plan to commit a crime. She couldn't have run very far in these four-inch high heels!"

(3) *The Inductive Fallacy of Inadequate Sampling.* The "fallacy of inadequate sampling" is the subject of the quotation from Sherlock Holmes that starts this chapter. The great detective said that "premature theories" based on insufficient data were the "bane of [his] profession." Often, we lazily infer a generalization from one or two examples, or else we use a larger sample that is unrepresentative. This is the fallacy of inadequate sampling. Bertrand Russell's chicken fell for it: Instead of surveying the fate of every chicken who ever had lived in the barnyard, but only on the basis of those whose necks hadn't yet been wrung (and indeed, from only one chicken's own idiosyncratic story), the chicken inferred erroneously that the farmer was trustworthy. Similarly, the inexperienced lawyer predicts a windfall from a lawsuit involving a barroom brawl because so many cases in the Torts casebook awarded damages for assaults. The experienced lawyer knows that a bigger sample of real-world assault litigation will involve trivial damages, insolvent defendants, and negative verdicts based on self-defense.

FALLACIES RESULTING FROM BIAS

(1) *The Fallacy of Availability: Flat-Earth Theory.* The "fallacy of availability" is a type of inadequate sampling in which one considers only the data with which one is familiar, or that which is close at hand. "When I look down the street or across all the fields in the countryside I know, everything

I see is flat." Therefore, because of this bias, "I inductively infer that the earth is flat." This reasoning is erroneous because it uses only the simplest evidence, and it ignores observations of seasons, climate, eclipses, and red-shifted sunsets. Thus, the fallacy of availability is a bias that tends to exclude data because it is unfamiliar or difficult to process.

In the law, this fallacy is pervasive. The inexperienced lawyer who hopes for a big verdict from a barroom brawl lawsuit is a victim of it. The cases in the Torts casebook are not typical; they are not supposed to be. They are unusual, by definition, because they are the cases that make new law. By realizing this and by considering how typical cases will differ, the experienced lawyer avoids the fallacy of availability--and avoids taking on most assault cases.

(2) *The Fallacy of Anchoring: The Example of the Ptolemaic Universe.* The "fallacy of anchoring" consists of a failure to adjust one's generalizations to accommodate later-acquired evidence. We cherish our theories, even the ones we build on small initial samples, and thus we are biased against abandoning the wonderful results of our early mental brilliance.

For example, in the Second Century A.D., the Alexandrian astronomer Ptolemy passed down a model of the universe in which the sun and all the other heavenly bodies revolved around a fixed earth, which was at the center of the universe. Unfortunately, planets sometimes backtracked, contrary to the way Ptolemy would have predicted. Nevertheless, into the 1500's, established scientists clung to the Ptolemaic theory and explained this "retrogression" of the planets by postulating "epicycles," or orbits within orbits (and when those didn't fit the observed facts, they invented still another generation of epicycles, or loops within loops within loops). The papal court convicted and punished Galileo for the crime of heresy because he asserted that the earth in fact moves in orbit around the sun. This history demonstrates the power of the bias that can underlie the fallacy of anchoring.

And it happens to lawyers too. A lawyer who has begun the process of advocating a client's position tends to believe that position and, paradoxically, may neglect to investigate all of the possibilities (such as the opponent's version). It takes conscious effort for an advocate to step out of this role and say, "We easily could lose this case. The settlement offer isn't what you want, but it's reasonable. Take it."

(3) *The Fallacy of Anchoring and Pam Tillis's Song About the Queen of Denial.* The speaker in Pam Tillis's song "Queen of Denial," which is quoted at the beginning of this chapter, seems to have fallen for an extreme form of the fallacy of anchoring. She is so unalterably attached to her boyfriend that she projects onto him good qualities that he does not possess. The anchor is the speaker's wishful thinking about "this perfect romance," which persists "even though I saw him dancing last night with a girl in leopard-skin pants" (as the song says in a passage immediately preceding the quoted lines).

(4) *Fallacies Based on Identity of Source or Interest.* The "fallacy of identity" is well known but hard to overcome. "Capital punishment is morally endorsed by the Bible," says the Christian, puzzled by the unpersuasiveness of this argument to a listener who (unbeknownst to the proponent) is an atheist. Or, children playing baseball heatedly discuss whether a batted ball was fair or foul "by a mile," and not coincidentally, members of the batting team are those arguing for "fair." A neighborhood kid who joins the game in mid-argument may even insist on affiliation with a team before opining on the fair-or-foul-by-a-mile question. Such is the fallacy of identity of source or interest. This is why a venire member who is prosecuting a case identical to the plaintiff's should not serve on the jury.

(5) *The Fallacy of Configuration (or Completion): Gestalt Psychology and the Trapezoidal Window.* The "fallacy of configuration" or "completion" can be illustrated by psychological experiments using trapezoidal windows. If shown a multipaned window shaped as an isosceles trapezoid, most people are fooled by it, especially if the distance precludes detailed inspection. The eye reads such an object as a rectangular window tilted away, because its non-parallel sides mimic visual perspective.

Our bias is such that we impose a familiar configuration on the perceptions received from the eye. In other words, we complete the picture with mental imaginings, instead of simply storing the raw data. The same thing happens in the law. We learn about a concept called a "contingent remainder" in the property course, and suddenly, everything looks like a contingent remainder, even executory interests or vested remainders, because they share some of the same aspects of form. This confusion is caused by the fallacy of configuration or completion. This is one of the findings of "Gestalt" psychologists (Gestalt means form, configuration or pattern).

(6) *Bunching or Clumping of Random Data So That They Look Like a Non-Random Pattern: The Configuration Fallacy of the "Losing" Baseball Team.* Here is an example of the fallacy of configuration or completion in a statistical setting. Imagine that a major league baseball team has lost fully eight out of its last ten games. (This happens often to bad teams.) Is this eight-out-of-ten-losing team going to end up at the bottom of the league? Is this a losing team?

Actually, no. The team in question is the 1998 New York Yankees, which set a then-existing American League record for the most games won in a season (114) and went on to sweep the World Series. Some pundits have labeled the '98 Yankees the best team of all time. There was one ten-game period, however, when the '98 Yankees happened to lose eight games.

This kind of statistical record fools people easily. The human mind is an excellent pattern-recognition device, but the problem is, it's so good that it recognizes patterns that aren't there. Statistically, it is not improbable at all for a winning team in a 150-plus-game season to lose eight out of ten at some point, just as a random effect. If you flipped a coin 150 times, the probability is quite high that you would produce a ten-flip sequence, somewhere along the line, with eight or more heads. A random distribution will not produce perfectly alternating heads or tails, except as an extremely rare occurrence, even though many people expect alternation. Instead, the data usually "bunch" or "clump" so that there are strings of heads, or strings of losses even for a winning team. And this data-bunching fools many people. (We shall consider this issue, together with related questions, in later chapters on probabilities and statistics.)

EXAMPLES AND PROBLEMS

(1) *Does Smoking "Cause" Lung Cancer (Is This the "Fallacy of Causation")?* Perhaps the correlation and the mechanism of smoking as a cause of lung cancer are clearly enough established so that it is appropriate to use the word "cause." But lung cancer occurs in some people who never have smoked (and therefore smoking didn't "cause" it for them), and many people who smoke never suffer from lung cancer (and thus it didn't "cause" it for them, either). Perhaps it is more precise to say that smoking "increases the risk" of lung cancer (or that it is "correlated" with it). Is it fallacious to say that smoking "causes" lung cancer, or is this merely plain language?

(2) *How Lawyers Can Fall for the Fallacies of Consistency and Inadequate Sampling: Do High-Power Transmission Lines Cause Disease?* During the early 1990's, people in some local precincts noticed that they suffered highly disproportionate rates of certain cancers. They also observed that they were close to electric transmission lines. Other precincts, further from power lines, reflected lesser rates of the same cancers.

With great fanfare, high-profile personal injury lawyers filed suits throughout the country against firms in the power transmission business. But a few years later, they quietly dismissed these cases, because the reasoning upon which they were based was fallacious.[2] Can you see why, by considering both the fallacy of consistency and the fallacy of inadequate sampling? (This problem is interesting from the perspectives of several different disciplines, and we shall return to the power transmission fallacy in later chapters.)

(3) *Dismissal of Power-Line Lawsuits as a Victory over the Fallacy of Anchoring.*   One can see the quiet dismissal of power-line suits as an overcoming of bias, or as a victory over the fallacy of anchoring. Can you see why?

(4)   *Racial Prejudice, the Fallacy of Availability, and the Law.* Sometimes racial prejudice reflects the fallacy of availability. Can you explain why? Note that opinion polls show that European-Americans and African-Americans subscribe to dramatically different definitions of what "racism" means: whites tend to see it as an intentional kind of wrongdoing, while blacks tend to interpret the word independently of wrongful intent. To African-Americans, "racism" describes a process that produces differential impact on the members of different races, not necessarily just intentional or

---

2   It would be equally wrong, however, to conclude that better reasoning showed that power lines near your home are "safe." In a late-breaking development while this book was being written, the National Institutes of Health formally reported that it could not declare power lines "completely safe." It cited evidence of a possible "weak association" between magnetic-field exposure and leukemia. *See* U.S. News and World Report, June 28, 1999, at 12. This weak association may be weak indeed, because the NIH put power lines in a category with other carcinogen suspects such as automobile exhausts, Asian pickled vegetables and coffee, and it considered it more important to reduce magnetic effects of household appliances. But the moral is, the universe holds secrets to which we simply must admit we do not know all the answers with assurance. Then, in 1999, the British medical journal *The Lancet* published an exhaustive study that included all of that nation's children diagnosed with leukemia in the last four years. The study concluded, once again, that power lines had no effect. Still, scientists from the World Health Organization commented that this was not the hoped-for "definitive" study.

conscious thinking. Does this perceptual difference have anything to do with the fallacy of availability?

(5) *The (Gestalt) Fallacy of Configuration or Completion: Friendly Fire from the F-16.* On April 15, 1999, an American F 16 pilot in the former Yugoslavia, whose mission from NATO was to interdict Yugoslavian military atrocities against ethnic Albanian civilians, "spotted a convoy of three dark green trucks moving from a burning house." He "became convinced the trucks were moving to the next house to set it on fire." These observations were made while the pilot simultaneously monitored anti-aircraft fire, enemy missiles, unfriendly aircraft, and mountains around him, in a heavily vibrating airplane not designed for slow speed. The pilot later explained that he "roll[ed] in on two passes" and used "my targeting pod, IR picture" as well as "my eyeballs." See Houston Chronicle, Friday, April 15, 1999, at 16A.

But after the pilot had destroyed the first truck with a laser-guided bomb (and another pilot had done the same to the second truck), it was learned that the three green trucks carried fleeing civilian refugees, many of whom died. Can you explain this error as an instance of perception bias, or of the fallacy of configuration and completion?

(6) *The Gestalt Fallacy in the Law.* One of the most difficult tasks a lawyer is called upon to perform is to read a dense standard document and tell whether anything is missing. Can you see why this task sometimes can be more error-prone than preparing the document, even if it is a familiar one?

(7) *Law, Public Policy, and the Fallacy of Seeing Patterns in Bunches of Clumped Events: Gun Deaths, Urban Myths, and Inferences From Data About Violence.* People tend to draw inferences about the rate of gun deaths in the United States from incidents reported in the newspapers, using what statisticians call "anecdotal" evidence. The bunching of repeated news reports, then, seems to support the inference that the death rate from guns is increasing. And so, for the year 2000 and beyond, we need a use-a-gun-go-to-jail law, now, more than ever. Right?

Wrong. In 1999, the Centers for Disease Control and Prevention reported that gun deaths had dropped from 15.4 per 100,000 to 12.1 per 100,000 from 1993 to 1999, reaching the lowest rate in 30 years. What do you think makes some people reason erroneously about such matters as the death rate from guns?

§ 2.03 Inquiry, Testing, Refinement, and Heuristics

[A] Inductive Methods: Generalization, Abduction and Retroduction

SUMMATIVE AND PREDICTIVE GENERALIZATIONS

(1) *Returning to Inductive Logic: How Can We Sharpen the Results?* In this section, we consider how we can evaluate our confidence in inductive generalizations. We begin with a simple distinction between "summative" and "predictive" generalizations. Which is due more confidence? We then consider whether the quantity or quality of observations contributes more to confidence. We introduce the term "heuristics," meaning rules of thumb for inquiry or testing. And finally, we consider the ideas of "abduction" and "retroduction" as systematic means for inferring generalizations.

(2) *Distinguishing between Summary and Predictive Generalizations.* Some inductive insights, called "summative" or "summary" inductions, are characterizations of known results in known populations. The objective is not to predict but to summarize. For example, if we test all the children in Mrs. Chenoweth's second-grade class for reading ability, we then can characterize the results with a summary generalization: "Most of the children in Mrs. Chenoweth's second-grade class read at the third-grade level." This generalization does not, however, tell us much that is reliable about similar scores in any given second-grade class at a different school. A "predictive" or "ampliative" generalization, on the other hand, amplifies our knowledge by extending the inference to yet-unknown events. "From many past observations, I predict that the sun will rise in the east tomorrow."

(3) *Is There Really a Difference in the Use or Reliability of Summary and Predictive Generalizations?* Imagine a national opinion poll showing that the President has a 55% approval rating. Is this likely to be a summary induction or a predictive one? The answer is that it partakes of both: It summarizes opinion data, and it predicts the President's leadership ability in the near future. The terms "summative" and "predictive" do help us test the validity of generalizations in the uses to which we put them, but they are only approximate labels.

Which type is more reliable? Summary generalizations are based entirely on known events, and therefore it might seem that they are more likely to be accurate. But this depends on the correctness of the sampling, observation, measurement, and expression that underlie the generalization. Some predictive generalizations merit high confidence, such as the forecast of an eastern sunrise. Therefore, summary isn't better; predictive isn't better; only better is better. Still, the distinction between summary and predictive induction helps remind you of the factors upon which reliable conclusions depend.

INDUCTIVE HEURISTICS: ENUMERATION OR VARIATION?

(1) *Heuristics: Inquiry or Testing.* The term "heuristics" means simply "inquiry" or "testing." A heuristic method (or, simply, a "heuristic") is a device for asking questions, as opposed to constructive logic that builds propositions. After a chain of deductions, if we lack complete confidence in the result, we test it by heuristic techniques. Or, a heuristic may point the way to new deductions or inductions.

(2) *Enumerative or Variative Heuristics.* Is confidence in an inductive generalization strengthened more by the sheer number of consistent observations, or by observations under differing conditions? There is a long-standing debate about this issue. The former is called the "enumerative" heuristic (lots of observations), the latter the "variative" (observations in varying circumstances).

Sir Francis Bacon endorsed the variative method, calling enumeration "childish," and so did John Stuart Mill, who railed against "unscientific enquirers" who "rely too much on number." But some modern logicians have emphasized enumerative confirmation, at least to the point that repetition can sometimes be more valuable than changed conditions. Here, we shall examine the uses of both, without choosing sides.

(3) *Enumerative Heuristics: The Calendar Problem.* Imagine that we pick five dates from a calendar, at random. Our results: September 29, June 5, February 15, March 12 and December 21. We begin to form a hypothesis: There is no such date as New Year's Day. Our calendar does not contain a January 1, or at least that is the initial inference from these (limited) data. We then proceed to test this dubious hypothesis by many more observations, then by still more. Sooner or later, we will succeed in falsifying this no-

New-Years-Day hypothesis, even if it takes thousands of random drawings, because sooner or later we'll draw January 1.

Would variative heuristics speed the process? Perhaps not: If we were to change conditions by performing this experiment in Hong Kong, or by drawing calendar dates in an airplane at thirty thousand feet, or at a time when the moon is in Capricorn, the odds of randomly picking January 1 would remain stubbornly unaltered, at 364 to one. Of course, if we were to concentrate all our random drawings in the month of January, this variation would improve our odds, but we would be unlikely to hit upon such an idea unless we already had detected the source of the falsehood. In this case, trying to determine whether January 1 exists, enumeration would be better, unless you happened to know in advance exactly what you were looking for.

(4) *Variative Heuristics: The Water-Boiling Problem.* But sometimes, variation is better. Imagine that we want to determine the boiling point of water, and so we perform an experiment in New York City. The result: The pot boils at exactly 100 degrees Centigrade. If we repeat the experiment a thousand times, we still obtain identical results. But then we vary the conditions. We boil water in Denver, the mile-high city, and presto! It boils at a lesser temperature, slightly below 100 degrees. We have falsified our initial hypothesis (formed by enumeration), that water always boils at 100 degrees, and we probably would have been unable to do so without the heuristic of variation.

(5) *A Refined Hypothesis: Water Boils at 100 °C, but Only in a Standard Atmosphere.* From these experiments, we can refine our hypothesis: The 100 degree boiling point is valid, but it depends on altitude (or standard pressure). We can verify this hypothesis by boiling water in Hong Kong, in London, and in Denver in a hyperbaric chamber pressurized at one atmosphere.

But then, we can falsify the refined hypothesis by varying the conditions in another way: Superoxygenated water boils below 100 degrees, even at standard pressure, and so we need to refine the hypothesis further. This process of inquiry can continue endlessly, because there are no stable hypotheses; there only are those that have been refined to the point that today's heuristics will allow.

ABDUCTION AND RETRODUCTION:
FINDING THE MECHANISM

(1) *Mechanism: An Explanatory Theory Consistent with an Inductive Generalization.* One way to inquire further into a generalization is to hypothesize a "mechanism" that shows how it works. For example, our observations of sunrise in the east justify more predictive confidence if we couple them with the theory that the earth's rotation is the mechanism. We then can test the mechanism-hypothesis by varied observations. For example, we can travel north of the Arctic Circle and observe the apparent trajectory of the midnight sun, or we can correlate our observations of the orbiting moon. (Even this mechanism of the rotating earth can be falsified by the different lengths of days and nights in different seasons, forcing us to refine it by postulating that the earth's axis is tilted.)

(2) *Testable Mechanisms as Part of the Scientific Method.* This methodology, which couples testable generalizations with testable mechanisms, provides a powerful means of justifying confidence in our inductions. Paradoxically, the mechanism also provides a powerful heuristic for falsifying the induction and refining it. We shall return to this idea in a later chapter on scientific method.

(3) *Abduction: C.S. Peirce's Term for the Process of Generating Hypothetical Mechanisms.* The philosopher Charles Sanders Peirce distinguished "quantitative" generalizations, or those that characterize statistical observations ("the sun has risen in the east for the last 1000 days"), from "qualitative" induction, which gives us the explanation or mechanism ("these sunrise observations are consistent with an earth that rotates").

Actually, this process of hypothesizing mechanisms (or "qualitative" inductions)--which Peirce labelled "abduction," to differentiate it from deduction and induction--is more complicated, because usually we must generate a series of competing hypotheses. Abductively, we might hypothesize that the sun is a chariot driven by an extraterrestrial named Apollo, as the ancients did. Or, as politically correct scientists did through the time of Galileo, our abduction might be that the sun revolves around a fixed earth. Such hypothesis-generation is useful (provided we don't exclude falsification), because it facilitates further inquiry.

(4) *What Does All of This Have to Do with the Law?* In the law, proof is done by an evidential hypothesis. "The reason this defendant fled from the scene is that he had a consciousness of guilt." Abduction of mechanisms figures heavily into the Evidence course in law school; in fact, it is important whenever we search for the policy underlying the law. And below, we shall consider enumeration, variation, abduction, and retroduction in the legal contexts of first-impression appeals, and in laws targeted at child abuse.

(5) *Retroduction: The Elimination of Falsified Hypotheses.* Abduction is complemented by a process that Peirce called "retroduction," the one-by-one testing of abductive mechanisms. Take the example of water boiling at less than 100 degrees in Denver. Abduction might result in a blizzard of unrelated hypotheses: Hypothesis 1, that the lower Denver boiling point is related to the high nearby concentration of environmental gold and silver in Colorado; hypothesis 2, that the lower boiling point is related to the presence of a high-profile professional football team, the Denver Broncos; etc.

But we promptly can falsify both of these mechanisms by boiling water in Tibet, where there is neither excess gold nor football. This is the process that Peirce called retroduction. Sooner or later, we stumble on a better hypothesis: The mechanism is the equalization of air and vapor pressure, which occurs at lower temperatures in higher altitudes.

(6) *Infinite Mechanisms and the Shortness of Life.* Theoretically, the abduction-retroduction process could take forever, particularly if we have to test even absurd mechanisms (like the hypothesis that the Denver Broncos lower the boiling point of water). But C.S. Peirce was an optimist. In fact, he waxed positively mystical, observing that humans have an "animal instinct" for generating useful hypotheses. "[T]he human mind is akin to truth, in that in a finite number of guesses it will light upon the correct hypothesis." Otherwise, abduction would be useless, because we never could eliminate all possible false hypotheses through retroduction.

EXAMPLES AND PROBLEMS

(1) *Enumerative and Variative Testing: A Problem Involving The Decision of a Novel Question by a State Supreme Court.* Let us imagine that the Colorado Supreme Court is considering a case that never has arisen in Colorado before. It is a difficult case, and the Colorado justices send their

law clerks to the library with instructions to find every similar case decided by any other state supreme court.

It turns out that the same issue has arisen repeatedly in Virginia. There is a series of eight (8) Virginia Supreme Court decisions that are squarely on point, announcing a rule of decision that the Colorado justices could apply directly to resolve the case before them. But there also are other decisions (one each) by eight other state supreme courts in Alaska, Delaware, Florida, Montana, Pennsylvania, New Jersey, Texas, and Wyoming, all setting forth different rules of decision, all squarely applicable to the Colorado case.

Now, the Court is faced with a problem of enumerative versus variative testing. The Colorado justices could reason enumeratively, considering all sixteen cases to be of equal persuasiveness. Or they could use the variative method, giving greater weight to the eight that are spread through the United States (or, for that matter, to the eight Virginia ones, which reflect treatments of different fact situations within the same court). What can be said for and against each method, enumerative and variative, here?

(2) *Public Policy and Child Abuse Heuristics: The (Hypothetical) Observation That Nonpaternal Males Are More Likely to Abuse Male Children.* Child abuse is a stubborn problem of public policy, one that the law has struggled to address. We understand the mechanisms of child abuse only imperfectly. For example, imagine that examination of voluminous hospital records produces the tentative induction that, nationwide, male children who are abused by men are far more likely to be abused by men who are not their fathers. This appears to be a summative induction. But can it also be used as a predictive one?

Further, this induction appears to rest on enumerative foundations (the "voluminous" hospital data). But perhaps the hospital records are skewed, reflecting disproportionate numbers of poor families. Can you see ways in which we might verify or refine the induction through variative heuristics?

(3) *Public Policy and Child-Abuse Heuristics, Continued: The Mechanism of Our Hypothesized Nonpaternal Child Abuse, as Developed by Abduction and Retroduction.* Notice that the mere quantitative induction of nonpaternal male-on-male child abuse is helpful by itself, provided it is sufficiently reliable when used predictively. We can reduce child abuse by such policies as alerting women, at least after the first signs of abuse, to the

perceived danger of unquestioned reliance on live-in boyfriends as babysitters for their boys.

But we might do better if we could infer a mechanism by abduction and retroduction: that is, by explaining why men might abuse male children who are not theirs. We begin with abduction of several hypothetical mechanisms: H1, that women who are separated from their children's fathers disproportionately may tend to find attractive precisely those kinds of men whose characteristics include disposition toward abuse of boys; H2, that live-in boyfriends resent the time and attention that women spend on their children instead of on the boyfriends, etc. Can you, through abduction, generate some other (possibly more promising) hypotheses, and can you suggest methods of retroduction that would identify the best ones?

(4) *Was Peirce's Optimism (and Near-Mysticism) about the Quality of Abduction Justified?: Inferences about Mechanisms in Science--and in the Law.* Maybe the reason humans are good at abduction isn't "animal instinct" but rather our use of analogy. Water vapor has something in common with air, and both vary in their characteristics according to pressure. Can you see how analogy rather than instinct might be the mechanism for our hypothesizing atmospheric pressure more readily than the Denver Broncos as the better abduction for Denver's different boiling point?

On the other hand, perhaps humans are not as good at this game as Peirce suggested. In the Sixteenth Century, people still believed that the sun revolved around a fixed earth in spite of massive data to the contrary, and they abducted complex orbits-within-orbits to confirm their false hypothesis. Why does this sort of fallacy occur?

As for legal rules, they are heavily dependent on abduction and retroduction, whether they are made by courts or legislatures. They reflect guesses about how human beings can best be induced to behave properly; i.e., they depend on hypotheses about the mechanism of peoples' motivations and about changes that can be produced by legal intervention. But unfortunately, the guesses of courts and legislatures often prove to be wrong, so that overruling of past decisions frequently is necessary. In *Plessy v. Ferguson*, 163 U.S. 537 (1896), the Supreme Court held that segregated facilities did not cast any implication of inferiority upon members of minority races. Later, of course, the Court dramatically reversed this inference in *Brown v.*

Board of Education, 347 U.S. 483 (1954). Does this example cast doubt on Peirce's optimism about people's "animal instinct" for correct abduction?

[B]   Holistic Approaches: Dialectics and Story Theory

THESIS, ANTITHESIS, DIALECTICAL SYNTHESIS, AND STORY THEORY

(1) *Holistic Approaches.* In previous sections, we have studied step-by-step logic, the kind that builds from premises to conclusion or from observation to generalization. In this section, we consider the opposite approach: looking at the logic as a whole. Dialectics, or competition among conclusions, and story theory, or evaluation of overall consistency, are two very different kinds of holistic approaches.

(2) *Dialectics and the Law: The Competitive Method.* One method of inquiry and testing, called "dialectics," is simply to debate the idea. The ancients used this method extensively, particularly in a variation that was a teaching technique (the Socratic dialogue). The concept is that competition calls forth, reciprocally, the best justifications of one's own theory, as well as the best criticisms of the opponent's. Dialectic is well known to the law. A murder trial is a dialectic, and in a different way, so is a real estate deal negotiated by a buyer and seller.

In the dialectical method, a proponent's theory, called a "thesis," competes with the opponent's "antithesis," from which observers form a refined hypothesis, called a "synthesis." The synthesis need not be an equal combination of the two; the thesis may be highly persuasive, requiring incorporation of only minor elements from the antithesis to produce a more refined theory, or, for that matter, the synthesis may result from total or near-total destruction of the thesis, leading to its rejection. The jury may convict the defendant of manslaughter by accepting pieces of both the prosecution's case and the defendant's.

(3) *Story Theory: Narratives, Rather Than Syllogisms.* Another method of testing is "story theory," which is what its name implies: the recounting of an event by narration, which gives a more complete rendition than any particular deductions from it. For example, consider what is known as "critical race theory," or the hypothesis that an oppressive white society uses ostensibly neutral but actually racist rules to dominate people of color.

Proponents of critical race theory have used story methods extensively in support of their thesis. Their idea is that no single generalization conveys what a narrative, or story, can demonstrate about prejudice and subordination. Another example of story theory is the frequent use of parables in the Bible and in other Scriptures.

(4) *The "Smell Test" in Law Practice: Using Story Theory to Demonstrate Factual or Ethical Fallacy.* One of the best methods for determining testimonial falsehood is to consider the coherence of the story. If a suspect charged with burglary were to explain his presence at two o'clock in the morning inside a locked building, while he was wearing gloves and standing at the cash register, by claiming that he simply wandered in off the street because he needed to use the bathroom, we would reject the story in its totality. "It just doesn't smell right." We probably would not pause to consider inductive generalizations about cash registers or gloves or to apply them deductively to the evidence. Instead, we would reach our conclusion simply because the defendant's story is spectacularly lacking in narrative coherence when compared to the alternative inference (that he is a burglar). (Criminal defense lawyers sometimes refer to this familiar story as the "wee wee defense," and they recognize its limitations.)

An alternate use of the smell test is as a check upon ethical or legal deductions. A loan officer for a mortgage company, whose debtor is an impoverished widow, considers foreclosure on her home and proposes an expeditious method that depends on the widow's lack of sophistication. More experienced mortgage officers reject the proposal on the ground that, although all of the proponent's deductive steps "sound" individually correct, taken together, the plan "doesn't pass the smell test." It "smells" unethical, contradicts the image the company seeks to publicize, and might even trigger a lawsuit for fraud or related violations.

EXAMPLES AND PROBLEMS

(1) *Scientific Theories and Legal Trials as Dialects or Debate.* When two different schools of scientists propose antithetical theories, the result tends to be dialectical. Thus, proponents of the Ptolemaic universe (sun orbits earth) marshalled observations and evidence to fend off supporters of the Copernican universe (earth orbits sun). They appealed to, and were assisted by, the papal courts, which convicted and punished Copernicans for heresy.

Likewise, an American criminal or civil trial is dialectic. Thus, O.J. Simpson was acquitted because, given the two competing theories of the case, the jury selected the option of not guilty. What do these examples show about the usefulness, or the limitations, of dialectics?

(2) *"A Syllogism Is Not a Story": The Supreme Court's Decision in the Case of Old Chief v. United States*, 117 U.S. 664 (1997). A criminal lawyer sometimes may seek to stipulate to certain elements in a charged crime as a means for arguing about the exclusion of embarrassing evidence related to the stipulated issues. For example, if a defendant is charged with possession of LSD with intent to distribute, the defense attorney may deny possession by this defendant, but agree to stipulate that whoever possessed this particular LSD must have had the intent to distribute it. The lawyer's objective is to exclude evidence of quantity--perhaps there were ten thousand (10,000) individual doses or "hits" found on the defendant's premises--and thus to prevent the jury from knowing anything more than that there was some quantity of LSD on the defendant's premises (although the defendant does not admit to having possessed it). Thus, the defendant is able to argue the best defense, but hopes to exclude all evidence about the 10,000 doses.

In *United States v. Old Chief*, the Supreme Court rejected this defensive tactic (except in certain special circumstances). The Court reasoned that a jury has "expectations" that it will hear testimony from witnesses rather than hearing the entire proof of some elements through brief agreements between lawyers. The prosecution has the burden of proving all elements of the crime to the jury's satisfaction beyond a reasonable doubt, and it therefore has a strong interest in providing "evidentiary depth" to the jury even on issues that the defense might prefer to stipulate.

The *Old Chief* Court added this pithy epigram: "A syllogism is not a story." What does the Supreme Court's reasoning say about story theory? (Is a story "better" than a syllogism, at least in some instances?)

§ 2.04 Epistemology and the Limits of Logic: From Poetry to Humor to Faith

[A]   Epistemology and Metaphysics

WHAT DO WE REALLY "KNOW" (IF ANYTHING), AND
WHAT IS THE NATURE OF THE THINGS WE KNOW ABOUT?

(1) *Knowing What "Ain't So."* "The problem isn't what people know," to paraphrase Mark Twain. "It's what they think they know that ain't so." Centuries ago, people "knew" that the sun orbited the earth. Even earlier, they "knew" the flat earth was traversed by a sun about the size of one of the Greek islands. And within the last decade, some people "knew" that high-power transmission lines caused cancer. Today, informed opinion says that none of these propositions is provable. But . . . how can we "know" this? For that matter, how can we really know anything?

(2) *Epistemology: From Skepticism to "Cogito Ergo Sum."* "Epistemology" is the philosophy of knowledge. How can we derive knowledge or verify it? One extreme position is called "skepticism": We know nothing. Our seeming perceptions of the universe may simply be a dream; moreover, we ourselves may not even exist, but rather we may cavort as cartoons in the imagination of some larger consciousness (or even as illusions in the absence of any material or mental existence). This is why Rene Descartes famously asserted, "Cogito ergo sum" ("I reason, therefore I exist"). This was a powerful reply to the skeptics. Thinking implied that something, at least, exists, even if it is only mental; if I doubt that I think, even that doubt is thinking, and so, I exist.

But does the "cogito" argument actually hold up? The committed skeptic would reply, "No, you only think that you think, and your appearance of thinking may be an illusion too." Refuting this position is not easy!

(3) *Alternatives to Pure Skepticism: Coherence, Empiricism and Rationalism.* Although skepticism is a useful reminder that all knowledge is uncertain, skeptics cannot take us very far. Most people still believe that there are principles to which we can ascribe some probabilities of truth. For example, the most doctrinaire skeptic might refrain from jumping off the Empire State Building, even though convinced that the law of gravity cannot be definitively established.

Therefore, philosophers have developed other epistemologies. "Coherence theory" holds that a system of logic need not be externally verifiable, but only must exhibit internal consistency to qualify as knowledge. The symbolic logic contained in an earlier chapter meets this coherence test because it "hangs together" (even if the skeptic can postulate a parallel universe where it might not hold true). Then, there are the "empiricists": All knowledge is derived from observation or experience. There are no pre-existing (or "a priori") principles that can be derived from reason; we derive everything from experience ("a posteriori"). Empiricists sometimes have been called "positivists."

Finally, "rationalists" believe that some knowledge is a priori, or derived from reason, independently of empiricism. Rationalists differ from empiricists in that they believe that reasoning can produce knowledge even without observation or empiricism.

(4) *Law and Epistemology: Coherence, Empiricism, and Rationalism.* We use coherence theory heavily in the law. The legal doctrines of Vermont may be different from those of Wyoming, but still, we study whether the decisions in each state are systemically "consistent" with each other and with the state's statutes. Thus, we sometimes may remain selectively skeptical, at least with respect to which state's policy is better (that's a political question, not a legal one).

Empiricism has an influential position in the law. The "logical positivists," as they are called, saw actual court decisions as the law itself, not just as evidence of the law; they rejected reliance on black-letter rules. This is an empiricist or positivist position. Finally, legal philosophers who advance a "natural law" viewpoint often argue that inherent rights and duties can be derived by reason, and this is a rationalist philosophy. We shall consider these ideas in greater depth below, in the Chapter on Jurisprudence.

(5) *Metaphysics.* "Metaphysics" is a branch of philosophy whose purpose is to determine the true nature of things. It differs subtly from epistemology, which attempts to determine what we know, in that the inquiry of metaphysics is to determine the structure, meaning or workings of whatever exists. Both claim to be the most "fundamental" or "comprehensive" bodies of knowledge, and often a given problem can be taken up by philosophers of both labels.

EXAMPLES AND PROBLEMS

(1) *Distinguishing the Views of Subscribers to Skepticism, Empiricism, Rationalism and Coherence Theory.* Imagine four philosophers who hold the

views that the truth of valid syllogisms is established, respectively, by (a) "our derivation of them through reasoning"; (b) "our observation that they always have held true"; (c) "our ability to fit them consistently within larger logical systems"; or (d) "nothing" (or in other words, "no reasoning or observations that humans can offer can verify syllogisms"). Which is the rationalist, the empiricist, the coherence theorist, and the skeptic?

(2) *St. Anselm's Ontological Attempts to Prove the Existence of God.* During the Middle Ages, one of the great efforts of philosophy was to prove the existence of God. St. Anselm's proof in the 11th Century, later known as the "ontological" proof, used an a priori method. "That than which nothing greater can be imagined," said St. Anselm, "must necessarily exist in fact and not merely in imagination." This was so, he explained, because *if* this "greatest thing" existed "only in imagination," something greater could be imagined, namely, the same thing existing "in fact." God is "that than which nothing greater can be" imagined, and therefore God necessarily must exist "in fact."

This is a rationalist argument (can you see why?). However, a skeptic would have little trouble refuting it, and even in the Middle Ages few philosophical theologians actually articulated it. Can you see the flaw (is it true that the greatest thing you can imagine must necessarily exist in fact)?

(3) *Thomistic Proofs of the Existence of God.* In the 13th Century, St. Thomas Aquinas offered this reasoning to prove the existence of God: (1) Since all observed motion has a cause, one must presuppose the existence of a "Prime Mover" to explain the existence of motion in the world, or in other words, one must presuppose God. As a second explanation of the same concept, St. Thomas argued that (2) the material world is contingent and dependent, and to account for its existence, the existence of a Being that is necessary and self-contained must be postulated. The third demonstration in this series of "Thomistic" proofs is that (3) the

St. Thomas Aquinas

world is harmonious and orderly, rather than chaotic, and hence, one must presume that a Creator organized it this way.

St. Thomas concluded each of these proofs (which are separate but parallel and intended to reinforce each other) with the words, "and this" [the Prime Mover, the Necessary Being, or the Creator] "is what all men call God." St. Thomas claimed that these were "empirical" proofs. Are they?

(4) *Hume's and Kant's Criticism of the Ontological and Thomistic Proofs.* In the 18th Century, philosophers David Hume and Immanuel Kant critiqued each of these attempted proofs. (The ontological flaw is discussed in note 2 above.) As for the Thomist arguments, Hume and Kant pointed out that they each depend upon inferring a "cause," which in each instance is God. Induction about events on earth may be valid, and even, in a sense, induction about causation, they reasoned. But when the proponent extends the earthly notion of "cause," which is within human experience, to a realm that is wholly outside of that experience, there is no reason to suppose that the same experience holds true. This was one of Hume's and Kant's skeptical criticisms of the Thomistic proofs. Is it valid?

[B] The Limits of Logic: Humor, Choice, Nonsense, and Faith

CHOICE, HUMOR AND NONSENSE

(1) *The Logic (?) of Nonsense.* The silly limericks of Edward Lear are examples of our taste for nonsense. So are the works of Lewis Carroll, with his delusional world in *Alice in Wonderland* and his made-up words in the poem *Jabberwocky*. At least in some contexts, such as these literary works of nonsense, it is clear that we humans enjoy vicarious experiences that break the rules.

But notice that although Lear's and Carroll's works may be "nonsensical," they are not "illogical." If *Jabberwocky* were a random string of guttural syllables unrelated to each other, it wouldn't be interesting, even as nonsense. Actually, *Jabberwocky* carefully follows the logic of language and poetry. *Alice in Wonderland* incorporates adventure-story logic and, furthermore, it fits the existentialist philosopher's vision of the great-but-ordinary person coping with and eventually overcoming a chaotic environment.

Perhaps this correspondence of nonsense with logic is not surprising. Carroll, who perhaps was our greatest writer of nonsense, also was one of the prominent logicians of his day. He studied, diagrammed and explained syllogisms. And so--logic and nonsense are related.

(2) *The Logic of Humor.* A joke, like a syllogism, is a logical construct. The setup of a joke contains two meanings or story lines in the same words, one obvious and one hidden. Then, the punch line departs from the obvious story line with an incongruous surprise, but one that has been there all along, because it is consistent with the hidden story.

For example, consider the (admittedly old and shopworn) joke that asks, "Did you hear about the rich Texan who took up golf, but he wasn't sure he'd like it, and so he only bought three clubs?" With these words, the story line deliberately nurtures an impression of a duffer too tentative to pay for more than a putter, a driver and perhaps a 7-iron. But then comes the surprise, in the punch line: "The clubs he bought were Lakeside, Golfcrest and the River Oaks Country Club."

The more dramatic the logical shift, the better the joke, and yet, the outcome must have been buried there all along (remember, our novice golfer was also a "rich Texan"). Comedians, then, need to be good logicians!

(3) Humor in the Law: The Mountain Man's Pancakes (Or, "In the Law, It Doesn't Even Have to Be Very Funny"). Sometimes humor can make a silly legal rule seem more sensible. Humor in front of a judge or jury can work too (provided it is carefully chosen). Imagine this: the defense lawyer, addressing the jurors for the first time, needs to counter the strong impression left by the prosecutor's opening. And so the defender begins with a (weak) joke: "This case reminds me of the story about the old mountain man who made pancakes every morning. And he used watery pancake mix. But he always said, 'No matter how thin I make 'em, there's always two sides!'" Now, this humor isn't very funny, but the point is, it doesn't have to be. It will draw broad smiles from the jurors. In the law, a little bit of on-point humor sometimes goes a long way; it can make the illogical more acceptable.

(4) *Choices, Impulse Purchases, and Variety--and When to Indulge in Them, in Law and in Life.* Occasionally, we come across someone who dithers with purportedly logical reasoning when making an inconsequential choice. "Nope. Not strawberry. Had that yesterday. But still, I like

strawberry. Maybe instead of considering what I had yesterday I ought to just get what I like. Let's see. . . ." The extreme of this indecisive behavior is associated with obsessive-compulsive personality disorder, in which preoccupation with orderliness obscures the point of the activity and decisionmaking becomes impaired.

Logic must give way to a certain sphere for random choices and for variety. It is a paradox: The person who is self-disciplined sometimes must exercise the self-discipline not to exercise self-discipline. But the key word, here, is "sometimes": An impulse purchase of strawberry over chocolate may be healthy, but the impulse purchase of a car, for most people, is not. It is important, and harder for some people than it sounds, to distinguish the two cases and to adjust one's behavior accordingly.

In the law, this dilemma is pervasive. In negotiating the purchase and sale of a valuable building, you encounter a blizzard of issues. You have to ignore some of them. But you have to focus on the important ones. It isn't always easy. And, of course, the lawyer on the other side will be trying to persuade you that the important issues really are inconsequential.

EXAMPLES AND PROBLEMS

(1) *What Is the Logic behind the Appeal of Magicians, Illusionists, and Too-Clever Lawyers?* The magician pulls a rabbit out of a hat through sleight of hand, saws an assistant in half by using a special apparatus, and makes an elephant disappear with smoke and mirrors. As reasoning beings, why do we happily sit through a show of this kind, when we know it all is illusion? [Occasionally, a lawyer can exploit this same human predilection. The jury knows the lawyer is a manipulator, but forgives this fact because the lawyer is charming--and talented at manipulation.]

(2) *Skeptics May Deny the Proof of Faith, But They Also Must Deny Its Disproof; So Where Does This Leave Us?* In modern times, religious philosophers have made sophisticated attempts to revive both the ontological and Thomistic proofs of God. Skeptics, of course, have responded with sophisticated refutations. Some people accept the skeptics' proposition that the ontological and Thomistic arguments about God are not "proofs," but they still regard these arguments as providing weighty evidence short of absolute proof.

Still other theologians have deemphasized logical proofs, regarding reason and faith as consistent but differently derived. Perhaps the skeptics' message was misunderstood in earlier centuries: Human inability to prove God exists does not prove the converse.

(3) *The Car Salesman (and the Negotiating Lawyer).* You have just finished test driving a beautiful red Pennoyer-Neff Scorpion convertible that costs about double the uppermost price that you thought of before coming to the showroom. "Just picture yourself tooling down the Harbor Freeway with the top down on this baby," the car salesman grins. "That Bose system's pumping out Beethoven or Garth Brooks, with your honey there beside you." He has a pen in his hand. "Now, which is the best financing plan for you?" See whether you can describe the car salesman's tactic and explain why it works.

Do you suppose an opposing lawyer will ever use this method with you during negotiations, to get you to agree to a continuance, a stipulation, or a contractual warranty?

PART II

Economics, Finance, and Markets

Chapter 3
Economics I

Prices, Markets, Economic Efficiency, and the Law

> *"It is not from the benevolence of the butcher, the brewer, or the baker, that we expect our dinner . . . . [Each] intends only his own gain, and he is . . . led by an invisible hand to promote an end which was no part of his intention."--Adam Smith, An Inquiry into the Nature and Causes of the Wealth of Nations*

> *"There is nothing more dangerous than to build a society, with a large segment of people in that society who feel that they have no stake in it; who feel that they have nothing to lose."-- Martin Luther King, Jr.*

§ 3.01 What This Chapter Is About

ECONOMICS, PRICES, MARKETS, AND EFFICIENCY

(1) *Basic Microeconomics: The Price System, Competitive Markets, and the Law.* The subject of economics is related to the logic of deduction and

induction covered in the previous first chapters in several ways. For example, the relationships among supply, demand and prices can be established empirically, through induction. From this induction, numerous other relationships can be established deductively. However, our emphasis here is not upon logic for its own sake, but on demonstrating economic relationships and their impact upon the law. Today, thinking people must be able to understand market economics both in reasoning about public policy and in making personal decisions, and there is a highly influential "Law and Economics" movement.

Modern economics began to take shape centuries ago. Adam Smith showed how the "invisible hand" of the market coordinated economic activity more efficiently than any rule or law or government program ever could. In this chapter, we consider such issues as supply and demand, "marginal cost," "marginal utility," "factors of production," and various measures of economic efficiency, all under the assumption of a competitive market without "externalities." These are issues usually dealt with in the subject called "microeconomics." We also take up "macroeconomics," as a counterpart to microeconomics.

The chapter will help you to understand the economic arguments that support our law of contracts, negligence, product liability, and the like. Even when it has been justified in rigorously formal terms, the common law usually has coincided remarkably well with economics.

(2) *The Tradeoff between Economic Efficiency and Distributive Justice (Equality).* But we shall see that there is an inherent problem in this kind of reasoning. The quotation from Adam Smith shows that a market system brings about economic efficiency in a remarkable, almost magical way. But it will not necessarily produce a fair and just distribution of wealth. The result may be a divided society in which a few wealthy "haves" uneasily confront masses of disaffected "have nots." The quotation from Martin Luther King describes this danger. How to reconcile this difficulty is a constant problem of law and public policy.

(3) *The Next Chapter: Market Imperfections and the Law.* As is indicated, this chapter deals with competitive markets, without imperfections. However, there are no truly perfect markets, and in the next chapter, we shall consider the limits of the theory that this chapter explores, including tradeoffs and legal interventions.

§ 3.02 The Market System and Its Alternatives

[A]   Markets, Equilibrium, and the Price System

THE EQUILIBRIUM PRICE IN A COMPETITIVE MARKET: SUPPLY AND DEMAND

(1) *The Concept of Perfect Competition.* A "perfectly competitive market" is one with so many firms that none has any control over prices and in which all produce an undifferentiated product. This situation sometimes is referred to as "atomistic competition." A familiar example is agricultural products, such as wheat or corn, of which even the largest firm produces only a tiny fraction of the supply.

(2) *The Efficiencies of Prices in a Market System with Perfect Competition: Avoidance of Intervention by the Law.* A market system, in which prices are not set by government or by law, exhibits a number of advantages when there is perfect competition. A economist would say that such a market has several different kinds of "efficiencies." For example, we shall see later in these materials that a perfectly competitive market causes firms to produce an efficient mix of goods and services (the mix that consumers' dollars overall would select), with efficient use of resources. It also distributes them efficiently.   The widely shared conclusion of economists, including both those who would self-describe as either conservatives or liberals, is that the law generally should not intervene in the setting of prices by a competitive market.

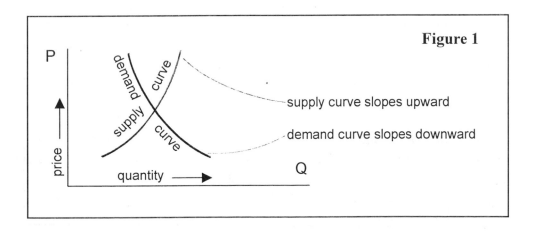

Figure 1

P

demand curve

supply curve

demand curve

supply curve slopes upward

demand curve slopes downward

price

quantity

Q

(3) *Supply and Demand Curves.* Figure 1 is a graph containing a hypothetical supply curve, as it is called. It is marked "supply curve." Let us say that this is the supply curve for the widget market, although it could be any product or service. It graphs the quantity, "Q," of widgets that firms in the widget industry are willing to produce at any given price, "P." The vertical axis in this graph is the price, P; the horizontal axis is the quantity, Q, that firms are willing to supply at a given price.

Notice that the supply curve slants upward in the relevant part of the graph. This is so because, at higher prices, firms are willing and able to produce more widgets than at lower prices.

The other curve is the "demand curve." This curve graphs the quantity Q of widgets that consumers will buy at any given price P. Unlike the supply curve, the demand curve slopes downward, because consumers will buy more quantity, Q, if price, P, is lower.

(4) *The Law of Supply and Demand and the Equilibrium Price.* We now are ready to consider the principle that sometimes is called the "law of supply and demand." This "law" is a naturally observed phenomenon in markets that approximate perfect competition. Remember that the supply curve slopes upward, because firms are willing to supply greater quantity at higher prices, while the demand curve slopes downward because consumers will buy greater quantities at lower prices. The point at which the two curves cross is called the "equilibrium price" and is crucial to a market system.

(5) *The Equilibrium Price.* Figure 2 shows the significance of the

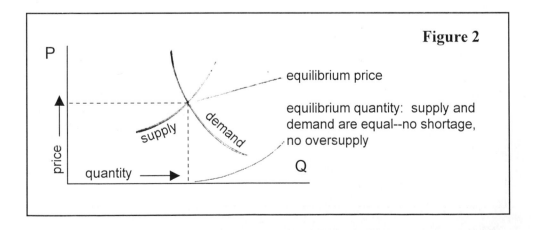

Figure 2

P

equilibrium price

equilibrium quantity: supply and demand are equal--no shortage, no oversupply

supply

demand

price

quantity

Q

"equilibrium price" and the corresponding equilibrium quantity. The equilibrium price is determined by the point at which the supply curve and demand curve cross. At this point, in a perfectly competitive market, widget firms are producing exactly the quantity, Q, of widgets that customers want to buy, no more and no less. There is no scarcity. There is no waste, either. Thus, the price system efficiently allocates the society's resources to produce widgets.

(6) *The Equilibrium Price and the Law of Contracts.* We can begin, now, to see why the common law of contracts is economically sound. A system in which each firm is free to make its own contracts, and can expect them to be enforced, will result in a price that approximates equilibrium.

THE "INVISIBLE HAND": MARKET ALLOCATION AS OPPOSED TO A CENTRALLY PLANNED, COMMAND ECONOMY

(1) *The Alternative of a Centrally Planned Economy: Making Production Decisions by Politics or by Law.* Theoretically, another way for a society to address supply and demand is to use central planning. In the not-too-distant past, several countries have used this system generally, as an alternative to markets, but few do so today. We therefore consider central planning, here, only as a means of explaining the market system, or as a contrast. The idea is not to scold or lambaste central planners, because that would be a bit tendentious. Few intellectuals even attempt today to substitute law or politics for markets in making production decisions. But the best way to appreciate markets, perhaps, is to consider the opposite approach of using law to decide how resources are allocated.

In a centrally planned economy, government officials would figure out quantities of all possible commodities that they think the society may need, from washing machines to rubber bands to television game shows, and they would instruct publicly operated firms to produce them. This was the method used by the former Soviet Union. Indeed, every nation still has at least some limited aspects of its economy that are centrally planned; in the United States, most highway systems as well as public educational services are allocated this way.

(2) *Inefficiencies of Central Planning: Law and Economics.* The most obvious difficulty with a centrally planned system would be that it would

depend on the ability of planners to accurately gauge the tastes and needs of consumers, as well as to understand all intermediate steps necessary to satisfy those desires. Worse yet, the system would be vulnerable to political influence. If the steel-plant manager happened to be an adept, powerful apparatchik, central planners might be persuaded to divert resources into excess steel production, away from more useful purposes, just so that the steel manager could run a bigger factory.

And there would be subtler difficulties: Central planners might not be innovative, and they might simply order the same old products rather than spurring invention of new ones. Ultimately, it might be necessary to allocate products among consumers by command (i.e., by law), rather than to allow consumers to make choices.

(3) *The "Invisible Hand" of the Marketplace: More Efficient Allocation?* But if central planning doesn't match quantities with our wants and needs, who will? The answer, in a competitive market, is everyone--and no one. The market, itself, does it.

If we consider the equilibrium price analysis of the previous section, and if we extend it not just to the widget industry but to every other product and service from washing machines to rubber bands to television game shows, we find that there is an allocation mechanism for all of them. The market, at

least if it approximates perfect competition, will pressure suppliers as well as consumers toward the equilibrium price and quantity for every commodity, and this is the price at which consumers want exactly the quantity that suppliers supply. Both scarcity and oversupply are minimized.

The great eighteenth-century economist Adam Smith elegantly described this feature of the market as an "invisible hand" directing the economy. The result is a system that is more efficient, in several respects,

Adam Smith

than central planning: in allocation, in production, in distribution, and in innovation.

(4) *One-and-a-Half Cheers for the Market: What Role Remains for the Law?* Many of the founders of the United States were enthusiastic scholars of the ideas generated by Adam Smith and his predecessors, and they repeatedly praised competitive markets as they ratified our Constitution. Today, we still favor markets more than most societies, and free enterprise ranks with apple pie as an American value.

But don't get too enthusiastic yet. In later sections, we shall consider the limits and dysfunctions of the marketplace. For now, suffice it to say that the market will not supply subsistence to a disabled person who cannot work, nor will it, alone, reduce accidents or air pollution, prevent recessions, adequately produce public goods such as national defense, or for that matter, prevent the ravages of consumers' bad taste. And remember, the theory in this chapter applies only to perfectly competitive markets. At some point, even the most ardent defender of unregulated markets will be forced to admit that there is a role for intervention by the law.

DYNAMIC MARKETS AND THE
EFFECTS OF PRICE CONTROLS

(1) *The Signaling Effect of Prices.* Let us imagine that widgets suddenly are in short supply. Either there has been an unexpected increase in demand for widgets (perhaps teenagers have discovered that widgets are "cool"), or supply is harder to come by (perhaps raw materials are scarce because of weather). The previous equilibrium price now no longer fits. Consumers, now, want to buy more than suppliers want to produce.

What will happen? Some consumers will pay more than the historically established price, and soon they bid up the price to higher levels. And now, what do suppliers do? The higher price motivates them to produce more. They take on new employees and buy more machines. This is the "signaling function" of the price system. It tells consumers that they must sacrifice more to buy a scarce item, thus lowering demand, and it tells producers that they will be rewarded for producing more of the item, thus increasing supply.

(2) *The Incentive for Price Controls.* Imagine, however, that consumers react with collective anger at what they see as "price gouging." The commodity may be an essential one: oil and gas during a worldwide boycott,

or medical services, or foodstuffs. (A peculiar, and yet familiar, example occurs when a store owner charges "market prices" for flashlights and candles in the aftermath of a hurricane.) Consumers watch in frustration as a few producers earn "excess profits" while threatening the consumers' own way of life. They complain to their elected representatives and ask for price controls.

(3) *The Effects of a Law Imposing Price Controls: Frustration of the Market's Signaling Function.* Figure 3 shows the effects of these price controls when the market actually is perfectly competitive. The government passes a law to regulate the price of (let us say) gasoline, at a level below what would be the equilibrium price, in order to "protect" consumers and prevent oil companies from collecting "windfall profits." (The United States government did exactly this in the late 1970's and early 1980's.) Point "C" is the controlled price, lower than equilibrium.

Notice that, at this controlled price, supply and demand do not match. Gasoline producers are not willing to produce as much; they scurry to lay off inexperienced workers and postpone buying additional machinery because their revenues won't justify paying for these factors of production. The signaling function of the price doesn't work.

(4) *Price Controls, Demand, and Shortage.* And that is not all: The demand side is affected too. Notice that at price C, because it is lower, consumers want to consume more of the commodity. They drive everywhere instead of using mass transit or carpooling, and in the longer run they want gas guzzlers instead of high-mileage cars. The signaling function is impaired

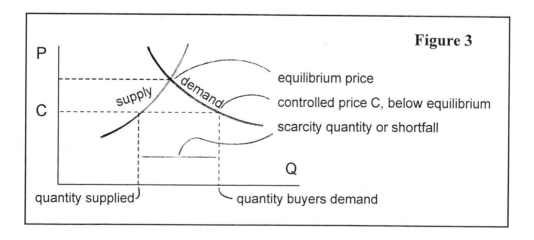

Figure 3

P

equilibrium price

controlled price C, below equilibrium

C

scarcity quantity or shortfall

Q

quantity supplied

quantity buyers demand

for both supply and demand, and the result is a scarcity of millions of gallons, shown on Figure 3 by the bracket labelled "scarcity quantity or shortfall."

Sometimes, on the other hand, government keeps the price higher than equilibrium, rather than lower. Thus, some kinds of commodities are the subject of price supports or of regulated minimum prices. This kind of intervention, instead of creating shortages, tends to motivate producers to enter the market or increase production beyond the level of demand, leading to oversupply. Either way, the signaling function of a competitive market is frustrated.

(5) *The Disadvantages of Nonprice Allocation under Price Controls: Statutory Commands.* In the face of scarcity, many consumers will want to pay premium prices rather than curtail their use of gasoline. But price controls make such a transaction illegal. Some consumers will simply violate the law, paying extra amounts "under the table" in black market purchases. Some suppliers will favor longstanding past consumers--or the brightness of the smile the customer flashes at the gas pump will determine the lucky recipient.

The government may respond by passing a statute outlawing "discrimination" (as indeed the government did with scores of thousands of gasoline stations in the '70's and '80's), but this law will be difficult to enforce. In fact, since some consumers who are long-distance commuters will want or need more gasoline than others, a law fixing everyone's allocation at the same amount, and prohibiting any deviation as "discriminatory," is inherently unstable. Ultimately, this regime will require a detailed, intrusive command society, a network of laws and bureaucracy, to enforce allocations among consumers.

(6) *How Does All of This Relate to the Law?* Hundreds of legal rules are affected by these considerations. Should a court refuse to enforce a price escalation term tying the contract to market price on the ground that it is unconscionable or against public policy? Courts have faced precisely this question on occasion, and they have consulted economic reasoning to decide. Every time we change the rules about contract enforcement, breach, or damages, we need to consider the resulting effects on the price system and the market.

CONSUMER SOVEREIGNTY AND WEALTH EFFECTS

(1) *Continuing Controversies over Legal Controls in the Event of Gouging or Windfall Profits.* For these reasons, most economists agree that price controls in competitive markets are generally unwise. But remember: we can only give one-and-a-half cheers to the market, because it may not carry out all of the values of our society. There are instances in which price regulation can be justified. One example is monopolistic industries such as some utilities, or industries in which consumer choice might be ineffective to prevent fraud or coercion, such as the market for taxicabs. Remember, we assume perfect markets in this chapter.

Beyond that, some people would argue that the government should intervene to prevent excess profits from concentrating wealth in a few persons, especially if the commodity is essential, the wealth transfer is large, or the scarcity is artificial. This argument, however, is controversial, because if we use price controls to prevent a few people from becoming wealthy, we will frustrate the price signaling system for everyone. A law controlling gasoline prices (or those for health care, electricity, etc.) may have desirable wealth distribution effects in the minds of some people, but these effects have to be balanced against the shortages that the law will cause.

(2) *Consumer Sovereignty through "Dollar Votes" in a Market System: Power to the People.* A market system with unregulated prices means that consumers make choices rather than laws or governments. Every consumer has his or her number of "dollar votes," or so the theory goes, and these dollar votes ultimately motivate firms to produce that mix of goods and services that the consumers, collectively, want to use their dollars to select. Alternative political systems have used the phrase, "power to the people," but market enthusiasts argue that politicians who accept this principle should get out of the way and let the unregulated market work, because the price system produces consumer sovereignty--the ultimate in power to the people. (Or so the argument goes.)

(3) *The Limits of Consumer Sovereignty: Rich People and Bad Taste?* But again, this notion is controversial for some kinds of products, because dollar votes are not like those in the political system, where votes are distributed among individuals according to notions of political equality. Instead, dollar votes in the marketplace are allocated more heavily to those who have more dollars. Should rich people determine the allocation of

lifesaving organ transplants, for example? Should their dollar votes pay organ donors?

And a more subtle argument concerns the unwisdom of some consumer choices. The marketplace inundates consumers with what some people think is trash, because others desire it: television's Jerry Springer Show, cop-killer rap, and pink plastic flamingoes used as lawn ornaments. In most instances, we tolerate these instances of bad taste because we believe government intervention would have worse consequences, or even that it is morally wrong. But there are limits: A forest of pink flamingoes may prompt neighbors to seek zoning laws to keep the offending sight from affecting them, and government policies may limit the ability of a welfare parent to spend everything on muscatel instead of baby food.

EXAMPLES AND PROBLEMS

(1) *School Vouchers: A Current Controversy in the Law.* As an alternative to government-managed schools, some economists and politicians have proposed a statutory voucher system. In recognition of the fact that education is (at least to some extent) a public good, the government still would allocate a dollar amount for each child--perhaps an amount equal to current per-pupil expenditures. But government would not spend the money or choose the school. Instead, it would transfer the funds in the form of vouchers to individual parents, who then would choose their own schools. Families would be free to add additional amounts of their own money if they chose more expensive schools.

Explain how the theory of prices and markets supports this (currently controversial) idea favoring school vouchers. Then, since the market cannot satisfy all societal values, explain the arguments that voucher opponents might use, and evaluate the two arguments.

(2) *Taxicab Fare Regulation by Law--Price Competition?* Imagine that the taxicab market in Capital City is perfectly competitive. If anyone happens to be unsatisfied with the price, cleanliness, or other qualities of a particular cab, the consumer immediately can choose from any of a large number of other cabs lined up at cab stands on every corner. Furthermore, assume that all consumers are sophisticated about taxicabs, and they completely understand all fares and routes. Explain the argument that, in such a situation, Capital City should remove price controls and leave fares

unregulated. Explain, also, the considerations that might persuade a real-world Capital City (where the market for taxicabs might not be so nearly perfect) to keep its fare regulation laws in place.

(3) *The Efficiency of Enforcing Contracts as Written.* Absent fraud, illegality or other unusual circumstances, the hornbook law is that the courts will enforce the parties' contract. To put the matter another way, a court usually tries to avoid rewriting a contract by law, to suit the court's own economic preferences. This principle of the common law is economically efficient, even though it usually is justified in formal terms rather than by economic arguments. See whether you can explain why the common law of contracts is economically efficient, considering (a) consumer sovereignty, (b) supply by firms, and (c) equilibrium prices.

[B]   Marginal Cost, Marginal Utility, and Factors of Production: The Components of the Supply and Demand Curves

MARGINAL COST, MARGINAL UTILITY, AND THE LAW

(1) *Marginal Cost: The Cost of Producing One More Unit of the Commodity.* Now that we have examined supply and demand, we turn to another, closely related subject: namely, the components that lie behind the supply and demand curves. One of the fundamental concepts in market economics is "marginal cost." Marginal cost is defined as the cost of producing just one more unit. The first widget that a new firm produces is very expensive, reflecting start-up costs, but the second unit costs less; and

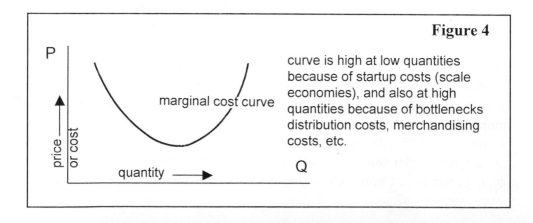

Figure 4

P

marginal cost curve

curve is high at low quantities because of startup costs (scale economies), and also at high quantities because of bottlenecks distribution costs, merchandising costs, etc.

price or cost

quantity ⟶

Q

for a time, the marginal cost falls with each additional unit. This effect is called "economies of scale." But then, at some point, costs for additional units go up. The firm runs out of efficient factory space, uses older machinery, pays overtime to workers, and has to advertise and merchandise more to sell more units.

(2) *The Marginal Cost Curve for a Typical Firm.* Figure 4 shows the marginal cost curve for a firm in the widget industry. Again, Price, P, is the vertical axis, and Quantity, Q, is the horizontal axis. As we have said, the curve is high at low quantities, because per-unit costs are high; it then slopes downward, as per-unit costs decrease; and then it rises again, as bottlenecks, merchandising costs, and the like increase the firm's per-unit cost.

(3) *Factors of Production: Their Marginal Costs as Components of the Firm's Marginal Cost.* A farmer uses land, labor, fertilizer, machinery, management, and entrepreneurship to produce wheat or corn. Each of these items is called a "factor of production." The sum of the marginal costs of all factors of production is the firm's marginal cost. The firm is motivated to reduce these costs to their lowest level for any given level of production. If fertilizer costs increase, for example, the farmer will shift to using less of it and will increase the use of other factors such as land or labor.

(4) *Marginal Productivity: The Usefulness of One More Unit of a Factor of Production.* We must also consider the concept of "marginal productivity." This is the usefulness of one more unit of a factor of production. For example, adding fertilizer has utility for producing crops. At medium levels, the marginal productivity, or dollarwise usefulness of one more unit of fertilizer, is high. But after a large number of pounds per acre, the marginal productivity of adding more fertilizer declines. (This principle sometimes is called "the law of diminishing returns.") The farmer will not add fertilizer beyond the point where its usefulness equals its cost--or, in economic terms, where its marginal cost equals its marginal productivity.

(5) *The Efficiency of Contract Law: Revisiting the Issue.* We now have new reasons to appreciate the efficiency of the common law. If a court were to rewrite the parties' contract, it would need to consider how the changed contract fit with marginal costs for the firm and industry. Theoretically, the court should also fit the changed contact to marginal productivity. It would need to do all of this at the same time that other factors of production fluctuated in price and thus changed the calculations, and while competitive

firms in the same industry continued to bid the price up or down. A solitary trial judge who is not an economist, not even familiar with the industry, cannot hope to juggle all of it. But--the market can!

§ 3.03 Economic Efficiency

[A]   Economic Efficiency in Production and Consumption

MARGINAL COST AND PRODUCTION EFFICIENCY

(1) *Efficiencies of the Market System in Production: Marginal Cost Curves, Supply Curves, and Marginal Utilities of Factors of Production.* We now are ready to consider the effects of perfectly competitive markets on production efficiencies. We can draw several remarkable conclusions. All of these conclusions can be demonstrated mathematically (and interested readers easily can find sources that contain the proofs), but here, we shall explore them verbally.

(2) *Profit Maximization Motivates a Firm to Choose the Mix of Factors of Production that Minimizes Its Overall Marginal Cost.* The farmer uses the mix of fertilizer, land, labor, management effort and entrepreneurship that produces a given quantity at the lowest marginal cost. Similarly, a widget factory uses an efficient mix of capital, labor, etc. Profit maximization within the market system motivates each firm to act in this way, minimizing marginal cost by using factors of production efficiently.

(3) *The Marginal Cost of a Factor of Production Tends to Equal Its Marginal Productivity.* As the farmer chooses among land, fertilizer and other factors, she decides how much of each to use by considering its usefulness in production against its cost. If the marginal productivity of fertilizer is higher than its marginal cost, she uses more of it, increasingly, up to the point where its marginal cost does not exceed its marginal productivity (because she does not want to pay more for it than it will return in production). Thus, the marginal cost of a factor of production tends to equal its marginal productivity. This is so because each firm is motivated to employ factors of production efficiently, up to the point where the cost of each factor counterbalances its productivity.

(4) *The Firm Attempts to Produce at That Level Where Its Marginal Cost Equals Its Marginal Revenue.* As long as each dollar of production cost

brings in more revenue than one dollar, the firm tends to produce more. It is willing to pay for more units of production until precisely that point where its marginal cost equals, but does not exceed, the price it receives for the last unit it produces (called its "marginal revenue"). Thus, each firm naturally desires, and therefore attempts, to produce at the output where marginal cost just equals, but does not exceed, marginal revenue.[1]

(5) *The Firm's Marginal Cost Curve in a Competitive Market Tends to Equal Its Supply Curve, if All Costs are Included.* Remember that marginal cost includes management cost and entrepreneurship cost (or profit). If we add up the marginal costs of all factors, they produce the firm's overall marginal cost curve. In a perfectly competitive market, each firm's supply curve equals its marginal cost curve[2] (remember, a normal profit must be included in marginal cost).

(6) *The Price System Tends to Induce Each Firm to Produce at Its Most Efficient Level and to Use the Most Efficient Mix of Factors of Production.* In a perfect market, the invisible hand of the market, through the mechanisms of marginal cost, marginal utility, and marginal revenue, creates these different kinds of efficiency, all without government intervention.

(7) *If We Cumulate the Curves of All Firms within an Entire Industry, We Obtain an Industry-Wide Supply Curve, with the Same Underlying Efficiencies as for an Individual Firm.* If we treat all the firms in an industry cumulatively as if they were one firm based in numerous centers, we get a picture of the entire industry, whether it be the wheat, the steel or the widget industry. For the entire industry, marginal cost (including normal profit) tends to equal marginal revenue, and the industry supply curve tends to fit the cumulative marginal revenue curve for all firms. Thus the price system motivates every individual firm, and indeed the entire industry, to operate efficiently.

---

1   Each firm will tend to approximate this result in a dynamic market. In long-run equilibrium, price approaches minimum average cost. Average cost equals total cost divided by output (or quantity). A plot of average cost against quantity is a U-shaped curve, just as marginal cost is, and minimum average cost is the lowest point of the U. Thus, in a competitive market in the long run, with a generic product and no dynamic effects, every firm is a price taker, every firm must be efficient, and every firm is forced toward the lowest cost--which is the lowest average cost, or the cost per unit that is lowest for the firm. (This footnote is included for technical accuracy, and if it doesn't make sense, don't worry.)

2   That is, it equals the ascending portion of the curve, where quantity is greater than for the minimum MC on the curve. However, if price increases, the theory predicts that more firms will enter the market, and price will return to equilibrium.

EXAMPLES AND PROBLEMS

(1) *How to Make a Business Decision about How Much to Spend in Your Own Law Practice.* Imagine that you have just acquired a building that you intend to use for your law practice. It is somewhat run down, and you conclude that if you spend a little money to improve it, your modest repairs will produce much more in fees than they will cost. Knowing this, you decide to fix the place up. But you know that if you spend an excessive amount on your new building, you won't get your money back--you'll lose money on those higher expenses. Therefore, the first question you face is, just how much should you spend?

The answer is, you should spend an amount up to and including that point where you expect that the last dollar spent on improvements in the facilities for your law practice will produce at least one dollar in additional revenue (or fees). Can you explain this conclusion?

(2) *Another Law Practice Decision: Where Do You Make Expenditures (on Which Factors of Production)?* In improving your rundown law office building, you have a number of choices: You can paint the exterior, replace the floor, set up a library, insert gold-plated fixtures, or do any of a variety of other things. How do you decide which? [The suggested answer: You should consider expending on each one up to that amount, if any, such that its marginal cost equals its marginal productivity, but not beyond that amount. Can you explain this conclusion?]

(3) *Applying This Reasoning to a Lawsuit: Decisions about Discovery, Experts, Jury Simulations, Etc.* One important issue that usually does not emerge from the cases in your casebooks is that prosecuting or defending a lawsuit is shaped by economic efficiency. In a modest-sized lawsuit, you can use only a limited number of processes, and today, a $100,000 dispute is a modest-sized one, with real cost pressures restricting every step an attorney makes. Do you file a motion for summary judgment, knowing that it has only a 20% change of success and will cost $15,000 to prepare and present? Do you take two depositions, or ten? Do you settle for $50,000 when you might (or might not) recover $100,000 (or zero)?

Describe how the economically efficient attorney would make these decisions, using the production-decision principles we just have finished studying. Consider marginal cost, marginal productivity, and marginal revenue.

(4) *Common Law Damages: Efficient Breach of Contract.* The common law rule is that punitive damages are not recoverable for a breach of contract, even an intentional breach (no matter how deliberate), and even though the breaching party by definition has breached a promise. Economically, there is such a thing as "efficient breach of contract," however odd that concept might sound in moral terms. Imagine that performance will impose enormous costs and losses on one party because of unplanned events, and it will provide only negligible benefit to the promisee. Can you explain the efficiency of the common law rule against punitive damages in this situation, using reasoning about factors of production and marginal cost/productivity?

CONSUMER UTILITY AND EFFICIENCY

(1) *Marginal Utility Applies to Consumers Just as Marginal Productivity Does to Producers.* When a consumer surveys all the products and services in the marketplace, the consumer decides whether to buy a unit of each by considering its usefulness in satisfying that individual's wants or needs. The satisfaction that each additional unit of a given commodity will produce, whether it be more square feet of housing, a porterhouse steak, or a video game, is the "marginal utility" of that commodity. Marginal utility is to the consumer as marginal productivity is to the producer; in fact, the concept is the same, because the marginal utility of a product unit to a consumer can be thought of as its marginal productivity in terms of consumer satisfaction. Marginal utility often depends upon the quantity of the item the consumer already has; if a person already has one basic-transportation Chevrolet automobile, it is unlikely that she will derive much more satisfaction or marginal utility from a second, third, tenth or hundredth identical Chevrolet.

(2) *Efficiency and Consumer Choice.* Consumers therefore tend to purchase items according to the balance of each items' marginal utility and its cost. For the same reason that producers use efficient mixes of factors of production, consumers tend to act so that the marginal utility of each unit of purchase equals the marginal utility of each other unit of purchase. To put it another way, a fully sophisticated consumer in a market economy is able to purchase precisely that mix of goods and services that produces the most satisfaction of that individual's wants and needs, within the limits of his or her budget.

EFFICIENT INNOVATION, PRODUCTION VOLUME, AND INVESTMENT

(1) *Innovation, Growth and the "Production Possibility Frontier."* The market is efficient in still other ways. Although the precise reasoning is beyond our scope here, the market system tends toward that mix of innovation versus stability that consumers overall would choose. It tends, also, to induce firms cumulatively to produce at the "production possibility frontier." This is an economic term that means the most that is attainable, given existing resources and technology and the mix of goods and services desired.

(2) *Present and Future: Consumption versus Investment.* Further, the market tends to induce efficiency in the mix of present consumption versus investment for the future. A student with a small nest egg needs to decide whether to continue straight ahead in getting an education or whether to buy a sailboat and travel around the world for a year. There is no need for a law or a government agency to tell the student what to do: The balance of costs and utilities, both present and future, will determine the choice.

(3) *Implications for Intellectual Property Law.* In order to ensure that innovation is paid according to its marginal productivity, we create rights in intellectual property. The resulting monopoly or quasi-monopoly has implications for efficiency in that it impairs atomistic competition in the patented or copyrighted good. Just how far should the protection of these rights extend? Efficiency questions about intellectual property call for careful balancing.

[B]   Distributional Efficiency: Pareto Optimality and Kaldor-Hicks Efficiency

THE CONCEPTS OF PARETO OPTIMALITY AND KALDOR-HICKS EFFICIENCY

(1) *Pareto Optimality: When All Beneficial Trades Have Been Made.* Next, we consider efficiencies in distribution among consumers. A "Pareto optimal" distribution is one in which no consumer can benefit from any voluntary trade with another. In other words, all trades that can increase utility already have been made. (This concept is named after Vilfredo Pareto,

an Italian economist who developed it.) If consumer A has two widgets but no thingamabobs and would prefer one of each, while consumer B has no widgets but two thingamabobs and also would prefer one of each, the distribution is not Pareto-optimal. The two consumers can produce a "Pareto-superior" distribution if A trades B a widget for a thingamabob.

Notice that a Pareto optimal distribution is not necessarily "fair" or "just," but only "efficient." If there is another consumer, C, who has nothing, neither widgets nor thingamabobs, Pareto optimality does not ensure that C gets anything. (Remember, the market can't solve all of our problems.)

(2) *How the Market Tends toward Pareto-Optimal Efficiency.* Pareto optimality is one measure of the distributional efficiency of an economic system. A perfectly competitive market tends toward this kind of efficiency, in that each consumer selects those goods and services that this individual wants, to the extent of his or her resources. Note, again, that Pareto optimality is a limited measure of efficiency. It deals only with trades that could increase utility, and it is not concerned with equality in the distribution of wealth.

(3) *Kaldor-Hicks Efficiency.* Sometimes, even though an exchange leaves some individuals worse off, it still may arguably be "efficient" to make the exchange if the total gain by those who gain exceeds the total losses of those who are disadvantaged. This is the concept of "Kaldor-Hicks" efficiency. In fact, such an exchange results in a Pareto-superior distribution, provided only that the winners compensate the losers for their losses.

Sometimes, compensation for a Kaldor-Hicks-efficient transaction is possible. For example, the Fifth Amendment to the Constitution requires "just compensation" whenever a majority of the people benefit themselves by taking private property for an exchanged "public use." But sometimes compensation is not practical because winners and losers are diffuse and the differences are small in amount. Our political system sometimes supports such an exchange and leaves the losses where they fall.

EXAMPLES AND PROBLEMS

(1) *How the Market Approximates Pareto Optimality, without Intervention by the Law.* Pareto optimality exists when all mutually

beneficial trades have been made among consumers. But the market tends to approximate Pareto optimality even without any actual trades between consumers themselves. In fact, markets for direct barter between consumers in the United States are insignificant in size compared to the general economy. Still, the market in which consumers buy from firms tends toward Pareto-optimal efficiency, using money as a medium of exchange. Can you explain why? Remember that each consumer buys goods by balancing marginal cost and marginal utility.

(2) *Law and Subsidies as Increasing Efficiency: The Factory that Has Lawfully Reduced Pollution, but Not as Much as Townspeople Want.* Imagine that a factory, under the law, is required to reduce its pollution to 100 pounds of effluent per month. To reduce that amount even further, to 50 pounds, would require an additional expenditure of $100,000, which the factory owner has no internal incentive to undertake. But assume that reduction to 50 pounds would be worth $500,000 to townspeople. The existing distribution is Pareto-optimal, but does Kaldor-Hicks efficiency explain why the townspeople might provide a subsidy of $100,000 in pollution control expense?

(3) *Contract Damages under the Law and Kaldor-Hicks Efficiency.* We considered the common law of contracts in the previous section, above. Breach of contract sometimes can be efficient, particularly if performance is costly and benefit is negligible. In this situation, the law allows the promissor to breach deliberately without punitive damages, so long as the promissor pays the promisee's damages. This common law rule can be justified in terms of Kaldor-Hicks efficiency. Can you see how?

[C]   Inconsistencies between Efficiency and Equality

EQUALITY VERSUS EFFICIENCY: THE TRADEOFF
AND THE LAW

(1)   *Economic Efficiency and Equality.* Notice that one arguable deficiency of the marketplace is that it does not tend to produce distributive equality. Consider individuals who control valuable factors of production, or who are themselves factors of production, such as skilled Fortune 500 CEO's or 20-game-winning pitchers in major league baseball. If these individuals are paid according to their marginal productivity, they will amass

more wealth than others. This result is tolerable up to a point, especially since it is associated with various kinds of efficiencies. Many people believe, however, that a grossly unequal society, with a few fabulously wealthy individuals and many desperately poor people, is unjust.

(2) *Wealth Redistribution by Law and Its Inconsistency with Economic Efficiency.* Given a sufficiently severe inequality, some citizens will vote for laws that will redistribute wealth, even if there is some loss in efficiency. Exactly where the line is drawn, where wealth disparity becomes so great that it justifies statutes favoring redistribution and the resulting interference with efficiency, is a political judgment to be made by each individual and ultimately by the society in a body politic.

(3) *Mechanisms of Wealth Redistribution through the Law.* In fact, the United States uses several means of redistribution. One example is the graduated income tax, by reason of which people with high incomes pay higher proportions of their earnings (or at least that is the theory). Notice that graduations in the tax arguably increase the resulting economic inefficiencies, because marginal revenues of high wage earners are depressed and do not correspond to their marginal productivities. Nevertheless, voters may consider that the tradeoff is worth it. (In fact, any tax on income, or on any commodity or service, artificially lowers its marginal utility or marginal productivity, whether the tax is graduated or not, and thus lowers efficiency. Can you see why?)

EXAMPLES AND PROBLEMS

(1) *What Legal Reforms Would You Consider if You Were Hugo Chavez, the Elected President of Venezuela, a Nation He Describes as a Society "Broken" Between Rich and Poor?* Hugo Chavez, President of Venezuela, described that country in 1999 as "broken in pieces." It was divided between "a small part of Venezuelans who have everything" and "a large majority who barely receive a drop to survive on."

What sorts of legal reforms might you consider if you occupied President Chavez's position? You would have to engage in a balancing act, because if your policies preserve the existing wealth distribution, then crime, rebellion, repeated coup attempts, and other civil disorders will foster an unstable society that may endanger everyone, including even the wealthy. But if your policies include efforts to redistribute wealth by taxation, transfer payments, or nationalization, they may impair economic efficiency so severely that they will destroy Venezuela's existing economy, aggravating both poverty and instability. How, then, do you proceed? (This problem raises issues not only of economics, but also of ethics and politics, which we shall consider in later chapters.)

(2) *Scarce Necessities as an Occasion for Laws that Redistribute Wealth.* Sometimes it happens that prices of scarce necessities are higher than those that poorer members of the population can privately afford (e.g., medical services, electricity, or elementary education). First, how should the society decide when wealth distribution should be addressed in this situation, and second, how should it set the level of redistribution or subsidy?

(3) *In-Kind or Unrestricted Subsidies: Which Should the Lawmakers Choose?* Should the law be written to provide these subsidies in-kind, as in the case of public education, food stamps, or Medicare? Or should it provide support with relatively unrestricted dollars, as in the case of welfare transfer payments like Aid to Families with Dependent Children? Or should there be a mix of both?

(4) *Redistribution by Price Controls as Compared to Tax-and-Transfer Systems.* Sometimes across-the-board price controls on fuel, health care or the like are justified on the ground that poor persons cannot afford these necessities. One can argue, however, that the alternative of general taxation that produces revenues for a system of transfer payments to the poor is more efficient, because it redistributes without distorting the signaling function of prices. Explain the economics that might support this argument, and also, explain the opposing arguments of those who might prefer price controls.

(5) *Does the Issue Lie Solely in Eradicating Severe Poverty, Or Does It Also Include Breaking up Enormous Fortunes?: The Estate Tax.* Some people believe that the upper end of the population (billionaires) is not the problem. They reason that the issue is whether there are individuals in severe poverty, rather than how wealthy some other people are. On the other hand, Americans sometimes have regarded enormous fortunes themselves as an evil to be combated by the law, even apart from poverty; for example, the estate tax, upon property passed down at death, historically has been justified not only as a revenue measure but as an alleged means of breaking up

concentrated economic power. Can you explain both of these opposing positions?

(6) *At Some Point, When the Wealth Gap Becomes Extreme, Doesn't Efficiency Depend on Passing Laws That Redress Inequality? Martin Luther King, Jr.'s View.* The quotation from Martin Luther King, Jr. at the beginning of this chapter suggests that it is "dangerous" to build a society in which a large segment feels "that they have no stake in it; . . . that they have nothing to lose." This disaffection also may lead to inefficiency, obviously. Wealthy people will experience these inefficiencies right along with poor people as they live behind barricades, worry about confiscation, lose confidence in investment, and find fewer available goods and services. There are many real-world examples. As of the time of

Martin Luther King, Jr.

this writing, for instance, squatters have taken over large sections of privately-owned land in Zimbabwe with the approval of the government, which advocates redistribution. The result is economic chaos. Thus, there is a paradox: insistence on laws mandating equality by wealth distribution will impair efficiency because redistribution distorts the market, but ignoring equality impairs efficiency too. Can you explain and reconcile this seeming contradiction?

§ 3.04 Macroeconomics: The Influence of the Larger Economy

MACROECONOMIC GOALS: GROWTH, EMPLOYMENT, AND STABILITY

(1) *Macroeconomics Compared to Microeconomics.* Up to this point, this chapter has concerned "microeconomics": the behavior of firms and consumers in the marketplace. Now, we shall introduce (although not in depth) what is called "macroeconomics": the behavior of the economy as a whole. Macroeconomic effects also influence markets. For example, the market for new home construction may experience severe dislocations during

a nationwide recession. Tax policy depends heavily on macroeconomic concerns, and so does regulation of international trade.

Actually, economists today are probably more occupied with studying macroeconomics--the economics of the entire economy--than with microeconomics, the study of firms within markets. There seems to be more "action," and perhaps more mystery today, in examining the effects of an intervention by the Federal Reserve Board, or of a recession in Indonesia and its ramifications for the North American economy, than there is in considering how markets affect particular prices and individual firms. Our coverage here, however, has placed greater emphasis on microeconomics, and it will treat macroeconomics briefly. Therefore, this coverage does not necessarily conform to the emphasis placed by expert economists. There are several reasons for this seeming discrepancy. First, macroeconomics tends to be more complex, and its mastery requires a thorough understanding of microeconomics.   Second, for the average lawyer a greater increase in reasoning ability for practical problems probably results from understanding microeconomics. But macroeconomics affects individuals' choices too, and therefore, we need to consider it.

(2) *The Three Competing Macroeconomic Goals: Growth, Full Employment, and Stability.* Unlike perfectly competitive markets, the macroeconomy is generally regarded as requiring governmental management. This management has several independent and sometimes conflicting goals, of which the most important are growth, full employment, and price stability. First, many market sectors depend on growth in the gross domestic product (GDP), and so does economic improvement. Second, stable prices (with limited inflation) are a key element of steady growth, because predictability is essential to capital markets. Third, a low rate of unemployment also is a macroeconomic goal, both for its own sake (for its distributional effects) and for its contribution to growth.

These goals are interrelated, and to some extent they compete with one another. Low unemployment, for example, tends to create inflationary pressures, because it produces labor shortages, which drive up prices. The compromise that a government makes among these sometimes inconsistent goals is one of the most sensitive issues of public policy that a society faces.

(3) *Measuring the Goals: GDP, CPI, and Unemployment.* What are our goals for employment? Some economists have considered approximately 4% to 5½% unemployment (the exact figure varies) as "full" employment, because there always are unemployed people between jobs due to job or market adjustments, and because very low unemployment aggravates inflationary pressures. As for inflation, classically, inflation under 3%, as measured by the consumer price index (CPI), has been the goal. Growth is measured by changes in the "gross domestic product" (GDP), or the total market value of goods and services newly produced domestically during the year.[3]

(4) *Macroeconomic Tools Provided by the Law: Monetary Policy and Fiscal Policy.* "Monetary policy" is government regulation that influences the supply of money and credit, under a system of statutes. The Federal Reserve System and its Board of Governors are dominant players in monetary policy. Restriction of credit, for example, may reduce inflation; an increased credit supply fuels growth and employment, but it may create inflationary pressures. "Fiscal policy" is effectuated by the respective levels of government spending and taxation. Higher spending and lower taxation are inflationary, although they may tend to stimulate growth and employment.

Although many people regard fiscal policy (government spending and taxation policy) as the more important and more difficult component, both components, fiscal and monetary, are essential. It is possible, through coordination of the two kinds of policy, to produce steady growth with low unemployment and low inflation, as the United States experienced in the latter 1990's.

EXAMPLES AND PROBLEMS

(1) *Are the GDP and the CPI Adequate Measures?* The gross domestic product (GDP) and the consumer price index (CPI) are such precisely defined concepts that they produce some odd results. For example, if you paint your own house and wash your own dishes, the GDP does not increase. But if you

---

3   A slightly different quantity, "gross national product" or GNP, includes foreign effects and hence is more accurate, but the United States, following other countries, recently switched to GDP. The difference between GNP and GDP is small for this country.

hire a painter and a housekeeper, it does. Consider whether the GDP, then, is a good measure of national output. Feminist lawyers often have criticized the GDP as a measure. Can you see why?

Also, the GDP fails to take account of the so-called underground economy, including unreportable and illegal transactions. Should it include these items? Finally, let us imagine that a firm uses a more expensive method of production so that it produces a less harmful environmental impact, and as a result its goods and services are reduced by $1 million--but the cleaner air and water are worth $2 million to the American public. This transaction will result in a $1 million reduction to GDP. Is this measure appropriate?

Similarly, the CPI is made up of a hypothetical "market basket" of consumer goods. Since consumer preferences change continuously, the CPI soon becomes dated, and so perhaps the mix of the basket should change annually. Can you see, however, why it should not?

(2) *A Public Policy Dilemma Involving the Unemployment-Inflation Tradeoff: What Is the Right Approach?* In the late 1970's, with double-digit inflation at a ruinous 12%, the Federal Reserve System slashed monetary growth rates from 8 percent to 5 percent in a two-year span. The rate of inflation declined to 6.2%, but unemployment soared from 6 to amounts on the order of 10 percent. Is such a draconian tradeoff of stability for unemployment "right"? Is it economically defensible, moral, and just?

(3) *Effects of Common Law Rules on Macroeconomic Goals.* A study by the RAND Corporation demonstrated that employment laws in different states produced dramatically different effects on unemployment. Specifically, states that allowed greater damage recovery in lawsuits for wrongful termination tended to have unemployment rates several percentage points higher than they probably would have otherwise. Can you explain why, using the microeconomic concepts of marginal cost and marginal productivity? Furthermore, if these damage rules were adopted nationwide, they ultimately would affect the other macroeconomic goals of growth and stability. Why?

CLASSICAL MACROECONOMICS AND THE
KEYNESIAN REVOLUTION

(1) *The Business Cycle.* Historically, GDP growth has fluctuated between upswings and downswings, or periods of more rapid than average growth and periods of shrinkage, even as overall growth has averaged two to three percent. This fluctuation is called the "business cycle." At times it has shown the regularity of a cycle and at times not.

(2) *The Failure of Early Macroeconomics.* Old-fashioned economics regarded the macroeconomy as similar to a market sector, but bigger and composed of consumers as well as firms. Consumers furnished land, labor and capital to firms, for which they were paid rents, wages and interest, and firms provided goods and services to consumers in exchange for consumer spending. This was the early view: the entire economy was regarded as resembling one big market, with consumer spending and income balanced against business spending and income.

But this simple, two-circled flow failed to explain the business cycle, particularly the Great Depression. The earlier theory predicted that with rising unemployment, wage rates would decrease, increasing firms' demand for labor and reducing unemployment. But as wages dropped during the Great Depression, unemployment actually increased. The old-fashioned theory had failed to account for government policy. For example, lopsided distribution of income, dysfunctional management of credit supply, high tariff barriers that closed foreign markets through retaliation, and budget-balancing by Congress during a severe downswing, all had their influences. The failure of early macroeconomics was in regarding the macroeconomy as just a bigger version of a microeconomic market and thus leaving out the role of laws, of government, and of foreign markets.

John Maynard Keynes

(3) *The Influence of John Maynard Keynes.* During the first half of the 1930's, the English economist John Maynard Keynes evolved his alternative to classical theory. To the simplistic picture of a circular flow between consumers and firms, he added the leakages and injections provided by financial intermediaries, foreign markets, and particularly, government.

Whereas earlier economists had envisioned macroequilibrium only at full employment, because they saw the relation between wages and labor demand as the sole determinant, Keynes postulated infinite equilibria, wherever the sum of leakages and injections balanced out. At that point, GDP = Y_e = C+I+G+F (where Y_e is total spending, C is consumption, I is investment, G is government, and F is foreign markets). [Note: If the equation makes your eyes glaze over, let's do it in words. The gross product is made up of what we consume plus what we have invested but not consumed. To this, however, we have to add the production and costs of government and of foreign markets, because both are too big to leave out. This was one of Keynes's insights.]

Keynes's theory changed the classical two-circle flow to something like Figure 5. Government, in short, could even out the business cycle by spending and reducing taxes during recession and following the opposing policies during an upswing. Government wasn't just the tail of the dog, it was *part* of the dog, and when government spent money or took it in taxes, it affected the rest of the macroeconomy. This issue of public policy could be managed so that the effects would be advantageous, or at least, this was the hope.

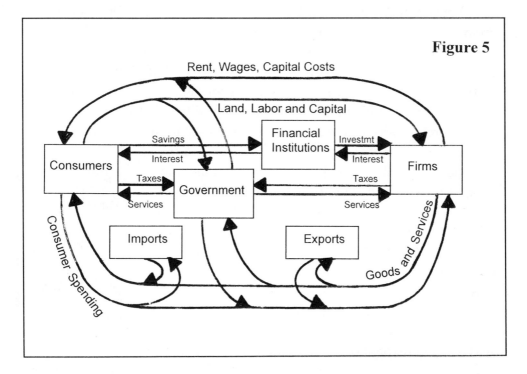

(4)   *Investment, MPC, and the Keynesian Multiplier.*   When the macroeconomy is at equilibrium, an increase in investment has an effect

greater than its absolute amount. Specifically, it is multiplied by what is called "the multiplier," or the "Keynesian multiplier," signified as k. The multiplier, k, is determined by a factor called the "marginal propensity to consume," MPC, which simply reflects the percentage of income that the average person in the economy will spend rather than save. In fact, k = 1/(1-MPC).

(5) *A Contractor Example Demonstrating Why the Multiplier Works.* Imagine that one of your clients, a restaurant, decides to build an addition to its building, costing $100,000. This investment will result in a $100,000 payment to the contractor. The contractor (and subcontractors and suppliers) now have an extra $100,000, which they will spend according to the MPC (marginal propensity to consume). Imagine that the MPC is 0.8, meaning that currently, people spend 80% of their income and save 20%. The contractor (and suppliers), then, will spend $80,000, which enters the income flow and becomes available for a second round of people to spend. They will spend 80% of the $80,000, creating $64,000 in income to still other people. The spending continues to echo through the macroeconomy, producing 80% of $64,000 (or $51,200) in the third round, $40,960 in the fourth round, $32,768 in the fifth round, and so on, indefinitely.

The reverberations of this spending add to the original investment an infinite series, mathematically expressed as [MPCxI + MPCxMPCxI + MPCxMPCxMPCxI...]. Although the mathematical proof is beyond our scope here, this infinite series yields a sum equal to 1/(1-MPC), and hence the Keynesian multiplier, k = 1/(1-MPC).

Thus, the restauranteur's original investment of $100,000, given a marginal propensity to consume, MPC, of 0.8, and given the equation for the multiplier, k = 1/1-0.8 = 5, results in increased total spending and GNP growth of five times (5 times) the original $100,000, or $500,000. Investment has growth effects that far exceed the absolute amount of investment.

(6) *Banking Law and the Money Supply.* Our country has a large apparatus for the regulation of banking, lending, and credit. Many lawyers work in this system. How much in actual resources must a financial institution keep when it lends out its funds? At what rates of interest can or will it lend? These are the questions we shall turn to now.

MONETARY POLICY, THE FEDERAL RESERVE SYSTEM, AND THE LAW

(1) *Money and Credit Markets and Their Regulation by "The Fed."* Now, let us shift from fiscal concerns to monetary policy. Just as there are markets for commodities, there are markets for money and credit. During times of growth and full employment, the demand for money and credit is high, producing inflationary pressures. Furthermore, these effects are influenced by government through the law, because although demand for money and credit can come from firms, the money supply is influenced by the Federal Reserve System ("the Fed"), which is the nation's chief instrument of monetary policy.

(2) *Banking Laws and the Fed's Three Legal Tools of Monetary Policy: The Rediscount Rate, Open Market Transactions, and Reserve Requirements.* Our banking laws provide the Fed with three main tools of monetary policy. First, the Fed's Board of Governors sets the "rediscount rate," or the rate at which a financial institution such as a bank can borrow from the Fed itself. This, however, is not the most frequently used law for close calibrations.

Second, the Fed engages in open market transactions, which consist of the Fed's buying government securities on the open market. In this way, the Fed regulates the "federal funds rate," which is a different item than the rediscount rate. The federal funds rate is the rate at which banks lend to each other on an overnight basis, and it is influenced in a predictable way by the Fed's open market purchases. This is publicly the most visible effect of the Fed, as capital markets and even the general public have learned. Securities and banking lawyers listen carefully to speeches by the Chair of the Fed (currently Alan Greenspan) for hints about a tightening or loosening of the federal funds rate by market transactions, which they know will reflect itself quickly in their client banks' own higher prime lending rates and other rates. And the contracts that these lawyers write must adjust, with flexibility, to the changes.

Finally, there is the reserve requirement. Each financial institution is required by law to keep a certain level of cash on its account at the Fed. This requirement serves two purposes: to help protect the financial solvency of the institution and as an instrument of monetary policy. Change in reserve requirements is the third factor influencing credit that the Fed can use as a legal tool.

(3) *The Exponential Effect of Changes in Reserve Requirements under the Banking Laws.* Financial institutions once attempted to balance lending against actual capital holdings. Today, however, they depend on various sources, including depositors and the Fed. Since their reserve requirements are only a few percent of their transaction accounts (with the upper requirements hovering about ten percent), financial institutions contribute to the money supply in a manner that resembles the Keynesian multiplier (but is slightly more complex). From a $1,000 deposit, if 10% (or $100) must be reserved, the banking system makes a $900 loan that produces further deposits, and in this manner, it may add $9,000 or $10,000 to the money supply from that small ($1,000) deposit.

(4) *Effect of Increase in the Federal Funds Rate: Increases in Interest Rates and Less Spending.* An increase in reserve requirements creates a reduction in loan amounts that reverberates through the banking system, producing an exponential reduction in the money supply. It is for this reason that the Fed's control over reserves is effective. It tends, however, to be a regulatory chain saw rather than a scalpel, and the Fed uses it sparingly.

EXAMPLES AND PROBLEMS

(1) *Adjustable Rate Mortgages: Indexes, Macroeconomics, and Real Estate Law.* Traditionally, home mortgages were lent for long periods (thirty years) at fixed rates. This method seemed economically inefficient (can you see why?). During the 1970's, the Fed allowed use of a wide variety of "adjustable rate mortgages" (ARMs). The interest rate was tied to an index; it might increase or decrease with the consumer price index (CPI), or more commonly, be set at two percentage points above the market rate for certain federal securities (Treasury Bills, or T-bills).

In advising a client about such a mortgage, a lawyer needs to be sure that the client understands the influence the macroeconomy of the future is going to have on the client's mortgage contract. Can you see why? Specifically, the client needs to know that the client's interest rate will increase automatically if the Fed decides to decrease the money supply by selling government securities (it thus takes in money and takes it out of circulation).

Can you explain all of this to a hypothetical client trying to evaluate an adjustable rate mortgage?

(2) *Refinements (Departures?) From the Keynesian Model: Deficit Concerns, Supply-Side Economics, and Income Tax Policy.* The Keynesian model has undergone continual change and criticism. For example, concern about the federal deficit grew during the latter 1980's and 1990's. At some point, the federal deficit can threaten the availability of credit. Can you see why?

Another perspective is that of supply-side economists, who argued during the stagnant, inflationary economy of the late 1970's and early 1980's that the entire burden of federal, state and local taxation and regulation, including progressive income taxes, stifled production. The net effect was that productive people, who otherwise would produce enough to lift the entire economy to another level and cure the existing "stagflation," declined to produce what they otherwise would. They substituted leisure for productive work, since they saw the rewards of work as too small, or so the theory went. Supply siders therefore called for large tax cuts and criticized Keynesian economics as maintaining high tax rates.

Critics of supply-side economics responded that tax reductions could not have the desired result because they would increase government deficits to ruinous levels, and they also argued that people were not likely to work more because of a tax cut--some might already be working harder than they desired because of the effects of taxes. Finally, critics argued that the wealth effects of the supply-siders' proposals would be unacceptable, increasing the incomes of a small percentage of wealthy persons while adding little to middle incomes and having negative effects on poor persons. Can you explain and evaluate these arguments?

(3) *The Fed's Response to the Stagflation Problem: A Demand-Led Recovery Rather than Tax Policy.* Rather than the supply-side (major tax cut) solution, the Fed increased the money supply in the early 1980's. Congress increased spending and undertook lesser tax cuts. This combination of policies produced a demand-led recovery, as opposed to the supply-side, production-led recovery. Can you explain?

(4) *Are We "All Keynesians Now?"* Despite the adjustments and criticisms, the Keynesian framework continued to serve as the basic model during the latter half of the 1900's. President Richard Nixon once said, famously, "We are all Keynesians now." Do you think this includes the supply-siders?

(5) *The Fed's Open Market Transactions.* Perhaps the monetary tool that is easiest to calibrate is for the Fed to buy federal securities (bonds and bills) to increase the money supply and to sell them to reduce it. Can you explain?

Chapter 4
Economics II

Redressing Market Imperfections: Structure, Externalities, and Transaction Costs

> *"Under perfect competition private and social costs will be equal."--George J. Stigler, The Theory of Price.*
>
> *A journalist, an engineer and an economist were stranded on an island, with all their food in cans. "But we can't open them!" wailed the journalist. "I could calculate how to do it, if only we had some steel!" lamented the engineer. "No problem," the economist smiled. "Let's just assume we have a can opener."--Anonymous*

§ 4.01 What This Chapter Is About

MARKET IMPERFECTIONS, ECONOMICS, AND THE LAW

(1) *The Assumption of Perfect Competition in the Preceding Chapter-- and the Need for Legal Intervention.* Stigler's famous statement, quoted above, depends upon "perfect competition." This simplifying assumption

makes the discussion of microeconomics in the preceding chapter possible. That chapter assumed perfectly competitive markets without externalities. But without perfect competition, "private and social costs" will not be equal. In addition, the preceding chapter sidestepped the question of wealth distribution.

Sometimes, economists' assumptions have to be idealized, and hence there is the old joke quoted above--in which the economist solves a practical problem by "assuming" a can opener when none exists. In real life, most economists are not so pointy-headed, and usually, they are aware that their assumptions have limits. In this chapter, we shall expand our economic analysis by examining market imperfections, and we shall consider other issues, such as distributive justice, in later chapters.

(2) *Where Does the Law Come In?: Externalities, Structure, Absent Markets, and Other Imperfections.* Some markets function differently from the theories in the previous chapter because they are monopolistic or oligopolistic. We refer to this imperfection as the problem of "market structure." Further, some production that is efficient at the firm level produces "externalities" or bad side effects, such as accidents, injuries and pollution. These issues, in fact, are the reasons we have many of our laws.

Sometimes, there are no economic markets for transactions that need to be treated in economic terms, and uncertainty also affects markets. These "information deficiencies" create imperfections in the theory. Finally, "transaction costs" are yet another type of market imperfection, representing factors of production beyond those required for production itself. This chapter introduces each of these concepts and explores how market-oriented political systems deal with imperfect markets, through the intervention of the law.

§ 4.02 Market Imperfections: Imperfect Competition, Externalities, Uncertainty, and Transaction Costs

[A] Market Imperfections, Part One: Industry Structure and the Antitrust Laws

INDUSTRY STRUCTURE, CONDUCT AND PERFORMANCE: MONOPOLY, OLIGOPOLY, AND THE LAW

(1) *The Assumption of Perfect Competition: Is It Valid?* Notice that our discussion thus far has assumed that all markets are perfectly competitive. This assumption does not fit the real world, since some industries are not perfectly competitive. Our earlier discussion probably describes the agricultural industry fairly well, but not your local electric company or the domestic steel industry. For that matter, even agricultural markets may be imperfect if large entities operate in any of them, or if buyers or sellers band together in cooperatives.

Furthermore, the assumption of perfect competition implies perfect buyers, who never make purchasing errors or become victims of misleading advertising. The consumer, it is assumed, is "homo economicus," or "the economic consumer," who knows every relevant fact about all conceivable products and who never hesitates in accurately chosing between vanilla or strawberry, sport utility vehicles or sedans. The very existence of advertising, particularly institutional or image advertising, shows the limits of this assumption. Brand loyalty and the creation of new demand through product diversification undermine it further. And in some instances, these phenomena are so disadvantageous that we limit them by the law.

(2) *Monopoly.* A "monopoly" is a market with a single large seller. (There also is a concept called "monopsony," characterized by a single purchaser, which raises different but analogous issues.) A rational monopolist does not act in the same way as a firm in a competitive market. The monopolist resembles the competitor in wanting to maximize profit, but the difference is, the monopolist actually maximizes by restricting output (quantity) so as to increase price. (This theory can be demonstrated with the same kinds of cost, supply and demand curves that we have seen above, although we shall not reproduce them here.)

(3) *The Disadvantages of Monopoly: How Should the Law Intervene?* Hence, the disadvantage of monopolies to an economist is not that monopolists are inherently evil people. Rather, the trouble is with effects of monopoly on resource use and production. The monopolist, if he or she acts rationally, restricts output. Society enjoys less of the monopolized good than consumers would want. At the same time, the monopolist uses resources disproportionately in production by receiving greater-than-normal profit.

The economist would see this performance as rational behavior, not as immoral; the monopolist has the same motivation as the competitor but adjusts strategy to maximize profit in the particular market. The question, for the economist, is whether and how the society should intervene in the market to prevent or reduce the monopolist's restriction of output.

(4) *Natural Monopolies, Governmental Franchises, and Monopolies from Industry Consolidation.* Monopolies can arise in several ways. The term "natural monopoly" refers to one in which capital requirements or physical factors dictate that there can be only one efficient seller. A toll bridge over a narrow strait might be an example. Your local energy distribution system, arguably, may be another, although recently we have discovered that some supposedly natural monopolies really can change so that they are not, and we have seen competition enter such industries as gas pipelines and long distance telephone service. Technology can destroy natural monopolies--and it changes the economic world in the process.

Franchise monopolies from government grants are exemplified by patents and copyrights. Du Pont's domination of the cellophane market is a consequence of a deliberate government policy, the issuance of patents. Finally, monopoly can result from industry consolidation. In each instance, lawmakers face difficult issues of antitrust policy.

(5) *Oligopoly.* "Oligopoly" refers to a market in which there are few enough sellers so that firms must take account of other firms' individual behaviors. A price cut or increase by one is likely to be matched by others. Therefore, rational behavior might involve a firm's refraining from a price cut that might otherwise be motivated by attempts to increase sales, because of the perception that other firms will match the cut, thus defeating the purpose and resulting in reduced profit for all. An oligopoly may be so tightly reciprocal that it resembles a monopoly, or it may result from an actual agreement, sometimes called a cartel.

(6) *Characteristics of Oligopoly; the Inconsistent Application of Antitrust Law.* Oligopoly often is characterized by "product differentiation," or brand differences. Remember that competitive markets involve undifferentiated products. Thus, there is no brand loyalty for the grains of wheat that make up a sack of flour, but there is for Chevrolets, Cadillacs and Fords. Another, related characteristic of oligopoly, then, is non-price competition through product changes, logos, and advertising.

A third characteristic is "barriers to entry," or large initial investment, often because of "economies of scale" or sharply declining initial marginal costs. And "oligopolistic competition," which can resemble a competitive market, may nevertheless be characterized by somewhat restricted output and greater-than-normal profit because of firms' reciprocal behavior. The courts have acted somewhat inconsistently in deciding whether this behavior violates antitrust laws, such as laws against price fixing.

(7) *Legal Responses to Monopoly and Oligopoly: Regulated Industries and Antitrust Laws.* Society often responds to monopoly by price regulation. We authorize the state public utilities commission (or the Federal Communications Commission, depending on the precise industry) to impose price controls. We thus attempt to establish motivation for the monopolist to act more like a competitor. In addition, we have laws against certain kinds of behavior--price fixing, market division between competitors, anticompetitive mergers, price discrimination, and so-called "tying arrangements" (by which a large seller bundles products to force buyers to pay for things they don't want). These antitrust laws are supposed to minimize the creation of monopolies or cartels and to force oligopolists to function more like competitors, although there is controversy about whether all of these laws actually serve the purpose.

EXAMPLES AND PROBLEMS

(1) *How a Monopolist Maximizes Profit by Restricting Output: The Example of a Professional Sports Franchise that Wants a Smaller (Not Larger) Arena.* A professional basketball team would want the city to build the largest possible arena so as to maximize its profit, right? Wrong. A metropolitan newspaper reported in 1999 that one NBA basketball franchise wanted its new arena to be *smaller* than the one that the local Sports Authority had proposed. The reason: "largely because they want to ensure selling out each game. Guaranteed sellouts make it easier to charge higher prices." Can you explain the economic theory behind the franchise owner's preference for a smaller arena?

(2) *Regulating the Monopolist's Price: What Should Be the Law's Response?* How should regulated prices be determined? The traditional method, under what is called the "*Hope-Permian* formula" (after two United States Supreme Court cases of those names), is to add up all the monopolist's historical costs of production, including an amount for use of capital that

reflects the entrepreneurial risk of the industry. Question: But what does this historical-cost regulatory approach do to the signaling function of prices? Note that this kind of regulation tends to freeze prices in the past.

(3) *Some Sources of Errors in Regulatory Law: Lag, Politics, Undercapitalization, and Non-Innovation.* Several kinds of problems are likely to arise in monopolist price regulation, including the possibility of "regulatory lag." (Rate proceedings last for many years, during which prices are not adjusted.) Also, political intervention may be a problem. (The public may seek to cut cost estimates unrealistically, or conversely, the monopolist may use influence to inflate them). Still another issue is under- or over-estimation of the rate that should be paid for capital. (The problem is that no one really knows the risk involved in investments in the regulated industry, because there is no precisely similar market by which to measure it.) A final problem is caused by regulators' failure to appreciate the need for innovation. (Perhaps a given utility would produce more efficiently if it invested now in differently fueled plants, but regulators may disallow the costs for distributive reasons.)

These kinds of regulatory errors ultimately produce disadvantages, such as brownouts, accidents, poor quality, etc., that somewhat resemble the effect of price controls in competitive markets. Can you explain why?

(4) *Denying Recovery of Some Costs under the Law: "Prudent" Cost Regulation versus "Used and Useful" Regulation.* What if the monopolist's costs are wasteful? For example, imagine that a utility pays each of its 500 vice presidents a ten-million-dollar bonus (or installs gold-plated faucets in all its plants). The traditional approach is to deny recovery of these "imprudent" costs. But notice that this "prudent cost" approach discourages only those expenditures that are so truly foolish that they demonstrably are "imprudent." It does not discourage below-average performance, nor does it encourage better performance in the way that a competitive market would.

Therefore, some regulators have invented the "used and useful" standard. This more complex approach disallows recovery of investment unless it results in used-and-useful machinery, or investment that actually aids in production. The utility's shareholders lose all of their investment in an abandoned nuclear plant, for example, even if its construction was prudent at the time. That's what would happen to shareholders in an unregulated firm, and so this approach is thought to increase efficiency.

But notice that a regulatory authority that imposes a used-and-useful requirement will have to allow a higher rate for the cost of capital. Can you explain why? (An analogy: Imagine that a car company, which must absorb all the loss for an abandoned product such as the Edsel, simultaneously is limited to "normal," or restricted, profit for a highly successful innovation such as the Mustang. Would anyone invest in such a company?)

(5) *"Conscious Parallelism" of Prices in Oligopolistic Markets as Proof of Price Fixing under the Law: Is the Inference Appropriate?* Laws against price fixing do not require proof of a written agreement or even an express one, because price fixers could evade such a requirement by nonverbal coordination or tacit collusion. It is not easy to define the types of purely behavioral cooperation that ought to trigger a finding of price fixing. Some of the court decisions make illegality depend heavily upon "conscious parallelism." They infer that an oligopolist that deliberately conforms its prices to those of other competitors is guilty of price fixing.

But other courts decline to base decision on conscious parallelism without proof of a "plus factor," consisting of some action that would be against the firm's interest in the absence of price fixing. Can you explain why?

(6) *Do Antitrust Laws Work Properly in a Heavily Political Environment? The Microsoft and Citicorp Examples.* In the latter part of the 1990's and early 2000's, the Department of Justice vigorously pressed its suit against Microsoft Corporation for antitrust violations that included monopolization (practices allegedly designed to drive out competitors of its Windows operating system), tying arrangements (bundling systems together so that the purchaser would have to buy them all together, including Internet access, word processing, and other possibly separable items), and other claimed infractions. Microsoft vigorously defended by offering evidence that its dominant position had resulted from skill, foresight, industriousness, and superior products; that it had acted only as a rational market actor would in its position; and that "bundling" systems together was not an illegal tying arrangement but a more efficient way to provide related services with less redundancy.

The trouble with these kinds of issues is that the concepts are vague, manipulable and unpredictable. Can you see why a future counterpart to Microsoft in a different industry might be deterred from useful innovation or efficiencies by concern for similar litigation? Also, because of their vagueness, some antitrust law enforcement seems to reflect political influence. For example, while it was pursuing Microsoft, the DOJ did not similarly pursue Citicorp, a major player in the financial markets, when some people thought that its conduct at least equally merited enforcement. Critics charged that Citicorp escaped because of political influence. What, if anything, do these considerations show about government's intervention in the form of law enforcement and regulation in economic markets?

DISTRESSED FIRMS AND OVERLY COMPETITIVE MARKETS

(1) *A Market in Distressed Firms or Their Assets.* Some firms do not survive, because they are poorly managed, undercapitalized or unlucky. In that event, efficiency depends upon the existence of markets for the sale of such a firm or its assets. Firms that purchase in this kind of market sometimes are called "vulture funds," although they serve useful purposes. In the worst cases, bankruptcy proceedings may aid this process through reorganization or liquidation.

(2) *Overly Competitive Markets with Low Barriers to Entry.* Some economists believe that there are industries in which chronic inefficiencies persist, ironically, from too much competition. In some cities, restaurants and bars arguably fit this description. Enthusiastic new entrants open up daily but fail after a short time, only to be replaced by other failures-to-be. Meanwhile, successful operators' ability to invest and expand is siphoned off by these marginal businesses--or so the theory goes.

EXAMPLES AND PROBLEMS

(1) *Growing Concentration, Shrinking Market: What Is the Appropriate Policy of Antitrust Law Enforcement?* Imagine that the second-largest widget manufacturer has offered to acquire the fifth-largest, which has not made a profit in recent years because of declining overall widget sales. The combined firm will become the industry's largest. The Justice Department's Antitrust Division must decide whether to challenge this merger as anticompetitive. Can you explain some of the considerations that should be balanced?

(2) *"Let's Start a Rock Band and Play All the Local College Bars!" (or, "Let's Start an Entertainment Law Firm!")* Suppose a friend makes this proposal to you, and adds, "We're good musicians; we'll have a blast and

make enough money to pay our tuition!" Evaluate this business venture in light of the industry into which entry is proposed. [Certain kinds of law practice can involve the same dangers. Should you become an entertainment lawyer, and represent movie stars?]

(3) *The Lawyer Who Helps a Client to Obtain Startup Funds from a Lender: Ingredients of the Business Plan.* As a lawyer, you may represent a borrower client, and your job will include drawing up papers to apply for a loan. A business plan sufficient to support a commercial loan probably will need to detail the characteristics of the industry, the extent of competition, potential customers and their demand, and the promoter's reasons for believing that consumers will purchase this firm's product. Explain why a lender might require this information. (In a later chapter, we shall consider how to prepare a business plan.)

PUBLIC GOODS

(1) *Public Goods, Hybrid Goods, and the Law.* Certain kinds of goods are called "public goods" because their benefits are so diffuse that no particular individual has sufficient incentive to invest adequately in them. This characteristic sometimes is called "non-rival use": there is no inconsistency in many people benefitting at the same time from the same thing. National defense is an example. Everyone arguably benefits from expenditures for the armed services, but few individuals would be motivated to buy an aircraft carrier so as to reap the protections of its patrolling the Mediterranean. Then, too, there are "hybrid" goods that benefit some people more than others or that provide private benefits as well as public ones. Law enforcement may be a public good, but shouldn't a rock concert performer have to pay for police-furnished security?

(2) *Free Riders and the Law of Trade Secrets.* A closely related issue involves "free riders," or persons who benefit from costs incurred by others without paying an amount corresponding to their marginal utility. If any individual did decide to pay for an aircraft carrier to help the United States patrol the Mediterranean, everyone else in the country would become a free rider. A new invention can benefit many people, perhaps; to prevent them from becoming free riders, we extend patent protection and thus provide for payment to the inventor according to the product's marginal utility. A new abstract idea, which is not patentable, may benefit many persons who do not

pay for it, and therefore firms often go to great lengths to keep trade secrets from competitors.

(3) *The Law and the "Tragedy of the Commons."* Public goods sometimes are not maintained because incentives are too diffuse. Individuals may litter parks or pollute the air because they derive less utility from the increment of cleanliness that they could contribute than the cost of modifying their behavior. This idea is related to the phenomenon of "externalities," which is covered in the next section, and it is a major challenge for the law.

EXAMPLES AND PROBLEMS

(1) *Education Funding: The Legal and Economic Arguments.* Some people believe that private education is superior to government-owned-and-operated schools. But still, most critics do not advocate that local governments de-fund the schools; they simply would redirect the public moneys through parents in the form of school vouchers. Explain how these people might argue that it is not inconsistent to favor a law providing government-funded education even though they argue against government-run schools.

(2) *The Economics of Laws Protecting Trade Secrets.* Each state has evolved various kinds of legal principles by which businesspeople may hold liable certain employees or competitors who misappropriate trade secrets. Explain how these laws might promote economic efficiency.

(3) *"Against Settlement": Lawsuits, Precedent as a Public Good, and Free Riders.* Professor Owen Fiss wrote an article called "Against Settlement," in which he argued against the encouragement of private dispute resolution. (Some other professors consider Fiss's position indefensible.) One of Fiss's arguments is that private dispute resolution does not contribute to the storehouse of publicly available explanations of legal principles that otherwise might be created by disputants and taxpayers paying to generate appellate court opinions. Evaluate this argument economically, using the ideas of public goods and free riders. [Who pays for the precedent bank that benefits everybody, under Fiss's idea?]

[B]   Market Imperfections, Part Two: Socioeconomics and the Critique of Homo Economicus

SOCIOECONOMICS: EXAMINING ECONOMIC ASSUMPTIONS

(1) *"Homo Economicus," or the Economic Person.* Recall our discussion of "homo economicus," or the economic human, in a previous section. Homo economicus is an idealized construct, invented to make economic theory workable. He or she is perfectly knowledgeable, never fooled, discerns utility infallibly, and always acts from pure self-interest, never from altruism.

(2) *Why Socioeconomics Instead of Economics?* Although economics obviously has useful predictive and normative applications, there are scholars who argue that it is incomplete and misleading. For example, Richard H. Thaler conducted an experiment demonstrating that real consumers are sometimes guided by their perceptions of social appropriateness or fairness rather than by economic factors such as market price or economic utility, even when they make ostensibly economic choices.

In *The Winner's Curse: Paradoxes and Anomalies of Economic Life* 31 (1992), Thaler reports that he asked a similar economic question of two groups: what was the most they would pay to buy a bottle of beer from a remote supplier? He varied the question, however, by describing the remote seller as an expensive resort hotel for one group and as a rundown grocery store for another:

> You are lying on a beach on a hot day . . . . For the last hour you have been thinking about how much you would enjoy a nice cold bottle of your favorite brand of beer. A companion . . . offers to bring back a beer from the only nearby place where beer is sold: [a resort hotel] [a cheap grocery store]. He says that the beer might be expensive and so asks how much you are willing to pay for the beer. He says that he will buy the beer [only] if it costs as much [as] or less than the price you state. . . . What price do you tell him?

Although most models of market economics would view the questions asked both groups as the same, Thaler's two groups actually responded significantly differently. Those who were told that the remote seller was the small grocery store were willing to pay an average maximum price of $1.50, but those who thought they were buying from the resort hotel were willing to spend much more, an average maximum of $2.65. Why? Perhaps because they thought it squared with a sense of justice to pay a high price to a glitzy hotel, but not to a cheap grocery store. Or perhaps they feared appearing foolish in paying an extravagant price to the grocer, but not to the hotelier.

One might attempt to explain these results by reference to the economic concept of consumer utility. One can speculate that the respondents assigned less utility to the beer from the grocery store, either because of the potential embarrassment of submitting to price gouging or because their feelings of injustice at providing excess profit to a firm with low marginal cost created a kind of negative utility. But this reasoning bends the economist's concept of utility into an unrecognizable shape. It seems more sensible to regard this influence as different from the usual comparisons studied by economists, and to seek the advice of other disciplines.

(2) *Socioeconomics as "Economics-Plus."* Thus, socioeconomics resembles economics in that it analyzes choices under conditions of scarcity. But socioeconomics regards economics, with its assumptions of consumer rationality, self-interestedness, and focus on efficiency, as inadequate to explain actual marketplace behavior. Professor Jeffrey L. Harrison puts it this way: "[S]ocioeconomics is not a closed system, as . . . economics tends to be. In other words, there are no questions to which the answer is, 'But that violates the assumptions.'" In a manner of speaking, socioeconomics is "economics-plus": it borrows from ethics, psychology, political science, game theory, and other disciplines to provide more complete analyses of economic behavior.

(3) *Socioeconomic Effects on Firms, Consumers and Workers.* The criticism of economics by socioeconomists is pervasive. In classical economics, for example, "business ethics" cannot be accounted for except as an oxymoron: the firm maximizes profit inexorably, regarding even the law as something that imposes penalties only on those who get caught, and seeing unethical but lawful conduct as a mere public relations issue. The fact is, however, many managers unquestionably do respond to notions of ethics in business. As for consumers, Thaler's experiment shows that they, as well as firms, sometimes defy conventional economic models. And Professor Harrison provides an example that applies to wage earners:[1]

> . . . suppose a person who has been abused, disadvantaged, or discriminated against is offered a wage of $4 to do a job that other

---

1   *Law and Socioeconomics,* 49 J. Legal Ed. 224, 227 (1999).

workers are paid $5 an hour to do. She may accept this exchange because in her world this is an improvement . . . . Another worker might reject the offer because it offends her sense of interpersonal justice. It would be a strange [theory] that would stop the analysis with the conclusion that both parties are better-off and no one is worse-off and, thus, the outcome is to be recommended as a normative matter.

Harrison concludes that these examples show two failures of economic theory. "[First,] . . . being better-off is not the same as *feeling* better-off. The second source of trouble . . . is related to the first, but concerns the fact that people differ in what makes them feel better-off."

EXAMPLES AND PROBLEMS

(1) *Crime, Economics, and the Law.* Economists have adapted their theories to explain how rewards and deterrents can influence criminal behavior. For example, in later chapters on jurisprudence and on statistics, we shall consider economist Isaac Ehrlich's use of utility theory and multiple regression equations to analyze the death penalty as a deterrent to murder.

Consider, however, the following example. Two employees, for whom the marginal utility of money is the same (they have equivalent needs, salaries and savings), each discover a virtually risk-free opportunity to embezzle $10,000 from their firm. One commits the crime, but the other refuses. Wouldn't a straightforward economic analysis predict that both would take the money?

(2) *Socioeconomics and Socialization.* Both economics and socioeconomics are involved, in differing ways, with questions about what is desirable behavior and how to encourage it. For example, aside from the question of distinguishing the nonembezzling employee in the previous problem from the embezzling one, we might concern ourselves with how we could motivate more people to follow the example of the non-embezzler. How would the answers provided by economics to this question differ from those provided by socioeconomics?

[C]   Market Imperfections, Part Three: Externalities, from Accidents to Pollution

WHAT ARE EXTERNALITIES? AND
WHAT IS THE LAW'S RESPONSE?

(1) *Profit Maximization.* The theory of the marketplace assumes that individual firms will maximize profits and that economic efficiency will result. But the theory we thus far have developed does not guarantee that firms will have any incentive to avoid side effects that harm society, such as accidents or pollution. We shall now examine this problem.

(2) *Externalities.* We call these kinds of byproducts "externalities" (or "external costs of production"). The reason that the unregulated market does not minimize them is that external costs are not directly incurred by the firms that cause them. Indeed, the market system induces firms to produce efficiently, with the least possible expenditure of resources. Even if the most internally efficient method causes huge external costs in accidents or pollution, prices drive the firm to choose this internally desirable but societally disadvantageous method. Thus firms are motivated to "externalize their costs," and in a sense, they become "free riders" on the costs borne by accident victims and people sickened by pollution.

There also are positive externalities: a company seeking to motivate employees pays an architect to design a beautiful business park. Passers-by benefit without having invested. They receive a kind of windfall. Sometimes we value these externalities so much that we provide subsidies: tax credits for research and development, or public funding for education or training. But perhaps people tend to notice negative externalities more!

(3) *Regulatory and Legal Responses.* Society can respond to this problem of negative side effects in several ways. For example, it can ignore a given externality and simply let the costs fall where they may ("The factory smells bad, but that's the smell of money"). In some instances, we can efficiently leave the producers and those who bear external costs to negotiate the best balance. (We shall return to this concept in the following sections, which deal with "transaction costs" and the "Coase Theorem.")

At the opposite extreme, society can regulate by prohibiting certain activities (such as trucking at over 55 m.p.h., net-fishing without turtle excluders) or by setting performance standards (such as by a law providing that emissions may not exceed five parts per million of sulfur dioxide). Another regulatory method is to use taxes, permits or subsidies to allow a certain volume of external effects but to cause firms to "internalize the costs." Finally, the law can require firms to pay damages to victims for the costs they externalize, which is another way of forcing firms to internalize the costs.

EXAMPLES AND PROBLEMS

(1) *Laws Imposing Prohibition, Standards, Financial Incentives, or Damage Liability: A Question of Efficiency.* In some instances, financial-incentive regulations or laws creating damage liability may be more economically efficient than prohibitions or performance standards. Explain why.

(2) *Laws that Internalize the Costs Exactly: Inducing Expenditures so That the Last Dollar Spent Produces Precisely "One Dollar's Worth" of Safety or Pollution Reduction.* Theoretically, the level of incentives to internalize costs is most efficient when the last extra dollar the firm spends on safety yields exactly one dollar's worth of accident cost reduction. It is inefficient, and generally unwise, to attempt to regulate so as to utterly eliminate all externalities. Explain why. (If you have difficulty answering, see the next section.)

ACCIDENTS, NEGLIGENCE LAW, AND ECONOMIC THEORY

(1) *Economic Analysis of the Common Law.* Economic analysis of tort law is a useful aid to its proper development, from age-old problems of trespass to modern issues of product liability. Even when the reasoning of the common-law courts has been ruthlessly formalistic, the results almost always have made sense in economic terms. The economic goal is to administer the deterrent effect of a damage remedy in the appropriate circumstances and at roughly the proper level. This level is that at which the last dollar spent on reducing externalities through accident prevention equals the loss in manufacturing value that it causes, because at this level, greater expenditures will cost more than they are worth.

(2) *An Example: Judge Learned Hand's Opinion in the Carroll Towing Case.* Occasionally, common-law judges have used explicit formulae that recognize this economic goal. Perhaps the most famous case is *United States v. Carroll Towing Company*, 159 F.2d 169 (2d Cir. 1947), in which Judge Learned Hand explained the basic negligence calculus. There, the issue was

whether a barge owner was negligent in failing to have an attendant on board while the barge was being towed, in case she broke away.

Judge Hand's analysis was "a function of three variables: (1) [t]he probability that she [the barge] will break away; (2) the gravity of the resulting injury, if she does; [and] (3) the burden of adequate precautions." Judge Hand observed that it might help to state the formula in algebraic terms, and he proceeded to do so: "[I]f the probability [of an accident] be called P; the injury, L; and the burden, B; liability depends upon whether B is less than L multiplied by P: i.e., whether $B < PL$."

(3) *Why Is Negligence Law an Economic Concept?* Stated as an equation in modern mathematical notation, Judge Hand's formula means that negligence liability begins to appear at the point where $B < PL$. That is, it appears whenever the societal savings from safety expenditures (PL, the "probable loss") begin to exceed the cost of accident prevention (B, the "burden"). This is an economic formula. Judge Posner explains the significance of Judge Hand's reasoning as follows:[2]

If the cost of safety measures . . . exceeds the benefit in accident avoidance to be gained by incurring that cost, society would be better off, in economic terms, to forego accident prevention. . . . [O]verall economic value or welfare would be diminished rather than increased by incurring a higher accident-prevention cost in order to avoid a lower accident cost. If, on the other hand, the benefits in accident avoidance exceed the costs of prevention, society is better off if those costs are incurred and the accident averted . . . .

In other words, if we impose damage liability in such a way as to induce modest expenses for safety that prevent deaths and costly injuries, we increase economic efficiency. But if we regulate so as to require automobiles to be equipped like Sherman tanks, to prevent accidents that produce injuries comparable only to a hangnail, we have acted unwisely.

(4) *A Graphic Depiction of Judge Hand's Economic Formula for Negligence Law.* Graphically, Judge Hand's reasoning can be illustrated by

---

2   Richard A. Posner, *A Theory of Negligence*, 1 J. Legal Stud. 29, 32-33 (1972).

a diagram such as Figure 1.[3]   The burden B (or cost due to accident prevention expenses) increases as the degree of care, or amount of money spent on safety, increases. Therefore the line representing B slopes upward. The probable cost due to losses from accidents, or the probability of an accident multiplied by the likely amount of the loss (P x L), produces the downward-sloping line PL, because the value of these losses declines as the degree of care increases.

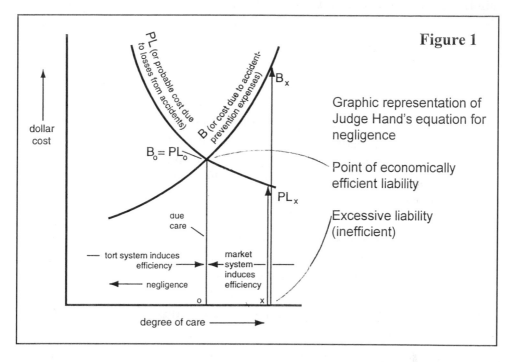

Figure 1

Graphic representation of Judge Hand's equation for negligence

Point of economically efficient liability

Excessive liability (inefficient)

The intersection of the two curves, where $B = PL$, is the optimal level of care, or "due care." At lesser degrees of care, the tort system threatens the producer with negligence liability, thereby inducing greater social efficiency through negligence liability for damages. At greater degrees of care, the producer wastefully invests safety expenses that cost more than they are worth in accident reduction; here, the market system should induce efficiency by forcing the producer to produce more inexpensively.

(5) *Excess Liability.* Figure 1 also allows us to illustrate the effect of excess liability. At safety level X, for example, the expense attributable to the

---

3   This Figure is similar to one in Richard A. Posner, Economic Analysis of Law 191-92 (3d ed. 1992), as are the three figures that follow. All figures are different in some respects, such as the addition of features that illustrate overdeterrence. These figures and part of this text first appeared, with differing text, in an article by the author in the Maryland Law Review.

degree of care is disproportionately high, well above the level of due care. At safety level X, the total safety expense (B_x) added to the probable accident loss (PL_x) greatly exceeds the total at the due care level (point O), $B_o + PL_o$. (That is, $B_x + PL_x > B_o + PL_o$.) At the higher level, to use our earlier analogy, an automobile producer is forced to manufacture a product that resembles a Sherman tank in order to avoid an accident that is the economic equivalent of a hangnail. This dysfunctional effect results from the response of a rational manufacturer to excess damage liability.

EXAMPLES AND PROBLEMS

(1) *Persons with Physical Disabilities and the Negligence Standard.* For a person with a physical disability, negligence consists of unreasonable behavior as judged for a person with that disability. Thus, a person with impaired legs is not negligent in driving a car that has hand controls but would be negligent, probably, if she drove a car that lacked these controls. Is this standard, for negligence for the disabled person, economically efficient? Explain.

(2) *The Vagueness of the Negligence Standard.* Notice that proper behavior by a firm requires the firm accurately to gauge the point at which B_o (the financial burden of all precautions) equals PL_o (the mathematically expected loss from accidents), all as valued by a jury some time in the future. Obviously, the firm will have to do a lot of guessing. Does this mean that negligence law is inefficient?

(3) *Safety Laws That Actually Decrease Safety: Judge Easterbrook's Example.* There are very few fatalities per million passenger-miles from airline crashes. Nevertheless, many people react to these deaths by saying, "even a small number is too many." Imagine, however, that regulators respond by ordering installation of a safety system that increases airline ticket prices nationwide by an average of $20 each. As Judge Frank H. Easterbrook has pointed out, this regulation will motivate some people to drive to their destinations by car instead of flying. The effect may actually increase fatalities, since the few lives saved by the airline safety systems may be outnumbered by automobile-accident deaths, which exceed those of airlines on a per-mile basis. The point is not that airline safety won't save lives, but that the resources dedicated to it must be evaluated to ensure that lives saved exceed lives lost, or more generally, that benefits exceed costs. Is the example persuasive? Consider the next two sections.

THE EFFICIENCY OF ACCIDENT LAWS:
THE EXAMPLE OF ACTUAL AND PUNITIVE DAMAGES

(1) *Compensatory Damages as Economic Deterrents.* In this section, we expand our analysis to consider damage liability, both actual and punitive. As we have seen, if a cheaper means of production results in environmental pollution or in an unacceptably large proportion of accidents and injuries, the unregulated price system functions counterproductively.[4] It forces firms to choose this privately-desirable-but-socially-dysfunctional method of production. The economist would see the imposition of damage liability as a corrective to these externalities. The desirable level of damage liability would be reached when it precisely balanced the consumers' desire for readily available products against the desire to avoid the harmful consequences, such as pollution or injuries, that result from cheap production.

In this view, deviations from the optimal level of damage liability are undesirable, irrespective of whether they are upward or downward. Too much damage liability results in an undesirable suppression of the production of goods or services; too little results in undesirably high levels of external effects.

(2) *Deterrence Rather than Compensation as the Goal.* Usually, the tort system provides the requisite deterrence through compensation to the plaintiff. This compensatory orientation, however, obscures the economic function of damage remedies. Although compensation is the measure the courts have adopted, the more significant aspect of compensatory damages to an economist is the deterrence of the defendant that results from the defendant's having to add the amount of potential damage verdicts to its production costs. The theory requires that the compensation be complete, including all of the costs or losses suffered by the plaintiff, whether explicitly monetary or not, and whether readily measurable or not; but if this level is reached, the tort system theoretically provides exactly the level of deterrence that is socially desirable.

(3) *Punitive Damages as Gap-Fillers in the System of Economic Deterrence.* The economist would see complete compensatory damages, at least in theory, as fulfilling this function of deterring accident cost

---

4   This section, together with the preceding section and the three sections that follow, parallel an article by the author published in the Maryland Law Review, although the writing here is adapted to this book.

externalization. The price system, in this view, induces the firm to produce goods and services efficiently, while the tort reparations system confronts the firm with the precise cost of losses to victims in the form of compensatory damages.

But the compensation-based theory is accurate only if *every* tort victim recovers *fully* for *all* losses. The trouble is, transaction costs (such as attorney's or experts' fees) and proof difficulties are such that not all injured persons will sue, let alone recover, exactly what they have lost. It is for this reason that punitive damages are useful. The economic function of these damages is not so much that of "punishing" an individual based upon "wrongful intent" as that of adjusting the level and locus of damage liability to take account of undervaluation of external costs by the tort system through compensatory damages alone.

(4) *Limiting Punitive Damage Liability to Avoid "Overkill."* At the same time, there is a need to limit punitive damages. Economic theory suggests that they can be harmful rather than helpful, if they are imposed in excessive amounts. Therefore, there is a need to compute their amounts so that they fit their respective deterrence gaps. The economist would see a threshold requirement of gross negligence, for example, as a rough means of limiting the availability of punitive damages to cases of underdeterrence. A more economically precise measurement would inquire about the deterrent adequacy of actual damages. The gross negligence threshold is a crude yardstick; nevertheless, it approximates this function. In addition, various means of measuring the proper amount of punitive damages have evolved in the law, such as by requiring proportional relationships to actual damages (or by imposing absolute limits, as some states have done).

EXAMPLES AND PROBLEMS

(1) *Actual Damages: An Example of Economic Reasoning by the Supreme Court.* In *Memphis Community School District v. Stachura,* 477 U.S. 299 (1986), the Supreme Court reviewed a damage verdict based upon the freedom-of-speech claims of a wrongfully suspended public school teacher. The district court had instructed the jury to award the plaintiff (1) compensatory damages, plus (2) punitive damages, *plus* (3) an amount of *additional* damages based upon the value or importance of the abstract constitutional right that the defendant allegedly had violated. Specifically, the district court stated, "The precise value you place upon any Constitutional

right which you find was denied to Plaintiff is within your discretion. You may wish to consider the importance of the right in our system of government . . . ." The district court entered a large judgment based upon a jury verdict that included this supplementary element, on top of the compensatories and punitives found by the jury.

The Supreme Court, however, held that these "additional" damages were unlawful. The Court expressly tied the function of compensatory damages (provided that all losses were fully compensated) to the deterrence purpose:

> ". . . damages in tort cases are designed to provide '*compensation* for the injury caused to plaintiff by defendant's breach of duty.' To that end, compensatory damages may include not only out-of-pocket loss and other monetary harms, but also such injuries as 'impairment of reputation . . . , personal humiliation, and mental anguish and suffering.' Deterrence is also an important purpose of this system, but it operates through the mechanism of damages that are *compensatory*--damages grounded in determinations of plaintiff's actual losses."

Excessive deterrence, such as that which would have resulted from the district court's gratuitous addition of a supplement to protect the abstract right in question, would have caused school districts to become excessively risk-averse, by retention of incompetent teachers and disruptive students. Can you explain why the Supreme Court's analysis of the function of compensatory damages was economically sound?

(2) *Punitive Damages: Another Example of Economic Reasoning by the Supreme Court.* In *Smith v. Wade*, 461 U.S. 30 (1983), the Supreme Court considered a suit against Smith, a prison guard, for having placed in Wade's cell two other inmates who beat and sexually assaulted him. Wade alleged that Smith violated the Eighth Amendment's prohibition on cruel and unusual punishment because the guard knew or should have known that assault was likely. The trial court instructed the jury that Smith could be liable for compensatory damages only if he acted with gross negligence, "defined as 'a callous indifference or thoughtless disregard for the consequences of one's act or failure to act.'" Smith thus could not be liable even for compensatory damages on a finding of simple negligence, because any liability finding required proof of gross negligence.

The trial judge also instructed the jury on punitive damages. But for punitive damages, the judge's instructions required no greater culpability than that required for compensatories: "[I]f the conduct of one or more of the defendants is shown to be a reckless or callous disregard of, or indifference to, the rights or safety of others, then you may assess punitive or exemplary damages in addition to any award of actual damages." Liability for compensatory damages thus automatically triggered the jury's power to impose punitive damages with no finding of any worse mental state, and this was what the jury did.

Smith argued that the punitive award should be reversed because the instruction should have limited punitive damages to situations involving "ill will, spite, or intent to injure." The Supreme Court, however, rejected this argument: "Smith's argument . . . is that an actual-intent standard is preferable to a recklessness standard because it is less vague. . . . [But the] need for exceptional clarity in the standard for punitive damages arises only if one assumes that there are substantial numbers of officers who will not be deterred by compensatory damages; only such officers will seek to guide their conduct by the punitive damages standard. The presence of such officers constitutes a powerful argument *against* raising the threshold for punitive damages."

This reasoning, although it does correctly characterize the deterrence function, is subject to criticism. Arguably, it is not just reckless officers who may be deterred, as the Court seemed to believe. Instead, *all* corrections officers now will need to trim their performance to avoid the prospect of vague punitive-damage liability, which can be inappropriately overimposed just as it can be underimposed, and it can be imposed even upon officers who believe they are acting reasonably, if a jury later disagrees. Thus, in his dissent, Justice Rehnquist, joined by Chief Justice Burger and Justice Powell, pointed out that "the uncertainty resulting from largely random awards of punitive damages will have serious effects upon the performance by state and local officers of their official duties." Explain why both arguments, majority and dissent, are economic in nature.

A CLOSER LOOK AT THE ECONOMIC THEORY SUPPORTING DAMAGES FOR ACCIDENT LIABILITY

(1) *Adjusting the Defendant's Cost Curves through Tort Remedies.* The economic theory sketched above can best be developed by an examination of

short-term marginal cost curves. Remember that marginal cost is the cost associated with each additional unit of output. Figure 2 shows a private firm's marginal cost curve (indicated by the dotted line), when the producer is not motivated to consider externalized accident costs. The society wishes that the producer actually would use a more expensive method of production, one that does not externalize the losses caused by accidents. Therefore, the socially desirable level of production cost is higher, even though this cost means higher product cost to the consumer.

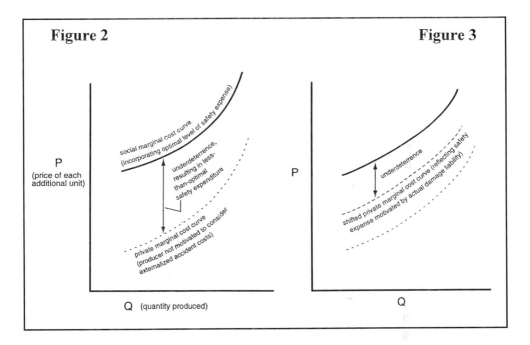

The social marginal cost curve (indicated by the solid line) is shaped somewhat like the private firm's marginal cost curve, but the cost level is higher because it includes safety-related behaviors that reduce accidents. The difference between the curves is the level of underdeterrence, or the degree to which the producer will externalize. The economic goal of the tort system, then, is quite simple: to force the producer to internalize accident costs by shifting the firm's cost curve.

(2) *Punitive Damages as Forcing Further Internalizing of Costs to Fit the Deterrence Gap.* Usually, however, compensatory damages leave a gap in deterrence caused by failures in detection, prosecution, proof, or remedy. Figure 3 illustrates this set of circumstances. The imposition of actual damage liability does partially force the firm to shift its marginal cost curve

upward, because the firm is motivated by the possibility that the courts may force it to compensate accident victims. But still, the shifted marginal cost curve (dashed line) is not socially optimal, because the failure of all accident victims to recover their costs fully results in a level of underdeterrence.

Punitive damages that fit this gap may force the proper shift. The firm's upward-shifted marginal cost curve would approximate the solid line (the social marginal cost curve) because it now would include expenses for safety features induced by the *combination* of compensatory and punitive damages.

(3) *The Economic Limits of Damages Laws: Costs, Benefits, Supply, and Demand.* There is a natural tendency to assume that if one dollar of accident-prevention expense is a good idea, two dollars are twice as good; consequently, there is a human urge to exaggerate the punitive award with the idea of perfectly deterring accidents. A decisionmaker in the form of a judge or juror may reason (erroneously) that the proper level of punitive damages is "whatever level is necessary to make these companies stop this behavior"-- i.e., to stamp out the offending behavior completely. This reasoning results in punitive damage overkill.

(4) *Punitive Damage Overkill.* The disadvantages of this overkill are illustrated in Figure 4. In an atomistically competitive market, the firm's

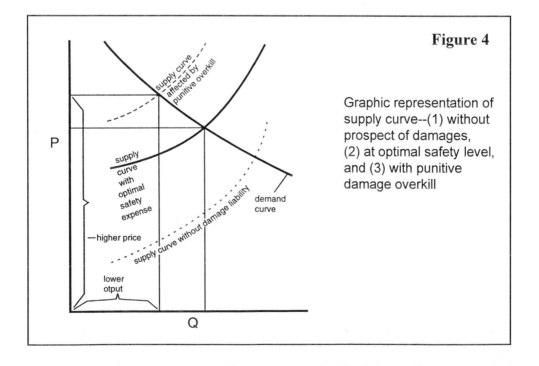

Figure 4

Graphic representation of supply curve--(1) without prospect of damages, (2) at optimal safety level, and (3) with punitive damage overkill

supply curve is identical to its marginal cost curve. This figure therefore labels the marginal cost curves as supply curves and couples them with a demand curve. The supply curves are sloped upward, because producers are eager to produce greater quantities when price increases; the demand curve, on the other hand, slopes downward, because consumers are willing to purchase greater quantities when price decreases. The intersection of the supply and demand curves is the market price.

Once again, the dotted line represents the firm's supply curve when the firm externalizes accident costs. This would be the supply curve if there were no prospect of damage liability. Producers would be willing to supply great quantities at low prices, but there is a catch: They cause a socially unacceptable number of accidents. The higher-level supply curve (solid line) is the social supply curve, reflecting optimal safety expense. The supply curve affected by punitive-damage overkill (dashed line) represents the supply curve that will result if firms are affected by an excess of punitive liability.

When firms face this sort of punitive-damage overkill, the tort system sends dysfunctional messages to producers. Consumers find that their purchases are more expensive, even in the case of crucially necessary products. If we apply an excess of punitive damages to producers of life-saving medicines, ambulance manufacturers, or health-care providers, we may find that we have both restricted the output of these goods and services and priced them out of the reach of some consumers.

[D]   Market Imperfections, Part Four: Informational Deficiencies and Transaction Costs

INCOMMENSURABILITY, IRRATIONALITY AND UNCERTAINTY

(1) *Economics in the Real World: The Uncertainty of Damage Liability.* The diagrams in the preceding section are useful because they clarify economic relationships. But they oversimplify things. For example, a real firm in a real marketplace cannot consult any handbook or web site that will show it the precise contours of the social marginal cost curve. Economic analysis must take account of incommensurability, irrationality, and uncertainty.

(2)   *Incommensurability of Values: What Is the "Worth" of a Human Life?*   When we compare accident losses and safety expenses, we are in a sense comparing apples   to   oranges.   This   is   the   issue   of "incommensurability," or lack of a common measure. Justice Antonin Scalia stated the problem well when he observed,   in   *Bendix   Autolite   Corp.   v.   Midwesco Enterprises*, 486 U.S. 888, 897 (1988), that the Supreme

Justice Antonin Scalia

Court often is called upon to decide "whether a particular line is longer than a particular rock is heavy."   Thus, in the abortion cases, the Court has undertaken to "balance" (a) the societal interests in preserving potential life against (b) individual abortion-related interests such as care of an unwanted child.   There is no common measure for these values, just as there is no common unit for apples and oranges.

It might be supposed that the balancing by the Court would be more reliable when one factor seems far more prominent than another, as if we compared a six-inch line with a thousand-pound rock. But what if the line is a chain of platinum, while the rock is only a half-ton of cracked limestone? In the tort arena, the risk of loss of life or paraplegic injuries may be weighed against the consumer's ability to choose an attractive convertible in the automobile market. In these kinds of cases, incommensurability becomes a serious problem.

(3) *Shadow Markets, or the Effort to Value the Unmeasurable.*   The economist usually "solves" the problem by assuming that each of these incommensurate values can be translated into dollar amounts. This is one of several assumptions that enables the economist to draw clear diagrams, but tradeoffs of incommensurate values must not be forgotten.   In some instances, the law recognizes the Herculean difficulty of placing dollar amounts on values--in fixing damages for the wrongful loss of a human life, for example--and the governing legal principles recognize the roughness of the result.   Still other values, such as love, achievement, or pleasure, are similarly difficult to quantify, although again the law does so when it is necessary, as when a tort plaintiff claims damages for the loss of these items.

Sometimes, we can construct hypothetical markets, or "shadow markets." For example, we can study how much of a premium in wages people insist upon to work in an occupation involving serious risk of death and compare it to a similar occupation without the risk. But the resulting calculation of the "value" of human life is crude.

(4) *Irrationality of Enforcement.* Even if we could derive clear, accurate curves by perfectly translating into dollars all accident losses, from hedonic pain to loss of life, and even if we could compare them to accurate totals of all safety expenses, we would face a second and related difficulty. Marginal cost curves are meaningless unless decisionmakers understand them. It would be necessary to educate every judge, and for that matter every juror, in economic theory.

Furthermore, we would need to ensure that the meaning of every verdict, present or future, would be adequately known to every firm. If a very high punitive award, for example, were to be based upon the jury's perception of a peculiar fact-bound instance of underdeterrence, every firm would need to perceive the limits on ways in which the verdict could be applied to that firm's (presumably different) circumstances.

(5) *Uncertainty of Factors in the Future.* Learned Hand's $B>PL$ formula assumes that such factors as the "probability" of accidents are known. But if so, they are known in only a very general way. Sometimes, recurring situations can be subjected to actuarial analysis, but even this science is imperfect, because it depends upon evaluation of past circumstances and their comparison to a different future. Thus, the firm that weighs production efficiency against safety expenses cannot precisely know either the probability that an additional dollar of safety expense will avoid an accident or the mathematically expected loss from the accident. For that matter, it cannot predict the evidence rules and legal principles that a future jury will apply to such a hypothetical accident years from now.

EXAMPLES AND PROBLEMS

(1) *An Appraisal for Purposes of the Eminent Domain Laws.* Imagine that the city has decided to take a narrow strip of a citizen's land to widen the road. It must pay "just compensation," or market value, to the landowner. Under the law, this compensation is valued by the price that a willing buyer would pay to a willing seller for the strip of land, with neither under compulsion to buy or sell. One way that an appraiser might determine this figure is to examine "comparable sales," or to investigate the "shadow market" of somewhat similar properties in recent years nearby, if there are

any. Can you see the uncertainties and incomparables that might enter into such an appraisal for this narrow strip? Is there really a meaningful shadow market for a narrow strip along the side of a particular property?

(2) *Can Cost Methods Determine Just Compensation under the Law?* A second method is to examine historical costs; i.e., to investigate how much the landowner paid per square foot for the property that includes the narrow strip (and if the transaction is old, to include a multiplier to bring it up to date). Critique this method, as compared to the shadow market.

TRANSACTION COSTS

(1) *The Concept of Transaction Costs, Including Legal Costs.* Next, we shall consider the market imperfection called "transaction costs." In virtually every transaction, the consumer pays more costs than those for the direct good or service desired, because there are costs involved in the making of the transaction itself. For example, the consumer may have to spend many hours looking at automobiles and talking to salespeople, as well as travel expenses. The market value of the consumer's time and expenses is part of the transaction cost. Or, imagine that a consumer seeks to sell, and another consumer seeks to buy, a home. The broker who puts the two together may charge a six percent (6%) commission (and a lawyer may charge a fee), which, together with the market value of the time and out-of-pocket costs expended by the two consumers, are transaction costs.

(2) *Gathering Information, Prevention of Fraud, Uncertainty of Performance, etc.* The "due diligence" that a purchaser undertakes in a complex transaction, in order to avoid loss caused by faulty information, fraud or nonperformance, also is properly to be considered as a transaction cost.

EXAMPLES AND PROBLEMS

(1) *The Costs of Litigation as Transaction Costs; Efforts to Lower Costs.* Notice that transaction costs can be very high; sometimes they are the costliest part of the package. In personal injury lawsuits, for example, less than half of the dollars that defendants pay is paid to accident victims, because plaintiffs' and defendants' attorney's fees and costs exceed half the total.

The law therefore has made many efforts to reduce transaction costs in these circumstances: no-fault insurance, "caps" or limits on recoveries in some kinds of cases, direct regulation of attorney's fees in some kinds of cases, etc. Note, however, that along with their hoped-for efficiencies, these methods of transaction cost reduction also produce certain kinds of inefficiencies. Can you explain? [What if reasonable real-world attorney's fees exceed the regulated maximum?]

(2) *Insurance Deductibles.* An insurance policy with low deductibles costs disproportionately more than one with high deductibles. Can you explain why, in terms of transaction costs?

(3) *The Transaction-Cost Justification for Class Action Suits.* Imagine that a consumer has a provable claim against a manufacturer for damages of approximately $5,000. But the claim is complicated, and the market value of attorney's fees to handle it is more than $25,000. There are several thousand other consumers who have very similar claims based upon the manufacturer's identical conduct. In terms of transaction costs, explain why a class action might be an efficient solution here.

§ 4.03 The Coase Theorem: If Transaction Costs Are Zero, Private Negotiation Treats Externalities Efficiently Regardless of Legal Rules

THE COASE THEOREM:
PRIVATE BARGAINS VERSUS LEGAL RULES

(1) *The Genesis of the Coase Theorem: The Problem of the Farmers and the Railroad.* Next, we shall consider an idea in law and economics known as the "Coase Theorem." The idea is related to transaction costs.

Professor Ronald Coase derived his famous theorem from contemplating a problem of contrasting legal rules. Imagine that a railroad runs through farmlands. Engines create sparks that burn nearby wheat fields. At least two legal rules are possible: one that would impose liability upon the railroad for damage to farmers, thus encouraging it to minimize sparks, and one that would place the loss upon farmers (by a rule of no liability for the railroad), thereby encouraging farmers to protect against sparks, such as by setting back their crops from the tracks.

Coase's insight was that, if there are no transaction costs, it is immaterial from an efficiency standpoint which of these legal rules one chooses, because the railroad and the farmers will themselves negotiate the efficient solution. This, then, is the Coase Theorem. It was further developed by Dean Guido Calabresi and economist George Stigler, among others. (Stigler's statement of the theorem is at the beginning of this chapter.)

(2) *Stating the Coase Theorem Generally: If Transaction Costs Are Zero, It Is Immaterial from an Efficiency Standpoint Which Legal Rule One Chooses with Respect to Liability, because the Parties Will Privately Arrive at the Efficient Solution by Negotiation.* If, for example, spark preventers can be placed on all engines for $10,000 per year, and the result will be that farmers can grow additional wheat worth $100,000 per year by planting closer to the tracks, the farmers collectively will pay the $10,000 even if there is a rule of no liability. (They will recover the cost of this factor of production through its inclusion in wheat prices, which efficiently will be paid by all who consume wheat, including the railroad and its owners.) This is so, that is, if transaction costs are zero.

On the other hand, if spark preventers cost $100,000 per year and the wheat crop gain from close-to-the-tracks planting is only $10,000, the railroad will pay the farmers to set their crops back so that it can save the higher cost of spark preventers, even if the legal rule imposes liability on the railroad. (The railroad will include the cost of this factor of production in its fares, which efficiently will be paid by all who ride the railroad or buy goods that are shipped on it, including farmers.) Again, this conclusion depends on the assumption of zero transaction costs.

(3) *The Coase Theorem as an Argument for Private Bargaining and for Reduction of Transaction Costs to Facilitate It.* The Coase Theorem usually is thought of as an argument in favor of private bargaining. The railroad and the farmers will reach an efficient solution if only government puts no obstacles in their path--and, of course, if transaction costs are zero.

And if there are other solutions--wetting the fields, using space close to tracks for strawberries instead, or relocating the rails--the parties will tend to find them and to negotiate them irrespective of the rule of legal liability, so long as their doing so is not legally prohibited and is free of transaction costs. The Coase Theorem thus is an argument for structuring things so that private bargaining is effective and for the reduction of transaction costs.

(4) *Distributional Effects May Remain.* This analysis does not mean that the farmers and the railroad are indifferent to which liability rule is imposed. The farmers may have to pay the railroad, or vice versa. Whoever pays will be forced by the market to include this cost in the product cost, reducing demand and creating wealth transfers. But the point is that allocative efficiency by the market is unaffected. Meanwhile, both sides may lobby the legislature for the entitlement in question--the right to emit sparks without consequence for the railroad, or the right to be compensated for the damage by farmers. Whoever gets this "property" right has obtained a political advantage, a wealth-enhancing entitlement, but it does not affect economic efficiency.

EXAMPLES AND PROBLEMS

(1) *The Assumption of Zero Transaction Costs: Does It Make the Coase Theorem a Useless Truism?* Notice that the Coase Theorem holds only when transaction costs are zero. This condition never can be met literally, because even the simplest transaction requires time and effort by the participants, and therefore it always costs something--some positive amount. The farmers would have to meet, agree, elect leaders, and negotiate with the railroads' representatives, who would have to do the same things. The parties would expend effort that must be subtracted from that available for farming and railroading.

Do you think that this real-world consideration makes the Coase Theorem useless? Or, if transaction costs are extremely small in relation to the production in question--if there is only one huge farmer in the valley, for example, and he and the railroad's president work out a solution in a 30-second telephone call--does the Coase Theorem, then, provide a useful analytical tool?

(2) *The Potential Superiority of Monetary Incentives over Laws Imposing Standards or Prohibitions in Some Cases.* Does the Coase Theorem suggest a reason why monetary incentives for (say) pollution reduction might be superior to absolute prohibitions or standards? Why might it be a bad idea for a government agency to mandate that all railroads install spark preventers (or, for that matter, for it to order farmers not to plant close to the tracks)?

(3) *Laws That Inhibit Dispute Settlements by Agreement.* For the most part, private settlements of lawsuits are not prohibited. In fact, contractual

resolution of disputes normally is encouraged. But there are some instances
when the law refuses to enforce settlement agreements: for example, claims
by minors, even if their parents consent, usually cannot be settled but require
a suit that is resolved by a judgment.

Does the Coase Theorem bear on whether this legal rule is efficient? In
practice, what lawyers usually do in the instance of a claim by a minor is to
negotiate a settlement, which by itself is ineffective, and then to file an
agrccd-upon suit called a "friendly suit," whereupon they present their
agreement to the judge, with the expectation that the judge will make it the
judgment of the court unless there is reason to disapprove it. Can you
analyze the efficiency of this solution?

Chapter 5
Finance

Risk, Return, and Valuation; Accounting and the Law

> *"Take my assets--but leave me my organization and in five years I'll have it all back."--Alfred P. Sloan, Jr., My Years with General Motors.*

> *"PV = 1/(1+i)^n."--Formula for the present value of a dollar, n years in the future at interest rate i.*
> *Therefore, the present value of each dollar regained by Sloan would be $1/(1+.1)^5 = 62$ cents, if all is gained at the end of five years, using a ten percent interest rate.*

§ 5.01 What This Chapter Is About

FINANCE AND ACCOUNTING

(1) *Management and Finance: The Sequel to Economics.* In this chapter and the next one, we shall consider the reasoning by which managers, investors, individuals, and governments make economic decisions, and we

shall see how those decisions interact with the law. No matter how good the idea is and irrespective of the nature of the organization, whether it is a corporation that is on the verge of discovering a cure for AIDS or a not-for-profit that promotes better race relations, it cannot produce without adequate financing. As the quotation above from the legendary Alfred Sloan indicates, good decisions produce results that cannot be obtained from raw materials alone. But as the present value equation shows, it is hard to evaluate the results without an understanding of finance. And a lawyer who represents either the corporation or the not-for-profit needs to understand finance and accounting.

These chapters are a natural companion to the economics chapters. In the economics coverage, we took a "top-down" approach, asking, "How does the market force firms to make efficient choices?" Here, the approach is "bottom-up": If you are the president of a firm in the marketplace, you must ask, "Given the market conditions facing me, how do I make efficient choices within the bounds of the law?" These chapters, then, are the "flip side" of the economics chapters.

(2) *Finance--Time, Risk, and Return: Why Do Lawyers Need to Know?* This chapter, on finance and accounting, will cover debt and equity financing as well as various aspects of time, risk, return, and valuation.

As a lawyer, you will find that your clients frequently need you to know about these subjects. If you want to help a client to obtain a loan (as lawyers frequently do), you will need to understand the lender's risks. Even in, say, a divorce practice, you frequently will face valuation issues, because often the first step in property division is to determine what the marital property is worth. And obviously, in a corporate or securities practice, finance is extremely important.

(3) *Accounting--and the Law.* But before considering these issues, we start with a more basic subject: accounting. Our first section considers fundamental accounting documents and methods. Again, a good idea, well financed, handled by good managers, cannot succeed without sound accounting. A not-for-profit entity that hopes to cure AIDS or bring racial justice needs accurate accounts as much as any profitable corporation does.

As a lawyer, you may have frequent interactions with accountants. Before settling a case with a marginally solvent defendant, for example, you probably will obtain financial statements from the defendant. You can make a better decision about settling if you understand the defendant's balance sheet. Major issues in a tax or securities practice depend upon accounting doctrines. In fact, some law schools have required that law students study accounting before graduating.

§ 5.02 Accounting

[A]   The Basic Accounting Documents

FROM JOURNAL TO BALANCE SHEET

(1) *Business Management and Basic Accounting Documents.* We begin, in this section, with accounting. We explain the basic accounting documents--the journal, the ledger, the balance sheet, and the income statement. We begin this chapter with accounting because it is fundamental to other issues in this and the next chapter, such as finance and business decisionmaking, and because unfortunately, although its basic concepts are simple, accounting seems foreign and forbidding to some people. It should not, as we shall see from the documents in this section. Later, we shall see how financial statements can be manipulated, and there, surprisingly, we shall see that the basic methods of manipulation also are simple. And, of course, we'll consider applications of accounting in the law, from tax to litigation.

(2) *Double-entry Bookkeeping: The Journal.* Accounting begins with bookkeeping. For an ongoing organization, each transaction is recorded sequentially as it occurs. Each trade, payment or acquisition is recorded in order. The document in which it is recorded, as it occurs, is called a "journal."

And if the journal is kept properly, it is done by "double-entry" bookkeeping. Double-entry does not mean keeping two sets of books. Instead, it means that whatever is traded away (or paid out) is reflected in the journal, and whatever is traded for (or bought) also is reflected separately. Each transaction creates two entries.

Double-entry accounting is one of the great inventions of modern finance. It facilitates the consolidation of journal entries into documents that provide an overall view, such as the balance sheet and income statement, which we shall consider below. Also, double-entry bookkeeping helps to create an audit trail by which the accuracy of accounts can be verified.

(3) *What a Double-Entry Journal Looks Like.* Imagine that our ongoing operation uses cash on hand to purchase office supplies worth $100. Then, it purchases computers worth $10,000, and it gives the seller a promissory note for this amount. Finally, it receives $1,000 from a customer for services rendered, with the $1,000 representing revenue. The journal entries for these three transactions would look something like this:

Figure 1 Journal with Double Entries			
Office Supplies	Cash	$100	$100
Computers	Note Payable	$10,000	$10,000
Cash	Revenue Received	$1,000	$1,000

(4) *Debits and Credits.* These journal entries are called "debits" and "credits," respectively. When part of an account is used in exchange for something else, so that it is reduced, we "credit" that account. Correspondingly, when we increase another item that the first account was reduced in exchange for, we "debit" that account. In the figure, for example, we have spent $100 cash in exchange for office supplies costing $100, so we "credit" cash $100 and "debit" office supplies $100. The concept can be expressed (with roughly accurate simplicity) by saying "You credit the account where the money came from, and you debit the account where the money went."

Notice that these terms are neutral; they do not convey any positive or negative judgment. Colloquially, a credit may sound "good" and a debit may sound vaguely "bad," but not in accounting. In fact, it's the account that decreases (here, cash) that gets "credited," while the account that increases (office supplies) is the one that gets "debited." But don't worry too much about keeping this confusing (and intuitively backward) terminology straight, because in reality what a double-entry bookkeeper does is to decrease one account and increase another in an equal amount, always with two entries, a debit and a credit. That's the real point.

(5) *Consolidating the Journal: Posting in the Ledger.* Remember, all the journal does is to record transactions as they occur in time. It does not collect together all the office-supplies transactions, or all the cash, or all the notes. If you want to tell what you've spent or what you've got, the journal isn't a convenient reference, because it's just a jumble of raw data.

Therefore, we need to consolidate all transactions involving each similar item. The document that results will sum up all changes by category: office supplies, cash, and notes payable (and every other asset or liability). We then can know how much more or less of each of these things the operation had at the end of the period than at its beginning. We call such a document a "ledger," and we "post" items from the (chronological) journal into the (itemized) ledger, which categorizes them.

By consulting the financial statements at the beginning of the period and adjusting them for the changes, we will be able to see, now, what the operation has, as well as how it has changed. With modern electronics, it is possible to prepare financial statements directly from a proper double-entry journal, and so this intermediate consolidation represented by the ledger sometimes is not explicitly printed; however, explaining it, here, makes the link between the journal and the overall financial statements easier to understand.

(6) *The Balance Sheet and the Income (or Profit-and-Loss) Statement.* The two most representative financial documents, after the journal and ledger, are the "balance sheet" and the "income statement" (also called the "profit and loss statement," or simply the "P and L").[1]

The balance sheet is a composite representation of the organization's assets, liabilities, and net worth. The income statement is a reflection of the changes in the various accounts, and in the bottom line, over a given period of time, such as a year. The next section will concern itself with these fundamental documents.

---

1   There also can be other statements, such as the "cash flow statement," but they are beyond our scope here.

THE BALANCE SHEET AND THE INCOME STATEMENT

(1) *The Fundamental Accounting Equation That Underlies the Balance Sheet.* The fundamental accounting equation is this:

ASSETS = LIABILITIES + NET WORTH (or EQUITY).

Simplistically, "assets" are the tangible or intangible things that you have that have value. "Liabilities" are what you owe to other people. "Net worth" is the amount by which what you have exceeds what you owe.

"Net worth" often is called "equity," as in "the equity in this business is $50,000." In a not-for-profit organization, it usually is referred to as the "fund balance." This last expression may help explain the concept; the fund balance (or the net worth, or equity) is the balance left over, after you have subtracted liabilities from assets. This simple equation is the essence of the balance sheet.

Figure 2
Balance Sheet of Bookstore Inc.
As of December 31, 2000

Assets			Liabilities		
Cash		$10,000	Accounts Payable	$5,000	
Equipment	$10,000		Note Payable	8,000	
Less:			Unearned Revenue	500	$13,500
Accumulated Depreciation	2,000	8,000			
Accounts Receivable	10,000		Equity		
Less: Reserve for Bad Debts	1,500	8,500	Capital Stock	$8,000	
			Additional Paid-in Capital	10,000	
Inventory		10,000	Retained Earnings	5,000	23,000
Total Assets		36,500	Total Liabilities and Equity		36,500

---

(2) *The Customary Format of the Balance Sheet.* It is customary for assets to be listed first, in the upper or left-hand part of the balance sheet. Separate entries are made for different sorts of assets: cash, accounts

receivable, furniture and fixtures, real estate owned, and the like. The last entry for assets is called "Total Assets" and is double-underlined.

Liabilities likewise are set out separately, with such items as accounts payable and loans payable. "Total Liabilities" is the next entry, followed by "Equity" or "Net Worth." Then, "Total Liabilities and Net Worth" is the last item and is double-underlined. This double-underlined figure, for liabilities and net worth, must equal the double-underlined figure for assets. Remember the fundamental equation: Assets = Liabilities + Net Worth (or Equity).

Figure 2 is an example of a simple balance sheet. This one happens to be for a corporation called "Bookstore Inc."

(3) *Summarizing the Balance Sheet: A Year-End Snapshot.* The balance sheet, then, is a "snapshot" of the financial condition of the business entity as of a given moment, such as the end of the year. It tells you how much the entity has, how much it owes, and how much what it has exceeds what it owes. And it's just that simple.

But there are questions that the balance sheet can't answer. How good has this past year been? Has the business made money or lost money? The balance sheet is static. It's possible that Bookstore Inc. gained most of its equity this year, and it's equally possible, from the balance sheet alone, that it started the year with much more, but lost money. To analyze these possibilities, we need a separate document, called an "income statement."

Figure 3
Income Statement for Bookstore Inc.
For the Year Ended December 31, 2000

Revenues			Office Expense	$2,000	
Sales of Books	$10,000		Insurance, Interest, Fees	1,000	
Less: Cost of Goods Sold	-8,000	2,000	Uncollectible Accounts Receivable	1,000	
Services Rendered		5,000	Total Expenses		$6,000
Total Revenues		$7,000	Net Income before Taxes		1,000
Expenses			Taxes		100
Depreciation	$2,000		Net Income after Taxes		$ 900

(4) *The Income Statement.* The income statement, or profit-and-loss statement, summarizes "revenues" (items received), "expenses" (costs paid), and "net income" (revenues minus expenses) over a given time period, usually a year. Net income may be separated into "net income before taxes" and "net income after taxes." Figure 3 is an income statement, again for the fictional "Bookstore Inc."

(5) *Summarizing the Income Statement: A Representation of Gains or Losses During an Entire Time Period, Such as a Year.* Thus, while the balance sheet is a snapshot taken at a given instant, the income statement shows the change over a period of time (often, a year). If the business has made money during this period, the income statement will tell us so, just as it will tell us if it has lost money.

EXAMPLES AND PROBLEMS

(1) *The Balance Sheet: Assets, Liabilities and Equity--and Their Relation to the Journal.* The assets all come either from last year's balance sheet or from the journal. The same is true of the liabilities; the sum of entries in each journal category is used to adjust the figure from last year's balance sheet. The total-equity figure then can be simply done by subtraction. Can you see why?

(2) *A Lawyering Problem Involving the Income Statement: Net Income, but What Relation to Equity?* Notice that the Income Statement above, for Bookstore Inc., shows positive net income before and after taxes. The corporation has "made money" over the last year. But this does not mean that buying it would be a good investment. Can you see why, considering that the net after-tax income as a percentage of equity is less than 5%? Imagine how you would advise a client who wanted to buy Bookstore Inc.

[B]   Adjusting to Account for Time Differences

ACCRUAL BASIS ACCOUNTING

(1) *Cash Basis: Payment or Receipt Date as Controlling, with Resulting Distortions.* So far, we have been discussing these issues as if only the "cash basis" for accounting were applicable. Cash basis means that an expense is recognized in its entirety when paid, and revenues in their entirety when received. But what if the organization receives an advance payment for

services that are to be rendered over the next five years? A cash basis income statement recognizes all of it immediately, even though it hasn't been earned. Similarly, a large capital expense ($10,000 for computers that will be useful for five years) is recognized at once, even though its benefits have yet to be realized.

(2) *Accrual Basis Accounting.* Another way to do it is to "accrue" income when it is earned (whether received or not) and to "defer" income that has been received but not earned. Similarly, one "accrues" expenses that have been incurred (whether paid or not) and "defers" those paid but not earned. This is "accrual basis" accounting, as opposed to cash basis.

For example, imagine that Bookstore Inc. receives $1,000 on July 1 of this year for services to be performed monthly for the local newspaper over the next twelve months. Cash basis accounting would recognize the entire $1,000 as revenue in this year. Accrual basis accounting, however, would recognize one-twelfth of the $1,000, or $87.50, each month; $500 in revenues would be attributable to this year, $500 next year. This treatment arguably is more accurate, because the second $500 hasn't been earned this year.

Individuals and small businesses often use cash basis accounting. It is simpler; the complexity and expense of accrual accounting may exceed the gain in accuracy. But larger businesses usually use accrual accounting. When properly done, accrual accounting may provide a more accurate snapshot of financial condition.

(3) *The Accounting Treatment of Deferred or Accrued Items.* How would accrual accounting treat the Bookstore Inc. contract we just discussed ($1,000 for yet-to-be preformed monthly services)? It would record the $1,000 in cash in the journal as having been received (it's in Writers League's possession and has to be recorded), but it would not record this amount as revenue. Instead, it would record a liability under the heading of "unearned revenue." Upon receipt of the $1,000, then, the Writers League would add an entry of "Cash . . . $1,000" and an offsetting entry of "Unearned Revenue . . . $1,000."

Then, each month, the journal would reduce the $1,000 in "Unearned Revenue" by $87.50 (one-twelfth), after the organization performed its services. It also would add an entry of $87.50 to revenue.

At the end of this year, if there were no other relevant transactions, the balance sheet would reflect the following changes from last year: Cash, changed by $1,000; Unearned Revenue, changed by $500; Equity, changed by $500. The balance sheet in Figure 2 shows these kinds of accounts, in fact. The income statement would be similarly affected (see Figure 3). Originally, in the journal, the entries would look like Figure 4:

Figure 4 Accrual Treatment of Cash Received, as Yet Unearned (Taken From Figure 2)		
Cash	$1,000	
Unearned Revenue		$1,000

Then, each month, there would be an entry of "Revenue, $87.50," and a separate entry reducing Unearned Revenue: "Unearned Revenue, $87.50."

(4) *Reserves: Bad Debts and Other Contingencies.* Accrual accounting creates another kind of problem: sometimes it recognizes revenues that haven't been received and may never be. When services are rendered or goods sold on credit, the account receivable is an asset. The total of all accounts receivable of a particular kind is reflected in that category on the balance sheet. Since the accounts receivable have been earned, their total is accrued as revenue. But will it all be collected?

The answer, for many organizations, is no. A certain percentage of buyer-debtors will default. The balance sheet, therefore, should subtract an estimated amount. This amount is called a "reserve," in this instance a "reserve for bad debts" (also sometimes called an "allowance for uncollectible accounts"). The balance sheet in Figure 2 shows an example of such a reserve or allowance. An excerpt is shown in Figure 5, which repeats the relevant part of Figure 2:

Figure 5 Treatment of Reserves Against Account (Taken From Figure 2)		
Accounts Receivable	$10,000	
Less: Reserve for Bad Debts	1,500	$8,500

(5) *When Reserves Are Required: The Principle of Conservatism.* In general, a reserve is mandated by "Generally Accepted Accounting Principles" ("GAAP's") whenever a contingent loss is likely to occur and can reasonably be estimated. We shall discuss GAAP's further below. The method of estimating bad debts is a complex matter dependent on the type of receivables, the company and industry history, etc.

This requirement of reserves for likely contingencies is part of the "principle of conservatism." Accountants aren't necessary gloomy people, but the rules they follow are conservative. The GAAPs often require a choice of the approach that would avoid inflating the books, even if the choice tends to deflate them.

By the same token, although contingent losses often require reserves, contingent assets, or probable future gains, usually are not as easily recorded. Accounting is a conservative profession. If you think you have taken steps that make you very likely to obtain revenues of $1 million a year from now, an accountant probably will not accrue it if significant contingencies to its entitlement remain.

(6) *Depreciation.* Yet another problem concerns the concept of depreciation. If the organization purchases computers for $10,000, and it pays in cash in advance, it expects the asset to remain useful for more than the year in which it is purchased--but not to remain useful forever. It gradually will be used up or become obsolete. This is a "capital expenditure" that is subject to an expense called "depreciation." (When the asset is an intangible, such as a patent, "amortization" is the equivalent term, and the term "depletion" is used for natural resources. The basic concept, however, is the same, and here, we shall concentrate on depreciation.)

Depreciation is an expense that is reflected on the income statement as such. On the balance sheet, it reduces the asset account. Typically, the "book value" or purchase price (also called the "basis") is shown on the balance sheet, and depreciation is shown as a subtraction from it. As a result, depreciation also reduces equity (although the latter effect is not explicitly shown, since depreciation is factored in with all other expenses). Figure 2 (the Bookstore Inc. balance sheet) shows an example, and Figure 6 is an excerpt that repeats the relevant part.

Figure 6
Treatment of Depreciation (Taken From Figure 2)

Equipment	$10,000	
Less: Accumulated Depreciation	2,000	$8,000

In this example, the basic or book value is $10,000. It is reduced by the accumulated depreciation of $2,000 so that total assets, and indirectly equity, will reflect net value of $8,000.

(7) *Accelerated Depreciation.* The simplest kind of depreciation is "straight line" depreciation, which expenses the same amount each year. The book value is divided by the "useful life" of the asset, after first being reduced by the "salvage value" (or value at the end of its useful life). If computers worth $10,000 have a useful life of five years and can be sold as junk for $5,000 after that time, each year's straight-line depreciation will be ($10,000 - $5,000) ÷ 5 = $1,000. This type of depreciation--straight line--is what is shown on the Writers League balance sheet and income statements in Figures 2 and 3, as well as in Figure 6, here.

But an asset may depreciate faster in earlier than in later years. (An automobile, for example, depreciates much more in the first year than the second.) Sometimes, then, "accelerated depreciation" may give a more accurate picture than the straight-line method. For example, the "double-declining balance" method is one among several depreciation models that depreciate faster than the straight line method. It doubles the straight-line amount in the first year. In the second year, it takes the basis less first year's depreciation and again doubles the straight-line amount for that balance, using the remaining useful life. No salvage value is used for the double-declining-balance method. The examples, below, show how it is done.

EXAMPLES AND PROBLEMS

(1) *A Tax Law Example: Sometimes Accrual Accounting May Result in Favorable Tax Treatment.* Imagine a service provider who collects fees in full in advance for services that will be rendered over several years in the future. (Some attorneys, as well as various other service providers, fit this description.) It generally is advantageous to have current use of cash but to defer taxes on it until later years. It is possible, therefore, that accrual

accounting would create better tax treatment for this service provider. Can you explain?

(2) *More Tax Law: Using Accelerated Depreciation.* Accelerated depreciation, too, can offer tax advantages. In our $10,000 computer-purchase example, with a useful life of five years, the double-declining-balance method, for the first year, would yield double depreciation of 40%, not 20% ($10,000 x 40% = $4,000). In the second year, we would begin by figuring the balance left after the first year's depreciation ($10,000 - $4,000 = $6,000), and we would again multiply by 40% ($6,000 x 40% = $2,400).[2]

In this example, accelerated depreciation has expensed $6,400, or sixty-four percent (64%) of the asset's $10,000 basis, in just the first two years. This sort of necessary and ordinary business expense may be deductible against gross income, reducing taxes. Can you explain the math--and explain why the use of accelerated rather than straight-line depreciation may give tax advantages?

[C]   The Use of Judgment in Accounting

STANDARDS, JUDGMENT, AND "COOKING THE BOOKS"

(1) *Legal Standards and Generally Accepted Accounting Principles (GAAP).* An entity called the Financial Accounting Standards Board ("FASB") has promulgated a set of accounting standards, usually denominated by the acronym plus a number (e.g., "FASB 66," pronounced "FAS-bee-66," which denominates the 66th standard). These FASB standards, together with certain other standards, make up what are called "Generally Accepted Accounting Principles" (which usually is abbreviated "GAAP" and pronounced, simply, "gap"). We already have seen one application of GAAP, above, when we described the allowance for uncollectible accounts. The applicable GAAP, as we saw, requires a reserve for any contingent loss that is likely to occur and subject to reasonable estimation.

---

2   There actually are different methods of calculating double-declining balances. Some readers may have learned a different one.

Certified public accountants are subject to a professional code that ties them to FASB, and many areas of the law depend on FASB and GAAP. The SEC, for matters within its jurisdiction, presumes that accounting not conforming to FASB standards is misleading (i.e., that it reflects securities fraud). In other instances, failure to follow GAAP accounting may subject a person to possible liability of various kinds. Therefore, GAAP accounting is important.

(2) *An Example of Accounting Judgment and the Law: The Treatment of Inventory and Sales.* But the standards leave a great deal of room for judgment. Let us consider one example here: the treatment of inventory. As we shall see, judgments about methods of valuation can make financial statements for the same business either gloomy or rosy, and they can create liability for your clients under the law.

Many kinds of businesses, especially sales businesses, deal in constantly changing inventories. The financial statements then depend on how the organization values its inventory at the end of the accounting period, as well as how it values the expense for the goods it has converted to revenue (called the "cost of goods sold").

(a) *Existing Inventory: Lower-of-Cost-or-Market.* If Bookstore Inc. has in stock two thousand reference books dated in the past year and bought at $10 each, but a new edition has just come out, should it value the existing inventory of these soon-to-be obsolete books at cost ($20,000) or at market value (which is much less, perhaps $2 per book, for a lower value of $4,000)?

The basic principle, consistent with the conservatism of accounting, is to use the "lower of cost or market." Here, the $20,000 valuation would be misleading. A purchaser of a business valued this way might have a valid lawsuit for fraud or breach of warranty. The lower-of-cost-or-market principle would require valuation, instead, at market value, or $4,000. A set of complex rules guide the accountant in deciding about this, but a great deal of judgment is required.

Often, the accountant's clients react negatively to this "writing down" of assets to a lower value, based on market value. They need to show positive equity, as high as possible, for various reasons: to attract capital or to declare a dividend, perhaps. The accountant's duty to avoid misleading can be difficult to stick to, in such circumstances. And notice one other thing: if the market value of the inventory has increased, the client does not get this increase reflected on the books. It's the "lower" of cost or market that the accountant must use. Again, the principle of conservatism is at work.

(b) *Book Value of Existing Inventory and Sales: LIFO, FIFO, Average Cost, Etc.* Next, let us consider a different kind of judgment about inventory. Let us assume that Bookstore Inc. also acquired two thousand of this year's reference books, half bought early at $10 each and half bought later at a more expensive price of $20 each, and it has since sold a thousand at $30 each. The question now arises, how does it value the revenue--and the remaining inventory?

First, it can adopt the "FIFO" method–"first in, first out"--and assume that all the sales were of the earlier-acquired books. This method would value the existing inventory of 1,000 books at $20,000, while attributing only $10,000 to "cost of goods sold" (the other 1,000 books, bought at $10 each). FIFO, in these circumstances, produces a high value for revenue and also for inventory. See Figure 7 for an example of how the choice between LIFO and FIFO would affect the account.

Figure 7
Comparing Effects of FIFO and LIFO on the Income Statement

Sales of Books	$30,000		Sales of Books	$30,000	
Less: Cost of			Less: Cost of		
Gods Sold,	10,000		Goods Sold,	20,000	$10,000
Using FIFO		$20,000	Using LIFO		

Alternatively, Bookstore Inc. can use 'LIFO"–"last in, first out." This means that its cost of goods sold is $20,000 rather than $10,000, lowering its revenue, and its inventory will be valued at only $10,000 (based on the cost of the earlier books) rather than $20,000. LIFO, in this situation, paints a gloomier, more conservative picture.[3]

(3) *Footnotes to the Financial Statements: How a Lawyer Should Read Them (and Should Insist That They Be Written).* For the reader of the

---

3   Yet another method is to average the valuations. This "average cost method" produces results between those of LIFO and FIFO.

financial statements, these different possibilities create difficulty in knowing what the statements mean. If FIFO has been used in this situation, the income statement paints a rosy picture, and so does the inventory portion of the balance sheet. If LIFO has been used, the picture may be artificially gloomy. The numbers themselves do not tell which of these different methods has produced them.

Part of the solution to this problem is disclosure. Footnotes to the financial statements are an important part of the statements. A footnote might explain, for example, that inventory was valued using the last-in-first-out method (LIFO), and it might indicate what difference this choice makes. Another part of the solution is consistency: The use of similar methods in related documents.

(4) *Cooking the Books: Legal (and Illegal) Manipulation of Financial Statements.* The above discussion suggests ways in which financial statements can be manipulated. Here, we shall catalogue various ways in which an organization wanting to present a rosy picture can "cook the books." As a lawyer, you will need to be alert to these devices in the books of companies with which your clients do business.

(a) *Characterization.* An organization using accrual accounting can record a cash receipt as earned revenue when it ought to be recorded, instead, as a liability under the heading of "unearned revenue." Sometimes, the issue is ambiguous, and the mischaracterization may not be readily detectable (or provable).

(b) *Inconsistency.* An organization may shift accounting methods (cash or accrual, for example) from year to year, each time choosing the one that pumps up its income and equity. Or, two subsidiaries that sell to each other might adopt LIFO or FIFO inconsistently, improving the picture for both. The solution, for the reader, is to study whether consistent methods are used in related statements. Alternatively, the reader can insist on consolidated financials from a holding company, including all its subsidiaries.

(c) *Valuation.* We already have seen that the failure to use market value for inventory, when market value is less than cost, can misrepresent near-worthless assets as valuable ones. Choosing FIFO over LIFO, in an inflationary economy, may overstate both income and assets.

(d) *Reserves and Depreciation.* A wholesale organization can puff its bottom line by adopting a 2% reserve for bad debts when the industry average is 15% (such a difference might wipe out all net income). An organization that uses the straight-line method with a long useful life and high salvage value, in computing its depreciation expense for exhaustible resources like automobiles, may succeed in overstating both income and equity.

EXAMPLES AND PROBLEMS

(1) *A Litigation Problem Involving Accounting: How an Organization Expecting to Be Sued Might Present Its Financials.* More often than not, an individual or organization has a motive to inflate the financials, such as when they are being used to obtain a loan, attract investors, or sell a going concern. But sometimes the motive is to understate equity and income. Imagine, for example, an organization that is threatened with suit, attempts to settle, and adopts the strategy of arguing, "Your demand far exceeds the net worth of this entire business, and if you insist on it you will recover less than if you compromise."

Often in this situation, the claimant demands financial statements. Imagine that the defendant organization prepares them for the purpose. Imagine that, in doing so, it systematically does all of the following: (a) adopts accrual methods to defer income, (b) characterizes revenue as unearned in ambiguous circumstances, (c) adopts high contingency reserves, (d) values inventory by pessimistic market methods, (e) shifts cash to sister corporations in exchange for assets of book value less than the cash, (f) values inventory and cost of goods sold by the LIFO method, and (g) uses double-declining balance depreciation with short useful life for all its capital assets. Can you explain why this lawsuit target has adopted each of these tactics?

(2) *A Lawyer's Reasoning About Financial Statements.* How can a lawyer reading such a set of financial statements put them into proper perspective? Consider how each of the following might help. (a) Look to see whether there are footnotes explaining the underlying methods in each of these instances, and if not, discount your reliance accordingly. (b) Read the footnotes related to these matters. (c) Consider the impact of reversing each of the indicated choices (i.e., make a guesstimate of the difference that FIFO or average cost would make if substituted for LIFO). (d) Insist on an explicit

representation that the financials conform to GAAP. (e) Insist on a representation to this effect by a solvent third-party accountant. (f) Insist on audited financials (see the next section).

[D]   Internal Controls and Auditing

CONTROLS (PREVENTING MISUSE)
AND AUDITING (VERIFICATION)

(1) *Internal Controls: Preventing Illegal Transactions.* One of the dangers suggested but not made explicit by the discussion above is the possibility of misuse of assets or liabilities by officers or agents of the organization. This possibility raises the issue of internal controls.

The key to rigorous internal controls is separation and duplication. Then, the custody of an asset is in one person's hands, the execution and recording of transactions is in another's, and the power to authorize the transaction is a third person's responsibility. It is difficult, then, for one individual to embezzle without detection.

But these controls are a balancing act. They are costly, both in terms of expenditures on the controls themselves and in terms of incursions on the judgment of the persons controlled. A flower shop run as a proprietorship, for example, might be better off without the same controls as a larger entity.

(2) *Internal Controls for Cash Receipts and Disbursements.* Cash is a favorite target of embezzlement. If an employee receives cash for sales, it is easy for the employee in some organizations to pocket it and simply fail to account for it. Similar results can occur with checks through the expedient of forged endorsements. In some kinds of businesses, such as bars and restaurants, internal controls regarding cash can make the difference between profitability and disastrous losses. The owner of a bar may need to be there, every evening.

One essential requisite is to account for cash immediately upon receipt. Setting up systems so that transactions cannot be completed without such an account (e.g., numbered customer receipts) is an example. Duplication also is a solution: a mail-order business may require two employees to open the day's receipts, set up an accounting document, and sign it.

As for cash disbursements, one control is to require all cash to be deposited, rather than dipping into the day's receipts for expenses. This means that there is a clearer paper trial: an employee will have to write a check to embezzle from deposited cash. But this alone is not enough. Backup documents for expenses must be generated, explaining each check-paid item, and must be reviewed by a separate person. In the absence of these controls, employees have been known to write checks literally for millions of dollars to shell entities that they controlled.

(3) *Auditing: Can Your Clients Rely on the Financials?* Preparing financial statements is one thing. Often, it is done by internal employees or by the proprietor of a small business. "Auditing" of financials is quite another thing. It may involve exhaustive verification of assets and liabilities if that is the auditor's charge; in that event, the auditor may insist on eyeballing the inventory, seeing each item of real estate, contacting customers to verify transactions, etc. At the other extreme, the auditor's task may be limited to relying upon and examining financial documents generated by the organization for the purposes of certifying that they conform to GAAP.

Certifying auditors usually are not internal employees but independent certified public accountants. Within their delineated task, they follow "Generally accepted auditing standards," or "GAAS" (the counterpart of GAAP). The potential liability of the independent auditor for losses due to misstatement is one reason lenders, investors, and other contracting parties place reliance on audited statements.

(4) *How a Lawyer Should Read the Audit Letter: Components and Qualifications.* Upon completing an audit, the independent auditor will provide an "audit letter." It typically contains three components. First, it delineates the responsibility of the auditor, protecting the auditor from claims outside this responsibility. "We have relied upon financial statements of income and equity that are the sole responsibility of the Corporation's management," for example, means that the auditors do not purport to have examined all the underlying documents or exhaustively verified the assets. The second component is a description of the performance by the auditor, usually containing the statement that the auditor has conformed to "generally accepted auditing standards." A typical representation also would state that the auditor has examined "evidence" on a sampled or test basis that provides "reasonable assurance" of freedom from material misrepresentation, even if not every document or asset has been examined.

The third component is an opinion, with or without qualification, that the financials "fairly present" the organization's condition, "in conformity with generally accepted accounting principles." Any qualification to the opinion detracts from the credence that a reader should place in the financials.

§ 5.03 Finance

[A]   Equity and Debt Financing

BEHIND EQUITY OR NET WORTH ENTRIES: CAPITAL ACCOUNTS AND RETAINED EARNINGS

(1) *A Lawyer's Knowledge of Finance: From Equity and Debt Finance to the Time Value of Money.* In this section, we consider finance. If an organization has a good idea, how does it fund the execution of the idea? As a lawyer, how do you help it deal with lenders or investors? We shall encounter such concepts as debt and equity financing, different methods of each, the time value of money, investment risk and return, and like concepts.

Again, these issues are universal to organizations with worthwhile operations. We have discussed the need of a corporation seeking to cure AIDS for good accounting; one reason is that it must secure financing. The same is true of a not-for-profit entity that intends to create better race relations. We need, therefore, to consider financing. We start with the financing reflected in the accounting documents we have seen above, for Bookstore Inc.

(2) *Legally Significant Components of Net Worth: Capital Accounts and Retained Earnings.* First, let us examine the "bottom line" of the Bookstore Inc. balance sheet in Figure 2: the equity or net worth item, or what the entity has that exceeds what it owes. For a small organization conducted as a proprietorship, the net worth or equity item is not complex and usually is not subdivided. For a partnership, different partners may have different equity accounts depending on their capital contributions and the partnership agreement. A corporation or similar organization, like the entity in Figure 2, is more interesting and will be our principal subject here. The equity item in Figure 2 and its components are excerpted here in Figure 8.

Figure 8		
Equity and Its Components (Taken From Figure 2)		
Capital Stock	$8,000	
Additional Paid-in Capital	10,000	
Retained Earnings	5,000	$23,000

The components of equity include "capital accounts" (capital stock and additional paid-in capital) and "retained earnings." These kinds of classifications can be crucially important to a lawyer, determining (for example) whether a corporation lawfully can pay a dividend under controlling statutes.

(3) *Capital Accounts: Capital Stock and Additional Paid-in Capital.* A corporation issues stock to shareholders in exchange for capital, cash or otherwise, or for other value. The amount of this capital is the "capital accounts" portion of the equity.

There is a technical distinction between two particular capital accounts. First, "capital stock" or "stated capital" denotes the par value paid for the stock. The definition of par value varies from state to state, usually is less than the capital paid in, and carries complexities that are beyond our scope here. In some states, the classification of equity as "capital stock" (or stated capital), may make legal differences, affecting taxes or other aspects of the corporation's existence.

The remaining capital contributions are called "additional paid-in capital," or "capital paid in in excess of par value," or "capital surplus." Again, see Figure 2. This is the amount paid in to the entity, for shares, in excess of par value of the shares. Thus, there are two components of the capital accounts. In the figure, capital stock (par value invested) is $8,000, and additional paid-in capital (investment above par value) is $10,000. The capital account portion of equity is $18,000.

(4) *Retained Earnings.* "Retained earnings" are exactly what their name implies: net income, after taxes, that has been retained rather than paid to shareholders in dividends. In the figure, the retained earnings portion of equity is $5,000. This means that the entity has earned this much net income after taxes, along the way, that it has not paid out.

DEBT AS CONTRASTED TO EQUITY FINANCING

(1) *Equity Financing in Our Example: The Lawyer's Role.* The balance sheet and income statement for Bookstore Inc., and the equity accounts repeated above, show it to be heavily financed by equity. There is at least one debt item, the $8,000 note payable (for equipment, probably), and there are accounts payable (but these are short-term). Equity, on the other hand, is $23,000, of which $18,000 is paid-in capital. This may be a poor way to finance an entity that has earned less than $1,000 during the past year. As a lawyer, you will need to understand these matters in helping your clients with lenders or investors.

(2) *Leveraging Through Debt Financing.* If, on the other hand, the corporation had $5,000 worth of equity and had financed the rest of its business through debt (a bank loan), a net income after taxes of $900 would provide a return of 15%. (It is not possible simply to convert an organization of this kind into a debt-financed entity with the same net income because interest expense will increase accordingly; the example, however, demonstrates the "leveraging" power of debt financing.)

EXAMPLES AND PROBLEMS

(1) *Financing Through Retained Earnings.* The Writers League accounts show retained earnings as $5,000, which are part of its financing. It would be atypical for such an entity to retain all earnings, as opposed to paying part of them out as dividends (which would be reflected on the income statement but, at least for this entity this year, are not). Financing with retained earnings sometimes is called "growing from within." This is a conservative method of business expansion. Can you see why?

(2) *The Corporate Lawyer's Concept of a Leveraged Buyout (LBO).* Suppose that Brenda Buyer agrees to purchase Bookstore Inc. for $40,000. (For this transaction to make sense, we need to imagine that Bookstore Inc. is returning, say, 25% on equity, equal here to $5,750 annually, or that it shows promise of producing such a return.) Buyer pays twenty percent of the purchase price, or $8,000, from her own funds and borrows the rest, $32,000, at eight percent 8% interest from a financial institution. Buyer has just completed a "leveraged buyout," or "LBO." (We usually think of LBO's as multi-billion dollar transactions, but the principle is the same. Also, usually

the assets and income stream from the purchased entity are used to secure or pay the loan.)

How has Buyer "leveraged" her investment? She can hope for net income of $5,750, reduced by her additional interest expense of $2,560, or $3,190 annually. On an investment of $8,000, the return is 40%. Can you see how debt financing "leverages" Brenda? (Notice that if she had paid the $40,000 purchase price from her own capital, her income of $5,750 would yield only 5,750 ÷ 40,000 = 14%, a much lower rate of return.)

(3) *Playing With Someone Else's Money: Why Shouldn't a Lawyer Advise the Client to Borrow It All (Debt Financing of 100%)?* One might wonder, then, why Brenda would not borrow all of the purchase price and complete the transaction with 100% debt financing. Brenda might like to, and indeed sometimes financing of this kind--with no money down--can be obtained. But the more responsive answer is that the lender is likely to insist on equity financing by Brenda to some degree. Can you see why a prudent financial institution might insist on this?

[B] Risk, Return, and Valuation

THE TIME VALUE OF MONEY

(1) *Why Must a Lawyer Consider the Time Value of Money?* One major consideration in finance is the time value of money, which has significance because the use of capital over time has value. A person who will owe $1,000 ten years from now has the use of the capital it represents for the intervening years and is financially better off than a person who owes the same $1,000 now. Conversely, the $1,000 is worth less to a recipient who will get it after ten years than it is to the recipient who gets it now.

To take a concrete example, consider our hypothetical corporation seeking to find a cure for AIDS. If it receives investments now, the corporation can begin research now. If its funding will not be available until ten years from now, any innovations it might produce will be delayed for ten years, and so will the income it might gain and the benefits it might produce. Similarly, a lawyer who settles a lawsuit for a twenty-year payout (a structured settlement) needs to understand that it is worth less than cash now, and the lawyer must know how much less.

(2) *Compound Interest.* Compound interest may more accurately reflect the time value of money than simple interest. A dollar at ten percent simple interest produces ten cents (10¢) each year. But if the ten cents is not actually paid to the creditor, the use of the dollar for a year makes it worth $1.10, and a truer picture of its time value for the second year would be obtained by adding ten percent of this figure--.10 x $1.10 = $0.11, or eleven cents-- producing a total value of $1.21.

In the third year, then, compound interest would add $0.121, to produce $1.331. At ten percent, a rough rule of thumb is that money doubles after slightly over seven years.

(3) *The Concept of Present Value: A Problem for the Personal Injury Lawyer.* At the beginning of this chapter, we saw an equation for present value, PV, of a dollar to be paid n years in the future at interest rate i. The formula is, $PV = 1/(1+i)^n$.

This relationship, in turn, tells you how much you would have to invest now, at interest rate i, to have $1 at a time n years in the future. The formula can be adapted to the valuation of a series of future payments or to computation of the future value of a present investment. Obviously, these are considerations that either debt or equity financiers would take into account.

This concept also will be important to a personal injury lawyer claiming future lost earnings and medical expenses. The jury makes a present-dollar award. Usually, the jurors will be told to discount to present value. The defense attorney, in particular, may use an expert witness to discount the damages.

(4) *What Rate of Interest?* Present value depends on the rate of interest one uses to do the discounting. At high interest rates, there is more discount, and this makes the present value less, for a given future value. To some extent, the selection of the discount rate (interest rate) requires judgment; it ought to represent the return a person might otherwise earn, if the money were available for use now. In most of the problems here, we use ten percent, partly because this is a return currently available on investments of moderate risk (and partly because it simplifies the math).

(5) *Yield, or Rate of Return.* Yield, or rate of return, is the interest rate that would produce a given income from an investment with a given cost.

We can use the present value equation, in fact, to derive a yield or rate of return if we know present value (purchase price), sale price, and the number of years the investment was held. We just solve for i in the equation $PV = FV/(1+i)^n$, where FV is the future value.

The solution involves the steps, $PV (1+i)^n = FV$; $(1+i)^n = FV/PV$; $1+i = (FV/PV)^{1/n}$; and therefore, $i = (FV/PV)^{1/n}-1$. The fractional exponent makes the calculation messy, but this is the equation. We shall see an example of the calculation in the examples and problems, below.

EXAMPLES AND PROBLEMS

(1) *The Present Value of Alfred Sloan's Capital.* At the beginning of the chapter, we considered Alfred P. Sloan's famous saying, "Take my assets–but leave me my organization–and in five years I'll have it all back." This statement exhibits a strong, and perhaps appropriate, confidence in the effectiveness of management and organization. But it also provides us an interesting finance problem. Assuming Sloan will "get it all back" exactly five years from now,[4] what is the present value of each dollar he will regain?

Again, let us use an interest rate of ten percent. Then, $PV = 1/(1+i)^n = 1/(1+0.10)^5 = 1/(1.10)^5$. Next, multiplying 1.10 x 1.10 x 1.10 x 1.10 x 1.10 gives us 1.61, and dividing $1 by this number gives $0.62.

Therefore, the present value of each dollar Sloan regains five years from now is 62 cents. Can you explain the reasoning?

(2) *Winning the Lottery: $1 Million Stretched Over Twenty Years.* Lottery face values usually are not present values. If you win $1 million, it may be payable in installments over twenty years. What is the present value of a lottery payment in the twentieth year on a $1 million jackpot? Stretched over twenty years, the $1 million becomes $50,000 per year. Then, $PV = \$50,000/(1+i)^n = 50,000/(1.10)^{20}$. We must multiply 1.10 times itself nineteen times to get 1.10^{20}; this produces 6.7275, which, when divided into the $50,000 payment, yields a present value of a measly $7,432 for the twentieth year's payment. This is what the last year's payment really is worth: $7,432, not $50,000.

---

4 The computation would be more complex if we assumed, as is probable, that he would rebuild a little at a time. But if we knew the timing of each dollar regained, we could do the calculation for each and then add them. The principle would not change.

We can similarly compute the value of payments in each of the other nineteen years. Upon adding them all together, a winner might be dismayed at what the $1 million jackpot is really worth, because its present value will be only a fraction of the total of the payments. There usually is a lump-sum option for the winner (discounted to present value), but can you see why lottery managers prefer to publicize the $1 million amount rather than its present value?

(3) *The Value of a Series of Periodic Payments: A Lawyer Evaluates a Client's Investment, or a Structured Settlement.* To compute the total present value of our hypothetical lottery jackpot, instead of computing each year and adding, we could use the formula for a present value of a fixed annuity. A fixed annuity simply means a periodic stream of equal payments. The equation is $PV = [1 - 1/(1+i)]^n/i$. For twenty years at 10%, this formula yields $[1 - 1/(1.1)^{20}]/0.1$, or 8.5136, which when multiplied by 50,000, gives $425,678 as the present value of the so-called "$1 million" jackpot. Can you explain how the reasoning gives this result?

Also, if a lawyer settles a personal injury suit for $1 million to be paid over 20 years, the client should be told that it is worth only $425,678 in present dollars at 10%. It can be difficult to explain this concept to some clients. How would you explain it?

(4) *Analyzing the Yield or Rate of Return.* Imagine that Brenda Buyer buys a stock for $1,000 and sells it 4 years later for $2,000. What is her yield or annual rate of return?

Our equation, where yield or rate of return is i, is $i = (FV/PV)^{1/n}-1$. (We figured this out in the section above, by deriving it from the present value equation.) This formula gives $i = (2,000/1,000)^{1/4}-1 = (2)^{1/4}-1 = 1.19 - 1 = 0.19$, or 19 percent.[5]

Can you explain the math in conceptual terms? Notice that this method enables us to compare two investments. Brenda Buyer's investment, in this case, has produced a much better rate of return than, say, a fixed investment at 10% annually.

---

5   Two to the one-fourth power $(2^{1/4})$ is 1.19. (We pointed out, earlier, that the fractional exponent is messy.)

(5) *Valuation of an Investment.* Imagine that a small corporation that hopes to help cure breast cancer offers an investment opportunity that would entitle Brenda Buyer to $10,000 per year at the end of each of the next fifteen years. The corporation badly needs Brenda's funds to conduct vital research, and so it wants to price the investment so as to attract her capital, but still to maximize the capital infusion from her.

Assume that we use, this time, an interest rate of eight percent, because this is the rate Brenda can obtain for other, similarly secure investments. How much should she be willing to pay for this fifteen-year, $10,000-a-year income stream? From note 3 above,

$$PV = \$10,000 \ [1 - 1/(1+i)^n]/i$$
$$= \$10,000 \ [1 - 1/(1+0.08)^{15}]/0.08$$
$$= \$10,000 \times 8.56$$
$$= \$85,600.$$

The present value of the fifteen payments, then, is $85,600 (even though they add up to $150,000). If offered this investment for $100,000, Brenda probably should decline; if offered it for $60,000, she might jump at the chance--but the corporation will be underfunded. Can you explain why?

(6) *Family Lawyers' Opposing Efforts to Value Assets upon Divorce.* Even in the average divorce, difficult valuation issues are likely to arise. It may be necessary to take into account a pension or profit-sharing plan, for example. This entitlement may be subject to division (or it may affect the division of other assets), and the first step in that endeavor is to value it. Usually, one party or the other is likely to receive the asset or the bulk of it. That party wants the asset to be given a low value, while the other party wants the value to be high. In more complex divorces, various kinds of income streams may require valuation. Can you explain the tactics that the parties will use about the discount rate, time of probable payment, etc., to make the value seem either higher or lower?

(7) *How Lawyers Argue about Different Valuation Methods.* In addition to divorce cases, lawyers must contend with valuation in contexts ranging from business litigation to tax law. The methods of valuation vary, and they include the following:

(a) *"Book value"* (or historical purchase value). This method resembles the accountant's thinking, and it may result in a conservative (i.e., low) valuation.

(b) *"Liquidation value."* This method values each asset at what it could be sold for.

(c) *"Going-concern" valuation; "goodwill."* A completely different method looks to the value of the ongoing business. It usually adds up the income stream in some manner, analogous to the valuation in note 5 above. For a successful business, this method often gives a higher valuation. It includes the business's "goodwill," or ongoing effectiveness.

A plaintiff's lawyer trying a case involving the destruction of a business may contend that the damages should be calculated by a "going concern" valuation, while the defense lawyer may argue for book value (or liquidation). Can you explain?

RISK AND RETURN

(1) *Risk and Return: The Risk Premium.* We now introduce another element: investment risk. In the last problem in the previous section, we tacitly assumed that Brenda would get her $10,000 each year as reliably as clockwork. But if the breast cancer laboratory funding her annuity becomes insolvent, or if contingencies or ambiguities in her investment contract defeat her expectations, she may receive less. This is what risk is: the probability of a return that is less than expected.

Higher risk usually means that investors must be attracted by higher returns. Risk-taking is a factor of production similar to other factors that we considered in the chapter on economics. It must be compensated for at a rate comparable to its marginal productivity. In a market economy, in fact, risk-taking investors will command a marginal cost (return for the investor) that equals their investments' marginal productivity (return for the investee). The higher return necessary to compensate for risk is referred to as the "risk premium."

(2) *Statistical Methods for Quantifying Risk: Measurement by Standard Deviation of Historical Returns.* Because of the relationship between return and risk, it becomes important to measure risk in order to evaluate differing returns. Sometimes it is possible to do so by using historical returns. One frequent method of risk analysis is to measure and compare what are called

the "standard deviations" of past returns on differing investments. The standard deviation, or SD, is a statistical concept. We shall consider it carefully later in this book, in the chapter on Statistics. You may not fully follow the method here yet (because you don't have the mathematical tools, unless you've studied statistics before). But still, we can show in general terms how the method works.

(3) *The X Bond and the Y Bond: Quantifying the Risk.* As an example of risk quantification, consider two securities, one issued by X Corporation and one by Y Corporation, that an investor is considering for purchase. Both have the same average return, but the risks are different.

Year	1	2	3	4	5
X Security's Return	8%	10%	-2%	8%	6%
Y Security's Return	4%	12%	-6%	12%	8%

Which is risker? Arguably, security Y is, because it exhibits greater fluctuation. It changes more, up and down. Financiers can quantify the risk by a statistical technique called the "standard deviation" method. (We'll consider the specifics later, in the Statistics chapter.)

The "standard deviation," put simply here, is just a mathematical measure of the fluctuation. By using this statistical factor, we actually can put a number on the amount of fluctuation, which corresponds to the degree of risk for each bond.

In this case, the average return for both securities is 6%. But the standard deviations differ sharply. The standard deviation for X Security, when calculated, is 4.1952.[6] For Y Security, it is 6.6933. The data are few (because we want to keep the example simple), and therefore the calculation is due less confidence than it would be if we had data over many time periods; the principle, however, remains the same. The Y security is riskier;

---

6   Here, briefly stated, is the method of figuring standard deviation: first, we sum the squares of the deviations from the average (expected) return; second, we divide this sum by the number of deviations (this gives us the average squared deviation); and third, we take the square root of the average squared deviation.

The deviations (difference from the 6% average) for X are 2, 4, 8, 2 and 0, which when squared are 4, 16, 64, 4, and 0; the squared deviations sum up to 88, which when divided by 5 (the number of deviations) is 17.6; therefore, SD = $\sqrt{17.6}$ for X. For Y, deviations are 2, 6, 12, 6 and 2; squared deviations are 4, 36, 144, 36, and 4; the average of the squares (their sum divided by their number) is 224÷5 = 44.8; therefore, SD = $\sqrt{44.8}$ for Y. But don't worry about this--until the Statistics Chapter.

its "changeability" factor is about 6.7, as opposed to a factor of only 4.2 for the X security. Even though each has an average return of 6%, the fact that the Y security is riskier may mean that it is worth less, on the open market.

(4) *Why Quantify the Risk? Because the Calculation Can Be Used to Quantify the Extra Return, or Risk Premium, That Investors Will Expect.* There are two reasons for a rigorous quantitative analysis of risk. The first is that, in a comparative situation, mere "eyeballing" can result in error. We might choose a riskier use of capital, prone to greater likelihood of loss, for no good reason.

The second reason is that measurement of risk can help to predict the risk premium, or additional return, that would be demanded by economically motivated investors in the marketplace. The methods are beyond our scope here, but they would help a bond seller to price an offer and a buyer to figure an appropriate bid price.

(5) *Real Return and Nominal Return.* Next let us consider another issue: What if there is a stable 4% inflation rate during the history of Securities X and Y? This factor will drastically reduce the "real return," which is defined as the "nominal return" (or face amount) minus inflation. For example, the first year's nominal return on Bond X is 8%, but it translates into a mere 4% real return.

One risk of fixed investments, such as ordinary debt (e.g., fixed-return bonds), is that their real return will decrease if inflation increases. Equities, such as common stock, tend to reflect inflation; that is, they tend to produce higher returns if prices increase generally through inflation. (Equities are subject to other business risks, however, to which debt is less susceptible.)

EXAMPLES AND PROBLEMS

(1) *When Inflation Goes Up, the Price of Fixed-Return Bonds Traded on an Exchange Goes Down.* Fixed return debt instruments issued by major corporations can be bought and sold on exchanges; what is being bought and sold, of course, is the right to receive the income stream. An increase in the rate of inflation usually reduces the price that a bond of this kind commands. Can you explain why?

(2) *Banking Law and Home Loans: Adjustable-Rate Debt Instruments Compared to Fixed Rate Debt.* One way in which capital can be obtained at lower cost is to shift some of the risk away from the investor. A "floating" or "adjustable rate" debt instrument, using an index that reflects inflation, is one method. The most familiar example to most people is adjustable rate mortgages ("ARMs"), by which homeowners finance their home purchases.

If a homeowner obtains a long-term, fixed-rate loan--say, 7½ percent over 30 years--the homeowner has shifted to the lender all of the risk of inflation. During the high-inflation years of the 1970's and early 1980's, these kinds of mortgages were a significant factor in the failures of financial institutions, particularly savings and loans. One result was a change to the widespread use of ARM's. Regulators changed laws, in fact, to facilitate this shift. Can you explain, in terms of risk, why ARM's are likely to provide a lower average rate of return to the lender and, conversely, to cost the borrower less?

(3) *Mortgage Lawyers Can Fine-Tune the Risk Allocation in an Adjustable Instrument.* Today, the risk adjustment in ARMs is even more sophisticated. ARMs usually set the interest rate at a figure that is, say, two percent higher than the current United States Treasury bill rate (which accurately reflects changes in inflation). Often, ARMs contain annual "caps": interest rate increases cannot exceed 2% in any one year. They also may contain overall "caps": the rate can never exceed 14% during the life of the loan. These clauses have the effect of shifting back to the lender some of the outlying risk that the borrower otherwise would have assumed, and in turn, the lender is likely to charge a slightly (but only slightly) higher rate to a borrower whose ARM contains these caps. Can you explain why a mortgage lawyer might use these devices?

Chapter 6
Management

Organization, Decisionmaking, and Marketing Theory for Lawyers

> *"If it doesn't make for faster circuits, happier customers, or more motivated employees, we don't spend a nickel on it."--T.J. Rogers, CEO, Cypress Semiconductor*

> *"Strive for long-term improvement more than short term profits. . . . At every stage of the process, strive to continually improve and satisfy internal as well as external customers."--W. Edwards Deming, advocate of Total Quality Management (TQM) (who, among other accomplishments, helped Ford develop its "Quality is job one" approach)*

§ 6.01 What This Chapter Is About

MANAGEMENT, ORGANIZATION, MARKETING AND DECISIONMAKING

(1) *Organizational Approaches and Decisionmaking.* This chapter is closely related to the preceding chapter and to the economics chapters. We

shall consider the reasoning by which management makes product, personnel, and process decisions in organizations. We shall also see how well-managed entities are structured.

(2) *Marketing Strategy, Leadership, and Human Relations.* We shall also consider marketing strategy. This study will involve cost and quality factors and the way in which product decisions can best be made in light of market factors. The quotations above from businessman T.J. Rogers and Professor W. Edwards Deming show different (but perhaps not inconsistent?) approaches to cost and quality. Briefly, then, we introduce ideas related to leadership and human relations.

(3) *Why Lawyers Need to Understand Management.* Legal decisions rarely exist in a vacuum. Often, they define risks that are part of a larger management issue. Whether to settle a lawsuit, for example, or whether to declare that a commercial lease has been forfeited, definitely involve legal questions, but only as risk factors that must be assimilated into a management decision by a decisionmaker who usually is not a lawyer. The lawyer's ability to communicate with such a decisionmaker is crucial. In fact, a large percentage of complaints about lawyers expressed by sophisticated managers concern lawyers' seeming inability to give useful advice for these decisions.

Then, too, there is the problem of the lawyer's own management. Lawyers notoriously are poor at running their own offices, at deciding on facilities, collecting, and treating their personnel. Almost certainly, bad management causes more unethical practices and more malpractice than bad intentions do.

§ 6.02 Management Approaches

[A] The Development of Organizational Management

CLASSICAL, MODERN AND CONTEMPORARY MANAGEMENT APPROACHES

(1) *Classical, Modern and Contemporary Management Approaches.* In this section, we turn away from financial considerations and look instead at a broader view of organizational management. Imagine that you have just inherited the presidency of an ongoing entity. It might be IBM, or AT&T; or it might be a small startup flower shop; or it might be a nonprofit

organization that seeks to improve racial relations or prevent breast cancer. How would you go about making decisions so that you maximize the effectiveness of your organization, through its policies, structures, personnel, finances, and output?

The answer to this question has varied over the years and remains in development. The "classical" approaches evolved during the 1800's and early 1900's, beginning with "rule-oriented systems," progressing to "scientific management," then to "administrative management," and next to "human relations theory." See Figure 1. The modern era saw "quantitative theory," "organization theory," "systems theory", and "contingency theory." Contemporary issues, as the figure shows, include "total quality management" and "just-in-time management." We now proceed to define and evaluate each of these innovations.

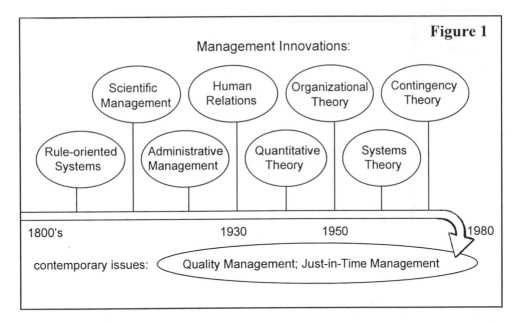

Figure 1

Management Innovations:

(2) *From Rule-Oriented Systems to Scientific Management.* During the 1800's, organizations systematically codified rules, duties and procedures. They wrote and permanently memorialized standard methods of production and detailed descriptions of workers' responsibilities. This *"rule-oriented system"* approach was an advance because it formalized management, led to an emphasis on economic efficiency, and facilitated the introduction of accounting controls. It was dysfunctional, however, in that it did not consider differences between management's goals and those of workers, or for that matter, the views of customers or regulators. What was lacking was a

decisional framework that focused on whether the detailed system of rules was achieving desirable results.

"Scientific Management" aspired to fill this gap, at least as to workers. It focused on finding the most effective, most efficient set of procedures, scientifically chosen, so that workers' actual goals and actual procedures would match the single best method of production.   For example, time studies could tell how long each step took so that processes could be modified, workers could be trained to be more efficient, and piece-rate pay (by which workers were paid according to individual output rather than by a fixed salary) would make workers' goals similar to those of management. See the figure, here.

The effects of scientific management were revolutionary. Ford Motor Company, for example, put chassis assembly onto a standardized line, adapted its machinery, and retrained its work force; it thereby cut chassis manufacturing time from more that 12 hours to 1½ hours-- and made automobiles affordable to middle Americans. But this "scientific " approach had its shortcomings, too. It made unwarranted assumptions about how workers' behavior would change in response to standardization and to production-oriented compensation. Also, it did not focus on external factors, such as customers. Ford, for example, was famous for the saying that you could buy a car in "any color, as long as it's black."

(3) *A New Focus on the Human Factor: Administrative Management and Human Relations. "Administrative management"* probably improved upon scientific management by clarifying hierarchies and enhancing equity. The most important single contributor to this concept was Henri Fayol, a French executive, who set out "14 principles" of management.   The greatest innovations in the fourteen principles included the notions (a) that authority needed to be delegated along with responsibility (a supervisor who had a given job to do should have all necessary authority to manage it); (b) that discipline needed to be based on clear expectations and sanctions; (c) that centralization, unity of command and unity of direction would create a single chain of command in which each employee had only one supervisor and would be oriented toward organizational objectives if all directives flowed through the single chain of command; (d) that equality would govern treatment of employees; (e) that rewards would be based on subordination of individual goals to organizational ones, as well as loyalty and longevity; (f)

that initiative would be encouraged; and (g) that esprit de corps was important.

The *"human relations"* movement took the focus on employees a step farther. This approach grew out of scientific psychological experiments that identified characteristics of informal work groups. Whatever the organizational goals, workers inevitably generated their own group norms that influenced productivity. For example, workers' behavior tended to conform to other workers' attitudes against both "slackers" and "rate busters." On the one hand, if you did too little work, you would be disdained as a slacker by those who had to make up parts of your job; on the other hand, if you were too much of an overachiever, so that you increased management's expectations for everybody, you were even more strongly condemned. And when the time-study man came around, slowdown techniques that fooled him, so as to lower expectations, were an art form.

The key insight of human-relations management, therefore, concerned the existence of informal norms and the ways in which group behavior influenced productivity according to status and cohesion. The prescription was for management to emphasize the job satisfaction, happiness and self-esteem of workers. Social welfare sometimes ranked higher than economics, or so the theory went, because workers would produce if their welfare was attended to.

The trouble with this approach was that it underrated employees' rational responses to rules, policies, rewards and discipline, all of which have their place. And there was an even deeper problem. Although people tend to assume that self-esteem, satisfaction and happiness are strongly correlated with productivity, subsequent studies showed that this assumption had limited validity. The research debunking satisfaction and self-esteem as uniform keys to achievement runs contrary to many people's cherished beliefs, but it is clearly established and continues to the present day. One striking study, for example, found that a random sample of prison inmates scored higher on tests for self-esteem than a sample of college students(!) In short, although group norms had important effects, and although employee happiness and self-esteem are intrinsically valuable for their own sake, increasing employee satisfaction and self-esteem, by itself, was not a prescription for productivity.

Classical management, then, contributed important insights. It still left unattended, however, the issue of how the organization relates to outside elements (e.g., customers). And it tended to adopt simplistic models of the motives of humans within the organization. We now turn to more modern innovations.

(4) *Quantitative Theory.* "Quantitative management" began during World War II and can be viewed as a modern outgrowth of scientific management. It used such quantitative techniques as linear programming, statistical studies, and computer simulations to choose among alternatives. Quantitative methods can be applied effectively to such diverse issues as production decisions, traffic analysis, investment evaluation, and inventory control. In a way, this approach may represent the polar opposite of human relations models, because it looks to inputs and outputs rather than to the inner objectives of workers.

The shortcomings of this approach include the tendency to overemphasize variables that are more readily quantifiable. The most important decisions, in fact, often involve unbounded variables in unique factual contexts. Also, managers untrained in quantitative methods tend to misunderstand them, and unpredictable worker behaviors in response to them may defeat them.

(5) *Organizational Theory.* At about the same time, a more modern, more sophisticated outgrowth of the human relations model developed, called "organizational theory." This approach adopts the fundamental insight of human relations, that employee productivity depends on informal group norms as well as on official command, but it avoids assuming that any one simplistic prescription will improve the mix, whether it be self-esteem, happiness or economic incentives.

For example, in the 1960's, Douglas McGregor contrasted two managerial models : "Theory X," which assumed that employees were undisciplined and required close supervision, and "Theory Y," which assumed that employees wanted to work and could discipline themselves to do it under the right conditions. Theory Y would lead to more worker autonomy, to varied functions rather than finely divided assembly-line duties, and to greater influence by workers upon management.

The shortcomings of this approach included its failure to emphasize technology. At some point, technology demands specialization and uniform process rather than autonomy and participation. Rapid turnover in work force, or differences in employee desires and schedules, might well mean that a shift toward Theory X, with its assumption that workers require supervision, would be better. And again, organizational theory did not emphasize matters external to the organization.

(6) *Systems Theory.* At about the same time, "systems theory" began to treat the organization as a whole that interacted with its environment. Classical management, as well as some modern approaches, viewed the organization in isolation; it was a closed system. Systems theory, in contrast, saw it as an "open system": as opposed to an entity that took in raw materials and other factors of production and refined or transformed them in a fixed way, it depended on feedback from the outside, particularly customers.

This insight led to several corollaries. Systematic study of the whole organizations's interaction with the environment would lead to "synergistic" results: the product not only would be modified but would be spun off into other consumables by "product extension," or the invention of related products. Nike may have begun with athletic shoes, but it readily could develop a variety of sports equipment and apparel from its basic expertise. At the same time, system theory facilitated thinking about multiple possible paths to expansion. Units within a system were "subsystems": shoe manufacturing at Nike is a subsystem of Nike, which in turn is a subsystem of the shoe-and-sports industry, with all subsystems being parts of an overall system ultimately tied to the consumer.

One advantage of system theory is that it focuses not only on internal efficiency but also on what managers call "effectiveness": accurate matching of the organization's production to market demand. The principal shortcoming of the theory was that it did not provide detailed direction on how to manage or coordinate the subsystems; for that, other managerial approaches were necessary.

(7) *Contingency Theory.* Modern management also developed "contingency theory," which focused on surrounding circumstances across wide varieties of industries. For example, a firm in a mature and stable market, such as steel production, needs different management from a firm in a new and rapidly changing market, such as Internet services. A firm in a growing industry (television production) needs different management than a firm in a declining industry (leaded gasoline). The history of the

organization, its size and resources, and the strength of its personnel are additional contingencies that should influence the managerial approach.

Contingency theory, in a different way from system theory, helped to adapt management approaches to the circumstances. Its shortcoming, again, was that although it provided a holistic view of the firm in its environment, it was short on specifics about how managers should react.

(8) Contemporary Approaches: Total Quality Management (TQM) and the Just-in-Time Approach. Notice that the philosophies outlined above emphasize cost, workers, and systems, but they say little about the quality of the product. The quality revolution began with Americans like W. Edwards Deming, but oddly, it began in Japan, while American management was concerned with other issues. Deming's "*Total Quality Management*," or "*TQM*," changed the phrase "made in Japan" from a mark of inexpensive manufacture to a symbol of excellence. Later, during the 1980's and '90's, TQM made its way to the United States.

TQM'S central focus is on customer satisfaction. It is the customer, not the manager, whose determination of quality counts. Deming articulated fourteen points that carried out the philosophy of TQM. For example, management should "Improve constantly . . . the system of production and service." At every stage, it should "strive to continually improve and satisfy internal and external customers." It should "break down barriers between departments" to facilitate responsiveness to customers, "eliminate slogans," and emphasize "training and retraining." It should "cease dependence on mass inspection" and "correct problems early rather than late," so as to "build quality into the process."

Earlier management approaches had assumed, tacitly, that quality had to be traded off against cost. Deming's TQM approach made it clear, instead, that both were simultaneous objectives, with the customer as the ultimate decisionmaker.

Another contemporary philosophy, called "*just-in-time*" management, is a system that mandates operations only when they are needed and will add value to the product. Instead of manufacturing a million identical automobile frames and storing them in inventory, the just-in-time approach would fabricate them in small lots when they are called for. Waste is eliminated, and so is unnecessary financing; meanwhile, workforce skills and communication must be enhanced to reduce cycle times, transportation distances, and setup delays. Obviously, just-in-time methods must be balanced carefully against economies of scale, but the point is to avoid large batches except to the extent required for efficiency.

Ultimately, the goal of just-in-time management is the same as that of TQM: to keep costs low and to assure quality. The latter goal, quality, results from careful attention to the customer, which can be achieved through just-in-time management because of cost savings and because fabricating only a few automobile frames rather than a million at a time allows for adjustments and choices that satisfy the customer.

EXAMPLES AND PROBLEMS

(1) *Identifying Flaws in Management Strategies.* Consider the following examples of management actions, which are paired with historical and classical management philosophies. Can you explain why, in each instance, the identified philosophy would consider the managerial action to be flawed?

(a) *Rule-Oriented Systems.* Imagine that the company has no employee policy manual. Customarily, employees have gathered at the gate before the time of opening of the plant, but recently, many have begun arriving a half-hour or more late.

(b) *Scientific Management.* Or, imagine that the company uses two different printers, one that specializes in slickly produced brochures (for sales documents) and one that specializes in large-scale black-and-white (for product instructions). The company has not investigated whether finding a single printer to do both would lower costs or improve service.

(c) *Administrative Management.* While entering the plant, the company president sees two workers, and she believes one of them is doing the job correctly, while the other is slacking. The president crosses the operations floor to praise the first and reprimand the second.

(d) *Human Relations.* A manager pays certain employees premium wages for working in an older factory that is unattractive, dirty, and bleak.

(e) *Quantitative Management.* The company has not re-examined the size of its inventory or the order of its manufacturing steps for more than a decade.

(f) *Organizational Behavior.* The company that pays workers a premium wage to work in its bleak, older factory also uses the same divisions of labor and supervisory systems there that it uses in all its other operations.

(g) *Systems Theory.* The company has not surveyed customers to discover whether the mail-order department understands the product sufficiently well to correct dissatisfaction in the event of mistakes.

(h) *Contingency Theory.* A manager hopes that the same management techniques she used to turn around a failing bank in a shrinking community will help her turn around an Internet services provider that is on the skids.

(2) *Management by Lawyers: Identifying Similar Flaws in the Law Office.* Lawyers are notoriously bad managers (at least, some of them are(!)) [Perhaps the reason lies in legal education, which teaches how to approach every problem as one of public policy instead.] Consider how each of the flaws in problem (1) above, could appear in a law office.

(3) *TQM and Just-in-Time Approaches: From the Law Office to the Hospital.* Next, consider the following types of businesses. Can you imagine ways in which contemporary philosophies, either TQM or the just-in-time approach, might improve the services they provide? (a) The office of an attorney who does a general practice. (b) A newly constructed rural hospital. (c) An apartment building that caters to college students.

[B]   Managerial Decisionmaking

CONDITIONS OF BUSINESS DECISIONS
(AND MOST LEGAL DECISIONS)

(1) *Unstructured and Uncertain: Business Decisions and Legal Decisions.* Next, we take up a related question: managerial decisionmaking. Decisions are influenced by the kinds of philosophies considered in the previous section. But they also are influenced by the decisionmaking *process* itself. Business decisions, at least the most important ones, rarely present themselves in clear packages with unambiguous solutions.

Instead, decisional situations often are unstructured. Choices may be infinite. In fact, even the need for a decision may not be obvious. The factors that should affect the decision may not be readily identifiable, and their significance often is uncertain.

(2) *Conflict and Conformity in Business and Legal Decisions.* As a result, decisions generate conflict, both within and outside the individual

decisionmaker. Psychological conflicts for the individual arise from contemplation of the consequences of bad decisions, as well as direct human consequences for those affected. Within decisionmaking groups (e.g., a board of directors or a team of lawyers deciding on a litigation budget) and consultative groups (subordinate advisers to a division manager or an expert witness in a medical malpractice case), overt conflicts may occur, in which decisions become skewed by the political influences of key individuals. Alternatively, conformity or "groupthink," as we shall see in a later chapter on psychology, may result in early oversimplification and failure to consider important issues or alternatives.

(3) *Due Diligence in Business and Legal Decisions.* At least for recurring kinds of decisions, the concept of "due diligence" is useful. Even if an appropriate decision seems clear, the manager, lawyer, or group goes through a fixed series of steps each time: collection of particular kinds of information, verifications, and predetermined consultations. Due diligence helps to mitigate the ill effects of conflict, politics, and groupthink. It also helps avoid the extremes of bad decisionmaking, and in some cases it minimizes fraud.

EXAMPLES AND PROBLEMS

(1) *An Example of an Unstructured Decision That Will Present Problems of Uncertainty, Conflict, Politics and Conformity: Addressing the Company's Falling Market Share.* The Widget Corporation has experienced declines in its market share for the past two years, which happen to be the first two years under its current CEO. Can you explain the ways in which the company's analysis of this circumstance is an occasion for unstructured decisionmaking under conditions of uncertainty, and why it might present difficult problems of conflict, politics and groupthink? In fact, the threshold decision may be deciding whether the decline requires any change in current policy (i.e., whether a decision really is called for). Why?

(2) *Due Diligence.* Can you explain why due diligence might be important in each of the following circumstances, and what steps it might entail? (a) A law firm seeks to replace its litigation section manager, who has retired. (b) A lawyer considers how to prepare the prospectus for a company that is about to make an initial public offering of shares. (c) A law firm considers whether to buy a parcel of land and build a new building there.

(3) *Due Diligence, Securities Laws, and Rule 10b-5.* Rule 10b-5, promulgated by the SEC, outlaws misleading statements about securities. In fact, it goes farther: it cam impose sanctions or liability upon a law firm for the issuance of a statement that *omits* information required to make it *not* misleading. This is a heavy burden. What happens to the lawyer whose *client* conceals information? The answer is that the lawyer or firm easily can be liable. To avoid this (disastrous) result, the cases say, a law firm must exercise "due diligence" in verifying the statements (particularly financial statements), *independently* of the client. If the client has a number of retail outlets, for example, the law firm had better have one of its personnel go see them all (and examine the leases for every one). As a beginning lawyer, the author of this book actually did this by looking at every one of a client's more than 30 fast food restaurants in Los Angeles and matching them to leases. Can you explain why it was important to "go through the motions" of doing this kind of due diligence?

STEPS IN FORMAL DECISIONMAKING, BUSINESS OR LEGAL

(1) *Diagnosis.* Now we go to a related subject: the actual process of decision. We describe here a relatively formal, deliberate, structured process of decision, involving seven steps. The first step is to recognize that there is an issue for decision. This recognition may be triggered by an opportunity: success that produces retained earnings that need to be reinvested, a prospective acquisition, etc. It may result from some dysfunctional change recognized by a comparison of present to past sales or a trend that threatens future falloff. Or, it may be an undefined combination of the two. Or, it may be a legal decision with management overtones, such as whether a distributor should file suit against a manufacturer or whether it should prematurely terminate its lease for bad maintenance.

(2) *Generating Options.* The next step is to generate multiple options. Even when the solution seems clear, the process should include this step. Some problems may have fixed solutions: hire another similar employee to replace the one who quit, or use lower-priced ingredients to compete with a successful price competitor. But there are alternatives. For example, the firm might abolish the employee's position, or establish a different market identity from the competitor's with a quality product. Instead of advising terminating a lease, the lawyer may advise steps to ensure better maintenance.

(3) *The Feedback Loop.* Frequently, the process of generating options helps to redefine the diagnosis of the issue for decision. Discussion of a problem about organization structure, for example, may lead to consideration of process or product issues. Therefore, each step in the process should be influenced by the "feedback loop," as Figure 2 illustrates. Arrows that lead from more advanced stages of decisionmaking to earlier stages represent the reconsideration of the earlier stages in light of information developed at later stages. Thus, after generating options, the decisionmaker(s) should consider their diagnosis against (and revise) their statement of the problem, if redefinition is called for.

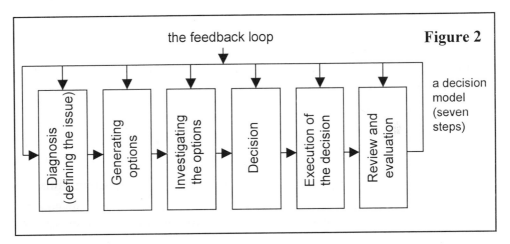

(4) *Investigating the Options.* Next, the options must be assessed, and for this, they must be investigated. The first substep is to gather information about each option. This information may be obtained through forecasting, surveys, simulation, or expert advice. But the information frequently will be incomplete and uncertain. Generating scenarios, which represent distinct possible outcomes for each option, may be a useful further step to show possible consequences.

(5) *The Actual Decision.* Next, the formal process of decision assigns probabilities to various alternatives, assesses how reliable the probabilities are, and chooses the apparent best option.

(6) *Execution of the Decision.* But we are not through yet. The decision should involve a plan for its execution. This plan should assign responsibilities, set up chronological steps, and estimate times required for each step. Also, it should describe the result of desired changes (or the appearance of the company after execution), with enough clarity so that

whether the decision has been executed properly can be objectively evaluated.

(7) *Review and Evaluation.* The desired result should be defined as objectively and quantitatively as possible, because the final step is review and evaluation. This step should be built into the process at the time of decision, with a fixed time or event triggering the review and evaluation. A bad evaluation indicates either a bad decision or incomplete execution, and it means review of the preceding steps. If, for example, the decision is to negotiate better maintenance rather than terminating the lease, objective measures of the accomplishment of the goal should be built in.

(8) *The Feedback Loop.* Throughout the process, the decisionmaker should formally consult the feedback loop. In other words, the process should include deliberate, conscious reassessment of previous stages at each step.

DECISIONMAKING AIDS AND TOOLS

(1) *Quantitative and Visual Tools.* What are some decisional aids that can assist in this process? For some kinds of decisions, payoff matrices and decision trees may be appropriate. (We shall see these devices in later chapters on strategy.) Consider, for example, a decision whether to temporarily employ two legal assistants or three to organize documents produced in a complex lawsuit, or to buy two machines or three. Buying three will result in more net income if demand is high but will produce a bigger loss if demand is low. The actual construction of a matrix that plots demand against revenues may be useful. A decision tree or chain may show the same thing.

Linear programming is another device for visual simulation. A simple example is the use of "Gantt charts," which reflect, in the manner of a bar graph, each of the steps in a manufacturing process. Comparative Gantt charts for alternative processes enable the manager to visualize where bottlenecks may occur. They also facilitate creation of potentially efficient variations, in that bars on the chart can be interchanged to simulate visually the possible changes in the process.

(2) *Formalism and Informality: From Brainstorming to Due Diligence.* Some steps in the process are enhanced by informality, or by tolerance and

encouragement of nonconformity. Generation of options, for example, may be made more complete by use of brainstorming, in which no idea is subject to criticism. In other areas, the following of formal decision processes, or the idea of due diligence, may help to avoid psychological traps, information deficiencies, and fallacy.

Sometimes the problem is structured and recurrent, so that a predetermined process of due diligence applies. In novel and unstructured decisionmaking, sometimes it is useful to design a process deliberately. "In considering what to do about this defaulted lease, we will generate at least four options. And then we will reconsider our definition of the problem, followed by reconsideration of the options. Then, we will gather such-and-such types of information about each option. . . ."

(3) *Explicit Consideration of the Possibilities of Bias and Fallacy: Why Lawyers Need to Overcome Occupational Hazards.* What else can we do to enhance decisionmaking? Recall our earlier chapter on fallacy. Formal decision processes can help to avoid fallacy, and so can explicit consideration of possible fallacies. In other words, in investigating options, the decisionmaker can explicitly evaluate the possibility that biases or psychological fallacies have produced a bad decision. "Am I engaging in anchoring, holding to a cherished but unjustifiable belief?" Or, "Am I falling for the fallacy of availability, overvaluing some options simply because they are familiar or because it's easier to collect information about them?" In litigation, where the tendency of the lawyer as advocate is to argue in support of the most desirable outcome, these fallacies are especially tempting.

(4) *Groups.* Group decisionmaking has significant advantages, ranging from generating more information to enhancing understanding and acceptance (and therefore execution) of decisions. Group decisions probably are superior on average to decisions made by average individuals. But individual decisions, on the other hand, may be superior to group decisions if made by superior decisionmakers.

Groups present certain problems that we shall see later, in the chapter on psychology: conformity and groupthink. The "information effect" may not be present, in other words, and the "conformity effect" may dominate, meaning that consensus solidifies behind an inferior option. There also may be "goal displacement," in which the group adopts a dysfunctional compromise between two positions, thereby adopting the goal of satisfying political constituencies rather than making the best decision. Likewise, goal displacement may take the form of efforts by a dominant player to win the argument, rather than to adopt a cooperative best solution.

EXAMPLES AND PROBLEMS

(1) *Decisionmaking Processes: The Formal Seven-Step Method.* Consider each of the following management situations. Can you identify ways in which they could formally be addressed by the seven-step method (consisting of (1) diagnosis, (2) generating options, (3) investigating the options, (4) actual decision, (5) execution, (6) review and evaluation, and (7) the feedback loop)?

(a) You are a member of the Joint Chiefs of Staff and are troubled by the low rate of reenlistment of experienced military personnel. (b) You are a member of a growing law firm that finds it has no room for storage and that its existing facility is uncomfortably crowded. (c) You are a lawyer on the defense team in a high-profile criminal case, and you must decide how to present the defense case--including the related question whether to advise the defendant not to testify at all.

(2) *Decisionmaking Tools and Aids.* In the second example above (the lawyers whose facility is crowded), consider how the decision might be enhanced by the aids and tools considered above. This question calls on you to evaluate the use of (1) visual and quantitative aids, (2) formal due diligence and informal brainstorming, (3) explicit considerations of fallacy and biases, and (4) group versus individual decisions.

§ 6.03 Marketing: Product, Competitor, and Customer Strategies

MARKETING AND THE BUSINESS PLAN

(1) *Marketing: It Isn't Mostly About Advertising, and Sometimes It's Constrained by the Law.* Next, we consider marketing. When some people hear the word "marketing," they think of advertising. Actually, advertising is only one small component. Marketing really means market analysis and competitive strategy. Should you fit your product with a new gizmo that involves costs and risks but adds a new function? Or should you replace parts of it with inexpensive ingredients and compete as to price? How should you serve which customers, and how should you react to competitors? Each

of these marketing strategies, incidentally, has legal ramifications: the cheaper product may breach warranties or cause injuries, and actions toward competitors can create antitrust or other liability.

(2) *The Business Plan: An Essential Document for Capital Formation, Strategy, and Evaluation.* Particularly for a new venture, the "business plan" serves an important marketing function. An entrepreneur begins with an idea: perhaps the entrepreneur sees an unserviced demand in the marketplace (or perhaps the entrepreneur nurtures a cherished dream that exists independently of any market for it). The business plan is the expression of this idea in a way that supplies information to financiers, guidance to management, and a useful checkpoint for evaluation. Law firms, just like other firms, need business plans.

(3) *Overall Components of the Business Plan: Market Analysis, Goals, Management, and Projected Financials.* A business plan should include (a) a market analysis as one of its most important ingredients. This component is described further below. In addition, the plan should contain (b) a statement of short-term and long-term goals, as well as (c) a description of internal assets that will be used: physical plant, management and personnel. Finally, it should propose (d) a budget, which will include "pro forma" financial statements: a projected income statement, cash flow statement, and balance sheet. Because these documents are projected, they are not likely to be closely accurate, but their estimation is an important exercise.

For lenders and investors, the business plan provides assurance that the entrepreneur has undertaken at least a basic level of strategic thought. For management, the plan provides something more than a vision statement, something less than a blueprint. And for future market analysis, the plan provides an objective basis for evaluating whether the initial analysis has achieved the goals or whether it needs to be changed.

(4) *The Market Analysis in the Business Plan.* The market analysis is the heart of the business plan. It usually begins with (a) an identification of the product or service, the needs it is designed to serve, and reasons for believing that it fills a gap--that it has an element of uniqueness. This uniqueness may be a simple matter of convenience, e.g. a grocery store in an underserved location, or it may be an electronic gadget no one ever has heard of before. Or it may be a law firm that offers particular services in a particular location. Next, the plan needs (b) a profile of customers or clients: who they are,

where, and how many. Related to that idea, (c) distribution mechanisms may be important. It does no good to identify thousands of potential customers if the only feasible distribution method is to set up independent retailing facilities that make the costs noncompetitive. And (d) a description of competitors is essential--who they are, how many, how they differ, and how they may respond to the new entrant. If the number of consumer bankruptcy lawyers in the region is already too large, a new entrant needs to consider the option carefully.

This material, above, identifies the sales market. Next, the plan should analyze the market for providing the product or service: (e) location (characteristics and costs), (f) suppliers (whether components are available competitively), (g) equipment (what it is; whether to lease, buy, or purchase in used condition), (h) human resources (what sorts of workers, at what cost, and with what supervision needs), and (i) the regulatory and legal environment (whether the innovation will require permits, reports, compliance programs, or liability minimization).

Figure 3 is a graphic representation of the ingredients of the market analysis in a business plan. Not every new business will require significant analysis of each element, but the entrepreneur should at least address each. A lawyer will need to understand this analysis in helping a client to obtain financing, as well as to properly plan the lawyer's own practice.

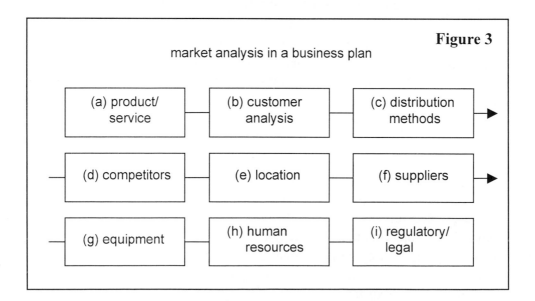

Figure 3

market analysis in a business plan

(a) product/ service	(b) customer analysis	(c) distribution methods
(d) competitors	(e) location	(f) suppliers
(g) equipment	(h) human resources	(i) regulatory/ legal

(5) *Quantitative Estimation.* Quantitative or semi-quantitative estimation is helpful for some of these variables. Thus, the customer base, competitors, and sometimes other factors, such as distribution channels and suppliers, need to be described in numerical terms as well as qualitatively. For example, a customer description may be helpful if it merely says that the product or service is "potentially desirable to any person who regularly engages in photography as a hobby." But the usefulness of the analysis will be enhanced if it adds, "Local photography clubs have assisted us in estimating that there are more than 15,000 regular photography hobbyists in the City of New Zenith, and they are served by only two full-service competitors."

EXAMPLES AND PROBLEMS

(1) *Identifying the Overall Components of Business Plans for Two Very Different Businesses: A New Lawyer and a Fortune 500 Client.* Consider the following two startup ventures: (a) A newly licensed lawyer who plans to move to the small town of Madisonville, which the lawyer believes is underserviced, and to start a general practice (doing everything from criminal defense to writing wills); and (b) An electronics manufacturer that has billions of dollars in annual sales and that is considering the formation of a subsidiary to assemble high definition television (HDTV) receptors for sale to consumers. How will the basic ingredients of the two ventures' business plans differ (market analysis, goals, management and projected financials)?

(2) *Market Analysis and Quantitative Estimation for the Newly Licensed Attorney.* Next, can you describe how the market analysis for either of these two ventures (e.g., the new lawyer) might address the essential marketing components (product/service, customers, distribution, competitors, location, suppliers, equipment, human resources, and regulatory/legal)?

Also, how can the planner develop quantitative estimates for some of the key marketing ingredients? (Be careful not to overlook the obvious: the federal Small Business Administration, local chambers of commerce, professional associations, the Yellow Pages, and consultation with local individuals in the same business. Even if they are competitors, these individuals may be cooperative. Can you see why?)

SOME FUNDAMENTAL TYPES OF MARKETING STRATEGIES

(1) *Recalling the Economic Analysis in Earlier Chapters: The Basis of Marketing Strategy.* In the chapters on economics, we did a "top-down" analysis: how the marketplace imposes efficiency. Here, our analysis is "bottom-up": we consider strategies for an individual entrepreneur trying to succeed within the discipline of the market.

(2) *Three Kinds of Product Strategies: Operational (Price), Quality (Differentiation), and Niche (Segment Focus)--and Adaptation by Lawyers.* A business can adopt any one of three basic product strategies. For example, it can serve the low-to-middle mass market with good operations that produce low cost, and its competitive position can combine uniform quality with an emphasis on price. The product of this "operational" or "price" strategy tends then to be relatively undifferentiated and generic. Chevrolet's Chevette might provide an example (or Kia might, at the lower end of the range). On the other hand, the business can adopt a quality strategy, with an emphasis on product differentiation, unique features, and appeal to the high-end customer to whom brand loyalty is focused more by the perception of excellence than by cost. Mercedes or Cadillac are examples.

Finally, there are "niche" markets, or "segment focus" markets, formed by "customer intimacy." The business targets a segment of customers defined not so much by quality or price as by attention to their narrower preferences. The Corvette, Porsche's products, and (at a different end of the

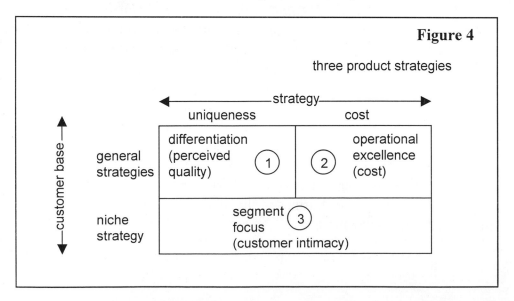

Figure 4

three product strategies

market) the Dodge Ram, are examples. To implement this strategy, the competitor needs constant close contact with, and adaption to, its consumer base, and hence the term "customer intimacy."

Figure 4 is a graphic representation of these three basic product strategies. It should be added that a law firm needs to consider which of these strategies it will adopt, and it needs to know its clients' strategies. An operational small business probably will squeeze the lawyer on cost, forcing the abandonment of various inquiries that the lawyer may consider essential.

(3) *Requirements and Risks in Implementing the Three Strategies: Will Your Business Clients Succeed, and How Will They Use Your Services as a Lawyer?* Each of these strategies has its own set of requirements. Low-cost, operational strategy rests on stable financing, structured organization, and careful labor and cost supervision. Conservatism about innovation is important. A changing legal or regulatory environment creates special difficulties. The perceived-quality differentiated product, on the other hand, requires innovation, creativity, research and development, merchandising (advertising), and (of course) quality control. The niche strategy requires all of these items, directed at the relevant market segment, with the addition of a close focus (intimacy) with customers.

The risks of the operational strategy include technological or societal change that may require expensive innovation; new competitors, particularly in industries with low barriers to entry; and cost pressures. Remember how Ford made automobiles affordable with such strict uniformity that the consumer could buy one "in any color, as long as it's black?" Ford's cost leadership caused it, early on, to relinquish market share to General Motors, which produced a series of more differentiated products.

But the quality or differentiation strategy also implicates risks, particularly as markets mature. If price differentials become too great, or if lower cost competitors learn inexpensive ways to duplicate the perceived quality features through invention, imitation or changing buyer preferences, the differentiating features may cease to command brand loyalty.

On the other hand, the risks of not following a clear strategy may be even greater. A competitor whose cost is too high for cost-sensitive buyers, but who does not project the aura of quality that high-end buyers of differentiated products demand, may be in a weak competitive position.

(4) *Market Share and Competitive Strategy.* Remember, from the chapter on economics, that the firm's marginal cost curve is U-shaped, at least in the short run. Marginal cost (the cost of producing one more unit of output) decreases at first with increasing output, as fixed costs are spread over more and more production. It rises eventually, however, when bottlenecks occur, labor shortages arise, and distribution or merchandising costs mount. Figure 5 shows this relationship, repeating the concept from that earlier chapter.

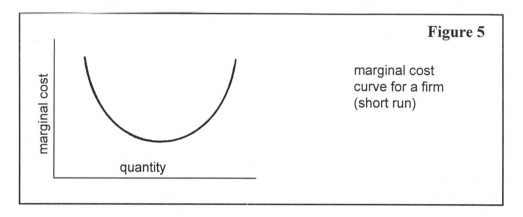

Figure 5

marginal cost curve for a firm (short run)

This relationship suggests that a firm needs to adopt not only a product strategy, but a market share strategy as well. It would be disastrous, for example, for a firm hoping to compete on price to gain only a small market share that left its marginal cost in the high range defined by low output. Conversely, a firm depending on a differentiated product, with a customer base insistent on perceived quality without price sensitivity, cannot define itself so that a large market share is required.

ANALYZING COMPETITORS: STRATEGY AND REGULATORY LAW

(1) *Competitor Analysis.* In an oligopolistic industry, an analysis of competitors is important to any strategic decision. Remember that oligopolistic industries are those in which competitors are few enough so that they must be individually considered. Many if not most markets have at least some oligopolistic features. For example, both of the industries that we considered in the preceding materials are oligopolistic. The HDTV manufacturing industry is limited to relatively few firms worldwide, and the newly licensed attorney relocating to Madisonville finds a market with a handful of other attorneys.

In these situations, one must consider the capabilities of all major competitors. Their financial strengths, management capacities, abilities to change quickly, abilities to grow, facilities in raising entry barriers against new entrants, and availabilities of exit strategies need to be assessed. Once these capabilities are assessed, possible offensive moves that competitors might make need to be considered. Does each competitor seem satisfied with its position, or is there one that is likely to attempt to increase market share? An HDTV competitor that has just done a public offering for this purpose, or a small firm in Madisonville that has made offers to two new associates, are examples. At the opposite end of the scale, there might be an HDTV manufacturer that is about to abandon the market, or a lawyer in Madisonville about to retire. The strategist must evaluate how these competitors might seek to influence the market.

(2) *Market Signals; Offensive and Defensive Moves.* In such circumstances, competitors spend considerable effort sending and analyzing market signals. Antitrust laws, as a general rule, prevent enforcement of contractual arrangements for cooperation (and indeed they make even non-contractual combinations illegal in most situations involving merchandising, territory and price). Instead, a competitor may pre-announce a price change. Other competitors cooperate by matching the leader's price increases, and not to do so, which is equivalent to a discount, becomes an aggressive stance.

Competitive moves can include cooperative strategies (the price increase described above is an example). The development of an underserved market or certain kinds of product differentiation, similarly, may be nonthreatening moves. But the examples of aggressive moves mentioned earlier, such as advertising increases, territorial expansion, price discounts, and indeed the entry of a new competitor in an already-served market, invite retaliation.

(3) *Retaliation, Discipline, Commitment, and Limits under the Law.* Retaliation may take the form of market "discipline": efforts that seek to alter the aggressive competitor's future behavior by educating and forcing the competitor to pay a price. Examples are reciprocal, targeted price discounts; similar but responsive expansion into the aggressor's territory; overmatching of advertising (or negative advertising); or attempts to use contacts with regulators to slow a new entrant.

Disciplinary defensive moves can be complex. Competitors have been known, for example, to develop retaliatory "fighting brands": new, branded products, differentiated from the competitor's own brand but relatively undifferentiated from the aggressor's, to compete in price. Denying the aggressor a base and demonstrating commitment to the retaliatory course also are possible components of disciplinary strategies. Thus, the firm might ostentatiously assemble resources, maintain a history of resolutely staying the course, undertake steps that prevent it from exiting from the disciplinary move (as advancing armies sometimes have burned bridges behind them), and otherwise communicate its intention not to back down. Obviously, laws against unfair competition, regulatory regimes, or antitrust laws may limit the availability of these alternatives.

EXAMPLES AND PROBLEMS

(1) *Product Strategies: Operational (Cost), Differentiated (Quality), and Niche (Segment Focus) Approaches.* Consider each of the following strategies and identify the approach (operational, differentiated or niche) represented by each. (a) A HDTV manufacturer standardizes to one size, produces at a uniform rate with standardized assembly, and thereby turns out the market's least expensive product. (Alternatively, a new lawyer in Madisonville announces fixed, low fees for certain frequently-needed services.) (b) Another HDTV marketer designs a set that "looks like fine furniture" and is "absolutely dependable." (Or, a small firm in Madisonville claims to offer highly responsive service: "We return your calls within the hour.") (c) A third HDTV marketer designs its colors, sound, controls, and sharpness to maximize the reception of sports events and designs a cabinet that will appeal to sports fans. (Or, a new attorney in Madisonville lets the retail community know that she spent years as a retailer before going to law school, and she claims to appreciate the peculiar problems of retailers.)

(2) *Risks of These Competitive Strategies.* Which of these strategies, outlined above, would be most clearly at risk from (a) technological, methodological, or social innovations that dramatically lower overall industry costs? (b) A widening cost differential between expensive and cheap products or services in the market? (c) The creation of alternative products by others, or major economic or sociological changes, that alter dramatically the composition and identities of groups within the customer base? (d) A failure to capture and keep sufficiently large market share to maintain low marginal cost?

(3) *Competitive Strategy.* Imagine that a quality-oriented HDTV manufacturer studies the idea of producing an alternative, low-cost standardized model, for which it would advertise, "You can have quality and price, too!" (Alternatively, imagine that an old-line small law firm in Madisonville, known for responsive, high-quality service, explores the concept of adding a new associate through whom it might offer low-cost standardized services.) In each instance, lower-cost competitors will perceive that they might lose market share and position as a result of what they see as prospective aggression.

What are some of the counter-moves and strategies that competitors might use to respond to these plans, and what dangers should be anticipated from them? Consider such strategies as market signals, discipline, denying a customer base, and commitment. Also, consider reciprocal discounts, territorial invasion, "fighting brands," and moves that might prevent market exit.

(4) *The Public Policy Perspective: A Preference for Vigorous Competition, but a Paradoxical Limit on the Ability to Force It.* Notice that the perspective of strategic firms in an oligopoly does not necessarily coincide with the public perspective. Laws (such as the antitrust laws) are designed to limit cooperation among firms in the same industry and to force competition. To put the matter another way, tacit adoption of a noncompetitive strategy may be best for the competitors themselves, but consumers may perceive this solution as allowing firms to recover excess profit by withholding output and limiting innovation in much the same manner as a monopoly. Therefore, public policy might be designed to force firms to compete aggressively even if it forces them into competition that they would rather avoid. Can you explain this conclusion?

But at some point, there must be a limit to such pro-competitive laws. It is difficult to enforce laws against contracts, combinations, or conspiracies when strategies of cooperation result not from coordination but from each firm's individual adoption of rational profit-maximizing goals. Likewise, it might be futile, as well as bad policy, to legislate so that firms are required to adopt self-destructive strategies. Can you explain?

§ 6.04 Other Aspects of Management: Human Relations, Leadership, Communications, Organizational Structure, Etc.

OTHER ASPECTS OF MANAGEMENT

(1) *Human Relations.* In this section, we shall mention, without describing in depth, a number of additional aspects of management. Complete treatment of these subjects would make the chapter unwieldy. Our hope, instead, will be to characterize the issues so that the reader can recognize problem areas.

"Human relations," today, refers to the systematic treatment of employees: how to hire them, terminate them, promote or advance, handle layoffs or reductions in force, evaluate them, discipline them, and manage their relations with each other. How, for example, should an employer go about testing prospective applicants for secretarial jobs so as to hire the best applicants? (At the same time, the employer is attempting to comply with the law and minimize litigation, since using the wrong kind of test can be a costly legal mistake.) Alternatively, how can an employer best minimize sexual harassment, investigate complaints, and address violations?

For the small business, one sometimes overwhelming aspect of being an employer concerns bookkeeping, paperwork and compliance requirements imposed by multiple government agencies. Imagine that the new attorney in Madisonville employs a secretary and a legal assistant. Social security and income taxes require accurate completion of forms and several different kinds of withholding. Compliance with immigration, benefits, unemployment, health and safety, wage and hour, and other laws requires additional accounting, office policies and forms. Efficient but accurate conformity to these requirements is a major component of small business success.

(2) *Leadership.* It is a mistake to think that leadership requires only innate charisma. Management study shows that there are leadership methods that can be learned. For example, strategic management may require conception and communication of "vision," consisting of general ideas that coordinate and motivate. Operations management, on the other hand, guides line workers and teams with rules and instructions that must be both uniform and flexible.

(3) *Communications.* Some kinds of communications should come from the top down. The organization's sexual harassment policy is a prototypical example. Others should carefully follow the chain of command, because the

authority of intermediate managers otherwise may be compromised. Different methods of bottom-up communication may be needed for workers' quality and efficiency messages, on the one hand, and for their grievances on the other. The nature, language and attitude of these communications is an aspect of management study.

(4) *Organizational Structure.* The shape of a firm's organizational chart has a major impact on its productivity. A manufacturing firm may have a broad, top-down management, with many employees supervised by relatively few managers. A service firm may have a narrower top-down arrangement, with more supervisors each managing fewer employees. A law firm owned and managed by five lawyers through a partnership may resemble a five-pointed star in its organizational structure. (In fact, it is likely to resemble this shape because of the lawyers' inertia or unwillingness to consider the issue, even if the structure is clumsy.)

These matters raise the issue of the "span of control": narrow, with few employees per supervisor, or broad and flat, with many employees per supervisor. There also is the question whether the structure is "mechanistic," meaning a defined bureaucracy with delineated responsibility, authority and reporting relationships, or whether it is "organic," meaning that it is evolutionary, changing, based on accommodation of suggestions and advice rather than orders and rules, decentralized, and informal.

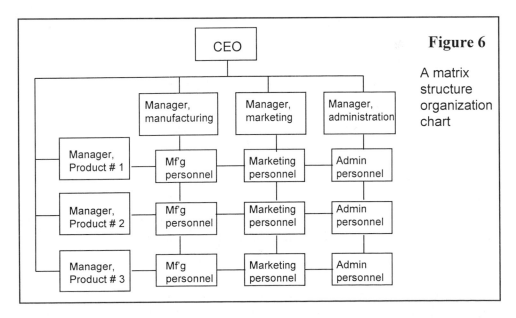

Figure 6

A matrix structure organization chart

Straightforward, centralized hierarchies contrast with firms that are departmentalized. For example, geographical departmentalization may be functional in a hotel chain with locations in different cities, while another firm may be departmentalized along product lines. A "hybrid" organization, on the other hand, combines functional and departmental leadership.

One important type of hybrid organization is the "matrix" structure, which actually subjects employees to control by multiple managers. Figure 6 diagrams this arrangement.

The most salient advantage of the matrix organization is the expertise of each manager. A less obvious factor is the greater efficiency of each manager, who accomplishes more within a sphere of responsibility with less effort. A major difficulty concerns conflict: conflict among mangers that creates conflict among workers.

EXAMPLES AND PROBLEMS

(1) *Human Relations Problems.* Reconsider the five-lawyer partnership, described above as resembling a five-pointed star in its organization. Assume that this firm has numerous support personnel, ranging from nurses and radiology associates to receptionists, bookkeepers, insurance specialists and custodians. Are there reasons for believing that a firm with this organization may have more (or less) in the way of human relations problems than one with a hierarchical structure?

(2) *Mechanistic and Organic Structures.* In fact, the rigidly hierarchical manufacturing organization we hypothesized above could probably benefit from greater tolerance of organic structure. By the same token, the five-pointed organization of the lawyer's partnership probably would benefit from some additional structure of a centralized, mechanistic type. Can you see why?

(3) *Matrix Organization, Leadership and Communication.* Imagine that the five lawyers, recognizing their limitations, decide to employ a new supervisory executive, to whom they plan to give the title of "law firm administrator." This reorganization will result in a hybrid structure, in a matrix configuration. Can you explain why, and can you foresee the types of problems that it is likely to generate?

What sort of leadership characteristics should the lawyers look for in this new director of administration? How should they arrange communications among themselves and the new director so that they will minimize the expected problems? (In fact, the five lawyers will probably need not only to establish new channels, but to undertake a whole new style of communication. Can you see why?)

PART III
ETHICAL AND POLITICAL REASONING

Chapter 7
Ethics

Teleology, Deontology, and Distributive and Procedural Justice

> *"There is, therefore, only one categorical imperative. It is: Act only according to that maxim by which you can at the same time will that it should become a universal law."--Immanuel Kant, Foundations of the Metaphysics of Morals*

> *"[T]he foundation of morals is 'utility' or the 'greatest happiness principle[,]' [which] holds that actions are right in proportion as they tend to promote happiness; wrong as they tend to produce the reverse of happiness."--John Stuart Mill, Utilitarianism*

§ 7.01 What This Chapter Is About

ETHICAL PHILOSOPHY AND POLITICAL THEORY

(1) *Contrasting Ethical Theories: Utilitarianism and Deontology.* This chapter makes another abrupt shift: from logic and economics to ethics and values. The chapter begins with a summary of a few historical developments

in political and ethical thought. No claim of comprehensiveness or depth is made. The treatment is very brief and it is included to give a basis for more contemporary ideas.

In particular, our effort is to distinguish "teleological" or consequentialist philosophies, such as utilitarianism, which emphasize the goodness or happiness that flows from moral actions, and "deontological" ones, which emphasize justice instead of happiness--the rightness or wrongness of actions, independently of consequences. The quotations above, from Kant and Mill, are the basic statements of these two opposing theories, written by the philosophical giants who gave them their most famous expositions. The impact of these views on the law has been profound. For example, utilitarian justifications produce theories of criminal sentencing that differ sharply from utilitarian ones.

(2) *Contemporary Ethical Theories and Problems.* The chapter then considers some contemporary issues. Is a combination of utilitarianism and justice-based philosophy possible? We look at the concepts of the "rule-oriented utilitarian," for example, and at the "limited deontologist." We also consider "ethical relativism," as well as the alternatives of "distributive" and "process" theories of justice. Again, the coverage is brief and there is no claim of completeness.

§ 7.02 Historical Developments in Political and Ethical Thought

HIGHLIGHTS IN THE HISTORICAL DEVELOPMENTS OF POLITICAL PHILOSOPHY, FROM THE ANCIENTS THROUGH THE FRENCH REVOLUTION

(1) *The Greeks and Romans: Virtue, Limits on Democracy, and Aristocracy.* Ancient Greece sometimes is called the cradle of democracy; in fact, the word "democracy" comes from the Greek. But at the same time, the most influential of the Greek philosophers, Plato and Aristotle, were skeptical of democracy, especially of direct and universal democracy, which they saw as rule by the uneducated. Greek democracy was fundamentally different from ours. Popular democracy was particularly distasteful; at times, the Greeks even disdained elections and chose their officials randomly.

These Greek philosophers particularly emphasized virtue, or the living of life according to duty, as opposed to freedom or pursuit of happiness. Plato's rejection of civil disobedience, for example, is an inflexible command to follow all laws without sorting those that are unjust. Aristotle favored rule by aristocracy as a better means of achieving virtue. Ironically, these influential ideas did not necessarily mandate, but were consistent with, regimes over the ages that demanded obedience and conformity from ordinary people while at the same time providing them little political input.

(2) *The Republican Era in Rome.* The Roman republic added to these philosophies a number of particularized concepts such as the law of wills, as well as the concept of a "res publica," or "public thing"--a republic in which each citizen had "natural rights," those arising from membership in the body politic. "Civis Romanus sum," or "I am a Roman Citizen," was a claim not merely of identity but of guarantees of fair treatment. It thus helped to preserve the ideal of citizens' rights as opposed to the pure ideal of virtue.

(3) *The Middle and Dark Ages: The Christian Influence; Universities and Cities; Arabic, Jewish and African Scholars.* The Roman Empire at first persecuted Christians and then embraced their faith. Some of the dominant philosophical questions in much of the ensuing millennium focused upon God and the church. For example, St. Thomas's proof of the existence of God was a centerpiece of Thomistic philosophy. Religious philosophy also was a heavy influence in secular politics and in science: Kings traced their power to God, bloodlines, and consent, and even after this period, the papal court convicted Galileo of heresy for his advocacy of the Copernican universe instead of the Ptolemaic (in which the sun and other bodies were thought to orbit in crystalline spheres around the fixed earth). However, religious centers also supported science and other aspects of civilization.

Several factors also contributed to this mix in some places: The medieval university (populated by clerics), which emerged as an institution dedicated to independence and academic freedom; royal power with secular goals as a sometimes countervailing force to religious institutions; and, in some places, the rise of cities, which produced the saying "Stadt luft macht frei" ("city air makes one free"). Jewish, Arabic and African scholars contributed independent voices in subjects ranging from mathematics to preservation of the ideas of the ancients.

(4) *Magna Charta: The "Law of the Land" as a Limit on the King.* In 1512, Magna Charta (the Great Charter) resulted in some limits on the power of the monarchy and protection of the individual rights of some people

(although they were a relatively narrow aristocracy). For example, some historians trace our Constitution's Due Process Clause, which guarantees fair treatment to all persons, to the king's promise in Magna Charta that no "free man" would be punished except "by the law of the land."

(5) *The 1600's and 1700's--Renaissance and Enlightenment in England: Hobbes's Social Contract, Locke's Concepts of Property and of Revolution against Tyranny, and Smith's Invisible Hand.* During the mid 1600's, Thomas Hobbes advanced the invention of the "social contract." Alone and in a state of nature, each individual's life would be, in Hobbes's famous phrase, "solitary, poor, nasty, brutish and short." In his major work, *The Leviathan*, Hobbes explained that the body politic consists of people banded together to defend against the dangers of nature through a "social contract," by which they seek the protection of a "leviathan" or sovereign, whose rule they accept.

Hobbes's preferred form of government was monarchy, since he saw democracy as dominated by rhetoric. But his was an enlightened monarchy, in which the power and riches of the monarch stemmed from the citizenry, with the interests of the monarch thus intertwined with those of the people.

In the later 1600's, John Locke accepted the idea of a social contract, but Locke differed from Hobbes in that he saw the state of nature as less dangerous and, indeed, he saw individual self-interest as a positive good. Acquisitiveness in commerce would mean more for everyone. A principal function of the state, therefore, was to protect property: "The great and chief end of men uniting into commonwealths . . . is the preservation of property." Locke thus saw the social contract as an agreement among equals, individual citizens,

John Locke

rather than a submission to a "leviathan" sovereign. Within the limits of the social contract, which were discernible from study and contemplation, individuals were to have natural rights to the greatest possible degree of freedom, and all were equal under the social contract. Thus, for example, Locke was a major proponent of the freedom of speech, as a result of his emphasis on natural rights within the context of the social contract.

Locke also insisted on the right of the people to revolt against a ruler who broke the social contract through tyranny. This sketch may support the inference that Locke's views may have had some influence upon the American Revolution and United States Constitution. The same can be said of Adam Smith's economic philosophy, as we have seen in an earlier chapter.

(6) *French, American and English Philosophers of the Later 1700's: The Social Contract, Commercialism, Romanticism, Revolution, and Reaction.* In France, Baron Montesquieu developed and refined Locke's ideas, and he also was quoted frequently by the founders of the American order. Rousseau, one of the romantic thinkers who influenced the French Revolution, emphasized a different view of the social contract, in which the collective will of the people, rather than commercialism or technology, would govern individuals in a spirit of equality and fraternity, and as a consequence, true liberty would flow from duties owed by all to the state. Rousseau's romantic idealism is illustrated by his statement that people in a state of nature were "happy and good," and that traditionally society "corrupted" them. His concepts of equality and fraternity may have helped to influence the cornerstones of the French Revolution, which, in the excesses of its aftermath, vividly demonstrated how a bloodthirsty republic of fear can result from romantic reason.

Meanwhile, Adam Smith developed a different philosophy in his *Wealth of Nations*: The "invisible hand" of the market would drive the allocation of goods more efficiently than Locke had imagined, thus setting the stage for modern microeconomics. Across the Atlantic, one of many forces supporting the ratification of the American Constitution was *The Federalist*, written anonymously by James Madison, John Jay and Alexander Hamilton. It advocated strong central government as a means of protecting property and commerce and maximizing

Edmund Burke

liberty, but the people would be safeguarded by separation of powers within three branches, as well as separation between central and state governments in a federal system (see the Politics chapter for more). Implicitly, though not inconsistent with concepts of equality (at least among landowning males of wealth), this American vision departed sharply from Rousseau's conception of state-imposed equality and fraternity.

Edmund Burke viewed with distaste the excesses of the French Revolution from across the English channel. Burke's political philosophy rejected the romanticized equality of Rousseau in favor of a tradition-based view of the social contract. Burke saw the social contract as extending infinitely into the past and future: Present society owed a duty to both forebears and posterity, who also were "contracting parties." This duty could be carried out better by respect for tradition, in which change is not to be sought for idealistic reasons and should be evolutionary rather than revolutionary, and where property rights, even if unevenly distributed, must be carefully respected.

EXAMPLES AND PROBLEMS

(1) *The Influence of the Ancients.* Burke's traditionalism differed sharply from Rousseau's romantic, fraternal equality and rejection of commercialism, but both derived their philosophies in part from the influence of the Greeks. Can you explain how this is so? (For example, both limited any sense of the importance of freedom and happiness by a strong sense of duty to community, i.e., virtue.)

(2) *Imagining the Property Ownership of a Major Communications Organ Such as a Television Network: How Would These Political Philosophers Have Allocated It?* None of these philosophers, of course, had television. But imagine the application of each of their philosophies, one at a time, to the ownership and control of television stations today (or to an equivalent imaginary resource in their own day). Should control be held by an aristocracy, by wealthy individuals, by a monarch, by the people collectively, or by the state--and with what conditions or limitations--under the respective philosophies of (a) the major Greek philosophers (Plato, Aristotle), (b) Hobbes, (c) Locke, (d) Rousseau or (e) Burke?

(3) *Tracing an Institution of Law through Philosophers of the Ages: Separation of Powers.* In Plato's Dialogues (Laws XI), 875-76 B.C., the wise

"Athenian Stranger" (a reference to Socrates) observes, "[If] [a person] be possessed of absolute and irresponsible power, he will never . . . persist in regarding the public good as primary [and his own] private good as secondary. The inference is that some things should be left to courts of law; others the legislator must decide for himself." Magna Carta chs. 12-18 (1215) does not recognize separation of the judiciary from the executive power (each of which then was exercised by a monarch), but does contain rudimentary protections: e.g., "Common Pleas (courts) shall not follow Our [the king's] Court, but shall be held in some certain place."

John Locke, in his Second Treatise § 159 (1689), wrote "[T]he Legislative and Executive Power are in distinct hands in all moderated Monarchies and well-framed Governments." 11 Montesquieu, Spirit of the Laws ch. 6 (1748), says "In every government there are three sorts of power: [1] the legislative; [2] the executive in respect of things dependent on the law of nations [which Montesquieu calls simply the 'executive']; and [3] the executive in regards to matters that depend on the civil law [which Montesquieu calls the 'judicialry' and describes as 'punish[ing] criminals and determin[ing] disputes']."

Notice how these concepts followed a consistent thread and contained more refinement as history developed.

(4) *Derivation of Various Political Institutions from Hobbes's Invention of the Social Contract.* The philosophers who adopted Hobbes's theory of the social contract used it to support a surprising variety of existing ideas, ranging from the separation of powers to the protection of private property to the enforcement of equality and fraternity. How could they justify each of these diverse concepts from the basic idea of the social contract?

HISTORICAL FOUNDATIONS OF ETHICAL PHILOSOPHY IN THE LAW: FROM UTILITARIANISM TO THE CATEGORICAL IMPERATIVE

(1) *Teleological Ethics and Consequentialism as Distinguished From Deontology.* One major divide in ethical philosophy is between "teleology" and "deontology." Teleology can be thought of as "purposive" philosophy, or the emphasis of behavior consistent with appropriate purposes or results, as opposed to an emphasis on justice. More broadly, teleological philosophy treats the universe and all its processes as possessing ultimate causes,

purposes, or ends. An acorn has a mission or purpose--to be an oak, perhaps, or to increase fertility of soil, or to provide nutrition to animals. When we justify behavior in terms of mankind's "nature" or purpose on earth, we speak teleologically. (We considered teleology briefly in the second chapter, on logical fallacies, when we evaluated a teleological "proof" of the alleged existence of Santa Claus. You may wish to review that passage if you are unclear on this concept.)

Consequentialism, or the ethics of producing good results, is a particular kind of teleological philosophy. In this view, murder is illegal because it destroys the social fabric, invites retaliation, and causes others to live in fear. In other words, murder is illegal because of the results it causes, which are harmful rather than good.

Deontology, on the other hand, refuses to total benefits and costs from results; instead, it emphasizes justice, or the rightness or wrongness of actions. In this philosophy, murder is illegal because it is wrong. It subordinates one human being, the victim, to the satisfaction of the needs of another, the murderer. In summary, teleological philosophies emphasize "the good," while deontological ethics emphasizes "justice."

(2) *Utilitarianism in the 1700's and 1800's: Bentham and Mill's Teleological, Consequentialist Philosophies--and Their Impact upon the Law.* Jeremy Bentham, during the late 1700's and early 1800's, developed an enormously influential philosophy of "hedonistic utilitarianism." In this teleological philosophy, the good, or pleasurable satisfaction, was the highest value, dominant over right or justice in the sense that those values were subservient to happiness. Bentham expressed his essential principle succinctly: "It is the greatest happiness of the greatest number that is the measure of right and wrong" (sometimes stated as "the greatest good for the greatest number"). "Hedonistic" utilitarians, like Bentham, differ from "idealistic" utilitarians, who seek to maximize a pluralism of values, such as knowledge, love, or aesthetics, rather than happiness alone. (Notice how this utilitarian philosophy would clash with the Greek preoccupation with virtue.)

John Stuart Mill, a student of Bentham, generalized the theory in the 1800's to include individual rights and justice. He used utilitarian reasoning to defend these concepts on the ground that without right and justice there would be no good or happiness. There also is a strong libertarian principle in Mill's philosophy: Personal autonomy is to be respected unless it results in harm to others, and moral offense does not count as harm. Mill puts this distinction in terms of "other-regarding harm," or hurting others, which can be suppressed, and "self-regarding harm," that which reflects disgust at another's self-destruction or lack of virtue, which may not be suppressed merely out of moral repugnance.

John Stuart Mill

(3) *The Consequentialist and Aggregative Nature of Utilitarianism.* Utilitarian philosophy therefore was a branch of "consequentialism," i.e., philosophy that depends upon the overall results of actions and rules. No government intervention was valid merely because of its intrinsic "rightness," but only if it resulted in greater popular happiness. Also, utilitarians looked to "aggregate" effects: Disadvantages felt by some people were not to be judged by whether they were intrinsically right or wrong but rather by whether they led to greater aggregate good. (Notice the sharp contrast with egalitarian philosophies, such as Rousseau's, as well as with the concept of social contract, which the utilitarians rejected.) When it is used to justify laws, utilitarianism is vulnerable to the charge that it disadvantages already disadvantaged minorities.

(4) *The Contrasting Deontological Philosophy of Kant: The Categorical Imperative.* In contrast to utilitarianism, Immanuel Kant in the latter 1700's developed an influential deontological philosophy. (Deontology is simply a large word for non-teleological, or morally-based philosophy, emphasizing right, duty and justice rather than purposive, result-oriented concepts such as utilitarianism.) Kant concluded that every individual had a duty to act in ways that could acceptably be imitated

Immanuel Kant

generally, as a "universal law." For example, if you accept a rule against falsehood, you cannot exempt yourself, and you cannot make exceptions for lies that overall might be beneficial (as utilitarianism might).

Kant called such a "universal" rule a "categorical imperative," a rule that should be rigorously adhered to without variation and regardless of consequences. Categorical imperatives, or invariable fundamental rules, were to be distinguished from "hypothetical" imperatives, or rules of thumb--the conventions or habits one follows as a matter of taste, such as, say, avoiding consumption of unhealthy foods.

(5) *Kant's Anti-Objectification Principle: All Humans Are Valuable Ends in Themselves, Never to Be Treated Only as Means to Others' Ends.* A separate test for a categorical imperative was that every such rule must treat each person as individually valuable, and not as an object to be used only as a means to ends preferred by others. Kant derived principles, for example, that required the keeping of promises no matter what the cost, and the telling of the truth regardless of consequences. One could not "use" another by lying or breaking promises--not ever. This was the nature of a categorical imperative.

(6) *Retributive Justice and Criminal Sentencing.* In addition, Kant developed a uniformly retributive philosophy of punishment. If we caught a burglar in a time of frequent unsolved burglaries, we could not use utilitarian philosophies such as deterrence to aggravate his sentence, merely so that we could advance interests of others, because that would involve "objectifying" him; we must sentence him only consistently with proportional justice. On the other hand, we would be forced to carry out justice even if a given sentence served no utilitarian purpose at all: In one famous passage, Kant concludes that even if a society's laws were to be abolished, such as by the disbanding of the entire society, the "last murderer" in its prisons should be executed first, so that "bloodguiltiness" would not remain upon the departing individuals(!)

(7) *Which Is the Value the Law Should Maximize: "Good" (Happiness), or "Right" (Justice)?* The debate about which was the superior or intrinsic value has existed since before the time of the Greeks. A short formulation of the difference in the utilitarian-Kantian debate is that utilitarians such as Bentham and Mill see the intrinsic values of the law as good or happiness,

with right and justice to be interpreted accordingly, while Kant sees duty, right and justice as the intrinsic values, dominant over good or happiness.

EXAMPLES AND PROBLEMS

(1) *The Trouble with Law Based on Utilitarianism, Part One: Slavery.* Utilitarianism leads to some results that we would reject today. For instance, a slave trader would like Bentham's utilitarianism in its simplest form, because it easily can be used to justify slavery. Can you see why? On the other hand, Kantian deontology squarely supports the modern rejection of slavery. Why? (Some utilitarians have responded to this problem by positing a minimum level of utility to be reserved to all members of the society.)

(2) *The Trouble with Law Based on Utilitarianism, Part Two: Vulnerable Minorities.* The Americans with Disabilities Act (ADA) imposes costs on the non-disabled majority so that disabled persons can partake of more of the benefits of society. What would utilitarianism make of the ADA? Wouldn't "pure" utilitarianism lead to a repeal of this statute? (Since one of Kant's categorical imperatives involved helping others, his deontology probably supports the ADA more easily.)

At the opposite end of the spectrum, imagine that a hardworking, inventive individual has built a valuable theme park. The population wants to confiscate and nationalize it so that everyone can use it without paying. What would "pure" utilitarianism say? (It might be used to argue in favor of the confiscation, mightn't it?) What would social contract theory (which the utilitarians rejected) say? Our Fifth Amendment Taking clause is designed to prevent short term utilitarianism of this kind.

(3) *The Trouble With Kant's View of the Law, Part One: Conflicting Categorical Imperatives.* But there also are problems with Kant's deontology. For example, imagine that you have entered into a contract (a promise, which categorically must be performed). But now you discover that your performance is prohibited by a later-passed law (compliance with which also is a categorical imperative). You have to obey the law and also keep the promise, but you can't do both! Does Kant's theory point to any resolution of this not-infrequent dilemma? Does utilitarianism?

(4) *The Trouble With Kant, Part Two: Inflexibility Disallows Balancing of Imperatives With any Other Value, Even When Losses Overwhelm Gains.*

Imagine that a terrorist is pursuing your neighbor, who is hiding in her closet. You would like to save her life by telling the terrorist, falsely, that your neighbor is at another location across town. What would be Kant's evaluation of this lie? What about Bentham's or Mill's?

Or, imagine that a corporate CEO signed a contract years ago that, because of bad luck, now will bankrupt the firm and abolish thousands of jobs if performed, while providing only minimal benefit to the other contracting party. If the CEO seeks to withhold performance, what would be Kant's answer? How would the utilitarians differ?

DIALECTICAL MATERIALISM, EXISTENTIALISM, AND SOCIALISM

(1) *Hegel's Dialectics and Communitarianism.* G. W. F. Hegel, in the 1800's, saw history as a constantly "dialectic" or evolving struggle between different views of right and wrong: a "thesis," or a given political theory, would compete with an "antithesis," or opposing theory, until a "synthesis," or selective combination of the two, emerged as the new thesis, to which an antithesis also would emerge. Contradiction was inherent in this view; the "absolute," or perfect truth, was the ideal toward which history struggled but would never attain.

The purposefulness of this dialectic struggle depended on its members' functioning as part of a community, not as autonomous individuals with separate existence. (This "communitarian" view is to be contrasted with "existential" philosophies of autonomous individuality, considered below.) Hegel saw the state as the dominant collective entity, dominant over the other "collectives" that he perceived as historically continuous (the family and society), and certainly dominant over the individual. The state, he concluded, would better moderate the dialectic struggle.

(2) *Marx's Dictatorship of the Proletariat.* Hegel's ideas led to at least one surprising turn. "A spectre is haunting Europe," Karl Marx wrote in *Das Kapital*, "the spectre of Communism." But this spectre was frightening mainly to "the bourgeoisie," the economically privileged, who kept workers, "the proletariat," mired in poverty for the bourgeoisie's benefit. Accepting Hegel's dialectical method, Marx changed its focus from materialism, a society in which the bourgeoisie could continue to rule, to a struggle that the workers would eventually win, establishing a "dictatorship of the proletariat."

The state then would own and control all means of production and would bring about a classless, equal distribution: "to each according to his needs; from each according to his abilities."

Das Kapital predicts the eventual proletarian victory, but it is much more than a description; it is a utopian call to action. "Workers of the world, unite!" Marx wrote. "You have nothing to lose but your chains."

(3) *Nietzche's "Ubermensch" and the Later Existentialists.* A very different vision came from Friedrich Nietzche. In the latter 1800's, Nietzche formulated a bleak view of society, full of conflict and alienation, fighting dark forces of nature. But Nietzche saw each individual as autonomous, each with a drive toward control and power. In the face of the irrational state and ever-repeating history, the "Ubermensch" (an untranslatable term, but perhaps best rendered as "the great person" or the "person above the crowd") was the one who followed his or her own stars, exercising the human will without undue conflict with others and unafraid of the bleakness of life, using an innate drive for power to triumph with new creations.

According to Nietzche, society would either evolve into an alienated mediocre crowd or be transformed by Ubermenschen to control its own fate. This viewpoint was a precursor to the philosophy of the later "existentialists" of the 1900's, who stressed the individual's position as a self-determining agent responsible for his or her own choices in a purposeless and irrational world.

EXAMPLES AND PROBLEMS

(1) *Hegelian Dialectic and Governor Bush's Self-Description in 1999 as a "Compassionate Conservative."* In the late 1990's, in positioning himself as a potential Presidential candidate, Governor George W. Bush adopted the label, "compassionate conservatism." Does Hegel's dialectic theory explain the combination of these two concepts into one political position?

(2) *The Growth of Marx's Influence--and Its Retrenchment.* Marx's philosophy influenced many other thinkers, from Engels to Lenin, and formed the philosophical basis for the economic, social and political systems of some of the most influential nations of the 20th Century, including the Soviet Union (of which Russia was the largest part) and China. But as the

Century ends, many of these countries have rejected Marx. Why? Can you see what specific problems or issues might have led to this result?

(3) *The Fascists and Nietzche.* Nietzche's philosophy may have led to the existentialists, but paradoxically, it also was a favorite of the Fascist nations of the 1930's and '40's, including Hitlerian Germany. Can you see how the concept of the Ubermensch might have been congenial to the Fascists? (Today, their interpretation generally is viewed as a corruption of Neitzche.)

§ 7.03 Classical   and   Modern   Notions   of   Liberalism and Conservatism

CLASSICAL LIBERALISM, MODERN LIBERALISM, AND DIFFERING CONSERVATIVE VISIONS OF THE LAW

(1)   *The Market-Oriented Classical Liberalism of Mill, Smith and Jefferson: A Term Whose Meaning Has Changed Sharply.* As we confront the emergence of modern political and ethical outlooks, we need to distinguish carefully between "classical" liberalism and modern liberalism. Originally, "liberalism" was associated with laissez faire economics and with the philosophy of J.S. Mill and Adam Smith. It was, in part, a reaction to earlier theories of statism, particularly to "mercantilism," which measured national wealth by state-owned gold bullion and sought to build it by repressive colonialism.

Liberalism comes from the Latin word "liber," or free, and classically it emphasized limited government and noninterference in economic markets. In other words, classical liberalism was close to the philosophy that today would be labeled, instead, by the term "conservatism." Some leaders in the new American democracy, in particular, embraced classical liberalism. As Thomas Jefferson put it, "That government is best that governs least."

(2) *Foundations of Modern Liberalism: Green's Positive Freedom and Bernstein's Democratic Socialism.* Modern liberalism, then, is different from classical liberalism. During the latter 1800's, the English philosopher Thomas Hill Green, the father of modern liberalism, favored government intervention to protect what Green called "positive" freedom. Earlier, classical liberalism had stressed laissez faire economics, free of government interference, and it had exalted private arrangements through contracts. But

what good was the right to negotiate contracts, Green asked, if you had no bargaining power? Your freedom to contract, then, did not amount to positive freedom.

For example, classical liberals preferred to let the market set wage rates. The invisible hand would say what a worker ought to be paid. But Green feared that the market rate might be too low, below a living wage. Therefore, he supported a minimum wage law, which he viewed not as government interference with freedom, but as a protection of "positive" freedom that made it more meaningful.

Later, at the turn of the century, Eduard Bernstein developed a related movement from a different direction. Bernstein articulated a philosophy of democratic socialism or, as he put it, "Evolutionary Socialism." In doing so, like Green, he spurred a movement related to modern liberalism, but unlike Green, Bernstein started not from classical liberalism but from Marxist socialism. Bernstein's innovation was to reject the necessity of revolution and to advocate evolutionary change through the ballot (thus earning himself the pejorative label of "revisionist" from committed Marxists).

Eventually, social democrats rejected the socialist label as well as the Marxist insistence on state ownership of production. What they retained was a concern for workers and for state-funded welfarism, so that welfare liberalism, rather than socialism, might be a better label than socialism for social democrats today. Thus, Green and Bernstein, coming from different directions, were founders of what we loosely call "liberalism" today.

(3) *Economic, Traditional, and Social Conservatives.* Classical liberalism, meanwhile, evolved into modern conservatism, particularly into "economic" conservatism. This philosophy generally opposes large-scale intervention in functioning competitive markets of the kind that modern economic liberals advocate for social welfare purposes, such as minimum wage laws, nationalized medicine, and government-funded pensions. Another, quite different kind of conservatism is the "traditionalist" version, traceable to Edmund Burke. This philosophy of traditional conservatism, which perhaps is more consistent with the concept of conservatism as "conserving" values of the past, argues for respect for tradition and for evolutionary change.

"Social" conservatism, like social liberalism, is more difficult to describe. Both philosophies would like to claim that they seek to maximize freedom and equality, but it is difficult to distinguish their respective claims on these grounds. Social conservatives tend to believe in such values as individual responsibility and parental independence, while social liberals tend to emphasize individual autonomy and communitarianism. But the coherence of these assertions is poor: social liberals may value autonomy in abortion decisions while social conservatives value community control to protect the right to life; but on the other hand, social conservatives value autonomy in gun ownership while social liberals value community control of guns.

EXAMPLES AND PROBLEMS

(1) *The Laws We Support: Are We All Economic Liberals Now, and Also, at the Same Time, Are We All Economic Conservatives?* The American people, apparently by a vast majority, seem to support the maintenance and stabilization of a social security system under government control. Furthermore, most seem to support legislation requiring minimum wages, fixed limits on work hours, family and medical leave, and governmental intervention in medical markets. Are most Americans, then, economic liberals?

At the same time, there seems to be greater reluctance in America than ever before to regulate competition in functioning markets, as is indicated by modern statutes deregulating industries from banking to airlines. Furthermore, our people obviously are suspicious of overregulation of medicine, and they seem to support a balanced federal budget. Does this mean that Americans are economic conservatives?

(2) *But It's All Relative: Comparing a More Heavily Welfare-Oriented Democracy (Sweden) With the United States.* In 1987, taxes in the United States were 30% of national output (GNP). But that same year, they were nearly twice that percentage in Sweden. There, taxes were 57% of GNP. In other words, for every five kronas earned, a Swede had to pay three of them to the government (in rounded figures). Is the United States, then, an economically conservative country? If so, that result is arguably consistent with "classical liberalism." Can you explain why?

(3) *The Ethical Implications of Economic Conservatism and Economic Liberalism.* The difficulty with the conservative rejection of welfare-state

liberalism is, arguably, that it unethically relegates the least fortunate members of society to a far lesser standard of living than the wealthy. In fact, it may tend to make the gap between the two increase. Imagine that you are severely disabled, so severely that you are unemployable and require constant attendant care. In the United States, your existence might be meager and shadowed by the fear of being unable to pay what it takes to stay alive. Or, imagine that you are one of the high percentage of American children living below the poverty line, or that you are a minimum-wage worker. Does America's distributive philosophy seem unethical from these vantage points? (Would you rather be Swedish, if you were one of these people?)

On the other hand, one can argue precisely the opposite: that it is Sweden's welfare liberalism, not the United States's relative economic conservatism, that is unethical. Sweden's tax rate is confiscatory, in this view; it denies Swedes the freedom to make fundamental choices about their lives and arrogates these choices, instead, to an overreaching state. Nobel-laureate economist Milton Friedman is one of the foremost exponents of this linkage between capitalism and freedom. Worse yet, one can argue, Sweden's welfarism creates a drag on the national economy that sacrifices the birthright of Swedes in generations to come, by suppressing economic growth.

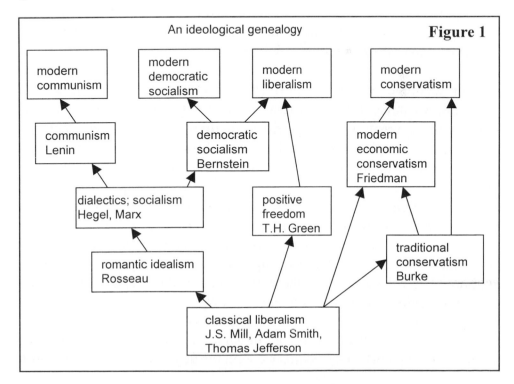

An ideological genealogy   **Figure 1**

Which of these two ethical conclusions do you consider more nearly correct? Are they both correct? (Since they seem to contradict each other, how can they possibly both be correct?)

(4) *A Genealogical Chart for Modern Political Ideologies.* Figure 1 is a graphic representation of the development of today's versions of liberalism, conservativism, democratic socialism, and communism. As do all summaries of this kind, the chart simplifies and arguably distorts the picture. Can you explain the genealogical lines traced in this figure, and state where you think it may misstate the relationships among philosophies?

§ 7.04 Some Modern Views of Ethical Philosophy

CONTEMPORARY LEGAL ISSUES OF CONSEQUENTIALISM AND DEONTOLOGY

(1)   *Comparing Consequentialist and Deontological Analyses of Economic Interventions.*   The economic arguments sketched in earlier chapters on economics are primarily utilitarian or consequentialist. They seek to maximize utility by market incentives or, when there is a market imperfection, by imposing a less costly deterrent to minimize costly behavior through the law. But there are other ways to evaluate interventions in the market by measures that in some instances have arguable claims to superiority over the marketplace view with which they may conflict.

For example, one may consider actual or punitive damages as a deontological device, concerned less with maximizing utility than with moral duty. In this alternate view, the justification for punitive damages is not their function in correcting market deficiencies. Instead, it is an expression of rightness and wrongness, of just deserts, or of moral blameworthiness.

(2) *Rightness and Wrongness in Economics?*   Whereas the consequentialist views the deterrent message perceived by uninvolved actors in the marketplace as the principal purpose of a penalty (even to the exclusion of compensation of persons unjustly injured), the deontologist emphasizes the individual moral positions of the participants in the event. The innocent accident victim, in this deontological view, deserves compensation not because compensation serves an economic function, but because it is "right." Similarly, the actor who is involved in what we refer to as causation of the injury is to be punished in accordance with the degree of that person's moral

blameworthiness, and not in a greater or lesser amount calculated by the need to communicate a corrective to the marketplace.[1]

(3) *An Example. "Zero Tolerance" Laws as Seen by Deontologists and Consequentialists.* The deontologist, then, seeks to accomplish retributive justice against morally blameworthy injurers. Closely connected to this retributive principle is the idea that penalties should be proportionally graded. To take an example from recent news stories, a school principal might seek to explain a severe punishment, such as expulsion, for a child who possesses Advil or Midol, on the ground that it carries out the school's policy of zero tolerance toward drugs. The consequentialist would ask whether this sanction produces more cumulative benefit in terms of its deterrent purpose than the total of costs or disadvantages attributable to it. The deontologist, on the other hand, would inquire whether the punishment has been triggered by a sufficient violation of moral duty and whether it is proportional to this individual's blameworthiness.

It is possible in such a situation that the consequentialist would see the means (i.e., the severe consequences borne by one individual) as justified by the end (i.e., the cumulative benefits to all others in the society). The deontologist would be troubled, however, by the sacrifice of the individual for the allegedly greater welfare of the many. Deontological reasoning thus includes asking whether the end justifies the means.

(4) *Expiation and Condemnation.* Still another deontological concept is that of expiation. Punishment serves the function of discharging the actor's moral debt and fits the wrongdoer for full acceptance back into the society. Punishment also may serve the purpose of condemnation. It thereby produces in morally upright people the satisfaction that justice is intact, expresses solidarity with innocent injured persons so as to assuage their suffering, and compensates for losses so that nonresponsible persons do not undergo the unfair burden of bearing them. Each of these considerations is related to deontological concepts or to retributive justice, although these ideas also may be related to consequentialist reasoning.

(5) *A Synthesis of Consequentialism and Deontology: The Kantian Who Defers to the Market and the Rule-Oriented Utilitarian.* Few people are

---

1 For example, the criminologist H. L. A. Hart posited three conditions for punishment: a voluntary act that is morally wrong, a punishment that is in some way equivalent in severity to the wrong, and that such punishment is just or morally right.

exclusively consequentialists, and few are pure deontologists. The deontologist, for example, cannot claim to use purely moral principles to derive all of the answers to production or pricing problems facing a firm in the workplace. Thus, even Kantians have to defer to the market for the answers to some questions. We have, then, the "limited deontologist," who may wish to impose categorical imperatives on some fundamental moral choices but not on others.

Likewise, the consequentialist cannot pretend that every decision can be based upon individualized determination of costs and risks, as opposed to relying for some decisions upon rules, norms or laws. Hence, there is the "rule-based utilitarian." Moreover, the consequentialist cannot persuasively defend a regime that unfairly imposes crushing burdens on random individuals to achieve general goals. In contemplating the need to deter drunk drivers, for example, even a person who predominantly is a consequentialist would be unlikely to advance an argument favoring the death penalty for slightly intoxicated offenders on the ground that theoretical economic calculations proved that the execution of the first unfortunate arrestee would produce deterrence powerful enough to result in a net benefit.

(6) *Continuing the Synthesis: Perhaps Deontology and Consequentialism Are Merely Different Ways of Seeing the Same Legal Issues?* In fact, it is possible to argue that moral retributivism is really a disguised form of utilitarianism. In this view, for example, proportional justice is beneficial because it adjusts the deterrent to avoid hidden costs such as public resistance or rebellion against punishments perceived as unfair. Likewise, condemnation and compensation produce utility in terms of better performance by the generally law-abiding population.

Perhaps it is equally possible to view some kinds of consequentialism as disguised forms of deontology. In this view, the retributive correctness of punishments is related to the marketplace, because moral blameworthiness is related to the calculus of risk, or to the excusability (or lack thereof) of the actor's particular resolution of the balancing of the likelihood of harm against the burden of precautions. To put it another way, moral judgments about what is right, and laws imposing liability, usually will be tied to the likelihood of causing benefits or harm to others and the magnitude of those effects.

EXAMPLES AND PROBLEMS

(1) *When Should You Use Consequentialism to Evaluate the Law--and When Deontology?: Professor Hurd's View.* The trouble with the "synthesis" described above is that sometimes utilitarian and deontological views still point to different solutions. When the answers conflict, which approach is superior? Professor Heidi M. Hurd, *The Deontology of Negligence*, 76 B.U. L. Rev. 249, 251-52 (1996), argues that, at least in the context of accident law, "[T]he principal payoff of deontological maxims is their ability to define and patrol the borders of consequential justification." To put it simplistically, the law should follow economic considerations (utilitarianism) in most applications, but it should be measured by moral concerns (deontology) in extreme cases. Mostly, we should think as utilitarians, but we should keep our deontological compass ready for those instances in which we might go overboard with utilitarianism. Do you agree?

(2) *An Example, from the Supreme Court's Restriction of Punitive Damages under the "Excessive Fines" Clause of the Constitution: BMW of North America v. Gore*, 116 S. Ct. 1589 (1996). In the *BMW* case, a jury found BMW liable for defectively painting a new vehicle after an accident and not informing the ultimate consumer. To the consumer's actual damages of $4,000 based on the jury's verdict, the state courts ultimately added a whopping $2 million in punitive damages. In an opinion by Justice O'Connor, the Supreme Court reversed, holding this

Sandra Day O'Connor

assessment excessive. To reach this decision, it consulted three morally oriented factors that were to limit punitive damages: (1) the "degree of reprehensibility," (2) the ratio of actual to punitive damages, and (3) the criminal or civil penalties available for comparable misconduct.

Commentators have regarded these factors as heavily deontological; can you explain? The Supreme Court's decision seems to reflect a borderline case, with an extreme ratio of punitive damages. What, then, will be the remaining function of consequentialism in assessing punitive damages?

(3) *Efficient Breach of Contract.* The generally established law is that a person cannot be liable for punitive damages for breach of contract. If the breaching party pays the other party's actual damage, the breacher may refuse to perform a contractual promise with no other legal consequences.

One reason for this legal rule is that there is such a thing as efficient breach of contract, when performance will be ruinous for one party and will benefit the other negligibly. Some would argue that one "ought" to breach in these circumstances. What would a Kantian deontologist say? A consequentialist? Are there occasions when "efficient" breach would nevertheless be immoral?

(4) *Sissela Bok's "Test of Publicity" for Morally Acceptable Falsehoods.* Sissela Bok's book, *Lying* (1978), proposes that rigid truth-telling cannot be a universal imperative, because lying is proper in some special circumstances. Recall the example in the previous section of the falsehood that saves your neighbor's life from a terrorist. Kant apparently would prohibit the lie, even in this case. As  **Sissela Bok** an alternative, Sissela Bok proposes a "test of publicity": Before deviating from the usual rule of truth-telling, a moral actor must consider whether the moral population would approve the lie if it were publicized.

Is Bok's reasoning deontological, consequentialist, a combination or compromise of the two, or something altogether different? Is it an improvement on Kant's categorical imperative? Consider whether Bok's test of publicity can tell us when to deviate from the categorical absoluteness of Kant's philosophy--or when to make an exception.

RAWLS'S THEORY OF DISTRIBUTIVE JUSTICE: EQUALITY AS THE PREMIER VALUE, INFERRED FROM THE "ORIGINAL POSITION"

(1) *John Rawls's "A Theory of Justice" (1971).* John Rawls's "A Theory of Justice" is one of the interesting philosophical works of the Twentieth Century. It also is highly debatable. Rawls presented his theory as an improvement upon social contract approaches and as an alternative to utilitarianism. His major theme sounds Kantian, at first blush: "Justice is the first virtue of social institutions . . . . Each person possesses an inviolability founded on justice that even the welfare of society as a whole cannot

override." But Rawls's approach is not that of Kant's universal imitation or categorical imperatives. It uses new methods and reaches different results.

Furthermore, Rawls's theory is sophisticated, with important defined places for market economics and civil disobedience, among a myriad of other institutions. But the thrust of his conclusion, as we shall see, is that justice is "fairness" to all, and as we also shall see, a major criticism of Rawls's theory is that it centerpieces what arguably may be a stultifying kind of equality, which some people think suffocates other values such as freedom and autonomy.

(2) *Rawls's Use of the "Original Position," "Perfect Knowledge," and the "Veil of Ignorance" as Devices from which to Derive Maxims of Distributive Justice.* Rawls replaces the social contract, Hobbes's great invention, with a similar but different tool, which he calls "the original position." This device is a hypothetical construct, just as the social contract was, to focus the thinking that derives Rawls's theory. Rawls's original position is the condition in which all of the members of the society would find themselves if they were transformed out of their current roles to a kind of planning conference for a new social order, to which they were to be returned in yet-unknown roles.

Rawls posits that all planners in the original position have "perfect knowledge" of the varieties of status into which they might return. But a key feature of the original position is that all the planning is assumed to be done behind a "veil of ignorance." None of the planners knows what the eventual role of any of them will be in the society--whether male or female, butcher, baker or candlestick-maker, disabled, gay, a member of majority or minority races, or for that matter, whether a merchant or a thief. Thus, the purpose of the veil of ignorance is to assure the planners' concern for the whole society. The device of the original position, then, is only that--a device--just as the metaphor of the social contract or Kant's universal imitation were devices, from which to derive the real theory.

(3) *Rawls's Simple Statement of His Two Principles of Justice: First and Foremost, Equal Liberty Consistent with Others' Liberty (The "Equality Principle"); and Second, Inequalities as Strictly Limited (The "Difference Principle").* Rawls concludes that the planners in the original position, with perfect knowledge of the society but with their own roles hidden behind a veil of ignorance, "would choose two rather different principles: the first

requires equality in the assignments of basic rights and duties, while the second holds that social and economic inequalities, for example inequalities of wealth and authority, are just only if they result in compensating benefits for everyone, and in particular for the least advantaged members of society."

These two maxims differ starkly from utilitarianism. As Rawls says, they "rule out" the argument that "hardships of some are offset by a greater good in the aggregate." Here is his basic statement of the two principles:

[1] First [Rawls's *"equality principle"*]: each person is to have an equal right to the most extensive basic liberty compatible with a similar liberty for others.

[2] Second [Rawls's *"difference principle"*]: social and economic inequalities are to be arranged so that they are both (a) reasonably expected to be to everyone's advantage, and (b) attached to positions and offices open to all.

The genius of this formulation, arguably, is that although its roots are deontological, it also accommodates limited versions of institutions more closely associated with utilitarianism, such as political democracy and market economics.

(4) *Priority Among the Equality and Difference Principles--What if They Conflict?: How Rawls Avoids Intuitionism.* Rawls's ambitious aim is to rank these two principles for all cases, even when they conflict with other principles or with each other. His formulation is that the first principle (the equality principle) is the first priority, and it must in all cases be satisfied. The second (the difference principle) is subordinate, and all other principles, in turn, are subordinate to these.

This priority avoids "intuitionism," in which the ethical decisionmaker is left with no basis to decide among conflicting principles other than intuition. One can argue that Rawls thus solves a problem that Kant did not solve. For example, if Kant's categorical imperative not to lie were to conflict with the imperative to keep promises, for example, there would be no rule of decision other than intuition because both are categorical. The utilitarians solved this problem by making aggregate utility maximization the priority principle, and thus their philosophy could be used to justify oppression of a minority (e.g., slavery) by its overall benefits. Rawls's solution is very different.

(5) *The First Principle: Equality under the Law.* The equality principle applies to "basic" liberties, says Rawls. And these "basic" liberties "are, roughly speaking, political liberty (the right to vote and to be eligible for public office) together with freedom of speech and assembly; liberty of conscience and freedom of thought; freedom of the person along with the right to hold (personal) property; and freedom from arbitrary arrest and seizure as defined by the concept of the rule of law." Equality in these matters, according to Rawls, is absolute and may not be subordinated to any other value. Here, Rawls differs sharply from the utilitarians, and, more subtly, he also differs from Kant.

(6) *The Second Principle: Justification of All Wealth and Social Differences by the "Worst Outcome" (the "Maximin" Principle).* Rawls's second principle is more complex. Outside of the absolute equality of basic political liberty, which has priority under the first principle, there are realms of wealth and social status where the final distribution can (and will) be unequal, even though in the original position all may have contemplated an equal chance. There must be leaders of certain institutions, for example, and they may enjoy higher status and rewards than others. An inventor or developer who through creation or hard work provides benefits to others will wind up with greater-than-average wealth.

But for Rawls, these inequalities must always depend on two rigorous conditions. First, the opportunity to enjoy these unequal benefits must be open to all. And second, no inequality is tolerable unless it makes everyone better off, not just the benefitted individual, or some people, or even the majority. In fact, the true criterion of an acceptable inequality, says Rawls, is that it must benefit "the least fortunate groups in a society." In other words, there can be no bonuses for high-performance executives unless they also make homeless persons better off.

Rawls calls this the "maximin" principle:[2] "We are to adopt the alternative the worst outcome of which is superior to the worst outcomes of others," he says--worst outcome meaning the impact on the least advantaged person in society.

---

2 "Maximin" is a term derived from game theory, as we shall see in a later chapter (the chapter on strategy). Maximin is the general name for a cautious strategy--in fact, the most cautious possible strategy--which might, pejoratively, be labeled pessimistic or even defeatist, in some competitive situations. It assumes the worst outcome and then adopts the approach that will result in the "best of the worst" outcomes--a "worst-case scenario" method of planning. As we also shall see, however, maximin strategy also maximizes total benefits in some cooperative games.

SOME CONTRASTING VIEWS OF DISTRIBUTIVE JUSTICE: FROM NOZICK'S LIBERTARIANISM TO CALABRESI'S TRAGIC CHOICES

(1) *Enterprise versus the Welfare State.* One way to view Rawls's views is as a reflection of overly optimistic times. In the 1960's, it seemed to some people that all things were possible, that production and increasing wealth were inevitable, and that fair distribution was a greater concern than incentives to efficiency. Rawls developed his theory at the height of this optimistic era. But then, the early 1970's saw the humiliating exit of the United States from a lost war in Vietnam and severe shortages of oil and gas aggravated by government policies and by foreign boycotts. The new sense of vulnerability produced a variety of views that differed from Rawls's theory. Can you see why Rawls's views might be seen as the product of overly optimistic times?

(2) *Nozick's Critique of Rawls's Equality Theory: The "Night Watchman" Theory of Law and the "Michael Jordan" Example.* A few years after the publication of Rawls's theory, Robert Nozick answered with a different philosophy emphasizing a natural human right to the fruits of one's own labors. Efforts to use government coercion to redistribute wealth through law were unjust and equivalent to forced labor, Nozick said, including taxation of the wealthy at higher rates.

In Nozick's libertarian philosophy, laws should be kept to limited roles such as preventing theft and enforcing contracts. Government should act as a kind of "night watchman" state. Perhaps Michael Jordan has made more money playing basketball and endorsing products than a person flipping hamburgers at minimum wage, but the law has no business addressing this inequality, said Nozick, because Jordan is entitled to the gain from his own body and his own efforts.[3] It also may be true that Jordan, by accident of birth, has physical endowments enabling him to be a high earner, but Nozick sees this concern as irrelevant to Jordan's entitlement to his earnings. Nozick's vision of government has been referred to as "the night watchman state," because it limits society's coercive force to a smaller role than other ethicists would allow. Is Nozick's view a persuasive counter to Rawls's theory?

---

3   Nozick actually referred to an earlier basketball player, Wilt Chamberlain, but the point is the same. In the future, maybe the current example will be football's Ricky Williams(?) (New Orleans) or baseball's Roy Oswalt (Houston).

(3) *The Law of "Tragic Choices": Calabresi and Bobbitt and the "Mickey Mantle Example."* Guido Calabresi and Philip Bobbitt saw the equality issue through a different lens: that of scarce essential resources. Consider the demand for and supply of organs for transplant and the legal regime for distributing them. In their book, *Tragic Choices*, Calabresi and Bobbitt effectively demonstrated that no single criterion of equality was inevitable in such cases. For example, should a scarce, life-saving liver be placed in the body of a person whose healthy life choices support an inference of longevity, even though the donor's match to the recipient is less than perfect? Or instead, should the recipient automatically be the one with the best tissue match, despite health or lifestyle?

Guido Calabresi

In the 1990's, after Calabresi and Bobbitt's book, baseball legend Mickey Mantle received a liver transplant even though his health, partly through neglect, made it unlikely that he would survive long. When Mantle died very soon after the transplant, many observers considered this scarce resource wasted, even though the decision ostensibly was based on tissue typing. And *Tragic Choices* likewise demonstrated that even if these decisions are supposed to be strictly controlled under the law, they often reflect subterranean, quasi-political influences, which many suspected in Mantle's case. Should the choice of Mickey Mantle as a recipient be directed by his fame, or the inspiration and entertainment he provided to millions, or for that matter, his ability to outbid others in the marketplace?

Tragic Choices examines various decision mechanisms, including the "aresponsible" agency (not "irresponsible," but "a-responsible," like a jury, in the sense that members are exempt from a duty to report to any sanctioning authority). Such a body might reduce political and economic influences. And further, *Tragic Choices* demonstrates the need for scarcity policies to take account of human strategies that are designed to exploit the criteria in those very policies. Imagine that an alcoholic promises never to drink again if only he receives the liver that will save his life; in such a situation, a rational decisionmaker must foresee and be able to counteract the likelihood of nonperformance that will be unredressable by any reasonable enforcement mechanism.

Is the problem of tragic choices, then, one that eludes solution by Rawls's absolute egalitarianism?

EXAMPLES AND PROBLEMS

(1) *Criticizing the Justification of Rawls's Principles: Perfectionism and Projection Rather than Achievable by Law.* One critique of Rawls's theory is that it is utopian. It assumes a complete, instantaneous ordering of society based on the plan from the original position, and thus it may not tell about the operation of an imperfect society or its evolution into a more just one. Rawls admits this limited objective: His thrust is not to consider "how we are to deal with injustice." Instead, "I examine . . . a well-ordered society . . . . [I] ask what a perfectly just society would be like."

But a real-world legislator operates in a society with an unequal wealth distribution (perhaps even with slavery). Would America's Founders have succeeded in promulgating the United States Constitution if they had tried to follow Rawls?

(2) *Does Rawls Exalt One Arbitrarily Chosen Value, Equality, at Too Much Expense to Other Values?* A separate criticism concerns Rawls's inference of his two principles as the necessary and inevitable results of the original position. He states that the planners, with their veil of ignorance, "would choose" these maxims (not "might choose," but "*would*.") Why? "The intuitive idea is that since everyone's well-being depends upon a scheme of cooperation without which no one could have a satisfactory life, the division of advantages should be such as to draw forth the willing cooperation of everyone taking part in it, including those less well situated." In other words, the welfare of all persons in the original position depends crucially on their benefitting the worst-off members of the society. From this, says Rawls, "we are led to these [two] principles."

But is it not possible that less risk-averse original-positioners would exalt other values, such as freedom, autonomy, or retention of the fruits of one's own labors? Is the inference of Rawls's two principles really as universal and inevitable as he argues, or is it merely a projection of Rawls's own idiosyncratic preferences?

(3) *Questioning Rawls's First (Equality) Principle and Applying It to the Law: Can There Be Deviations for Supermajorities, Unequal*

Representation, Prohibitions on Contract Abrogation, or Accommodation of Unequal Practices by Religious Groups? If Rawls's first principle allows no deviation from equality in political liberties such as voting, can there be supermajority requirements (as the Constitution requires for a constitutional amendment--two-thirds of the Congress, three-fourths of the States)?[4] Under Rawls's theory, is it "unjust" that people in a sparsely populated state like North Dakota elect the same number of senators as California, whose more numerous citizens thus have lesser votes?

Or, imagine that the founders of a society decide in their constitution to prohibit contract abrogation for reasons of economic efficiency (in fact, the United States Constitution imposes this prohibition on the States). Later, the voters, by a majority, decide that they wish to abrogate contracts of a certain kind that they believe have become politically repressive because of their wealth effects, but they are prevented from doing so because of the constitutional prohibition. Is this prohibition unequal and therefore unjust, since it prevents the majority from acting politically on a given subject when a different majority would be able to act politically on another chosen subject? Also, can one argue that the contract-abrogation prohibition violates Rawls's priorities, since it uses economic efficiency, a matter governed by the second principle, the difference principle, to govern political voting, which is supposed to be inviolable to economic arguments because of the priority of the first principle of equality?

Finally, imagine a clash of two political liberties: a religious practice that conflicts with others' equality. A church might allow only men, not women (or vice versa!), to perform its sacraments. This practice denies the equality of one gender or the other, but if the law required the church to do otherwise, it might violate the members' most sacred tenets and deny them equality in matters of religious conscience. How would Rawls resolve this dilemma (or does his theory resolve it at all? Does it leave it to intuitionism)?

(4) *Rawls's Second Principle: The Full-Employment, Welfare, and Minimum Wage Law Examples.* A society with roughly five percent (5%) unemployment is, by some economists' conclusion, at "full employment," because efforts to reduce employment below a certain level are likely to produce ruinous inflation as well as other economic disadvantages. But five

---

4   This is the requirement if the amendment is accomplished by Congressional resolution (the most common route).

percent unemployment, low as it may be, still means that some individuals do not have jobs. In fact, the unemployment rate for teenage African-American males consistently is much higher, so that a five percent rate means more than five percent joblessness in this disadvantaged group.

Since the "worst outcomes" or "least fortunate" are the key to Rawls's "maximin" principle, would Rawls's philosophy require the society, then, to use whatever draconian means it can, to push unemployment literally to zero--and to suffer whatever drastic economic consequences may befall all other citizens?

Note that Rawls's principle, taken to its literal limit, requires a focus on the one, single worst-off individual in the society. If only one individual is unemployed, must governments' policies be reordered to make sure this one individual gets employed? Perhaps the society might solve the problem by transfer payments (welfare). But can it do so if there are even a few welfare recipients who would rather work? (Refinements added by Rawls to his second principle do enable a welfare system to operate.) But can government set necessary conditions on welfare, such as time limits, if it knows that even a few individuals will not comply (indeed, some through their own willful nonperformance)?

Finally, consider a minimum-wage law, which will mean that some low-paid workers will be better off. Imagine that a marginal employer is able to pay only a wage one dollar less for a potential job opening that unemployed workers would line up to seek, but the transaction is prohibited by the minimum wage law. Since every minimum wage law benefits some of the poor but inevitably hurts others, doesn't it violate Rawls's second principle?

(5) *Defending Rawls against Nozick: Must the Law Accept the Disadvantages of the Marketplace When It Is Society, after All, That Enables the Marketplace to Function in the First Place?* Nozick's view, in rejecting Rawls, implicitly assumes that marketplace results are just, to the exclusion of other values that society may prefer in a given instance. At its logical extreme, Nozick's arguments would prevent transfer payments even to the most disabled citizens, because they have to come from taxes imposed on what other people have earned.

But the laws of society, as well as the individual or firm, are essential to the functioning of the market. Nozick tacitly recognizes this by permitting government to enforce contracts. As we saw in the preceding chapter, it is possible for an unregulated market to result in small groups of haves confronting larger numbers of have-nots, or even in a few extraordinarily wealthy persons, who own most of the society's resources, living with many desperately poor ones. One can argue that society may use the law to order its participation in the market so that it avoids such a result as unjust. Is this argument persuasive? Does it answer Nozick's critique of Rawls? If not, is a synthesis of these different views possible?

A MODERN ETHICAL CONUNDRUM:
THE TROLLEY PROBLEM AND ITS FALLOUT

(1) *Tragic Choices, Rawls, and the Trolley Problem.* Now, let us examine the problem of distributive justice from another angle. The famous "trolley problem" stretches views of egalitarianism and justice. Imagine that a runaway trolley is rolling down the hill toward six people whom it inevitably will kill if not diverted. A switch manager is standing beside a switch that will shunt the trolley onto a different track, where it equally inevitably will kill only one person, a different person, one who will live if the switch is not thrown.

The question posed by the trolley problem, then, is whether it is ethical for the manager to throw the switch, killing the one person rather than the other six. What would the utilitarians say? Or Kant, Rawls, or Calabresi?

Often, people confronted by this problem try to avoid it by saying, "The manager should shout at the six to get out of the way," or by using similar extrinsic solutions. Perhaps this instinct is good (or even correct), but the trolley problem depends on imaginary circumstances in which the deaths of either the one or the six are inevitable and the only possible intervention is to throw the switch. If persuaded to accept this assumption, most people justify throwing the switch and killing the one unfortunate person on the other track instead of the six who are in the trolley's path. Why? Are most people utilitarians? (Still, some people may persist in the deontological view that a human being can't intervene to "play God" by choosing who lives and dies, not even to the extent of choosing one death over six.)

(2) *The Trolley Problem and the Law of Capital Punishment.* Some justifications of capital punishment are based upon the projection that executions of a few people guilty of heinous crimes will deter murders and

thereby save many more innocent lives than the people who are executed. (There even have been quantitative calculations of the numbers saved per execution, as we shall see in another chapter.) Does the trolley problem provide any insight into this argument? Do you suppose that people who justify throwing the switch to divert the trolley also may be the same people who accept this deterrence rationale for capital punishment?

(3) *Variations of the Trolley Problem (Including the Involuntary Organ Donor).* Next, let us consider a variation on the trolley problem. Imagine that the switch manager knows that all six people on the trolley's track are convicted felons under sentence of capital punishment, all to be executed next week, while the one person on the diversion track is a revered national leader. Could there be some ethical switch managers who would conclude that these facts should change the outcome?

And finally, let us imagine a partly different but perhaps analogous problem. There are six people who will die within days unless they receive organ transplants that will make them healthy. One needs a heart, one a lung, another a liver, another a kidney, etc. The hospital locates one healthy individual whose tissue typing allows him to be a donor to all six, saving all their lives. The question is whether society may sacrifice this individual to harvest his or her organs.

Is this "involuntary organ donor" problem different from the trolley problem? Isn't it closely analogous? But most people, even if they would divert the trolley, refuse to allow the state to kill the involuntary organ donor. Why? Do most people reject utilitarianism in favor of deontology?

SOME OTHER VIEWS OF LAW AND JUSTICE: INDETERMINACY, PROCESS, AND SOCIAL THEORY

(1) *Indeterminacy: From Rule Utilitarianism to Limited Deontology.* Kant, Mill, and Rawls each sought ways to avoid indeterminacy by positing categorical rules or priority principles. Although their systems were different, all three tried to provide clear guidance to lawmakers rather than to allow reliance on "balancing" of values or what Rawls calls "intuitionism."

Other schools of thought, however, frankly admit that it is impossible to avoid ethical indeterminacy. The trolley and organ-donor problems in the previous section suggest the reason: Most people think sometimes deontologically, sometimes in utilitarian terms. There are various ways to make compromises. The so-called "rule-oriented utilitarian" sees the same principles that the deontologist does, regards them as essential to utilitarian goals as well, and accepts the contribution to utility made by defined norms rather than universal balancing for every question. The calculus about the wrongness of committing murder, then, does not require a situational balancing of utility to a greater number from the murder of a particular person, but rather the utility-maximization of complying with the defined norm embodied in the murder statute. Similarly, a deontologist may define realms of justice in which consequentialism is more appropriate (as Rawls did, in accepting economic markets).

A quite different approach is to accept a particular philosophy generally, but to abandon it in borderline cases, or breakdowns, when an opposing philosophy provides better guidance. Professor Hurd's proposal, referred to in an earlier section, that accident law should be governed primarily by consequentialist theory (utilitarianism), with deontology reserved for "patrolling the borders," is an example.

(2) *Pervasive Indeterminancy: Westermark's Ethical Relativism.* Fuller moral "relativism" gives a greater play to indeterminacy. Various ethical positions may each be justifiable in any given situation, and there is no real way to rank them objectively, says the ethical relativist. One of the most articulate spokespersons for this view is Edward Westermarck, whose principal work is called "Ethical Relativism." Here is Westermarck's summary: "None of the various theories of normative science can be said to have proved . . . that moral judgments possess objective validity, that there is anything truly good or bad, right or wrong, [or] that moral principles express anything more than the opinions of those who believe in them." Westermarck goes on to assert that not only can no one prove any objectivity, but further, that it cannot exist.

Is there any substance to ethics at all, then? Do our laws rest on any moral foundation? Only on pragmatism, according to Westermarck: "It may, of course, be a subject for scientific inquiry to investigate the means which are conducive to human happiness or welfare, and the results of such a study may also be usefully applied by moralists, but it forms no more a part of ethics than physics is a part of psychology." This does not mean that there can be no law, or no morals; dialectic among morally concerned people may produce a system of rules for a society. But Westermarck insists that it is no more than this--a system of rules for one society--and not any objectively verifiable truth about ethics.

(3) *Process Theories of Law and Justification by Debate.* Because of the indeterminacy problem, some have suggested that process, rather than outcomes or substantive rules of decision, is what justice is about. Imagine that a jury has rejected a person's claim that another owes damages for negligence, or has convicted the person of murder over a claim of self-defense. Except for the basic rules in the judge's charge, which are nebulous, there are no binding laws for decision. And for both cases, the legal issue boils down to one highly indeterminate concept: whether the defendant acted "reasonably." Literally, that is the key word the judge will use in both the negligence and the self-defense case, and on it, the entire outcome depends. Yet, we do not control (or even examine) the myriad conflicting points of view, maxims, rules of thumb or inductions that the jury may use in interpreting this ambiguous standard, or for that matter how jurors accept facts to believe or fit them to the law.

Instead, we concentrate on providing a fair process, and this is fine with the process theorist. But if the process were unfair, if jurors known to be irreparably biased were allowed to serve, or the plaintiff were denied an opportunity to present evidence, then the result would be unjust. This sometimes is so, to the process theorist, even if the outcome is clear; irrefutable eyewitnesses, physical evidence and a confession squarely fitting the murder statute cannot justify summary punishment without a trial under the law.

At a more abstract level, a different kind of process theorist, the "meta-ethicist," attempts to construct principles of argumentation that should govern the derivation of ethical principles. Meta-ethics accepts indeterminacy in norms and concerns itself with the types of derivation, or processes, by which the substantive principles should be defined.

(4) *The Formation of Legal Norms: If One "Should" Refrain from Stealing, "Why"?* Another approach to argumentation seeks to uncover the justifications underlying norms or laws as a guide to their interpretation. Why "should" a person not steal? The response that stealing is wrong is "tautological," or in other words it assumes the conclusion. Tautology can justify any position that the speaker accepts: If the speaker defines abortion as wrong, then it is unethical, whereas another speaker may define

restrictions on abortion as wrong, in which event the opposite position is true. (This is the "fallacy of definition" explored in Chapter 1.)

The mere existence of a law or a norm, then, is not its justification; instead, the justification depends on the separate question of why it "ought" to be the law. One may, for example, argue that "stealing is wrong because it threatens orderly exchange" (utilitarian) or that "stealing is wrong because it subordinates the victim to the thief's own uses" (deontological). From this kind of analysis, we can analyze whether the justification is persuasive; if, for example, it turns out that a given kind of stealing does not interfere at all with market exchange, a utilitarian can redefine the definition of theft to omit it. For example, is it wrong for a poor person to steal a loaf of bread if it is the only available means to avoid starving? Many states have accepted a limited defense of necessity to resolve this problem (Kant would disapprove!) The utilitarian calculus (but perhaps not the Kantian categorical) changes in this situation, if we recognize a diminished threat to the marketplace and the offsetting utility of a saved life, and thus we can redefine the law of theft to exclude an instance of strict necessity. (But the states usually do not allow necessity as a defense to murder, even very severe necessity, proving that there still is a place for deontology.)

(5) *Social and Developmental Moral Theorists.* Still others regard ethics as dependent upon the social structure in which a particular person is immersed. To these social theorists, there are no absolute moral principles. Instead, everything depends upon the culture of the society in which one lives. In the United States today, it is murder, and immoral, to kill a person who has harmed one's kin; in early England, on the other hand, the same practice was ethically appropriate and, indeed, sometimes was the principal means of law enforcement.

Finally, there are developmental theorists. Beginning with Swiss psychologist Jean Piaget's *The Language and Thought of the Child*, developmental theorists have observed that, from childhood, people advance through stages of moral consciousness. The lowest stages are simplistic: versions of entitlement ("That's mine!") moderated only by result-dependent rules of strict liability ("It broke, and I'm in trouble"). Cultural principles of greater complexity replace these early perceptions (I need to apologize because it was my fault, but I wouldn't need to if it weren't my fault). The top stages of moral development involve more complex balancing, and developmental moral theorists posit that they are not reached by the average person.

EXAMPLES AND PROBLEMS

(1) *Polygamy in Southwestern Utah: Moral Indeterminacy or Failure of Law Enforcement?* Polygamist families, sometimes with dozens of children, live communally in southeastern Utah in open violation of bigamy laws, according to deeply rooted religious traditions. Local sheriffs can justify their failure to arrest bigamists by reference to higher enforcement priorities, such as violent crime, and by comparisons to other laws against fornication or adultery, which rarely warrant enforcement.

At a different moral level, sheriffs could point out that breaking polygamist families is ruinous for children, that past efforts at enforcement have proved futile because general public outrage results in impossibility of conviction as well as widespread disrespect for law, and that the law actually conflicts with divine commands sacred to the polygamists. On the other side, many members of the public regard polygamy as criminal, exploitive of women, productive of other crimes such as incest and statutory rape, and harmful to children precisely because it traps them in an illegal regime. Some groups of former polygamist wives are particularly vocal in denouncing polygamy.

How would a traditional ethicist, (1) Kantian or (2) utilitarian, analyze these moral conflicts? (3) A rule-oriented utilitarian? What about (4) a moral relativist, or (5) a process theorist, or (6) a social theorist?

(2) *The Trouble with Indeterminacy: Slavery and Sex-Selection Abortions as Seen by Self-Interested Decisionmakers Using Manipulable Criteria.* Slave owners justified slavery by pointing out that it had existed throughout history: "It is natural for one person to own another." Would the moral relativist succeed either in recognizing immorality in this argument or in constructing persuasive counterarguments? What about the utilitarian who accepts deontology in extreme cases (to "patrol the borders")? What about the process theorist or social theorist?

For a hypothet closer to today's situation, imagine a widespread practice of aborting girls as a means of selecting gender at birth. Large numbers of women, let us suppose, support each other in electing abortions solely to avoid birthing girls, justifying the decision by explaining that they have concluded boys have "higher social status" and by pointing out that the law provides each of them the exclusive choice. Imagine that others (perhaps including some who are usually pro-choice) oppose this practice as immoral, barbarous, sexist, and ultimately, bad eugenics, even if it is not prohibited by today's laws.

How would (1) utilitarians and (2) Kantians react to this gender-selection abortion issue? (3) Moral relativists, (4) process theorists, or (5) social theorists? (Notice that some of the arguments on both sides are tautologous, including the sex-selectors' appeal to the existing law of choice--does that mean that one "should" engage in this behavior? On the other side, consider the opponents' "barbarousness" label).

Chapter 8
Politics

Democratic Institutions, Tradeoffs, and Public Choice

> *"In the United States, then, that
> numerous and turbulent multitude does not
> exist, who, regarding the law as their
> natural enemy, looked upon it with fear and
> distrust."--Alexis de Tocqueville, Democracy
> in America*

§ 8.01 What This Chapter Is About

DEMOCRACY, ITS INSTITUTIONS, AND ITS TRADEOFFS

(1) *Why a Constitutional Democracy With Separated Powers?* The chapter begins with a contrast between democracy (particularly constitutional American democracy) and other forms of government. It considers the theory that a democratic system tends to preserve a number of widely shared values, and it examines different varieties of democratic structures.

(2) *Conflicts Within Democratic Institutions.* But whatever legal form a society chooses, there will be internal conflicts, and so the chapter goes on to consider these conflicts. For example, it examines a concept called

"Arrow's Theorem," which deals with one of the basic problems in voting and public choice. Further, there is the "Madisonian dilemma": the problem of protecting minority rights within a regime of majority rule. Neither of these problems can be perfectly solved, but we shall look at alternative methods for addressing them.

(3) *Democratic Structure and Tradeoffs Among Values in the Law.* Next, the chapter considers the structure of democracy. It compares the theory of separation of powers with its democratic opposite, the unified parliamentary system. It also covers the question of political parties (should there be one, two or many?). Finally, it considers tradeoffs among the values that underlie the law: the relationships between property and freedom, between freedom and equality, and among different political concepts of equality.

(4) *Assumption of Familiarity With American Political Institutions.* This chapter assumes familiarity with the content of a basic civics or government course. Also, it does not cover politics in the sense of partisan conflicts, or how to conduct political campaigns. Instead, it covers more general questions: What are the institutions that sustain a democracy, and what tradeoffs, problems or imperfections will they generate for lawmakers?

§ 8.02 American Constitutional Democracy and Its Alternatives

COMPARING AUTHORITARIANISM TO DEMOCRACY

(1) *Examining What Is Right About Our System: The View of Secretary of State James A. Baker, III.* The section you are about to read did not exist in the original draft of this book. But after reviewing the chapter, former Secretary of State James A. Baker, III, wrote the following commentary:

> . . . I agree wholehearted that there is a need to teach [readers] how to think independently about the great subjects in your [book].
> . .
> However, . . . I see that you have assumed that your [readers] are familiar with American political institutions.
>
> . . . Yes, they are familiar with the fact that we have a President and a Congress and a judicial branch. But I see evidence that too few in our culture understand . . . , for example, what distinguishes democracy from other forms of governance . . . .

Maybe I am mistaken, but I fear that, partly as a result of being taught more in our schools about the imperfections of democracy than about its immense benefits, partly as a result of cynical journalism, and partly as a result of the distrust in our government that some politicians engender for their own benefit, many citizens believe that our system is corrupt and oppressive. . . .

You face a difficult problem in your book. Clearly, you cannot teach basic civics, from the ground up. And you also should not be expected to provide an entirely uncritical look at our institutions.

But I do believe this--the first tool that should come to hand in any discussion about politics and government is an exposition of what's right about our democratic system and an appreciation of the exquisite privilege we have, living in the United States with our system of representative democracy.

The earlier version, omitting these considerations, may have been too scholarly in the ivory tower sense that it assumed too much and focused on aberrational matters. This section therefore is included in response.

(2) *Authoritarianism Compared to Democracy.* "Authoritarianism" refers to a variety of different types of government in which power is exercised by persons or small groups who do not derive it from the people at large, as they would in a democracy. By this definition, Hobbes's "leviathan" model of the state run by a benevolent monarch was authoritarian. So were some of the Greeks, who preferred an aristocracy. Authoritarian power may be oligarchic (wealthy families) or exercised by an army commander or group of officers after a coup.

Authoritarianism need not exhibit the pervasive repression that characterizes totalitarianism, which we consider below. There may, in fact, be a considerable range of private personal freedom in cultural, social, and economic matters. But order and conformity to duties to the state are emphasized in the public arena, where the individual has no control over the laws but is expected to obey them carefully. There may be democratic institutions, but in authoritarian governments they exercise little power, as the national legislature did in the Soviet Union, where the party was the real institution of power.

Some political scientists have suggested that in newly independent third world countries, authoritarianism is likely to develop even after the establishment of a fragile democracy. The everyday struggle for subsistence limits popular participation. A multiple-party system may degenerate into cultural animosities, violence and terror. A strong authoritarian leader may be able to maintain stability and may be acceptable to a needy people even though it comes at a high price in political freedom and the rule of law--or so the argument goes.

(3) *The Evolution of Authoritarianism: Democracy or Totalitarianism?* It is possible for an authoritarian society to transform itself into a democracy. A classic example is Spain, which emerged from an authoritarian regime under Generalissimo Franco. What is required for such a transition? It appears that a stable middle class (as opposed to a wide gap between rich and poor) is a factor, as are education and a minimum level of economic development.

The possibility also exists, however, for an authoritarian regime to transform itself into a totalitarian one. Authoritarianism sounds confusingly similar to totalitarianism, but the two are conceptually distinct. Totalitarian regimes are by definition authoritarian, but there is more to them than that.

(4) *Totalitarianism.* "Totalitarian" systems, as described (for example) by Carl J. Friedrich and Zbigniew Brzezinski, exhibit six fundamental characteristics: (1) an all-encompassing ideology (such as Communism or Fascism), (2) a single political party (later we shall consider the central function that multiple, competing parties play in democratic government), (3) organized terror (such as the Blue Guards in post-revolutionary France, the Gestapo, or the Soviet NKVD), (4) exclusive control of communications (state radio, television, and other news media are the only ones, or nearly so), (5) exclusive control of weapons (there is no maintenance of private arms, making rebellion difficult), and (6) a controlled economy (such as Soviet-style centralization). Perhaps the ultimate, anti-utopian version of totalitarian government is that of the fictional Big Brother in George Orwell's novel *Nineteen-Eighty-Four*.

(5) *The Character of Democracy: Facilitating Dignity, Change, Growth, and the Rule of Law.* The character of democracy is exhibited by several factors that differ from these authoritarian models. Laws are made through power derived from election. Lawmaking officials are accountable by

election, and they must, therefore, have popular support.   There is competition for votes, and elections provide real choices among alternatives. There is broad openness in the right to seek public office, but at the same time, government officials are in a position such that they are motivated to learn about public opinion.   The majority rules, but there is a sphere of protection for minority rights, and there is careful protection of rights of expression, petition and dissent.

These characteristics are thought to serve a number of values that authoritarian regimes do not. A democratic system creates confidence in the dignity and autonomy of the individual. Its preservation protects substantial levels of freedom and equality. Less obviously, it facilitates the rule of law, because the legitimacy of government induces more cooperative, voluntary compliance with standards of conduct. (The quotation from de Tocqueville that begins this chapter supports this conclusion.) Democracy also allows a mechanism for peaceful transfer of power (not always available in authoritarian systems).   It probably encourages individuals to hope and therefore to plan for the future, and therefore, it arguably fosters a predictability that induces economic benefits.   In summary, democracy advances the ideals that Thomas Jefferson described in the phrase, "life, liberty, and the pursuit of happiness."

INTEREST GROUP COMPETITION
AND CIVIC REPUBLICANISM

(1) *Civic Republicanism as an Alternative to Laws Won by Competing Interest Groups.* One vision of democracy is that it reflects contests between inconsistent voter preferences, or competitions among interest groups, which are to be resolved by majority rule or by political power. But as an alternative to this model of competition and struggle, some political philosophers have advanced the idea of "civic republicanism."   These philosophers point out that the preferences of bare majorities with political power may contradict solutions that are better for the community as a whole. Civic republicans therefore prefer a process that depends more upon debate, reflection, negotiation, and agreement, or upon decisionmakers or agencies charged with considering all interests, as opposed to a winner-take-all model of competitive democracy.

This description is simplistic, and it omits the many differences among civic republicans about ways to achieve a better society. In general, however, civic republicans agree that government should include the kind of representative democracy that is characteristic of a "republic," with an elected legislature, for example. They tend, however, to place faith in institutions that derive from democratic representation, but are insulated to some extent from the political forces inherent in democratic competition. Simplistically, then, civic republicans might prefer a greater role for the judiciary, which enforces laws passed by the legislature, but still is independent of the legislature. Or, perhaps, civic republicans might prefer to entrust to independent agencies, boards, or commissions questions that others might prefer to have decided by legislatures.

(2) *Critiques of Civic Republicanism: Communitarianism--or Displacement of Democracy by Authoritarianism?* Opponents of civic republicanism see it as overly idealistic. The insulation from competitive political forces that civic republicanism emphasizes is only partly a good thing, the critics argue. This insulation may lead to an elitist, out-of-touch bureaucracy that is responsive to its own idiosyncratic preferences rather than to the popular will. Or, the insulation may result in insensitivity to the rights of a minority, from whose political power the decisionmakers also are insulated. Both individual rights and popular sovereignty may suffer from these effects, the critics argue. In summary, the opponents of civic republicanism see it as reflecting some of the defects of authoritarianism.

CONSTITUTIONALISM AND SEPARATION OF POWERS

(1) *Constitutionalism.* A constitution is a set of fundamental rules that creates stable processes by which a government conducts its affairs. In a sense, every nation has a constitution of some kind, since even unwritten rules qualify (for example, there is the British model). There are, however, great variations in the degrees to which different nations enforce their constitutions, the structures they create, and the laws they permit.

What does a constitution contain? (a) It may set forth a formalized statement of national goals that is largely symbolic but nevertheless influential. (b) It creates a defined structure of government. (c) It may provide a specific procedure for the creation of laws, and as a related purpose, (d) it may state what kinds of laws are (and are not) within the power of government to pass. This may be done either by authorization (a grant of power that contemplates certain categories of laws but not others) or it may be expressed by prohibition or limits on power (a Bill of Rights, for example). The American Constitution contains elements of each of these limiting features.

It is also important, however, for a constitution (e) to be flexible, because it must allow solutions to the unforeseen, unknowable problems of the future. It should provide for (f) orderly change, both through transfers of power within government structures and in its own terms, by amendment. And a major purpose of a constitution is (g) to define, and therefore establish, the legitimacy of government.

(2) *Separation of Powers in Constitutional Democracies: Federal Systems, Executive and Legislative Functions, Independence of the Judiciary, and Representation.* Obviously, the mere existence of a constitution does not guarantee the preservation of democracy. Totalitarian regimes often promulgate constitutions that contain appealing provisions. Instead, constitutional democracy depends on the kinds of structures set up to enact and enforce laws, the protections of the powers of these institutions, and the limits upon them. It also depends on the civic polity and social institutions.

"Federalism" refers to a divided sovereignty in which there are sovereign units, such as states or cantons or provinces, as well as a sovereign national government. The smaller entities are not merely subdivisions (like counties in a state, which may be non-autonomous administrative units). In a federal system, they have protected spheres of power, separate from national power. In addition to the United States, such diverse unions as Switzerland and Australia have federal systems.

The American union has a federal system partly for historical reasons. The newly independent thirteen colonies predated the union, and they originally banded together in a relatively weak confederation; later, the people within these thirteen states, in state conventions, ratified a stronger national government for mutual political, defense, and economic reasons. In doing so, however, they established constitutional protections of the existence and powers of the states (although scholars disagree widely about the extent of these protections).

(3) *Federalism as a Part of the Separation of Powers.* But American federalism is not a mere historical accident. This division was part of the thinking of some of the Founders about the separation of powers. In the earlier chapter on ethics, we considered the historical justifications for the

tripartite separation of legislative, executive and judicial powers as a means of limiting government, as articulated by such giants as Plato, Locke and Montesquieu.   The point here is that limited government also was a consideration underlying the federal division in the American union. The national government, it was expected, would forge an economic and defensive union, and its size and representative government would "cool the passions" of contending "factions" within the smaller units, the states. But the power of the states also was thought to be important, as a bulwark against authoritarianism. The states were seen as a kind of balance wheel against the national government.

EXAMPLES AND PROBLEMS

(1) *The Claims of "People's Democracies."* Some societies would say that their "people's democracies," rather than ours, are the genuine variety. Western democracies have tended to adopt as their ideal a democracy aimed at achieving the greatest degree of freedom consistent with the general good; some other nations' theory, by contrast, is that a classless, socialistic democratic society is an overarching goal.

Imagine, for example, that you are negotiating with a diplomat from the People's Republic of China. It is important for you to understand and achieve rapport with this Chinese diplomat. In response to your expressed preference for American democracy, the diplomat politely says:

"But in America, you have thousands of homeless people who sleep on subfreezing sidewalks. China may not have the same per capita income, but everyone has a place to sleep. Your urban schools are decaying, while rich politicians send their children to elite private enclaves. But our premier's children go to schools qualitatively no different from those that poorer children attend. Chinese citizens have more equal access to medical care, public safety, and every other societal good than Americans do."

Consider what you might say in response. What values do the "People's Democracies" sacrifice to preserve their claims of equality? Is it possible that some democracies under-emphasize the goal of equality and create dysfunctional class and wealth differences? Or are you suspicious of this theory?

(2) *Was the Democratization of Russia Inevitable Given Technological Advances?* Russia was a part of the former Soviet Union, an authoritarian regime. Technological advances and changes in government policy produced a citizenry that had somewhat broader access to information. Some people have theorized that this factor inevitably led to the democratization of Russia. Do you agree (or would other factors, as well, have been necessary)?

(3) *How Much Separation? A Tripartite Executive?* One of the proposals debated but rejected at the American constitutional convention called for a three-member executive. Instead of a President, a three-person committee would have enforced the laws. Historically, there have been several examples of three-person heads of state ("troikas" and "triumvirates"). Might this idea, in America, have furnished an additional desirable protection against authoritarianism? (If so, would it have entailed countervailing disadvantages that justified its rejection? See the discussions of Arrow's Theorem and of parliamentary systems, below.)

(4) *An Independent Judiciary.* Perhaps it can be argued that the independence of the judiciary is a more important kind of separation of power than the separation of the executive from the legislative. Why do you think this argument might have support? Is it because the judiciary is the branch that most fosters adherence to the rule of law? Or that preserves the structure of the other branches? Or that protects minority rights within a regime of majority rule? Or is it simply because the judiciary is the "least dangerous" branch to political liberties (as one of the Founders wrote), or in other words because it arguably is the weakest branch?

(5) *Unelected Officials in Democratic Regimes: From Life-Tenured Judges to the Problem of Bureaucracy and the Administrative State.* The Founders certainly did not create a complete democracy in the sense of requiring election for every important official. For example, federal judges are appointed, and they have life tenure, subject only to impeachment. But many States subject judges to election and have definitively rejected the federal model, believing that it reduces judges' incentives to excel in public service.

Then, there is the problem of bureaucracy. The Founders do not appear to have anticipated the modern administrative state, and indeed, it presents a conundrum for supporters of democracy. Being unelected, the individuals in appointive agencies do not have a direct elective tie to the citizens, and the chain of responsibility that traces back to an elected official may be so long that it is ineffective. Thus, American citizens frequently complain about the unresponsiveness of bureaucrats who are their main contacts with government. On the other hand, there may be a need for a degree of insulation of administrators from electoral politics. Independence of judgment, consistent treatment of similar issues, continuity in the face of electoral change, and recruitment of competent personnel, all arguably depend to some degree on this insulation. To what extent, then, do you think bureaucracy and civil service are inconsistent with democratic theory?

(6) *Interest Groups, Majorities, and Alternatives: How Much Civic Republicanism?* Perhaps the preceding questions indicate that civic republicans differ only in degree from their critics. Neither wants to abolish the kind of representative democracy that characterizes an elected legislature, but neither wants to remove judicial independence altogether. Would you agree, then, that the relevant question is not whether civic republicanism has merit, but rather, it is, "How much civic republicanism should we incorporate into our governance, and where?"

(7) *Whose Democracy? (Who Is a Member of the Electorate?): The Problem of Child Abuse, Constituencies, and the Right to Vote.* At the time of adoption of the original Constitution, the electorate was limited. It did not include, for example, women, most African-Americans, and in some states, poor people (because of property ownership requirements). Amendments to the Constitution have changed each of these practices, and the right to vote now is more nearly universal. Does this mean that everyone's interests are adequately protected? Well, there is at least one nonvoting minority-- children--that is high in poverty and low in some kinds of protection under the law.

Child abuse is a far too frequent problem in America. Agencies responsible for addressing child abuse have inadequate resources. Parents vote, hire lawyers, and have constitutional rights respecting their termination for abuse, but children generally do not. "Drive-by" checkup visits in which abused children are not physically inspected are a regular feature in many states; abused children regularly are returned to the parents who abuse them because there is no place else to put them; and case workers are underpaid, burned out, and subject to frequent turnover. In summary, we do what democracies frequently do with unrepresented groups who don't vote: we have neglected and underfunded the needs of abused children.

Obviously, most people would conclude that votes by children are not a realistic option, but consider the thought as a means of analysis through fiction (like the social contract, or Rawls's original position). There is a group that is unable to vote, because it is not practical to allow it to vote. Do we therefore have a special responsibility to address this problem of democracy? If we conclude that there would be less child abuse if children voted, but we decide we cannot and should not extend the franchise (as we indeed have decided), how should we set up our institutions to treat this vulnerable non-voting group--children--fairly in our democracy?

§ 8.03 Conflicts Within Democratic Values

ARROW'S THEOREM OF DEMOCRATIC "CYCLING": THE BENEFITS OF LEGISLATIVE LOGROLLING AND THE INEVITABILITY OF APPELLATE INCONSISTENCY

(1) *Arrow's Theorem as an Explanation of Certain Tradeoffs in Majority-Rule Democracy.* In this section, we shall consider Arrow's Theorem, which illuminates an important kind of inherent difficulty in democracy. Arrow's Theorem explains why democratic choice through voting may be an imperfect mechanism for public decisions.

The theory is best understood through an artificially simplified example involving three decisionmakers and three choices, although the theorem holds true for larger numbers of decisionmakers and for a wider variety of choices. Imagine that Huey, Louie and Dewey visit the grocery store for the purpose of purchasing a quart of ice cream. Huey's choices, in rank order, are vanilla, strawberry and chocolate; Louie's are strawberry, chocolate and vanilla; Dewey's are chocolate, vanilla and strawberry, each in that order. Symbolically, Huey: $V > S > C$; Louie: $S > C > V$; and Dewey: $C > V > S$.

If the issue of chocolate versus strawberry is put to a vote, Huey and Louie will vote for strawberry. But the trouble is, depending upon the pairing of the two items selected for the vote, it also is possible to produce majority votes for either vanilla or chocolate given this set of choices and voters!

(2) *"Cycling": The Disturbing Result of Arrow's Theorem.* This result of Arrow's Theorem sometimes is referred to as "cycling." A binary vote produces a choice that actually is misleading. This consequence is disturbing: It demonstrates the fallibility of majority rule systems, ranging

from democratic elections of public officials to the likelihood of inconsistency in opinions of courts of appeals deciding the law. It need not seem so disturbing as to destroy our faith in democracy, but it points to a problem that we should be aware of, even if voting systems do approximate majority preferences much of the time.

(3) *Public Policy and Arrow's Theorem.* In public policy, Arrow's Theorem explains why inconsistent opinions or decisions by a court of appeals are not only likely, but unavoidable as a practical matter. It shows that a multi-member zoning board is inevitably going to produce decisions about variances that will be in conflict. And a legislative body, or a city council, will sometimes vote unpredictably in a departure from prior votes. Arrow's Theorem also explains why single-vote democratic elections may not be the most complete method for some public choices. For example, the three-way race in which President Clinton was elected in his first term, in which no candidate gained a popular vote majority, exhibited this defect. A run-off election might have produced more reliable results, but our system did not provide for it. Furthermore, even with a run-off election, Arrow's Theorem implies that the result may not accurately reflect voters' true preferences, because it is possible that the third candidate, who did not make the runoff, might beat both runoff candidates in head-to-head contests. But a runoff is one partial "solution."

Still other approaches, such as reliance not on elections but on markets (which depend upon what sometimes are called "dollar votes") may be better solutions for some kinds of choices. Non-majoritarian political decisionmaking, such as supermajority requirements, multiple votes by different constituencies, cumulative voting, or even appointment rather than election, may be options for some kinds of situations. Perhaps some people would view Arrow's Theorem as casting doubt upon the constitutional inevitability of the one-person one-vote result in *Reynolds v. Sims*, 377 U.S. 533 (1964).

EXAMPLES AND PROBLEMS

(1) *The Virtual Inevitability of Appellate Court Inconsistency, Given Arrow's Theorem: Judge Easterbrook's Theory.* Imagine a case before a three-member appellate court. Justice First would choose a rule that would cause the plaintiff to win (P), but in any event, she believes that it is important for the court to decide the case, and she therefore prefers a rule that

would cause the defendant to win (D) over a holding that the court has no jurisdiction (N). Justice Second would choose a rule under which the defendant wins (D), but failing that, she prefers for the court not to decide the case, but instead to hold that there is no jurisdiction (N) than to have the plaintiff win (P). Justice Third thinks that the court has no jurisdiction (N), but if the court does decide it, she would adopt the pro-plaintiff rule (P) rather than the one that makes the defendant win (D).

Symbolically, then, we can depict the three judges' conflicting views as follows. Justice First: P>D>N; Justice Second: D>N>P; and Justice Third: N>P>D. What will happen, now, when the justices attempt to decide this case? They will "cycle." Can you see why? Judge Frank Easterbrook, in his writings about public choice, points out that Arrow's Theorem means that inconsistency is virtually inevitable in the decisions of appellate courts. Can you explain why?

(2) *How the Order of Decision Changes the Outcome.* Now, imagine that this particular court follows the rule that the court must first consider whether it has jurisdiction over the case, before deciding the merits of the case. In other words, the judges first must decide whether to accept the outcome of N (don't decide) over either P (plaintiff wins) or D (defendant wins). Let us suppose that each must vote for only one of the three alternatives, the one most preferred; thus, First votes P; Second, D; and Third, N. And so, N loses. Next, the court must decide either P or D, and now P wins. Can you explain the effect this rule about the order of decision has on the outcome?

Note that it is possible, once again, to cause any one of the three possible outcomes to occur, depending on the order in which the binary choices are made. In fact, whenever cycling occurs, this result also occurs; one of the corollaries of Arrow's Theorem is that it is possible to determine a decision path for each of the possible results in this situation!

(3) *Perhaps a Court Can't Be Blamed for Inconsistency(!)* We are accustomed to thinking of inconsistencies among opinions as a criticism of the court that rendered them. Arrow's Theorem suggests a different analysis: Inconsistencies are virtually inevitable when justices go about their individual roles in a consistent manner.

(4) *Strategic Voting: How Justice Second Can Avoid Losing by Negating the Conditions for Arrow's Theorem.* Now, imagine that Justice Second, in the problem above, foresees the result. If he votes his true preference, D, then P will win, which is his least preferred outcome. Therefore, he declines to vote his real conviction and votes N (no jurisdiction) instead. This way he salvages his second choice, N, and avoids the worst alternative, P. This tactic is known as "strategic voting."

Strategic voting has many manifestations. Among judges, on courts, strategic voting sounds distasteful, because we want to have faith in each judge's commitment to "follow the law," or in other words to state a true preference, honestly. For this reason, strategic voting in courts may be less frequent than in legislatures. If so, ironically, courts may produce more inconsistency than legislatures (a conclusion that seems counterintuitive since courts are supposed to follow precedent, i.e., to be consistent). Strategic voting sounds more congenial, of course, in a legislature. What really happens when there is strategic voting is that Arrow's Theorem no longer applies because its conditions are negated. In the next note, we will see why. Let us, then, reconsider Justices First, Second and Third to see what the limits of the Theorem are.

(5) *The Limits of Arrow's Theorem (or, the Arguable Benefits of "Log Rolling").* What happens if Judges First and Second caucus first (because they both are Democrats, and Judge Third is a Republican)? Or, what if they compromise in a coordinated effort to reach consistent rules?

Then, Arrow's Theorem does not apply. In fact, Kenneth Arrow postulated five necessary conditions for the validity of his theory. The three most interesting of these are (1) unrestricted choice--individuals must be free to rank alternatives in any order that they choose; (2) independence--the choice must not be influenced by other votes, or by vote-trading (or in other words, by strategic voting); and (3) transitivity--if vanilla is preferred by a voter to strawberry, and strawberry to chocolate, then vanilla must be preferred to chocolate as well.

Notice, then, that the prediction of cycling from Arrow's Theorem does not hold if the Majority Whip in the legislature enforces party loyalty, or if vote-trading (pejoratively known as "log rolling") occurs. Is enforcement of party loyalty, then, a good thing? (Or, log rolling?) The instinctively held theory of most people in a democracy is that partisanship is bad in politics, but doesn't Arrow's Theorem tend to demonstrate that a certain amount of partisanship is good (or even necessary)?

THE MADISONIAN DILEMMA:
HOW TO PRESERVE MINORITY RIGHTS
WITHOUT DESTROYING MAJORITY RULE

(1) *Bickel's Theory: Protection of Minority Interests Is Necessarily Anti-Democratic.* In the 1960's, Professor Alexander Bickel considered another kind of democratic imperfection: the problem of majority rule and minority rights. The executive and legislative branches were political and responsive to the majority. The judiciary, which was the prominent entity to prevent the overriding of minority rights, was not political or responsive to the majority.

Therefore, whenever the courts protected minority rights by invoking the Constitution, the immediate result was an incursion upon democracy. "Nothing can finally [be allowed to] depreciate the central function that is assigned in democratic theory and practice to the electoral process," Bickel wrote. "[N]or can it be denied that the policy-making power of representative institutions . . . is the distinguishing characteristic of this system. Judicial [power] works counter to this characteristic." He added, "[D]emocracies do live by the idea . . . that the majority has the ultimate power to displace the decision-makers and to reject any part of their policy. With that idea, judicial review must achieve some measure of consonance."

(2) *Is Judicial Power to Protect Minorities Really "Anti-Democratic?"* Justice Robert H. Jackson called the Supreme Court "anti-democratic," and Justice Felix Frankfurter wrote that the Court's "stupendous powers" of judicial review were a "limitation on popular government." Justices (and all federal judges) have life tenure (Art. III, § 1), subject to removal only by impeachment (Art. II, § 4). Thus, says Edward Levi, when the Court strikes down an act of Congress, "we are confronted by the fact that the one non-elective and non-removable element in the government rejects the conclusion of the two elective and removable branches."

(3) *The Madisonian Dilemma: Reconciling Minority Rights with Majority Rule.* The central problem of judicial power is related to this anti-democratic characteristic. It concerns the resolution of what has been called the "Madisonian dilemma." A Madisonian democracy, such as the United States, emphasizes that majorities generally are entitled to rule simply

because they are majorities. But it also emphasizes that individuals, even when in the minority, must have some protection from majority control.

The dilemma is that neither the majority nor the minority can be trusted to draw the dividing line, because tyranny either by one or by the other inevitably would follow. If the majority is given the right to decide whenever there is a conflict, no minority rights can

James Madison

exist, but if the minority is given a veto, there no longer is majority rule.

(4) *One Attempt to Resolve the Madisonian Dilemma: United States v. Carolene Products Co.,* 304 U.S. 144 (1938). There have been numerous attempts to reconcile this conflict. One famous attempt is called the "*Carolene Products* formula." The *Carolene* opinion hinted, in dictum, at a means by which enforcement of the Constitution might generally honor majority rule but emphasize protection of minority rights in those cases in which protection is most needed. Justice Stone's opinion for the Court upheld a statute regulating commerce in milk. The Court determined that the statute had a "rational basis." In a famous footnote, however, Justice Stone distinguished certain kinds of situations in which a rational basis might be insufficient to support the majoritarian action, and stricter scrutiny might be warranted. In so doing, he arguably provided the basis for two different levels of judicial review--one applicable to cases generally, and a stricter kind applicable to three special cases of minority rights, defined as follows:

There may be narrower scope for operation of the presumption of constitutionality when legislation appears on its face to be within a specific prohibition of the Constitution, such as those of the first ten amendments. . . .

[A second situation is presented by] legislation which restricts those political processes which can ordinarily be expected to bring about repeal of undesirable legislation, [and this situation may] be subjected to more exacting judicial scrutiny . . . than are most other types of legislation. . . .

[Third,] . . . similar considerations may enter into the review of statutes, directed at particular religious, or national, or racial minorities . . . ; [so that] prejudice against discrete and insular minorities may be a special condition, . . . which may call for a correspondingly more searching judicial inquiry.

EXAMPLES AND PROBLEMS

(1) *"Discrete and Insular Minorities:" Does the Carolene Products Formula Work Well for Resolving the Madisonian Dilemma?* The *Carolene Products* formula would protect, first, minority rights contained in a "specific prohibition of the Constitution. . . ." Thus the right of citizens in tiny Rhode Island to two senators should prompt closer scrutiny if larger states formed a majority sufficient to remove Rhode Island's senators by act of Congress.

Further, *Carolene Products* would scrutinize "legislation which restricts [the] political processes." If the majority votes for laws that make it difficult for some citizens to vote, these laws would not be entitled to the usual presumption of validity. And finally, *Carolene Products* would protect "discrete and insular minorities," such as religious, or national, or racial groups.

This last provision protecting "discrete and insular minorities," however, is subject to varying analyses. For example, in the abortion context, which group is the appropriate discrete and insular minority for protection, if any: women? pregnant women? fetuses/unborn children? persons who care deeply about the right to life? In other contexts, could it happen that white males might be considered a discrete and insular minority? Consider whether it is possible to apply this framework in a reasonably specific way, or whether every case will involve competing claims of people arguing that they are discrete and insular minorities.

(2) *Ely's Thesis That the Courts Can Counteract Failures of Democracy by Safeguarding the "Process": J. Ely, Democracy and Distrust* (1980). Dean Ely argues that judicial review actually can be representation-reinforcing--that is, it can enhance, rather than frustrate, democracy. It can do

so, Ely argues, if it defers to the political branches when they would naturally be expected to further the democratic process, but provides for a stricter standard to check what might be called failures of democracy.

As Ely puts it, "The approach to constitutional adjudication recommended here . . . intervenes only when the 'market,' in our case the political market, is systematically malfunctioning. (A referee analogy is also not far off: the referee is to intervene only when one team is gaining unfair advantage, not because the 'wrong' team has scored.)."

Is this thesis persuasive, or does it break down in the face of criticism? First, consider who is to determine when "representation-reinforcing" intervention is needed, and what form it should take. Ely says that only judges are "in a position objectively to assess claims--though no one could suppose the evaluation won't be full of judgment calls. . . ." Is this correct? Or will judges, by countermanding political results on the ground that they are reinforcing representation, wind up simply substituting other political processes and outcomes merely because the judges personally prefer them?

Secondly, by invoking principles outside the Constitution to interpret it, how can Ely insure that judges will stop there rather than reading in other extra-constitutional principles that reflect their personal preferences? *Cf.* R. Bork, *Styles in Constitutional Theory,* 26 So. Tex. L. Rev. 383, 390 (1985), who argues: "Some theorists . . . would have courts make democracy more democratic. [Dean Ely], who is a non-interpretivist whether he knows it or not, takes this tack. The difficulty is that there is neither a constitutional nor an extra-constitutional basis for making the Constitution more democratic than the Constitution is."

§ 8.04 Democratic Structure and Alternatives

COMPARING SEPARATION OF POWERS TO PARLIAMENTARY SYSTEMS: DIFFERENT THEORIES OF DEMOCRACY

(1) *Separation of Powers versus Parliamentary Democracy.* In this section we shall consider some of the solutions that different democracies have used to address these problems, beginning with the difference between a parliamentary system and the separation of powers. The American model is to separate the executive, judicial and legislative powers to create checks

and balances and thereby prevent an imperial government. The English democracy is quite different, being a "parliamentary" democracy, in which an elected Parliament in turn chooses the Prime Minister, who has both legislative and executive duties. See Figure 1. Parliamentary democracy arguably is no more or less "democratic" than separation-of-powers democracy, but it may be more coherent in policymaking.

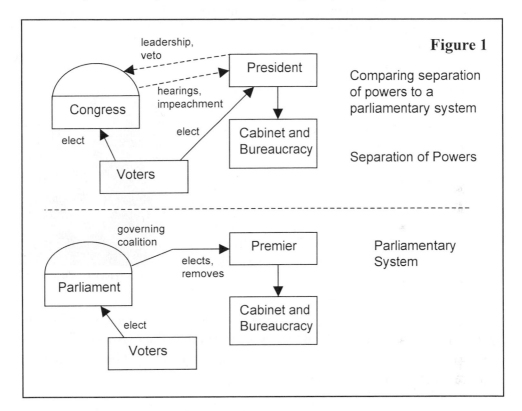

Figure 1

Comparing separation of powers to a parliamentary system

Separation of Powers

Parliamentary System

(2) *Is Separation of Powers Beneficial, or Is It Disadvantageous?* The impression that an "imperial" President or Congress is dangerous assumes that the concept of separation of powers is an essential prerequisite to democratic government. This argument is periodically rebutted by constitutional reformers who argue that today the United States cannot afford the separation of powers and its dispersal of control and the consequent loss of efficiency and ability for a quick action. Consider the following, from Schlesinger, *Shielded from an Imperial President*, Outlook, May 20, 1986, at 1:

[H]igh-minded and capable Americans argue today for reforming the Constitution. [T]he most basic challenge [c]omes from those reformers who challenge [t]he separation of powers. . . .

The Committee on the Constitutional System, co-chaired by three distinguished Americans, Sen. Nancy Landon Kassebaum, R-Kan., Douglas Dillon, the former secretary of the Treasury, and Lloyd Cutler, a former counsel to President Jimmy Carter, mounted a thoughtful re-examination of the whole question. "The checks and balances inspired by the experience of the 18th century," the Committee declares, "have led repeatedly, in the 20th century, to governmental stalemate and deadlock, to an incapacity to make quick and sharp decisions in the face of urgent problems."[1]

In domestic policy, the separation of powers, it is argued, inhibits concerted action by the executive and Congress to deal with the budget deficit, the trade deficit and other agonizing questions. In foreign policy, some add, the consequences may be even more disastrous.

Senator Nancy L. Kassebaum

(3) *The Founders' Justifications for Separation of Powers.* Consider the justifications for the separation of powers posited by the Framers. Can these reasons answer the charge that the technological realities of the 20th century require an executive to act quickly?

> *The Federalist No. 47 (1787) (Madison).* "The accumulation of all powers, legislative, executive, and judiciary in the same hands, whether of one, a few, of many and whether hereditary self-appointed, or elective, may justly be pronounced the very definition of tyranny. [But this does] not mean that these departments ought to have no *partial agency* in, or no *control* over, the acts of each other. . . . [It only means] that where the *whole* power of one department is exercised by the same hands which possess the *whole* power of another department, the fundamental principles of a free constitution are subverted."

---

1 Professor Schlesinger has cautioned, here, that he was reporting the views of others.

The Federalist No. 48 (1787) (Madison). "It is agreed on all sides that the powers properly belonging to one of the departments ought not to be directly and completely administered by either of the other departments. It is equally evident that none of them ought to possess, directly or indirectly, an overruling influence over the others in the administration of their respective powers. [The] most difficult task is to provide some practical security for each, against the invasion of the others. . . ."

EXAMPLES AND PROBLEMS

(1) *Pre-Constitutional Proposals: Separation of Powers or Parliamentarianism?* The Founders of the American constitutional order did not have a unified pre-existing sense of the government they wanted (indeed, some initially contemplated a monarchy with George Washington as king). One proposal would have had the Congress, rather than the people, elect the President. What effect would this proposal have had (how would it change our democracy)?

(2) *Madisonian Democracy and the Separation of Powers.* The American model, embodying what we have called "Madisonian" democracy after one of the principal architects of the Constitution, James Madison, uses a general scheme of majority rule but restricts it to protect minority rights. It sometimes is argued that better resolution of the Madisonian dilemma results from separation of powers because of checks on decisionmaking and, particularly, because it increases the independence and therefore the power of the judiciary to protect minority rights. But is this really a "better resolution" of the Madisonian dilemma, or is it instead a tilt toward minority veto?

(3) *Does Separation of Powers Contribute to Inefficient Spending or Pork-Barrel Politics?* In 1999, when the United States and its allies were involved in military conflict in Yugoslavia, the President asked for $6 billion to replenish weaponry and for other military objectives. Congress, however, passed a $12-billion dollar spending bill. It included funding for people in States that had suffered natural disasters, foreign aid for Central America, and loan guarantees for certain businesses. Executive branch spokespersons decried the "pork barrel" nature of the spending, but most items, it appeared, could be defended as in the national interest. Well, then, the response went,

bring them up separately so each one can be debated individually on its merits.

But perhaps the answer to that argument is, sometimes the only way in America to address a real problem, a critical need, is to attach legislation about it to a bill about an unrelated subject--because of the separation of powers. Can you see why?

(4) *The Line-Item Veto.* Pork-barrel complaints sometimes trace to the principle that the President's veto power must strike down an entire bill, not just part of it. Various attempts have been made in Congress to confer upon the President the ability to veto individual items in a bill passed by Congress.

This "line-item veto" would increase the legislative powers of the President, and although it would not convert the United States into a parliamentary democracy, it would bring it closer to the parliamentary model. Can you explain? [The Supreme Court has held one such model unconstitutional.]

(5) *Separation of Powers and Military Conflicts.* During the 1999 Yugoslavian conflict, President Clinton pledged not to use American ground troops.   This pledge unquestionably was unwise as a matter of military strategy. Former Chairman of the Joint Chiefs of Staff Colin Powell criticized the President's public statement: "If I had been part of the decision process, I would have argued strongly not to tell him [the Yugoslav commander] what we might or might not do with ground troops. Why tell him?"

Colin Powell

But perhaps the separation of powers forced the President to give away his strategy, as a political rather than a military matter. Perhaps a parliamentary system would not require this strategic sacrifice. Can you see why?

(6) *Separation of Powers and Frustration of the Orderly Declaring of War.* Some people believe that the constitutional mechanism for declaring war is so unworkable that it never will be used again--except possibly in cases so obvious as to trivialize it. Since World War II, Congress has avoided declaring war in the Korean "police action," the Vietnam "conflict," Operation Desert Storm, and the Kosovo-Yugoslav engagement. Has the United States, de facto, adopted a parliamentary system for declaring war, to replace the mechanism in the Constitution?

(7) *Arrow's Theorem and the Separation of Powers.* As we have seen, Arrow's Theorem explains why cycling blocks rational decisionmaking. Consider what effect separation of powers will have on the problems predicted by Arrow's Theorem. Will separation of powers aggravate cycling?

(8) *How Should Venezuela's New Constitution for the 21st Century Be Set Up?* In an earlier chapter, on economics, we considered Venezuela, whose president described it as a "broken" society, divided between a few fabulously wealthy Venezuelans and a much larger majority "who barely receive a drop to survive on." Among other measures addressing this issue, President Hugo Chavez advocated a new constitution for Venezuela. Consider how the new structure should be shaped to allow this unstable nation its best chance of success. Consider whether a parliamentary system or separation of powers is preferable. The draft of the new constitution, in fact, was the subject of highly fragmented disagreement among the Venezuelan populace, including disagreements over concentration of powers, individual liberties, control of the military, and many other issues. What might Arrow's Theorem tell you about its contents and chance of passage?

POLITICAL PARTIES

(1) *The Importance of Political Parties to Democracy: The Antidote to Arrow's Theorem.* This section considers an arguably necessary democratic institution that many people love to hate: political parties. "Partisan politics" turns a lot of people off. But it is difficult to overstate the importance of political parties to modern democracy.

Arrow's Theorem gives us many insights, but perhaps none is more important than the understanding that it provides of the need for political parties. The Theorem tells us that the gridlock, indecision and paralysis due to cycling is inevitable if every vote is independent (and if the other conditions of the Theorem are met). Parties provide the aggregation of interests that overcomes this blockage. When the Speaker of the House, for example, tells the majority leadership to "whip" the party members for an upcoming vote, the cycling phenomenon is reduced because the independence of this immediate decision vanishes. Party members know that their constituents will be affected in future issues by their allegiance to the party in this vote. Legendary Democrat Speaker Sam Rayburn put it simply: "To get along, you've go to go along."

(2) *What Do Political Parties Do?* But aggregation of interests is only one of the tasks of political parties. As a second function, they recruit citizens and interest groups into the political process. For example, a disaffected environmentalist movement may learn to use political influence rather than violence or sabotage by coming under the tent of one of the major parties (or by starting its own party, as the "Greens" did in some European countries). Yet a third function of political parties is to provide an initiation, a political education, to new voters. Government as such has less incentive than partisans do to reach out to new voters.

Fourth, parties form a "bridge" function: They translate the actions of government into terms that citizens who are not professional politicians can understand, and they convey the messages of voters back to candidates and representatives. Fifth, they generate coherent political ideas, such as crime, tax or education packages, in which the different parts are coordinated to achieve desired results. And sixth, they mobilize voters for elections.

Seventh, they organize government. To use the example again of the Speaker of the House, they facilitate the election by a majority of members of a single individual to hold this leadership position. Eighth and finally, this organizing function provides an incentive for energetic electoral participation by politicians, since policymaking power follows.

(3) *One Party, Two, or Many?* Governments in a few countries have attempted to abolish political parties or to legalize only one. Spain is an example; Generalissimo Franco's abolition of parties gave way to a "National Organization" that really performed the same functions, and after Franco's

death the political system produced the same exuberant cornucopia of parties that exists elsewhere in Europe.

The United States has traditionally functioned with two major parties, although splinter organizations ranging from the Socialist Labor Party to the Vegetarian Party consistently have operated. Occasionally, third parties have had real influence, as in the election of 1992, when Republican George Bush, Democrat William J. Clinton and Reform Party Candidate Ross Perot split the popular vote three ways, with no candidate receiving a majority.

The principal alternative is to have many political parties. In some countries, the result is not significantly different from two-party systems because stable coalitions form among the parties. Then, two or more coalitions form government and opposition groups. On the other hand, fragmentation in some countries, such as Israel and Italy, is so pronounced that coalitions remain unstable, and governments change frequently. See Figure 2, which shows the Israeli Knesset after the election of 1999. This proliferation of small parties partly explains the tendency toward changes in government.

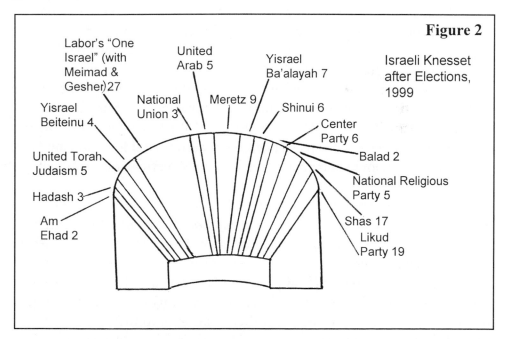

(4) *Party Strength as Dependent on Parliamentary or Separated Power, Centralization of Elections, Discipline, and Spoils.* Other things being equal, parties are likely to be stronger institutionally in parliamentary than in

separated-power systems. A parliamentary system tends to mean that one party (or one coalition) is in power, whereas separation of powers increases the likelihood that power will be fragmented among parties. Even if there are numerous parties, a parliamentary system means that the majority coalition does not have the same compulsion to compromise as Republicans and Democrats do when one holds the Senate or House, the other the Presidency.

Centralization of elections is another factor strengthening parties. In some countries, national parties select local candidates and run centralized campaigns. This model means greater ideological consistency than the American method of local candidates, who largely control their own fundraising and electoral campaigns. Party structure and discipline on the one hand, and the availability of spoils for reward to allegiant members on the other, are further factors that contribute to party strength.

EXAMPLES AND PROBLEMS

(1) *The Relative Weakness of American Political Parties.* Political parties in America tend to be weaker and less ideologically coherent than those in some countries. Considering the parliamentary-versus-power-separation, decentralization of elections, discipline and spoils factors, can you explain why? In addition to these factors, the major American parties tend to act as mass or catchall parties with big-tent philosophies. In countries with more political parties, ideologies may be more distinct, arranged according to left-right orientation, issues (such as environment, labor or security), religion or ethnicity. In the United States, the Libertarian Party follows this model of greater internal consistency. Such parties tend to command more intense loyalty from members than the big-tent American ones. Why?

(2) *The Costs and Benefits of Party Weakness: Voting, Party Platforms, Special Interest Vulnerability, Stability, and Local Control.* Voter turnout in American elections tends to be much smaller than in some other countries. Some political scientists theorize that low turnout results from the relative weakness of America's political parties. Can you see why? Additionally, some political scientists attribute the relative inability of America's political parties to articulate clear visions in their platforms to their weakness, and some believe that this weakness creates vulnerability to special interest influence that is connected with campaign financing. Why? On the other hand, relatively large, weak national political parties may contribute to local control and to stability. Why?

(3) *American Tension Among Party Loyalty, Constituency, and Independence.* A representative in the United States is affected by party discipline but has greater ability to respond to constituency (broadly defined to include supporters, voters and actual constituents) as well as to vote independently on the basis of independent decision than do representatives in some other countries. This phenomenon arguably may result in better constituent representation by locality (if not by ideology), but it also may create a greater tendency toward pork-barrel politics. Can you see why?

PLURALISM AND ELITISM

(1) *"Direct" and "Representative" Democracy.* The "town meeting" style of democracy still is popular in some places. Each voter votes directly upon each immediate question. But such a process of "direct" democracy requires each voter to know the details, and what is harder, to negotiate with all other voters, in a depth that is not attainable by people incidentally involved.

"Representative" democracy is a kind of division of labor by which one person votes in the stead of many and has greater opportunity to learn and negotiate issues. Historically, representative democracy also has been used by democracy advocates who distrust uneducated, persuadable masses, just as the Greeks preferred aristocracy. The trouble with representative democracy is that it may be wasteful, especially in smaller entities, adding a sometimes unnecessary formal bureaucracy; furthermore, the motivations and perceptions of the professional-politician representative may diverge from those of voters and may make the representative vulnerable to lobbying that direct voter action would resist.

(2) *Pluralism and Elitism.* A closely related question is whether a political society should further hands-on participation equally by all members, from the most to the least informed or capable, or whether some mechanism, whether structural, legal, or self-selective, should result in emphasizing the influence of the most informed and capable. Greeks such as Plato and Aristotle had a clear elitist preference for aristocracy. In the United States, the playing field is much more tilted toward pluralism.

But does the United States also institutionalize elitism? Electoral politics, campaign funding, lobbying, political parties, and other mechanisms contribute to a regime in which some active, informed, wealthy individuals have more influence than others.

EXAMPLES AND PROBLEMS

(1) *Direct or Representative Democracy?: From Voter Initiatives to the Electoral College.* Some states allow voters to vote directly upon propositions to become law ("initiatives"), while other states do not provide this mechanism. Imagine that you are in a state where no such process exists, but there is a proposed amendment to the state constitution that would create it. What arguments would supporters and opponents use?

As another example, consider the electoral college. The initial idea of the Constitution was that the people would not vote directly for the President but instead for "electors," members of an "electoral college," who then would elect the President. Why did the Founders invent this strange device, the "electoral college?"

(2) *Skinner's Walden Two: Is There an Argument That Sensible Members of a Society Might Turn Over Government Participation to Others Who Are Specialists in It?* The great psychologist and philosopher B. F. Skinner also was a novelist. His *Walden Two* was the story of a utopian society that had advanced to the point where participation in government was not customary for the average citizen. Consider the following statement:

"The government of Walden Two," [Frazier] continued, "has the virtues of democracy, but none of the defects. . . .

"In Walden Two no one worries about the government except the few to whom that worry has been assigned. To suggest that everyone should take an interest would seem as fantastic as to suggest that everyone should become familiar with our Diesel engines. . . ."

Walden Two is a novel, and it would be wrong to attribute to Skinner all of the opinions his characters expressed. But in a later nonfictional work, *Beyond Freedom and Dignity*, Skinner expressed some of the same views. Is there anything to these ideas?

(3) *De Tocqueville's View.* Consider the quotation from de Tocqueville that begins this chapter about the uniqueness of American democracy in producing a citizenry that does not hate and fear the law. Is this the result of an anti-elitist government? Note that relatively few people were allowed to

vote at that time. Is de Tocqueville's view inconsistent with the views of Skinner's characters in *Walden Two*?

(4) *The Governance of Business and Social Organizations and the Problem of Democratic Effort: The Problem of Partnership A and Partnership B.* These problems are not confined to governments. The question of direct or representative democracy, and of full participation by each constituent or of professional management, applies also to business and social organizations.

For example, consider two business partnerships, each with two hundred (200) partners. The two organizations are similar in most respects, but they differ sharply in their management. In Partnership A, the partners elect a three-member management committee that decides most important management issues. In Partnership B, most important management questions, instead, are submitted to a general vote of the partners.

In Partnership B, direct democracy may mean that every partner has to be fully informed on every management issue. Worse yet, every partner must spend time bargaining, persuading and politicking with other members about every management issue. Is it possible that Partnership B might actually produce a regime in which the partners cannot do their work efficiently because they become preoccupied with electoral campaigns about management?

(5) *Business and Social Organizations, Continued: Apportioning the Stock in a Close Corporation.* A related, but different, problem arises in the small, three-person corporation. Is it best for four friends who are shareholders to divide the shares, one-fourth to each? This arrangement might contribute to a cycling problem. Can you see why?

Perhaps then, it would be better for the friends to contribute in unequal portions, so that one has 40% of the stock and each of the others has 20%. This arrangement would reduce cycling and stalemate. It might result in the dominance of one shareholder, but the alternate coalition of the three 20% holders limits this dominance. We shall consider this problem in greater depth in a later chapter, on game theory.

§ 8.05 Tradeoffs Among Democratic Values

PROPERTY AND FREEDOM

(1) *Lesser Protection for Economic Rights?* Next, we examine another institution, private property, and its relationship to democracy. The view often is expressed that such economic rights as the right to enforce contracts or to protect property are of lesser status than individual and political rights. In this view, the freedom from invasion of personal security, the right to vote, and the freedom of speech are more deserving of protection.

Milton Friedman

(2) *The Argument That Personal and Political Rights Depend Upon Economic Rights: Professor Friedman's View.* The contrary view is that the ability to protect capital in private hands is necessary to other freedoms. According to this theory, if individuals can transform their accumulated wealth into printing presses, ink, and paper, they may be able to begin a newspaper; without the ability to protect wealth from government invasion, they may not be able to do so. One of the principal proponents of this view is Professor Milton Friedman, who argues that it is necessary only to convince a few wealthy people to publish any idea, in a capitalist society, no matter how novel. In a socialist society, however, only the state owns printing presses. It is all-powerful, and ideas must be approved by government to be published. Friedman adds:

> Let us stretch our imagination and suppose that a socialist government is aware of this problem and is composed of people anxious to preserve freedom. . . . It could establish a bureau for subsidizing subversive propaganda. But how could it choose whom to support? If it gave to all who asked, it would shortly find itself out of funds. . . .

> But we are not yet through. In a free market society, it is enough to have the funds. The suppliers of paper are as willing to sell it to

the *Daily Worker* as to the *Wall Street Journal*. In a socialist society, it would not be enough to have the funds. The hypothetical supporter of capitalism would have to persuade a government factory making paper to sell to him, the government printing press to print his pamphlets, a government post office to distribute them among the people, a government agency to rent him a hall in which to talk, and so on.

M. Friedman, *Capitalism and Freedom* 17-19 (1962); *see also* M. & R. Friedman, *Free to Choose* 65-69 (1980). Friedman concludes that no one who favors both socialism and freedom has faced up to this issue.

(3) *The Argument Against Equivalent Protection of Economic Rights.* There also are many commentators who would oppose or qualify Friedman's theory. In the first place, there is the argument that capitalism produces such serious harm to the common environment, because it does not motivate people to serve the common good, as to outweigh its putative advantages, at least in some instances. *Cf.* J. K. Galbraith, *The Affluent Society* (1958). Another view is that the capitalist claim of market superiority is exaggerated in that the market requires much more participation by government to produce regularity and predictability than market-supporting economists would admit. *Cf.* J. K. Galbraith, *The New Industrial State* (1967).

Furthermore, a market economy by itself produces (and cannot redress) severe inequalities of income, including extremes of poverty. *See* R. Dorfman, *Prices and Markets* Ch. 9 (3d ed. 1978); P. Samuelson & W. Nordhaus, *Economics* ch. 34-35 (12th ed. 1983); *cf.* R. Posner, *Economic Analysis of Law* ch. 16 (3d ed. 1986). Finally, the agglomerations of wealth that Friedman sees as leading to political freedoms are seen by others as leading instead to the permanent oppression of a powerless underclass, with whom the wealthy have too little in common.

EXAMPLES AND PROBLEMS

(1) *Tushnet's View: Tushnet, A Note on the Revival of Textualism in Constitutional Theory*, 58 S. Cal. L. Rev. 683, 694 (1985). In critiquing Laycock's theory of liberal textualism, Tushnet points out that Laycock identifies objects which the Constitution positively values (such as national unity, individualism, personal autonomy, and private association) as well as "bad" values (such as state sovereignty). Tushnet says: "I would add private

property and the social control thereof to the list" of values that the Constitution regards as "bad."

Is Tushnet's proposal capable of justification, given that the Constitution expressly prohibits taking of property for public use without just compensation, makes property an object of the due process clause, and prohibits contract impairment by the states? Is Friedman correct in arguing that Tushnet's view would lead to a loss not only of property rights but of other freedoms as well?

(2) *The View of the Current Supreme Court Majority: Economic Protection is Not a "Poor Relation."* One of the Supreme Court's pronounce-ments regarding the constitutional status of "economic rights" is *Dolan v. City of Tigard*, 512 U.S. 374 (1994). In the *Dolan* decision, the Court, per Chief Justice Rehnquist, stated that "[w]e see no reason why the [rights under the] Taking Clause of the Fifth Amendment, as much a part of the Bill of Rights as the First Amendment or Fourth Amendment, should be

William H. Rehnquist

relegated to the status of a poor relation in these comparable circumstances." Are the Chief Justice's views correct, or are those who disagree with him correct?

(3) *Zapata's View: La Tierra Appartiene a Quien La Trabaja.* Still another question is whether and how property rights may or should be involuntarily redistributed. A regime that protects property absolutely from such a transfer (or to put it pejoratively, from confiscation) may theoretically face a dilemma. Remember, the market does not assure fair distribution, and it may result in a kingdom of the few lavishly rich confronting a horde of the

desperately poor. In one society that tended toward this model, the revolutionary Emiliano Zapata redefined how property was acquired and thus called for its involuntary transfer. "Tierra y libertad!" he said, and he added that "the land belongs to whoever works it."

Is it possible that land reform periodically is necessary, along with other modes of wealth redistribution, so that there can be a just (and indeed,

Emiliano Zapata

an efficiently functioning) society? In fact, the concept that Zapata expressed has been borrowed in the United States. As one among many examples, the Hawaii Land Reform Act of 1967 set up a condemnation system whereby renters could request that the state use its power of eminent domain to purchase the property they occupied for subsidized resale to the renters. The state paid compensation to the owners, but it used general revenues from taxes disproportionately paid by those same owners to do so. The purpose was to reduce the perceived evils of a land oligopoly traceable to early Hawaiian high chiefs. The Supreme Court upheld this system as constitutional in *Hawaiian Housing Authority v. Midkiff*, 467 U.S. 229 (1984). Does such a system differ, in reality, from Zapata's call for redistribution?

These arguments lead to a paradox. The protection of private property from involuntary transfer arguably is necessary for both economic efficiency and political freedom. But the society's ability to force involuntary transfer as a means of wealth redistribution may also be necessary to secure these same values against a lopsided structure threatened by implosion and rebellion. Are these conclusions accurate?

COMPETING THEORIES OF EQUALITY

(1) *What Does the Word Equality Mean?* In this section, we consider another type of tradeoff: the tradeoff among different concepts of equality. What does the word "equality" mean? We shall look at one particular problem to illustrate the issue, called the "stockholder's problem."

(2) *The Stockholder's Problem.* The stockholders' problem involves three individuals named Abe, Babe and Cabe, who each are employees and stockholders in a corporation that is about to be dissolved. Abe owns 50% of the stock, Babe 30%, and Cabe 20%. Unexpectedly, the corporation receives 30 gold bars, and now, Abe, Babe and Cabe must decide how to divide them. Should they each receive 10? This solution would reflect "individual" equality. It would treat all of the players identically as individuals.

But this individually equal division might be unfair to Abe, who invested more initially and who owns half the stock. Individual equality may be "unequal." Shouldn't Abe, then, receive 15 gold bars, with Babe receiving 9 and Cabe 6, so that the division reflects their ownership percentages? This is a different concept of equality from "individual" equality. It might be called "investment" equality.

(3) *Equality as the Avoidance of Invidious Criteria Such as Race, Gender, and the Like: Equality as a "Freedom From" Concept.* Another view of equality would hold that either the individual or the investment view is acceptable, because both avoid "invidious discrimination." Both individual and investment equality are rationally defensible in these stockholders' circumstances. This notion of equality underlies laws against racial, gender and other kinds of discrimination.

(4) *Yet Another Concept of Equality in the Stockholders' Problem: A Game Theory or Voting Rights Approach.* But we are not through yet. There is another, completely different way to look at equality in the stockholders' problem, and that is to equalize in proportion to each player's contribution to a majority voting coalition, since the outcome depends on the votes that each brings to the issue. The results of this concept of "equality" will be surprising, but game theoreticians defend the approach as more equitable, in fact, than either individual or investment equality as described above.

This new concept of equality begins by asking, "Who is most valuable to any voting coalition that can muster a majority?" The answer is that Abe is essential, but neither Babe nor Cabe is, because Abe could form a majority with either of them. In this situation, game theorists have devised several means of computing what might be called "coalitional" equality, which is equal treatment with respect to each player's contribution to a prevailing coalition.

One such method of computation involves a technical concept called "Shapley values" (which we shall consider in a later chapter on game theory). Shapley values quantify the contribution of each stockholder to a voting majority by examining the ways that each can complete a majority coalition. The concept is technical, but we shall learn how to compute simple Shapley values in a later chapter. For now, it suffices to understand that one concept of "equality" is to treat each player according to the player's contribution to a majority solution.

It turns out that a Shapley value solution in this case would distribute a whopping 20 gold bars to Abe, but only 5 each to Babe and Cabe. Is this, then, "equality?" Yes, a game theorist might say, because it reflects precise equality, in proportion to the contribution of each to a solution(!)

EXAMPLES AND PROBLEMS

(1) *Is the Coalitional Equality Theory Really a Legitimate View of Equality?* Game theorists argue that a coalitional division, based on voting strength, is a more "equitable" solution than either individual or investment equality. It treats each player equally in the sense that it distributes to each in proportion to that player's contribution to the majority coalition. But is this really a legitimate view of equality, given that, in our stockholder example, coalition theory distributes 2/3 of the gold to Abe, who owns only half the stock, and only 1/6 to Babe, who owns 30% of it?

In some circumstances, the answer may be yes, or so game theorists would argue. Consider the following possibilities. In a close corporation, Abe, Babe and Cabe probably set up their voting shares with voting control in mind. And it also is possible that Abe paid an extra amount for his 50% vote. Such a payment is common; it is called a "control premium." Isn't it "equal," then, to divide the prize according to the principle of equality that is inherent in the expectations the parties initially adopted?

(2) *Equality of Result--or Equality of Opportunity?* If you were to ask people which was more appropriate, equality of "result" or equality of "opportunity," it is likely that a large majority would choose opportunity. But do they really mean it? In the stockholder's problem, the Shapley value solution reflects one way in which nature might produce an "equal" outcome, and presumably each of the three shareholders had equal opportunity to obtain stock in the beginning. Thus, one can argue that the Shapley solution--20 to Abe, 5 each to Babe and Cabe--represents equality of opportunity. But many people would regard this solution as unequal. Why? Is it because, although pretending to prefer equality of opportunity, American people really prefer equality of result, at least to some degree?

(3) *Needs-Based or Efficient-Use Equality.* In the stockholder's problem, imagine that Cabe has a terminal disease and no other assets, and he needs 12 gold bars to obtain the medical treatment that will save his life. But Cabe has only 20% of the stock. Cabe therefore advocates a "needs-based" division: the three stockholders should canvass the uses to which each would put the gold and then distribute it where it will be put to the most efficient uses.

Arguably, this is the method by which some scarce resources are allocated, such as organ transplants, public education of Americans with Disabilities, and (to a lesser extent) health care generally. Can you explain why?

(4) *Invidious Discrimination, Non-Invidious Criteria, and Theories of Equality.* Next, imagine that Abe and Cabe form a voting coalition to exclude Babe from recovering any of the gold, because they strongly disapprove of his behavior. Let us say that Babe has murdered the corporation's plant supervisor, or run away to join a commune, or registered as a Republican (which distresses Abe and Cabe, who both are lifelong Democrats). Given that none of these criteria appears on the usual lists of prohibited discriminants, is a resulting distribution of, say, 22 gold bars to Abe, none to Babe and 8 to Cabe defensible as "equal?"

(5) *The Equal Protection Clause of the Constitution.* The Fourteenth Amendment to the United States Constitution provides that no State shall "deny to any person . . . the equal protection of the laws." But it contains no definition of the term "equal." Should it?

(6) *One Person, One Vote: Reynolds v. Sims*, 377 U.S. 533 (1964). In the *Reynolds* case, the Supreme Court interpreted the equal protection clause to require that votes be equalized by legislative apportionment, so that approximately the same numbers of voters reside in each legislator's district. This "one person, one vote" principle is thoroughly ingrained now in popular culture.

But is the *Reynolds* solution of one person, one vote, really the only legitimate voting arrangement under the Constitution? Several dissenting justices argued that the Court had opted for one narrow theory of equality and had left out other, just-as-legitimate concepts, such as those based on geography (for example, the United States Senate is equally apportioned by States, but not population) or those based on balancing of rural and urban areas (imagine a State with one large city, in which urban and rural voters, wary of each other, set up two legislative chambers in their Constitution, one for urban districts and one for rural). Both of these arrangements would be unlawful under the majority's reasoning. Can you see why, and can you articulate the argument that one-person-one-vote rejects concepts of equality that are just as valid as the one the Court chose?

FREEDOM AND EQUALITY

(1) *The Tradeoff Between Freedom and Equality: Reconsidering the Stockholder's Problem.* Imagine that the parties in the stockholders' problem wind up dividing the 30 gold bars according to a coalition formation theory of equality. Abe, with 50% of the stock, gets 20 bars; Babe, with 30% (3/5 of Abe's), gets only 5; and Cabe, with 20%, gets 5, the same as Abe. This division, however, is reached through the votes of only Abe and Cabe, because Babe dissents. He sues, and a court orders an individually equal distribution. In other words, the court says that each player must get 10 bars, regardless of stock percentages.

(2) *Protections of Equality as Requiring Selection Among Theories of Equality, and Also as Inevitably Reducing Freedom for Some People.* Every governmental intervention to secure equality, if it is to be effective, must select among competing theories of equality. The stockholder's problem illustrates the reason. Also, every intervention to secure equality must, to a greater or lesser degree, reduce freedom and autonomy for some people.

Again, the stockholders' problem shows why an enforcement of equality may conflict with freedom for some. Here, the court's enforcement of an individual equality solution (10 bars each) removes the freedom of Abe and Cabe to opt for a coalitional equality division (20, 5 and 5) and it also prohibits their choice of investment equality (15, 9 and 6). Furthermore, it prohibits all future stockholders from structuring their relations as Abe, Babe and Cabe attempted to do.

EXAMPLES AND PROBLEMS

(1) *The Religious Landlord, the Unmarried Couple, and California's Unruh Act.* California's Unruh Act is a broad guarantee of "equal accommodations" for all people in any business arrangement. It has been interpreted as a general prohibition against any kind of "unreasonable" distinction by a business among persons. In one case, a small landlord, because of religious objections to unmarried cohabitation, refused to rent a residence to an unmarried couple. This case, although very different from the stockholders' problem, also involves a tradeoff between freedom and equality. Can you explain why? (The California Supreme Court has considered a similar case but avoided the Unruh Act question.)

(2) *The Justification for Protections of Equality: When They Outweigh the Loss in Freedom.* When a political system opts in favor of a principle protecting equality, the reason may be that it values any loss of freedom in the circumstances less than the gain in equality. For example, the freedom of a large employer to discriminate on racial grounds seems of little value compared to the interests of individuals not to be discriminated against. Thus, the Civil Rights Act of 1964 prohibits racial discrimination in employment.

But on the other hand, the public accommodations section of the 1964 Act, which prohibits discrimination in places of lodging, contains an exception allowing racial exclusion by "an establishment located within a building that contains no more than five rooms for rent or hire and which is actually occupied by the proprietor of such establishment as his residence." Why might some members of Congress have considered the freedom-equality tradeoff in voting for this provision, which explicitly allows racial discrimination in spite of the Civil Rights Act of 1964?

Chapter 9
Science

Scientific Method and the Law; History and the Social Sciences

> *"Scientific methodology today is based on generating hypotheses and testing them to see if they can be falsified; indeed, this methodology is what distinguishes science from other fields of human inquiry."--Sir Karl Popper, Conjectures and Refutations: The Growth of Scientific Knowledge*

> *"[H]ypotheses non fingo (I don't generate hypotheses)."*
> *--Sir Isaac Newton, Principia Mathematica*

§ 9.01 What This Chapter Is About

FROM NATURAL SELECTION AND THERMODYNAMICS TO SCIENTIFIC METHOD

(1) *Scientific Principles That Are Useful in Reasoning about Law and Policy.* Now, we make a major shift, from politics to science. We begin this chapter by reviewing selected scientific principles, both contemporary and

historical. The principles are selected from fields as diverse as biology and physics. They share little in common beyond their derivation through scientific method. However, these are principles of fundamental importance, and the peculiar characteristic that has inspired their inclusion here is that each of them can be used heuristically or directly in other kinds of reasoning.

Why should lawyers learn about scientific principles? The question almost answers itself. Most litigation involves expert witnesses. The admissibility of expert testimony under the rules of evidence depends on principles based on scientific reasoning. This is true not only for "hard" scientific disciplines; the criteria for those have been adapted, also, to all other kinds of experts. See *Kumho Tire Company, Ltd. v. Carmichael*, 119 S. Ct. 1167 (1999). And this is not all. Knowing how the world works, in the way that scientific principles can show, will make you better at reasoning about law and public policy. You will be able to detect more issues and to use more analogies.

(2) *The Philosophy of Science and So-Called "Soft" Sciences.* In addition to selected scientific principles, the chapter also covers scientific methodology and scientific models. What makes a given field a "science"-- what methods or goals? As the quotations above from Popper and Newton show, the question is not easy to answer. The "empiricists" or positivists, such as Popper, hold a narrower view, emphasizing observation and testing, than the "rationalists," like Newton, who instead see science as conceptual reasoning. How does this issue connect with the law? In a later chapter on jurisprudence, we shall see a very similar split between positivists and rationalists about the law.

(3) *Lawyers and History: Is History a Science?* The concept of empirical testing applies most rigorously to "hard" sciences, such as physics. But the same principles also characterize some so-called "soft" sciences, such as economics, history, and the behavioral sciences. The chapter therefore evaluates the extent to which these fields can be called scientific, and it discusses their methodologies. Again, the law of evidence about expert witnesses depends heavily on these issues--and so does (for example) interpretation of the Constitution.

§ 9.02 Physical and Life Sciences: Some Principles That Are Useful in Legal Reasoning

[A] Biology: Natural Selection and Competing Theories, from Lamarckian Evolution to Punctuated Equilibrium

NATURAL SELECTION ("EVOLUTION") AND CONTRASTING HYPOTHESES

(1) *Natural Selection or "Evolution": Not Purposeful, but Resulting from Mutation and Environmental Selection.* Natural selection is a biological hypothesis that most biologists accept as empirically proven. Living organisms are subject to genetic change, and any given mutation may or may not improve the individual's rate of propagation. (In fact, the vast majority probably are dysfunctional, leading to premature death.) The theory of natural selection is that these random alterations,

Charles Darwin

coupled with the environment, produce a natural selection of those individuals that reproduce. The phenomenon sometimes is referred to as "evolution" or as "Darwinism," after Charles Darwin, who first articulated it fully.

Popular reasoning about "evolution," however, is subject to a variety of errors, of which probably the most prevalent is inferring purpose in mutation. For example, it would be fallacious to infer that leopards have spots "because" spots provide camouflage and assist in hunting. (Biologists would call this a "teleological" statement, meaning that it infers a purpose to the underlying mutation. We considered teleology in the second chapter, on logical fallacy, and we also encountered it in the chapter on ethics.) Instead, natural selection is scientific, rather than moralistic: it sees the spots as a change that occurred randomly in an individual or individuals, and these individuals then propagated as a result of natural selection. Without this reasoning, we would not be able to explain the exuberant diversity of our biota (or in other words, it is difficult scientifically to explain the duckbilled platypus or the HIV virus by inferences of purpose).

(2) *The Fallacy of Lamarckian Evolution and Spontaneous Generation.* Historically, the road to our understanding of natural selection was littered with false hypotheses. For example, before the widespread acceptance of

natural selection, a biologist named Lamarck proposed that evolution occurred through the inheritance of acquired characteristics. An individual organism that grew stronger through exercise would produce stronger offspring--or so Lamarck theorized. (If you study architecture, perhaps Lamarck would predict that your lineage would include plenty of architects, too.) But observations have discredited this "Lamarckian evolution" (it simply doesn't describe the experimental facts) and, simultaneously, observation tends to support natural selection.

Then there was the theory of spontaneous generation, which today seems even more outlandish: it was thought that life appropriate to its surroundings would appear spontaneously. For example, a neglected barn with food scraps and hiding places was supposed to "spontaneously generate" rats and other vermin (certainly true!) and the theory was inferred from these kinds of evidence.

(3) *Creation Science, Catastrophism, Alleged Gaps in the Fossil Record, and the Theory of Punctuated Equilibrium.* There are other opposing theories, one of which, frequently discredited, is the creationist or creation-science hypothesis. This theory depends upon such factors as system-wide disasters, such as the possibility of a world-wide flood (remember Noah's ark?) Creationism tends to suggest (but in its most abstract form need not depend on) the existence of a purposeful supernatural creator.

Creationists debunk natural selection by pointing to alleged gaps in the fossil record, or the "absence of transitional forms." The evidence tends to suggest that, rather than gradually evolving from one type of organism to another, very different fossil types appear relatively suddenly, without the in-between types that one might expect from the evolutionary hypothesis. From this and other evidence, creationists infer the non-evolutionary appearance of forms or "types" of biota, as opposed to their selection through mutation.

But biologists who accept natural selection have addressed the fossil record, and as a result, we have the more sophisticated evolutionary theory of "punctuated equilibrium": Natural selection produces changes more dramatically at some times than at other times, particularly those involving catastrophic environmental change. If an ecosystem-wide or worldwide disaster occurs--an ice age, or the avulsion of a continent--the change may instantaneously alter the factors that influence selection. It is to be expected, then, that the transitional forms one would look for as a result of slow, orderly evolution would not be there--because natural selection simply is not always slow or orderly!

EXAMPLES AND PROBLEMS

(1) *Natural Selection, Public Decisionmaking, and the Law.* How would knowledge of natural selection affect public policy thinking? First, it is directly relevant to public health decisions and to a variety of other legal issues involving biological, medical or scientific processes. At another level, it might help to understand the nature of competitive environments. It might even be related to some of society's deepest taboos, e.g. incest or human cloning. Can you see why?

(2) *Vancomycin-Resistant Pathogens.* For some usages, vancomycin has sometimes been thought of as the last antibiotic line of medical defense for germs whose mutation allows them to resist other antibiotics. But the emergence of vancomycin-resistant organisms also is not only possible, but predictable (and has occurred). Can you explain why (and also explain why theories other than natural selection might not help to recognize this possibility)?

(3) *The Law, Public Policy, and Antibiotics: What Should Be Done About Resistant Pathogens?* What does this reasoning suggest about responsible limits on use of antibiotics by an individual physician (or about whether limits should be imposed by public health authorities)? [Perhaps the law should tell you that you cannot use a strong antibiotic for a trivial infection? Notice, also, that humans are not the only organisms treated by antibiotics, which also are used for animals, particularly in feedstocks; should the law counteract this usage?]

(4) *Laws about Child Abuse, Animal Behavior, Natural Selection, and Public Policy.* Among some animal species, some behavioral biologists argue, non-paternal males tend to kill young that are not their own lineage more frequently than those that are. Is this phenomenon, if it exists, related somehow to natural selection? There also is the hypothesis, referred to in an earlier chapter, that male child abusers are more prone to abuse children who are not their own. Is this hypothesis suggested by natural selection? Consider whether this idea, if true, might influence our decisions about law and public policy in combating child abuse.

(5) *It Isn't Really Survival of the Fittest, but Instead It's Natural Selection: The Analogy of the Three-Way Duel, or "Truel."* Natural selection sometimes is described as "survival of the 'fittest.'" But the metaphor is misleading, unless one remembers that it is "Darwinian fitness," or natural selection, that really is at stake. The strongest, fastest, or abstractly fittest may not be selected for long-term reproduction.

To see why, consider the following analogy from game theory. Abe, Babe and Cabe are participants in a three-way duel, or "truel." Abe is the best marksman and hits his targets 100% of the time. Babe is second with an 80% rate, and Cabe is last with only 50%. They draw lots to determine the order of shots and shoot one at a time. Who has the best odds of survival?

Paradoxically, the answer is . . . Cabe, the worst shot of the three! If either Abe or Babe goes first, their best strategy is to ignore Cabe and shoot at each other. If Cabe goes first, his rational strategy is to shoot deliberately to miss. Thus "fitness" depends on all the rest of the characteristics in the environment, and it really signifies a superior ability to cohabit with the ecological whole. Does this three-way-duel analogy help to illustrate why the survival-of-the-fittest metaphor is misleading?

(6) *Is the Common Law the Product of "Natural Selection" (Is Law's Evolution Analogous)?* Perhaps the common law is the product of a process analogous to natural selection. Judges evolve new doctrines. The ones that are useful survive. Those that are not, disappear. A new doctrine creates an alternative or exception to the failed doctrine, and thus the law grows in the manner of natural biota. Is the analogy apt? If so, what are its limitations? Note that law is created by purposive agents, unlike natural mutations.

[B]   A Few Concepts from Physics: The Inverse Square Relationship and the Heisenberg Uncertainty Principle

THE INVERSE SQUARE RELATIONSHIP

(1) *What Is an Inverse Square Relationship?* Many geometric formulae require exponents, such as squares. Thus, you learned in elementary or middle school that the area A of a circle is given by "pi-r-squared": $A = \pi r^2$. Many other physical relationships also depend on exponents, as in $E = mc^2$.

What, then, is an "inverse square" relationship? As its name implies, an inverse square results from a reversal (or inversion) of the usual squared formula. If we know the area A of a circle and its radius r, and we want to calculate the value of pi, π, we can back-calculate it from the equation $A = \pi r^2$. We multiply both sides by $1/r^2$, and we get $A \times (1/r^2) = \pi$. The factor $(1/r^2)$ is an "inverse square."

And now, a slightly more complex problem: Suppose we know the radius r and volume V of a sphere (for which the formula is $V = 4/3\ \pi r^3$), and we want to calculate the circumference c of a section sliced through its center (for which the formula is $c = 2\pi r$). We can multiply both sides of the volume equation by 3/2 and then multiply both sides by $1/r^2$ (the inverse square of the radius), and we get $3V/2r^2 = 2\pi r$. Since $c = 2\pi r$, the circumference of the slice through the center is $c = 3V/2r^2$. This, too, is an inverse square relationship.

(2) *The Fundamental Forces of Gravity and Electromagnetism as Reflecting Inverse Square Relationships.* Here is one reason why this relationship is important. The most familiar forces in nature, forces that we encounter every day, are gravity and electromagnetism. Both are subject to inverse square relationships. One way to understand this relationship is to remember that both forces are unidimensional (they exist at a certain magnitude, given two bodies at a fixed distance), but they propagate in three dimensions. The effect is like back-calculating the unidimensional circumference (measured in feet) from a three-dimensional sphere (measured in cubic feet).

Figure 1 attempts to picture this relationship. Another way to visualize

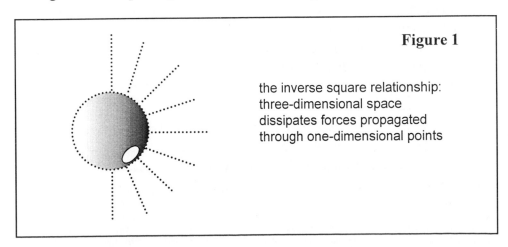

Figure 1

the inverse square relationship: three-dimensional space dissipates forces propagated through one-dimensional points

it is to consider forces as radiating in concentric spheres, dissipating rapidly as the spheres expand. The result is that the falloff in force strength is more rapid than the extension of distance, because it is inversely geometric, or inversely dependent on the exponent.

The figure represents lines radiating uniformly from a point. If we imagine multiple concentric spheres centered on the point, then the same number of lines will intersect each sphere. But the surface area of each sphere is a two-dimensional factor, and so the lines intersect larger and larger areas at greater distances. The intersections are not as dense. This "density of the crossing lines" is proportional to the perceived "intensity" of the lines. For example, if the lines represent light, the example shows that the perceived intensity diminishes in proportion to the square of the distance from the light source.

(3) *Newton's Gravitational Law:* $F_g = G(m_1m_2)/r^2$. Now, we shall apply this concept concretely. First, let us examine the fundamental force known as gravity. Sir Isaac Newton deduced that the gravitational attraction of two bodies was proportional to the inverse square of the distance r between them. Thus, $F_g \propto 1/r^2$. (The symbol, $\propto$, means "is proportional to.") The gravitational force also is proportional to the mass of each body, m_1 and m_2, so $F_g \propto m_1 \times m_2$. Putting these together, then, the force of gravity, F_g, quals the mass of each body multiplied together (m_1m_2), then multiplied by the inverse square of the distance r between them, or $F_g = m_1 \times m_2 \times 1/r^2$. Finally, to convert the number to measuring units (e.g., metric units), we must add a conversion factor G, called the gravitational constant.

Thus, Newton's complete equation is $F_g = G(m_1m_2)/r^2$. The meaning of the equation can be illustrated by an example. Imagine that the masses of two spheres are 2 kilograms and 4 kilograms respectively, and their centers are 2 meters apart. Then, the gravitational force F_g attracting them is $G(m_1m_2)/r^2 = G(2 \times 4)/2^2 = G \times 8/4 = 2 \times G$ kilograms per square meter. Since the unit of force in the metric system is called a "newton," abbreviated "N," the gravitational force is two G newtons, or (2G)N.[1]

---

1   As we shall see below, the gravitational constant G is 6.7×10^{-11}, or 67 with ten zeroes in front of it. The gravitational force in newtons in this example, then, would be twice this number, or 13 with nine zeroes, or 13 trillionths of a newton. Since a newton is defined as the force that will accelerate a kilogram at the rate of one meter per second per second, if these two spheres are by themselves out in space away from a gravitational field such as the earth's, the two will come together imperceptibly slowly at first but with gradual acceleration.

(4)   *Coulomb's Law of Electromagnetic Force:* $F_e = k(q_1 q_2)/r^2$. Next, we shall look at the other frequently observed fundamental force, which is electrical force.   Charles Augustin de Coulomb was the first to deduce the equation for electromagnetic forces, which really is identical to the gravitational equation.   The electromagnetic force F_e between two point charges is proportional to the inverse square of the distance between them: $F_e \propto 1/r^2$. It also is proportional to the product of their magnitudes, $q_1 x q_2$. These

Charles A. Coulomb

magnitudes are measured in "coulombs," the unit of electrical charge. (Except for measurement of electrical charge rather than mass, this is the same as Newton's equation.)

Thus, $F_e = (q_1 x q_2)/r^2$. But because this relationship does not give measurements in metric equivalents, it must be multiplied by a constant, k, to convert it: $F = k(q_1 x q_2)/r^2$.[2] If you compare this equation to the gravitational one, you should be able to see that it is precisely analogous.

(5) *Other Inverse Square Relationships: Apparent Magnitude of a Light Source, Etc.* Another inverse square example, as we have seen, is the apparent magnitude or brilliance of a light source. When you see a star (such as the magnitude 1 star Sirius, which is in Canis Major), the apparent magnitude that you see is proportional to its actual magnitude, but it also is proportional to the inverse square of the distance between the observer and the star. The light travels in one dimension to you, but it dissipates in three

---

2   The conventional notation is more complex yet, because it is easier to derive other equations that actually are used more frequently by adopting a peculiar form for the constant, k. Thus, Coulomb's law usually is written, $F = (1/4\pi\epsilon_o)(q_1 q_2/r^2)$, where ϵ_o is a number called the "permittivity constant." But if you don't follow this equation, don't worry. This footnote is included just so that knowledgeable physics students will recognize the formula. Since $\epsilon_o = 8.85 \times 10^{-12}$ coul^2/N-m^2, the constant, k, actually is $1/[(4\pi)(8.85)(10^{12})]$ newton-meters-squared per square coulomb, which equals .009 x 10^{12}, or k = 9.0 x 10^9.

dimensions. And there are still other inverse-square relationships in the physical world.

Are there inverse square relationships in the legal world? We'll see about that.

EXAMPLES AND PROBLEMS

(1) *The Gravitational Force Attracting the Proton and Electron in a Hydrogen Atom.* A hydrogen atom has one proton and one electron. What is the force of gravitational attraction between them?

We apply Newton's law, $F_g = (m_1 m_2)/r^2$. Thus, we need the masses of a proton and an electron (m_1 and m_2) and the distance between them (r), as well as the gravitational constant, G. The mass m_1 of a proton is 1.7×10^{-27} kilograms (kg). The mass m_2 of an electron, roughly two thousand times smaller, is 9.1×10^{-31} kg. The distance r between them varies but is about 0.53 angstrom units, or 5.3×10^{-11} meter on average. The gravitational constant G is 6.7×10^{-11}.[3]

Therefore, the calculation of the gravitational attraction between a hydrogen proton and its electron is:

$$F_g = G \frac{m_1 m_2}{r^2} = (6.7 \times 10^{-11}) \frac{(9.1 \times 10^{-31})(1.7 \times 10^{-27})}{(5.3 \times 10^{-11})^2} = 3.7 \times 10^{-47} N.$$

In other words, the gravitational attraction between this proton and electron, in newtons, is 37 preceded by forty-six zeroes. A pretty small number!

(2) *Comparing the Electrical Force to the Gravitational Force in the Hydrogen Atom.* Now, just for comparison, let us compute the electrical force F_e between the same proton and electron. Coulomb's equation is exactly analogous to Newton's: $F = k(q_1 \times q_2)/r^2$. We need the values of q_1, q_2, r, and k.

---

3   Strictly speaking, it is 6.7×10^{-11} newton-meters squared per square kilogram, or 6.7×10^{-11} N-m²/kg². This dimension is necessary to make the dimensions work out to newtons, the basic measure of force. But don't worry about this either.

The electrical charge on a proton is the same as that on an electron; it is 1.6 x. 10^{-19} coulombs for each. The distance between them, once again, is about 5.3 x 10^{-11} meters. The constant, k, for Coulomb's Law is 9.0 x 10^{9}.[4]

The calculation of the electrical force between a hydrogen proton and its electron, then, is:

$$F_e = k \frac{q_1 q_2}{r_2} = \frac{(9.0 \times 10^9)(1.6 \times 10^{-19})(1.6 \times 10^{-19})}{(5.3 \times 10^{-11})^2} = 8.1 \times 10^{-8} N.$$

And so the electrical force, in newtons, is 81 with seven zeroes in front of it. This electrical force is stronger than the gravitational force by a factor of 2 x 10^{38}, meaning that it is 2 with 38 zeroes times as strong the gravitational force. The gravitational attraction between a proton and electron, therefore, is negligible compared to the electrical attraction. Can you explain the math?

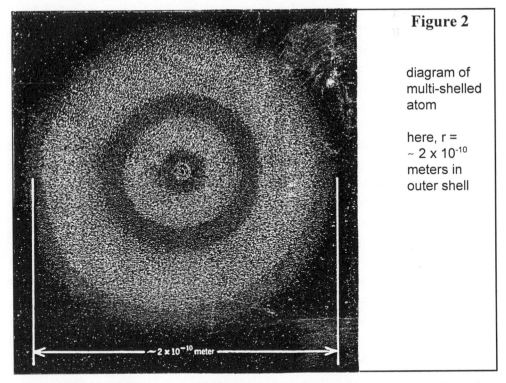

Figure 2

diagram of multi-shelled atom

here, r = ~ 2 x 10^{-10} meters in outer shell

~2 x 10^{-10} meter

(3) *What About Forces on Electrons in a Larger Atom?* Next, imagine a larger, more complex atom, such as the one (simplistically) represented in

---

4   Again, with dimensions, it is 9.0 x 10^9N-m^2/coul^2, but again, that's not important.

Figure 2.[5] How does the force attracting an outermost electron to a given proton in the nucleus compare to the force attracting an inner-shell electron (which is equivalent to an electron in a hydrogen atom)? This problem will show us what the inverse square rule really means: that the force falls off inversely with distance much faster than a linear falloff.

Electrons orbit at different levels, or shells, and not in planar circles, but in smears or electron clouds that sometimes are like fuzzy spheres (or other shapes). In this particular atom in the figure, the maximum distance, X, for the outer shell from the nucleus is about 2×10^{-10} meters. The distance Y in the hydrogen atom (equivalent to the inner shell here) was, as we saw, 5.3×10^{-11} meters. The ratio of the two forces equals the ratio of the squares of the distances, or $X^2/Y^2 = (2 \times 10^{-10})^2/(5.3 \times 10^{-11})^2 = (2 \times 10^{-10})^2/(0.53 \times 10^{-10})^2 = 2^2/(0.53)^2 = 4/0.28 = 14$.

Therefore, for this particular atom, the attractive force asserted by a nuclear proton on an inner electron is about fourteen times that asserted on an outermost one. An inverse-square force falls off exponentially faster than distance. Can you explain the math?

(4) *Electrical Force Holds Solid Matter Together.* Coulomb's Law not only affects the relationship between electrons and protons, it also is the force that holds together atoms to make molecules and molecules together to make solids. If a bridge is held together by a steel tie beam, it actually is held together by electrical forces, because it is these forces within the crystalline structure that hold the steel beam together. We ourselves, our bodies, also are held together by electrical forces that obey Coulomb's Law.

(5) *An Analogy in the Law: Is There an Inverse Square Relationship Between Conformity to a Disagreeable Rule and the Magnitude of One's Disagreement?* Now that you understand the physics of the inverse square relationship, it may be interesting to apply it to another, completely different field, by analogy. Is it possible that the inverse square rule could be applied to human behavior about the law?

For example, one might hypothesize that perhaps there is an inverse square relationship between a person's conformity to a disagreeable rule and

---

5   The diagram is idealized. Electron orbits are not necessarily spherical; some are shaped like figure 8's, and indeed the entire notion of an "orbit" may be misleading because the concept is better described by references to clouds or probability maps. But this caveat does not affect the usefulness of this example or problem.

the magnitude of disagreement, at least when the actor will suffer no tangible ill effects from violation of the rule. For example, if President Clinton had seen that accurate findings under a law passed by Congress would result in Presidential findings of fact that would produce a $1 increase in the minimum wage, he would have been likely to make the findings accurately--because his disagreement with the law would be minimal. But if a law had required President Clinton to make a factual finding about whether Mexico has made progress in reducing drug trafficking, he would have been likely to "fudge" the finding by stating that it has, when in fact it has not, so as to avoid decertification of Mexico--a result with which he would have strongly disagreed.

If this analogy is correct, the President's honest compliance with the laws would be inversely proportional not to the magnitude of his disagreement, but to the *square* of this magnitude. The theory likewise would predict that judges' decisions and rulings would deviate from evenhanded conformity to law according to the squares of their disagreements with the principles in question. As the disagreement increases, the tendency not to conform increases even faster, with an exponent. Is there anything to this hypothesis?[6]

(6) *Science and the Law: Reconsidering the Earlier Problem of Lawsuits About Power Transmission Lines (in the Fallacy Chapter).* In an earlier chapter, we considered a problem about people who claimed their cancers were caused by transmission lines. The inference was based on finding that one or a few particular areas near power lines reflected higher-than-average cancer rates while some other, more distant areas did not. The lawsuits quietly were dropped because they were based on bad statistical reasoning. They also may have been based on poor science.

It turns out that the electromagnetic field around a power transmission line falls off rapidly with distance. Within a few inches of a power line, the field is significant, but a few dozen feet away, it falls to insignificance. The relationship is not an inverse square relationship, because the magnetic field created by a line of charge is determined by a different equation than the field around a point charge. But it still falls off rapidly, so that the force may be less than that from sitting by your television set.

---

6 Note that it is only a hypothesis, and before crediting it, we should require experimental testing. But maybe it would be worthwhile for a psychologist to devise an experiment that would correlate disagreement and nonconformity.

This problem illustrates another, more general point, too. You should be suspicious of any statistical inference of causation for which there is no discernible causal mechanism.[7]

THE HEISENBERG UNCERTAINTY PRINCIPLE: MEASUREMENT INHERENTLY INVOLVES TRANSFORMATION

(1) *Heisenberg's Principle in Quantum Mechanics.* Here is another, separate concept from physics. The "Heisenberg uncertainty principle," named after German Physicist Werner Heisenberg, is one of the philosophical foundations of quantum mechanics. It explains that it is impossible simultaneously to determine the location and momentum of a particle such as an electron.[8] Proof of the principle requires familiarity with quantum physics and is beyond the scope of this book.

Werner Heisenberg

(2) *The General Statement of the Broader Principle.* But the (fascinating) general statement of the broader principle is that it is impossible to observe anything without interacting with it and therefore affecting it, and thus all measurement is inaccurate because it changes the measured object. A speedometer uses a tiny portion of the car's energy, for example, and it furnishes only a close approximation of what the velocity would be without the speedometer. And so, if we disconnect the speedometer but depress the accelerator identically, the measurement given earlier by the speedometer no longer will be precisely accurate.

---

7   But the possibility of a weak association between power lines and cancer, according to the National Institutes of Health, cannot be ruled out completely by the statistics. See Chapter 2, above. The possibility (likelihood?) that all indications of "association" are due to confounders also exists; for example, power-line neighbors might be less wealthy than others and live in lower-rent areas with attendant causal factors.

8   Or even a "particle" such as a baseball. The theory is general; the effect with an electron is noticeable because of the mathematics, but the relative size of the effect in the case of a baseball is infinitesimal.

EXAMPLES AND PROBLEMS

(1) *Heisenberg's Principle and the Law: Official Opposition to Court-Ordered Prison Monitors.* This problem applies Heisenberg's principle, by analogy, to a social problem. Court-ordered prison reform decrees have touched nearly every state with provisions about crowding, discipline, medical care and other issues. Some courts have appointed "masters" to oversee implementation, and some have authorized these masters to employ many other individuals as "monitors" to enter prisons and continuously verify progress toward compliance. The result is that a large number of allegedly neutral individuals not connected with existing prison policies have come into correctional facilities.

Outside critics see these monitors as mere neutral "eyes and ears of the court," but prison officials have opposed monitors with a vigor that surprises the critics. Perhaps, though, this opposition is not so puzzling. See whether Heisenberg's principle, as an analogy, can help you to infer a legitimate reason why a prison warden should be concerned about the entry of court-ordered monitors to interact with inmates on the inside. (Suggestion: What is a monitor likely to do upon receiving a confidential disclosure of a regulatory violation by a prisoner, e.g., one who shows a monitor an allegedly defensive but prohibited homemade "shank?" What effect might the monitor's tacit tolerance of the violation have?)

In fact, the phenomenon of effects on human behavior caused by external examination is well known to psychologists. Subjects may conform to their perceptions of the experimenter's expectations or otherwise alter their behavior as a "demonstration effect" of the experiment. In medical experiments, the same phenomenon sometimes is called the "placebo effect." These phenomena are, of course, distinct from Heisenberg's principle because they involve human behavior rather than physics. But is the analogy useful?

(2) *Cameras in the Courtroom.* Does Heisenberg's principle help to explain, by analogy, why some courts exclude television cameras or disallow them from photographing jurors? (Might cameras change behaviors?)

(3) *Lawyers' Uses of Focus Groups: How Focus Groups Are Influenced by Heisenberg's Principle.* In one national Sunday political talk show during 1999, former presidential adviser George Stephanopolous narrated a segment in which focus groups were asked questions related to presidential

preferences. The members of Stephanopolous's groups knew they were being videotaped and might appear on television. Therefore, on this popular television show viewed by millions, Stephanopolous cautioned that, in his words, because of "Heisenberg's principle," the expressions of opinions by the focus group members might be distorted. It seems unlikely that most viewers understood Stephanopolous's reference to "Heisenberg's principle," but can you explain why his observation made sense? How might a lawyer preparing for a jury trial minimize this effect? (Lawyers use focus groups as preparation for jury trials, and the issue developed here also arises there.)

[C]   Thermodynamics: The First and Second Laws of Thermodynamics and the Concept of Entropy

ENTROPY AND THE SECOND LAW OF THERMODYNAMICS

(1)   *The First Law of Thermodynamics as a Helpful Means of Understanding the Second Law: Conservation of Energy.* In this section, we shall turn to a different scientific issue. We shall consider the field of thermodynamics, which is the science of heat transfer as connected to mechanical work. Actually, the "second law of thermodynamics" helps to explain many of the physical processes that we rely upon in our daily lives, ranging from the internal combustion engine to air conditioning. (Can we use it, by analogy, to help us to reason about the law? In some instances, yes, we can!)

In order to understand the second law, it is necessary first to understand the "first law of thermodynamics." Although capable of intimidatingly squiggled mathematical expression, the first law at its core is simply the law of conservation of energy. Within a closed system, the sum of mechanical work, heat, and electrical energy (assuming no other kinds of energy are at issue) must be the same as it was before the process began. In other words, energy is conserved, neither created nor destroyed, although it may be transformed from heat to mechanical or electrical energy or vice versa. The first law explains, for example, that if we use a heat engine to do mechanical work, the heat energy loss must exactly equal the mechanical energy gained. And conversely, if we apply mechanical energy (a paddle stirrer) to a liquid and let it settle, the expended mechanical energy will be replaced by equal heat energy.

(2) *Why the Second Law Is Necessary.* The second law of thermodynamics is more complicated. Like the first law, it is an empirically derived principle, from experimentation and observation of the universe.

The second law was devised because the first law does not explain why some processes take place. For example, if we connect two bodies such as two balloons full of water (or two "reservoirs," as chemists tend to call them), and one is hot and one cold, heat will flow from the hot to the cold one, and not from the cold one to the hot one. Empirically, we know this pattern so well that it seems obvious. A toddler learns not to touch a hot stove. But the first law (conservation of energy) cannot explain this result. The simple explanation of the second law, then, is very, very simple: heat flows from a hot object to a cold one.

(3) *The Concept of "Entropy" in the Second Law.* The second law postulates a quantity called "entropy," which is a characteristic of every system. (A "system," in this language, is just a collection of objects or atoms, such as a volume of gasoline vapor in an automobile cylinder, that is subjected to a process.) It is useful to conceive of entropy as a quantity roughly representing the molecular "disorganization" of a system. The second law predicts that a closed system that undergoes any chemical process tends toward increase in "disorganization," or entropy, at least for real-world processes.

Thus, if a gas volume pushes against a piston, expands, and then absorbs heat, its "disorganization" or entropy increases. Compression followed by cooling of the gas, resulting in a reduction of system entropy, requires external energy and an increase in the total entropy of the universe for real-world processes. Thus, the second law is the empirical observation that system entropy, roughly corresponding to molecular disorganization, tends toward

Rudolf Julius Emanuel Clausius

maximization in a closed system, and that energy and entropy are oppositionally related.

(4) *Another Conception of Entropy: The Number of Possible Physical States.* More technically, entropy is a measure of the total number of microscopic states potentially available to a system. In this view, entropy usually is changed by processes, such as heat transfer, performed upon a system. Some theoretical processes can be done slowly and carefully so that they return the entire system (i.e., the whole universe) to precisely the same state at which it began, preserving the entropy at the same level as before the process started. Real-world processes, though, leave the universe with more possible states (increased entropy), because exact restoration to the initial status is impossible.

Thus, in the example of a gas volume pushing a piston, expanding, and absorbing heat, the increase in volume and energy (from the heat) increases the number of potential positions and velocities that each atom can have. The system has gone from a collection of closely packed, slowly moving atoms whose velocities and positions are less different to a frenzy of fast and slow, more expansively located atoms. The potential number of microscopic states has increased (and less precisely, we might say its disorganization has increased). Its entropy, therefore, has increased.

(5) *Clausius's Statement of the First and Second Laws in One Elegant Sentence.* The great German physicist R. J. E. Clausius often is considered the founder of thermodynamics. Clausius put the first and second laws elegantly in one sentence, this way: "Die energie der Welt [World] ist konstant; die entropie der Welt geht immer zu [always increases]." And that is the essence of both laws: "The energy of the universe is constant; the entropy of the universe is always increasing." This one sentence says it all.

(6) *Mathematical Expression of Entropy.* Entropy is "a quantity that is the measure of the amount of energy in a system not available for doing work, numerical changes in the quantity being determinable from the ratio dQ/T where dQ is a small increment of heat added or removed and T is the absolute temperature." Webster's Third New Int'l Dictionary 1280 (1986). Therefore, for the mathematically inclined, entropy S is defined by the following equation:

$$dS = dQ/T$$

where dS is an infinitesimally small change in entropy, dQ is the corresponding infinitesimal heat energy change, and T is temperature.

(7) *Multiple Equivalent Statements of the Second Law.* The second law is capable of many different equivalent statements. For example:

"The second law is expressed mathematically in terms of the concept of entropy. When a body absorbs an amount of heat Q from reservoir at temperature T, the body gains and the reservoir loses an amount of entropy $S = Q/T$. . . . If an amount of heat Q flows from a hot to a cold body, the total entropy increases; because $S=Q/T$ is larger for smaller values of T, the cold body gains more entropy than the hot body loses. The statement that heat never flows from a cold to a hot body can be generalized by saying that in no spontaneous process does the total entropy decrease. In all real physical processes entropy increases; in ideal reversible processes entropy remains constant." Columbia Encyclopedia 2730-31.

"Entropy [is a] thermodynamic quantity which always increases for irreversible processes, giving a direction in time for processes which might otherwise appear reversible from energy considerations alone; symbol S, units J/K (joule per kelvin). Freezing water to ice decreases the entropy of the water, but at the expense of increasing the entropy of the total system, such as the refrigerator and the room containing it. Entropy may be understood as a measure of disorder at a microscopic level, caused by the addition of heat to collections of atoms. The second law of thermodynamics states that for all processes entropy either is constant or increases." Cambridge Encyclopedia 412 (1992).

(8) *Simple Uses of the Entropy Concept in Language.* J.R. Newman said that "entropy is the general trend of the universe toward death and disorder." Webster's, *supra.* Entropy also is a useful expression for describing social disintegration. David Bidney said that "cultural diversity and heterogeneity counteracts the tendency to cultural entropy." *Id.*

EXAMPLES AND PROBLEMS

(1) *A Simple Demonstration of Entropy and the Second Law, Using a Rubber Band.* The concepts in this section can be vividly illustrated with a

simple experiment using a rubber band. A thick, heavy (but flexible) band is best. Hold the band with your forefingers and touch it to your forehead, or better, to your lips (which are more sensitive). Note how hot or cold it feels. Next, stretch the band with your forefingers and immediately touch it again to your lips. You should feel a slight increase in the output of heat compared to the unstretched band. Here's why: in the stretched band, the rubber molecule chains line up side by side in an organized fashion, requiring external energy (from you), and the mechanical energy from you is converted into heat.

Now, keep the band stretched and expose it to the air for one minute, so that it cools to room temperature. After a minute, quickly unstretch the band by bringing your fingers together, and immediately touch it to your lips. It feels colder than before. Here's what has happened: The heat associated with the stretched band has dissipated into the larger environment, lowering the band's entropy and increasing the atmosphere's (the increase of atmospheric entropy is greater than the decrease in the rubber band's entropy, and that's why the universe always increases in entropy).

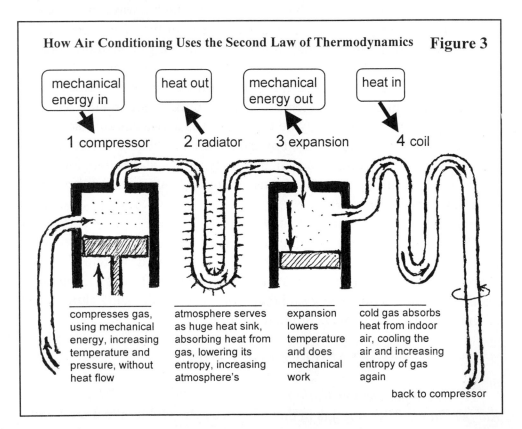

How Air Conditioning Uses the Second Law of Thermodynamics   **Figure 3**

mechanical energy in → 1 compressor

heat out ← 2 radiator

mechanical energy out → 3 expansion

heat in → 4 coil

compresses gas, using mechanical energy, increasing temperature and pressure, without heat flow

atmosphere serves as huge heat sink, absorbing heat from gas, lowering its entropy, increasing atmosphere's

expansion lowers temperature and does mechanical work

cold gas absorbs heat from indoor air, cooling the air and increasing entropy of gas again

back to compressor

The cooling of the band in its stretched condition results in decreased entropy because the rubber molecules are lined up and cooled. Once unstretched, the system composed of the rubber band is now capable of absorbing heat from the environment rather than giving it off, and its entropy increases with the heat flow into it.

(2) *How Air Conditioning Works: Putting the Second Law to Practical Use.* If you understand the rubber band demonstration, you're halfway there in understanding air conditioning. See Figure 3. Rather than a rubber band, an air conditioner uses a special gas such as freon, selected for its entropy characteristics. First, the gas is compressed by external electrical and mechanical energy supplied by a compressor (Step 1). It now is hot. This hot, compressed gas, comparable to the hot, stretched, rubber band, next will go to a radiator for cooling by exposure to the outside atmosphere (Step 2). The atmosphere is a giant heat sink, and it cools the gas by absorbing heat from it. The entropy of the gas decreases, and the entropy of the larger universe increases.

These two steps, compression and radiation, take place out of doors. Next, the compressed-but-cooled, low entropy gas is pumped to indoor coils where it quickly is expanded and made to do mechanical work (Step 3). Finally, the coils are exposed to indoor air (Step 4). After its expansion, the gas absorbs heat from the indoor air, thus cooling the indoor air while increasing the entropy of the gas again. See the figure for these four steps.

Then, the gas is pumped outside to the compressor again, and the cycle begins once more. The entropy of the air inside the house has decreased, with an input of external electrical and mechanical energy from the compressor. Meanwhile, the entropy of the total system, the house plus the external atmosphere (and indeed the entire universe), has increased.[9]

(3) *Why Lawyers Should Care: Entropy in Reasoning about the Law-- The Example of Measuring Industry Concentration Under the Antitrust Laws.* What about the usefulness of the second law of thermodynamics in law and public policy? If the answer is not obvious to you, that is not surprising. However, there are some important applications. For example, in antitrust

---

9 The figure idealizes and simplifies the cycle, depicting it as a "reversible" process. If the step 3 expansion is a free expansion and not one that does work, there will be an entropy increase in that step which is unbalanced, and thus entropy will increase in the universe. This is the case with real-world refrigeration systems.

law, mergers are unlawful in some circumstances if they would injure "competition." Courts often apply this provision of the Clayton Act by defining a relevant market and then measuring the concentration of that market by examining the largest four, largest eight, or similar groups of firms. Actually, what the courts are doing by this reasoning is to examine the "disorganization" of separate firms, or entropy of the marketplace.

There have been proposals for the actual, direct use of entropy computations to measure concentration in this situation. Perhaps judges who understood the second law, and the concept of entropy, could better apply the merger laws in the Clayton Act; for example, if there is a single very large firm but no close second, and then there is a large number of other, smaller firms, an entropy theory might show greater entropy (and lesser concentration) than, say, in a market with four twenty-five percent firms. This result may not be intuitively obvious.

(4) *Use of Analogies Built on Entropy and the Second Law.* But perhaps a more broadly useful conception of the second law in our thinking would involve the use of analogy. One concept attributed to criminologist James Q. Wilson, and put into effect with ostensible success in New York City by Mayor Rudolph Giuliani, is to enforce relatively minor laws against quality-of-life offenses, not only for their own sake, but as a means of indirectly reducing the incidence of more serious crime.

For example, if vandals break a window in an abandoned building, the solution of immediately causing the window to be fixed and pursuing the offenders dissuades other vandals from freely breaking other windows, or so the theory goes; and control of this kind of fraying of the social fabric may even result in a lessening of other categories of crime such as drug offenses or assaults. The theory is difficult of proof, but Giuliani points to evidence that appears to support it. An understanding of the phenomenon of entropy and disorganization, coupled with an understanding of the opposing role of energy (application of law enforcement to smaller offenses), may provide an aid in understanding the theory.

(5) *An Example about Law, Justice, and Entropy from the Star Wars Myths: Bounty Hunter Boba Fett and His Use of the Concept of Entropy.* In the wonderful Star Wars myths, Boba Fett is a bounty hunter. Doing a job that may be needed but is not respected, he accepts contracts to "collect" wanted people (or rather, wanted *creatures*) in the name of an uncertain

justice, depending on which society has contracted for his services. Boba Fett has a highly developed vocabulary, in which he expresses a precise (if cramped) philosophy of evil. It is a frontiersman's amalgamation of individual responsibility with fatalism:

> . . . Evil exists; it is intelligence in the service of entropy. When the side of a mountain slides down to kill a village, this is not evil, for evil requires intent. Should a sentient being cause that landslide, there is evil; and requires Justice as a consequence, so that civilization can exist. . . .

Daniel Keys Moran, *The Last One Standing: The Tale of Boba Fett*, in Star Wars: Tales of the Bounty Hunters 277-78 (Bantam Books, Kevin J. Anderson ed. 1996). Can you explain what Boba Fett means by "entropy," and evaluate whether you agree with his philosophy?

§ 9.03 Scientific Methods and Models

[A]   Scientific Method (and the Law of Expert Witnesses)

OBSERVATION, CONCEPT AND QUANTITATIVE THEORY

(1) *The Law--and the Battleground of Scientific Philosophy.* Now, let us shift from our examination of specific scientific principles to the broader question of the philosophy of science. What is science, and what makes a proposition more or less "scientific"? As we shall see, there are at least three parts of the scientific endeavor: observation, concept, and quantitative theory. Throughout the history of science, different ones of these three issues have been pushed to the forefront, and they have been the battleground of the philosophy of science.

How will this help us study the law? Courts often must deal with scientific evidence, and they must decide what science is. But there also is another important connection. Jurisprudence sometimes is referred to as the "science" of the law, and some of the same issues that distinguish good science have been advanced by legal philosophers to distinguish good jurisprudence--as we shall see in a later chapter.

(2)   *Observation or Measurement as the Core of Science: The Empiricists or Logical Positivists.* To some philosophers, observations are

the core of science. In this view, a concept or theory--for example, Boyle's Law relating the pressure, temperature and volume of a gas--always is inaccurate. In fact, this criticism is literally true of any scientific theory; to use the same illustration, Boyles' Law applies only to an "ideal" gas, a hypothetical concept that does not really exist but was invented by theoreticians so that the numbers for Boyle's Law would work out. (Boyle's Law, incidentally, is that $P_1 x V_1/T_1 = P_2 x V_2/T_2$, or the pressure of a gas multiplied by the volume and divided by the temperature is constant.)

For empirical philosophers, science consists of measurement, observation, and experimentation. A slavishly literal empiricist might say that a concept such as Boyle's Law, which produces only approximations when used with real gases such as oxygen or ammonia, is unscientific because experimentation proves that although it gives approximations, it always gives false values. It ultimately requires empirical observation anyway, to tell what the real numbers are. Although few empiricists would push the primacy of observation to the point of rejecting Boyle's Law, this example may show why the empiricist must, at some point, compromise with conceptualists, if we are to avoid conceiving of science merely as a jumble of unrelated observations.

(3) *The Idea of "Falsifiability."* Thus, the empiricists see experiment as the core of science. Experimentation or observation, with measurement, can exhibit consistency with (and inductively support) a theoretical relationship, or it can disprove (or "falsify") it. This view limits science to that which is "falsifiable."   The British-Austrian philosopher Sir Karl Popper has been a leading proponent of this view of "generating hypotheses" that can be "tested" empirically, or of science as defined by "falsifiability."   A famous quotation from Popper, to this effect, is at the beginning of this chapter.

Karl Raimund Popper

(4) *Concepts as the Core of Science: The Rationalists.* Others disagree, seeing the core of science as concepts rather than observations. A series of

observations of a gas such as oxygen or ammonia would allow us to provide charts of the relationships among pressure, volume or temperature, but if the strict empiricist is correct, we could not predict other data points. We could not even interpolate between observed data points, because this would require a concept or theory. Furthermore, unless linked by a concept, our measurements would remain as nothing more than raw data. Boyle's Law, by contrast, provides a model, or a concept, that organizes the data, even if it is imperfect.

Sir Isaac Newton

Sir Isaac Newton, for example, was more a rationalist than an empiricist. He deduced numerous relationships in the physical world, producing what now is referred to as Newtonian mechanics, as a conceptual exercise, although subject to verification. While recognizing the need for revision if the concepts he postulated proved empirically wrong, he saw science largely as concept, or as rational rather than purely empirical. Newton's famous statement, "[H]ypotheses non fingo," or "I don't generate hypotheses," which is at the beginning of this chapter, clashes sharply with Popper's theory that science is hypotheses and testing. Newton did not generate hypotheses because he deduced his ideas conceptually.

(5) *Science as Quantitative Theory.* A third part of the puzzle is mathematics. There are those who say that formal quantitative theory is the heart of science. You cannot understand a phenomenon, they insist, unless you can assign numbers to its inputs and derive numbers from those for its results. Boyle's Law, for all its imperfections, fits this conception.

(6) *In Some Measure, Science Consists of All of These Factors.* Few philosophers of science today would regard any of these ingredients as irrelevant. A concept that does not fit the facts at all is not useful, and neither is a jumble of raw empirical data correlated by no concept. The philosophers differ primarily in how they emphasize these ingredients.

EXAMPLES AND PROBLEMS

(1) *What Are the Consequences of Using Falsifiability as the Test for Science?: The Example of Biological Taxonomy--and the Law of Expert Witnesses.* Popper's theory of falsifiability, that experimental verification is the defining element of science, would make some branches of what is thought of as science unscientific, if applied with excessive rigor. Consider the example of biological classification or taxonomy. It is difficult to "prove" observationally that a whale is a mammal, or that a spider is not an insect. We can "prove" these facts by resort to definitional characteristics, such as that mammals are warm-blooded and insects have six legs, but this is merely a concept, not falsifiable in itself; it might be equally possible to construct a definition by which a whale is a fish.

The concept of a "mammal" or "insect" is like all concepts; it is designed to show relationships, and the test of its validity, arguably, should be whether it is useful for that purpose, not whether it is capable of experimental proof. The point is that we can predict other characteristics of whales and trace their evolution better by treating them as mammals. Still, our classification of a whale as a mammal remains conceptual, not experimentally verifiable. It is not possible to falsify the statement that a whale is "like" a horse, when the whale is like a horse in some respects and unlike it in others.

Is the classificatory biologist, then, wrong in claiming to be a scientist? Or is Popper's theory wrong? And now, a key legal question: If an empiricist says the taxonomist isn't a "scientist," does this mean the taxonomist can't testify in court? (Maybe it does! See below.)

(2) *The Prediction of "Tachyons" by Relativity Theorists: Is It Scientific?* Another test of Popper's philosophy is the relativity construct of tachyons. Nothing we know of can move faster than the speed of light, because the energy required to accelerate it would exceed all the energy that exists in the universe. This concept, however, has led relativity theorists to postulate the existence of "tachyons," which travel faster than light ("tachy" is taken from a Greek word meaning fast). Just as nothing else can exceed the speed of light, tachyons cannot slow down to light speed, because the energy they would give off would exceed what the universe could absorb.

Many of the predictions of relativity theory have been verified by observation, but we never have seen a tachyon. It's hard to catch them. We may never observe them. Question: Does this mean that theories contemplating tachyons are unscientific, under Popper's theory? If so, were all of the predictions from relativity, that since have been experimentally observed, "unscientific" when conceived?

(3) *The United States Supreme Court Has Opted for Popper's View in Qualifying Expert Scientific Evidence: Daubert v. Merrell Dow Pharmaceuticals, Inc.*, 509 U.S. 579 (1993). In the *Daubert* case, the Supreme Court defined the circumstances in which an expert witness may testify to a conclusion based on scientific principles. The Court's concern was with so-called "junk science," or with witnesses whose testimony could not be traced to valid principles. "Ordinarily," said the Court, "a key question [is] whether the principle can be (and has been) tested." It then quoted Popper: "'Scientific methodology today is based on generating hypotheses and testing them to see if they can be falsified; indeed, this methodology is what distinguishes science from other fields of human inquiry.' [K.] Popper, Conjectures and Refutations: The Growth of Scientific Knowledge 37 (5th ed. 1989). '[T]he criterion of the scientific status of a theory is its falsifiability, or refutability, or testability.'" Although the court allowed for balancing with other criteria, such as peer review, error rates, and general acceptance, the Court seems to have emphasized the falsifiability criterion more than others.

Does this decision, that science "is" falsifiability, legalize only one narrow-minded view of science in the face of other arguably correct views? Will it make the qualification of some kinds of true experts (e.g., a good biological taxonomist) unreasonably difficult? Notice that Newton, Einstein and Freud would have had difficulty qualifying under the Supreme Court's current view if they had been called as expert witnesses in their times, even if they could assist in discovering truth.

(4) *Is Law, or Justice, a Science?* Most people would say that law and justice are not scientific. Concepts or models exist in law and justice just as they do in science. But the validity of these models depends upon their derivation from a proper authority (in the positivist view) or from natural justice (in the opposing view) and not from anything that can be tested by experiment or observation.

(5) *Use of Scientific Reasoning in Legal Opinions: Brown v. Board of Education*, 347 U.S. 483 (1954), *overruling Plessy v. Ferguson*, 163 U.S. 537

(1896). The early Supreme Court decision in *Plessy* upheld segregation laws, reasoning that separate but equal accommodations did not create any "badge of inferiority" unless "the colored race [chose] to put that construction on it." In *Brown*, however, the Court overruled its 1896 decision and held that "separate . . . facilities are inherently unequal." Among other reasons, the Court stated that "[a] sense of inferiority affects the motivation of a [segregated] child to learn." The Court added, "Whatever may have been the extent of psychological knowledge at the time of *Plessy v. Ferguson*, this finding is amply supported by modern authority," and it cited seven psychological and sociological publications, experimental or survey-based, all demonstrating the point.

Was the Court's statement, then, that "separate . . . facilities are inherently unequal" a scientific pronouncement or an interpretation of the law (and if the latter, what place did the science have in the opinion)?

[B]   Scientific Models and Mechanisms

SCIENTIFIC MODELS AND THEIR LIMITS

(1) *The Uses of Models.* Much of science consists of deriving "models" from observations or experiments. Boyle's Law, as we have seen, is a concept, or model, superimposed upon our observations of gases. Likewise, the "meatball" vision of an atom, with ball-shaped electrons orbiting a nucleus composed of bigger balls that are protons and neutrons, is a model. It is useful in some ways, inaccurate in others. Models help us, first, to understand the phenomenon that they represent, and second, to predict its characteristics.

(2) *The Map Is Not the Territory, and the Model Is Not the Physical Reality.* Models are to physical reality as maps are to the earth. Good maps distort less than bad ones, but all distort. The standard mercator projection map, showing the earth as a rectangle, enlarges Greenland because it is closer to the pole. Other projections, keeping areas consistent in size, are possible, but they chop the earth into pieces and distort shapes in other ways.

Even a road map fails to capture the shape, size and appearance of intersections, so that it is possible to miss a connection. In the same way, the meatball atom, even as it helps us to see the nucleus in relation to electrons, is inferior to a model recognizing electrons in shells or layers, or better yet, in slurred clouds.

(3) *Occam's Razor: Other Things Being Equal, the Model with the Fewest Number of Arbitrary Elements Ordinarily Is Preferable.* The model must accurately reflect reality, and to the extent it does not, it is defective. But of two models, one containing a large amount of complexity and another less, the simpler is preferable if it describes the territory equally well. This principle sometimes is referred to as "Occam's razor," after the philosopher William of Occam.

(4) *Multiple Models.* In spite of Occam's razor, some phenomena require multiple models. The map-of-the-earth problem mentioned above is an example. A serious geographer might want to keep several projections around for consultation in different situations. Newtonian mechanics, or the classical physics of motion in which matter and energy are conserved and F = ma (force equals mass times acceleration), works well in most earthly conditions but poorly in other conditions, e.g., extreme gravitational fields, in which effects predicted by the theory of relativity become significant.

(5) *The Limits of Models.* At extreme pressures, Boyle's Law may cease to operate even as an approximation. Likewise, at very high or at cold temperatures, the gas may undergo a phase change (oxygen becomes a liquid, for example). One of the characteristics of models is that they cease to operate, even as analogies, beyond their limits of application. Perhaps a better way to put it is that models must be used within their constraints.

EXAMPLES AND PROBLEMS

(1) *How Bad Can a Model Be, and Still Be Useful?: The Example of Light Waves and Photons.* Imagine that a concept gives valid results only part of the time. Is it useful, then? To take a specific example, we have two radically different concepts of light: the wave theory and the particle theory. Wave theory is useful for some purposes, such as explaining color and interference. But particle theory, which conceives of light as a stream of particles called "photons," is better for understanding other phenomena, such as the photoelectric effect.

How can light be a wave, like those that we see in the ocean, and a stream of particles like tiny baseballs, both at the same time? The answer is that it isn't really "like" those things, and waves and particles are mere analogies. These physical analogies to particles and waves are merely the best that human minds can do, to understand this unique phenomenon. We probably will never see either a photon or a light wave, since the required resolution almost by definition makes it impractical to see them using light itself. But how do we know which model to use? Is the choice of which model to use really "scientific?"

(2) *Multiple, Competing Models in Legal Reasoning: The Example of the so-called "Erie Doctrine" in the Law.* In *Erie RR. v. Tompkins*, 304 U.S. 64 (1938), the Supreme Court required federal courts to use federal procedural rules, but for substantive rules of decision, to use state law. The trouble was, it soon turned out that it was hard to tell exactly which laws were "procedural" and which "substantive." The Supreme Court then embarked upon a series of decisions in which it adopted multiple, inconsistent models for distinguishing procedural rules from substantive ones.

First, the Court suggested that any rule that was "outcome determinative" would be substantive. But this didn't work in some cases, because sometimes rules that are obviously procedural can determine the outcome. (They're supposed to.) Later, the Court used a "balancing" of state and federal interests. If the federal interest in having federal law control was stronger, the matter was procedural; if the state's interest, then substantive. But this model worked poorly in some cases, because the balancing was too indeterminate. Since then, the Court has used many other models, including considering all the policy factors underlying its original *Erie* opinion. Question: Is this legal, multiple-model

Ptolemy

reasoning analogous to the multiple-model theories of light?

(3) *Ptolemaic, Advanced Ptolemaic, and Copernican Universes.* In the Second Century A.D., the Alexandrian astronomer Ptolemy publicized a concept of the universe with a fixed earth at its center and the sun, moon, planets and stars rotating about it. Was this model "scientific," given that a great deal of observation could be offered to support it?

In later years, the earth-centered model was refined: The heavenly bodies all were embedded in concentric balls of crystal, to reflect their different distances from the earth. And their rotation (believe it or not) was thought to produce "the music of the spheres." Was this theory scientific?

For a long time, politically correct scientists postulated "epicyclic" orbits for the planets. These were necessary because observations showed that planets sometimes backtracked in the sky. An epicycle is the shape traced by a point on a circle that rolls about the circumference of another circle, and it explained the so-called "retrogression" of the planets. But again, it failed to account for observations, leading scientists to construct epicycles within epicycles. One factor driving this conceptualization was the church, which preferred the existing earth-centered model over the sun-centered Copernican model to such an extent that it punished heretics, including Galileo, for efforts to challenge it. Was the use of epicycles, then, "scientific"?

(4) *The Copernican View: Was It More Scientific?* Finally, Nicolaus Copernicus's model won out, featuring a solar system that had the sun at its center. But some scientists still erred in seeing planetary orbits as circular, whereas today we know them to be elliptical. Was the basic Copernican model, then, unscientific? And, of course, Copernicus failed to adjust orbits for such phenomena as gravitational influences of close-passing bodies or solar wind. Does the lack of an accounting for such future knowledge make our current view unscientific?

Nicolaus Copernicus

(5) *If We Were to Revise the Earth-Centered Ptolemaic Universe With Mathematics Such That It Accurately Conformed to Planetary Motions, Would the Result Be Scientific?* The Ptolemaists were justified in the sense

that all motion is relative. It makes as much sense from the standpoint of mechanics to regard the sun as moving with respect to the earth as to regard the earth moving with respect to the sun. It also makes for more complicated mathematics to describe the "motion" of the sun "around" the earth, but theoretically, it could be done. And if that could be done, then theoretically, we could describe the motions of the planets "around" the earth, with still more complex mathematics. Would such a view of the solar system make a good model, and would it be scientific?

(6) *The Use of Models in Other, Very Different Fields: Accounting and Law.* Accountants use "Generally Accepted Accounting Principles" (GAAPs) to determine what is a fixed and what is a contingent liability (and to determine many other questions). But with many GAAP's, the application may be imperfect, because GAAPs are just models, with which accountants must struggle when they do not fit the real financial picture. (Accounting probably is not a science, but the point is that it uses models.) Likewise, the law uses models. Negligence law is defined by "reasonable" conduct--the type of conduct that a reasonable person, in the exercise of ordinary care, would exhibit. Law is not scientific either, but this hypothetical construct of the reasonable person is a model, resembling the kinds of models that are used in science.

MECHANISM: ABDUCTION, RETRODUCTION, AND CHANGE IN SCIENTIFIC THEORY

(1) *The Concept of Mechanism.* Some scientific models are concerned with the "mechanism" of an observed phenomenon, or why it works. But other models are not. Boyle's Law tells us how we can calculate a new pressure for a quantity of gas, for example, if we have changed the volume and temperature. But it does not tell us how or why the relationship exists. Similarly, a chemist might synthesize a benzene derivative using smaller-chain hydrocarbons but know little about intermediate products. And the Copernican model of the solar system does not tell us why the earth maintains such regularity in its path around the sun as opposed to spinning off into interstellar space or crashing into the sun. These questions require a further model, called a mechanism, that explains the observed model.

"Phenomenological" models are those that explain single phenomena (or small ranges of effects). "Fundamental" models, on the other hand, apply universally, or at least to a broad range of phenomena. Kepler's laws of planetary motion, which described the speeding and slowing of these bodies in their elliptical orbits, were phenomenological; Newton's mechanics, which explained why Kepler's laws held true, were more fundamental. The search for mechanisms is, in a sense, an effort to link a phenomenological truth to a fundamental one.

(2) *Abduction and Retroduction.* The models of abduction and retroduction that we encountered in Chapter 1 describe the search for a mechanism. In the case of Boyle's law, we might abduce, for example, that gas molecules at higher temperatures exert more pressure because of faster motion and more collisions, and this concept might lead us to the field called statistical mechanics. This reasoning will lead us to the mechanism underlying Boyle's Law. The mechanism is itself falsifiable, and it leads us to further questions and insights.

WHAT MAKES A GOOD SCIENTIFIC (OR LEGAL) MODEL?

(1) *Tractability, Simplicity, and Empirical Validity: A Basic Theory of Scientific Modeling (or of Other Modeling, Including in the Law).* A basic theory might describe three characteristics of a good scientific model: tractability, simplicity, and empirical validity. The first factor, "tractability," means the amenability of the model to coherent treatment, or its workability. A jumble of uncorrelated experimental results might be empirically accurate, but it would not provide a good model because it would not be tractable. "Simplicity" is the concept related to Occam's razor, above. "Validity" means correspondence to empirical observation.

Notice that this multi-factor theory avoids the trap of exclusive reliance on the views of either the rationalists or the empiricists. It recognizes that a model may be bad because it badly fits the empirical data. But it also recognizes that a model may be bad even though it mirrors reality perfectly, if it is not tractable--particularly if there is a more workable model that entails only an insignificant loss in validity.

After developing this idea, we shall apply it to models in the law.

(2) *Refining the Theory of Scientific Modeling: A Six-Factor Approach.* Perhaps this three-factor approach can be further refined. Tractability consists of at least two factors: communicational tractability, or how well the model can be used to convey ideas from one person to another, and

computational tractability, or the amenability of the model to calculations. Simplicity also involves at least two factors: Occam's razor, or the preference for the fewest number of arbitrary elements, and generality, or the propensity of the model to organize larger rather than smaller amounts of data. Finally, validity consists of at least two elements: close correspondence to empirical observation within the range of its correct application, and clear demarcation of its limits or constraints.

EXAMPLES AND PROBLEMS

(1) *The Uneasy Scientific Relationship Among Correlation, Mechanism, and Causation.* An observed correlation between two variables does not establish a mechanism, and a mechanism does not establish a cause. For example, from a series of observations, we can infer a correlation, such as that the reaction of an acid with a base tends to end in a more neutral solution and a dissolved or precipitated salt. Thus, if calcium hydroxide (CaOH) in water solution is added to sulfuric acid (H_2SO_4), it produces a more neutral solution containing more water molecules (HOH), and it precipitates calcium sulfate ($CaSO_4$). By abduction we can hypothesize a mechanism for this reaction, and we can retroductively test the hypothesized mechanism by experiment: The mechanism, we infer, is that the acid and base dissociate in water to produce hydrogen (H+) and hydroxyl (OH-) ions on the one hand and (Ca++) and (SO_4--) ions on the other, and the last two form the precipitate while the first two produce either combined or dissociated water.

But neither the observed correlation nor the mechanism tell us the "cause" of this reaction. Causation simply is a dicey concept, much more manipulable than either correlations or mechanisms. Does the acid "cause" the reaction? Or the base? Or the water in which they are dissolved?

This example shows why scientists tend to avoid using words such as "cause," preferring to describe correlations and mechanisms. But sometimes scientists do speak in terms of causation, or of "dependent" variables that are influenced by "independent" ones; they usually use these terms carefully, however, and with an awareness of the distortion that can result from them.

(2) *Mechanism as a Heuristic Check Upon Statistical Inferences of Causation in the Law: Comparing the Power-Transmission-and-Cancer Example to the Smoking-and-Cancer Example.* This section is a reminder, once again, of the usefulness of mechanism inquiries as a heuristic for

checking inferences of causation.   Recall the example of high-power transmission line lawsuits based on the fallacy of inferring causation from cancer rates in a few precincts.   As we have seen, it is difficult to perceive reasonable mechanisms for such an inferred relationship. The absence of a reasonable inference of any mechanism by which power lines could have any effect on nearby residents, much less a cancerous one, should have created suspicion about the inferred correlation.

On the other hand, mechanism is only an inference, a heuristic, and it may be improper to debunk a strong inference of correlation merely because the mechanism remains elusive.[10] The smoking-and-cancer example illustrates the fallacy.   For years, tobacco manufacturers resisted any inference of connection between smoking and cancer. What was true, early on, was that absolute proof of a mechanism was lacking, and the tobacco companies therefore vehemently denied that smoking "caused" cancer.

Can you explain why this tobacco strategy might have worked? And can you explain why the inference of correlation between smoking and cancer may have been valid, even without proof of the mechanism, whereas it was not valid in the case of power lines and cancer?

(3) *Applying the Six-Factor Analysis of a Good Scientific Model: Some Examples.*   As we have seen, a scientific model is good if it is readily communicable, suitable for calculations, based on relatively few elements, generally applicable, consistent with observed data, and subject to a clearly defined range of application.   It is a poor model if it is difficult to communicate, hard to calculate, bristling with arbitrary elements, narrowly applicable, inaccurate, and unclear in the limits of its applicability. Consider the following examples and determine whether you agree with them.

(a) *Communicability.* Quantum physics, such as the forest of squiggles known as the Schroedinger Wave Equation,[11] provides a more accurate

---

10   Once again, recall that the National Institutes of Health has left open the possibility of a weak association between power lines and cancer. See Chapter 2, above.

11   The Schroedinger Wave Equation computes energy levels in electron shells. Are you ready?

$$\epsilon\psi = -\frac{h^2}{8\pi^2 m_e}\sum_{i=1}^{n}\left(\frac{\partial^2\psi}{\partial x_i^2} + \frac{\partial^2\psi}{\partial y_i^2} + \frac{\partial^2\psi}{\partial z_i^2}\right) - Ze^2\psi\sum_{i=1}^{n}\frac{1}{r_i} + e^2\psi\sum_{i,j>i}^{n}\frac{1}{r_{ij}}$$

The Schroedinger method uses what my Physical Chemistry text calls "familiar mathematics"(!), although it also says that this "simplified" equation is "such a bad approximation that it is of no value."

description of the behavior of electrons than does the simplistic ball-and-stick or "meatball" model of an atom. Nevertheless, the meatball model may be better for some uses. Why?

(b) *Calculability.* Pi (π) is an irrational number, and therefore all we can do in the real number system is to approximate or model it. For some uses, we might need a precisely refined model of π, with lots of decimal places, such as 3.141628 . . . , although even if we were to calculate it out to a hundred decimal places it still would be provably wrong (can you see why)? For many other uses, it is customary to model π by using the simple fraction, 22/7, which is close to 3.141628 but less exact, because it is simpler to use in calculations. When, then, might 22/7 sometimes be a better model for π, than the more accurate 3.141628?

(c) *Simplicity.* As we have seen, it might be possible to develop a series of equations that accurately would describe the solar system using the Ptolemaic model, i.e., with the sun circling the earth. Why would this model be inferior to the Copernican model, even if we used equations sophisticated enough to accurately describe the actual celestial motions?

(d) *Generality.* Even assuming we could develop an accurate description of how known, existing solar system bodies move by sophisticated equations built on the Ptolemaic theory, this model might function poorly in describing other phenomena, such as the motion of a newly discovered comet. Can you explain why this makes it an inferior model?

(e) *Validity.* For some usages, Newtonian mechanics, in which F = ma (force equals mass times acceleration) and in which energy is conserved within closed systems, may be highly accurate. But Newtonian mechanics are a poor model when relativistic effects are significant, such as close to a black hole. Why might this be considered a defect in the Newtonian model?

(f) *Demarcation.* The taxonomy of classifying a whale as a mammal along with a horse is valid in some respects, in that it allows us to infer that the two are alike: they are warm-blooded, hairy, and viviparous. Beyond the definitional characteristics, however, the mammal model does not tell us very precisely which other characteristics may or may not be similar: the whale's size and ability to remain under water, the horse's hooves, mane, and running ability. We can't really know whether any given prediction we make about the whale, based on the horse, is going to prove true. Why might this be considered a defect in the model?

(4) *Models in the Law: Definition, Quality, and Scientific Method.* When we articulate a legal doctrine, in a sense we are using a model, just as scientists do. The definition of negligence, based on the reasonable person,

is a model. The general-rule model doesn't work in all instances (e.g., when we try to evaluate the negligence of a disabled person). Knowing how to apply the model, how to measure real facts against it, and when to reject the model, is indispensable for a lawyer. In this respect, law resembles scientific method. And how do we tell whether a legal doctrine is "good" or "bad"? Perhaps by the same three criteria (or the six we have derived here from the three): tractability (can it be applied by courts and by those subject to it?), simplicity (are its effects and meaning relatively non-complex?), and accuracy (does it get people to behave as society aimed for them to?).

§ 9.04 Sciences and Humanities: The Examples of History, Ethics, and Economics

HISTORICAL METHODS AND LEGAL REASONING: IS HISTORY SCIENTIFIC?

(1) *"Soft" Sciences and Nonsciences.* Next, let us consider some fields of knowledge that conform less rigorously to scientific criteria. We shall concentrate most heavily on the study of history, since it has a particularly rich record of comparison to, and distinction from, the scientific method.

(2) *Historical Views of History: As Linear, as Purposive, as Cyclical, as Dialectical, and as Comparative.* One way to view history is to see it simply as reporting a series of happenings in time. This "linear" model, sometimes called the "speculative" theory of history, is a first-order view that reports events as purely empirical data, unconnected to each other. A second-order model, sometimes called the "critical" or "analytical" approach, uses procedures and categorizations in an effort to infer causes, effects, relationships and even "laws" of history. One early view was that of St. Thomas Aquinas and other theological historians who, up to the time of the Enlightenment, expressed a "teleological," or purposive, theological theory of history, which was dependent on human development by a higher wisdom. In this view, humankind continuously advances owing to God's plan. This theological view is not common among academic historians today, but arguably it represented a step from purely speculative or linear history toward the integration of events.

Yet another view of history is that it is "cyclical," with civilizations going through predictable cycles of growth, stability, decline and decay. In an earlier chapter we saw Hegel's and Marx's views of history as "dialectical" struggle. Finally, history as a "comparative" endeavor sees events not necessarily as cyclical or dialectical but as comparable across time, so that two civilizations acted upon by similar internal or external influences can be expected to exhibit similar effects.

(3) *The Scientific View of History After the Enlightenment: From Mill to Spengler and Toynbee.* Sir Isaac Newton and his contemporaries profoundly influenced all disciplines, not just the physical sciences. During the Enlightenment, therefore, historians rejected linear and purposive approaches in favor of a history that would frame and test hypotheses in the manner of the sciences, evolving laws of history as a result. John Stuart Mill adhered to this view. So did Giambattista Vico, who labeled his historical work Scienza Nuova, or "New Science," and he even claimed that history could be better understood scientifically than the physical world that God had created (since the world of nations had been created by humankind, who therefore could "hope to know" it). Vico's was a cyclical view of history, but with a tinge of theology, seeing historical development as progressive overall because of a divine providence.

In contrast, Oswald Spengler's *Decline of the West*, published in the early 1900's, borrowed even more clearly from science. Spengler's cyclical view of history was quasi-biological, with civilizations deterministically passing through stages of establishment, growth, stability, decline and death. Yet another scientific view was that of Arnold Toynbee, who published his enormous *A Study of History* in multiple volumes from 1934 to 1961. While rejecting linear and progressive views as well as cyclical theories, Toynbee's work was inductive, in that it compared civilizations by

Oswald Spengler

observation of similar causes and effects. This comparative approach, Toynbee claimed, enabled him to induce hypotheses and support them as laws according to a "scientific approach to human affairs."

(4) *The Counter-Scientific Movement: Explaining History as Interpretations of Thoughts and Actions by Purposive Human Agents.* Other philosophers of history rejected both the linear and the scientific views in favor of an "interpretive" idea of history. History can be understood, they

argued, only in the sense that historians can explain it, and this interpretive function, rather than scientific analysis, is what makes history meaningful.

British historian R. G. Collingwood, for example, argued that history should be liberated from "pupilage to natural science." The subject matter, he maintained, was the actions of humans as purposive agents, and therefore the historian's task was to illuminate the thinking behind these actions, or the climates of opinion that brought historical events about. According to Collingwood, this task required imagination and interpretation, not scientific induction.

(5) *The Twentieth Century: Comparing the Positivists or Logical Empiricists to the Empathy School of History.* Thus, there has been and still is a struggle about the discipline of history, featuring on one side those who see it as borrowing the methods of the sciences, and on the other side those who view it as imaginatively interpretive. Nineteenth-century Scottish philosopher David Hume, for example, argued that inquiry into historical causation could only mean that two events stood in a relationship so that they could be compared by induction to other, similar pairs of events. During the 1900's, the "positivists" carried this idea forward: An inference of cause and effect had to be based on a general inference of relationships between analogous historical events. This positivist, logical-empirical, or quasi-scientific view attempted objectivity and tried to avoid imaginative interpretation.

On the other side were the "empathy" historians, who attempted an understanding ("Verstehenung") of the thinking behind human actions. Positivists regarded this empathy method as anathema, while the empathy school objected to the positivist's assumption of a high degree of regularity in human events that obliterated the particularity of individual events. Empathy, the empathists explained, was not a touchy-feely concept, as the word might sound, but rather dealt with ascertaining the intellectual climate that produced events. Despite the positivist's disdain, these historians argued, this kind of understanding could be inquired into as objectively as comparisons between cultures and events, but without ignoring their uniqueness.

(6) *Historical Method: Sources, Documentation, Principles of Explication, and Objectivity.* Modern views of historical method emphasize documentation and the reliability of sources. Because of the interpretive

function, original sources are preferred. Modern views also govern principles of explication: provable hypotheses, defended with evidence in a way that accounts for opposing inferences. Some philosophers have argued that "objectivity" comes from these methods. Others argue that objectivity, if attainable at all, is a matter of degree and is specific to a given work, because the historian's predilections inevitably influence the result, and they may be a greater determinant than the method.

EXAMPLES AND PROBLEMS

(1) *Is History, Then, "Scientific"?: The Answer Depends Upon One's Concepts of History and of Science--and Can Influence Our View of the Philosophy of Law.* The positivists' or logical-empiricists' view of history is that it objectively uses empirical data to make generalizations by induction. This sounds like scientific method. Is it? The empathists, on the other hand, see the imposition of interpretation as a departure from scientific criteria. But one also can argue that empathy theory also is scientific, but that it just has a greater conceptual ingredient than the positivists would prefer. Is this view correct?

In a later chapter, we shall consider jurisprudence, or the philosophy of the law. Certain divisions among legal philosophers resemble divisions among historians.

(2) *Evaluations and Moral Inputs into History.* The positivists regarded evaluative inputs, such as moral evaluations of events, as inappropriate. Can you see how this view conforms to the positivist philosophy? (Other historians have seen evaluative inputs as useful, and indeed, as inevitable.)

(3) *An Example: The Fall of the Roman Empire.* Some historians have concluded that the fall of the Roman empire was caused by internal factors such as cultural or economic weaknesses. Others have seen it as the result of external influences, including the ascendancy of Vandals, Goths and Visigoths who overran the Empire. How might individual historical philosophies and historical methods determine which of these views a particular historian happens to hold?

(4) *Normative and Interpretive Studies, From Law to Game Theory to Ethics to Economics: Are They Scientific?* Later chapters in this book will look at game theory, which studies rational strategies of players in interactive

situations. Although it is logical and mathematical, game theory is not testable or falsifiable, because it prescribes what a rational actor in a given situation ought to do as a matter of strategy, not what the actor will do. In other words, game theory is "normative" (ought) rather than "descriptive" (will). Therefore, an empiricist holding Popper's view would regard game theory as nonscientific, whereas a rationalist, regarding concept as more important than empiricism, might disagree. Can you explain these conclusions?

To make matters more complex, psychologists have studied how experimental subjects conform or deviate from game-theory strategies. These experiments seem to fit even the empiricist's concept of science, even if the underlying game theory does not. Can you explain why?

Ethics is another kind of normative study, exemplified by the works of Mill or Kant. Most people would not call ethics "scientific." But could it be so considered? And finally, economics is yet another field that occupies the gap between the sciences and the humanities. To what extent, then, is economics "scientific"?

(5) *Uses in the Law of Empathetic History: Originalist Interpretations of Texts, Including Constitutions.* One way to interpret ambiguities in a text is to consider the thinking, climate of opinion, and intentions of the drafters or framers of the text. In a later chapter, we shall see that this historical method is not the only way to resolve questions about a document. Some scholars argue, however, that historical interpretation based on original intent is the superior manner of interpreting the United States Constitution. This view gives weight to the empathy theory of history that the positivists so disparaged. Can you explain why this theory of originalism arguably depends upon an empathetic theory of history?

(6) *The Hearsay Rule of Evidence, the Court's Insistence on Perceptual Knowledge, and Historical Method.* The courts enforce a general rule against the reception of hearsay as evidence. Although it has many exceptions, this rule buttresses a requirement of first-hand knowledge. Other rules force most witnesses to testify about their perceptions, with no more interpretive input than is helpful to understanding. Can you explain how these rules of inquiry parallel the ideals of historical method? Perhaps this conclusion is tautological, since a major task of the courts is historical: the accurate reconstruction and causal analysis of past events.

Chapter 10
Jurisprudence

Legal Theory, Rules, and Interpretation

> *"[L]aw, when it merits the synonym justice, is based on reason and insight."*-- *Justice William J. Brennan, Jr., Constitutional Adjudication and the Death Penalty.*

> *"The life of the law has not been logic. It has been experience."--Justice Oliver Wendell Holmes, Jr., The Common Law*

§ 10.01   What This Chapter Is About

LAW, JUSTICE, RULES, AND TEXTS

(1) *Jurisprudence: Formalism and Instrumentalism, Positivism and Natural Rights--and Contemporary Issues.* We now shift from scientific reasoning to legal reasoning. Jurisprudence sometimes is said to be the "science" of the law, although it hardly is scientific; "theory" of the law might be a better statement. In this chapter, we examine certain historical perspectives on jurisprudence, and we examine some contemporary views, from what is called "critical legal studies" to "feminist jurisprudence." Just

as science has felt the tug-of-war between empiricists and rationalists, so has the very different field of jurisprudence, as the statements of Justices Brennan and Holmes demonstrate above.

(2) *Legal Interpretation of Texts and Documents.* A closely related, but technically separate, part of the chapter concerns interpretive methods. These range from "hermeneutics" or literary techniques (particularly those used for reading Scriptures) to extra-textual reasoning from history, doctrine, policy and ethics.

§ 10.02   Some Basic Concepts of Jurisprudence

[A]   Formalism and Instrumentalism

DISTINGUISHING BETWEEN FORMALISM
AND INSTRUMENTALISM

(1) *"Instrumentalism" or "Functionalism" Is a Basic Jurisprudential Approach, as Distinguished from "Formalism."* Formalism conceives of law as pre-defined rules to be rigorously applied in accordance with deductive logic. If the definition of a legal concept is clearly set out, the formalist would apply it exactly, undistracted by purposes or consequences. On the other hand, the instrumentalist or functionalist feels less rigorously bound by the formal elements of the definition and seeks instead to discern the purposes, intent, consequences, or values underlying a legal doctrine and to interpret the doctrine in accordance with those indications.

(2) *An Example from the Supreme Court's Separation-of-Powers Cases.* For example, in *INS v. Chadha*, 462 U.S. 919 (1983), the majority of the Supreme Court used a jurisprudence of formalism when it struck down a law providing for a "legislative veto," by which a single House of Congress could countermand an administrative decision. Chief Justice Burger's majority opinion held that the legislative veto was inconsistent with literal clauses in the Constitution that required bicameral action in both Houses of Congress, coupled with presentment to the President for veto, to change a law. This approach of Chief Justice Burger can be characterized as literalist or formalist.

This is especially so when it is compared with Justice White's dissent in the same case, which instead used a functionalist or instrumental approach.

Justice White concluded that the purposes of the separation of powers were satisfied by the particular legislative veto in question, in that the result was that each of the Houses of Congress as well as the executive necessarily had to concur in countermanding the administrative decision, even though not through the traditional bicameral and presentment methodology. And therefore, Justice White's more instrumental or functional approach would have upheld the legislative veto.

EXAMPLES AND PROBLEMS

(1) *A Murder Statute, Considered by Formalists and Instrumentalists.* Imagine that your state has a murder statute that resembles the murder provision of the Model Penal Code. This Code defines murder as "recklessly causing the death of" another person (see Chapter 1). In an appeal to the state supreme court, the defendant argues that his act does not constitute murder. Contrast the approaches that might be used by a formalist and by an instrumentalist and evaluate the legitimacy of each approach.

(2) *The "Penumbra" Reasoning in Griswold v. Connecticut*, 381 U.S. 479 (1965). Justice Douglas's majority opinion in the *Griswold* case struck down a statute that banned birth-control devices. Justice Douglas examined the First, Third, Fourth, Fifth, Ninth and Fourteenth Amendments; he then reasoned that these created "penumbras" or shadows that "help give them life and substance;" and from these penumbras, he derived a broad "right of privacy" that is not expressed in the Constitution.

Justice Black dissented: "One of the most effective ways of diluting or expanding a constitutionally guaranteed right is to substitute for the crucial guarantee another word or words, more or less flexible and more or less restricted in meaning." Can you characterize the *Griswold* reasoning of Justices Douglas and Black as either formalist or instrumentalist?

[B] Natural Law and Positivism

THE DISTINCTIONS BETWEEN NATURAL LAW AND POSITIVISM

(1) *Natural Law: Discernible by Reason, Independently of Particular Political Processes.* Natural law duties and natural rights are a legacy of Roman law, among other sources. The concept is that people are endowed

with rights and subject to duties that transcend the political regime in which they find themselves. "[A]ll men are created equal," says the Declaration of Independence, and they are "endowed by their Creator with certain inalienable rights," including "life, liberty and the pursuit of happiness."

These words of Thomas Jefferson did not depend upon the promulgation of rights by any sovereign, because they were "inalienable," established by the "Creator." In other words, they were natural rights. Precisely which duties and rights are "natural" is a matter for deduction by reason, and the details always will be subject to debate. But reason will discern certain basic rights as natural rights--or, so goes the theory.

(2) *Positivism.* Positivism is a contrasting view, in which legal norms proceed not from nature or reason but from a command issued and enforced by a duly recognized sovereign. The mere statement by a person or group of norms that they accept through reason does not convert their claims into law; that path leads to self-interestedness, amorphous argumentation, conflicts, and ultimately anarchy, or so a positivist would reason. Instead, an edict by an established king, or better yet a bill passed by Congress, signed by the President and containing penalties for violation, has the better claim to obedience. Such a norm has the status of "positive law."

EXAMPLES AND PROBLEMS

(1) *Supreme Court Justices Iredell and Chase: Their Debate About Natural Law and Positivism.* In *Calder v. Bull*, 3 U.S. (3 Dall.) 386 (1798), Justice Chase set out an expansive philosophy: "The people of the United States erected their constitutions, or forms of government, to establish justice. . . . An act of the legislature (for I cannot call it a law) contrary to the great first principles of the social compact, cannot be considered a rightful exercise of legislative authority. . . . It is against all reason and justice for a people to entrust a legislature with such power; and therefore, it cannot be presumed that they have done it."

But Justice Iredell differed sharply: "[s]ome speculative jurists have held, that a legislative act against natural justice must, in itself, be void; but I cannot think that any court of justice would possess a power to declare it so. . . . The ideas of natural justice are regulated by no fixed standard; the ablest and the purest men have differed upon the subject. . . . There are then but two lights, in which the subject can be viewed. 1st. if the legislature pursue the authority delegated to them, their acts are valid. 2d. if they transgressed the boundaries of that authority, their acts are invalid. . . ."

What are the difficulties of Chase's position? Perhaps less obviously, what are the defects in Justice Iredell's position (can one properly read a Constitution without natural law, if its drafters believed in natural law)?

(2) *Chase as the "Better Prophet," Iredell as the Better Rhetorician?* Consider the following: "In form, the Supreme Court has adopted the views of Justice Iredell and ruled that it only may invalidate acts of the legislative and executive branches on the basis of specific provisions of the Constitution. In substance, however, the beliefs of Justice Chase have prevailed as the Court continually has expanded its bases for reviewing the acts of other branches of government." J. Nowak, R. Rotunda & J. Young, *Constitutional Law* 426 (3d ed. 1986). Do you agree?

(3) *Individuals' "Right" to Define "the Meaning of Life" and of "the Universe" as a Basis for Their Right to Abortion--Natural Law or Positivism? Planned Parenthood v. Casey*, 505 U.S. 833 (1992). In the *Casey* decision, Justices O'Connor, Kennedy, and Souter's Joint Opinion for the Court upholds the general right to abortion which earlier had been established in *Roe v. Wade*, 410 U.S. 113 (1973). Part of the Court's reasoning inferring this right as a Constitutional requirement was the assertion that individuals have a right to define "the meaning of life" and of "the universe."

Is this natural law reasoning, and can it be justified as such? Or is it positivist, in that it is promulgated by a recognized branch of government, interpreting a positive constitutional provision (the flexible Due Process Clause)? Another question: Is the Court's pronouncement about the meaning of life likely to be accepted by skeptics as sound, or is it sophistry?

[C]   The Legal Realists and Their Antecedents and Posterity: Early Twentieth Century Jurisprudence

FROM LANGDELL'S FORMAL LOGIC TO HOLMES'S EMPHASIS ON EXPERIENCE

(1) *What Is Jurisprudence: A "Science" or "Sociology" of Law?* Jurisprudence sometimes is seen as the study of the origins of law or of its

historical roots. More grandiose claims center on a "science" of law, in which study produces empirically derived principles. Similarly, "sociological" jurisprudence studied actual social effects of legal principles and attempted to shape them so that they reflected the true goals of the society. A more modest view of jurisprudence is that it analyzes differences in the results of thinking by different lawgivers or judges.

(2) *Langdell's Case Method (or Rather, Court-Opinion Method) and the Derivation of Formal Principles from Significant Decisions: Does the Court Opinion Method Shortchange Law Students?* During the late 1800's, Christopher Langdell, Dean of the Harvard Law School, led a revolution against the textual-exposition method by which, instead of learning from books that set out explanations of principles in the manner of a college geography or algebra text, law students instead would study a series of actual court decisions. They would infer legal principles from actual observations of their operation in court decisions, much as a scientist would infer empirical laws from observations of experiments.

For Langdell, this meant observing consistent formal principles. If there was a perceived inconsistency between a court's decision in *Smith v. Jones* and that in *Brown v. Green*, it was necessary to discover a principled difference. In this view, the common law was a constant, predictable set of principles that judges discovered and applied, rather than an evolutionary process that depended on individual facts.

A debate is beginning about whether Langdell's method shortchanges students. Perhaps its persistence in law schools is a historical accident. Listen to Dean Nancy Rapoport, of the University of Houston Law Center, in her leadership of her law school: "[W]e need to rethink our approach to legal education . . . . [T]he old (i.e., 'Harvard') way of teaching law is not the right way to train Twenty-First Century lawyers, and . . . we're sending our graduates out into the real world without the [competencies] lawyers need." UH Law Center Dean's Report 2001.

And even during Langdell's time, there were critics, although of a different kind.

(3) *Critiques of Langdell's Court-Opinion Formalism: Pound's Sociological Jurisprudence and Holmes's "Experience" Model.* On the one hand, Langdell's approach arguably improved over existing methods by

studying the "real" meaning of the law. On the other hand, Langdell's rigorous formalism was unrealistic. Its contrived efforts to explain all differences by syllogistic logic from formal first principles obscured the importance of fact differences, as well as the evolutionary, self regenerating nature of common law adjudication. A later Harvard Dean, Roscoe Pound, developed a sociological approach that recognized the need to change legal rules over time to achieve the effects that society needed: a kind of social-engineering approach.

Professor and later Justice Oliver Wendell Holmes laid the foundation for the later legal realists with several succinct, felicitously written criticisms of Langdell. "A page of history is worth a volume of logic," Holmes wrote. And, famously, "The life of the law has not been logic. It has been experience." He explained: "The felt necessities of the times, the prevalent moral and political theories, . . . even the prejudices which judges share with their fellow men, have a good deal more

Oliver Wendell Holmes

to do than the syllogism in determining the rules by which men should be governed."

EXAMPLES AND PROBLEMS

(1) *Inductive and Deductive Logic in Langdell's Formalism: Syllogistic Approaches.* Langdell's method appears to use induction to derive first principles from judicial opinions, then it applies these principles syllogistically to new cases. Can you explain these observations, using the exposition of logic (and the "IRAC" method) contained in Chapter 1 above?

(2) *Is Holmes Anti-Logical, or Nihilistic? Holmes's Positivism.* Holmes generally is regarded as a positivist rather than a natural-law exponent. Can you see why, from the quotations above? Also, it perhaps appears that Holmes is more opposed to formal logic than Langdell, or perhaps more nihilistic. Is this so, or is his logic simply different?

THE LEGAL REALISTS AND THE PROCESS SCHOOL

(1) *Llewellyn and the Legal Realists of the '20's and '30's.* The legal realists took Holmes's critique of Langdell even farther. One of the leading realist scholars, Professor Karl Llewellyn, for example, wrote that what "officials do about disputes is, to my mind, the law itself." The realists' view was that external influences shaped the law, rather than first principles. A judge was not qualitatively different from a legislator, in that the judge's life experiences determined outcomes.

For example, the Supreme Court's decisions of that era tended to invalidate restrictions on free enterprise, labor legislation, and other democratic enactments favored by the working class. The legal realists' view was that such outcomes resulted not from an excess of formalism that could be cured by sociological jurisprudence, but instead, from the membership of the Justices in the upper social class, their life experience as beneficiaries of capital, and their educations in institutions of similar values.

(2) *The Influence of the Legal Realists.* The realists criticized the formalists as unrealistic and, in return, were themselves criticized as anarchists and nihilists. But their influence, as they expanded through the academy and into the judiciary, was enormous, even upon today's world. Now it is commonplace for Presidents and senators to investigate thoroughly the background of a nominee to the Supreme Court. Our recognition of the outcome-determinative effects of the justices' culture, beliefs and experiences traces to the legal realists.

(3) *The Process School's Response to (or Refinement of) Legal Realism.* The realist movement had been centered at the Yale Law School. (Still today, Yale perhaps is more concerned with multidisciplinary approaches to legal theory than some other schools, and arguably less with preparation for entry into the profession, although the extent of this observation is debatable.)

From Harvard, the home of Langdell and Pound, came the counterrevolution of the legal process theorists. These thinkers recognized the contribution made by the legal realists, but they saw great danger in accepting a jurisprudence of indeterminacy that left decisions to judges' idiosyncratic preferences. Even if judges' backgrounds were influential, as the realists claimed, that did not mean that nakedly political decisionmaking by judges was tolerable. Later historians have traced this insight partially to the influences of the World Wars, to the political behavior of fascist judges, and to the concern that similar jurisprudence could arise here.

Professors Henry Hart and Albert Sacks proposed "process" limits to obviate these results: procedural rules that could be followed with universal regularity, formal constraints on decisionmaking, and requirements of explanation by authoritative principles. The process school reintroduced formal constraints through procedural mechanisms.

EXAMPLES AND PROBLEMS

(1) *The "Brandeis Brief"--Using Legislative Facts to Influence Judicial Decisions: The Example of Brown v. Board of Education*, 347 U.S. 483 (1954). How does a legal realist write a brief for the Supreme Court? Not by mere citation of authority. Instead, the "Brandeis brief," named after successful Supreme Court practitioner and later Justice Louis Brandeis, also includes "legislative" facts. It marshals statistical, economic or sociological materials to influence the justices' extra-legal thinking.

Perhaps the most famous use of this technique was in *Brown v. Board of Education*, which rejected separate-but-equal schools. As we saw in the preceding chapter (on science), the plaintiffs in *Brown* used psychological studies demonstrating that segregation was not equal but rather a badge of inferiority. The Court agreed and cited the sociological studies in its opinion. Can you trace this kind of advocacy to the legal realists? Later commentators, however, have criticized the Court's reliance on sociologists' conclusions. Can you guess the critics' arguments?

(2) *Federal Sentencing Guidelines and the Legal Process School.* Today, the Federal Sentencing Guidelines provide rules for determining sentence lengths, depending on aspects of the crime and of the offender. For example, the magnitude of the victim's loss, managerial participation in a group crime, and the defendants' prior criminal record, as well as numerous other specified factors, each influence the sentence in quantitatively defined ways. The trial judge still has limited discretion, but this discretion over sentencing is constrained by the guidelines.

This present system differs sharply from earlier federal sentencing, in which the judge had discretion to sentence any offender to any sentence within the broad legislatively defined range for the offense, such as from five years' confinement to life imprisonment. The earlier regime produced large apparent disparities in sentences in similar cases, which seemed to depend on judges' personalities. In addition, it widely was suspected that disparities might reflect differences in race or other unacceptable criteria. Can you see how the Federal Sentencing Guidelines might be viewed as an outgrowth of the process school's response to the legal realists?

§ 10.03   Contemporary Jurisprudence

[A]   "Critical" Movements: Feminist Jurisprudence, Critical Legal Studies, and Critical Race Theory

FEMINIST AND CRITICAL JURISPRUDENCE

(1) *One of the Historical Beginnings of Modern Feminine Jurisprudence: The Reaction to Kohlberg's Experimental Observation of Statistical Differences in Moral Thinking among Men and Women.* Social Psychologist Lawrence Kohlberg was an exponent of the moral development school, discussed in an earlier chapter. His experiments consisted of confronting subjects with moral dilemmas and characterizing the nature of their responses to determine their moral developments. From these observations, he determined that there were several fixed stages of moral development, from the lowest, simplistic egocentrism, to the highest, more complex views.

And Kohlberg noticed a statistical difference between men and women. Despite individual differences, he concluded that men statistically were more likely to reach what he saw as the higher, more complex levels of moral development. Women, in larger numbers, avoided the use of abstract moral determinants. For example, when confronted with the trolley dilemma or organ-donor problem of a preceding chapter, women tended to compromise the constraints, suggesting such solutions as the removal of all the threatened individuals from the trolley tracks. If asked whether a starving person could steal bread, greater percentages of women could be counted on to respond by avoiding the dilemma--by advocating a visit to a soup kitchen, or the like.

(2) *Gilligan's Feminist Response: A "Different Voice."* There were several possible ways to disagree with Kohlberg's conclusions, including rejecting his observations. For example, one could take the position that the differences reflected social influences upon girls, whose families and cultures

still treat them differently from boys, even though Kohlberg had made efforts to control this variable.

Carol Gilligan, one of Kohlberg's co-workers, also disagreed with Kohlberg, but in a different way. Her insight was that women's thinking was not "inferior" to men's, merely because women tended to avoid or compromise moral dilemmas, or because they emphasized personal relationships rather than absolute rights. Instead, such thinking merely reflected women's "different voice."

Carol Gilligan

(3) *The Varieties of Feminist Jurisprudence, from Relational Concerns to Anti-Subordination.* Gilligan's psychological insight was an inspiration for a movement reflecting a wide variety of legal approaches. Some feminists emphasize the effect of law on relationships, seeking to preserve institutions that foster communication, compromise, interdependence and tolerance rather than abstract rules or absolute rights. A different concern is that of feminists who seek to avoid subordination on the basis of sex or gender. Professor Catharine MacKinnon's feminist anti-pornography proposals are an example: Although the existing definition of obscenity requires the absence of serious literary, artistic, scientific or similar value, MacKinnon would additionally define illegal pornography in terms of graphic sexual subordination.

It should be added that most feminists do not advocate the use of gender as a discriminant, nor do they usually justify their principles by appeals to outcomes benefitting individual women over individual men. MacKinnon's proposal, for example, would suppress pornography that sexually subordinates men as well as women. What is "feminist" about this jurisprudence is the difference in moral voice, such as the argument that freedom of pornographic speech should not be absolute but rather balanced by relational concerns such as opposition to sexual subordination. Another qualification is that one does not need to be female to accept any given feminist theory.

(4) *Critical Legal Studies and Critical Race Theory.* Critical Legal Studies ("CLS") is a jurisprudence that seeks to "deconstruct" existing law. To deconstruct means to demonstrate that a given set of legal principles really

is a political tool used by powerful members of society to protect their positions against disadvantaged citizens. Deconstruction includes demonstrations that various legal rules actually are indeterminate despite their appearance of formalism, that they include imbedded preferences for politically established parties despite facades of neutrality, that they are designed to disguise their true meanings so as to preserve their one-sidedness, and that they embody concealed contradictions and false dichotomies.

Critical Race Theory, as its name implies, is a variant that deconstructs laws with reference to their tendency to preserve white dominance over persons of color.

(5) *The Reaction to CLS.* One might see the "Crits" as carrying the work of the legal realists to another level. One might also see them as facilitating a more egalitarian version of the law. Instead, CLS has had little discernible influence on legal institutions.

Perhaps this is so because, as its name implies, the thrust of Critical Legal Studies has been deconstruction rather than the synthesis of alternatives. Interestingly, however, the reaction to CLS seems to run deeper than this, in that some of the most vigorous denunciations have come from academics. Dean Paul Carrington, for example, suggested in the mid-1980's that CLS adherents should resign from law school faculty positions because they allegedly rejected the discipline that they purportedly taught. Even professors who countered Dean Carrington, on the ground that academic freedom prohibited efforts to exclude Crits, usually made plain their disagreement with CLS on the merits.

EXAMPLES AND PROBLEMS

(1) *"Relational" Contracts and Alternate Dispute Resolution: Are They Related to Feminist Jurisprudence?* Long-term contracts that require frequent adjustment and reinterpretation sometimes are called "relational" contracts. For example, twenty-year energy supply contracts have been common through certain periods in American industry, requiring adaptation to changed circumstances. Perhaps a relational interpretation of such a contract is appropriate, favoring ongoing compromise rather than hard-edged entitlements that might financially destroy one party or the other.

An agreed child custody decree is another kind of contract that may control the parties over two unpredictable decades or more. Is a relationship-preserving reading of these long-term, necessarily adjustable contracts justifiable by reference to feminist jurisprudence? Another example, perhaps, is mechanisms of alternate dispute resolution such as mediation, which promotes communication, cooperation and compromise rather than coercive adversariness. Is this device consistent with feminist jurisprudence?

(2) *Will Feminist Jurisprudence Disproportionately Hurt Women?: Collecting the Child Support.* The most frequent kinds of contract disputes, in which women of modest means are likely to find themselves, involve child support and alimony enforcement. (The support duty generally is embodied in a judicial decree but usually is also contractual.) The opposing disputants disproportionately are men with greater resources who can resist enforcement by such ambiguous, relational and contextual defenses as estoppel, ratification, novation, offset, substantial performance, reformation, or a host of other fact-dependent defenses that are expensive to litigate.

Perhaps women collecting child support would benefit from more hard-edged, rights-bound, formal rules of contract enforcement. Is it possible that feminist jurisprudence, paradoxically, might hurt women?

(3) *The Subjects of CLS Positions: Property, Contracts and the Elusive Public-Private Distinction.* A CLS adherent might attempt to demonstrate that protections of private property or contract entitlements really involve public rights because the state defines and enforces them; given this state involvement, the public-private distinction is a false dichotomy, which can be unmasked as a political device to perpetrate concentrated wealth. There certainly is at least some degree of truth that some people would see in such a position, isn't there? How, then, can one account for the lack of widespread acceptance of CLS?

[B]　Economic Analysis of Law

THE LAW AND ECONOMICS MOVEMENT

(1) *Calabresi's Economic Analysis of Tort Law.* Economic analysis has had an important place in the law since the turn of the century, because of the antitrust laws. Then, during the 1960's, Dean Guido Calabresi analyzed risk, tort law and the cost of accidents by using economic theory. Within the same

decade, Ronald Coase developed his famous theorem, which we have seen in an earlier chapter on economics.

These events were catalysts for a movement, the Law and Economics Movement, that was enormously influential and remains so today. The analysis differed from that of, say, Critical Legal Studies, in that it both explained existing legal rules and, perhaps more importantly, persuasively prescribed improvements or advances. The analysis of actual and punitive damages in the preceding chapter is an example.

(2) *The Chicago School: Judges Posner and Easterbrook.* Professor (now Judge) Richard Posner applied economics to subjects throughout the law, from crime and punishment to family law. The University of Chicago Law School became the center for law and economics, as Professor (now also Judge) Frank Easterbrook, together with Posner, wrote about economics and public choice theory.

EXAMPLES AND PROBLEMS

(1) *Applying Economic Analysis to Criminal Law: From Vicious Murders to Computer Viruses.* Instead of viewing crimes without apparent motives as senseless or irrational, Chicago School economists assumed that the actors were like everyone else in seeking to maximize their utility. In this view, a serial killer (and the creator of the Melissa virus) act as they do because they derive a perverse economic utility from their crimes. To be effective, sanctions must capture this perverse utility.

Some members of the Law and Economics school, then, argued that we can develop an economic equation that compares the criminal actor's utility to the mathematically expected deterrent of the sanction, including factors for defects in detection, apprehension, adjudication and application. With statistical techniques such as multiple regression analysis, economists have considered even such apparently non-economic subjects as the deterrent effect of the death penalty. In fact, one researcher, Isaac Ehrlich, used calculations to produce a result of eight (8) deterred murders from the first execution (although admittedly, statistical "noise" exceeded this figure and gave it low reliability).

Isaac Ehrlich

Ehrlich used an equation of the following kind as the basis of his regression analysis, an equation for the prospective criminal's expected utility:

$$EU = (1\text{-}PCON) \, U(C_0) + PCON(1\text{-}PE) \, U(C_1) + PCON.PE \, U(C_2)$$

where EU = expected utility,
    PCON = probability of a murder conviction,
        PE = conditional probability of execution given a murder conviction,
        $U(C_0)$ = utility to the individual if not convicted of a murder,
        $U(C_1)$ = utility to the individual if convicted but not executed,
        $U(C_2)$ = utility to the individual if executed.

Is this kind of analysis useful? Also, would these kinds of analyses be useful in discovering the defects in criminal sanctions generally (e.g., might they demonstrate how enhanced detection rather than severity could produce bigger payoff in a given situation)?

(2) *Public Choice Theory: The Application of Economics to the Actions of Voters, Lawmakers, and Public Bodies.* If economists could explain criminals, why not lawmaking too? Public choice theory examines legal decisionmaking through analysis of institutional effects on political actors' utility or self-interest. We considered portions of public choice theory in an earlier chapter when we encountered Arrow's Theorem.

(3) *Criticisms of the Chicago School's Consequentialism.* Can you anticipate the reactions of critics to the Chicago School? Its earliest products were heavily utilitarian, converting issues of law and justice into matters of economics. Would there be a point at which this approach would cease to be persuasive? Further, the approach emphasized limiting guidance by law and general reliance on private motives. Distributive justice, or more equal allocation of wealth, was not the principal thrust. Such was the power of economic analysis, however, that many critics of the Chicago School themselves used economics to demonstrate how goals such as redistribution could be built into the models.

§ 10.04   Interpretive Jurisprudence

[A]   Approaches to Interpreting Texts

SOME SELECTED MAXIMS OF TEXTUAL INTERPRETATION

(1) *Textual Interpretation--Why Does It Matter?: The Famous "Chicken Contract" Dispute and the Jurisprudence of Interpretation.* As contrasted to our discussion of jurisprudence, above, this section goes in a different direction, examining how lawyers and judges go about interpreting rules, contracts, and other texts.

Why does interpretation matter? It determines one person's entitlements against another. For example, in one famous lawsuit, the contract required delivery of "chickens" by the seller. The buyer claimed that the seller had breached by delivering fryers rather than broilers, which were what the buyer thought the language should be read to require. (The buyer lost, but both sides had credible arguments.)

In such a situation, it is good to have neutral rules for guidance. Some people argue that this is the real stuff of jurisprudence, where the rubber hits the road. How does one resolve a dispute that is based on interpretation of language?

(2) *"Ejusdem Generis" and "Exclusio Alterius": How to Read a List.* The principle of "ejusdem generis," or "similar type," is one of these principles of interpretation. It restricts global language to include only "other" devices that are similar in kind to those listed. Statutes and contracts often contain global lists, which are drafted to include unforeseen specifics by concluding with a general phrase such as "or any other device . . . ."

Thus, imagine that a statute prohibits the personal possession of "a pistol, firearm or other weapon." The defendant is charged under this statute with possessing a device that expels tear gas, and a court must decide whether the statute covers this tear-gas gun. Application of the "ejusdem generis" maxim focuses the inquiry: Is the tear-gas gun analogous to, or "similar in kind," to, a "pistol" or "firearm"? Notice that the maxim does not definitively solve the problem, and both prosecution and defense can make credible arguments by analogy, but it does focus the inquiry.

A separate Latin maxim, "expressio unius exclusio alterius," translates as, "the expression of one excludes the other." Thus, if a contract covers "chickens, ducks, and turkeys," there is a sound argument that it doesn't cover an eagle, because the expression of three other classes of animals that don't include eagles is an implied exclusion of eagles.

(3) *The Entire Document, Non Contradiction, Meaning for Each Word, Specific versus General, and Reasonableness.* In considering whether fryers or broilers are called for, the interpreter should consider the "entire" document. If, for example, a separate clause outside the delivery specifications makes it clear that the "chickens" are for a use that only broilers can fulfill, this clause is an indication that "chickens" should be read to mean "broilers." In other words, one does not read words or clauses in isolation.

A related concept is "non-contradiction": The document is to be read so that internal contradiction is avoided, if that is possible. Also, the interpreter should assume that no clause was inserted uselessly, and therefore an interpretation that gives meaning to each word is preferred. If the seller were to argue, for example, that the use-as-broilers clause should be ignored ("That's just window-dressing"), the meaning-for-each-word maxim contradicts this argument.

Yet another maxim is that the specific controls over the general. If a clause provides that the seller shall deliver "chickens," its generality is overridden by a later clause that says, "all chickens shall be broilers."

Finally, the document is to be interpreted so that it does not produce an unreasonable result. Imagine that the contract language, as a whole, makes clear that the buyer and seller both understood that the buyer had no possible use for fryers, only for broilers. The seller argues, "Well, even if it's clear everybody contemplated broilers, the delivery clause doesn't say so, and it's the buyer's tough luck." This kind of "gotcha" argument is refuted by the interpretation-as-reasonable maxim; it isn't reasonable to interpret the document the way the seller claims.

(4) *Plain Meaning, Extrinsic Evidence, Ambiguity and Merger.* It often is said that the interpreter should follow the "plain language" or "plain meaning" of the text, if there is such a meaning. Why? The parties agreed on the text, but they did not agree on everything they discussed during their negotiations, or on everything that other people in the business might do. Also, resolution on the basis of the text simplifies disputes: The interpreter does not have to go to the (often prohibitive) expense of investigating every

possible conflicting argument. Therefore, "extrinsic evidence," or evidence outside the text, is prohibited if the meaning is plain.

But another maxim says that, if the language is "ambiguous," having two or more reasonable meanings, then the decisionmaker shifts to considering evidence outside the text. Finally, what do contracting parties do if they want to reduce the amount of outside evidence that can be used in interpretation? This can come about, for example, if one party does not fully trust the other and believes that that party may ignore the language and use rejected negotiations to justify an after-the-fact variation. Then, the suspicious party can insert a "merger clause," which provides that the written document is the entire agreement. This "plain language" cannot be contradicted by evidence outside the document and limits the degree to which the other party can claim terms outside of it.

(5) *Intent of the Drafters; Maxims Only; Type of Instrument.* It often is said that these maxims are designed to carry out one overriding goal: to give effect to the intent of the drafters (as opposed to a rewriting of their document by the interpreter). Notice that the maxims are mushy, and they may not produce unambiguous answers. In fact, they often conflict. All they do is focus the interpreter's reasoning.

Also, sometimes it is said that the use of these maxims should depend on the type of document that is being interpreted; a statute passed by Congress to set up an administrative agency, for example, may require a more flexible reading than a mortgage instrument.

EXAMPLES AND PROBLEMS

(1) *The Ninth Amendment and "Expressio Unius."* The Ninth Amendment to the United States Constitution says that the "enumeration . . . of certain rights" in the Bill of Rights "shall not be construed to deny or disparage others retained by the people." Why do you think this Amendment was included? (Which maxim would apply, possibly, to limit the people's rights, if it were not included?)

(2) *"We Must Never Forget That It Is a Constitution We Are Expounding."* These words were written by Chief Justice John Marshall in *McCulloch v. Maryland*, 17 U.S. (4 Wheat.) 316 (1819), to justify an expansive, instrumentalist reading of the powers of Congress. What did he

mean? Why did it make a difference that the language came from "a constitution" rather than from the tax code?

John Marshall

(3) *Gays, the Bible, and the Law: St. Paul's Observation that "Men Committed Shameless Acts with Men and Received in Their Own Persons the Due Penalty for Their Error."* In the Bible, a passage from St. Paul reads as follows: "Men committed shameless acts with men and received in their own persons the due penalty for their error." What does this mean? This phrase is among those cited by some clergy to argue that homosexual behavior is sinful and wrong. Others disagree with this interpretation, believing that the passage means something else.

How can the first group of clergy, those who oppose gay activity, defend their interpretations by using the maxims indicated above? How can those who disagree use the same maxims to defend their opposing views? (Note: You may be inclined simply to conclude that the answer doesn't matter. Who cares about this phrase? But that response is dubious, because this Biblical passage is highly influential; it has affected both public and private reasoning.) Furthermore, as you will see in the next section, interpretation of scripture sometimes has been claimed to be analogous to interpretation of law.

HERMENEUTICS, HOLISTIC APPROACHES, AND THE LAW AND LITERATURE POSITION

(1) *"Hermeneutics" and the Law and Literature Movement.* "Hermeneutics" refers to literary interpretation, particularly of the Bible or other Scriptures. The Law and Literature movement seeks to use methods of interpretation that apply to other kinds of language, particularly literature, in interpreting legal texts or doctrines. Thus, for example, a particular word may not be meant literally but may be broadly symbolic or metaphorical; intent or meaning may be present in broad implications from disparate and seemingly unrelated provisions; a case decision or constitutional provision

may have a larger significance in the manner of an allegory or parable, etc. In this view, one searches for deeper meanings in legal texts just as one reads Milton's poetry, the plays of Shakespeare, or the Book of Genesis.

(2) *Holistic or Clause-by-Clause Interpretation: Dworkin vs. Posner.* To Professor Ronald Dworkin, the whole of a document is more than the sum of its parts; it stands for more than the literal meaning of its clauses. The Constitution, for example, expresses great themes such as liberty or equality that stem not merely from the precise words but from the whole. This approach justifies a broad reading of natural rights. Dworkin's theory, furthermore, is that one necessarily uses a holistic approach, in that one must be using some general philosophy of interpretation to approach the text.

On the other hand, Judge Posner advocates a clause-by-clause approach. He recognizes that context may be determinative and that multiple-clause readings may be illuminating, but he insists that one must interpret the text of say, the Equal Protection Clause by reference to its language, rather than discerning a grand theme of equality and interpreting it independently of the Clause.

EXAMPLES AND PROBLEMS

(1) *In the Law, What Does "the Age of Thirty-Five Years" Mean?: Tushnet's Hypothet.* Imagine that, with his saffron robes flowing in the wind, a twenty-one-year-old guru announces the formation of a Presidential Exploratory Committee. Television reporters ask why he thinks he is eligible to be President of the United States, given the Constitutional language that restricts the Presidency to persons who have attained "the age of thirty-five years." That's easy, replies the candidate; the provision isn't to be read literally. It merely is designed to ensure sufficient maturity, which the twenty-one-year-old guru certainly possesses, especially in light of all his years in previous incarnations. (This hypothet is adapted from Professor Mark Tushnet.) Is there anything to the guru's reasoning?

(2) *But It Doesn't Pay to Reject All Anti-Literalist Interpretations.* The Constitution also refers to the President as "he." Imagine that a reporter or opponent suggests to a woman candidate who meets all other requirements that this language restricts the Presidency to men. If we reject the non-literal reasoning of the twenty-one-year-old saffron-robed guru, must we also accept the "men only" literalist reading? If not, what is the difference?

(3) *Posner v. Dworkin, Continued.* Posner argued that to use holistic interpretation, in which one discerns and applies general themes from the document as a whole (as opposed to clause-by-clause reading), is "to enter cloud cuckooland." For example, the constitutions of the former Soviet Union, the United Automobile Workers, and the Daughters of the Confederacy probably all contain provisions from which a holistic interpreter can tease out notions of "equality." If one applies this and other similar themes, will all these differently worded constitutions become the same?

On the other hand, Dworkin continued to insist that a point of view, or in other words a holistic approach, was necessarily present in any interpretation. According to Dworkin's reasoning, even Posner himself used a holistic approach, without admitting it; specifically, Posner's holistic approach was to restrict legitimate readings to those that reasoned clause-by-clause. This approach had interpretive consequences such as restrictiveness and predictability that might appeal to a formalist, positivist viewpoint, but it was not the only way to reason about the document. Is this reasoning persuasive?

[B]   Going Outside the Text: Other Interpretive Methods

PROFESSOR BOBBITT'S "SIX MODALITIES"
OF INTERPRETIVE ARGUMENT

(1) *Bobbitt's Description of "Six Modalities of Constitutional Argument" (Which Actually Are Applicable to Other Legal Texts, Not Just to the Constitution).* Professor Philip Bobbitt has described six methods, or six "modalities," of constitutional argument. Philip Bobbitt, Constitutional Fate (1982). Professor Bobbitt's methods are adaptable to virtually any constitutional question, and in fact they are adaptable to questions of statutory construction or to the interpretation of other kinds of legal instruments and, indeed, to any kind of text. *See, e.g.*, Sanford Levinson, *The Embarrassing Second Amendment*, 99 Yale L.J. 637 (1989) (applying Professor Bobbit's six modalities to the interpretation of the Second Amendment militia clause and right to keep and bear arms).

(2) *Definitions and Demonstrations of the Six Modalities.* Professor Bobbitt's six modalities are:

(a) *Textual:* argument that considers the words and language of the text. For example, an interpretation of the First Amendment to the Constitution as absolute (or as establishing "preferred" rights), because it provides that "Congress shall make *no* law" abridging the freedom of speech, is based upon a textual argument. Likewise, if a lease says that it "shall terminate" when the tenant does any act that is illegal, a landlord's claim that it has terminated, because the tenant used the space for illegal gambling, is a textual argument.

(b) *Historical:* argument that relies upon the intention of the drafters, the events that produced the provision, or similar kinds of appeals to history. ("Originalism," or the reading of the Constitution according to the Founders' original understandings, is identified with this modality.) For example, an interpretation of the First Amendment as limited rather than absolute, because the Founders arguably saw it as more restricted in scope than modern readers might, or because their public interpretation arguably did not protect certain kinds of utterances (e.g., defamation or sedition), would be based upon historical arguments. Likewise, an argument that the lease mentioned above did not terminate because both landlord and tenant knew in advance of the tenant's plans to gamble and did not contemplate that they would be a breach of the lease, is a historical argument.

(c) *Structural:* argument that infers relationships among the entities set up or recognized by the document and interprets its provisions accordingly. Thus, the Constitution assigns roles to different branches of government, to the States, to the people, etc. An interpretation of the First Amendment that gives political speech a preferred position because it enables the people better to perform their function in electing, guiding and checking the government, for example, uses a structural argument. An argument that the lease should not terminate for illegal gambling, because that would give the landlord too much power to force pretextual evictions, would be a structural argument, too.

(d) *Doctrinal:* argument that refers to the tradition of received wisdom, often to the precedential implications of decisions by courts or other bodies. For example, an argument that First Amendment freedoms are preferred rights because the Supreme Court said so in a given case is a doctrinal argument. An argument that the lease should not terminate for gambling because no other landlord has ever evicted anyone in the face of thousands of known cases of gambling (or that this particular landlord never has) is likewise doctrinal.

(e) *Prudential:* argument that depends upon the practical consequences of differing interpretations, or in other words, "consequentialist" or "policy" argument. An interpretation of the First Amendment that allows prosecution of child pornography, on the ground that its protection is not necessary to robust public debate, can be called a prudential argument. An interpretation of the lease that disallows termination for gambling, on the ground that it would lead to too much homelessness of evicted gamblers, is also a policy (or consequentialist, or prudential) argument.

(f) *Ethical:* argument that relies on moral or ethical grounds. This modality sometimes may seem indistinguishable from the fifth modality, that of prudential argument; there is, however, a difference. Whereas prudential argument emphasizes the consequences of an interpretation in the practical sense, ethical argument emphasizes the rightness-or-wrongness of its moral content. For example, a reading of the First Amendment that excludes child pornography on the ground that its protection by the government would be immoral, either because the material damages children or because viewing it is wrong, is an ethical argument. An argument that lease termination for gambling is morally wrong, because such a large forfeiture for such an assertedly trivial infraction simply is unjust, is an ethical argument.

EXAMPLES AND PROBLEMS

(1) *Different Modes of Argument as Applied to the Constitutionality of the Death Penalty.* Supreme Court Justice William H. Brennan has taken an absolutist's position on the unconstitutionality of the death penalty. He argues that it is unconstitutional no matter what the circumstances, on the grounds that it constitutes "cruel and unusual punishment" (which the Eighth Amendment prohibits), is contrary to the principles allegedly found in past Supreme Court

William J. Brennan

decisions, denies the executed individual's humanity, and violates the "right to have rights."

Consider ways in which each of the suggested modes of argument-- textual, historical, structural, doctrinal, prudential, and ethical-- could be used to support Justice Brennan's view, or, for that matter, the opposing view. (Note, on the other side, that several amendments refer to "capital cases," several Supreme Court decisions uphold the death penalty, and many people consider it a deterrent or a necessary implement of justice in heinous cases-- although this question isn't about who's right or wrong, but about the categories of argumentation types.)

(2) *Reading the Bible--What Does It Mean?: The Abortion Example.* Imagine that one theologian interprets the scripture to mean that abortion is sinful, while another interprets the same scripture to mean that abortion is not sinful. What produces these disagreements (do Bobbit's six modalities help to understand it)?

(3) *Are Some Modes of Legal Interpretation Sometimes Superior to Others? A Couple of Examples.* The Uniform Commercial Code provides that the text of a sales contract is normally controlling over other interpretive methods, such as doctrinal concepts like trade usages or historical modalities such as course of dealing. Does this make sense? And in interpretations of the American Constitution, historical study of original intent ("originalism") appears to have broad appeal among scholars, although its acceptance is not universal and the extent of its persuasiveness differs widely among them.

A reader who insists on relatively strict originalism probably will regard the historical approach as controlling and consider other approaches as often inferior. Such a view might see prudential considerations as generally disfavored and ethical arguments as almost always disfavored (since ethical arguments, especially when contrary to original intent, arguably seek to promote propositions preferred by the reader even though more definite interpretations oppose them). Can you explain the apparent paradox that many people, even though they might consider the Constitution with a degree of reverence reserved for an important ethical statement, nevertheless might regard ethical arguments about its interpretation as suspect?

[C]   Different Kinds of Legal Rules: Categorical Rules, Balancing Rules, and Multi-Step Rules

CATEGORICAL RULES AND BALANCING RULES

(1) *Categorical Rules: If All the Elements of Murder Are Present, the Murder Statute Categorically Defines the Result.* A "categorical" rule defines elements that, if present, mandate a given result. Our earlier example of murder as set forth by Model Penal Code § 210 provides an illustration of a categorical rule. The elements of murder are present if a person (a) causes the death of (b) another human being (c) recklessly and (d) under circumstances manifesting extreme indifference to the value of human life. If these elements all are present (and if there are no defenses), the defendant's act categorically is murder; if not, it is not. The rule is syllogistic, definitional, and categorical.

(2) *Balancing Rules, as Contrasted to Categorical Rules: The Negligence Example.* On the other hand, there are "balancing" rules. These rules tell the judge or jury to weigh two factors against each other and determine the result by the balance.

For example, some formulas for explaining the concept of negligence use balancing rules. One such approach is to direct the decisionmaker to evaluate the burden of the defendant's undertaking a given precaution (such as employing a security guard or checking the brakes once a year) and to balance that cost against the cost of expected or probable loses without the precautions (such as robberies of customers that could have been prevented by a security guard or accidents caused by defective brakes). If the result of this balancing is that the value of probable losses exceeds the cost of undertaking precautions, the defendant is negligent.

(3) *The Merits and Defects of Both Balancing and Categorical Rules.* Which are better, balancing laws or categorical ones? The answer is both-- and neither. Balancing rules may take into account more of the context. They sometimes allow the court to focus on the truly determinative issue, which often involves the clash of two competing values, in a way that a categorical rule might not.

On the other hand, the values that are balanced often are incomparable and unmeasurable. For example, a court hearing an automobile death case may be required to weigh the aesthetic and sensual benefits of driving a convertible against the increased risk to human life from a rollover accident in a convertible. Balancing rules sometimes exhibit an unpredictability and mushiness that categorical rules may help to reduce. Categorical rules mean that a person trying to comply with the law can better know how to avoid violation, and perhaps a court can apply a categorical rule more consistently.

(4) *But the Difference between Categorical and Balancing Rules Shouldn't Be Overstated, because Many Laws Incorporate Features of Both.* A categorical rule often includes balancing requirements hidden in its elements. For example, the murder statute referred to above contains a requirement of "recklessness." Hence, the seemingly categorical murder statute ultimately depends on what arguably is a balancing test, concealed within its terminology.

As for the balancing-based definition of negligence, after the balancing is performed, the rule operates categorically. If the cost of precautions outweighs expected losses, the omission is not negligent. Thus, the reasoning is categorical, after the balancing is done.

(5) *But Still, the Difference Matters.* And so, most balancing rules have categorical aspects, and vice versa. Still, it is wise to know the difference between categorical rules and balancing rules, since particular laws often are more of one type than the other in their crucial steps.

COMPLEX LEGAL RULES: MULTIPLE STEPS OR FACTORS

(1) *A Multi-Step Rule of Law: The Example of the Supreme Court's Commerce Clause Interpretations.* Article I, section 8 of the Constitution gives Congress power to regulate interstate commerce. One implication of this Clause is that state laws affecting interstate commerce may sometimes be unconstitutional. This rule is complex, as interpreted by the Supreme Court, in that it uses multiple factors and two separate steps.

First, if the state law discriminates against interstate commerce, then it categorically is unconstitutional unless it is the least discriminatory means of achieving the state's purpose. Second, if the law does not discriminate against interstate commerce, it is constitutional, unless the burden on interstate commerce heavily outweighs the benefits of the state law. This is a two-step rule.

(2) *Why Have a Two-Step Rule?: To Apply Two Different Types of Rules to Different Circumstances.* In this Commerce Clause example, the first step

is a categorical rule. If the law discriminates, it is unconstitutional, by definition. This is so unless it meets the least-discriminatory-alternative criterion, which is hard to meet. Therefore, this part of the two-step process gives a straightforward result, with all of the benefits of a categorical rule, in one type of case, which involves the most suspect kind of state law: the kind that targets interstate commerce for unfavorable treatment.

On the other hand, if this discriminatory effect is missing, and if the burden on interstate commerce is incidental to the state's goal, perhaps there should be greater deference to the state law. And under step two, there is. The state law is examined by a balancing test, and it will be upheld if the burden doesn't grossly outweigh the possible benefits of the state law.

Thus, the two-step methodology enables the Supreme Court to apply two different methodologies to two different kinds of cases. The worst state laws, those that target interstate commerce for discrimination, are screened out by a categorical rule, but more debatable laws are treated by a balancing test.

(3) *Unevenly-Weighted Balancing Rules.* Sometimes it may be wise to use a balancing rule that is unevenly weighted. For example, in the case of a nondiscriminatory state law that produces only unintended side effects on interstate commerce, there arguably should be a strong presumption that the law is constitutional. The judgment usually involves a comparison of unmeasurable and incomparable values, such as the benefits of unregulated commerce weighed against the state's effort to protect its environment or the safety of its people. For all these reasons, it makes sense to hold a nondiscriminatory state law unconstitutional only in a clear case.

And in fact, this is how the Supreme Court's balancing test is written: it invalidates a nondiscriminatory state law only if the burden on interstate commerce is "clearly" excessive in relation to local benefits. In other words, only if the burden is very heavy and the benefits are slight. This is an unevenly weighted balancing test. It is "loaded" in favor of upholding the state law.

(4) *Multiple-Factor Balancing Rules.* Sometimes the law directs a judge or a jury to consider a variety of factors and to balance them all against each other, without any particular factor necessarily controlling. An analogy taken from everyday life may help to understand this approach. Let us imagine that you have been accepted by five colleges and you are trying to decide which

to select.   You might consider such factors as tuition costs for each, reputations of the faculties, living accommodations, proximity to home, available curricula, and courses in your intended major.   No one of these factors would be necessarily determinative.

(5) *An Example of Multi-Factor Balancing in the Law: Taking of Private Property and the Fifth Amendment's Requirement of Just Compensation.*   The Fifth Amendment to the Constitution says that if government takes private property for a public purpose, it must pay just compensation. But this clause can be difficult to interpret when regulations merely reduce the value of property rather than confiscating it. In other words, when is a regulation so onerous that it really amounts to a "taking"?

For instance, if you own a piece of land that is zoned so as to limit your use of it, the zoning category probably reduces its value. Nevertheless, if the zoning plan is fair and extends equally throughout the city, it probably isn't a taking of your property. But the conclusion might be quite different if, say, the zoning category prevents any economically valuable use of property, or if it requires you to let the public enter the land to use it recreationally.

The Supreme Court's approach to this problem has been simply to list a number of weight factors, such as the economic impact of the zoning law, the degree of physical invasion, the breadth of the public purpose, the comprehensiveness or uniformity of the city's zoning plan, and other factors. These issues simply are weighed against each other in an unquantifiable way. The advantage of such a rule is that it enables the court to consider all of the factors that operate in the real world and to give them the weight that the context justifies.   But the mushiness of a balancing rule is magnified manyfold if we add multiple factors weighed in unspecified ways. In the Supreme Court's balancing cases, the reasoning frequently looks unconvincing because the factors often support opposite conclusions equally.

Chapter 11

Psychology

Psychological Disorders, Learning Theory, Intelligence, and Social Psychology--and How They Affect Lawyers

> *"[The ego] has the task of self-preservation. [I]t performs that task by . . . storing up experiences about [stimuli] (in the memory), by avoiding excessively strong stimuli (through flight), by dealing with moderate stimuli (through adaptation), and finally by learning to bring about expedient changes . . . (through activity). . . . [I]n relation to the id, it performs that task by gaining control over the demands of the instincts."--Sigmund Freud, Outline of Psychoanalysis*

> *"[We can] replac[e] intelligence with instinct"-- muttered Frazier. . . . "When [a person] behaves as we want him to behave, we simply create a situation he likes . . . . Technically it's called 'positive reinforcement.'"--B.F. Skinner, Walden Two*

§ 11.01   What This Chapter Is About

PSYCHOLOGY, SOCIAL PSYCHOLOGY, AND THE LAW

(1) *The Science of Psychology: Disorders, Learning Theory, and Intelligence.* Psychology is a varied field, ranging from perception to group diversity. Here, we cover only a few subjects of widest interest. First, we consider psychological disorders, from psychoses to anxiety disorders, together with their origins and treatments. In the course of this coverage, the chapter also exposes the reader to "learning theory," or the connection between stimulus and response. We also consider intelligence.

Is psychology scientific? The rationalist, arguably unscientific views of Freud quoted above, who nevertheless made a giant contribution, contrast sharply with the rigorous empirical work of Skinner in learning theory.

(2) *Social Psychology.* The chapter also covers selected issues dealing with social psychology, or psychological relations of persons to other persons. It explores the concepts known as attribution, attraction, dissonance, conformity, and authority. One of the goals is to understand persuasion.

(3) *Why Is This Chapter of Interest to Lawyers?* First, in some fields, psychological evidence is frequent and important. Family law probably is the prime example. Criminal law, personal injury practice and employment law also use psychologists. Second, understanding persuasion is particularly useful for lawyers. (Persuasion fits both here and in the Rhetoric chapter, and the coverage is split.) Third, the methodology of psychology is not exactly that of the hard sciences and not exactly that of the soft ones. This discipline builds models that are empirically supportable but that fit individuals and circumstances only stereotypically. You will think better generally if you can master this additional type of model-building, which sometimes resembles the way lawyers think.

Furthermore, psychological issues are capable of arising in virtually any case. Consider, for example, *In re Tiffany Green*, 1996 LEXIS 16812 (E.D. Pa. 1996), in which a juror suddenly refused, in the middle of a complex commercial trial, to serve further. The district judge ordered Green to show cause why she should not be held in contempt. At the show cause hearing, the principal evidence came from Green's treating psychiatrist, who diagnosed and explained her "anxiety disorder," clinical "depression," and other conditions. The judge had to understand (and in his opinion, explained) the diagnoses and effects of both of these conditions.

(4) *Your Own Mental Health: Lawyers and Depression.* Another reason for knowing something about this material is your own mental health. It may shock you to learn that, according to the American Bar Association, "[l]awyers have the highest depression rates of any group in the workplace,"[1] Even if you think you're exempt, it may behoove you to understand this material, if only so that you can understand other lawyers.

§ 11.02   The Scientific Claims of Psychology

IS PSYCHOLOGY SCIENTIFIC? FROM FREUD TO DSM-IV

(1) *Why Does It Matter to a Lawyer?* If you handle litigation, sooner or later you will have to cross examine a psychologist or other mental health professional. You will be immensely helped by understanding the method of psychologists, whether you present one by direct or whether you cross examine.

B. F. Skinner

(2)   *The Extent to Which Psychology Is Scientific Depends on One's Concept of Science: Rationalist, Empiricist, and Computational Perspectives.* To the extent we define science by falsifiability, testability or replicability, we reduce the stuff of psychology.   There are, however, many aspects of the subject that are scientific by the most rigorous standards, such as B.F. Skinner's learning-theory experiments with pigeons that responded replicably to rewards or the social psychology experiments of Asch and Milgram described in a later section of this chapter.

On the other hand, psychology includes some theories, such as Howard Gardner's typology of seven different kinds of intelligence (described below), which depend more on concept and classification than upon anything that truly is falsifiable. A rationalist might accept Gardner's "radical" (his word) description as scientific, but an empiricist would be less likely to.

---

1   *See* Jefferson, *But What Role for the Soul?*, ABA Journal, Dec. 1991, at 60.

(3) *Freud.* It is almost impossible to discuss psychology without mentioning Sigmund Freud, who is one of psychology's (and history's) towering figures. His seminal book, *The Interpretation of Dreams*, characterized dreams as censored, symbolic stories that camouflaged their "latent content," which expressed unconscious drives that would be too frightening to confront if made explicit.

Sigmund Freud

Furthermore, Freud asserted that psychoanalysis could trace most dreams to sexual issues or, as he put it, "to erotic wishes." A knife, umbrella, or airplane in a dream, for example, might really symbolize a penis. A cave or bottle, Freud said, symbolized female genitalia. Freud's elaborate theory of dream process, which is diagrammed in Figure 1, did depend on repeated empirical observations of patients in psychoanalysis, but it depended more heavily on Freud's non-replicable interpretation of those observations.

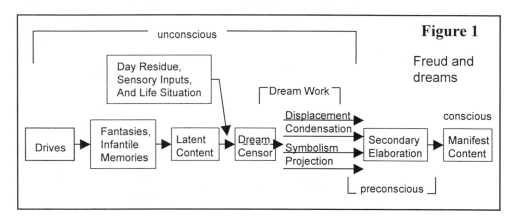

Figure 1

Freud and dreams

(4) *But Freud Is Only an Example; There Have Been Many Other Influential Pioneers and Contemporary Explorers.* We use Freud as an example here, but his contemporaries included such other giants as Alfred Adler (who emphasized a more direct, purposeful kind of therapy, a forerunner of what today would be called cognitive therapy), Karen Horney (who also differed from Freud, in her case with a more holistic approach), and Erik Erikson (who studied the human life cycle and empirically identified eight passages, or "stages" of personality development, from infanthood to maturity, each with its own crisis or conflict of values). Contemporary psychologists, some of who are mentioned in this chapter, continue to develop the field.

(5) *The Subjects of Psychology.* Today, psychology includes such different studies as child development (the stages, or passages, from birth through adulthood) and perception (visual or other stimuli and how we interpret them). It also extends to learning theory (stimulus and response), theories of personality, intelligence, cognition (thinking), language, emotions, psychological disorders, psychoanalysis, and social psychology (which studies conformity, group behavior, and like issues). Some of these fields probably deserve the label of sciences more than others.

EXAMPLES AND PROBLEMS

(1) *Was Freud's Work Scientific? Contemporary Attitudes.* Many contemporary psychologists have no use for Freud. His work did not pretend to be predictive, and therefore it was not uniformly replicable. But Freud and his contemporaries created the framework of modern psychology by seeking to explain the irrational, the disordered, and the unconscious.

Some of Freud's testable hypotheses have been rejected by observation. His idea that personality development was concentrated in childhood stages, such as the "oral" and "anal" stages, is contradicted by research indicating instead that development is lifelong, and his theory that gender identity emerges from an "Oedipal complex," or a five-to-six-year old child's resolution of sexual attachments to the opposite-gendered parent, is refuted by evidence that gender identity emerges much earlier, and emerges in households without opposite-gendered parents.

Yet some of Freud's ideas have survived. To what extent, then, was Freud's work "scientific?" (And to what extent does it matter?)

(2) *From Mind to Behavioral Empiricism and Back to Mind Again.* Although recognizing that this sequence is subject to exceptions, psychologist Richard Evans traces the history of the field, generally, as beginning with models of the mind that were highly conceptual (Freud and his contemporaries) and progressing to behavioralism that was empirically replicable (such as Skinner's learning theory experiments). But today, the pendulum seems to have swung back to include conceptual studies of the mind, which are not divorced from empirical support but depend more on rationalist modeling. Do you think it is possible that the human mind requires us to adopt this lesser fidelity to empiricism if we are to study all of it?

(3) *Courts, Psychologists, and the Rules of Evidence: Would Freud (or Howard Gardner) Be Allowed to Testify as an Expert Witness Under Current Supreme Court Rules?* In an earlier section, we saw that the Supreme Court definitively has opted for the empiricist's view of science and has made expert witness qualification depend upon it. Would Freud have been qualified under this standard, if he had been called in his time to testify about dream processes in a lawsuit about, say, nightmares following a traumatic event? Would Howard Gardner be permitted to testify to his theory of intelligence in a suit in which it was relevant? If not, consider whether the exclusion of such evidence is appropriate.

§ 11.03   Psychological Disorders and the Law

[A]   The Diagnostic and Statistical Manual (DSM) and How It Changes

THE APA'S DIAGNOSTIC AND STATISTICAL MANUAL (DSM)

(1) *Family, Criminal, Personal Injury, and Employment Law.* Several bread-and-butter areas of law practice feature psychologists as witnesses. If you practice in these areas, you are likely to encounter the classificatory system that psychologists refer to as "DSM."

(2) *Taxonomy or Classification: Labels by Analogy.* The classification and diagnosis of psychological disorders arguably bears more relationship to biological taxonomy than to most experimental science, and it may appear to some to proceed more by analogy than by scientific induction. The definition of obsessive-compulsive personality disorder, for example, combines such diverse diagnostic criteria as irrational attachment to worthless objects and overly conscientious moralism (see Figure 2, below). The definition rests, in part, on the correlation of observation of these characteristics in individuals with observations of their manifesting some or more defined symptoms. Obviously, one can argue about the extent to which this kind of classificatory and diagnostic endeavor is "scientific."

(3) *The APA's Diagnostic and Statistical Manual (DSM).* The American Psychiatric Association's *Diagnostic and Statistical Manual of Mental Disorders* (Fourth Edition), called "DSM-IV," is the authoritative system for this classificatory purpose. It has gone through four or, depending on how

you count them, five revisions. Consider, for example, DSM's treatment of sexual orientation, which has followed a zigzag course. See below.

EXAMPLES AND PROBLEMS

(1) *The DSM's Historical Treatment of Sexual Orientation as a Dubious Example of Its Classificatory Method: Science, Morals, Law, or Politics?* The APA's initial classification of homosexual orientation was as a "sociopathic personality disturbance." Later, DSM-II softened this diagnostic category to "sexual deviation," under the general classification of "personality disorders and certain other nonpsychotic mental disorders." Then, in 1974, the APA decided that homosexual orientation no longer was a disorder, and it changed the concept: "Sexual orientation disturbance" was defined as homosexual orientation coupled with "disturbance" or "conflict" about that orientation (to be fair, there are parallel kinds of heterosexual pathologies too). What do you think motivated these earlier classifications and changes?

(2) *Today's Treatment of Sexual Orientation in DSM-IV: Law, Politics, and Public Policy.* Finally, DSM changed this category to "sexual disorder not otherwise specified," which includes "persistent and marked distress about one's sexual orientation." See DSM-IV. Does this history of classificatory changes reflect simple empirical advancement (the march of science), or is it just confused ethical or political thinking? [What implications might it have for law and public policy?]

(3) *Pedophiles, Law, and Politics.* In an earlier chapter (on Logic and Fallacy), we considered the APA's pronouncement that pedophiles generally were psychologically "normal." We also considered the denunciation of this view by a prominent political figure, House Majority Whip Tom DeLay, who apparently concluded that the APA's statement was supportive of pedophiles(!) An APA spokesperson responded by saying that psychological normality did not mean that the conduct was excusable; in fact, the spokesperson added that sex with a child "is a crime. It should be."

Perhaps the APA's refusal to impute mental illness to pedophiles, and its view that they may be psychologically normal, actually support our imposing legal responsibility for the behavior, rather than detracting from it. Can you see why? (What if "abnormality" in the sense of delusions or compulsion were attributed to pedophilia?)

[B]   The Classificatory Scheme of DSM-IV: The Example of Personality Disorders

PERSONALITY DISORDERS, DSM-IV, AND THE LAW

(1) *These Labels Are Useful in Many Kinds of Litigation or Evaluation, but They Should Be Applied With an Awareness That They Are Imperfect.* The reader should cultivate an elastic attitude about the labels in DSM-IV, or for that matter in any type of psychological modeling. These labels, complexes, syndromes or models are useful, both in litigation and elsewhere, but only if the user remembers how tricky they are. Experienced clinical psychologists, in fact, use the labels we are about to study with an awareness that they fit imperfectly and indeed may not fit well at all.

For one thing, diagnostic labels may describe characteristics that are "situational": Present in the individual in some circumstances but not others. For another, the diagnostic criteria should be regarded as approximations, prototypes or stereotypes. Some stereotypes have predictive value (physicians on average are wealthier than tailors; people who claim to be poets usually are good with language), but such generalizations must be discounted for exceptions (some physicians are not wealthy, and some self-identified poets may not be good writers). Finally, the labels categorize characteristics that do not exist in absolute amounts but rather across a spectrum, so that a person with a labeled "disorder" may differ from other people only as a matter of degree.

One error that beginners make is to regard these labels, instead, as having an absoluteness, or a precision, that they do not possess. Given the radius and the value of π, one can specify the circumference of a circle with perfect accuracy. But imagine trying to describe the human personality in the same way! Can we categorize people who are "friendly," "smart," or "diligent" in an absolute way? Obviously not; these characteristics exist in degrees and situations. So it is with the labels described here. If this is borne in mind (and only then), these concepts are useful.

(2) *Personality Disorders.* In this section, with the caveat above in mind, we shall consider psychological pathologies, beginning with what are called "personality disorders." These disorders are, in a sense, milder than what are called anxiety disorders, in that they do not depend on dysfunctional anxiety, and milder than psychoses (which we shall consider next), in that they do not

involve disturbance of reality perception. Personality disorders consist simply of inflexible, enduring behavior patterns that are "maladaptive," or that impair functioning in society.

The "narcissistic personality disorder," for example, consists of pathologic exaggeration of one's own importance, rage or shame in response to mild criticism, and fantasies about one's success. A "dependent personality" needs support, guidance, initiative, or assumption of responsibility by others, to an extent that the need interferes with ordinary life. The APA's *Diagnostic and Statistical Manual* (DSM-IV) defines several other personality disorders. Here, we concentrate on two, called the obsessive-compulsive personality disorder and the antisocial personality.

(3) *Obsessive-Compulsive Personality Disorder.* Figure 2 reproduces DSM-IV's diagnostic criteria for the "obsessive-compulsive personality." Notice the long list of characteristics for which the diagnostician is to probe, coupled with a required number of positive observations from among the larger number of criteria. The DSM uses this method consistently. The obsessive-compulsive personality is characterized by dysfunctionally rigid adherence to abstract rules and unattainable standards of perfection, to such an extent that purposeful activity chronically is inhibited. The unhappiness, demands and anxiety of the obsessive-compulsive tend to drive family members to distraction. You should take a moment to read the criteria in the figure, so you can understand what DSM is like, in general.

Figure 2

■ **301.4 Obsessive-Compulsive Personality Disorder**

A pervasive pattern of preoccupation with orderliness, perfectionism, and mental and interpersonal control, at the expense of flexibility, openness, and efficiency, beginning by early adulthood and present in a variety of contexts, as indicated by four (or more) of the following:

(1) is preoccupied with details, rules, lists, order, organization, or schedules to the extent that the major point of the activity is lost

(2) shows perfectionism that interferes with task completion (e.g., is unable to complete a project because his or her own overly strict standards are not met)

(3) is excessively devoted to work and productivity to the exclusion of leisure activities and friendships (not accounted for by obvious economic necessity)

(4) is overconscientious, scrupulous, and inflexible about matters of morality, ethics, or values (not accounted for by cultural or religious identification)

(5) is unable to discard worn-out or worthless objects even when they have no sentimental value

(6) is reluctant to delegate tasks or to work with others unless they submit to exactly his or her way of doing things

(7) adopts a miserly spending style toward both self and others; money is viewed as something to be hoarded for future catastrophes

(8) shows rigidity and stubbornness

(4) *Law School: Does It "Teach" Obsessive-Compulsive Characteristics?* Does law school inculcate some characteristics that might coincide with this disorder? Nobody is saying that law school "makes you into" an obsessive-compulsive personality. It probably *can't* do that. But maybe it creates habits that can be dysfunctional at times(!) "[P]reoccupation with details, rules, [etc.]" definitely is one thing that law school teaches. So is "[p]erfectionism that interferes with task completion." Law school creates a profession "excessively devoted to work," with "rigidity" about being "reluctant to delegate." [Again, nobody is saying law school is going to stamp you with a diagnosable obsessive-compulsive personality disorder.]

(5) *The Antisocial Personality Disorder.* Another type of personality disorder, the antisocial personality disorder, affects relatively small numbers of people, but they demand disproportionate attention from society, because violent criminals disproportionately are antisocial personalities. Narcissistic and hedonistic, antisocial personalities are grossly selfish, irresponsible and impulsive, with interests that concentrate on satisfaction of immediate desires. DSM-IV, in one diagnostic criterion, puts it in terms of "lack of remorse, as indicated by being indifferent to or rationalizing having hurt, mistreated, or stolen from another."

Antisocial personalities often have superficial charm and good intelligence and are not subject to delusion or neuroses, but they are chronically untruthful, offering rationalizations or blaming others for their behavior. A lack of empathy for others' suffering, often reflected in cruelty to animals in childhood, makes the antisocial personality less inhibited about violence. DSM cautions that a long criminal record, although often exhibited by this disorder, is not alone diagnostic: "A mere history of repeated legal or social offenses is not sufficient to justify this diagnosis."

EXAMPLES AND PROBLEMS

(1) *Your Own Mental Health as a Lawyer: Are Some of the Characteristics Inculcated by Law School Dysfunctional?* Consider again the overlap among law school, the legal profession, and some characteristics of obsessive-compulsive personality disorder. Should a person suffering this disorder, or on the borderline, go to law school? (Maybe they would fit in well?) Again, no one is saying that law school will (or even can) create such a personality. But consider whether it inculcates some habits that you will

need to limit, at least in your own personal life. [Reconsider what we discussed earlier: lawyers' mental health, as a group, is troubling.]

(2) *A Diagnosable Obsessive-Compulsive Personality Disorder? The Example of the Driven Doctor.* Imagine that the following case is presented to a clinical psychologist. The subject is a physician whom everyone describes as a perfectionist. She works long hours and is committed to and adored by her patients, but she tends to berate her loyal staff for minor deviations from prescribed procedures. She recalls one incident in which her longtime office manager planned to microfilm and then dispose of twenty-year-old records, and the doctor "overreacted" (her word) by dressing the office manager down with four-letter words. She believes that the decision not to microfilm was correct because "some data always gets lost when you reconfigure," and she wants the office manager to "do it my way because that's what he's hired to do." But she has become aware that her life, as she puts it, "doesn't have balance," and she doesn't get along with people as well as she might. Is this subject a diagnosable obsessive-compulsive, or just a typical good doctor? [The answer is "No, she is not diagnosable," based on this information. See whether you can explain why--and see the next note.]

(3) *Differences of Degree; Maybe Some Obsessions and Compulsions Are Good(!)* Perhaps the question of diagnosing the obsessive-compulsive personality disorder is one of degree. One tirade about microfilm probably doesn't make it, and the picture is complicated by the benefits of some of these behaviors. The doctor may be "obsessed" with professional excellence because this is what she wants to do, and her "compulsion" about by-the-book procedures is what she learned as good practice in medical school. Are the DSM's diagnostic criteria too mushy?

(4) *Intervention in This Case.* Imagine that, after collecting more data, one psychologist would diagnose the obsessive-compulsive disorder in this subject, whereas another would not, seeing the subject's dysfunction as real but milder than the disorder diagnosis would call for. But both psychologists think that clinical intervention in the form of cognitive therapy (see below) is indicated. Does this mean that the diagnostic criteria, for all their mushiness, are useful? Perhaps they are the best that anyone can do, in prescribing universal, repeatable criteria.

(5) *Consistency in Diagnosis: A Scary Example.* How consistent would you expect clinicians to be, in diagnosing psychological disorders?

Obviously, there is great room for judgment. Some tests in the past have produced more disagreements than agreements among independent diagnoses, although the refinement of DSM through its revisions is said to have increased consistency.

In one (scary) experiment reported in 1989, twelve ordinary people with no ostensibly diagnosable disorders were sent to psychiatric hospitals. They gave assumed names and complained of hearing voices that repeated single words such as "empty" or "meaningless"; otherwise they provided correct information. On this evidence alone, all were diagnosed as either schizophrenic or suffering from bipolar (manic-depressive) disorder, and all, over their requests for release, were involuntarily hospitalized. No one ever detected the diagnostic inaccuracy. Why do you think this result occurred?

(6) *Sociopaths, Sociopathic Personality, and Antisocial Personality.* The APA has applied several different labels--"sociopath," "sociopathic personality," and "antisocial personality"--to sequential revisions of one particular disorder. Individuals first were said to be sociopaths, then to reflect the sociopathic personality, then to suffer from the antisocial personality disorder, all with slight differences in diagnostic detail. Does the change reflect an underlying lack of scientific method, or is it the result of scientific advancement?

(7) *A Diagnosable Antisocial Personality Disorder: Henry Lee Lucas.* Henry Lee Lucas confessed to murdering varying numbers of women, men and children, possibly as many as 360, many of whom he brutally mutilated. Later evidence demonstrated, however, that some of his confessions almost certainly were false, including one that had produced a death sentence (which the State's governor, George W. Bush, commuted). Lucas admitted that at age 13 he had strangled a woman because she refused to have sex with him, and apparently his last murder was the stabbing and dismemberment of his 15-year-old common-law wife.

As Lucas explained, he wasted no time on regret: "Once I've done a crime, I just forget it." Does it make sense to characterize Lucas as subject to a psychological disorder, or is he simply a violent criminal?

(8) *The Law and Drug and Alcohol Dependency, as Related to Personality Disorders: Is the Disorder Label Meaningful When It Fits Such a Large Percentage of the Population?* At one time, DSM classified drug

dependency and alcoholism under the heading, "personality disorders and certain other non-psychiatric mental disorders." Was the relationship of these categories appropriate? Note that a large percentage of the population, across a broad spectrum, fits this combined classification. One survey in 1991 reported that 13.8% of American adults had experienced alcohol abuse or dependence disorders at some time in their lives, and 2.6% had experienced the antisocial personality disorder; therefore, the Americans under this tent of combined disorders must have been very numerous.

Note that it matters, under the law, whether there is such a diagnosis. One frequent example is in employment law, where drug-and-alcohol-related disorders create a category of individuals protected under the Americans with Disabilities Act, whom the employer must "accommodate."

Is it appropriate to use the label "disorder" for such a large and amorphous group? Perhaps the study of psychological disorders really includes the study of a range of normal people, who sometimes experience pathologies? The obsessive doctor depicted in note 1 above also illustrates this point. (Now, the DSM classifies alcohol and drug dependency under the separate heading of "substance use disorders.")

[C]   Psychoses, Anxiety Disorders, and Other Disorders in DSM-IV

PSYCHOSES, SCHIZOPHRENIA, DISSOCIATIVE DISORDERS, AND AFFECTIVE DISORDERS

(1) *Psychoses and the Law: Delusional or Affective Interferences from Organic Brain Syndromes or From Functional Origins.* Now, we shall consider some more profound kinds of disturbances. "Psychoses," of which schizophrenia is a major type, are characterized by impaired cognitive or mental capacity. They reflect "delusion" (which is incapacity to perceive or test reality) or inappropriate "affect" (which means disjointed emotional response) to such an extent that ordinary living is impaired. The term once included all types of psychoses resulting from "organic brain syndromes" (medical conditions affecting the brain), such as certain kinds of poisoning or intracranial infection by agents such as encephalitis, but DSM-IV excludes delirium or dementia resulting from substance abuse or general medical conditions. Those disorders are separately categorized.

Psychoses also include those of "functional" origins, or in other words from psychological effects. The common denominator is impaired cognitive or mental processes that are reflected in poor reality testing or in impaired affect. Some psychoses can result from both organic and functional origins; in fact, the "etiology," or causation, is imperfectly understood.

In the law, these kinds of disorders obviously are among those most likely to result in excuse from criminal liability (or reduction through diminished capacity). They also are among those that lead to involuntary commitment.

(2) *Schizophrenia.* "Schizophrenic" psychoses reflect distortion of reality by delusions and hallucinations. These can result in incoherent speech (sometimes called "word salad"), dissociation, impaired affect, flat ambivalence, apathetic withdrawal or bizarre behavior. These manifestations vary, however, with the type of schizophrenia.

(3) *Types of Schizophrenia: From Catatonic to Paranoid.* Stuporous catatonic schizophrenia sometimes manifests itself in immobilization or "catalepsy," an odd frozen position that the individual may maintain for hours, punctuated by bursts of disorganized, violent activity. The "excited" catatonic, on the other hand, engages in continuous psychomotor activity which is dangerous both to the individual and to others, accompanied by disconnected verbiage or shouting.

The "paranoid" schizophrenic is usually older than catatonics or disorganized schizophrenics and suffers from delusions of persecution or of grandeur. Paranoids exhibit less breakdown of mental processes, less physical agitation and fewer instances of bizarre behavior; their intelligence and social skills may remain generally intact. But paranoids are tense, guarded, hostile and aggressive.

There are other kinds of schizophrenia, including the "undifferentiated" type (which is a catchall for a long-term schizophrenic pattern that does not fit other diagnoses).

(4) *Dissociative Disorders: From Dissociative Amnesia to Multiple Personality Disorder.* A related but separate family of disturbances is called "dissociative disorders." "Dissociation" refers to the splitting of some of a person's mental states or processes from the rest of the person's thinking, as in the unconscious defense mechanism that occurs in "hysterical

dissociation," in which an idea is separated from its accompanying affect. Amnesia, for example, may be caused organically by brain injury or alcohol abuse, but "dissociative" amnesia, a dissociative disorder, typically begins as a defense to an intolerable trauma or stress.

"Dissociative fugue" is closely akin to amnesia but also involves flight from one's identity, often by physical relocation and assumption of a new persona. The rare phenomenon of "dissociative identity disorder," formerly called "multiple personality disorder," is a massive dissociation from one's identity, resulting from severe psychological trauma, and usually involving one or more timid and restrained personae alternating with one or more that are impulsive and uninhibited.

(5) *Major Mood (Depressive) Disorders.* "Major depressive disorder" is an affective or mood disorder. Most people experience depressive symptoms in response to profoundly sad events or life circumstances, but the diagnosis of clinical depression requires persistence, in the absence of any discernible basis for bereavement, for more than two weeks. "Bipolar disorders," formerly referred to as manic-depressive disorder, result in an individual's alternation between states of depression and sharply contrasting states of "mania," which are characterized by euphoria, unjustified optimism, and frenetic activity. Some especially creative people are bipolar. They accomplish extraordinary feats in short periods of mania, during which they also need but resent restraint from reckless, impulsive conduct.

ANXIETY DISORDERS OR NEUROSES

(1) *Generalized Anxiety Disorder.* Another kind of serious disturbance is "anxiety disorders." "Generalized" anxiety disorder is simply severe, incapacitative anxiety that has no recognizable association with any particular situation. Freud said that in such a "neurosis," as anxiety disorders then were called, the anxiety is "free-floating." One of the most disturbing results of generalized anxiety disorder is that since triggering situations cannot be identified, they cannot be avoided, either. Without warning, the anxiety may intensify into a "panic attack," with symptoms of fainting or chest pain.

(2) *Phobias: Irrational, Incapacitative Fears.* In a "phobia," the anxiety is associated with a specific situation. Most people have situational anxieties--one of the most common fears is of snakes, shared by a majority of the population, followed by heights, mice, flying and closed spaces, in that

order--but clinical diagnosis of phobia requires irrationality and incapacitative severity. "Agoraphobia," for example, is an irrational, incapacitating anxiety associated with public places.

The good news is that since triggers for phobias are identifiable, they can be avoided, but the bad news is that they sometimes restrict major activities. Agoraphobics, for example, may refuse to leave their homes.

EXAMPLES AND PROBLEMS

(1) *The Common Cold and the Cancer of Psychological Disorders.* Depression is so widespread that it sometimes is referred to as the "common cold" of psychological disorders. It also has been said that, by comparison, schizophrenia is the "cancer" of these disorders. Can you explain these analogies?

(2) *The Layperson's Metaphor of a Split Personality.* The expression, "split personality," often is applied--erroneously--to schizophrenia. Although the word schizophrenia originated in Greek words meaning split mind, this concept actually fits dissociative disorders better. Can you explain?

(3) *Suicide and Depression.* Of all the "indicators" or predictors of suicide, depression is the most powerful. Studies consistently show that around 90 percent of suicides are accompanied by serious depression. Can you see why? Other indicators include talking about suicide, previous suicide attempts, disposition of possessions, and ideation about death, all of which may be related to the underlying depression. Why?

But despite the correlation of these indicators with the act, it is very difficult to predict suicide because of the large population of depressed individuals, most of whom do not commit the act. Can you explain? Another reason for the difficulty is that, oddly, on the eve of the suicide, one indicator is serenity, relief, and apparent purposivity. Can you surmise why?

When a person talks about suicide, some people have a tendency to respond with flippancy--"well, you gotta do what you gotta do"--which may precipitate a "promise-fulfillment" suicide. A better response might be to express strong wishes to the contrary, accompanied by statements of personal involvement, and to encourage or seek intervention. Can you evaluate this advice? Today, underlying depression usually responds to biomedical (pharmaceutical) treatment.

(4) *Some Other Psychological Disorders.* Consider the following syndromes and their appropriate classifications in DSM. (a) "Postpartum disorder" once was classified as an organic (non-brain) psychosis. It consists of abnormally severe affective disturbance in women after giving birth. Should this syndrome have been classified as organic or as a "psychosis"? The DSM-IV categorization is to treat manifestations as either major depressive or bipolar disorders if they fit and to add a "'postpartum onset' specifier." Is this classification more appropriate? [See the note about the Andrea Yates, case, below.]

(b) "Post-traumatic stress disorder" first was used to describe war survivors who had experienced terrifying combat experiences such as nearby death or dismemberment, and later it was extended to such diverse groups as some prisoners and some rape victims. It may exhibit itself in fixated memories, nightmares, anxiety, avoidance behavior, and social withdrawal. Should this syndrome be called an anxiety disorder, as DSM-IV treats it? Or as a psychosis, or a personality disorder? [If you practice personal injury law, you undoubtedly will deal with this diagnosis, and you may, also, if you practice employment, criminal, family, or disability law.]

(5) *Psychological Disorders, Insanity, and Criminal Responsibility Under the Law.* Imagine that a person who has committed a homicide is examined by mental health professionals, who categorize the person as suffering from "undifferentiated schizophrenia, type: severe."

Remember that the meaning of this diagnosis depends on questions of label and degree, and it may not even be reliably predictive of the person's behavior in any comprehensive way. Also, notice that the diagnosis does not resolve the issue of this person's criminal responsibility at law. Classically (but with modern differences that vary by State), the defense of excuse by insanity has required that the defendant not understand the nature of his or her conduct, or not understand that it was wrong. Can you explain why the mental health diagnosis does not resolve this issue? And as a more difficult question, can you explain how the diagnosis might be related to the legal question whether this defendant should be acquitted by reason of insanity?

(6) *The Andrea Yates Murder Case: What Level of Responsibility under the Criminal Law?* Andrea Yates methodically drowned her six children, one after another, in a bathtub. Then she called 911 to confess what she had done, and her confession indicated with clarity that she knew what she was doing and knew it was wrong. The state law followed the *M'Naughten* test: insanity had to be proved by the defendant by a preponderance of the evidence, and it excused only those who did not know the wrongfulness of their actions. But Yates repeatedly had been hospitalized for severe depression, and at least one diagnosis attributed not mere depression but postpartum "psychosis" to her. The local district attorney obtained an indictment against Yates for a death penalty offense. Many citizens, however, especially womens' groups such as the National Organization for Women, offered support for Yates--and raised money to help her.

Similar murders have produced widely differing results in the courts. Once case that also involved multiple filicides by drowning resulted in a probationary sentence with not even a day in custody. Another resulted in a 60-year sentence. How should our society handle crimes committed by severely depressed individuals who are *not* delusional, in the sense that they know right from wrong? Consider why the results are so disparate.

§ 11.04   Psychological Intervention: From Psychotherapy to Learning Theory

ETIOLOGY AND TREATMENT MODALITIES FOR MENTAL DISORDERS

(1) *Models of Etiology (Origins) of Mental Diseases: Biological and Medical Models for Anxiety Disorders.* Next, let us examine the "etiologies" (cause or origins) of these mental diseases. Many are poorly understood. Often, several independent co-variables may be involved. Different models have evolved, ranging from the biological to the psychoanalytic.

The biological or genetic model sees mental disorders, like some physical ones, as influenced by heredity. Thus, for example, it has been observed that when one of identical twins develops a phobia, the other often develops the same phobia, even when the two are raised separately. The medical model is related in that it sees mental disorders as organic, but not necessarily genetic. Debilitating illnesses or brain trauma may, for example, be associated with some disorders.

(2) *Learning Theory Models: The Executive Monkey Experiment.* A "learning theory" perspective is very different. The learning theory model of anxiety disorders sees them as conditioned responses to psychological trauma. Learning theory, here, is not limited to education in the usual sense. Rather, it refers to the association of stimulus and response. For example, experimenters have produced chronically anxious rats by subjecting them to unpredictable electric shocks (predictable electric shocks are much less anxiety-producing). The effects last long after the conditioning period.

The famous "executive monkey" experiment, shown in Figure 3, paired two monkeys, both of which were subjected to a series of electrical shocks, but one of which, the executive monkey, controlled the timing for both. In this picture, note the rigid anxiety of the monkey on the right, as compared to the relaxation of the executive monkey on the left. The resulting anxiety response suggests comparable results in humans. Thus, stimulus and response, or learning theory, may help explain the etiology of some psychological dysfunctions.

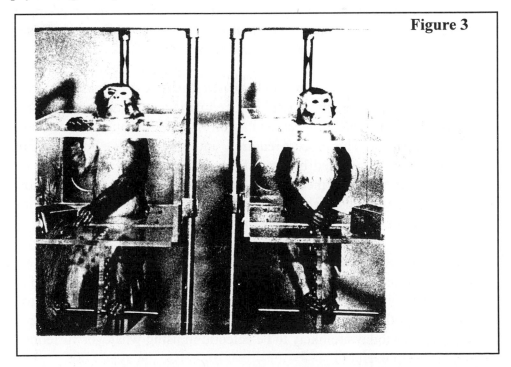

Figure 3

(3) *The Psychoanalytical Model of Anxiety Disorders.* Yet another theory of etiology is the psychoanalytic model. Psychoanalysis is based on the concept that, from childhood on, terrifying drives are repressed, and yet

they survive as anxiety, depression or other symptoms. Freud, for example, saw anxiety disorders as expressions of repressed psychosexual urges.

(4) *Treatment Modalities: Conditioning Therapies Based on Learning Theory.* Next, let us consider intervention and treatment of psychological disorders, beginning with "learning theories." Again, learning theory here implies stimulus and response. For example, "aversion therapy" has been used with mixed success in alcohol abusers, by giving them drinks laced with nausea-inducing drugs, and in pedophiles, by subjecting them to electric shocks while viewing pictures of children.

A more frequent behavioral therapy is "systematic desensitization." An agoraphobic (a person with a phobia about public places), for example, may be given relaxation training, and then may be asked to imagine a relatively nonthreatening public place. The exercise is repeated and gradually escalated until the patient can tolerate actual public appearances. "Behavior modification" is more intensive, moment-to-moment reward and punishment, and is used in treatment of aggression, for example, or in programmed parental supervision of autistic children. A "token reward system," using imitation coins or gold stars, can be used to reward.

(5) *Psychotherapy, or Assisted Historical Analysis.* Psychotherapy is yet another treatment modality. Freud induced patients to "free associate": to express whatever thoughts appeared in their minds, even inconsequential or embarrassing ones. This process required "interpretation," or guidance from the therapist, accompanied by "transference," or closeness and trust that allowed a transfer to the therapist of anxieties attached to other emotions, such as attitudes toward parents, to overcome "resistance" or unconscious blockage. Over a long period, the patient gains insight.

Today, more psychotherapists use "humanistic" therapies, dealing with present and conscious thoughts, reflecting a lesser confidence than Freud's in determinism by childhood sexuality. Another type of therapy called group therapy uses other people with related diagnoses as parallel therapists. In fact, therapists today are likely to be eclectic in using whatever varieties of therapies seem useful.

(6) *Cognitive Therapy, or Rational-Emotive Approaches.* At the opposite end of the spectrum from Freudian psychoanalysis, "cognitive" therapies attempt rational intervention in the patient's conscious mind,

analogously to educational information transfer. A therapist treating a depressed or anxious patient, for example, may trace the immediate manifestations (feelings of rejection and low self-esteem) and help the patient to recognize psychological traps and to generate strategies to avoid them.

(7) *Medical Therapies.* "Electroconvulsive therapy" still today is used as a last resort for severely depressed patients. "Psychosurgery," today, has been largely abandoned, although the prefrontal lobotomy earned its developer, Egas Moniz, the Nobel Prize for its ability to quiet violent and agitated patients such as excited schizophrenics.

Today, chemical or pharmacological therapy is far more likely to be the treatment of choice. Drugs such as phenothiazines (thorazine) have revolutionized the treatment of psychoses such as agitative schizophrenias, and clozaril treats withdrawn ones. Valium and Librium treat anxiety. Prozac, Zoloft, and a variety of others treat depression, and lithium salts have proved successful in evening the moods of bipolar disorder.

(8) *The Frustrating Inexactitude of Psychological Knowledge.* It is worth emphasizing, again, the inexactitude of all of these concepts. Those who have a conception of psychology as precise, like the physical or even the medical sciences, are likely to be disappointed. Diagnostic labels frequently are debatable and are fuzzy in meaning anyway. Causes and origins are incompletely known. Treatment modalities are subject to differing preferences, and they may not have uniform results.

It would be equally unfortunate, however, if the reader were to go to the opposite extreme by concluding that the mushiness of the subject deprives it of value. Diagnostic criteria do mean something, behavior does correlate with DSM categories, causes and origins sometimes can be identified, and treatment modalities sometimes are efficacious. The key is not to expect absolutes. Psychologists work in an area in which the received wisdom is not valueless, but its value depends in part on recognizing its imperfections.

EXAMPLES AND PROBLEMS

(1) *Are Lawyers Analogous to "Non-Executive Monkeys?"* Lawyers suffer more from stress than most professionals in the workplace. From the executive monkey experiment, can you speculate about the reasons? Note that lawyers have difficulty exercising control over their own schedules and

over the results of their efforts, which often are imposed by judges, clients, legal deadlines, and the cumulation of responsibilities all at one time.

(2) *The Law and Systematic Desensitization: Television Effects and Use by Lawyers During Jury Selection.* It has been hypothesized that television and video game treatments of violence produce a systematic desensitization that removes some people's inhibitions against engaging in violence themselves. Does the therapeutic use of systematic desensitization provide a model that can be extended to this situation?

In a very different situation, personal injury defense lawyers have been known repeatedly to expose potential jurors to gruesome photographs that they expect the opposing (plaintiff's) lawyers to display, while questioning the array of potential jurors about their attitudes toward the defendant and the governing legal principles. Does the therapeutic use of systematic desensitization lend any support to these defense lawyers' tactic?

(3) *Learned Helplessness, Learning Theory, and Personality.* One of the most interesting series of learning theory experiments is that of M.E.P. Seligman, who studied the relative abilities to escape electric shocks of dogs who had been exposed to unescapable electric shocks and "naive" dogs who had not been so exposed. Although naive dogs quickly learned to jump a barrier, the previously shocked dogs tended to exhibit "learned helplessness." They simply lay down, whined and passively waited for the shocks to end. But there were some experimental dogs who did not react this way and who managed to jump the barrier.

It has been suggested that these experiments may be useful in understanding depression, which is characterized by reduced initiative and hopelessness. Can you explain why? Furthermore, studies on humans (by survey rather than shocks) have produced insights into the type of personality that is less susceptible to learned helplessness, like the dogs that jumped the barrier. These personalities tend to attribute failures to situations rather than to inner defects in themselves, to avoid universalizing failures to situations generally, and to regard blockages as temporary. Can you explain these observations and speculate about how they might be useful in cognitive therapy?

(4) *Borderline Personality, Child Sexual Abuse, and the Supreme Court.* In such cases as *Maryland v. Craig*, 497 U.S. 836 (1990), the Supreme Court

has decided that substitutes for a child's live, in-court testimony about sexual abuse, such as real-time closed-circuit testimony, cannot be used unless there is a "particularized showing" of unusual need to prevent harm to the individual child from testifying. Evaluate this requirement.

In particular, a condition called "borderline personality disorder" (reflected in impaired self-image, sexual dysfunction, poor impulse control, substance abuse and related effects) is correlated with childhood sexual abuse. But psychiatrists disavow any ability to predict which abused children will succumb to borderline personality, no longitudinal studies exist, the factors are thought to range from trauma to genetics, and some of them depend on future events. Is it rational, then, to charge judges with the task of recognizing which individual children will be harmed by testifying?

Indeed, since denial and repression are part of the pathology of child abuse, ironically, it may be precisely those children who appear tough, and *least* likely to suffer harm from testifying and being cross-examined, who are *most* at risk. The result of the Supreme Court's approach may be a judge's decision, then, that is opposite from reality. Can you explain?

(5) *Another Legal Application--How People Sometimes Ridicule Mental Health Experts: "Cross-Examining the Shrink."* The indeterminacy of diagnosing psychological disorders sometimes tempts people to cross-examine them by exploiting this indeterminacy, which is endemic to the discipline, and to make it appear to be the responsibility of a foolish "shrink." "Doctor, are you telling us that two people might be schizophrenics, but they might have no similar characteristics at all in common?" "It's true, isn't it, that there's no unified definition of what a 'schizophrenic' is?" "And as for predicting who's dangerous and who's not, you can't tell from that kind of label?" "And this list of diagnostic questions asks you just to pick five out of eleven characteristics, right?" "And the experts disagree on any one of these a large percentage of the time, right?"

To counteract this attack, the lawyers calling the "shrink" will need to carefully avoid overpromising and introduce the judge or jury to the subject in a way that conveys its value, despite inexactitude. The witness needs to be unusually capable at explaining complexities to lay people. Can you explain?

§ 11.05   Intelligence and Psychological Testing

INTELLIGENCE TESTING AND THE LAW

(1) *Intelligence, Job Performance, and Employment Law: Racial Discrimination and Other Issues.* Intelligence measurement is crucial to many kinds of human endeavors. Your presence in law school, for example, is due to tests of both "aptitude" and "achievement" that you have taken. (We'll consider these ideas below.) The law regulates both the validity and use of intelligence measurement. In employment law, for example, any such test having disparate impact upon ethnic groups, as intelligence tests are prone to do, must be business-justified. There is renewed concern, today, that intelligence testing can possibly become unfairly discriminatory. (We'll consider this too.)

(2) *The Wechsler Adult Intelligence Scale-Revised (WAIS-R).* The "Wechsler Adult Intelligence Scale-Revised" ("WAIS-R") is one widely-used method of intelligence testing. It requires such tasks as rearranging jumbled cartoon pictures and substituting numbers for symbols ($\triangle = 1$, $\circ = 2$, etc., with the subject required to translate the symbols). See Figure 4.

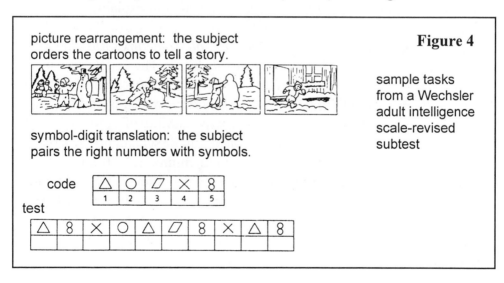

picture rearrangement: the subject orders the cartoons to tell a story.

symbol-digit translation: the subject pairs the right numbers with symbols.

Figure 4

sample tasks from a Wechsler adult intelligence scale-revised subtest

(3) *Validity, Reliability and Standardization: From IQ to Statistical Distribution.* The "validity" of the WAIS-R, meaning its accuracy in measuring what it purports to measure, is increased by its reduced dependence on language and cultural factors. But no test is perfectly valid; for example, is it possible that the "build-a-snowman" story in Figure 4 could be biased against people in tropical climates? Or could an intelligent person with an undeveloped vocabulary produce a lower score because of poor

understanding of instructions? There has long been a debate, and it continues today, concerning whether the test is biased toward lowering scores of African-Americans, recent immigrants, or other cultural or ethnic groups.

Second, the "reliability," or repeatable precision, of the Wechsler test also is imperfect but high. Third, a test must be "standardized," meaning that raw scores must be translated into a comparative scale. Early scales used "intelligence quotient" (IQ), or the quotient of mental age divided by chronological age multiplied by 100. This made some sense for children, but it distorted adult measurements. The Wechsler scale is standardized by its centering upon a statistically normal distribution, depicted in Figure 5, with the mean raw score producing a result of 100 and raw scores within one standard deviation (about 68% of people) ranging from 85 to 115.

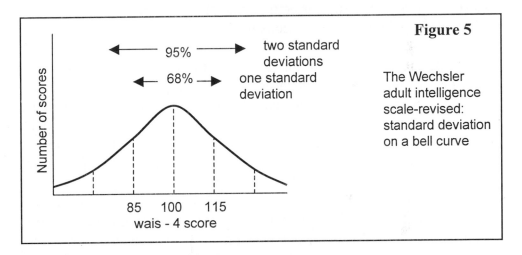

Figure 5

The Wechsler adult intelligence scale-revised: standard deviation on a bell curve

(4) *Other Tests for Other Purposes.* "Aptitude" tests are designed to predict how well a person will do in mastering new skills or knowledge, while "achievement" tests measure current mastery. An intelligence test is more akin to an aptitude test, while an examination at the end of a college course is an aptitude test.

But the two types tend to overlap. Intelligence tests that heavily emphasize vocabulary or mathematical ability may be acceptable for people of similar culture and achievement opportunity but might lack validity otherwise. Tests that reduce this kind of bias also have been devised; for example, in the "draw-a-man" test, the subject draws a figure and the interpreter uses a point scale to figure intelligence. But the arguable validity gain from reduction of cultural bias is offset by losses in reliability.

THE MEANING OF INTELLIGENCE

Howard Gardner

(1) *Gardner's Seven-Typed Theory of Multiple Intellectual Competence: The Rejection of Traditional Measures of Intelligence.* There are critics who maintain that intelligence testing, and indeed the concept of intelligence, are not useful. Harvard paleontologist Stephen Jay Gould wrote that "determinist arguments for ranking people according to a single scale of intelligence . . . have recorded little more than social prejudice." Harvard psychologist Howard Gardner also flatly rejects any general intelligence concept: "I place no particular premium on the word intelligence, but I do place great importance on . . . various human faculties."

Gardner identifies seven distinct "intellectual competencies": (1) linguistic, (2) musical, (3) logical-mathematical, (4) spatial, (5) bodily-kinesthetic, (6) intrapersonal intelligence (or personal intellectual competence in social interaction), and (7) intrapersonal intelligence (or competence with respect to one's own personality). His argument is that there is no one phenomenon of intelligence, although people differ in these competencies.

(2) *Gardner's Critics: The Insufficiency of Empirical Evidence.* Gardner does not defend his theory with quantitative data, or indeed with uniformly testable reasoning. Critics point out, furthermore, that general intelligence testing shows a significant correlation with high competence in each of his seven models, suggesting that there is, in fact, a general intelligence concept that unifies all of Gardner's types. Gardner responds by declining to accept the correlation, on the ground that current tests are biased.

(3) *General Current Agreement on the Existence of Cognitive Ability or Intelligence.* Despite these differing theories, today there is widespread but not exclusive agreement among psychologists that there is such a thing as intelligence and that it systematically varies among people. Psychologists also tend to agree that standardized aptitude and achievement tests all measure intelligence to some degree. Nevertheless, some people prefer the term "cognitive ability" to avoid the political baggage that the term "intelligence" carries, and there also is general agreement that this factor has limited value in assessing any given individual.

EXAMPLES AND PROBLEMS

(1) *Employment Testing, Discriminatory Impact, and the Supreme Court's Requirement of Demonstrable Validity Under Title VII: Griggs v Duke Power Company*, 426 U.S. 229 (1976). Let us say that a private firm wants to administer an intelligence test to clerical job applicants. Even if valid, the test may result in some degree of gender, age or racial impact. Why?

Furthermore, if the impact is significantly disparate, the law (Title VII of the Civil Rights Act) has been interpreted to require that the employer demonstrate a relationship between the test and actual performance of the job at issue. This burden of proof probably will require a statistical analysis of scores and performance ratings that demonstrates a significant correlation; it will not be enough for the employer's representatives to testify that they think an intelligence test is just generally a good idea for any job. Can you see why the law imposes this burden on the employer?

(2) *The Deliberate Use of a Bell-Shaped Standardization for the WAIS-R, Compared to Percentiles.* If the WAIS-R were done in percentiles, a score of 1 would mean that the individual fit in the lowest 1%, 50 would mean that the person was at the median, and 99 would mean that the individual scored higher than 99% of the population. A graph of numbers of people versus percentile scores would be a flat line.

Why, then, does the WAIS-R use a bell curve instead? Consider whether (a) political concerns oppose attaching the label of either 99 or 1 to an individual, (b) the dramatic difference in bell-curve scores at the upper and lower ends is useful (i.e., very high or very low scores are identifiably extraordinary), or (c) the ease of conversion to percentiles makes the question less important.

(3) *"If Boxcars Are Up, What's Down?": Avoiding (Reversing?) Illegal Discrimination in Intelligence Tests.* Allegations of latent bias in some intelligence tests have prompted critics to suggest that the "build-a-snowman" story test in Figure 4, as well as other kinds of traditional questions, should be supplemented by problems posed in the language and with the cultural assumptions of non-mainstream groups, such as disaffected youth. Perhaps these questions, then, should assume knowledge of the perceived advantages of body piercing or strategies in violent video games. One question that has

been suggested, half-facetiously: "If boxcars are up, what's down?"[2] Is there anything to these suggestions?

(4) *Does Gardner Have a Point (and Should the Law Acknowledge It)?* The idea of multiple intellectual competencies is intuitively appealing. Certainly, we all have known logical people with relatively little in the way of social skills, musicians who weren't very logical, and linguistic people who weren't good at introspection. Is there anything then, to Professor Gardner's seven-part model? If so, does it refute the concept of general intelligence sufficiently so that the law should require testing of specific competencies instead?

(5) *Herrnstein and Murray's "The Bell Curve" and Charges of Racial Discrimination in Intelligence Psychology: What Should Be the Response of the Law?* Richard J. Herrnstein and Charles Murray's book *The Bell Curve* produced a firestorm of criticism. The book maintained that psychologists shared general agreement that heredity was a major determinant of intelligence, with an influence somewhere between forty and eighty percent. It also reported, on the basis of standardized testing, that intelligence was differently distributed in racial groups. The bell curve of intelligence for African-Americans largely overlapped that of Caucasian Americans, according to Herrnstein and Murray, but they maintain that the mean of the curve for African-Americans is lower.

The book also says that, for most purposes, "We can tell you nothing with any confidence" about the actual competence differences between two individuals from different scores, that intelligence scores are a "limited tool" that must be evaluated together with information about "personality, talents and background," and that "cognitive ability" may be a preferable term. But, says the book, "received wisdom in the media is roughly 180 degrees opposite from" generally agreed views among educational psychologists.

The Bell Curve was attacked repeatedly as racist. How would you evaluate this criticism?

(6) *What, Then, Is Intelligence?* Is "intelligence" the score that results from a test? Or is it the ability to perform well at a task or problem in the future, which the test may not predict very well? The trouble is, we would

---

2 The answer: snake eyes.

like to have a reliable predictor of future capabilities at intellectual tasks, but since we cannot predict this factor reliably, we use intelligence tests, which do give repeatable results but which are not as closely related to the ultimate issue (future performance) as we might like. Can you explain this?

§ 11.06　Some Concepts From Social Psychology

[A]　Attitudes:　Dissonance, Attribution, Attraction and Persuasion

FESTINGER'S THEORY OF COGNITIVE DISSONANCE

(1) *Social Psychology and the Law.* Next, in this section, we shall consider some concepts of social psychology, which is the psychology of social situations. Festinger's theory of cognitive dissonance is one of the more important developments in this field.

This (very simple) theory applies to many disciplines, including the law. It explains how people "rationalize" bad behavior. It shows why examining jurors about their attitudes is difficult. And it may even explain why your professors in law school teach you the way they do.

Leon Festinger

(2)　*Cognitive Dissonance: Integration of Cognitive Attitudes to Fit Behavior.* Leon Festinger's theory of "cognitive dissonance" posits that there is a mental tension created by contradictory perceptions. The theory, which can be summarized as "behavior determines attitudes, as well as the other way around," is that individuals are motivated to reduce this tension (or "dissonance") by modifying their attitudes or perceptions to fit other cognitive inputs, including their perceptions of their own behavior. The mind, in other words, rationalizes nonconforming behavior and justifies it by changing the cognition (attitude) that conflicts with it.

(3) *Implications of Cognitive Dissonance for the Law: Examples of Cognition Changes to Reduce Tension, in Settings Involving Violence, Collaboration, and Investment.* The implications of Festinger's theory are wide-ranging, and observed effects from varied settings support it. For example, a subject who has been caused to harm another person with electric shocks during an experiment tends to begin disparaging the victim. This attitude reduces the dissonance. Prisoners who initially despise "snitches" tend to see crime prevention as noble after they have begun to collaborate with prison authorities.

Also, game theorists have noted that subjects induced to bid in auctions tend to value the prize more if they have heavily invested in it. Even such mundane experiences as a long wait at a bus stop can be analyzed in dissonance terms. The longer one has waited, ironically, the more one is motivated to wait even longer, to reduce the tension between a perception that one has invested heavily in waiting and the attitude that the investment is not worthwhile(!)

(4) *Role-Playing and the Dissonance Phenomenon: Zimbardo's Prison Simulation.* Psychologist Philip Zimbardo designed a disturbing experiment related to dissonance theory. He designated randomly-chosen students as "guards," provided them with paraphernalia such as uniforms and clubs, and gave them a set of "rules" to enforce. Other students were "prisoners," restricted to cell-like spaces and wearing jail clothing.

After an initial tentativeness, both groups began to behave as if the simulation were real. Guards imposed increasingly degrading punishments upon prisoners, who rebelled or passively endured. The experiment had to be terminated prematurely. Role-playing, it appears, tends to induce attitudes that conform to the role; the guards tended to elevate the importance of the "rules" and to disparage perceived infractions by prisoners. Dissonance theory may explain the reason. The guards revised their attitudes to justify their oppressive behavior.

(5) *Consistency and Hypocrisy: To What Extent Do Expressed Attitudes Influence Behavior?* It also is true that attitudes sometimes influence behavior. But the leakage in this phenomenon, or hypocrisy, is significant. For example, people who firmly express beliefs in gender and racial equality tend to downgrade work product identified by gender or race in double-blind experiments.

The psychological experiments indicate that people are more likely to conform their behavior to their attitudes when, first, negative external implications are minimal (a Senator is more likely to vote independently the year after election than in the ninth year while running for reelection), second, when the attitude is directly related to the behavior (health attitudes tend to influence exercise), and third, when the actor is fully cognizant of the attitude (attitudes that people have thoroughly studied and discussed are more predictive than less considered attitudes). But just as attitudes may influence behavior, dissonance theory explains that the opposite is also true. People revise their attitudes to justify their own behavior.

ATTRIBUTION AND ATTRACTION

(1) *How the Law Is Related to Attribution and Attraction.* "Attribution" theory helps to show us how human beings explain other people's behavior to themselves. In picking jurors or devising themes to present to a jury, a lawyer needs a feel for attribution theory. Attraction is important in persuasion, as well as in other contexts.

(2) *Attribution Theory: How People Ascribe Others' Behavior to Situations or to Personality.* What is "attribution theory?" Imagine that John, a person you slightly know, has just treated you in what you perceive to be an abrupt and insulting manner. To what do you attribute this behavior? One response is "situational" attribution: for example, you could infer that John is under stress. Alternatively, there is "dispositional" attribution: You might infer that John is just a mean person.

Experiments show that the mind's overwhelming tendency is to adopt the dispositional attribution, or to infer that John is mean rather than stressed. This is so even if adequate information is lacking or even if the evidence is to the contrary. This response is so familiar that it is called the "fundamental attribution error": the error of ascribing behavior to personality rather than to circumstances.

Ironically, this is not the case with our own behavior; we usually are aware of how it changes with the situation. But with other people's behavior, the fundamental attribution error is surprisingly seductive.

One striking experiment by Napolitan and Goethals involved a woman who alternately was instructed to act in a friendly manner or coldly. Two groups of students, a control group that falsely was led to believe that the woman's behavior would be spontaneous and a test group that was explicitly told the woman's instructions, individually interacted with her, and then they were asked what they inferred about the woman's real personality.

The astonishing result: there was no statistically significant difference between the groups. Even the subjects who were told openly that the woman would be acting, still, were just as prone as other subjects to infer that she really had a "cold" or a "friendly" personality. The fundamental attribution error is so powerful that even explicit evidence of situational origin did not influence the tendency to attribute behavior to personality!

(3) *Attraction: Exposure, Physicality, Attitudinal Similarity, and Reward.* Next, we consider interpersonal attraction. What attracts two people and makes them friends? First, familiarity and proximity. The "mere exposure factor" has at least a limited influence; indeed, experiments show that repeated encounters with unfamiliar forms of music or art tend to increase their attractiveness. Second, physical appearance has a surprisingly large effect, sometimes disproportionate to less superficial factors such as intelligence, compassion or sincerity. Experiments demonstrate that employers prefer attractive, well-groomed people who "dress for success."

Third, attitudinal similarity increases attraction. The theory that opposites attract makes good theatre, but similarity in attitudes, status, interests and the like is the experimentally valid predictor. Fourth, attraction is increased by reward. You're more likely to like someone who likes you back.

PERSUASION: SELECTED THEORIES AND LEGAL APPLICATIONS

(1) *Persuasion as Technique, as Reason and as Situation.* Now, let us apply some of these theories, plus some other observation, to the phenomenon of persuasion. There are many theories, and a huge number of theoretical models, of persuasion. They depend heavily on situations; for example, conducting a political campaign with a popular candidate is different from conducting a campaign for the newcomer opponent, and it also is different from short-term selling or lawyers' trial tactics. Furthermore, logic and reason enter into it. This, of course, is what we would hope: that persuasion is a reasoned endeavor, a factor often forgotten when we consider persuasion techniques. But the psychology of persuasion also is important.

(2) *Ingratiation: The Audience-Reward Theory and Its Use in the Law.*
One experimental finding is that a speaker's praise of the listener increases
the listener's reception of the message. This finding is predicted by the
attraction-reward theory. "You're the type of person who can appreciate this
Pennoyer-Neff Scorpion convertible," says the car salesperson. "You've got
superior intelligence."

One might worry that the listener would be put off by this apparently
insincere contrivance. But not necessarily, because of the fundamental
attribution error. Even when evidence suggests that the ingratiating behavior
is situational (after all, this is a car salesperson), the listener tends to attribute
the kind remarks to the speaker's real, sincere disposition.

Ingratiation also works in the law. We'll see how in a moment.

(3)   *A Familiar and Physically Attractive Spokesperson.*   When
Publisher's Clearinghouse wanted to publicize its magazine-related contests
to middle-aged and older consumers, it employed former Tonight Show
personality Ed McMahon and disc jockey Dick Clark as its spokesmen.
These were people one could expect to be attractive to the audience: familiar,
well groomed, and similar to the audience. Attraction theory supports the
inference of their persuasiveness.

(4) *Similarity: Identification as Attractiveness.* The speaker attempts to
emphasize similarities with the audience: "It's good to be back here in my
hometown (or home state)." Linda Tripp, who surreptitiously taped Monica
Lewinsky while she talked to a supposed friend about her relationship to
President Clinton, attempted to spruce up her image by telling the American
people she was similar to them: "I am you."

(5)   *Framing: How Lawyers Use It.*   The setting of the agenda, or
"framing" of the issue, influences the decision. In a later chapter, for
example, you will see that psychological experiments in game theory show
different play if identical strategic situations are differently labelled.

And imagine a lawsuit involving a vehicular collision with a child in a
school zone. The plaintiff's lawyer's one-sentence introduction is, "The
defendant was speeding recklessly through the very place we expect children
to do the unexpected." The defendant's version is, "The little girl darted out,
and you wouldn't have been able to stop either." Whichever side succeeds in

getting the jury to accept its framing is well on the way toward winning this suit. This side has furnished the lens through which the jury will view all the evidence.

(6) *Small Steps: How Cognitive Dissonance Works in Persuasion.* Observation confirms that it is easier to get individuals to shift attitudes if they already have taken steps in the desired direction. One experiment involved asking homeowners to post large, ugly signs saying, "Drive Carefully." Fewer than 20% consented. Those who refused were asked to display a tiny, three-inch sign, and nearly all agreed. Later, these homeowners who had accepted the tiny sign were asked, again, to accept the big, ugly sign, and nearly 80% agreed. Their earlier acceptance of small signs had changed their attitudes toward the entire question of signs.

As another example, political regimes that have used torture have recruited torturers in the same way: first, by having newcomers stand guard, then by having them observe, and then by inducing minor participation. Perhaps cognitive dissonance, in part, explains why this "small steps" technique works. Having "bought into" the behavior, the subject adjusts cognition (attitudes) to justify the behavior, even when it consists only of small steps.

(7) *Negative Effects of Dissonance on Persuasion: Horrible Consequences as Unpersuasive.* Overstatement of unpleasant consequences can be dysfunctional in persuasion. One experiment depicted hideously ugly gums and teeth from bad hygiene, in an effort to induce subjects to use better oral hygiene. These horrible-consequence pictures were less persuasive than other approaches. Apparently, the subjects resolved cognitive dissonance by rationalizing that such brutal effects could not happen to them.

(8) *Positive Effects of Dissonance on Persuasion: Obtaining Commitments.* "If I come back again tomorrow, will you try my product?" asks the salesperson. The hope is that dissonance will prevent the prospect from dishonoring the promise. Similarly, a wise employer may enter into an express contract with employees that specifies job duties and sets high standards. The purpose is not merely legalistic, but also persuasive.

(9) *Conformity and Authority.* In the next section, we consider conformity and authority, which also have roles in persuasion.

EXAMPLES AND PROBLEMS

(1) *The Use of Cognitive Dissonance in Interrogation: Law and Psychology.* Manuals on interrogation of criminal suspects suggest immediate confrontation of a lying subject with proof of the falsehood. The interrogator adopts an attitude of omniscience, implying that all that is asked is for the subject to confirm details. Above all, the interrogator suggests mitigating circumstances, such as provocation or need, that make the behavior less unattractive. Can cognitive dissonance theory explain why these techniques might work?

(2) *Persuasion by Lawyers in Trial.* Can you explain the following trial techniques or observations of trial situations? (a) Observations show that jurors form scenarios about a case very early, before hearing any witnesses, and that these form the basis for their perceptions of all the evidence. (b) Persuasion guides suggest that lawyers begin the case by stating one or two very clear themes, or three at the most, containing unifying predictions about the evidence, keyed to their preferred outcomes.

(c) Final argument often begins with a strong statement of belief in the jury system and thanks to jurors for their careful attention to the case. (d) Although one might think that unusual and severe injuries would induce juror sympathy, they sometimes instead cause jurors to blame the injury on the plaintiff's behavior. (e) Lawyers often obtain commitments from jurors during jury selection: "Even if there is a crime proven, and even if you strongly suspect John did it, can you promise me, and promise John here, that you'll acquit him if there's a reasonable doubt?"

(f) A lawyer cross-examining an adverse witness may start with issues with which the witness will likely agree, even if the issues are relatively small in the context of the entire case. (g) In defending a corporation, a lawyer often will have a personable officer sit through the trial, introduce her, and refer to it as "Sarah's company." (h) Sometimes lawyers repeat an explanation of a key legal concept, such as negligence, from the beginning of the trial to the end, beyond the point necessary for the jurors to understand it.

[B]   The Influence of Groups and Leaders: Conformity and Authority

CONFORMITY AND AUTHORITY

(1) *Conformity, Authority, and the Law.*   Why do lawyers need to understand conformity and authority? First, as we shall see, because they effect persuasion, and lawyers need, above all, to be persuasive. Second, because conformity and authority have significant effects on obedience to laws or norms. Groups can exert good influences on peoples' behavior in response to rules, and they also can exert surprisingly bad influences.

(2) *Asch's Conformity Studies: Disheartening Implications for Thinking or for Resistance to Group Lawbreaking.* Next, let us consider the social psychology of conformity and authority, of which Asch's conformity studies are a classic. Solomon Asch used a diagram with a test line and three comparison lines of differing lengths, combined with three "stooges," to test suggestibility toward conformity from group influence. See Figure 6.

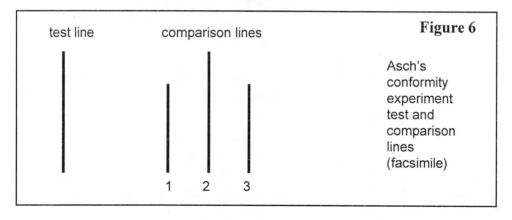

Figure 6

Asch's conformity experiment test and comparison lines (facsimile)

After the stooges each identified one of the comparison lines, which obviously did not fit, as matching the test line, Asch invited an experimental subject's response. In one experiment, 75% of the subjects conformed to the stooges' staged behavior, selecting the obviously wrong line in at least one trial (whereas control groups erred less than one percent of the time). Subjects often reacted to the stooges' choices with astonished looks and puzzled squinting, even as they conformed to the stooges' implicit suggestion. Asch's conclusion was that "intelligent, well-meaning" subjects were surprisingly willing to conform to erroneous group suggestion.

(3) *Norms, Normative Group Influence, and Informational Group Influence.* A "norm" is an accepted rule for proper social behavior. The "normative influence" of a group is its suggestion of conformity (which may

be good or bad, as Asch's experiment shows). The "informational" group influence, on the other hand, reflects the greater experience or knowledge of several people rather than one.

Imagine, for example, that a group is asked, "What foreign country do you first enter if you start at the center of Detroit and travel due south?" When one member of the group persuades the others that the answer is Canada, because the waterway separating that country from the United States makes a reverse-S shape immediately below Detroit, the informational influence is at work. But if a member of the group who knew the correct answer (Canada) were to adopt an erroneous answer (Mexico) because all other group members chose that response, the normative group influence would have won out.

(4) *Authority, Obedience, and Law: Milgram's Experiment.* The social psychology of authority and obedience has produced some disturbing results that have serious implications for lawyers. Stanley Milgram's authority experiment is a classic. Milgram set up a phony "experimenter" in an official-looking white lab coat, who actually was a stooge, and who instructed subjects to administer electrical "shocks" to a strapped-down "learner" whenever the learner made errors. The scale for the "shocks" began at "15 Volts ('Slight' Shock)" and went through 150 Volts ("'Strong' Shock"), all the way to 450 Volts.

But in reality there were no shocks, and the learner also was a stooge, who both erred intentionally and grunted or gasped in pain at the lower settings. At 120 volts, the stooge playing the part of the learner protested that the shocks were painful; at 150, the stooge (through a voice recorder) shouted, "Get me out of here! . . . I refuse!"

If the subject faltered, the experimenter responded firmly that "the experiment requires that you go on." At "180 volts," the learner shouted that he "couldn't stand" the pain; at 300, responses stopped, and the experimenter told the subject to treat a non-response as a wrong answer. Most subjects who "prematurely" terminated this charade were highly agitated, and so were those who continued, protesting all the way, to 450 volts. The white-jacketed "experimenter" used a simple technique, simply telling the subject that "the experiment requires you to continue," or words to that effect.

But astonishingly, more than 60% of the subjects continued to the end of the scale, hearing agonized cries from the stooge. Milgram's conclusion was that "ordinary people" were sufficiently obedient to purported authority that they could be readily engaged in a "terribly destructive process." It does not take much extrapolation to see that some people can be similarly influenced to violate the law, even when harmful results are clear.

(5) *Ethical and Legal Limits Upon These Kinds of Experiments.* No reputable experimenter is likely to replicate these results today. Milgram's work is, indeed, a classic. Ethical limits, not to mention legal liability to subjects, prevent certain experiments with human subjects.

(6) *The Factors That Increase Conformity to Suggestion and Obedience to Authority.* Subsequent experiments have shown that conformity to group suggestion is stronger if a sense of inferiority or insecurity is induced in the subject. The absence of prior commitment against the suggestion, as well as belonging to a culture that values conformity, also are strengthening factors. Unanimity of the group makes for more powerful suggestion than if the subject has an agreeing companion, and so does a high-status group, or a group with expertise. Group size also matters, but the effect seems to level off at a size ranging from three to seven, depending on the experiment. And, of course, ambiguity of the correct response increases conformity.

Similarly, Milgram's experiments showed that a high-status authority and the absence of a disobeying role model strengthened obedience. Physical factors, such as close proximity of the authority and distance of the person harmed (e.g., by walling the learner off in another room), also reinforced obedience. Subsequent experiments have show that depersonalization of the actor, such as by wearing a mask, makes the subject more obedient to group or authority suggestions that otherwise might be resisted.

EXAMPLES AND PROBLEMS

(1) *Non-Unanimous Juries.* Some states allow verdicts to be returned by nine or ten members of a twelve-person jury. But few states use eleven-member verdicts. Perhaps this is sensible, since theory predicts that eleven-member majorities are more likely than lesser majorities to persuade the lone dissenter and to result in unanimous verdicts. Can you see why?

(2) *Group Aggression: The Crowd Effect, Deindividuation, and Illegal Violence.* Members of a crowd are more likely to engage in aggression than individuals acting alone. British soccer violence is one egregious example of this crowd effect. Can you explain this "deindividuation" phenomenon by reference to the normative group influence?

(3) *Closeness and Touching as Criminal Interrogation Techniques.* Some police officers maintain that an interrogator's sitting very close to a subject face to face, so that the two pairs of legs even interlock, and reaching out to touch the subject, are effective inducements toward confession. Can you explain why this might be so?

(4) *Groupthink, or the Failure to Generate Dissenting Views.* One danger in a decisionmaking team is that even when there is no express suppression of contrary views, normative group influence may suppress them. The Bay of Pigs disaster is one famous example. President Kennedy expressed his support for the invasion of Cuba, and high morale, optimism and group dynamics fostered harmonious agreement. Then, after a CIA-financed force of Cuban exiles suffered a crushing defeat with severe casualties, many people, including the President, wondered how the decisionmaking process could have gone so badly wrong. Can you explain?

Chapter 12
Probabilities

Probabilistic Reasoning in the Law, Bayes' Theorem, and the Interval Distribution

> *"[S]ocial science . . . must be satisfied to test the validity of its conclusions by the logic of probabilities rather than the logic of certainty."--Justice Benjamin N. Cardozo, The Growth of the Law*

> *"Probability cannot be made the measure of progress in the dispatch of business . . . [A] wide variation from the average rate of progress may occur. Indeed, it is always probable that something improbable will happen."--Judge Logan E. Bleckley, Warren v. Purtell, 63 Ga. 428, 430 (1878)*

§ 12.01　What This Chapter Is About

PROBABILISTIC REASONING AND THE LAW

(1) *Probability Theory, Combining Probabilities, and Bayes' Theorem.* This chapter covers the estimation of probabilities, the combining of

probabilities for chain events, and the adjustment of probabilities for later evidence. A "probability" is a number between 1.0 (representing certainty) and 0.0 (representing impossibility) that roughly corresponds to a gambler's notion of the "odds" of a chance event. The laws of probability are deductive in nature, in that they can be considered by mathematical equations (of which we shall explore only a few), but estimates of probabilities, as well as predictions about events from estimates of probabilities, are inductive.

One equation that is particularly useful is called "Bayes' Theorem," after the person who developed and explained it. Bayes' Theorem is a means of adjusting probabilities for later evidence. More practically, it allows us to use an existing probability estimate (which may be intuitively or holistically derived), together with a later piece of evidence, to infer cause and effect.

(2) *The Interval Distribution.* The chapter also considers the way in which random variables tend to "bunch" or "clump." This issue is related to one of our greatest sources of fallacy, in that the human mind is such a powerful pattern-recognition device that people tend to infer patterns from this bunching or clumping, even when it is merely a product of randomness.

(3) *Statistical Reasoning (Next Chapter).* An additional reason to study probabilities is that they are an essential part of statistical reasoning, which we shall take up in the next chapter.

(4) *The Law: Why Do Attorneys Need Probabilities and Statistics?* Now, let us consider why it might be worth your while to understand this material. First, settlement of lawsuits is a probabilistic exercise. Mediators often use probabilities and mathematical expectations to help adverse parties analyze settlement offers. Since you will settle many times as many cases as you will try, this factor alone is reason enough. But there is more. Second, today more than ever before, probabilistic and statistical evidence is used to prove facts in litigation, ranging from civil rights to paternity cases. Third, legislation often is based on probabilistic and statistical evidence. For example, statistics can give rise to new laws that combat antisocial behavior better. Fourth, some of the methods of jurisprudence, particularly in the influential law and economics movement, rely on probability analysis. Finally, intuition about coincident events often produces fallacious reasoning about law and public policy. If you understand probabilities and statistics, you are less likely to fall victim to this kind of thinking.

§ 12.02 Probability Theory

WHAT ARE PROBABILITIES AND HOW ARE THEY USED?

(1) *Probabilities, From 0.0 to 1.0.* Mathematicians have devised a number system for what are called "probabilities." Zero, or 0.0, corresponds to impossibility, while 1.0 is certainty. Thus, if you flip an ordinary coin, the probability of getting both heads and tails at the same time is 0.0; the probability of getting one or the other is 1.0 (assuming it can't land on its edge). Usually, then, a probability is a number between 0.0 and 1.0, which sometimes is expressed as a decimal (0.5), sometimes as a fraction (1/2). An event with a probability close to one, such as .9999, is very likely to occur. A probability near zero, such as .0001, designates an event that is unlikely.

(2) *"Odds" and Probabilities.* Many people are used to a different numbering system, called "odds," but it corresponds to probability theory. One-to-one odds (or 1:1) refers to an event that is equally likely to occur or not to occur (such as heads in a coin flip). The corresponding probability is 0.5 (the probability of heads is the same as tails; both are 0.5). In the preceding paragraph, a probability of .9999 is the same as odds of 10,000:1, with rounding.

(3) *Converting Odds to Probabilities.* To convert odds to probabilities, divide the first number in the odds by the sum of the two numbers. Thus, for a coin flip, the odds of heads are 1:1; the probability is 1÷(the sum), or 1÷(1+1), or 1÷2, or ½, or 0.5. For the example of odds of 10,000:1, the corresponding probability is 10,000÷10,001, or 0.9999.

(4) *Why Use Probabilities When Most People Understand Odds Better?* Most people understand odds, if only because they've heard about the Kentucky Derby. You may wonder why we use probabilities, since some people are less familiar with them. The answer is, a probability is a single number, which we can use to figure other probabilities. We can add or multiply them. When the concept is expressed as odds, it's still possible to do it, but for some uses, it's clumsy.

(5) *If the Probability of an Event Is P, then the Probability of Its Nonoccurrence Is Easy to Figure: It's (1-P).* Remember, 1.0 means certainty. An event must either occur or not occur; therefore, the probability of occurrence plus the probability of nonoccurrence must add up to 1.0. This

means that if the probability of an event is P, then the probability of its not occurring must be (1-P). The probability of heads is 0.5, and so the probability of tails must be 1.0-0.5=0.5.

And here's another example: If we draw a sock at random from a drawer that has one red sock and two blue ones, the odds of drawing a red sock are 1:2, and the probability is 0.33. The probability of drawing a blue sock, then, must be 1.0-0.33=0.67.

(6) *Probability and Statistics.* One important use of probability theory is in statistical analysis, which pervades many fields, from sociology to medicine to law. In the next chapter, we consider statistics, but we take up probability theory first because it is necessary for statistical analysis, as well as important for its own sake.

EXAMPLES AND PROBLEMS

(1) *Mathematical Expectation: The Lottery Example and Lawsuit Settlements.* The concept of "mathematical expectation" is easy once you understand probabilities. Mathematical expectation is the probability of success multiplied by the payoff in the event of success (or, for multiple events, it is the sum of the products of the probabilities times their payoffs).

Thus, if the lottery payoff is $4 million, and the odds of winning it are 100 million to one, the probability of winning it is 1÷(100 million+1), or approximately (1÷(100 million)). Your mathematical expectation, then, is ($4 million) x (1÷100 million) = (4 million) ÷ (100 million) = 4÷100 = 0.04. The lottery ticket that you buy for $1 is "worth" four cents. Can you explain?

Settlement of a lawsuit can be analyzed by a similar kind of reasoning. Imagine that attorney Dewey Cheatham has filed a million-dollar lawsuit. He has pled for $1 million, that is; but he figures that his probability of winning is about one-third (a realistic figure for some lawsuits). Furthermore, it will cost him $250,000 just to try the case (also realistic). If he wins, he wins $1 million less $250,000 expenses; if he loses, he loses the $250,000 expenses. His mathematical expectation, then, is (1/3 x $1,000,000) - $250,000 = $333,333 - $250,000 = $83,333. It would be fallacious to look only at the $1 million jackpot, but it's easy to find yourself seduced into doing just that.

Now, assume that the defendant agrees with Dewey about the probabilities, and the defendant also faces expenses of $250,000. It is rational for both to settle. The plaintiff's mathematical expectation is less than the defendant's mathematically expected payout. Can you explain?

(2) *The Probability of a "Right" Quick Decision by a Court, Versus the Probability of a "Wrong" One.* Imagine that a court is presented with a request for a temporary restraining order. A developer is destroying trees on land that the plaintiff claims is his. It is an emergency request, and the judge can't hear all the evidence before deciding. The order needs to be decided upon today so the judge can either stop the construction or allow it to continue, but a full-blown trial would take a month.

Let us imagine that the judge listens to the plaintiff's attorney and, from experience and hunches, he estimates the likelihood of the plaintiff's winning at 2:3 odds, or in other words, the plaintiff's probability of winning is $[2\div(2+3)] = 2/5 = 0.4$. (Yes, judges do sometimes have to make these sorts of seat-of-the-pants estimates.)

First question: Can you explain why there is a probability of 0.6 that the defendant, the developer, will win instead? (Remember, the formula is 1-P.) Second question: What other information should the judge take into account in deciding whether to grant the injunction? (Notice that each party will suffer an unfair loss if there is a mistaken decision against it--the landowner will lose trees, the developer will lose investment and construction costs--but the sizes of their losses, and hence their mathematical expectation, may not be the same.) If you can't see the answer, go to the next note.

(3) *Judge Posner's Formula, Using Probabilities, for a Temporary Injunction Decision: American Hospital Supply Corporation v. Hospital Products Ltd.*, 780 F.2d 589, 593 (7th Cir. 1986). The traditional approach to the temporary restraining order and preliminary injunction question is for the judge to "balance the equities." That is, the judge considers the plaintiff's likelihood of success on the merits (a probabilistic concept), the harm to plaintiff if the injunction wrongly is denied, the harm to the defendant if it is wrongly granted, and the public interest. Assuming that the dispute is private, such as our landowner-developer dispute, and the public interest is not affected, there are three factors: the plaintiff's probability of success (P), the potential harm to the plaintiff (Hp), and potential harm to defendant (Hd).

In the *American Hospital Supply* case, Judge Posner translated these factors into an algebraic equation to tell a judge when to grant the injunction, using probabilities and mathematical expectancies. The judge should grant the injunction if PxHp>(1-P)xHd. (The symbol > means "is greater than.") Can you explain this simple equation in terms of probabilities and expectation, and can you compare it to the traditional balancing approach?

COMBINED PROBABILITY FOR MULTIPLE EVENTS: THE PRODUCT RULE

(1) *The Product Rule in Probability Theory: What Is the Probability of a Sequence of Independent Events?* The "product rule" allows us to calculate the likelihood of a series of different events. The rule is simple: The combined probability of multiple events is the *product* of their individual probabilities, provided that all events are independent. In other words, you simply multiply all of the probabilities together. For example, if you flip a coin three times, the probability of producing heads all three times is $0.5x0.5x0.5$, or $(.05)^3$, or 0.125. The probability of turning up heads four times in a row is $0.5x0.5x0.5x0.5$, or $(.05)^4$, or 0.0625.

(2) *Requirements for the Product Rule: The Events Must Be "Independent."* Notice that the product rule applies only if the events are "independent," or in other words, if the probability of each is not dependent upon or related to the occurrence of any of the other events. If, for example, the probability of the second event were to be increased by the occurrence of the first, the product rule would not apply.

(3) *The Law and the Product Rule.* Different, reinforcing items of circumstantial evidence vastly increase the reliability of a conclusion. Circumstantial evidence is probabilistic evidence, and it cumulates according to the product rule. Thus, the product rule is fundamental to legal proof. But it only applies if the evidentiary facts are independent. Let us see, now, what this means.

EXAMPLES AND PROBLEMS

(1) *Independence, Non-Independence, and the Product Rule: Drawing a Spade Twice from Two Decks of Cards, Either Shuffled or Not.* The probability of drawing a spade from a deck of cards is ¼, or 0.25. The

probability of repeating this draw of a spade twice from two different decks is $\frac{1}{4} \times \frac{1}{4} = \frac{1}{16} = 0.0625$. Can you see why?

But, consider a different scenario. Imagine that we know that the decks are arranged in identical order instead of shuffled, and we already have drawn the first card from the first deck and it is a spade. Now, the second event is not independent, because we already know how it is going to come out. In fact, the probability of drawing the second spade dramatically increases, from 1/4 to 1.0 (certainty). Can you see why the product rule no longer applies with the identical (non-independent) deck?

(2) *A Controversial Criminal Case Containing Product-Rule Reasoning: People v. Collins,* 68 Cal.2d 319, 438 P.2d 33 (1968). One controversial example of the use of the product rule in legal analysis is provided by the criminal case of *People v. Collins*, in which the conviction was reversed by the California Supreme Court. In addition to eyewitness identifications, the prosecutor offered the eyewitnesses' evidence of the characteristics of the individual defendants, together with expert testimony from a mathematician who explained the product rule to jurors. During final argument, the prosecutor used the product rule, together with estimates of the frequency of the defendants' characteristics in the population (blonde hair, yellow convertible, man with mustache, who also had a beard, etc.) in an effort to demonstrate that the eyewitnesses' descriptions of these characteristics would be unlikely to have occurred if the defendants were not guilty.

The California Supreme Court reversed, stating among other reasons that the factors were not independent (for example, two of the characteristics were a bearded man and the same man with a mustache; but perhaps men with beards are more likely also to have mustaches).[1] Can you see how this reasoning shows that the product rule could not give exact results, given the lack of independence? On the other hand, it seems unlikely that a jury would have thought that the prosecutor really claimed exact results, as opposed to merely illustration. Can you, therefore, critique the Court's reasoning? In fact, the prosecutor told the jury his figures were illustrative only. You should consider, for example, whether knowing about the product rule could be useful in these circumstances, even if it is understood that it gives non-quantitative results, as well as whether it might produce fallacious results.

---

1 The court gave other reasons, including the criticism that the claimed probability did not give a probability of guilt but only a probability that a random couple would share these characteristics. See the court's opinion for full treatment. This argument also remains controversial.

(3) *Conditional Probabilities as a Means of Increasing the Usefulness of Probability Theory: Solving the Beard-Mustache Problem.* One way to overcome the problem of non-independence is to use what are called "conditional probabilities." As the name implies, a conditional probability is simply the probability of a dependent factor, assuming a particular condition for another factor on which it depends. For example, we could solve the beard-mustache dependency problem, above, by substituting the probability of a person, known to have a beard, also having a mustache. In other words, we use the probability of a mustache, *conditioned on* the person having a beard. Can you explain why this adjustment of the theory would overcome objections based on non-independence?

(4) *The Product Rule and DNA Identification.* DNA analysis has become a powerful tool for identification of criminal suspects, as well as for other uses. The technique is essentially a determination of probabilities or odds, using the product rule. What the DNA analyst does is to isolate a particular DNA sequence from an unknown sample (taken usually from the crime scene) and to compare it to a corresponding sequence from a known sample (taken from the suspect). The analyst makes several comparisons of this type, using different sequences, to see whether each sequence from the unknown sample matches the corresponding sequence from the known one. Then, a statistician estimates the probability of each match occurring if the unknown sample were compared to a sequence from a random member of the population. The product of the probabilities for all sequences, then, is the probability of all the discovered matches occurring in the case of a person selected at random. Often, the numbers are astronomical, in the hundred millions or billions.

The final estimate depends, however, on several kinds of assumptions-- including the assumption that all the matches are independent. If a match in the first sequence happened to be correlated with the likelihood of a match in the next sequence, the use of the product rule and therefore the astronomical numbers, would be fallacious. Can you see why? For this reason, the assumption of independence has been debated extensively. It seems unlikely, in nature, that perfect independence could be taken for granted. Nevertheless, there is general agreement that proper analysis of DNA is reliable. Can you see how this conclusion depends on a conclusion that the probabilities, even if not perfectly independent, are sufficiently close to independence so that any error is small?

(5) *Variations of the Product Rule: What About One Tail in Five Flips?* We have seen how to figure the probability of five heads in a row. From the product rule, it's $\frac{1}{2}\times\frac{1}{2}\times\frac{1}{2}\times\frac{1}{2}\times\frac{1}{2}$, or $(\frac{1}{2})^5 = 1/32$. Now, let's vary the problem. What is the probability of throwing exactly one tail in the five flips (four heads and one tail)? We can't use the same formula for this problem, because it's slightly more complicated (but only slightly).

There are five (5) ways to get exactly one tail in five flips: on the first flip, or on flip 2, or 3, or 4, or 5. Each of these five ways is exactly the same in probability as five heads; we've just substituted a tail for one of the heads, and the tail also has the same $\frac{1}{2}$ probability. So, by the product rule, the probability of the first flip being tails and the rest heads is $\frac{1}{2}\times\frac{1}{2}\times\frac{1}{2}\times\frac{1}{2}\times\frac{1}{2}$, or $(\frac{1}{2})^5 = 1/32$. (It's the same as the probability for all heads.)

And the same probability applies to throwing tails on the second flip but heads on the four other flips. So it's also $(\frac{1}{2})^5$. Furthermore, the same probability applies to one tail on toss 3, on 4, and on 5. The probability of one tail in five flips, then, is $5\times(\frac{1}{2})^5 = 5/32$.

Now, we can do the same with one tail in ten flips: The probability is $10\times(\frac{1}{2})^{10} = 10/1024$. In fact, the probability of one tail in n flips is $n(\frac{1}{2})^n$. Can you explain the math? (You will need to recall and apply this formula in the next chapter, when we examine statistics.)

§ 12.03 Bayes' Theorem and the Law: Applying New Evidence to a Subjective Probability to Infer Causal Linkage

CALCULATING A NEW PROBABILITY WHEN THERE IS NEW EVIDENCE: BAYES' THEOREM

(1) *What Bayes' Theorem Demonstrates.* Given an initial probability, Bayes' Theorem provides a mathematical equation for computing a revised probability, resulting from an independent additional piece of information. In other words, Bayes' Theorem provides a quantative method for adjusting the computation of a probability, based upon new evidence. The theorem is named after Reverend Thomas Bayes, who discovered it during the 1800's. Today, Baysean analysis is used for some kinds of legal problems.

If the new information is such that its random occurrence is extremely unlikely (e.g., DNA characteristics that fit only one in several thousand members of the population), then the adjustment to even a moderate initial probability, such as 0.5, may produce a probability surprisingly close to 1.0. Without going through the exercise represented by Bayes' Theorem, one might underestimate this probability. Similarly, if the initial probability is low, say 0.1, and the additional information is such that its random occurrence is not unlikely, the probability, as adjusted, will likely still be low. Intuition might cause one to overvalue it.

(2) *The Practical Use of Bayes' Theorem in the Law (and Our Development of the Theorem Here).* The most practical use of Bayes' Theorem, however, is to correlate cause and effect. The Theorem is useful when there is an initial inductive estimate of a probability of the correlation, coupled with a highly specific piece of evidence. For example, Bayes' Theorem is used to calculate a probability of paternity of a child by a particular man, after an uncertain identification of the man is combined with a highly suggestive piece of evidence such as a blood chemistry or a DNA match. (We shall return to this example later in the Chapter.)

For now, we shall use simpler examples, in an effort to develop the mathematical relationship that expresses Bayes' Theorem. All you need to understand are probabilities, odds, multiplication, and division. We shall begin, in fact, with a trivially simple example. What are the odds of throwing two heads in a row, if we know that the first toss has turned up heads? Intuitively, we know that the odds are 1:1 (or a ½ probability), because these are the odds of the second coin turning up as a head. But we shall use a methodical calculation here, just to illustrate Bayes' Theorem.

(3) *Mathematical Expression of Bayes' Theorem in Terms of Odds: Multiply the Initial Odds by the "Likelihood Ratio" of the New Information.* Let "$\text{Odds}_{initial}$" stand for the initial odds of an event, those that existed before the new information. For example, if we are trying to figure the odds of two separate coin flips both coming up heads, the initial odds are one to three. That is, $\text{Odds}_{initial}$ = 1:3. (There is one way to throw two heads, heads-heads, but three ways not to: heads-tails, tails-heads, and tails-tails.)

But now, imagine we get a key piece of new information: The first coin flip has turned up heads. Now, what are the new odds, or "Odds_{new}" of two heads? The answer is that we simply multiply the old odds (Odds initial) by something called the "likelihood ratio" to compute the new odds, or Odds new:

$$\text{Odds}_{new} = (\text{Likelihood Ratio}) \times \text{Odds}_{initial}.$$

In other words, it is intuitively obvious that the odds change when we get new information. How much do they change? The answer also is intuitively obvious: The odds change in proportion to the likelihood of the new information turning up (the first head) if the event (two heads) were going to happen, as versus if it were not. This proportion is what we call the likelihood ratio.

(4) *Stay with This, Even if You Have to Read the Next Few Paragraphs Several Times.* Don't give up here. Don't let your eyes glaze over. This principle is important to your understanding of how evidence in lawsuits cumulates, particularly when scientific evidence such as blood chemistry or DNA is involved. Most modern evidence casebooks contain sections that depend on Bayes' Theorem. The next few paragraphs are the key to understanding it.

(5) *The Likelihood Ratio: A Number Equal to the Probability of the New Information Appearing if the Event Were GOING to Happen, Divided by the Probability of the New Information Appearing if the Event Were NOT Going to Happen.* This is the likelihood ratio: the ratio of two probabilities of the new information. Let $P_{eviftrue}$ be the probability of this new evidence appearing if the proposition were true (if the event is going to occur).[2] Let $P_{evifnot}$ be the probability of the new evidence if not (if the event is not going to occur). Then:

$$\text{Likelihood Ratio} = \frac{P_{eviftrue}}{P_{evifnot}}.$$

And Bayes Theorem becomes:

$$\text{Odds}_{new} = \frac{P_{eviftrue}}{P_{evifnot}} \times \text{Odds}_{initial}.$$

---

2   This symbolism, using "$P_{eviftrue}$" and "$P_{evifnot}$," is not standard. I invented it for this book because I think the customary notation is confusing. Standard symbolism includes, e.g., using $P(E|X)$ for "the probability that evidence E would appear if proposition X were true" and $P(E|\sim X)$ for "the probability that evidence E would appear if X were not true."

     I simply think $P_{eviftrue}$ and $P_{evifnot}$ help to keep the right quantities in mind. The symbolism doesn't change the effect of the equation.

This simple, four-factor equation is all there is to Bayes' Theorem. In English, it means that to compute new odds of the truth of a proposition based on new evidence, you multiply the old odds by the ratio of the probability of seeing the new evidence if the proposition is true to the probability of seeing the new evidence if it is not.

Recall our example: What are the odds of two coin flips both turning up heads if we know that the first flip already has turned up heads? The initial odds of two flips both turning up heads were 1:3. But we now know that the first flip has turned up heads. So, $P_{eviftrue} = 1$, because if we were going to get two heads in two flips, it must be true that the first flip would be heads (remember, 1 represents certainty). And $P_{evifnot} = 1/3$, because if we were *not* going to get two heads, there are three ways to do it--heads-tails, tails-heads, and tails-tails--only one of which involves heads on the first flip). And so, now we can compute $Odds_{new}$:

$$Odds_{new} = \frac{P_{eviftrue}}{P_{evifnot}} \times Odds_{initial}$$

$$= \frac{1}{1/3} \times 1:3 = 3:3 = 1:1,$$

which is the same as a probability of 0.5.

This result fits intuitively, because we already have gotten heads from the first flip, and we have one more flip, for which the odds are 1:1 (and the probability is 0.5). The example, thus, is trivial, but we have used it for this computation because it is simple.[3]

---

3   *Stating Bayes' Theorem in Terms of Probabilities Instead of Odds.* The equation also can be put in terms of probabilities rather than odds, but it becomes more complex:

$$P_{new} = \frac{P_{initial} \times P_{eviftrue}}{(P_{initial} \times P_{eviftrue}) + (P_{initial\text{-}not} \times P_{evifnot})}$$

This is one place where odds are easier to use than probabilities. From here on, we shall use the odds form of the equation. (You need not understand the probability-based formula in this note; it is included merely for completeness, for experienced users of Bayes' Theorem who have encountered it in this format.)

(6) *When and Why Would We Use Bayes' Theorem? Another Card Example (Although Proof of Causation Is the Premier Use in the Law).* When would we use Bayes' Theorem, then? The answer is that we would use it in any situation in which we have an initial probability or odds that are affected by new evidence, and we want to know the new probability or odds. For example, imagine that we draw two cards face down. We turn over one card, and it is a spade. What are the odds that the other card also is a spade?

For the first card, it was easy; since there are four suits, the probability of a spade was 1/4, or 0.25, corresponding to odds of 1:3. But now, we know that there is one less spade in the deck, because the first card was a spade. How does this fact affect the odds that the second card is a spade? (This is the kind of calculation that gives card-counting blackjack players their edge. See the Examples and Problems, below, for an analysis.)

(7) *A More Practical Example of the Use of Bayes' Theorem in the Law: The Paternity Suit Problem.* As a more realistic example, imagine a paternity suit in which there are two men who have equal odds of having been the father. Let us say that, from the testimonial evidence, we estimate subjectively the initial probability for each is 0.5. But then, from blood tests, we discover new information. The first man's blood is compatible with his fatherhood, and only one in 1000 random males in the population would produce offspring with this child's blood characteristics. We have not been able to locate the other man, and we assume he has no greater likelihood than random of having these blood characteristics.

What is the new probability, now, of the first man being the father? This is a practical use of Bayes' Theorem, and indeed it is a frequent use. See the Examples and Problems, below, for the actual computation of odds and the "probability of paternity," as it is called.

EXAMPLES AND PROBLEMS

(1) *Applying the Bayes Equation to the Spade-Drawing Example, Above, Part I: Computing the Initial Odds and the Likelihood Ratio.* Now, let us work through the card problem, above. We drew two cards from the deck, one of which we have turned face up, and it is a spade; what, then, are the odds of the other card also being a spade? There is one less card (and one less spade) after we have drawn a spade from the deck. How does this new information affect the odds of drawing a spade on the second draw?

See whether you can follow this reasoning (and verify that it is correct). $Odds_{initial} = 1:3$, because one suit of the cards, 13 of them, are spades (and three suits, 39 cards, are not).

Next, we must compute the likelihood ratio, or $P_{eviftrue} \div P_{evifnot}$. The probability of having drawn a spade the first time, if we were going to draw one the second time, is 12/51, because subtracting the second card gives one less spade, 12, and one less card, 51. Thus, $P_{eviftrue} = 12/51$. The probability of drawing a spade the first time if we were *not* going to draw a spade the second time is 13/51, because we would not have eliminated any spades (so there still would be 13), but we would have eliminated one card (leaving 51). Thus, $P_{evifnot} = 13/51$. Therefore, the likelihood ratio, $P_{eviftrue}/P_{evifnot}$, is $(12/51) \div (13/51) = 12/13$.

(2) *Applying Bayes to the Spade-Drawing Problem, Part II: The Equation Itself.* Now that we have the likelihood ratio of 12/13, we easily can apply Bayes' Theorem to the initial odds of 1:3:

$$Odds_{new} = (\text{Likelihood Ratio}) \times Odds_{initial}$$

$$= \frac{P_{eviftrue}}{P_{evifnot}} \times Odds_{initial}$$

$$= (12/13) \times 1:3 = 0.923:3.$$

The new odds, 0.923:3, are slightly less than 1:3, and this makes sense, because we know there is one less spade. These odds are less by a ratio of 12/13, because this is the ratio of one less spade to the full complement. Can you follow and explain the calculation?

(3) *Bayes and the Law: Applying the Bayes Equation to the Paternity Suit Example Above.* Remember the paternity suit example that we saw. What is the effect of blood evidence on the probability of paternity? In our example, the initial odds of the first man's paternity are 1:1, if he is one of two with whom the mother was intimate (and if this is all the information we have). Thus, $Odds_{initial} = 1:1$.

But then we discover the additional information that only one out of 1,000 random males would have compatible blood characteristics with this child, as the first man does. $P_{eviftrue} = 1$, since it is certain that this individual must have compatible blood if he is the father. $P_{evifnot} = 1/1000$, or .001, because this is the random chance of this blood characteristic in the population (i.e., of its occurring in the child if this man is not the father). The likelihood ratio, $P_{eviftrue}/P_{evifnot}$, is $1/(1/1,000) = 1,000$. Then, we apply Bayes' Theorem:

$$\text{Odds}_{new} = (\text{Likelihood Ratio}) \times \text{Odds}_{initial}$$

$$= 1,000 \times 1{:}1 = 1,000{:}1,$$

which corresponds to a "probability of paternity" of $1000/1001 = 0.999$.

Therefore, this new information has taken us from a 0.5 probability, or 50% likelihood, to a probability of 0.999, or 99.9% likelihood! Without doing the Bayes' Theorem calculation, many people underestimate the impact of the new blood characteristic evidence.

FALLACY FROM BAYES' THEOREM;
ITS USE IN LAW AS A HEURISTIC

(1) *Fallacy from Bayes' Theorem: The Result Depends on the Accuracy of the Initial Estimate and the Accuracy of the Likelihood Ratio.* To use Bayes' Theorem, you must have an initial probability. Herein lies one of the major problems with this otherwise useful equation. Blood chemists cannot give a probability of paternity unless they assume that there already is some initial evidence of paternity. Therefore, they usually begin the calculation by assuming a probability of 0.5, or even odds (1:1), that the man is the father. Then, they can apply Bayes' Theorem.

Notice that we made this assumption in our problem, above, by assuming that there was one but only one other man who was a possible father. Even this assumption is not likely to justify exactly 1:1 odds (can you see why, because of the timing and frequency of relations with the mother?). In addition, we assumed that the other man had no better than random odds of being the father, but this assumption may be invalid if the mother tends to choose the same physical types of men (can you see why?).

Without the assumption of 0.5 probability, all the blood chemist can give is a "paternity index," which tells us the odds against a random person in the population being the father. But the paternity index is difficult to use, and lay people tend to misunderstand it (they tend to apply it as the odds of fatherhood by this person, when all it really represents is the odds against a random person being the father).

(2) *Using Bayes' Theorem as a Heuristic Device.* One way to correct for this problem is to make a chart that lists a range of initial odds in tenths, and then to apply Bayes' Theorem to combine the new evidence with all of the possible initial odds in the chart. Thus, in our earlier example, there were only one in 1,000 odds that a randomly chosen man would fit the blood evidence, and the initial odds were one to one. What if we think the initial odds are only one to nine? Or two to eight? We can apply Bayes' Theorem to each possible set of initial odds. And so, we construct Figure 1:

Figure 1: Chart for Heuristic Use of Bayes' Theorem	
Initial Odds of Paternity	New Odds (rounded), after applying Bayes' Theorem to 1:1,000 Evidence
0:1 (certainty of nonpaternity)	0:1 (zero probability)
1:9	111:1 (111/112 probability = .99107)
2:8, or 1:4	250:1 (250/251 probability = .99602)
3:7	429:1 (429/430 probability = .99767)
4:6, or 2:3	667:1 (667/668 probability = .99850)
5:5, or 1:1	1000:1 1000/1001 probability = .99900)
6:4, or 3:2	1500:1 (1500/1501 probability = .99933)
7:3	2333:1 (2333/2334 probability = .99957)
8:2, or 4:1	4000:1 (4000/4001 probability = .99975)
9:1	9000:1 (9000/9001 probability = .99989)
1:0 (certainty of paternity)	1:0 (1.0 probability)

This chart enables us to use Bayes' Theorem as a heuristic, or investigative device. It shows us visually the impact of the 1,000:1 random-selection blood evidence. What is striking is that even with very low initial odds, such as one to nine, we get more than one-hundred-to-one new odds. This is because of the power of the new evidence: 1,000 to one against a random person having the characteristics at issue. Without Bayes' Theorem, we might underestimate the new probability.

(3) *Use of Bayes' Theorem in Law and Public Policy.* Bayes' Theorem may provide guidance in evaluating increments of circumstantial evidence. For example, imagine that eyewitness identifications are strong but uncertain, leading to a 0.7 probability that the defendant is the perpetrator. But imagine, also, that the defendant was apprehended shortly after the crime in possession of an item of property corresponding to one taken in the robbery, an item that only one in a thousand people in the general population usually possesses.

This additional, circumstantial piece of information produces a higher revised probability than one might guess. In fact, the probability is .99957 (see above). In some legal applications, it may even be possible to use Bayes' Theorem in mathematical form to produce evidence that a party might wish to offer in court.

(4) *The True Power of Bayesian Analysis in the Law: Inferences About the Past, Based on Updating Subjectively Estimated Probabilities With New Evidence.* Our "drawing two spades" example concerned a prediction (the future probability of drawing two spades). But prediction is not the most practical use of Bayesian analysis, and we used the two-spades example mainly because it involved mathematically computable probabilities.

Actually, our "DNA and paternity" example is a better illustration of the practical use of Bayes' Theorem, which is to explain the past rather than to predict the future. The true power of Bayesian analysis, then, is to update a subjectively estimated probability (such as the human-brain-based estimate of 1:1 initial odds of paternity) with new probabilistic evidence (such as evidence of blood DNA compatibility in only 1 in 1,000 men).

(5) *Why Study Probabilities? Because Our Lives Depend on Them--and Because of Their Use in Statistics.* The question remains, why study probabilities? The answer is, our lives literally depend on clear reasoning about them. From deciding to require people to wear seat belts to limiting cholesterol intake, we deal with probabilities. Also, probability theory is a prerequisite to the next Chapter, which concerns classical statistics. First,

however, we shall turn to an important application of probability theory, called "the interval distribution."

§ 12.04   The Interval Distribution: How Gaps and Clumps Appear in Either Random or Correlated Data

THE BASIC CONCEPT OF THE INTERVAL DISTRIBUTION

(1) *The Interval Distribution: A Probabilistic Measure of the Tendency of Random Data to Bunch Together or Create Clumps.* In this section, we consider a probabilistic concept called "the interval distribution." This is a subject that we have encountered informally throughout this book. The interval distribution is a measure of the degree to which observed data can be expected to "bunch" together or to "clump" on the one hand, or to exhibit gaps or intervals on the other.

For example, in an earlier chapter, we considered a baseball team that has lost eight out of its last ten games. A losing team? Hardly. As we saw, the 1998 New York Yankees lost eight out of ten games in one particular part of that season, even though they won a (then) record number of games, swept the World Series, and are considered by some observers to have been the greatest team of all time. There was a finite probability, related to the interval distribution, that an eight-out-of-ten-loss clump would occur, despite the team's record number of wins. And that probability is much greater than intuition would tell you.

We also have seen other examples of the same problem in this book. For instance, we have examined the heavier concentration of cancers in some precincts near power lines.

(2) *Why Should the Interval Distribution Matter to a Lawyer?* The interval distribution is important in legal reasoning because human beings have an almost irresistible tendency to generalize patterns from bunched data. Remember the "fallacy of configuration or completion" that we considered in an earlier chapter? The Gestalt psychologists showed how people tend to see patterns rather than individual data, even when the patterns are slight or coincidental.

In a similar manner, lawmaking tends to be driven by clumped events in the newspapers. Have there been three accidents of a certain kind in the last three weeks? Then lawmakers will react by trying laws that compromise other interests, and that may actually decrease safety. Have crimes of a certain kind made news recently? Then lawmakers will shift enforcement resources to combat them, meaning that these resources will not be available to address other (perhaps more serious) crimes. But these decisions may be poor ones, because the reasoning upon which they are based may be poor, just as major changes by the '98 Yankees' manager might have made a bad decision.[4]

(3) *What Is the Interval Distribution?* An "interval" is the time or space, or other gap, between similar events. In our baseball example, if there are two losses in a row, the interval is zero; if the sequence is loss-win-loss, it is one; if two losses are separated by eight wins, the interval is eight. Or we can look at intervals between accidents or crimes. The interval, put simply, is the gap between observed events.

What, then, is the "interval distribution?" This term refers to the distribution of all possible intervals that could occur in the particular population. We might expect that an interval of one (loss-win-loss) would be more common than an interval of ten (a ten-game winning streak) if the team, like any baseball team, has any substantial percentage of losses.

The interval distribution, in its simplest terms, is like a bar graph that shows the number of times in a given season we should expect a gap of zero wins, or one, two, or three wins, etc., between losses. More generally, it is a graph or curve that shows how intervals or gaps are distributed in any sort of random series.

(4) *The Technical Designation of the Interval Distribution Described Here: The Distribution of Interarrival Times for What Is Known as a "Poisson Process."* The interval distribution described here is the result of what is known as a "Poisson process." This distribution is named after the French mathematician Simeon Denis Poisson, who first published its derivation in 1837. The derivation of the equation is beyond our scope here,

---

4   It is not likely that Joe Torre, the '98 Yankees' manager, did the mathematical calculations discussed in this section. It is more likely that experience had taught him to expect a certain amount of clumping of losses. The problem, however, is that you may face choices in situations in which you do not have a lifetime of experience, and that is why you need to understand the interval distribution.

although the formula for the Poisson distribution is set forth in the margin (for mathematically inclined readers only).[5]

(5) *The Practical Significance of the Poisson Distribution (the Interval Distribution Described Here).* The interval distribution described here has many applications. For example, in addition to predicting the intervals between random baseball-game losses, it describes:

(a) The minutes between arrivals of random calls to a switchboard;
(b) The timing of random emissions from certain radioactive materials;
(c) The distances between random nubbly imperfections in a raw cloth;
(d) The times between random accidents in a workplace;
(e) The numbers of words between random typographical errors in a text;
(f) The arrivals of random automobiles at a freeway entrance; and
(g) The number of days between similar accidents or crimes.

To see why it is important to reason correctly about this kind of distribution, imagine the following example. The manager at a law office with a 9 a.m. to 6 p.m. switchboard must decide whether to hire only one telephone operator or whether to spend twice as much money to hire two. The incoming calls from potential clients occur randomly, and a study has shown that they average 3 per hour and five minutes in length. Imagine that it is very important not to miss any calls, because the expected revenue lost from only one or two unanswered clients-to-be greatly exceeds the cost of paying another operator. Nevertheless, the lawyer may be fooled into concluding that the second operator is a waste of money. This mistaken conclusion will result if the manager reasons--erroneously--that the "15 minute average spacing" that appears to exist between calls in the five-minute, three-calls-per-hour average means that overlapping calls will be rare. (Wrong!)

In fact, overlapping calls are highly probable in this example. The lawyer made an error in assuming periodicity: that the calls will be spaced equally. The actual interval distribution is quite different, and it produces a high

---

5 The Poisson distribution, for the mathematically inclined, is given by $f(x) = e^{-\lambda} \lambda^x / x!$, where x is a discrete random variable and λ (the Greek letter lambda) determines the exact shape of the curve and is called the "parameter" of the distribution. For low values of λ, the Poisson curve resembles a "decreasing exponential function," meaning that the number of short intervals is very high and approaches infinity, while longer intervals become increasingly scarce (see the figures below). There are in fact other possible distributions, but this one is unique for certain properties of randomness. But if you don't follow this footnote, don't worry. It is included only for completeness.

probability of short intervals and close events--or in other words, a high incidence of overlapping calls. In the following materials, we shall see why.

(6) *An Example to Work With, from Environmental Law. Legal Responses to an Epidemiologist's Analysis of Birth-Defect Observations Clumped in a Given Month.* Here is another example that will be quantitatively easier to work with. Imagine that a given city has experienced thirty (30) instances of an unusual birth defect during the last ten years. Suddenly, along comes one particular month in which there are three (3) instances of this defect, whereas the past rate averages not three per month, but three per year. Alarmed and frightened, the local citizenry looks for a cause. "Bad things," they tell themselves, "tend to happen in threes!" Political leaders note that nearby manufacturers produce a large volume of water pollutants, and they infer that the three-in-one-month bunching of defects is the result of this pollution.

This example parallels a real-life tragedy (although the numbers are simplified): the distribution of anencephalic infants' births in certain regions of Texas's Rio Grande Valley. Each instance of this defect is heartrending, but these data do not show a correlation.

(7) *What Should This Example of Interval Data Show to a Lawyer?* In fact, the likelihood of three defects in one month is about 1 in 500. (We shall consider the mathematical reasons below.) Once every 500 months (or once every forty-two years), we should anticipate a clump of three defects in a month. In ten years, then, there are roughly one-to-three odds, or there is a probability of about 0.25, of the clumping together of three birth defects in one month. This 25% likelihood means that the three-defects-in-a-month occurrence does not even come close to statistical significance, because one out of every four comparable cities can be expected to show the same effect!

In fact, for reasons that we shall explore below, a random variable with these background data could be expected to produce at least one interval of less than 0.0113 years, or four days. In other words, if there are three defects per year distributed randomly over ten years, the likelihood is that somewhere in the ten years, there will be two occurrences less than four days apart. In addition, a random variable, on average, would produce another pair less than eight days apart. Thus, it would be consistent with random effects for a three-per-year rate of occurrences, over ten years, to be distributed so that there would be at least one pair within four days of each other and another pair within eight days. It would be fallacious to infer a correlation from either (or both) of these coincidences of events.

(8) *Rational Legal Responses Based on Characteristics That the Data in this Birth-Defect Example Do Not Exhibit: Periodicity, A Large Aberrant Sample, or Temporal Coincidence.* Notice the characteristics that these data do not exhibit. First, they do not show exactly three instances in each year. That would be an improbable distribution; it is much more likely that the 30 birth defects in the last ten years reflect some years in which there were more than three and some in which there were fewer. In fact, the regularity of exactly three defects in each year for ten years would be strong evidence that the effect was not random but instead reflected some sort of time correlation. The law would be justified in intervening.

Likewise, our data for the previous ten years do not reflect precisely one defect each four months, all exactly four months apart. Such a precise periodic distribution would be strong evidence of a correlation. The "periodicity" of the data over such a large sample would cause us to inquire what was occurring exactly once each four months that could be correlated with the birth defects. And we might do well to address the causal variable by deterring it with the law.

Further, the data do not show a time correlation between sudden onset of pollution and the three-in-one-month observation of defects. Even that ground for attribution to this hypothesized cause, though stronger, would be weak without a larger sample size.

(9) *Correlational Clumping versus Random Clumping.* Finally, the clumping of the data, three in one month, does not demonstrate a sharp, concentrated departure from the background of thirty per decade. If, instead, the background were only one defect per decade, and suddenly a hundred (100) defects appeared in one month, our conclusion would be quite different. In other words, it is not necessarily fallacious to infer a correlation from a clumping of the data so extreme that it is unlikely to be a random effect.

Instead, what is fallacious is to infer correlation from the mere fact that the data clump at all, since a random variable usually results in clumping. This false inference, however, is a common error, because of the pattern-recognition tendency of the human mind. And so, innocent clumping sometimes creates irrational calls for new laws.

THE GRAPHS BEHIND THE INTERVAL DISTRIBUTION

(1) *What, More Precisely, Is the Interval Distribution?* The "interval distribution" is the distribution of interval lengths between successive random events. In simple terms, it is depicted by a bar graph that shows how many times a gap of each possible length will occur between two of these successive events, if they are distributed at random.

(2) *The Shape of the Interval Distribution: A Decreasing Exponential Curve.* How should we expect this graph to be shaped? If asked to draw a graph of the distribution of time intervals between successive random events that occur at an average rate of one every six months, most people will assume that a six-month interval is the typical, or usual, gap. In other words, they tend to assume that randomness means periodicity (an erroneous assumption). And as a result, they draw a "normal" curve or bell curve, like the one in Figure 2a.

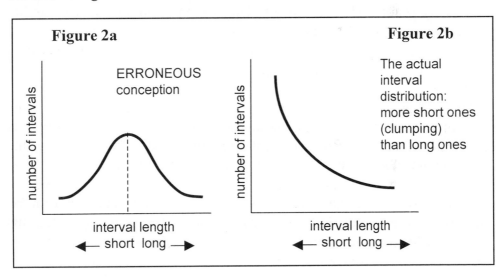

Instead, the correct answer is a decreasing exponential curve like the one in Figure 2b, which reflects exponentially more short gaps than long ones. One way to understand this matter, intuitively, is that precisely because shorter gaps are shorter, it takes more of them to "make up for" the longer gaps. An average rate of three events per year means that if there is a year-long gap (a year with no events), then six events must occur the next year to make the average work out.

This explanation bears repeating, because it is contrary to what people expect. The distribution of interval lengths *does not* cluster around an average length. Instead, at random, there tend to be many more short intervals than long ones. The best way to understand this is to remember that, if the average rate is three per year, and if there is an interval of one year with no events, there must be five events in the next year to "make up" for that year. Long intervals must be offset by more short intervals, precisely because the short intervals are short.

And this, in turn, is why random data tend to clump together. Short intervals mean precisely this: that the data will bunch together in clumps.

(2) *The Equation for the Distribution of Intervals of a Given Length in a Random Distribution.* Now we are ready to examine the equation that will tell us the percentage of each interval length to expect, on the average, from a given random distribution of events over time. Let I_T be this number (the percentage of intervals of length T). Then the equation for "I_T," the number of intervals of length "T," is:[6]

$$ I_T \propto \frac{1}{e^{(TR)}}, $$

Where "T" is the interval length (in years or fractions of years), "R" is the rate of occurrence (in events per year), and the symbol $\propto$ means "is proportional to." (The constant, e, is a number familiar to scientists as the base of natural logarithms; it is approximately equal to 2.71838.)

At this point, you should remember our discussion, in an earlier chapter, of "inverse square" relationships. We saw, for example, that gravitational attraction is proportional to $1/r^2$, where r is the distance between the two bodies in question. Now, you should notice a similarity between the inverse square relationship and the equation above. It also involves an inverse exponent, although the exponent, here, is not a fixed square, but instead is the product of the interval length, T, multiplied by the rate of events, R.

---

6   The form in which the equation usually is written is different from this formula. It usually is shown as an equality (=) rather than a proportional relation ($\propto$). This is accomplished by asserting a constant, denominated as I_o. And the inverse exponential usually is treated simply as a negative exponential rather than a dividend. As a result, the equation becomes $I(T) = I_o\, e^{-(TR)}$. The form used here is equivalent in showing the concept, but it may be easier to read. This note is inserted for readers who happen to know the equation in its customary form.

(3) *What the Equation Means: Short Gaps Between Random Events Are More Common Than Long Ones.* Here is what this relationship means. For high values of T (very long interval lengths), there are very few intervals (few long intervals). The denominator of the fraction, $1/e^{(TR)}$, increases as T, the interval length, increases, so $1/e^{(TR)}$, the number of intervals, decreases; and all of this happens at an exponential rate. Gaps of very long lengths are scarce. Shorter intervals, on the other hand, are far more numerous--because it takes more of them to "average out against" the long ones. The denominator $e^{(TR)}$ decreases as T (the interval length) decreases, and hence $1/e^{(TR)}$ increases, again exponentially. Recall the example given above: if there is a year with no events, the next year must have six events, with six shorter intervals, to average out against the one year interval, if the rate of events is three per year. It takes more short intervals to counterbalance long ones. In fact, as interval length approaches zero in the theoretically ideal curve, the number of intervals of this length approaches infinity!

This, in turn, is why events tend to "clump" or "bunch" more than people expect. Short intervals are more common than people expect, and therefore, so are clumps in the data.

EXAMPLES AND PROBLEMS

(1) *The Seeming Paradox of the Interval Distribution.* Why does it seem paradoxical that for truly random and absolutely uncorrelated events that the most likely time of occurrence of the "next" event is immediately after the last event? Perhaps the reason is that our minds are accustomed to patterns (such as periodicity)--or is it because we want to look for causation?

(2) *Is a Copycat Crime Really a Copycat Crime (i.e., Due to Publicity), or Is Its Occurrence a Reflection of the Interval Distribution?* Consider the terrible problem of student in-school violence, of which the Columbine High School incident near Denver in 1999 was a particularly sad example. That event, in which two students shot and killed a number of individuals on campus, was followed in relatively short order by other in-school shootings in different parts of the country. One theory was that the latter were "copycat" crimes, precipitated by the massive national media coverage of the Columbine incident. Some people charged that the resulting crimes were attributable to an irresponsible, sensationalist press.

But were these other shootings really "copycat" incidents? Or were they independent, timed at random, consistently with the theory of interval distribution? Columbine was not the first in-school shooting; similar incidents had happened at various times before (and happened after), in various countries, and with varying intervals. During the 1960's, a deranged individual named Charles Whitman killed more people at the University of Texas than were killed at Columbine. What, then, would we need to know in order to infer that recent, closely spaced school-shooting tragedies probably were related as copycat events, or whether they were random?

Principally, we would need to know T and R in the equation, $I_T \propto 1/e^{(TR)}$. "T" stands for the interval length (let us imagine that two recent shooting events are about a week apart, or 1/52nd of a year, which is approximately 2/100ths of a year; thus T = 0.02 year). "R" stands for the background rate of occurrence (let us imagine that there have been 3 such events per year on average in recent years, so that R = 3). Although the precise calculation is beyond our scope here, suffice it to say that a pair of week-apart incidents of a kind that occurs three times per year is not improbable. These data would not justify an inference of a copycat crime. Can you explain?

(3) *A Different Example: Carjackings.* Within a short time during the 1990's, the incidence of carjacking crimes (the taking of an automobile by robbery from the possession of the owner) increased from virtually zero per year to many per year. This observation differs sharply from the example (school shootings) given above, and it arguably justifies the inference of a causal agent as opposed to randomness. Can you explain the different inference? [One possible mechanism was that anti-theft devices made the simple stealing of automobiles more difficult and turned criminals toward forcible carjacking instead--although this inference is not demonstrable from these data, and it is not the point here.]

Chapter 13

Statistics

Sampling, Interpretation, Statistical Significance, and Regression Analysis in the Law

> *"[T]he [person] of the future is the [person] of statistics."--Oliver Wendell Holmes Jr., The Path of the Law*

> *Three statisticians went duck hunting. The first one shot two feet above the duck. The second shot two feet below it. The third one excitedly shouted, "You got him!"-- Anonymous*

§ 13.01   What This Chapter Is About

STATISTICAL ANALYSIS

(1) *Statistics and Sampling.* Statistics is a branch of mathematics that provides numerical measures that characterize populations or events, or that attempts to generalize numerical descriptions of them from samples. This chapter considers sampling techniques, including such questions as whether

the sample is random, representative, controlled, or biased, as well as the methods of treating imperfect samples.

(2) *The Interpretation, Presentation and Significance of Statistics: Law and Public Policy Uses.* The chapter also considers the interpretation of statistics in law and public policy. This coverage includes such concepts as "p-values," "correlation coefficients," and other measures of correlations. This coverage will show that statistical analysis is a powerful tool in law and public policy, as Justice Holmes implies by saying that the person of the future is the person of statistics; but statistics also can be misleading, as is shown above by the allegory of the duck-hunting statisticians.

(3) *Regression Analysis.* Often it happens that several "independent" variables combine to influence another variable, called the "dependent" variable. "Regression analysis" is a means of determining the effect of one independent variable from observing how the dependent variable changes with changes in it. A technique called "multiple" regression analysis enables us to calculate the effect of one among a combination of independent variables, if we know the effects of the other independent variables. The technique can be a powerful means of linking effects to their causes.

§ 13.02   Statistical Analysis

[A]   Displaying Statistical Data

BAR GRAPHS (HISTOGRAMS) AND
THE NORMAL DISTRIBUTION

(1) *An Example of a Statistic: A Baseball Player's Batting Average.* Statistics is the study of producing numerical information from multiple data. In baseball, a batting average is a familiar statistic. If the player has had many at bats, it is a useful statistic. We would say that it reflects every "unit," meaning every official time at bat, in the "population" of objects, which in this instance is the total official at-bats. (It is possible for statistics to be misleading because of sampling errors, which we take up later, but for now, we assume accurate population information.)

(2) *Display of Statistical Data in a Bar Graph or "Histogram": The Heights of Incoming Freshmen Plotted Against the Number at Each Height.* We all are familiar with bar graphs. The fancier word "histogram" means the

same thing. Figure 1 is an example of a bar graph; this one happens to show the heights of incoming freshmen at West State University, displaying the number at each height.

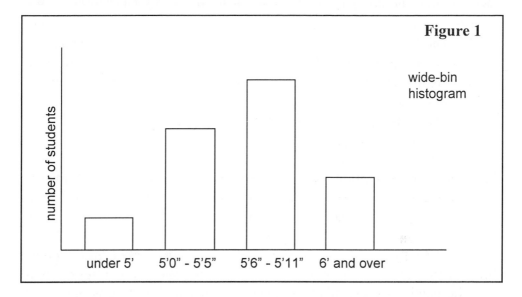

Figure 1

wide-bin histogram

number of students

under 5'   5'0" - 5'5"   5'6" - 5'11"   6' and over

(3) *The Concept of "Bin Width" and Its Influence on Statistical Analysis.* Figure 1 makes West York students look as though they are relatively tall. This may be the result of the choice of "bin width." In treating statistics, we sometimes round the numbers or assign them to artificial categories called "bins." Figure 1 uses a relatively large bin width; it's actually six inches wide. What if the biggest group of new freshmen were 5'6", and there were relatively few at 5'11"? Then, although this wide-bin histogram would be "accurate," people's minds are such that they might infer a misleading picture, compared to Figure 2, in which bin width is one inch. Statistical presentations can be manipulated by bin designations, as this one has been.

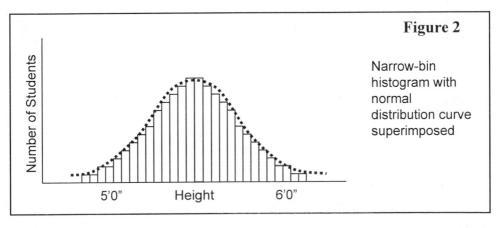

Figure 2

Narrow-bin histogram with normal distribution curve superimposed

Number of Students

5'0"   Height   6'0"

The point is not that more (or smaller) bins are better. In a given case, more might not be better, because they might give a false impression of precision. The point is that bin width, like all other aspects of statistical presentation, should be tailored to the sensitivity of the data.

(4) *The Bell-Curved Normal Distribution: Median, Mean and Mode are the Same.* Notice the shape of the dotted line on Figure 2. This is the well known "bell curve" that traces what is called a "normal distribution." A normal distribution makes a symmetrical pattern around a central mean or average. Data approximating normal distributions occur frequently in nature, because this is the expected pattern when data reflect the aggregate effect of a large number of small and independent influences, producing a bell curve. For a normal distribution, the "mean" (or average), the "median" (the data point where half the units are greater, half lesser) and the "mode" (the point corresponding to the greatest number of units) all are the same.

(5) *A Non-Normal Distribution: The Rocks-for-Jocks Class Example.* Imagine that, instead of plotting the heights of all the incoming freshmen, we plot the heights of students taking Geology 1 instead. It turns out that, in addition to students interested in the subject, Geology 1 includes most of the basketball team, because it is known as an easy course for athletes. Informally, the course is called "Rocks for Jocks."

Our distribution for the population in Geology 1, therefore, looks like Figure 3, because there is a disproportionate number of tall students. In this population, the "mode," or height of the largest number of units, is about 6'5"; the "mean," or average height, is about 6'1"; and the "median," or the height

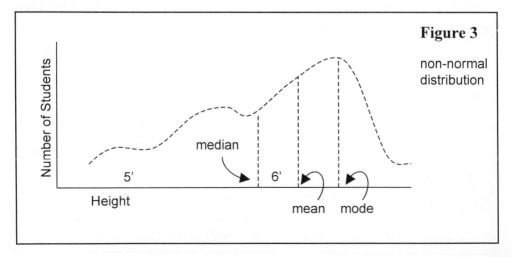

Figure 3

non-normal distribution

at which half of the units (students) are shorter and half taller, is about 5'11". If the only information we were given were the mean or average, we might form a misleading picture of the distribution in Geology 1, because it is not a normal distribution.

(6) *There Is Nothing Theoretically Wrong With a Non-Normal Distribution (but We May Need More Statistics to Understand It).* Despite the nomenclature, there is nothing theoretically wrong with a distribution that is not "normal." Such a distribution is not "abnormal," either. Sometimes, we expect a distribution that is not normal, as we would in the Rocks-for-Jocks class.

But the "wavy bell" curve in Figure 3 is more complex than a normal distribution, and we need more information to describe it. If we were to tell someone only that the mean (average) height of the Rocks-for-Jocks class is about 6'1", this statistic might create a misleading impression, with listeners picturing a normal distribution that has all the units clustered proportionally in a bell shape around the mean.

EXAMPLES AND PROBLEMS

(1) *Bin Width Manipulation That Produces a Misleading Impression.* The histogram in Figure 1 makes students seem taller than they really are. Perhaps this manipulation is not too offensive, because few people care about height distribution at a college. But let us imagine that West State University wants to misrepresent a more sensitive data set, such as the scores of the freshman class on standardized (SAT) tests. In other words, West State wants to "cook the books" statistically so that donors and prospects will be impressed with its new class.

Let us say that there is a cluster of students at the 86th and 87th percentile, but very few in percentiles above the 90th. The University therefore rejects the idea of a bar graph with bins displaying the 71-80, 81-90, and 91-100 percentile ranges. Instead, it constructs a histogram with ranges of 75-84, 85-94, and 95-100, because this bin designation makes its data look better. Can you see why the college prefers this bin designation?

(2) *Normal Distributions and Distributions That Are Not Normal.* Assume that West State University's only criterion for admission is the applicant's high school grade point average (GPA). If we assume that high

schools graduate few students with either very high or very low GPA's, we might predict (although without assurance) that a plot of percentile rankings versus the number of applicants would approximate a bell curve or normal distribution. Can you see why? But if West State has a cutoff GPA number, and it does not admit students who score below that GPA, the distribution of admitted students will not be normal. Can you see why?

[B]   Correlations: The Correlation Coefficient, r, and the p-Value

SCATTER CHARTS AND CORRELATIONS

(1) *A Scatter Chart Exhibiting a Relatively Close Association between Two Variables.* As an alternative to a bar graph, we can use a "scatter diagram" or scatter chart to display the relationship between two variables. Imagine that West State University uses many factors, including high school grades, activities, honors, etc., to determine admission. The biggest single determinant, however, is the applicant's percentile score on a standardized test (SAT), which makes up 70% of the composite "applicant index number" that West State uses to admit students. We might, then, produce a scatter chart like Figure 4. This chart obviously displays a close association, or "correlation," between the standardized test score and the applicant index number. This is what we would expect, since the test score is the most significant variable that influences the index number. The example therefore is somewhat artificial, but useful as an illustration.

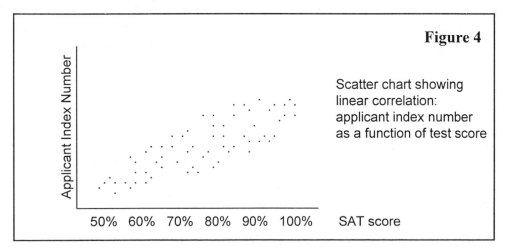

Figure 4

Scatter chart showing linear correlation: applicant index number as a function of test score

(2) *Independent Variables, Dependent Variables, and Correlations.* In Figure 4, the test scores are the "independent variable." This variable

influences, although it may not alone determine, the "dependent variable," the index numbers. The association of the two variables, so that they increase or decrease together, means that they are "covariates," or variables that vary together. In statistical terms, we say that they are "correlated."

This example is idealized for illustrative purposes. Often the independent variable is a factor that we conceive of as "causing" the dependent variable in a time sequence. For example, whether smoking is an independent variable correlated with the dependent variable of lung cancer, or whether childhood sexual abuse is an independent variable correlated with the dependent variable of borderline personality disorder, are more practical examples. But the test score example is useful precisely because it is simple.

(3) *Confounding Variables.* When we hypothesize a correlation between two variables, we have to watch for "confounding variables" or "confounders." Confounding variables are other variables that may influence the dependent variable. We particularly need to be careful about inferring cause and effect when there are confounders. In this instance, let us assume that the test scores are the independent variable of interest; the other factors (high school grades, honors, activities) are confounding variables that also may have effects on the applicant index, which is the dependent variable.

(4) *"Cause" and Correlation.* An inference of cause and effect is different from a correlation. To see why, consider whether it would be appropriate to say that the applicant index number "causes" the test score (SAT). This reasoning would be backward: It would confuse the effect (dependent variable) with the cause (independent variable). In fact, it is clumsy here even to say that the test score "causes" the index number, since other factors (the confounding variables) also "cause" it.

There may be a "cause behind the causes": Test scores and high school grades may be covariates, both associated with a separate factor, the applicants' intelligence (which also may be associated with the other confounding variables of honors and activities). All of these associations may reflect true correlations, but cause is a more vague concept.

(5) *The Closeness of a Correlation to a Linear Relationship: The Correlation Coefficient, r.* Statisticians have invented a statistic called the "correlation coefficient" to measure how closely the correlation fits a straight line. The correlation coefficient usually is signified by the letter "r." The

coefficient varies between -1.0 and 1.0, with -1.0 and 1.0 each meaning absolute linearity. (The negative coefficient just means that the line slopes down instead of up.)

If the scatter chart displays a nonlinear cloud of dots, dispersed randomly because there is no correlation, the correlation coefficient, r, is zero (0.0). For a very close linear correlation, r is close to 1.0. Thus, a mildly linear scatter cloud might produce a correlation coefficient r = 0.5, while a closer correlation might produce r = 0.9. Again, for dots arranged along a perfectly straight, upwardly sloped line, r = 1.0.

EXAMPLES AND PROBLEMS

(1) *Is There a Linear Correlation Between a Number and Its Square?* Imagine that we plot the whole numbers (integers) from one to ten, and then we plot their squares (1, 4, 9, 16, 25, 36, 49, 64, 81 and 100) on a scatter chart above them. Is there a linear correlation between the independent variable (the numbers, 1 to 10) and the dependent variable (the squares)?

The answer is, yes, there is, because we could draw a straight line that would (sort of) fit amongst the ten data points. We always can find a line of best fit for correlated data. But in this case (an attempt to draw a straight line to "fit" ten numbers to their squares), it would be a poor fit. The linear correlation coefficient, r, would be much less than 1.0. Can you see why? (This problem shows that there also are correlations that are nonlinear. If, instead, we were to use a different kind of correlation coefficient, one reflecting a square function, we could get a coefficient of 1.0.)

(2) *Correlation Coefficients and the Law: The Cold-Medicine Problem Produces Two Scatter Charts With Different Correlation Coefficients.* The Food and Drug Administration is charged by law with deciding whether a given drug is not only safe, but also "effective." Effectiveness generally is measured by statistical studies that compare correlations. Imagine that we test two groups to determine whether a particular zinc compound is effective in shortening the duration of the common cold. We plot two scatter charts, one showing the effectiveness of various amounts of a placebo on the first group (control group), and the other showing effects of various doses of zinc on the second group (the test group). The result is Figure 5, which shows that this zinc compound has a high linear correlation with reducing the duration

of the common cold--in fact, the correlation coefficient is -0.8. (Remember, closeness to -1.0, as well as to +1.0, means strong linearity.)

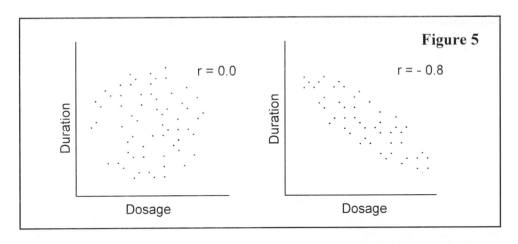

Figure 5

r = 0.0

r = - 0.8

Can you interpret the two scatter charts in this Figure to determine which is the zinc group, which the control group? (Incidentally, this is a "negative" correlation, because the dependent variable, cold duration, *decreases* with increases in the independent variable, the dosage.[1]

THE NULL HYPOTHESIS AND THE p-VALUE: WHAT IS THE SIGNIFICANCE OF AN OBSERVED CORRELATION?

(1) *Statistical Significance: The Problem of High Correlation Coefficients from Small Sample Size.* Next, we consider "statistical significance." Reconsider the experiment above, in which data for reduction of cold duration by zinc produce a correlation coefficient of -0.8. This sounds impressive. But imagine that we ask the experimenter about sample size, and we are informed that there were only four people each in the test and control groups!

Even though the correlation coefficient is high, we suddenly realize that we should not attribute too much significance to the experiment, because a couple of aberrant data--two zinc-taking subjects who happened to get well fast, but who might have done so with or without zinc--could have made all the difference. We call these aberrant data "outliers," as is illustrated in

---

1 Some people, therefore, might prefer to represent r by a negative number, r = -0.8. However, we could produce a chart with r = 0.8 by plotting days *reduced* (from a fixed outer duration) instead of duration.

Figure 6. The law may require withholding of an effectiveness finding in this case. We need a measure of the "statistical significance," as it is called, of the apparent correlation we have observed.

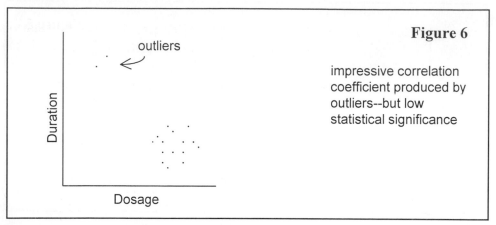

Figure 6

outliers

Duration

Dosage

impressive correlation coefficient produced by outliers--but low statistical significance

(2) *The Difference Between the Correlation Coefficient, r, and Statistical Significance.* The correlation coefficient, r, tells us how strongly linear the observed correlation is. But it does not tell us how sure we can be that a statistically significant relationship really exists.

If we took only two data points, for example, we could draw a straight line perfectly through them, giving the impression that the apparent "correlation" is highly linear, with r = 1.0. The problem is, with two data points, we would get this result even if there were *no* correlation. We would be more confident that the correlation existed if we had many data points. This is why, in addition to the correlation coefficient r, which measures linearity, we also need a statistic that tells us how "significant" our experiment is--or how much we can trust it.

(3) *The Null Hypothesis: The Assumption That No Correlation Really Exists, and That Observed Effects Are Random.* To measure statistical significance, we first introduce the "null hypothesis." This hypothesis is the possibility that the observed effects really are random, even though they seem (erroneously) to reflect a correlation. In other words, the null hypothesis is the assumption that our data sample has produced a false positive. We then can measure statistical significance by determining the probability that the null hypothesis could have produced the observed correlation as a false positive, from random effects.

(4) *The p-Value: The Probability That the Null Hypothesis Might Have Produced Similar Results, at Random.* The "p-value" is the probability that the null hypothesis could have produced similarly strong data implying a correlation. Another name for the p-value is the "observed significance level." A high p-value of 0.3, or 30%, means that the observed correlation is due little confidence, because the data are highly compatible with the null hypothesis.[2] Thirty percent of the time, random events would produce an equally apparent or stronger observed correlation--even if the relationship doesn't exist. Thus, the p-value is the likelihood of a random "false positive."

On the other hand, a very low p-value of, say, 0.001 (one-tenth of one percent) undermines the null hypothesis. It means that if a correlation did not exist, we would expect to see a data distribution this strong or stronger only once in every 1,000 experiments. A low p-value, therefore, increases our faith that the observed correlation really exists.

(5) *Statistical Significance, or Alpha (α): The .05 Level and the .01 Level.* Customarily, an apparent correlation is said to be minimally "statistically significant" if the p-value is .05 or less. This means that the odds are 95 to 5 against similarly strong evidence of a correlation appearing without a correlation (that is, if the null hypothesis were true).[3] Statisticians describe this result as "significance at the five percent level." Significance at the "one percent level" means that there is a probability of only 0.01 of similarly strong data arising under the null hypothesis. This result typically earns the label, "highly statistically significant."

Of course, the precise level of significance to be demanded depends on the circumstances, although it often is pre-set at either 0.05 or 0.01. The "alpha" value, α, is used to signify the level of significance demanded. If we have determined that we will not accept the results unless the p-value is 0.05 or less, then $\alpha = .05$. If we demand significance at the 1% level, then $\alpha = .01$.

---

2 Technically, the p-value cannot tell us the probability that the null hypothesis is true or false. It always is *possible* that the null hypothesis has produced whatever experimental data we have observed (even if it is *improbable*). And although some distributions would suggest a correlation and some would not, the null hypothesis remains either right or wrong throughout all the different distributions. Measuring statistical significance, therefore, does not avoid the possibility of a false positive. All it tells us is how often this particular false positive would occur if the null hypothesis were true.

3 Once again, it does *not* mean that there is a 95% likelihood that the null hypothesis is false. Such an inference is seductive but erroneous. Our observed data still may have resulted with the null hypothesis being true (i.e., the apparent correlation we think we have observed is illusory, and there really is no relationship). All the p-Value tells us is that such data, showing an apparent correlation, will appear 5% of the time--a false positive.

(6) *The Alpha Value as a Pre-Set, Somewhat Arbitrary Standard for Reliability.* In fact, this standard (the alpha value, α) reflects a somewhat arbitrary, nonstatistically based judgment about how certain somebody should be before drawing a conclusion. In real life, we often draw valuable inferences on less significant data. Setting an alpha value, α, beforehand is a way of insisting on greater formality or precision, because we fix a standard for reliability before performing our study or experiment.

(7) *Type I Errors (False Positives) and Type II Errors (False Negatives).* Sometimes, a study erroneously shows a correlation when none exists. It may even show it at a statistically significant level, meeting the alpha level, even though the null hypothesis is in fact true--there is no correlation. This is called a "type I error" or a false positive. The data makes it seem that there is a correlation, but there isn't. On the other hand, if the study fails to produce statistical significance, the possibility remains that the experimental hypothesis actually is true--a correlation does exist--but the analysis did not detect it. We call this a "type II error": a false negative. A correlation does exist, but our experiment missed it.

(8) *The Tradeoff Between Type I and Type II Errors: Setting the Legal Proof Standard for Criminal Conviction.* Notice that we cannot simultaneously minimize both type I and type II errors. That is, we cannot decrease the likelihood of mistakenly inferring a correlation (type I, or false positives) without increasing the likelihood of mistakenly failing to detect a correlation (type II, or false negatives). The only way to improve both is to get better data.

In a criminal case, for example, we minimize type I errors (false positives, or conviction of innocent people) by requiring proof beyond a reasonable doubt, thus greatly increasing type II errors (false negatives, or acquittals of many more guilty people). Setting a high alpha value (such as 0.01) has an analogous effect: it increases reliability in inferring an actual correlation at the expense of risk that a real relationship may not be detected.

(9) *The "Power" of a Statistical Analysis: The Likelihood of Its Detecting an Existing Correlation.* This leads us to the statistic called "power." The power of a statistical study, β, is the probability of its rejecting the null hypothesis when the alternative hypothesis--the hypothesized correlation--actually exists. In other words, "power" is the probability of avoiding a type II error.

Power depends on the strength of the correlation and on the sample size (as well as the alpha value chosen). If the correlation is slight and the sample small, power will be low. If both the correlation and the sample are large, then the power is high. If we are trying to detect a weak correlation, we need a large sample to have a sufficiently high power to be useful.

EXAMPLES AND PROBLEMS

(1) *Statistical Techniques in Law and Public Policy: The Bush Administration's Evaluation of Regulatory Standards for Drinking Water.* Statistical methods and statistically derived evidence appear frequently in modern litigation. They also figure in administrative (e.g., environmental or safety) determinations and in legislation. For example, the EPA under President Bush, in 2000, reconsidered environmental regulations proposed by the Clinton administration to ensure that the standards were based on "sound science," by which it meant appropriate statistical evidence. We shall return to law and public policy later. For now, let us nail down our understanding of correlation coefficients, null hypotheses, p-values, statistical significance, and power. For this, we consider some simpler illustrations.

(2) *Testing for a Loaded Coin by a Five-Flip Study: Does a Result of Four Heads and One Tail "Prove" the Correlation (That the Coin Is Biased)?* Imagine that we have a coin, which we suspect is "biased" or "loaded" to favor heads. We decide to flip it five times as a statistical experiment. The result: four heads and only one tail. We might, now, feel more psychologically justified in our suspicion (hypothesis) that the coin is biased.

But consider whether the result of our five-flip study is statistically significant. The answer is, although it may look convincing, it isn't significant. Can you see why? (If not, read on.)

(3) *What Is the Null Hypothesis for Our Five-Flip Experiment?* First, what is the null hypothesis? Remember, the null hypothesis is the hypothesis that there is no correlation, and that our experimental data have been produced by random effects. In our example, the null hypothesis is that the coin is *not* loaded, or in other words, that this seemingly skewed result of four heads and one tail actually came about by chance. Can you explain?

Notice that if we were to repeat the five-flip experiment a hundred times with an ordinary (honest) coin, we would produce some instances of four-to-one heads, the same as our test result. In fact, the composite results of the 100 experiments would approximate a normal distribution, with a few all-heads or all-tails results, somewhat more four-to-one results, and still more three-to-two results--as in Figure 7. Can you see why?

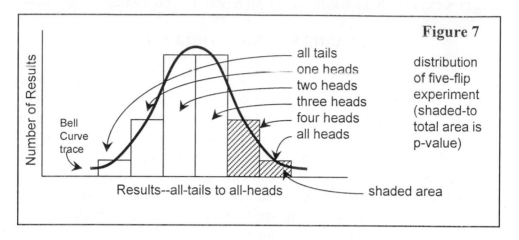

Figure 7

distribution of five-flip experiment (shaded-to total area is p-value)

all tails
one heads
two heads
three heads
four heads
all heads

Bell Curve trace

Number of Results

Results--all-tails to all-heads   shaded area

(3) *The Result of the Five-Flip Experiment: What Is the p-Value, and Is It Statistically Significant?* Remember, the statistical significance is determined by the p-value, which is the probability that the experimental result would be produced if the null hypothesis were true. Therefore, the p-value for our five-flip experiment is the probability that five flips of an honest coin would produce four heads and one tail (or five heads).

The probability for five heads is given by the product rule as $(\frac{1}{2})^5 = 1/32$. The probability for four heads and one tail resulting at random from an honest coin for our five-coin-flip experiment is given by a variation of the product rule, as $5 \times (\frac{1}{2})^5 = 5/32$. Therefore, the p-value for our five-flip test is 6/32 or .187, meaning that producing four heads is not unusual, since it would happen 18.7 times out of 100 (or approximately one-fifth of the time) simply by chance, even with an honest coin! Can you see why?

Thus, this five-coin flip result is not very significant. It exceeds both the five percent and the one percent levels of significance, and if we have set $\alpha = .05$ or $\alpha = .01$, the five-flip experiment fails. It simply is inconclusive. We cannot tell whether the coin is biased. (Notice that many people, given four heads out of five, would jump to the conclusion that the coin is biased, when the data do not justify much confidence in this. Why?)

(4) *A Graphic Representation of p-Value: The Ratio of the Shaded Area in Figure 7.* If you would rather not do the math for the five-flip experiment, you can approximate the result by eyeballing Figure 7. The shaded bars in this bar graph represent the times that four or more heads would turn up if we repeated the five-flip experiment many times. The unshaded bars represent the times that fewer than three heads would turn up.

The ratio of the shaded area to the total area is the p-value (the probability of producing four or more heads by chance). Can you explain why? The ratio looks like a little less than one-fifth of the total area, or a little less than 20%, and in fact the calculation (as we have seen) is 18.7%.

(5) *Changing to a Ten-Flip Experiment: More Power, More Statistical Significance.* Now, imagine that instead of five times, we flip the suspected coin *ten* times. We turn up nine heads and one tail. Notice that the greater sample gives us more power in the study. Can you see why?

Now, what is the p-value of a nine-heads-one-tail flip sequence? It is the probability that the null hypothesis is true, or the probability of turning up nine or more heads in ten flips with an honest coin. If we have the patience to flip an honest coin many thousands of times, we eventually will turn up several strings of nine heads out of ten, even ten out of ten. But the null hypothesis will produce such a result less often than for four heads out of five.

The probability of ten heads out of ten is given by the product rule as $(½)^{10} = 1/1024$. For the probability of nine heads out of ten, a variation of the product rule gives $10 \times (½)^{10} = 10/1024$. The p-value is therefore $11/1024 = .0107$. Can you see why?

Thus, by going from a five-flip to a ten-flip sample, we have improved the significance from a non-significant 18.7% level to better than the 5% level, almost the 1% level, and there is a statistically significant result, assuming $\alpha = 0.5$. And now, it is statistically likely (but by no means certain!) that the coin is biased.

(6) *One-Tailed and Two-Tailed Tests of Significance.* So far, we have been considering what is called a "one-tailed" test of significance. If you look again at Figure 7, you will see why. Our p-value has focused on only one end, or one "tail," of the normal curve, since we have considered only the

possibility of four heads, and not the possibility of four tails (which is an equally skewed result, but equally probable under the null hypothesis).

Some statisticians, for some purposes, believe that what is called a "two-tailed test of significance" is more appropriate. In our example, a two-tailed test would mean that the p-value would be the probability of randomly throwing *either* four or more heads *or* four or more tails. If the distribution is normal, a two-tailed test simply doubles the p-value, which would be .0214 in our example. Can you see why?

(7) *The Influence of Power.* Remember, the power, β, is defined as the likelihood that our experiment will avoid a Type II error (i.e., that it will not produce a false negative). What is the power of our ten-flip experiment with nine heads? The mathematical equation is beyond our scope here, but remember that it is determined by the alpha value (α), by the sample size, and by how strong the observed correlation is. Can you see why nine heads out of ten gives the study a greater power than four out of five?

(8) *A Case Using Statistics to Prove a Violation of the Gender Discrimination Laws: Does a Positive Linear Correlation Coefficient Make Good Evidence?* A friend of yours represents the plaintiffs in a gender-discrimination-in-employment lawsuit under Title VII. Your friend excitedly says, "The statistical study shows a positive correlation coefficient between salaries and whether the employee is a man or a woman. In fact, the linear correlation coefficient for males and higher salaries is 0.6. This is strong evidence of sex discrimination!"

Unfortunately, your friend's reasoning is wrong. Can you explain what else a statistician might want to find out before evaluating the result of this study? Consider (a) the null hypothesis, (b) the factor that estimates the likelihood that the correlation is real, (c) the pre-set value against which that factor is compared, and (d) how all of these factors are determined.

[C]   The Theoretical Normal Distribution (or Bell Curve) and the Standard Deviation

**THE IDEALIZED NORMAL DISTRIBUTION
AND THE STANDARD DEVIATION**

(1) *The Normal Curve, the Standard Deviation, and Confidence Intervals: Additional Methods of Describing Statistical Distributions and Testing Hypotheses.* In this section, we shall reconsider the normal distribution or bell curve in its theoretical or ideal form. We also shall describe what are called "standard deviations." Later, we shall use these concepts to consider the testing of hypotheses about real-world statistical populations.

(2) *The Standard Deviation as a Measure of Dispersion: A High, Peaked Graph or a Broad, Flat One?* Earlier, we considered the mean, median, and mode, which are indicators of the "central tendency" of a group of data (or in other words, of where and how their curve is centered). The standard deviation is different: it is a "measure of dispersion." It tells us how much the distribution tends to clump in the middle (that is, to make a high, narrow peak on a graph) or to spread out (forming a broader, flatter graph).

For example, consider Figure 8, which graphs the distribution of grades in two different college English classes of 60 students each. In Class 1, the professor awards 10 B's, 40 C's, and 10 D's, but no A's or F's. On a four-point basis, the mean or average of the grades in Class 1 is 2.0 (or C). In Class 2, a different professor produces the same mean, but with a wider dispersion: There are 8 A's, 12 B's, 20 C's, 12 D's and 8 F's.

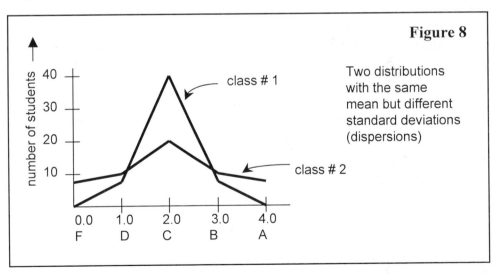

Figure 8

Two distributions with the same mean but different standard deviations (dispersions)

Thus, the mean (or average) is 2.0 (or C) for both classes, but we readily can see that the distribution is quite different. The graph for Class 1 shows a relatively sharp peak at the mean, whereas the graph for Class 2 is relatively broad and flat. These two graphs differ because they have different degrees of dispersion, even though both have the same mean and both are symmetrical. This degree of dispersion is what is described or measured by the standard deviation.

(3) *Reconsidering the Normal Distribution (or Bell Curve): A Theoretical or Idealized Graph Defined by Its Mean, μ, and Its Standard Deviation, σ.* We already have introduced the "normal distribution" as a symmetrical bell-shaped curve for which the mean, median, and mode[4] are all the same. The normal distribution is probably the most widely studied distribution in statistics. It is useful because it approximates many distributions that actually occur in real life, including large-scale samples. Of course, there is no advance guarantee that any particular natural function will follow the normal distribution, and those that do follow it may not conform to it exactly. The "perfect" normal distribution is a theoretical concept--an idealized model. But its usefulness lies in the tendency of many large-scale processes to produce results that come close to it (including large samples even from non-normal populations).

The mean of a distribution usually is symbolized by the Greek letter *mu*, or "μ." It corresponds to what most people call the "average" of a distribution. This number--the mean or μ--tells us where the graph of a normal distribution is centered. What we do not know from the mean, however, is whether the bell-shaped curve of the particular normal distribution will be relatively sharp and tall or whether it will be relatively

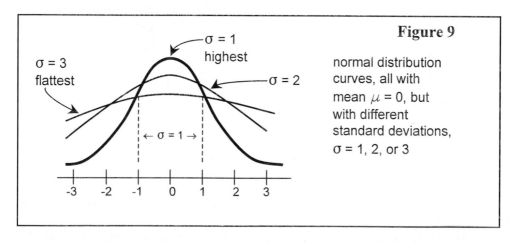

Figure 9

normal distribution curves, all with mean $\mu = 0$, but with different standard deviations, $\sigma = 1, 2,$ or 3

4 Remember that the "mean" is what most people call the "average." The "median" is that n umber for which half the units in a population are larger and half smaller. The "mode" is the number that fits the largest number of units. If a distribution is not normal, these factors differ. But for a normal distribution, all three are the same: the graph is symmetrical and bell-shaped.

broad and flat. For this, we need the standard deviation, which is symbolized by the letters "SD" or by the Greek letter *sigma*, or "σ.")

(4) *How the Standard Deviation Determines the Normal Curve: The Bigger the σ, the Flatter the Graph.* In Figure 9, we have graphed three normal distributions that have the same mean of zero ($\mu = 0$), but they have different standard deviations (σ = 1, 2, or 3). The one with σ = 1 and $\mu = 0$, marked by the heaviest line, happens to have the highest arch of these three. This one is called a "standard normal distribution." It is centered on a mean of 0 and has a standard deviation of 1. In other words, for a standard normal curve, $\mu = 0$, and σ = 1.

Next, compare the distribution in the middle, which has standard deviation σ = 2. It is flatter than the one with σ = 1. And the shortest one, with σ = 3, is flatter still. In general, the bigger the standard deviation, the flatter the curve. The standard deviation, in a manner of speaking, measures how "spread out" or flattened the curve is, or how much it is dispersed.

(5) *The Equation for the Standard Normal Distribution.* The equation for the normal distribution was first published in the seventeen hundreds (in 1733, to be precise) by French mathematician Abraham de Moivre. Later, the theory was further developed by Carl Friedrich Gauss, and in his honor, it sometimes is called the "Gaussian distribution."

Although the derivation and use of the equation for the standard normal distribution are beyond our scope here, the formula is set out below in a footnote[5] for the mathematically inclined.

(6) *Quantifying the Meaning of the Standard Deviation: The Area Within One Standard Deviation Approximates 68% of Total Area Under a Normal Curve; Within Two It Approximates 95%; and Within Three, 99.7%.* Let us imagine two vertical lines drawn to mark the standard deviation for a

---

5   The formula for the standard normal distribution is

$$f(x) = \frac{1}{\sqrt{2\pi}} \, e^{-x^2/2} \quad ,$$

where x is a continuous variable such that $-\infty < x < \infty$. For technical reasons, the letter "z" usually is used instead of x in describing the standard normal distribution. For the general (not standard) normal distribution, the equation is slightly more complex. But don't worry: it isn't necessary for you to understand these formulas; you can understand this chapter without them.

theoretical normal curve. (See Figure 10, where these two markers are the dashed lines at -1 and +1.) It turns out that these two lines will cover approximately 68% of the area under the curve. In other words, for a theoretical normally distributed population, we can expect to find about 68% of the units within one standard deviation of the mean. This relationship results from the curvature of the graph for a normal curve and the definition of the standard deviation (and it can be mathematically calculated, although that is beyond our scope here).

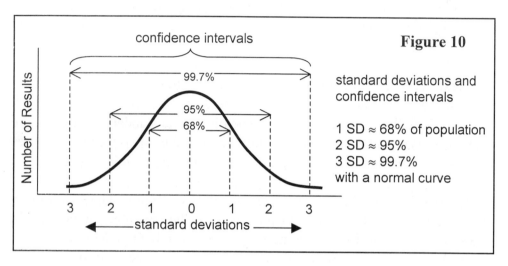

If we extend our interval to two standard deviations, we produce an even greater area bounded by the verticals. In the figure, this interval corresponds to the distance between the dashed lines at -2 and +2. The area under the bell curve, now, approximates 95% of the total. Thus, in a theoretical normal distribution, 95% of the population is within two standard deviations of the mean. And if we extend the boundaries to three standard deviations, approximately 99.7% of the area is covered. Therefore, approximately 99.7% of an idealized normally distributed population lies within 3 SD of the mean.

(7) *Why Should Lawyers Care about Normal Curves?: Sample Validity and Standard Deviations.* All of this may seem abstract. It may not appear to have much to do with your role as a lawyer. The connection will become clearer, however, if you consider that statistical evidence in litigation often depends upon samples, and sample validity sometimes can be measured by reference to the normal curve. Therefore, the usefulness of statistical evidence may depend on your understanding of this material. We now proceed to nail down the determinants of the normal curve (mean and

standard deviation). After that, we shall introduce something called the "central limit theorem," which will let us evaluate samples.

EXAMPLES AND PROBLEMS

(1) *Comparing the Shapes of Normal Curves to Their Standard Deviations, σ.* Our discussion of the normal distribution has emphasized the standard normal distribution (in which the mean, μ, is 0 and the standard deviation, σ, is 1). We did this because the standard normal curve is simpler than other normal curves.

Let us imagine other curves drawn over a standard normal curve, with the same center or mean ($\mu = 0$), but with different standard deviations, σ. For example, imagine a curve for which σ is one one-thousandth (σ = 0.001). Compared to the standard normal curve (for which σ = 1), this curve will resemble a tall, thin, needle-like spike with very low tails on each side. Or, consider a curve for which σ = 1,000; this one will look like an almost straight, flat line when viewed against the center of the standard normal curve. This is so even though all three curves have the same mean. Can you explain why, in terms of the meaning of standard deviation, σ, the curves with σ = 0.001 and σ = 1,000 will differ from the standard normal curve?

(2) *The Influence of the Mean, μ.* Changing only the mean, on the other hand, does not change the curvature of the graph, but merely shifts it horizontally. For example, if we measured the heights of a random sample of players on college basketball teams nationwide, and we compared them to a random sample of all college students, who do not play basketball, the results would approximate two different normal distributions. The most striking difference would be that the center of the curve representing the basketball players would be farther to the right (meaning taller heights) than the center of the curve representing the ordinary college students. Can you explain why this rightward shift of the basketball players' curve would occur, in terms of the mean, μ?

(3) *Professional Basketball Players, Mean Heights, and Standard Deviations.* Most players in the National Basketball Association, obviously, are taller than the mean height for adult members of the population of the United States. In fact, most of their heights probably would lie outside three standard deviations (σ = 3) from the mean of the adult population. Can you

explain why (remembering that exceeding three standard deviations means falling outside about 99.7% of the population)?

Furthermore, the center usually is the tallest member of any team, and the Los Angeles Lakers' Shaquille O'Neal is taller than most NBA centers. Can you guesstimate by how many standard deviations Shaquille O'Neal's greater-than-seven-foot height might differ from the mean of heights in the U.S. population? (Would you guess that the answer would be *more* than 3 SD, perhaps even 5 or 6?)

[D]   Sample Standard Deviations and Confidence Intervals: Methods of Hypothesis Testing

REAL-WORLD DISTRIBUTIONS, SAMPLES, AND THE CENTRAL LIMIT THEOREM: EVALUATING THE VALIDITY OF EVIDENCE IN A LAWSUIT

(1) *Real Distributions: Recalling the Rocks-for-Jocks Example.* Sometimes distributions in the real world closely mirror normal distributions. But many populations do not. Recall the Rocks-for-Jocks example graphed in Figure 3, above. There, the curve representing the distribution of heights of students in Geology 1 was skewed because it was known as an easy course for athletes, and members of the school's basketball team flocked to it.

Again, remember that the idealized normal distribution is a theoretical concept. In real life, distributions may be messy: they may be "bimodal" (with two peaks), or they may lack a median, or they may reflect "discrete" (fixed-value) variables rather than "continuous" ones. In fact, the non-normal Rocks-for-Jocks example may be more "normal" (in the vernacular sense) than a very-close-to-normal bell-shaped distribution.

(2) *The Central Limit Theorem: A Large Sample Approximates a Normal Distribution, Even if the Population From Which It Is Taken Is Not Normal.* What would happen if we sampled heights from the non-normal, skewed population of heights in the Rocks-for-Jocks class? With a small sample, we might get an almost equally skewed distribution. But imagine, now, an infinitely large population of students distributed exactly the same way as the Rocks-for-Jocks class. And imagine, further, that we take a very large sample from it. What will the sample look like?

The answer is surprising. Even though the sample is taken from a population that has a *non-normal* distribution, the sample itself will approximate a *normal* distribution, if it is large enough in relation to the degree to which the population is skewed. This insight is called the "central limit theorem." Since this result is counterintuitive, it bears repeating: even if the population is not normally distributed, a sufficiently large sample from it will still approximate a normal distribution. This important theorem allows us to make useful inferences about real samples, as we shall illustrate below.

(3) *The Usefulness of the Normal Distribution in Evaluating Statistically-Based Hypotheses in a Lawsuit, as a Consequence of the Central Limit Theorem.* Again, here is the central limit theorem: Large numbers of data points sampled at random from a given population tend to produce a normal distribution. Thus, if we take a random sample and measure each unit, we will approximate a normal distribution, at least if our sample is large enough. Even if its graph is skewed, a sufficiently large sample will approach a normal distribution. This theorem has implications for testing hypotheses from statistics in litigation.

SAMPLE STANDARD DEVIATIONS
AND HYPOTHESIS TESTING:
USING STATISTICS IN THE LAW

(1) *Statistical Samples in Real-World Litigation.* In the real world, we frequently do not measure the entire population of interest (that is called a "census"), because to do so would be impractical. Imagine, for example, that we are trying to determine the per capita wealth of the world's population. We cannot practically survey all individuals on the planet to do so.

For these reasons, we sample. We know from the central limit theorem that with a sufficiently large sample, we will approximate a normal distribution. We then can calculate a sample standard deviation for the sample, and we can consider "confidence intervals" to test hypotheses. We would do the same to test hypotheses in a lawsuit.

(2) *Hypothesis Testing: The Null Hypothesis and the Alternative Hypothesis.* Recall our earlier discussion of hypotheses and statistical significance, done in connection with correlations. In that earlier section, we were concerned with hypotheses about whether a given dependent variable was correlated with a given independent one. But in a broader sense, a

hypothesis is simply a theoretical statement about a population or about its relationship to another population. In addition to hypothesizing about correlations, we can hypothesize about the mean of a population (e.g., that the average typing test score of secretarial applicants at Ajax Corporation is greater than 40 words per minute) or about the dispersion of the population (e.g., that the standard deviation σ of the population of typing speeds among secretarial applicants at Ajax is between 10 and 20 wpm).

The null hypothesis is the hypothesis that is tested. Remember, for example, that in testing for a correlation, we would arrive at the alternative hypothesis that the correlation exists by rejecting the null hypothesis (which is that the correlation does *not* exist). If our hypothesis is that μ, the mean of typing test scores at Ajax, is greater than 40 wpm, our null hypothesis is that it is *not* greater than 40, and we seek to accept the alternate hypothesis (that it is) by rejecting this null hypothesis.

(3) *Setup of Experiments, Samples, or Surveys to Reject the Null Hypothesis if Possible; Degree of Confidence in the Alternative Hypothesis.* Remember: the null hypothesis is the hypothesis that we seek to reject. We then can accept the alternative hypothesis with the required level of confidence. We usually pre-set this level, α, as a matter of formal decisionmaking (because to set it later might lead to result orientation or "fudging"). But once again, a rejection of the null hypothesis does not definitively mean that it is false, but only that it is sufficiently improbable to allow us to accept the alternate hypothesis.

(4) *An Employment Law Example: Evaluating Typing Test Speeds of Secretarial Applicants at Ajax Corporation So as to Avoid Illegal Discrimination.* Here is an employment law example to work with. Suppose we are in the human relations department at Ajax Corporation, and we want to know about typing test speeds of applicants for secretarial positions. Specifically, we want to set a minimum typing speed so that we can reject lesser applicants quickly, but we want to establish this minimum speed carefully, so that we do not end up with too few qualified applicants, and so that our standard will be in compliance with the law (so that it can avoid producing illegal discrimination, for example).

Ajax employs scores of thousands of secretaries and gets thousands of applications per year. Our alternative hypothesis H_1 is that the mean typing speed of this year's applicants is above 40 words per minute. If valid, this hypothesis will enable us to set a minimum score in a rational manner. Let us say that we demand a significance level of α = 0.05 to reject the null hypothesis, H₀ (which is that the mean μ is *not* above 40 wpm). If we can reject the null hypothesis, we think we will have a sound legal and practical basis for establishing a minimum typing speed of (say) 40 wpm as a requirement for any applicant to be considered.[6]

Suppose we take a random sample of thirty of this year's applicants, and we produce the following array of typing test scores, all in words per minute (Ajax rounds them all to the nearest multiple of 10):

A Sample Consisting of Thirty Test Scores (in wpm, Rounded)

40, 40, 30, 40, 40, 50, 50, 70, 30, 70,

40, 30, 40, 50, 30, 40, 40, 50, 70, 70,

30, 50, 40, 30, 40, 70, 70, 50, 40, 40

We shall now proceed to compute the "sample mean," $\bar{x}$, for this sample, as well as the "sample standard deviation," s. These will serve (we hope) as estimators of μ, the population mean, and σ, the population standard deviation. After that, we shall proceed to consider the significance levels of our results and compare them to α = 0.05.

(5) *Computing the Sample Mean.* First we compute the sample mean, $\bar{x}$. (The mean of a sample is symbolized by a bar drawn over the symbol for the variable in question; here, x stands for the typing speeds in the sample, and therefore $\bar{x}$ stands for the mean of the sample.) This computation of $\bar{x}$, the mean, is easy: we simply average the thirty numbers (by adding them and dividing by 30). The result, as we shall see below, is 46. Thus, $\bar{x}$ = 46 words per minute. This is the sample mean.

This result "looks like" support for our alternate hypothesis, that the mean of Ajax's typing test scores exceeds 40, since the sample mean is 46. But does this reasoning really enable us to reject the null hypothesis? No, not yet.

---

6   Of course, this policy alone may not be enough to avoid liability for illegal discrimination. We also may be required to show that the typing test has business justification, i.e., that it is sufficiently related to job requirements. But having a valid sample may let us set an objective requirement that we can apply uniformly, and this too will help to refute illegal discrimination.

The sample mean is only an *estimator* of the population mean, and we need to know how good an estimator it is.

(6) *We Aren't Done Yet: We Still Need to Calculate the Significance Level and Compare It to a Pre-Set Value.* And so, we still can't reject the null hypotheses. Our null hypothesis is that the population mean is not greater than 40. Just because we have taken a sample and calculated a sample mean greater than 40 does *not* mean that we can reject the null hypothesis. For that, we need to see whether our result is statistically significant, using the pre-set α value of 0.05.

To test significance, however, we need another concept, called the "sample standard deviation." The central limit theorem tells us that if our sample is large enough, it will approximate a normal distribution. These concepts will enable us--in a later section--to test significance, after we have considered the sample SD.

(7) *Computing the Sample Standard Deviation for Our Employment Law Sample.* To calculate the sample standard deviation, we first must understand the "deviation" of each individual data point (or each typing test score) from the mean. This concept is simple: the deviation for each data point is just the difference between each individual value and the mean. For example, the first test score in the array above is 40 wpm. Given our mean of 46 wpm, the deviation for this first individual data point (the first typing test score) is minus six (-6) words per minute, because 40-46 = -6.

Now we are ready to define the sample standard deviation, symbolized by s, for the sample composed of Ajax's 30 typing speed scores above. It is defined as the square root of the mean of the squares of all the deviations, or:

$$s = \sqrt{\frac{\text{sum of (deviations)}^2}{\text{number of data}}}$$

This equation computes, from the sample, an estimator of σ, the population standard deviation (although the derivation of the equation is beyond our scope here). Below, in the examples and problems, we do the computation for these thirty typing speeds. The sample standard deviation, as we shall see, is s = 13.5 words per minute, and this gives us a sound basis for accepting our hypothesis. Now, let us proceed to see why.

EXAMPLES AND PROBLEMS

(1) *Employment Law, Human Relations Practices, and Statistics: Computing the Sample Standard Deviation for Our Thirty Typing Speed Tests.* Now, let us go through the calculation of s (the sample SD) for our 30 typing speeds. The array in the sample includes 6 scores of 30 words per minute, 12 scores of 40, 6 scores of 50, and 6 scores of 70.

To calculate s, we first must calculate the sample mean x̄. Then we must figure the deviations for all data points and sum the squares of all the deviations.

$$\text{sample mean} = \bar{x} = \frac{(6)(30) + 12(40) + 6(50) + 6\,(70)}{30} = 46.$$

deviation = 30 - 46 = -16 for all scores of 30 (deviation squared = 256).
40 - 46 = -6 for all scores of 40 (deviation squared = 36).
50 - 46 = 4 for all scores of 50 (deviation squared = 16).
70 - 46 = 24 for all scores of 70 (deviation squared = 576).

summed squares = (6 x 256) + (12 x 36) + (6 x 16) + (6 x 576) = 5520.

Now, we have the sum of the squares of the deviations; it is 5520. Next, we apply the equation for the sample standard deviation, s:

$$s = \sqrt{\frac{\text{sum of (deviations)}^2}{\text{number of data}}} = \sqrt{\frac{5520}{30}} = \sqrt{184} = 13.5$$

Thus, the sample standard deviation for our 30 typing test scores is s = 13.5. This number may not be exactly equal to the standard deviation for the population (σ), but it is an estimator of it. Can you explain the math?

(2) *An Employment Law Conclusion: The Meaning of the Sample Standard Deviation and Its Relationship to the Central Limit Theorem.* What this sample standard deviation of 13.5, above, means is that the sample fits the conditions for accepting our hypothesis that the true mean is greater than 40 wpm. Let us see why. If our sample is sufficiently large, the central limit theorem tells us that we should expect about 68% of the sampled typing speeds, or roughly 20 of the 30, to be within 13.5 words per minute of the mean of 46. (Actually, 18 out of 30, or 60%, fit within this interval of one standard deviation--and 18 is reasonably close to 20.) Also, we would expect

roughly 95%, or 28.5 of the 30 typing speeds, to be within two standard deviations. (Actually, all 30, or 100%, fit within two standard deviations-- and 30 is reasonably close to 28.5.) Our data are reasonably consistent with the central limit theorem. Can you explain this conclusion?

CONFIDENCE INTERVALS AND SIGNIFICANCE

(1) *Confidence Intervals: A Measure of Confidence in a Statistical Estimator, or of Statistical Significance, Analogous to the p-Value.* Next, we shall test the statistical significance of our sample mean, $\bar{x} = 46$, as an estimator of μ, the population mean. We shall use what are called "confidence intervals" to do this. An "interval estimate" is an interval that we are able to say, with a given level of confidence, includes a given statistical variable in a population, such as μ (the population mean) or σ (the population SD). The sample mean $\bar{x}$ and the sample SD s are merely estimators of these factors, and we need to know how closely they probably fit the real μ and σ. To do this, we use an interval of an estimated amount. Then, we say that the actual value is estimated at a certain amount, "plus or minus" the estimate. An example: "We estimate the mean of this population to be 46 ± 5."

Wide intervals of this kind are very likely to include the correct numbers for the actual variables, but wide intervals are not very useful. For example, we can estimate with very strong confidence that the mean age of all Americans is included within the interval from 20 years old to 90 years old-- but that does not give us a very specific idea of the average American age (as contrasted to, say, learning that the mean is between 35 and 36 years old).

The point is that we can construct a "confidence interval" for any percentage confidence level we wish. A confidence interval is just an interval estimate expressing our percentage confidence that the interval contains the targeted statistic. The broader the interval, the greater the confidence. Thus, the tradeoff for a narrower, more useful interval is a reduction in confidence that it really contains the statistical element we are trying to estimate. To put it another way, a wide interval creates more confidence but tells us less; a narrow interval helps to pinpoint the statistic but is due less confidence.

(2) *The Relationship of Standard Deviations to Confidence Intervals.* As we have seen, approximately 68% of a normally distributed population is within one SD of the mean, 95% is within two (2) SD, and 99.7% is within three (3) SD. Therefore, we can say with roughly 68% confidence that a

random variable will have a value within one SD of the mean (this is true for an unbiased sample large enough so that it approximates the normal distribution). We call this the "68% confidence interval," with "confidence limits" of one SD, and its "confidence level" is 68%.

Similarly, we have 95% confidence that if we pick a unit at random, its value will fall within *two* SD of the mean (the 95% confidence interval, with confidence level 95%). And if we expand the confidence limits to 99.7%, at *three* SD, we have a confidence level of 99.7% that a random variable will be within this interval.

Figure 11, which is a repetition of an earlier figure, illustrates this idea. Since approximately 68% of the units are within one SD in a normal curve, the confidence level for finding a random unit within this range is 68%. (The 68% corresponds, incidentally, to the area under this part of the curve, which is 68% of the total area under the curve.) Within two SD's, the probability of finding a random variable is 95%, so that the figure illustrates the 95% confidence limits by the verticals at -2 and +2. Similarly, the verticals at -3 and +3 show the span of the 99.7% confidence limits.

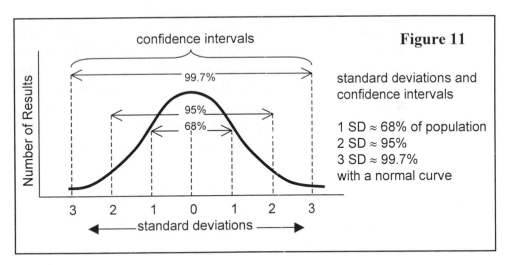

(3) *The Relationship of Confidence Intervals to p-Values and α Values.* Recall our discussion of p-values and their comparison to pre-set α values in determining statistical significance for a correlation. If we set α = 0.05, a p-value of 0.04 indicates statistical significance. Confidence intervals make the idea more general. A confidence interval of 95% means that we can express 95% confidence that the true value of the mean falls within a defined range

of the estimate we have calculated. A 99% confidence interval has an analogous meaning, at the 99% confidence level.

EXAMPLES AND PROBLEMS

(1) *Validity for Employment Law Purposes: Computing a 95% Confidence Interval for Our Earlier Example of Ajax's Sample of Thirty Typing Test Scores: Confidence Limits of ± 5.0.* The computation of the 95% confidence interval for the sample mean of 46 for our thirty typing test scores is beyond our scope here. (The standard method uses a statistic called "t"[7] to estimate the confidence interval; an explanation is set out in the margin for the mathematically inclined.[8]).

The computation yields a value of approximately 5.0, and hence the 95% confidence interval around our sample mean $\bar{x}$ of 46 is 5, or 46 ± 5. In other words, we can be 95% confident that the mean μ of the population of all of Ajax's applicants' typing scores lies between 41 and 51, or within 5 wpm of our estimate of 46 (the sample mean), assuming that our sample is appropriate.

In summary, this confidence interval means that we can reject (barely!) the null hypothesis H_0, which was that the true mean μ of Ajax's typing test speeds was *not* greater than 40 wpm. Thus, we accept the alternate hypothesis H_1, that it *is* greater than 40. We now feel that we are on sound ground in adopting 40 wpm as a minimum score for applicants. Can you explain how this conclusion follows? But if we had hypothesized a slightly higher mean, such as 45 wpm, we would not have been able to accept the hypothesis. Can you explain?

(2) *Reconsidering Our Earlier Loaded-Coin Experiment (Nine Out of Ten Flips Turning up Heads), Using Confidence Intervals.* In a previous section,

---

7   The distribution of the t function was first reported by William Sealy Gosset in the early 1900's. Gosset used the pen name "Student," and hence the distribution of t is referred to as "Student's distribution." It roughly resembles, but differs from, the normal distribution. It approaches the normal distribution as sample size increases, however, and this is why it can be a reliable estimator.

8   [Read this footnote only if you are interested in the more technical aspects of the mathematics.] In simplified form, the formula is $t \cdot s/\sqrt{n}$, where n is the number of data in the sample (here 30), s is the sample standard deviation (here 13.5), and t is a statistical value depending on n-1 and α, which statisticians usually get from a table (here, it is 2.0, when obtained from such a table). Thus, the confidence interval around our mean of 46 is approximated by $\pm t \cdot s/\sqrt{n} = \pm 2.0 \cdot 13.5/\sqrt{30} = \pm 2 \cdot 2.5 = \pm 5$, and thus our confidence interval is 46 ± 5, or 41 to 51. It should be added that t, in the equation, usually is notated as "$t_1 - \alpha/_2$" to signify that it depends on α and is two-tailed. But if you don't follow this, or the rest of this footnote, don't worry; it is included for completeness.

we considered the problem of a coin that we suspected was "loaded" or biased. It produced nine (9) heads in ten flips. By calculating the p-value, we noticed that this result was statistically significant at the 5% (nearly the 1%) level, meaning that if $\alpha = 0.05\%$, we indeed could reject the null hypothesis and conclude that the coin was biased. Let us say that we now wish to reconsider that experiment, using a confidence interval approach. If we did the ten flips many times with an honest coin, we would approach a sample mean of five heads. We want to see whether, with α set at 0.05, we can reject the null hypothesis that the coin is honest by constructing a confidence interval.

What, then, is the 95% confidence interval for ten flips of an honest coin (that is, the range of numbers of heads in which we would expect 95% of ten-flip experiments to fall)? It turns out that the 95% confidence interval ranges from approximately 2 heads to 8 heads.[9] Ninety-five percent of the time, we would expect to see at least 2 and at most 8 heads, with an honest coin. In other words, our experimental result of 9 heads out of ten is outside the 95% confidence interval, which ranges from 2 to 8 heads. If $\alpha = 0.05$, then, we can reject the null hypothesis (an honest coin) and adopt the alternate hypothesis (the coin is biased). Can you explain why this reasoning means we have used this confidence interval to reach the same result obtained by our earlier p-value computation?

(3) *How Backward Reasoning About Confidence Intervals Creeps Into Practical Problems: The Decision in Cimino v. Raymark Industries, Inc.,* 751 F. Supp. 649 (E.D. Tex. 1990). Here is a real-life example of difficulties in statistical reasoning. Cimino v. Raymark Industries, Inc. was a massive lawsuit, consisting of more than 6,000 asbestos-injury cases, all related but different. Realizing the impossibility of handling each case separately, the judge commendably attempted to use statistical techniques. He drew certain random samples from the cases, tried those cases, and then used the verdicts to estimate the total award for all 6,000-plus plaintiffs. He then held a hearing to determine whether the result was statistically significant.

---

9   This result actually was obtained with the use of a standard table that gives probabilities for what is called the "binomial distribution" (the distribution that results from repeated either-or events, such as coin flips). From the table, the probability of eight or fewer heads out of ten flips, with 0.5 probability for each, is 0.9893. The probability of fewer than two heads out of ten (or in other words, one) is 0.0107. Therefore, the probability of throwing at least two but fewer than eight heads in a ten-coin sequence with a fair coin is 0.9893 - 0.0107 = 0.9786. The range from two heads to eight heads, then, is the 97.86% confidence interval. It approximates the 95% confidence interval.

The judge appointed an educational psychologist as the court's own expert to assist in this investigation. The expert opined that the sample of cases mirrored the entire population of cases on such characteristics as race, percentage of survivors, etc. The problem was, the confidence limits for these findings were at the 99% level. The judge concluded that this level justified high confidence, better than the 95% confidence level. "The [sample] cases tried . . . produced a 99% confidence level [that] the [sample mean] would be comparable to the average result if all cases were tried [i.e., to the population mean]." 751 F. Supp. at 665.

Unfortunately, according to the Federal Judicial Center's *Reference Manual on Scientific Evidence*, "this is backwards." Can you explain why the reasoning was backward? (Notice that it is not very convincing to be correct with a 99% confidence interval, because that means that the interval is broad enough to ensure that the targeted statistic is within the range 99% of the time, even if the sample is completely uncorrelated with the population! Proper reasoning might have proceeded by constructing a 99% confidence interval for the null hypothesis--i.e., the hypothesis that no correspondence between sample and population existed--and then by finding out whether the experimental result was *outside* this interval.)

§ 13.03   Sampling and Data Collection: What if the Data Are Biased?

POPULATIONS, SAMPLES, AND BIAS

(1) *Reconsidering the Baseball Statistic: The Example of an Accurately Computed, but Biased, Batting Average.* So far, we have not considered the possibility of errors in the data collection. We have assumed that our study has used the entire population, or that whatever samples we took were representative. But often, we must sample, because the population is larger than our resources will allow us to measure. Sampling introduces the possibility of several kinds of errors.

Imagine, for example, that we want to figure a player's batting average for the season. Being lazy, we decide to take just the player's at-bats during the month of May, assuming that the resulting average will reflect the entire population. But what if the player was on a hitting streak in May? Then, the data will be biased, producing an erroneously high average. If we wanted to be lazy, we might do better to randomize our sample (by taking every fifth at-bat, for example).[10]

(2) *Errors in Data Collection: Validity, Reliability, and Recording.* Could there be any error, then, in a batting average? Yes, because the collection of some units may reflect measuring or recording errors. Imagine that there is a famous player named Babe Cardozo, for whom the official scorers have recorded only four hits out of twenty official at-bats, for a batting average of .200. Imagine further that two of the other at-bats really were hits, but the official scorers mistakenly recorded errors. Correction means that Babe's average zooms to a more respectable .300.

How could such errors occur? First, the measurement may lack "validity," meaning accuracy. It's possible that the official scorers couldn't see the plays, and they merely guessed. Second, the data may lack "reliability," meaning consistency. It's possible that the scorers have different mental standards for what is a hit, compared to an error. Finally, the scorers may have recorded their conclusions wrong in the box score, or statistical collectors may have misread their handwriting. Thus, errors of validity, reliability and recordation can affect many kinds of statistical studies.

(3) *Censuses versus Surveys: The Sampling Frame, from Convenience Samples to Random Samples.* A "census" measures every unit in the population. Thus, a major league player's batting average, or the United States Census, are true censuses. A "survey" or "sample," as its name implies, measures only some units in the population.

A key initial issue concerns the "sampling frame," or the method of identifying the portion of the population from which the sample is drawn. At one extreme, there is what is called a "convenience sample." The surveyor goes to a mall and questions people who congregate in a particular spot. The result of a convenience sample may be satisfactory if the sampling error can be ignored. At the other extreme, a census or a "random sample" may be taken from the entire population, in which each unit is selected by a method that gives each unit a theoretically equal probability of being sampled. One

---

10 Technically, we must begin collecting data at a randomly selected number from one to five for the sample to be a true probability sample, because only then will every member of the population have an equivalent chance to be included in the sample. But if you don't see why, don't worry; this note is placed here only for technical accuracy.

might, for example, measure every fifth unit, randomly chosen, or every one whose number pops up in a given number of lottery-machine runs.

(4) *Selection Bias and Nonresponse Bias.* Imagine, however, that we are trying to sample a population that is hard to frame. Let's say we want to poll amateur baseball players across the United States. There is no central registry, and it rapidly becomes apparent that defining the sample frame will be the biggest problem for our poll.

In fact, our amateur baseball poll will be affected by at least two kinds of errors. First is "selection bias." If we define the population by approaching known amateur organizations and begging for their mailing lists, we will generate one possible population. If we take every thousandth name from several big-city telephone books and poll those who self-identify as baseball amateurs, we will get a different selection-biased sample.

In addition to this selection bias, there is a second kind of error, which results from the fact that humans are uncooperative, and many will not respond to our survey. This is called "nonresponse bias." A large nonresponse weakens confidence even in a well-framed sample, because we cannot know the extent to which the nonresponse units have different characteristics, differences that may be correlated with their nonresponse.

DEALING WITH SELECTION AND NONRESPONSE BIAS

(1) *Compensating for Selection and Nonresponse Bias: Quotas, Secondary Measurement of Nonrespondents, and Reporting.* One way to compensate for selection bias is to use "quotas." We figure out which different categories of units might give different measurements, and we set a percentage for each. For example, in a poll about a political candidate from a sample known to be affected by selection bias that undercounts Democrats, we can refine our sample by discarding randomly selected Republicans. The trouble with this method is that it assumes we already know the categories and size of the selection bias and how to correct for it, when in reality, not knowing these things is precisely the usual problem.

For nonresponse bias, we sometimes can do a secondary measurement of nonresponsive units selected at random. For example, we make special efforts to obtain responses from every tenth non-respondent and compare those to our earlier responses. Here, the trouble is that we may change the measurement by the different (special) technique, and we still will be left with nonresponse bias because of units that resist measurement. In the alternative, particularly with cause-effect studies, we sometimes can compare the causal characteristics of the nonrespondents with those of respondents to determine the likely effect of nonresponse.

But in the end, reporting is the solution. Accurate disclosure is an essential part of a statistical analysis.

(2) *Controlled and Double-Blind Experiments.* The testing of new drugs is done with a population known to reflect sample bias (among other reasons, everyone must have consented). Therefore, the population is divided by random or probabilistic means into two groups, one of which is the "control" group. We then vary one specific condition between the two (in this case, by administering the actual drug to one, a placebo to the other). The most accurate results depend on each unit or person being "blind," that is, ignorant of the group assignment and therefore unable to conform responses to expectations. Ideally, the controlled experiment is "double-blind," meaning that neither the experimental subjects nor the data collectors know which are members of the control or test group.

(3) *Control as a Means of Minimizing Confounders.* Another way of thinking about this problem is to remember our discussion of "confounders." Selection and nonresponse bias increase the danger that confounders may confuse the inference, particularly if they are overrepresented or underrepresented in the sample. The use of a control group increases the likelihood that differences truly reflect the experimental group, because both groups are chosen from the same sample.

(4) *Observational Studies When Controlled Experiments Are Impossible.* Sometimes, controlled experiments are impossible because they are impracticably expensive or unethical. If we wanted to study the effects of denial of medical care during pregnancy upon newborns, theoretically the most accurate way would be to sample expectant mothers and deny medical care to a randomly selected control group. Such an experiment would be unacceptable. Many of our statistical insights, therefore, must deal with selection and nonresponse biases.

EXAMPLES AND PROBLEMS

(1) *The Misleading Batting Average.* Babe Cardozo seems to be on a blazing hitting streak. His batting average, so far this season, is exactly .750. Last season, he batted only .283. Can you explain a possible reason why his .750 average might be misleading?

(2) *A Litigation Example: Suits Based on the Theory That Electrical Transmission Lines Caused Cancer.* This is an example that we have considered several times already in this book. During the 1980's and early 1990's, people in some precincts close to power lines noticed that they had much higher cancer rates than there were in some precincts distant from power lines. In fact, calculations comparing these selected precincts' cancer rates with their distances from power lines would have produced both high correlation coefficients and good statistical significance. Several high-profile lawyers, nationwide, brought suits on behalf of landowners against power companies for the "damages caused" by transmission lines.

But the lawsuits later were dismissed, often at the instances of the attorneys filing them, because of sampling bias. Can you see why? In fact, the null hypothesis (no effect from transmission lines) would be expected to produce some precincts with strikingly high cancer rates close to transmission lines and some precincts with strikingly low ones.

(3) *The Hite Report: A Classic Case of Dubious Conclusions After a High Nonresponse Rate.* In 1987, Shere Hite published "Women and Love: A Cultural Revolution in Progress," which became known as the Hite Report. She sent out a hundred thousand questionnaires and received roughly five thousand responses, including a very large group of women who wrote at length about their disillusionment with love and marriage. Hite's conclusion was that this "outcry" against the injustices of marriage showed that its reflection of the exploitation of women was "just and accurate."

But even if it is true that marriage is unjust, the conclusion is not supported by Hite's data. Can you see how the roughly 95% nonresponse rate undermines the conclusion? For example, consider whether women who were not disillusioned with love may have had less motive to respond.

(4) *Avoidance of Selection Bias May Not Remove Nonresponse Bias.* Hite defended her report by the observation that the respondents "closely

mirror[ed]" the United States population in "age, occupation, religion and other variables." Perhaps this was an effort to demonstrate the absence of selection bias. If so, it does not compensate for nonresponse bias. Why?

Alternatively, Hite may have been trying to compare respondents with nonrespondents, to show that they did not differ, as a means of demonstrating that the nonresponse probably did not affect the results. If so, many readers would not be persuaded, and would remain concerned about nonresponse bias. Can you see why?

(5) *Examples of Bad Statistical Reasoning, from Spanking to Health Care.* A study a few years ago documented children who had been spanked and children who had not. A few months later, the study showed that the behavior of the spanked children was worse than that of the non-spanked ones. The media promptly reported these results as "demonstrating" that spanking was harmful. Can you explain why the absence of a control group and the presence of selection bias made this conclusion dubious? (Consider, for example, the possibility that children whose behavior was bad to begin with may have been more likely to be spanked in the first place.)

As another example, people sometimes mistakenly evaluate doctors and hospitals by comparing their patients' mortality rates. This approach may seem sensible at first glance, but can you explain why it is bad statistical reasoning? (Imagine a doctor who operates only on the highest-risk patients, and who therefore produces dismal mortality rates in spite of good skills.)

§ 13.04 Regression Analysis

LINEAR REGRESSION ANALYSIS: THE LINE OF BEST FIT

(1) *Simple Linear Regression Analysis; Multiple Regression.* Up to this point, we have considered whether a linear statistical relation exists: How linear is the relationship, and how sure can we be about it? Now, we shall consider how to describe the relationship quantitatively by setting up an equation for it. This is the task of "regression analysis."

In a later section, we shall consider "multiple regression," which concerns the analysis of multiple independent variables. If we are able to compute the effects of all other independent variables through regression analysis, we may be able also to figure out the effect of a single variable under study. This is the power of multiple regression analysis. It can demonstrate whether a given variable is correlated with the effect in a real world with multiple variables: a suspected carcinogen that we wish to analyze as related to a certain cancer, or the death penalty, which we wish to analyze as a deterrent to murder. First, however, we must consider simple linear regression.

(2) *Using Regression Analysis in the Law: From Environmental Causation to Employment Law to the Death Penalty.* Since regression analysis gives quantitative results, environmental lawyers use regression experts to figure out which of several potential compounds may be toxic and at what level. But this is only one example. Among other uses, regression also is featured in employment litigation and in analysis of the death penalty.

(3) *The Form of a Linear Equation and Its Slope and Intercept:* $Y = a+bX$. A basic algebra course teaches that the form of a linear equation is $Y = a+bX$. For example, the equation, $Y = 1+2X$ is a linear equation. It is graphed in Figure 12.

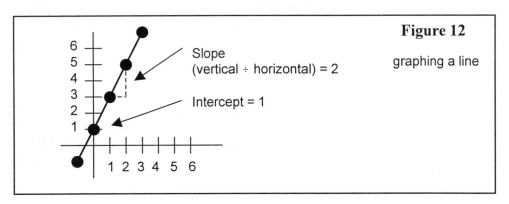

Figure 12

graphing a line

Slope (vertical ÷ horizontal) = 2

Intercept = 1

Notice that when X is zero, Y is 1. This number, 1, is called the "intercept" because it is the point at which the line intercepts the Y axis (where $X = 0$). See the graph. In this equation, $Y = 1+2X$, the "slope" of the line is the other number, 2. The slope is the vertical increase in the line relative to the horizontal increase; here, Y increases two units for every unit of increase in X.

In the general form of the equation, $Y = a+bX$, the "a" signifies the intercept, and "b" is the slope. For two linear variables, this is the form of the equation, and therefore it is this form that we use for linear regression analysis.

(4) *Linear Regression Analysis: Finding the Regression Line, or Line of Best Fit.* Linear regression analysis is an effort to find the "regression line" or "line of best fit": a straight line that best fits the data points. This line then gives us an equation that allows quantitative calculations.

In Figure 13, the line of best fit is drawn as a solid line among four data points, representing employees' salaries, which are graphed against their years of experience. The one-year employee has a salary of $50,000; the two-year $100,000, the three-year $80,000, and the four-year $130,000. There is an upward trend, or apparent correlation. (There would be poor statistical significance here because of the small number of data, but that is not the point; we have deliberately kept the data set small, to simplify.)

The equation for the fitted line in Figure 13 is Y = $40,000 + $20,000(X), where Y is salary and X is years of experience. Such a line always will cut a path between two sets of data points, which will fall above and below the line. The equation for the regression line or line of best fit allows us to predict the dependent variable quantitatively. This particular regression equation, in Figure 13, gives us an estimate of salaries for employees after they have been with the company for a given period of time.

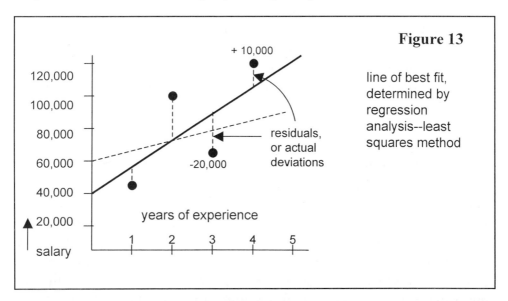

(5) *How the Equation for the Line of Best Fit Is Defined: The Least-Squares Method.* The line of best fit usually is figured by the "least squares" method. This method begins with the concept of "residuals," or deviations from the fitted line. Two of the four deviations are identified on Figure 13:

For the employee with 3 years' experience, the deviation is -20,000 (the calculation is $80,000 minus $100,000); for the four-year employee, the deviation is +10,000 (the calculation is $130,000 minus the regression-line prediction of $120,000).

One way to conceptualize the line of best fit is to consider that it minimizes these residuals or deviations. But the actual approach used by statisticians is slightly more complex. It minimizes the *squares* of the residuals or deviations. The reason is that this approach converts all the residuals to positive numbers; notice that it also gives greater weight to larger deviations. In the examples below, we show the computation.

EXAMPLES AND PROBLEMS

(1) *Computing the Squares of the Residuals for the Regression Line or Line of Best Fit; and, Comparison to Another Line.* In Figure 13, we have four data points, with residual values or deviations of -10,000, +20,000, -20,000, and +10,000 for the respective employees. For convenience, consider these to be -1, +2, -2, and +1 (in ten thousands). The sum of the squares, then, is $1+4+4+1 = 10$.

Figure 13 also includes another line--a dashed line--which is not the best fit. This dashed line, which traces the equation $Y = $60,000 + $10,000X$, yields residuals of -20,000, +20,000, -10,000, and +30,000 (or -2, +2, -1, and +3, in ten-thousands). The sum of the squares for the dashed line, then, is $4+4+1+9 = 18$.

The regression line is the one that produces the smallest sum of the squares of its residuals. Can you explain the mathematics, here?

(2) *The Usefulness of This Analysis in the Law: What if the Employer Wants to Compute a Nondiscriminatory Salary for a New, Totally Inexperienced Employee (or, for a Lateral Hire With Five Years' Experience)?* If the employer hires a new, inexperienced employee, the regression line shows that a salary of $40,000 would be consistent with other employees' salaries. If the employer hires a new employee from another company with five years' experience, the predicted salary is $140,000. Can you explain? This pair of examples shows one way in which an employer can determine terms of employment objectively and thus evidence the avoidance of illegal discrimination in salaries.

(3) *Regression Analysis as a Means of Proving Recoverable Damages in Business Litigation, Employment Discrimination and Antitrust Lawsuits.* The usefulness of regression analysis, then, is that it provides quantitative data. In the law, its greatest use probably has been in calculating damages for business, antitrust and (especially) employment discrimination cases.

It may be possible, for example, to produce a regression line based upon a comparison of comparably situated women and men in the form, $Y = A + bX_2$, where X_2 is a "dummy variable" of 1 (male) or 0 (female), for the employee's gender. The factor b, then, would represent the difference between women's and men's salaries due to the gender difference.

MULTIPLE REGRESSION

(1) *Multiple Regression: Using the Same Kind of Equation, but With Multiple Coefficients and Variables.* Now that you understand regression lines with one independent variable, we can generalize this approach to an infinite number of variables. Statisticians usually designate the estimated regression variable (the dependent variable) with the symbol $\hat{Y}$ (Y with a caret or "hat" on it). The independent variables, or causal variables, are designated as $X_1, X_2, \ldots X_i$, up to however many variables there happen to be.

Then, the coefficients or multiplying factors are designated by the Greek letter beta, with subscripts: $\beta_0, \beta_1, \beta_2, \ldots \beta_i$. Using these symbols, the general form of the linear multiple regression equation is

$$\hat{Y} = \beta_0 + \beta_1 X_1 + \beta_2 X_2 + \ldots \beta_i X_i + \varepsilon,$$

where β_0 is the "intercept" number and β_i is the coefficient or multiplier for X_i, which is the ith linear variable. The symbol "ε" is an error term, which recognizes the possibility that there may be undiscovered causal factors; ε, then, is the total effect of any omitted variables. For each independent variable, the line of best fit minimizes the sum of the squares of the residuals of all data, and hence the regression equation will minimize the total sum of all the squares of residuals for all variables.

(2) *The Usefulness of Multiple Regression: Isolating One Independent Variable to Study Its Relationship to a Dependent Variable.* As we have seen, regression analysis enables us to treat statistical relationships

quantitatively, not just to show that some relationship exists. But what if there are multiple factors at work? Here is the true power of regression analysis: with the right data, we can isolate and study a single independent variable.

Once we have derived the multiple regression equation, we know the quantitative impact of all variables that are built into our model. We can study the effect of a single epidemiological variable on cancer rates, for example, or compute the impact of an economic indicator on the national economy, or evaluate the effect of a particular crime control measure on homicide rates.

EXAMPLES AND PROBLEMS

(1) *Ehrlich's Use of Multiple Regression Techniques in Measuring the Deterrent Effect of the Death Penalty, Cited by the Supreme Court in Gregg v. Georgia*, 428 U.S. 153 (1976). In 1975, economist Isaac Ehrlich challenged existing statistical analyses of the deterrent effect of the death penalty. Ehrlich focused upon the relationship between execution risk (the fraction of convicted murders put to death) and homicide rates in the nation as a whole. He attempted to control other causal variables by using multiple regression analysis, so that the coefficient β_i for the execution risk, X_i, could be isolated. The other causal variables included such factors as detection and conviction rates. (Ehrlich's equation is set out in an earlier chapter on jurisprudence.)

Ehrlich's tentative conclusion was that β_i was approximately 8, meaning that each new execution would deter 8 homicides. The Supreme Court cited Ehrlich in upholding the death penalty in *Gregg v. Georgia*, although the dissenters cited a number of criticisms. Other studies on both sides of the debate have been made since that time.

(2) *The Major Criticism of Ehrlich's Study: It Is Dependent on the Time Series Chosen.* The most salient criticism of Ehrlich's study was that it combined time periods during which executions took place with periods in which none took place. If one considered only the time series during which there *were* executions, the analysis showed no deterrent effect; when the time series when there *were not* was added, however, the deterrent effect appeared. Does this mean that it was the design of the model rather than the

mathematics that fueled the criticism? Of what significance should this factor be?

(3) *Analyzing Probable Statistical Validity in Regression Analyses: Standard Errors (Deviations) and Confidence Intervals.* Standard deviations and confidence intervals can and should be used to evaluate regression results as well as correlations. Can you see why? It should be possible to calculate the precision of a given regression coefficient β_i in this manner, so that we know the degree to which we can rely on each factor in the analysis.

PART VI
Game Theory and Strategy

Chapter 14
Game Theory I

Zero-Sum Games, Competitive Tactics, and the Law

> *"Consider an ordinary tactical choice, of the sort frequently made in war . . . [A] bad road can be good precisely because it is bad and may therefore be . . . left unguarded by the enemy . . . . [T]he paradoxical logic of strategy reaches the extreme of a full reversal."--Edward N. Luttwak, Strategy: The Logic of War and Peace*

> *"Everything in war is very simple, but the simplest thing is difficult. The difficulties accumulate and end by producing a kind of friction that is inconceivable unless one has experienced war."--Karl von Clausewitz, On War*

§ 14.01   What This Chapter Is About

STRATEGY IN COMPETITIVE SITUATIONS

(1)   *Defining Game Theory: Players, Strategies and Payoffs.* Game theory is the study of interactions among two or more decisionmakers

("players"), each of whom is faced with multiple decisional choices ("strategies"), which in turn determine outcomes ("payoffs") for which the players have sufficiently clearly defined preferences so that they can be numerically evaluated. Under this definition, checkers and tic-tac-toe are games, but foot races and cowboys and Indians are not. A game in this sense does not mean a pastime; what really is being studied is socially interactive decisionmaking. The aim is to determine how rational actors ought to develop their strategies, as a matter of purely self-interested reason.

This chapter considers purely competitive interactions of the kind called "zero-sum games." The chapter exposes the reader to such concepts as "payoff matrices," "decision trees," "mixed strategies," "equilibrium" or "saddle" points, and the "minimax" principle.

(2) *Why Lawyers Need Game Theory.* Perhaps it is obvious that lawyers use strategy, but let us develop some nonobvious uses for these next two chapters.[1] First, principles of strategy are used in every competitive encounter. A trial is an example, and at the end of this chapter we shall directly analyze trial strategy. Perhaps less obviously, negotiation is an exercise in game theory. Third, the policy issues underlying civil discovery, divorce, and international agreements are amenable to game theory analysis. We shall see those applications. Fourth, legislation and other kinds of social incentives depend heavily on considering the responses of rational self-interested humans, which is to say, they depend on strategy. Finally, game theory can help us analyze deep philosophical issues about justice. Remember Rawls's "A Theory of Justice," discussed in an earlier chapter? Rawls's "minimax" strategy, proposed for his ideal society, was borrowed from game theory--as we shall see in this chapter.

---

1 *A Feminist Critique of Our Coverage Here.* One pre-publication reader wrote about these two chapters that they "felt more male, with lots of military and war examples." This critique is interesting; in fact, it is valid to the extent that the study of purely competitive strategy historically has been largely a male pursuit, and it still may feel that way. Feminist jurisprudence, as we have seen, favors accommodation and conflict resolution instead.

The next chapter will emphasize values more consistent with feminist jurisprudence when we study cooperative and mixed-motive strategies. But first, this chapter does indeed confront theories that were developed from conflicts such as military campaigns. Today, both genders study battle tactics at once male military institutions, and our armed services depend absolutely on women combatants. And here is the real point: for lawyers of both genders, this subject is important, because a trial (or a motion hearing) is a strictly competitive, zero-sum undertaking. Insights from other strategic settings, as we shall see, can help to understand trial tactics. Meanwhile, the preference of feminist jurisprudence for conflict resolution should be kept in mind, because sensible lawyers settle cases if they can--without turning them into zero-sum games!

(3) *Application of Game Theory to Psychology.* Although game theory is logical, it differs sharply from most kinds of logic, as Luttwak's statement quoted above about the "paradox" of strategy indicates. The existence of a thinking, self-interested adversary makes obvious answers sometimes wrong. Therefore, this chapter also considers the psychological insights that have resulted from game theory.

(4) *Competitive Strategy in War, Chess, Football--and Law.* Many kinds of military, political and economic situations can be modeled usefully by game theory, but others, because of their complexity, cannot. Nevertheless, there are strategic principles that apply to these more complex games, including assessment, intelligence, deception, coordination, and application of force. The classic theory of strategy in war was developed by Clausewitz, who is quoted above, and it still has value today. This chapter considers examples from such diverse fields as football, war, and chess, and it culminates, of course, in applying them to the law.

(5) *Cooperative and Mixed-Motive Games.* There are other kinds of games than strictly competitive ones. The next chapter will consider "cooperative" games. It also will take up "mixed motive" games, in which mixtures of competitive and cooperative strategies may be most rational.

§ 14.02   Simple Two-Person Zero-Sum Games

[A]   The Tools of Game Theory

PAYOFF MATRICES AND DECISION TREES

(1) *Zero-Sum Games: A Trial under the Law Is a Zero-Sum Game.* A "zero-sum game" is a "strictly competitive" game. In other words, it is one in which anything one player wins must be lost by the other player, and there is no prospect of mutual gain by cooperation. A game of chess, an election campaign between two political candidates, and a battle between two competing armies, all are examples of two-person zero-sum games. So is a lawsuit between two litigants that is to be decided by a jury's verdict.

(2) *An Example: Applying Game Theory to the Battle of the Bismarck Sea.* Here is an example of a zero sum game, based on a famous naval battle. (This is not a legal example, but it has been analyzed frequently by game theorists, and it will help us to develop the tools of game theory.) During the middle years of World War II, Allied intelligence learned that the Japanese

intended to sail a major convoy around the island of New Britain to supply Japanese forces in New Guinea. The Allied Commander, General George Kenney, had to decide whether to send his reconnaissance aircraft north or south of the island, and similarly, the Japanese admiral, Hitoshi Imamura, had to decide whether to sail north or south.

Kenney knew that if Imamura sailed north, north-stationed reconnaissance would detect the Japanese convoy in time to allow for two (2) days of Allied bombing. But if Kenney stationed his reconnaissance to the south, it would detect the north-sailing fleet in time for only one (1) day of bombing. On the other hand, north-stationed reconnaissance still would detect the fleet in time for two (2) days of bombing if Imamura sailed south, but if Kenney stationed reconnaissance to the south, the Allies could bomb a south-sailing Japanese convoy for a full three (3) days. Thus, Kenney and Imamura faced each other in a zero-sum game.

(3) *A Payoff Matrix for This Game.* A "payoff matrix" is a visual display of strategy combinations and their resulting payoffs. Two players each with two strategies will produce a two-by-two matrix with four payoff squares.

Figure 1 is a payoff matrix for the Battle of the Bismarck Sea. Customarily, player 1 (Kenney, here) is listed to the left, and his strategy is shown by the horizontal rows; player 2's (Imamura's) strategies are reflected by the vertical columns. Thus, if we want to see the outcome (payoff) when Kenney searches north and Imamura sails north, we look to row 1 (horizontal) and column 1 (vertical) to see the payoff, which is two (2) days of bombing.

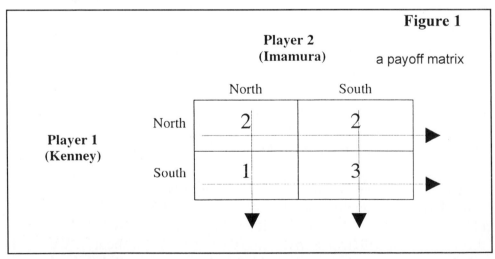

(4) *A Decision Tree for the Same Game.* A "decision tree" is an alternate method of visualizing strategies and payoffs. Figure 2 illustrates a decision tree for this game. The two circles represent decisions to be made by Kenney and Imamura, respectively; the circles also mean that both decisions are made with what is called "incomplete information," in that neither knows the other's decision until after he is committed on his own strategy. The dots, or "nodes," represent moves in decisional logic. The payoffs are given by the numbers beside the rightmost set of nodes. A decision tree, like a payoff matrix, enables each player to trace the payoffs for all available strategies.

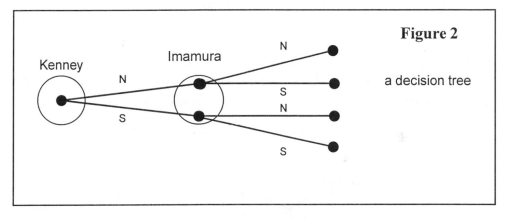

Figure 2

a decision tree

(5) *How Game Theory Offers Solutions.* It might seem that, without knowing the opponent's intentions, neither side would have a clear strategy in the Battle of the Bismarck Sea. Paradoxically, this is not true; there is a single rational strategy for both parties.

(6) *The Outcome, the Concept of a Saddle Point or Nash Equilibrium, and the Value of the Game.* The outcome was that Kenney sent his reconnaissance to the north, Imamura sailed north, and the Allies bombed the Japanese fleet for two days. The battle resulted in the worst Japanese naval loss up to that time (twenty-two ships and fifteen thousand troops).

But this outcome was dictated by rational strategies on the part of both players. The payoff matrix for this game, as we shall see, contains what is called a "saddle point" or "Nash equilibrium," or in other words, there is a single payoff square that is dictated by the rational strategies of both parties. The structure of the payoff matrix, with higher and lower payoffs encompassing this square to make it resemble a saddle, is what dictates the outcome. We say, therefore, that the "value of the game" is 2--two days of bombing. We proceed, now, to examine saddle points or Nash equilibria.

[B]   Saddle Points and the Minimax Strategy

SADDLE POINTS OR NASH EQUILIBRIA

(1) *Saddle Points or Nash Equilibria.* In the Battle of the Bismarck Sea, the strategies that minimize the worst outcome for each player coincide in the upper left box of the payoff matrix, the north-north box. This point is called a "saddle point" because it is equal to the highest point in one direction, its column, and equal to the lowest one in another, its row (just as a saddle sits at the highest point between the horse's flanks and at the lowest point between its neck and hind).

A saddle point is also called a "Nash equilibrium," after John Nash, who contributed importantly to the theory. Figure 3 shows this concept with a three-dimensional projection, demonstrating visually the saddle.

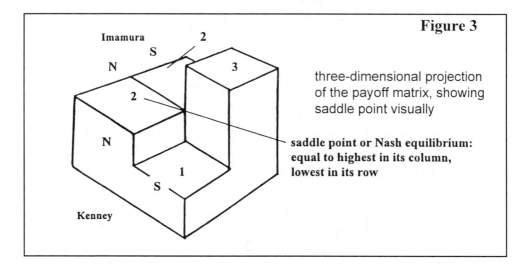

Figure 3

Imamura

three-dimensional projection of the payoff matrix, showing saddle point visually

saddle point or Nash equilibrium: equal to highest in its column, lowest in its row

Kenney

(2) *Dominant and Inadmissible Strategies; Previewing the Minimax Strategy.* Game theory in this situation specifies what is called a "minimax" strategy: the minimization of opportunity loss against an equally rational opponent. We shall explore this "minimax" strategy in the next section. For now, let us examine each player's options and the outcomes.

We first consider Imamura's options. Imamura wants low numbers (fewer days of bombing). His north boxes are (2, 1) and his south boxes are (2, 3). If he sails north, Imamura will suffer either two days of bombing or one, depending on Kenney's choice; if Imamura sails south, he will suffer either two days or three, depending on the same choice. The north column is in all instances either equal to or better than the south column for Imamura. In game theory terminology, therefore, we say that the north column "dominates" the south one for Imamura, and that south is "inadmissible." Imamura must sail north; any other strategy is irrational.

For Kenney, neither column is dominant in the same way, but the minimax strategy, of minimizing opportunity loss, indicates that Kenney's correct move is north. This is so because if Kenney contemplates a rational Imamura, he knows that Imamura must choose north, the dominant strategy, since south for Imamura is inadmissible; therefore, Kenney must choose north, which is dominant (where he will have two days of bombing) against south (only one day, which is worse for Kenney and therefore inadmissible).

(3) *The Saddle Dictates the Strategy.* This reasoning leads to the conclusion that if a zero-sum game has a unique saddle point, that point dictates the strategy of both players. A saddle point, or Nash equilibrium, is a point that is equal to both the highest level in its row and the lowest in its column, as Figure 3 shows visually. Rational play by both players makes this point dominant.

(4) *Value of the Game.* We say that the saddle point or Nash equilibrium fixes the "value of the game," or the outcome of reciprocal rational strategies. Here, the value of the game is 2 (two days of bombing).

MAXIMAX, MAXIMIN, AND MINIMAX STRATEGIES

(1) *Three Abstract Strategies: Maximax, Maximin, and Minimax.* Now, we proceed to consider three abstract forms of strategy: "maximax," which might be regarded as the most optimistic; "maximin," which is pessimistic; and minimax, which might be viewed as a conservative in-between strategy. It is the third of these, the minimax strategy, that is rational for both players in the Battle of the Bismarck Sea. But first, let's look at the others.

(2) *The Maximax Strategy (or Maximizing the Best Possible Outcome): The "Bet the Company on the Lottery" Plan.* If General Kenney had been a romantic, perhaps he would have chosen the "maximax" strategy, or "maxi"mizing the "max"imum, the best possible outcome of all rows. In this event, he simply would have chosen the row that contained the highest possible payoff. He would, then, search south, seeking a payoff of three (3) days of bombing. In doing so, he would ignore the other box in the row,

which forecasts the worst possible result, only one (1) day's bombing. Maximax might be called the "bet the company on the lottery" strategy.

In zero-sum games or in any real event with similar parameters, maximax is a poor strategy. Kenney's romantic thoughtlessness, if he had searched south, would not have given him the maximum return; it instead would have given him the worst possible result, only one day (since Imamura rationally could only sail north). The optimistic maximax strategy does, however, coincide with the romantic behavior of some people who play the lottery when its payoff is at a maximum, even though the number of other players may reduce mathematical expectation. Maximax sacrifices strategy to wishful thinking.

(2) *The Maximin Strategy (Choosing the Best of the Worst Possible Outcomes): Avoiding Risk at All Cost.* The opposite strategy is to search out the worst possible outcome of each possible move, and then to make the move that would select the best of all the worst possibilities. This is called the "maximin" strategy, because it "maxi"mizes the "min"imum payoffs. A few commentators have embraced this principle, but just as maximax may be too optimistic, maximin may be excessively pessimistic.

Consider the payoff matrix in Figure 4. Assume that "Player 2" actually is chance,[2] with one to one odds of selecting either column A or column B. The maximin strategy would tell Player 1, irrationally, always to choose row Y so as to obtain a sure one-cent payoff, in preference to risking a zero payoff by choosing Row X, even though Row X also contains a $100 million payoff that has a 50% likelihood of being realized! In fact, the maximin strategy

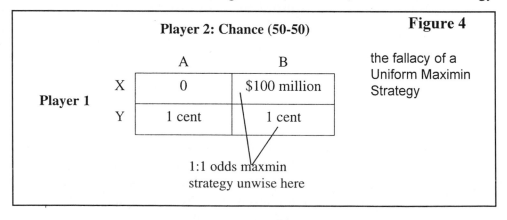

Player 2: Chance (50-50)   **Figure 4**

		A	B
	X	0	$100 million
Player 1			
	Y	1 cent	1 cent

the fallacy of a Uniform Maximin Strategy

1:1 odds maxmin
strategy unwise here

---

2   There must be two players for game theory to be implicated, but one of them can be nature, or chance. In this sense, solitaire is a "game."

will always select Row Y, even if the payoff is only a fraction of a cent, no matter how high the alternative to zero gets in Row X.

Still, it is impossible to dismiss maximin categorically in all circumstances. Sometimes, when it is important at all costs to avoid the worst-of-the-worst outcome, the maximin strategy may make sense.

(3) *The Minimax Strategy (Minimizing Opportunity Loss from the Opponent's Strategy): Taking Account of the Rational Adversary.* Game theorists consider the "minimax" strategy, as it is called, to be generally superior in the circumstances we are discussing.[3] (The key word here is "generally"; later, we shall see that the minimax strategy has its limits.) To see why, it is useful to transform the payoff matrix into a "loss matrix" (sometimes called a "regret" matrix). Instead of payoffs, each square in the matrix contains the "opportunity loss," or payoff reduction from some maximum, that is represented by that combination of strategies. The player then "mini"mizes the "max"imum loss in the available choices to follow the "minimax" strategy. As we shall see, this strategy is dictated by the strategy of a rational opponent.

(4) *Visualizing the Minimax Strategy with a Loss Matrix.* Figure 5 is a loss matrix for Kenney in the game represented by the Battle of the Bismarck Sea. Because the maximum payoff is 3, we call the corresponding opportunity loss zero (0), for "zero opportunity loss." (The reason: If Kenney gets three days of bombing, this is the best he can possibly do, and there is *zero opportunity loss.*)

Figure 5

Imamura

	A	B
X	1	1
Y	2	0

Kenney

loss matrix for the Battle of the Bismarck Sea

We also replace each "2" with a "1" (because two days, for Kenney, is one (1) day less than the best possibility of 3 and so the opportunity loss is

---

3　　That is, in strictly competitive two-player games with perfect knowledge (i.e., zero-sum games where each player knows the payoff matrix).

1), and we replace the "1" with a 2 (because it is two less than 3). The result, then, is the matrix in Figure 5.

If he follows the minimax strategy, Kenney makes the choice that will *minimize* his *maximum opportunity loss*. The maximum loss, here, is 2, which is contained in row Y; therefore, the minimax strategy for Kenney is to choose Row X, for which the maximum loss will be only 1.

(5) *Why Minimax Is Preferable for Rational Two-Person Zero-Sum Games With Perfect Knowledge.* The wisdom of the minimax choice for Kenney is confirmed if we consider the independent strategy of Imamura. Column A dominates for him. Imamura therefore must choose A, or north (column B, south, is inadmissible), and if Kenney had chosen Y, or south, he would suffer his worst possible outcome--an opportunity loss of 2. Below, we explore the limits of minimax, under conditions of risk and uncertainty.

EXAMPLES AND PROBLEMS

(1) *Reframing: Changing the Battle to Cops-and-Robbers Without Changing the Game.* Imagine that instead of the battle scenario we have been studying, we use a cops-and-robbers frame. In other words, we shall consider the same payoff matrix as the Battle of the Bismarck Sea, but we shall call the game by another name and explain the payoffs by a different analogy: cops and robbers. Imagine that the Chicago police are trying to catch Bad, Bad Leroy Brown. But because of limited resources, the Chicago police have two choices in their manhunt for Bad, Bad Leroy. They can concentrate their search on the north side or concentrate it on the south side.

If the police concentrate south and Leroy is hiding south, they will find him in two days (the south side is Leroy's home turf). If they concentrate south and Leroy is hiding north, they still will find him in two days (Leroy is not familiar with the north side). On the other hand, if they concentrate north and Leroy is hiding north, they will find him in one day, but if Leroy is hiding south (his territory), a northern search will take three days.

This cops-and-robbers game, you should recognize, is theoretically identical to the Bismarck Sea game. It has the same saddle point and solution. The only difference is the story line (or as game theorists would say, the only difference is the "framing"). Can you explain?

(2) *The Psychological Impact of Framing.* Nevertheless, the "frame" of the game is not a matter of indifference. It influences how well people understand the assumed game structure and, psychologically, how they perceive it. People who strongly favor an Allied victory in World War II scenarios, enough so that they discount the deaths of thousands of Japanese soldiers, will feel one way about the strategies in the Bismarck Sea game. Pacifists who regard bombing as unacceptable under any circumstances will feel differently. People who think bad guys should be arrested will identify with the police when the frame is cops and robbers, while those who identify with the outlaw underdog will root for Leroy.

In the next chapter, we will encounter a scenario that can be described as the game of "chicken" just as well as it can be called "stand up for your rights," even though the theoretical strategies do not change. What relevance does the framing have, then, if we try to extend our theoretical reasoning from games to real-life strategy?

(3) *Lawyers and the Framing of Lawsuits.* In a manner similar to the framing of games, opposing lawyers try to frame their positions in a lawsuit when they first talk to the jury. They often compete vigorously to do this. "This is a case about a plaintiff who got broadsided in an intersection and is horribly injured." "This case really is about a defendant who was proceeding cautiously and who couldn't avoid the other party who shot in from of him." Studies of jurors show that the winner usually is the one whose framing is accepted--and the acceptance usually occurs in the earliest moments(!) Can the results be explained by what you have learned about games?

(4) *The Influence of Utility: Reducing the Game to Triviality, or a Caged-Turkey Shoot.* One complicating factor is that the expected "utility" of a given absolute payoff may not be the same for each person. For example, imagine that Admiral Imamura knows that two days of bombing will completely destroy his fleet in the Battle of the Bismarck Sea. In terms of utility, then, three days is no worse for Imamura than two; the utility of both is the same to him.

Imamura then has only one strategic choice: to sail south and risk three days of bombing in the hope that he will get only one day (the only payoff that has any positive utility for him). Can you explain this? But notice that this transformation of the battle makes the "game" uninteresting, and one might argue that it isn't a game any longer (for the same reason that a turkey shoot is not a game if the turkeys are in cages). Can you see why?

(5) *Revising the Payoff Matrix to Conform to Utilities.* Another point illustrated by this issue is that the payoffs must conform to utilities. Imamura's payoff matrix, if three days' bombing really is the same as two, looks like Figure 6, where "1" is acceptable and "0" is not. But this matrix depicts a game that is theoretically uninteresting, or that really is not even a game, because Imamura has only one sensible strategy (column A) and so does Kenney (Row X). This is a caged-turkey shoot. Can you see why?

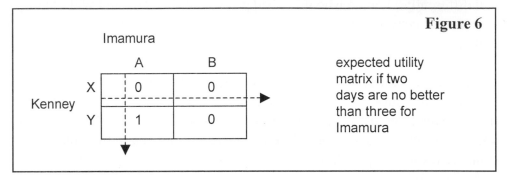

Figure 6

expected utility matrix if two days are no better than three for Imamura

(6) *Lawyers and Utility-Based Strategies.* Sometimes, in either litigation or transactions, structural problems prevent resolution--because one party's utility dictates a blockage. For example, if the plaintiff will be forced into bankruptcy unless it recovers $10 million, the plaintiff may refuse a reasonable lesser settlement offer and try the case even if it has poor odds. Can you see how understanding the opponent's utility is important?

(7) *Psychological Effects That Undermine Rational Strategies: The Maximizing Difference Game and the Surprising Way in Which Real Players React to It.* The scenario above, the one-choice Bismarck Sea battle, is uninteresting to game theorists, then, because it involves no real strategy. Again, it resembles a caged-turkey shoot. But would it be interesting to psychologists to find out how real people would play? (The results might be disgusting. Might there be some perverse human beings who would shoot with gusto at caged turkeys?) The point of the question is: Game theory is normative rather than predictive, and real human beings may not follow it.

One striking example is provided by studies of the so-called "maximizing difference" game. The game is simple. Two players are provided a payoff matrix that gives each his maximum possible payoff if both (in effect) choose the "north" column. This is not a zero-sum game, and the theoretically best strategy is for each player to cooperate with the other by choosing north, every time. To a game theorist, therefore, the "game" is trivial.

But to a psychologist, the maximizing difference game is interesting. Here's why: Psychological experimenters have had subjects play the game a series of times, with cash payoffs. One might think that players would cooperate and choose north each time, because they would maximize the cash they receive. But they don't. A surprising percentage of the time, one or another player chooses the opposite column, even though it is obvious that a lower payoff will result! Can you guess why? (We shall return to this game, later.)

(8) *The Law and the Maximizing Difference Game: Perverse Lawsuit Behavior.* This is all very bad news for a legal system that assumes rational behavior from litigants. The psychology of the Maximizing Difference Game tells us that litigants very well may forego opportunities to cooperate for mutual advantage (e.g., by courteously scheduling a deposition at a convenient time for both), and they instead may insult each other or attempt to maneuver to obtain a trivial symbolic gain at the cost of greater loss for both. Can you explain?

THE LIMIT OF MINIMAX: GAME THEORY, LAW, AND LITIGATION

(1) *The Limit of the Minimax Strategy: Introducing Risk and Uncertainty.* Now, let us introduce another element into the picture, to show a fundamental problem with the minimax strategy. Suppose it is known that Admiral Imamura is deeply superstitious. Inevitably Imamura will consult his magic Ouija Board, which produces perfectly random results, and then he faithfully will follow whatever it tells him to do. Thus, it is the Ouija Board that really is in control, nature (or chance) is the real second player, and the odds are equal that Imamura will sail either north or south.

Now, there no longer is any reason for Kenney to consider Row X dominant. His mathematical expectancy from the (1, 1) payoffs in Row X is $(\frac{1}{2} \times 1) + (\frac{1}{2} \times 1) = 1$, and from the (2, 0) payoffs in Row Y it is $(\frac{1}{2} \times 2) + (\frac{1}{2} \times 0) = 1$. The two expectancies are the same, and therefore the choice is a matter of indifference in terms of expectations. The minimax strategy simply does not matter, here, because we have replaced a strategic opponent with chance. Can you see why?

(2) *When the Minimax Strategy Is Inferior.* Furthermore, if we assume a still different game, one in which the Ouija Board is "loaded" to prefer a southern trip for Imamura, the minimax strategy becomes decisively inferior.

If, say, the odds are 3 to 1 that the Ouija Board will tell Imamura to sail south, then Row X (north) gives Kenney a mathematically expected loss or regret of $(1/4 \times 1) + (3/4 \times 1) = 1$, while Row Y (south) produces $(1/4 \times 2) + (3/4 \times 0) = ½$, which actually is the better choice. The minimax strategy, erroneously, would have sent Kenney north (Row X), decreasing his expectation. Can you explain why?

(3) *Conclusion: Use the Minimax Strategy Against a Rational Opponent in a Zero Sum Game with Perfect Knowledge, but Not Necessarily Otherwise.* The minimax strategy is not necessarily best in conditions of uncertainty. Also, it does not necessarily fit cooperative games or mixed-motive games of the kind that we shall see in the next chapter. It generally is superior for zero-sum games against a rational opponent where the payoff matrix is known to both players (perfect knowledge), but otherwise it has its limits.

EXAMPLES AND PROBLEMS

(1) *A Time for Choosing Maximin in a Lawsuit (Avoiding the Worst of the Worst)?: The Greedy Father's Child Custody Gambit.* When would a rational player use the pessimistic maximin strategy? The answer is, when a major loss must be avoided at all cost. The mother's response to the "greedy father's child custody gambit" is an example--a sad one.

Mary and John Smith are embroiled in a divorce proceeding. Mary would like her share of the assets and child support, but above all else, she needs to win custody of the children. John's desires are to obtain a large share of the assets and to keep support as low as possible. John therefore seeks custody himself but tells Mary that he will drop this claim if she accepts his proposed division of assets and child support amount.

Mary does not think John has much chance of winning custody, perhaps only one chance in ten, but even this risk is unacceptable. Can you see why it might be rational here for Mary to adopt the maximin strategy, or the avoidance at all cost of the worst possible outcome? (Unfortunately, this "game" is played daily in family courts throughout the nation.)

(2) *Recalling Rawls's Choice of the Maximin Strategy in His Theory of Justice.* In an earlier chapter, we considered John Rawls's landmark book, *A Theory of Justice*. Rawls's "equality" principle and "difference" principle were set up according to what Rawls described as a "maximin" principle: maximizing the pie for the least-well-off member of society. In game theory,

maximin is the most pessimistic strategy, choosing to make the best of the worst possible outcome. Is Rawls right to choose this principle for a just society? Or will his theory stifle growth, knowledge, art and creativity?

Notice Rawls's borrowing of a game theory term for use in law, politics, and ethics. Game theory has a great deal that is useful to say in these fields.

(3) *A Lawsuit Choice for Maximax: Rolling the Dice for the Biggest Possible Payoff.* Imagine that attorney Joe Schlemeil represents a client in a negligence suit. The defendant, recognizing the possibility of an adverse verdict, has offered to pay $100,000 to settle. Schlemeil figures that he could lose too. He estimates that only five out of ten juries would return a verdict in his favor (i.e., there is a probability of 0.5 of a plaintiff's verdict). But if he does get a favorable verdict, Schlemeil thinks his chances are one in ten of obtaining $500,000; the nine other estimated verdicts would average $100,000, exactly the amount offered. Schlemeil knows that the offer will forever be withdrawn if he doesn't accept it now.

Notice that Schlemeil's mathematical expectation from going to trial is $(.05 \times 0) + [0.5 \times (9/10[\$100,000] + 1/10 [\$500,000])] = \$70,000$, which is less than the settlement offer of $100,000. Nevertheless, what might push a person toward a foolish maximax strategy in this situation? Is a minimax solution, then, preferable in such a situation?

§ 14.03 Other Strictly Competitive Games: Games Without Saddle Points, with Larger Matrices, with Multiple Saddles, and with Uncertain Payoffs

GAMES WITHOUT SADDLE POINTS: MIXED STRATEGIES

(1) *Games Without Saddle Points: Adapting the Strategy by Randomizing.* What we have said up to this point has concerned games with saddle points. What if there is no saddle? Well, then, the rational strategy changes. A player no longer may use a "pure" strategy, as it is called. As strange as this seems, the player's best strategy is to resort to a randomizing device, such as flipping a coin(!) This is called "mixed" strategy--partially random. The game of the burglar and the security guard is an example.

(2) *The Burglar and the Security Guard's Game.* The burglar-and-security-guard game involves a company that has two safes in different parts of its factory, east and west. Each night, it keeps $10,000 in the eastern safe

and $20,000 in the western one. A burglar plans to steal from one of the two safes, knowing that the security guard will not be able to guard both at the same time. If the burglar tries to steal from the safe that is guarded, his payoff is zero; if the safe is unguarded, the burglar gets the contents.

In this situation, what strategy would a burglar familiar with game theory follow? And what should be the counter-strategy of a rational security guard? Again, the answer will seem strange. There is no pure strategy here, and both players should adopt a "mixed" strategy that involves randomizing.

(3) *A Matrix Without a Saddle Point: Is Minimax a Rational Pure Strategy?* The payoff matrix for the burglar and the security guard is shown in Figure 7. It has no saddle point, because there is no box that is both highest in its column and lowest in its row. And therefore, as we shall see, the pure minimax strategy does not work, either. Let us consider why.

		Security Guard's choices		**Figure 7**
		east .333	west .667	a two-by-two
Burglar's choices	east .667	0	$10,000	game without a saddle point:
	west .333	$20,000	0	burglar and security guard

First, the burglar has no minimax strategy, because either row has an equally bad worst outcome of zero (that is what the burglar gets if the safe that is burgled happens to be guarded). Second, although the security guard has what appears to be a minimax strategy--he can guard the western safe, which has $20,000 in it, limiting the burglar's gain to a maximum of $10,000--this pure strategy actually will not work either. If it really were true that the guard's "best" strategy was to camp out at the western safe, the burglar could count on a rational guard going singlemindedly to the west, and the burglar simply would make the opposite choice, breaking into the eastern safe and automatically collecting $10,000.

Then, like a dog chasing its tail, the efforts of the players to guess each others' strategies would begin to go around in circles, as the guard anticipated the burglar's choice of east and considered going there, except that the burglar simultaneously would anticipate the guard's shift to the eastern safe and would switch, himself, to the western one--and so on, ad infinitum.

(4) *The Rational Solution: A Mixed Strategy, Dictated Partly by Chance, Rather Than a Pure One.* A "pure" strategy is one dictated purely by reason. Paradoxically, the rational approach in a game without a saddle is a "mixed" strategy, one dictated partly by chance.

This strategy is shown by the .333 and .667 probabilities written into Figure 7. Both parties act rationally by using these probabilities. As crazy as it sounds, the burglar should place two red coins and one blue coin in a pocket and draw one at random. Then, if red comes up, the burglar goes to the eastern safe ($10,000); if blue, to the western one ($20,000). His mathematical expectations, then, are [.333 x 0 + .667 x $10,000 = $6,670] (if the guard chooses west) and [.667 x 0 + .333 x $20,000 = $6,670] (if the guard chooses east). The burglar thus has improved on the pure maximin strategy, increasing his expectancy to $6,670 from zero.

The guard, for his or her choice, should use the same three coins but with the opposite probabilities: red to west (probability .667) and blue to east (probability .333). These are the probabilities indicated in Figure 7.

(5) *A Paradox: Twice as Often, the Guard Should Watch the Safe With Twice as Much, but the Burglar Should Break in There Only Half as Often(!)* Thus, these probabilities result in the security guard watching the western safe, which contains twice as much money, twice as often. This strategy fits intuitively. But on the other hand, a rational burglar goes twice as often to the safe that contains only half as much money(!) This strategy is less intuitively obvious. But paradoxically, this is the strategy that maximizes the burglar's expectation against a rational opponent.

(6) *Is It Really Essential to Use a Coin-Determined Decision in a Non-Saddle Point Game?* Is it really necessary to use two red coins and one blue one? Obviously, the answer is no. The use of a coin is not the point. What is essential is inscrutability in choosing the options.

The real point, in other words, is to choose in a one-third-two-thirds ratio without the other player being able to anticipate the choice. If two players were to play the burglar-guard game nine times, and if the burglar were to adopt the strategy of choosing east twice and then west once, and then repeat the sequence two more times, east twice and then west, east twice and then west, this strategy would have results comparable to randomizing. This predictable pattern for the burglar would work just as well--that is, until the guard recognized the pattern and adapted his or her own strategy to it!

(7) *Perfect Knowledge and Imperfect Information: The Tactic of Maintaining Inscrutability (or Even of Creating a Diversion).* The terminology for this kind of game is confusing: perfect knowledge, but imperfect information. Both players know the payoff matrix, and this awareness is called "*perfect knowledge*." But both are ignorant of each other's move. This uncertainty is called "*imperfect information*."

In such circumstances, both players work hard to maintain inscrutability, and hence the use of randomizing devices. In real life, the players may even attempt diversions or other means of deception, as we shall see in more complex strategic situations such as football, or war--or litigation.

§ 14.04   The Psychology of Competitive Games

EXAMPLES AND PROBLEMS

(1) *Experimental Subjects Are Much Better at Strategy in Saddle-Point Than Non-Saddle-Point Games.* Next, let us consider a very different issue. What do real people who are not game theorists do when they are playing these games? Experimental psychologists have induced subjects to play saddle-point games against each other. The most interesting results concern "iterated" play, in which the subjects repeat the game (say) a hundred times.

Although the results are not uniform, and there are some experiments that show the opposite effect, many studies observe that subjects can learn to adopt rational strategies for saddled games. That is to say, they approximate, or tend to converge upon, the minimax strategy in games with saddle points.

But the results are dramatically different in games without saddle points. Some experiments have observed no statistically significant tendency for the subjects to converge toward optimal strategies, even after many iterations, and other experiments have produced only slight tendencies toward the probabilistically weighted "mixed" solution. Why do you think this difference exists in people's learning of saddled and non-saddled games? Of course, the computing of probabilities in non-saddled games adds a layer of complexity. But is this the real and complete explanation?

(2) *Framing Effects: Two Equivalent Questions, Differently Framed, Produce Different Results--as Do Differently Framed Games, and as Happens in Litigation.* We observed framing effects in an earlier section, when we reframed a naval battle into cops and robbers. We noted that,

although the two frames were identical in terms of game theory, they might elicit different responses from players. The same thing happens in litigation.

Both psychological experiments and opinion polls demonstrate these effects. For example, American people polled about whether ground troops from the United States should be sent to intervene militarily in Yugoslavian ethnic cleansing in the Kosovo region, after a period of heartwrenching television portrayals of deportees, strongly favored the action. But when the frame of the question was changed to explicitly include the possibility of even a handful of American deaths, the rate of positive responses dropped dramatically, even though American deaths were a clear inference from the first question. Again, framing a lawsuit strategically is crucial.

Similarly, psychological experiments have been done with reframings of game matrices similar to our naval-battle-or-cops-and-robbers example, with similar, though less dramatic, changes in results. People play the same game differently with a different name and framing situation attached to it, even though game theorists would construct the same payoff matrix. Do these observations show that people are poor at strategic choices? Or do they reflect subtle ethical differences (like the difference between the trolley problem and the involuntary organ donor, in an earlier chapter)?

§ 14.05   Multi-Player Competitive Games

MULTI-DIMENSION MATRICES, THE DOLLAR AUCTION, AND SOCIAL SITUATIONS

(1) *Multi-Dimensional Payoff Matrices for Competitive Games With Many Players.* How do we create payoff matrices for indefinite numbers of players? With three players, each having two move choices, the matrix is a cube with $2x2x2 = 8$ boxes. The matrix still may contain a saddle point: highest in a line of any direction, height or width or depth. In larger games it is customary to construct $2x2$ matrices for each player.

(2) *Auction Games: The Dollar Auction.* One multi-player competitive game that has generated significant research is the "dollar auction." An auctioneer announces that he will exchange a $1 bill for a payment from the highest bidder. The catch is that the next-highest bidder also must pay his or her bid. Therefore, as the bidding closes in on $1, players scramble to avoid becoming the next-highest bidder, a phenomenon that often sends the bids up to amounts exceeding $1.

There are three crucial junctures in the dollar auction: the second bid (which means that there now is going to be a loser), the first bid over 50 cents (which means that the auctioneer will profit from the players), and, of course, the "magic moment" (the first bid that exceeds $1).

(3) *The Entrapment and Escalation Phenomena in the Dollar Auction: The Concorde Fallacy, or Too Much Invested to Withdraw.* The "Concorde fallacy," as it is called, takes its name from the supersonic airliner produced by a British-French consortium, for which costs escalated. Even after it would have been apparent to an objective observer that the economically sound strategy was to cut and run, both governments increased their levels of commitment because they had "too much invested to withdraw."

A similar psychological trap has been observed in dollar auction experiments, with astonishing results. Experimenters typically give subjects sums ranging from $2.50 to $20 to bid, and often the escalation continues until the limit is reached. In some experiments, the subjects have become distraught to the point of crying. This "entrapment" phenomenon occurs in high percentages of experiments.

EXAMPLES AND PROBLEMS

(1) *The Optimal Strategy in the Dollar Auction and the Lock-in Strategy.* One of the saddle points in the dollar auction is for one player to be willing to bid up to 99 cents and for all other players to bid zero (to refuse to bid). The bidder then gets the dollar for one cent. Can you explain?

It might make sense for the bidder to discourage all others by a "lock-in" or "commitment" strategy (which we shall see again in the next chapter on cooperative games). The bidder locks in by tying some catastrophically self-destructive event to his or her failure, such as by executing a certificate of deposit for $10,000 payable to the auctioneer if the bidder does not get the dollar. Can you see why this tactic could work?

(2) *Motivational Differences: The Psychological Mechanism of Entrapment in the Dollar Auction.* One group of experimenters surveyed subjects during dollar-auction play and found that a change in motivation develops. The initial economic motivation, which is to obtain something for less than its value, gives way to a competitive urge that obscures the player's initial economic goals. Another group of experimenters tied the motive to face-saving, and they also produced evidence tending to demonstrate that

men are more susceptible to entrapment in escalation than women.[4] Can you explain these observations?

(3) *The Dollar Auction and the Uneconomical, Yet Unresolvable Lawsuit or Dispute: From Industrial Strikes to Small Claims Litigation to the Arms Race.* It sometimes occurs that parties to a lawsuit spend more in pretrial preparation than the amount at issue and still find themselves unable to settle their dispute short of a trial that will more than double the expenditures of each. Likewise, it sometimes happens that lawyers representing labor and management are unable to end a strike that has produced losses far exceeding any possible gains. And the arms race between the United States and Russia (the old Soviet Union) has often been analyzed by game theorists.

Can you explain how each of these phenomena might be related to the dollar auction?

§ 14.06   Competitive Strategy in Complex Situations, Including the Law

MILITARY BATTLES, CHESS, FOOTBALL, AND LITIGATION: STRATEGIES OF ASSESSMENT

(1) *Strategy Outside Game Theory.* So far, we have been considering games that fit game theory, with defined strategies and unambiguous payoffs. Next, we consider more complex strategic situations that do not admit of such simple treatment. Nevertheless, there are certain strategy considerations that apply across different competitions. We shall consider examples from military battles, football, chess, and (of course) law.

(2) *Why Should Lawyers Consider Military Strategy?* Military strategy is a great deal more relevant to the actual behavior of litigants in a lawsuit than, say, the analysis of appellate opinions in a typical law school class. As we shall see, strategies of deception, concentration, maneuverability, simplicity, and the like--military strategies--are used by lawyers in legal battles, in a way that is closely analogous to that of military battles.

(3) *Strategic Assessment: The Army's M-E-T-T-T Checklist--and How It Affects Lawyers.* "M-E-T-T-T" is an acronym used by the United States

---

4   But neither gender should claim superiority, because the next chapter discusses a different game in which men experimentally demonstrated more cooperative behavior than women.

Army for "mission, enemy, terrain, troops and timing." *See* Tom Clancy (with General Fred Franks, Jr.), *Into the Storm* 2-10 (1997) (providing a commander's view of the war in Iraq). The *mission* cannot be something uselessly general such as to win the battle; instead, it may be (say) to destroy Iraqi troops in the area of operations and stand by to defend Northern Kuwait (a paraphrase of the mission statement for VII Corps in Desert Storm). Or, in football, the mission may be to stop John Elway from connecting deep with Shannon Sharpe while containing the Denver Broncos' ground game (a defense mission in the 1998 Superbowl). And a lawyer handling a lawsuit should know the mission.

The next factor in the METTT acronym is the *enemy*. In Desert Storm, the Iraqis were arrayed in several layers behind a defensive line of mines and trenches, with the least will-to-fight troops in front and the elite Iraqi Republican Guard behind them. Analogously, the opponent in chess may be known to alternate among the Sicilian Defense, the French Defense and the (very difficult) Lange Attack.[5] In lawsuits, there are no "enemies" as such, but there certainly is an opponent!

Third, the *terrain* in Desert Storm, beyond the initial defenses, was undifferentiated desert, passable by armored vehicles as the ocean is by ships, meaning that pinpointing locations would be difficult, so that one unique problem created by terrain was a greater-than-usual need for abstract coordination. Likewise, a football team that faced Denver in its own Mile-High Stadium would need to adjust for wind, altitude, crowd noise, grass and field curvature. A lawyer needs to know the court, the jury, and the judge.

Fourth, *troops* includes technology, command and control as well as personnel. VII Corps had a 97 percent complement of major assets and full-strength troops as it started the invasion of Iraq. Similarly, chess players who have exchanged their queens play differently than before, and a football team must adjust for absent players. And as we shall see, lawyers need to adjust for the characteristics of their clients and support.

Finally, *timing* in Desert Storm was a carefully guarded secret, meticulously planned. VII Corps would begin on G+1, the day after Go Day (when other units' maneuvers began), at BMNT (the beginning of morning

---

5   The reader does not need a knowledge of chess, or for that matter of football, to understand this material. All that is needed is an appreciation that different strategies are well enough established to have names, that intelligence about opposing strategies is important, and that this principle is universal to competitive situations.

nautical twilight). In the Superbowl, Denver might decide to use a suicide pass pattern only in the third quarter, and a chess player (or a lawyer) might openly reveal strategy only after a certain number of moves.

(4) *Intelligence and Discovery: Appraising Clues About the Opponent's Strategy and Tactics.* Appraising the opponent's METTT and tendencies through intelligence and analysis is fundamental to competitive games without clear optimal strategies. Recall the burglar-guard game: either side could win by, say, observing the outcome of, or tampering with, the opponent's randomization device (by, say, stealthily observing the color of the coin drawn or clandestinely substituting one of the opposite color).

In Desert Storm, intelligence ranged from such simple tactics as interrogation of Iraqi deserters to AWACS aircraft. Similarly, a chess player puts together clues from which to infer whether the opponent really is playing the Gruenfeld Variation rather than the King's Indian Defense. A football coach studies game films and takes polaroid photographs during the game.

And obviously, lawyers amass clues about lawsuits.

(5) *Inscrutability, Maneuverability and Camouflage.* Other things being equal, the military commander retains flexibility and maneuverability and attempts to frustrate the enemy's intelligence. The best chess openings (other things being equal) are those that permit transposition into other styles (e.g., the Bishop's Opening). In football, modified T formations provide more options than the old-fashioned single wing did, even though the single wing gave greater concentration of power. The option play, in football, carries the strategy of flexibility to the last instant.

Because the opponent is not nature but other human beings, strategist Edward Luttwak speaks of the "paradox" of "full reversal" in the quotation that begins this chapter. The "reversal" comes about because of inscrutability: what may seem a bad strategy becomes a good one, and a good one may be bad, precisely because it is rational and therefore is what the opponent expects. A "bad" strategy may be good, because it creates surprise.

(6) *Deception.* Deception, as a tactic, is related to the inscrutability tactic discussed above, in that both are designed to frustrate opposing strategies. But deception differs from inscrutability in that it affirmatively misleads. In Desert Storm, General Schwartzkopf began with a famous feint or diversion

that reinforced Iraqi beliefs about where the Allies were likely to strike. Lawyers use deception and diversions, sometimes, in lawsuits.

Indeed, the tactic of using diversions is age-old. The Normandy Invasion on D-Day was preceded by diversions and by radio traffic and other clues contrived to deceive German forces. Similarly, a football team shifts formation at the last instant and may execute a play-action pass (with a fake to the running back, who decoys through the line). And the chess player works as long as possible to disguise the variation being played.

TACTICS OF MANEUVER IN COMBAT OR IN LAWSUITS

(1) *The Principles of Tactical Encounters--and Their Use in Lawsuits.* Principles of war developed more than a century ago are applicable to military conflicts today. Similarly, they are applicable to other kinds of tactical encounters, such as chess, football--and litigation.

(a) *Concentrated Use of Force:* The military commander seeks to concentrate troops and fire at a strategic point. Similarly, the offensive coordinator for a football team seeks to mass the blocking where it is needed, and a chess player seeks to combine the attack with multiple pieces at a decisive square or area on the board. And the litigator puts effort (and money for expert witnesses) into the crucial issues. But: There is a caveat. This goal has to be balanced against other goals.

(b) *Maneuverability:* The military commander seeks to gain positional advantage (see below). In football, the quarterback reads the defense and audibly signals a new formation and play. The chess player develops the center of the board, where flexibility is maximized. The trial lawyer keeps multiple claims alive and maintains flexibility.

(c) *Simplicity and the "Friction" of Combat:* A battlefield is disorganized. Command and control cannot reliably adjust in real time for complex strategies. The same applies to the football field, and, counterintuitively, to the chessboard (that's why there are relatively few basic defenses and attacks). A structurally simple strategy is preferable, other things being equal, to a complex one that requires many elements to be brought together. The great military strategist Karl von Clausewitz, in the quotation at the beginning of this chapter, spoke famously

Karl von Clausewitz

about the "friction" of war, in which "the simplest thing is difficult." Similarly, in litigation, unnecessary complexity can be a problem.

(d) *Unified Command, With Coordinated Command and Control:* There should be one overall commander for the tactical encounter. This idea is related to the simplicity goal.

(e) *Surprise and Paradox; Doing the Unexpected Even When It Seems Unstrategic:* The military commander seeks to conduct the operation at a time, in a way, and at a place where the enemy does not expect it. So do the football coach and the chess strategist. This consideration usually involves compromise of other tactics such as timing, concentration or maneuver. As Luttwak puts it, "At least some paradox will be present in . . . most competent military actions." And, one might add, in most litigation!

(f) *Economy of Force:* The largest possible force should be retained for the major objective. A separate maneuver, such as a diversion, should be accomplished with the minimum force necessary.

(g) *Protection--Refusing the Flank:* The military commander curls his front line back at the ends to prevent flanking maneuvers or encirclement. This tactic is called "refusing the flank." Command and control are protected. In football, the offensive line similarly curls in at the ends, and the quarterback is protected by a pocket of blockers. In chess, the castling move is similar although it should be avoided if the opponent can bring a forceful attack on the file where the king is located.

(h) *Focus on the Objective; Center of Gravity:* Clausewitz used the term "center of gravity" to denote the enemy's main source of power. A continued focus on this objective, avoiding distractions, is tactical.

(i) *Initiative:* Other things being equal, purely reactive strategies are undesirable. This is true in litigation, as well.

(j) *Attrition:* The commander studies the enemy's scarcities and exploits them. Is the enemy short of troops, air defenses, supplies, vehicles, or gasoline? The tactics differ depending on which is the enemy's shortage.

(k) *Timing--Hasty Attack, Meeting Engagement, and Deliberate Attack:* A hasty attack is one in which forces cannot properly be arrayed or coordinated because considerations of surprise require prompt action. A "meeting engagement" occurs when the location of the opposing force is known only in a general way, requiring search tactics and producing an engagement when the forces meet. A deliberate attack is one involving time and setup, particularly when surprise is not likely to result from early action. The commander, coach, chess strategist, or litigator needs to know the considerations underlying each of these possibilities.

(2) *The Culminating Point: Exhaustion or Limits of the Strategy.* Clausewitz invented the phrase, "The culminating point of victory." Luttwak refers to "culmination and reversal." There is a point beyond which troops, strategies and enemy weaknesses cannot be pushed. Napoleon and Hitler, for example, in invading Russia, both extended their armies beyond the culminating point, which was deep into Russia but short of Moscow. And both experienced disaster as a result.

Sheer exhaustion, supplies, communication, morale, and enemy advantages dictate the reversal upon passing the culminating point. Again, there is a paradox: the commander must press with determination--but must stop the advance in time, too. The chess master must watch for traps after a successful strategy, and so must the football coordinator--and although it's less obvious, so must the trial lawyer who is tempted to ask that (fatal) one question too many.

(3) *Frontal Attack: An Age-Old Maneuver.* Many battles in the Civil War were fought by opposing lines that marched toward each other, each hoping to overcome the other by sheer will, numbers and firepower. This is not really "strategy." In the Battle of Chancellorsville, by contrast, Robert E. Lee authorized General Stonewall Jackson to take his entire corps around the face of the opposing Union troops and to attack them from the exposed flank. Lee remained with two divisions, as the "fixing force," which kept the enemy in place while Jackson's "flanking force" enveloped them. The ultimate result was a decisive victory over General Hooker's much larger Union force.

Today, a military watchword is, "Fight outnumbered and win." The old frontal attack by brute force is no longer always the strategy of choice-- except that sometimes, it still may be.

(4) *Modern Maneuvers.* The direct frontal attack is only one of several forms of field maneuver that include--

(a) *Envelopment (Flanking):* circling about one or both flanks so as to attack from the side or rear, usually while another force keeps the enemy fixed to the front. The "fixing force" keeping the enemy occupied needs to be as small as possible, and the "flanking force" that undertakes the actual attack needs to be as large as possible, for the tactic to work best.

(b) *Infiltration:* sending forces in small units undetected through gaps in the enemy's line, then massing them to attack from the rear.

(c) *Penetration:* massing force at a concentrated point in the enemy line, usually a point of weakness, so as to break through and attack from the rear.

(d) *Turning Movements:* maneuvering the entire force to the enemy's flank, forcing the enemy to turn (useful if the enemy's terrain defenses are set in a certain direction).

EXAMPLES AND PROBLEMS

(1) *Tradeoffs Among Tactical Principles.* Tactical principles cannot always be maximized simultaneously. Concentration of forces, for example, may reduce maneuverability. Maneuver may reduce command and control. Maintenance of initiative may sacrifice other objectives, and so may proper exploitation of timing and surprise. Luttwak, for example, talks about the "costs of surprise": the loss in preparation or in forces used for diversion, which the commander hopes will be outweighed by the advantages of surprise. The best strategy maximizes the combination of all these tactics. Can you explain the tradeoffs?

(2) *Choice of Maneuver Tactics.* The choice among maneuver tactics depends upon such factors as the METTT assessment (see above). For example, a turning maneuver may be tactical against an enemy dug into defensive positions. Infiltration may be preferred if the enemy lines are punctuated and if terrain allows for stealthy advance. Can you explain these conclusions, and can you identify circumstances in which envelopment (flanking) and penetration would be preferable?

(3) *Lawyers' Tactics in Litigation.* In litigation, why might a lawyer undertake each of the following tactics, and how do they correspond to the tactics suggested above? (a) Including more than a dozen claims covering the same conduct in the complaint or petition (by pleading for substantially overlapping recovery on multiple theories of negligence, express contract, implied contract, quasi-contract, breach of fiduciary duty, common law fraud, statutory fraud, deceptive trade practices, unfair competition, violations of state and of federal securities laws, etc.). (b) Withholding anything more than minimal research and investigative expense on the bulk of the claims.

(4) *More Lawyering Tactics in Litigation.* Also, consider how these tactics relate to military principles. (c) Buying his adversary a drink at the airport bar while discussing the case. (d) Answering discovery requests such as written interrogatories with the minimal information necessary to respond (Q: "Explain in detail why and how the accident happened." A: "It happened because your client was negligent.") (e) Answering in a way that is literally truthful and responsive but misleading.

(5) *Still More Lawyering Tactics.* Here are some more litigation moves that Clausewitz might have approved. (f) Hiring multiple expert witnesses to support one particular claim instead of multiple experts supporting different claims. (g) Presenting only one, two, or three basic themes during opening statement at trial. (h) Having one single trial lawyer do all presentations and questioning before the jury.

(6) *The Litigation Example of a Culminating Point.* Sometimes a lawyer whose strategy has proved successful in a trial pushes a claim or issue beyond its credible limits and thus overshoots the culminating point, much as a military commander might. Can you see how there might be a natural human tendency to overshoot the culminating point by engaging in overkill? What sort of reversals do you think a lawyer would invite by overshooting the culminating point in an adversary proceeding?

(7) *The Line of Least Expectation: The Israeli Example--and Litigation.* Luttwak suggests that doing the unexpected is so important that some armies consciously attempt to adopt the most unexpected strategy, even if it is "unstrategic." Notice that this will compromise other goals, but the gain in surprise may be worth it. Luttwak calls this strategy the "line of least expectation." The best modern example is Israel. Luttwak observes that "Israeli forces much weaker materially than they need have been (because of secrecy, deception, improvisation and overextension) and operating with so much self-imposed friction that their condition bordered on the chaotic, have regularly defeated [larger] enemies caught by surprise . . . ."

Ironically, the success of this national strategy has alerted enemies, who now discount expectations about Israel. During the 1982 Lebanon War, Syria anticipated a seemingly irrational Israeli attack along bad mountain roads. But Syria failed to anticipate the Israeli move for which that mountain attack was a diversion: a direct, old-fashioned frontal attack on flat ground by massed forces, which overwhelmed the unprepared Syrians! Can you explain why this "obvious" move was nevertheless unexpected?

In litigation, pleading and discovery rules limit the surprise tactic. But they do not eliminate it. Lawyers sometimes struggle to conceal such matters as (1) which defendant is the "real" target defendant, (2) what the major thrust of the claim will be, (3) which witnesses actually will be called, etc.

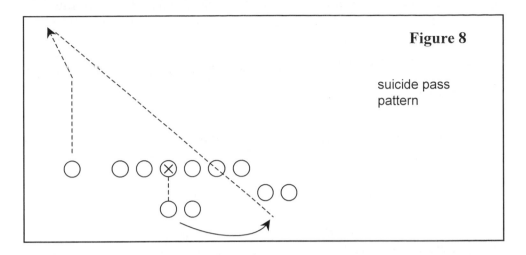

Figure 8

suicide pass
pattern

(8) *Suicide Pass Pattern.* Imagine that a football coach plans to build his strategy around frequent use of the play diagrammed in Figure 8. The quarterback begins in shotgun formation (with a snap or toss-back from the center, rather than a handoff under the center) and runs right, where he turns and passes across the field to the wide receiver on the left (weak side), who runs a deep pattern that angles to the left (called a flag pattern).

How would you advise the coach about this "suicide pass" tactic in terms of principles of concentrated force, maneuverability, protection, simplicity, timing, and surprise? Could the use of such a play be improved by adjustment of tactics (such as using it infrequently, having the quarterback move less far to the right, and including the option of right side receivers)?

§ 14.07 The Laws of War: Rules, Ethics, Civility and Strategy

THE STRATEGY OF RULEMAKING:
HOW COMBATANTS BREAK LAWS--
AND HOW TO WRITE THEM

(1) *Laws of War.* There are laws of war, and there are rules in football, chess, and litigation. In this section, we shall examine these rules. One of our goals will be to consider a strategy for writing rules about combat.

(2) *Clandestine Cheating.* In some competitive environments, cheating is readily detectable. A chess player who tries to move a knight along diagonals like a bishop usually cannot conceal the violation. But two members of a bridge team in a major tournament made national news during

the 1970's when they got caught using finger signals while holding their cards. Military commanders sometimes violate the Geneva Convention while interrogating prisoners of war, and football players hope for nondetection of an illegal block in the back. One famous pitcher denied putting any "foreign substances" on the baseball: "Every substance I put on the ball was from the good old U.S.A."

(3) *Open Violation of Rules of Engagement.* But violations do not need to be clandestine to be successful. Iraq under Saddam Hussein used poison gas in the Iran-Iraq War in clear violation of international law. Basketball teams playing against the Los Angeles Lakers sometimes adopt a strategy called "hack the Shaq": They aggressively foul huge center Shaquille O'Neal, who is notoriously bad at foul shooting. And what if a chess player insists on illegal moves in an unsupervised amateur situation?

(4) *Strategies for Writing Laws and Dealing With People Who Break Them: An Uncertain Art.* This leads to two questions. What does one do, strategically, when others break the rules? And how can we write and enforce the rules so that proper strategic behavior is not prohibited, but so that violations effectively can be deterred? These things are not easy.

EXAMPLES AND PROBLEMS

(1) *How to Write an Unenforceable Law, Part I: The Surf City Animal Ordinance.* Surf City, like many cities, has an ordinance that prohibits the keeping of various animals. But Surf City's ordinance is oddly written: "A person who keeps within the territory of the city any number of chickens, goats, swine [and here follows a detailed list of beasts], *and who is not in the business of boarding animals,* is guilty of a misdemeanor."

As a practical matter, Surf City's ordinance is unenforceable. Even if someone violates it by openly keeping 27 goats, the city cannot reasonably hope to obtain his conviction. In fact, this problem is based upon a real city ordinance under which local law enforcement officials declined to prosecute. Can you see why (bearing in mind that all elements of the crime, not just some, must be proven beyond reasonable doubt, that certain information such as the defendant's version is unavailable as privileged, and that prosecution of this traffic-court misdemeanor cannot exceed reasonable costs)? [Note: consider the "not in the business of boarding" clause.]

(2) *How to Write an Unenforceable Law, Part II: Intentional Grounding.* In football, a penalty for intentional grounding theoretically results if a passer within the pocket area avoids being sacked by throwing the ball away deliberately. Strong-armed quarterbacks easily evade the penalty by overthrowing covered receivers. Could the rule be rewritten to make its enforceability coincide more closely to violations (and if so, would the revision be a good idea)?

(3) *Law, Justice, and Morals: Do Failures of Law Enforcement Mean That the World Is Simply a Less Moral Place Than We Learned in Kindergarten?* Consider whether the following people did, could have or might have gotten away with violating the rules: (a) Saddam Hussein's use of mustard gas against Iranians and against Iraqi Kurds; (b) A lawyer who repeatedly asks witnesses in front of a jury questions that seek evidence already ruled admissible (a common occurrence); (c) A defensive lineman in football who repeatedly slaps the opposing lineman in the helmet and face mask (a common occurrence); (d) President Clinton, who testified under oath that he could not recall ever having been alone in the White House with Monica Lewinsky (among other whoppers). What should be the response of the immediate actors to these events? Of the larger community?

William J. Clinton

(4) *Strategies for Writing Enforceable Laws and Rules in Competitive Situations.* Evaluate the following advice for rule-writing in competitive environments, and consider how you might add to or subtract from this list:

(a) Make violations readily detectable. For example, include in the Geneva Convention a requirement of visitation by the International Red Cross for prisoners of war. [There is such a requirement in the Convention.]

(b) Make sure each element of each violation is readily provable. Eliminate intent requirements when they serve no purpose. Require a permit for people in the "business of boarding animals" in the Surf City ordinance mentioned above (or eliminate this ambiguous element).

(c) Make sure rules are both principled and perceived as fair. Rules that serve only game-related purposes (e.g., intentional grounding, in football) cannot be as draconian as, say, safety rules (illegal blocks).

(d) Create an automatic or otherwise credible enforcement mechanism. For example, consider the enforcement of property taxes. The lender's lien is inferior to the county's tax lien, and so the lender, by escrow, ensures that real estate taxes are paid whether the borrower would pay them or not.

(5) *What Strategies Can You Adopt for Avoiding Unethical or Illegal Behavior in a Competitive Environment (Such as a Law Firm)?* Evaluate the following advice for avoiding unethical behavior yourself, and consider how you would add to or revise this list: (a) Cultivate mentors outside your immediate competitive group; (b) Do not try to outdo the unethical opponent; (c) Learn better to deal with loss and failure; (d) Do not expect all rules to be fully enforced against all competitors as a condition of your compliance; and (e) Learn how to say no tactfully to peers or superiors who propose violations.

Chapter 15
Game Theory II

Cooperative Moves, Mixed-Motive Games, and Legal Strategies

> *"What accounts for [a particular cooperative strategy's] robust success is its combination of being nice, retaliatory, forgiving, and clear. Its niceness prevents it from getting into trouble. Its retaliation discourages the other side from persisting whenever defection is tried. Its forgiveness helps restore mutual cooperation. And its clarity makes it intelligible to the other player, thereby eliciting long-term cooperation."*
> *--Robert Axelrod, The Evolution of Cooperation*

> *"Major Strasser's been shot. Round up the usual suspects."--Claude Rains, in the movie Casablanca*

§ 15.01   What This Chapter Is About

COOPERATIVE AND MIXED-MOTIVE GAMES

(1) *Interdependent Strategies: Coordination and Mixed-Motive Games.* The previous chapter explored strictly competitive or zero-sum games. This chapter also involves game theory, but in what are called "coordination"

games and "mixed motive" games. We still assume a rational, self-interested actor, but in a different framework. The issue can be phrased as, how can a player maximize her own position in a game where multiple players rise and fall together? The quotations above, from game theorist Robert Axelrod[1] and actor Claude Raines, demonstrate that the answers are not always obvious.

Mixed motive games, arguably, may be even more interesting that competitive games. Reality television shows such as "Survivor," as well as quiz shows such as "The Weakest Link," command huge audiences because of their dramatic and thrilling combinations of mutuality, treachery, support, and ruthlessness, which result from the mixed-motive games upon which they are based.

(2) *Lawyers and Mixed-Cooperative Games.* In this chapter, we shall apply Axelrod's theory to the behavior of lawyers in civil discovery, which is a mixed-motive game. We shall see how divorce decrees can reflect a different mixed-motive game. And we shall see how game theory helps to analyze shareholder voting, as well as other kinds of problems in the law.

§ 15.02   Game Theory and Cooperative Strategies

[A]   Coordination and Mixed-Strategy Games

PURE COORDINATION GAMES VERSUS
MIXED-MOTIVE GAMES

(1) *An Example of a Pure Coordination Game: "Oncoming Trains."* Imagine that two trains are headed toward each other on the same track. There are, however, tracks on each side that provide shunts, but only if both trains turn to opposite sides. If either stays in the center or if both go to the same side, both drivers lose. "Winning" consists of passing without collision.

This is a simple example of a "pure coordination" game. The goal of both engineers is the same, there is no competitive element, and the strategy is purely one of coordinating the players' (hoped-for) cooperation to prevent collision.

---

1   Axelrod made this statement in relation to a programmed strategy called Tit for Tat, which despite its simplicity and inability to win any individual game, won repeated computer tournaments involving the iterated Prisoners' Dilemma (discussed in this chapter).

But "Oncoming Trains" isn't an interesting game. The strategy is trivial. There are some interesting coordination games, although we won't study them here. In this book, the only reason for introducing the Oncoming Trains game (and coordination games generally) is to show that there are other games than purely competitive ones. Sometimes cooperation is called for, but it can be hard to achieve. And coordination (cooperation) games are not the only alternative to competitive games: there are games that combine the two. This may be the most real-world type of game, and it is the type that is of most interest to lawyers, who often cooperate while competing (however odd that may sound).

(2) *Mixed-Motive Games: "Centipede."* This "combined" category of games involves a different kind of interdependence than "Oncoming Trains": partly cooperative, partly competitive. These are called "mixed motive" games, and they probably reflect more real-life situations than competitive games do. And as we shall see, they are of great interest in the law.

Figure 1 is a decision tree for a game called "Centipede." (If you imagine this tree extended to, say, 100 moves, you will see where the name comes from.) Centipede's rules are simple: A player who wishes to move must pay $20, and the opposing player is paid $100. The players alternate their moves, but either player may stop the game at any time. Therefore, cooperative play will enrich both players (the $100 payments) but rational strategy is competitive also (because of the $20 loss with each move).

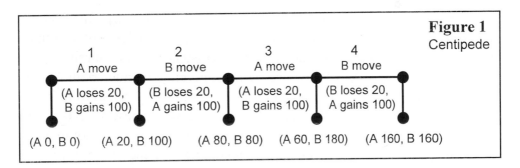

Figure 1
Centipede

1	2	3	4
A move	B move	A move	B move
(A loses 20, B gains 100)	(B loses 20, A gains 100)	(A loses 20, B gains 100)	(B loses 20, A gains 100)

(A 0, B 0)   (A 20, B 100)   (A 80, B 80)   (A 60, B 180)   (A 160, B 160)

(3) *The Paradox of Centipede: Rational Play Stops the Game Before the First Move, Even Though Both Players Lose by This Strategy(!)* The paradox of Centipede can be illustrated by "backward induction," or by starting at the last move and working back. If B is rational, Figure 1 shows why B will not make the last move, the one marked "4." That move earns A $100, but B

loses $20 (and is reduced from $180 to $160). Therefore, B will not make move 4.

For similar reasons, knowing that B will not make move 4, A contemplates move 3 and sees that while it earns B $100, it costs A $20. A, being rational, will stop before making move 3. This same logic extends to the very first move, which A, being rational, will not make.

The paradoxical "conclusion": Neither makes any moves, even though they each forfeit $160 that could be earned from these four simple plays!

(4) *The Law--and the Role of Contracts: To Avoid the Centipede Disaster by Enforcing Promises.* There is a simple solution: each party's promise to the other to cooperate. But what good is this promise? As we shall see below, psychological experiments are not encouraging. In other mixed-motive games, the ability to communicate and promise doesn't seem to enhance cooperation or welfare. But if we add a rule that the players *must* cooperate, and if we enforce it, we can avoid the Centipede disaster. It becomes rational to make the last move, the next-to-last, etc., because otherwise, a faithless player faces damage liability. This, in a nutshell, is what the law of contracts is all about!

EXAMPLES AND PROBLEMS

(1) *Even in the Law, Somebody Has to Trust Somebody: Playing Centipede a Hundred Times--Do People Act Rationally by Behaving Irrationally?* Ask yourself whether the backplay analysis of Centipede would change if we played a hundred moves instead of four. Surely, you tell yourself, A would begin by making a move, given how much both A and B stand to gain, and with the end so far away. But no: Backward induction leads to the same non-start, because both players know that B, acting rationally, will not make the 100th move, and therefore A will not make the 99th, B will not make the 98th . . . and so on, back to the first non-move.

This reasoning means that A and B give up a mutual $ 8,000, and it leads to the question, "Is this really 'rational' behavior?" One suspects that, instead, in the hundred-move case, A will, in fact, make move 1 if A is sensible, whereupon we suspect that B will make move 2. Does this mean that a degree of irrationality is essential to the rational play of some games?

Even in the law, there has to be someone who takes a risk and trusts the other player. In fact, lawyers frequently work with arrangements where there is risk that the other party will turn into a betrayer. Likewise, there will come a time when the mutual advantage ends--and a lawyer must expect that the other party may terminate the arrangement even if to do so causes loss. Can you see how these conclusions are illustrated by Centipede?

(2) *Why Lawyers Need to Understand Mixed-Motive Games Like Centipede: Clients with Divergent Interests Who Need to Cooperate.* Lawyers often are in mixed-motive situations. A group of businesspeople make an agreement in which their interests are divergent but each gets something out of it. Or, in a lawsuit, two defendants must decide whether to stick together in denying the plaintiff's claim or whether to point fingers at each other (and the plaintiff considers whether to form an alliance with one defendant against the other). Can you explain why these situations have something in common with Centipede? Other games in this chapter model lawyering circumstances more closely, but for now, the point is to understand mixed-motive games.

[B]   Two-Person Mixed-Motive Matrix Games

MATRICES FOR "BATTLE OF THE SEXES" AND "CHICKEN"

(1) *Matrices With Differential Payoffs.* In order to understand this next section, we must recognize that a given payoff may be different for different players. This can happen either because the absolute payoffs are different or because the players derive different utilities from them. In the Centipede game, for example, we saw that the rules specify that the payoffs for each move are different (+100 for one player, -20 for the other).

(2) *Lawyers, Litigation, and Matrices for Mixed-Motive Games.* We now proceed to develop three matrix games, which game theorists know as "Battle of the Sexes," "Chicken," and "The Prisoners' Dilemma." These colorful names describe payoff structures that model many situations in the law, as we shall see below.[2]

---

2   There is a fourth game with a related payoff matrix that is sometimes called "Leader," but it is less interesting than the other three.

		A	B	**Figure 2**
		Player 2 (Bogart)		"Battle of the Sexes": a mixed-motive game
Player 1 (Bacall)	X	2, 2	4, 3	
	Y	3, 4	1, 1	

(3) *"Battle of the Sexes."* Figure 2 is a payoff matrix for another game with differential payoff. This game classically is known as "Battle of the Sexes." The matrix shows independent payoffs for each player in each square. For example, if Player 1 chooses Row Y and Player 2 chooses Column A, the payoff square in the lower left applies, and the payoff is (3, 4): 3 to Player 1, and 4 to Player 2.

(4) *Battle of the Sexes: A Mixed-Motive Game.* Figure 2 also differs from previous payoff matrices in that it presents a mixed-motive, partly cooperative situation, rather than a zero-sum game. Classically, the game in Figure 2 has been called "Battle of the Sexes," although it might as well be called "partial coordination of the sexes."

Player 1 is the wife, who wants to watch the movie *Gone With the Wind* (her choice "X"), while Player 2, the husband, wants to watch *Casablanca* (his choice "A").[3] They have two VCR's and can retire to their own separate entertainments, but this produces less-than-optimal utilities of (2, 2), because they would prefer to watch together.

If husband sacrifices and watches *Gone With the Wind* with his wife (her choice "X," his choice "B"), the payoffs are (4, 3) (four to wife and three to husband), and husband gets to be the hero. If wife watches *Casablanca* (her choice "Y," his choice "A"), the payoffs are reversed (3, 4), and wife is the one to make the sacrifice. These optimal results occur, that is, unless both sacrifice by making their unfavored choices, leaving husband watching *Gone With the Wind* (which he doesn't like) while wife watches *Casablanca* (which she doesn't like) (payoff 1,1).

---

3   In the originally developed version, husband's choice was a boxing match, wife's choice, the ballet (the classic analysis was done during the 1950's). But the substitution of two romantic war movies makes the "battle" less "sexist," and it does not change the analysis.

(3) *An Interesting Insight Into Value Conflicts: Battle of the Sexes and the Concept of Equality under the Law.* The "Battle of the Sexes" game presents a situation in which equality must be sacrificed if the players are to obtain maximum mutual satisfaction. Equality is attainable, but ironically, not preferable, for either party, to an outcome that places one party in a less satisfactory position than the other. The best payoffs for an equal resolution are (2, 2). Higher payoffs result from inequality: (4, 3) or (3, 4).

Thus, the interesting inference from "Battle of the Sexes" is that if one party is willing to suffer inequality in the form of inferior satisfaction, both parties may emerge with higher payoffs, including the one who sacrifices, at least in some situations. To put it another way, sometimes equality conflicts with other important values.

(4) *Chicken (Or, Stand Up for Your Legal Rights): Another Mixed-Motive Game.* Here is another mixed-motive game, one that is framed in foolishly juvenile terms but nevertheless is fascinating to study. Two cars race at each other. The driver who turns is a "chicken." This stupidly risky game has been played with cars for decades, and it helped immortalize James Dean in the movie *Rebel Without a Cause.* It also is of significant interest to game theoreticians.

Figure 3 is a payoff matrix for the game of Chicken. It bears a superficial resemblance to the Battle of the Sexes, but the 3's and 2's are reversed, with perverse effects. If Player 1 proves his machismo and does not turn but Player 2 does, Player 2 is chicken but alive, and the payoff is (4, 2). If driver 1 turns but driver 2 does not, the payoff is reversed (2, 4). If both drivers turn, both are chicken, but neither feels as bad about it (3, 3). The worst outcome is that both players drive into and kill each other (1, 1).

		Player 2 (Dean)		Figure 3
		C	D	"Chicken": a perverse mixed-motive game
Player 1 (James)	C	**3, 3**	**2, 4**	
	D	**4, 2**	**1, 1**	

(5) *Litigation Analysis through Game Theory: Reframing Chicken as "Stand Up for Your Rights."* If the framing of the game as Chicken puts you off, it can be reinvented as "stand up for your legal rights in a too-small lawsuit": Two litigants are embroiled in litigation over a nondivisible trophy, but if they both insist on a trial, the trial will cost more than the trophy is worth to either. This framing may sound more appealing, but strategically "stand up for your rights" is identical to Chicken. Can you explain?

EXAMPLES AND PROBLEMS

(1) *Laws Regulating Marital Roles: What Can Battle of the Sexes Tell Us?* Sometimes there have been suggestions for the law to intervene during ongoing successful marriages in order to secure equality. For example, there have been equal rights advocates that have suggested limiting the ability of the breadwinner spouse to spend money, so that the other spouse can be protected. In fact, in the past, "coverture" laws that were designed to "protect" the wife actually limited what either party could do with property. The Battle of the Sexes game should show why we should be suspicious of efforts to mandate precise equality among partners. Can you explain why?

(2) *Contrasting These Mixed Games to Strictly Competitive Games.* There is no saddle point in either Battle of the Sexes or Chicken. Minimax (minimizing regret) does not uniformly optimize; for example, in Battle of the Sexes, it leads to a (2, 2) payoff, although there are two other squares that are better for both players (3, 4) and (4, 3). Maximin, or avoiding the worst possible outcome at all cost, is not a good strategy either, because again, in Battle of the Sexes, it leads to the (2, 2) non-equilibrium, which is not optimal.

(3) *The Madman and Lock-in Strategies: Games Lawyers Play.* Also, these games differ in another way: irrationality may be strategic. A player of Chicken (or for that matter, a maximizer in Battle of the Sexes or a lawyer in a lawsuit) might rationally adopt a "madman" strategy. By acting drunk, crazy and suicidal, the skilled Chicken enthusiast makes clear that his opponent's only rational strategy is to turn away. The former premier of the Soviet Union, Nikita Khrushchev, pounded his shoe on his table at the United Nations and may have obtained bargaining leverage from the madman strategy. Can you see why?

Another strategy is to "lock in." The husband, for example, destroys the video of *Gone With the Wind*, leaving only his choice, *Casablanca*. (Obviously, this strategy is not advisable for most husbands.) Or, the Chicken player tears the steering wheel out of his car in mid-game and throws it out the window where the opponent can see it. Similarly, advancing armies have been known to commit themselves by burning bridges behind them.

(4) *Lawyers, Madmen and Lock-Ins.* Lawyers use the madman strategy at times. The lawyer who credibly threatens to foreclose on a defaulted property in a mutual-loss situation, or the litigator who seems hell-bent on trying a small case in spite of a reasonable settlement offer, gets concessions from the opponent. Craziness is an effective tactic during negotiation, including lawyer-to-lawyer negotiation. And in more complex situations, lawyers use the lock-in tactic as well. Corporate takeover strategy is an example.

(5) *The Worst Kinds of Litigation: Reframing Chicken as "Child Custody Suit."* The Chicken game can be reframed by imagining two divorced parents litigating child custody and attempting to settle their differences. If one relinquishes the claim and the other does not, one will have a big payoff, the other a lesser one (4, 2) and (2, 4). If both relinquish, the judge will split custody (3, 3). The worst outcome will occur if they litigate through trial, which will damage both, and the children too (1, 1).

Does this frame change your perception of the game? Is there any credible way that either party in the "child custody game" can use the commitment strategies of "madman" or "lock-in?"

(6) *Bankruptcy Litigation Strategies and the Chicken Game.* In a bankruptcy liquidation situation, there is a limited estate--not enough to go around. How can a greedy lawyer get the lion's share? By threatening (usually impliedly) to make the process so cumbersome that it will consume all of the bankrupt's estate, and by acting crazy enough to do it. Other litigants, unfortunately, probably will defer to this tactic if they act rationally. But the tactic backfires if two or more greedy-threatening-crazy lawyers are involved. Does the Chicken game help explain these observations?

§ 15.03 The Prisoners' Dilemma: The Most Interesting Mixed-Motive Game

THE PRISONERS' DILEMMA AND THE
ITERATED PRISONERS' DILEMMA

(1) *The Prisoners' Dilemma: Cooperate or Defect?* The "Prisoners' Dilemma" is another mixed-motive game, closely related to Battle of the Sexes and Chicken, but it is the most interesting and most frequently analyzed problem known to game theory.

The game usually is framed in the following way. Two prisoners who have been charged with the same offense, and who are being separately interrogated in isolation, know that if neither confesses or inculpates the other, each will get a sentence of one (1) year. But if one confesses and inculpates the other, the confessing prisoner will receive a sentence of two (2) years, whereas the non-confessor will be sentenced to four (4) years. If both confess, they will receive a sentence of three (3) years.

Thus, the cooperative choice, which is for both to remain silent, would provide the best result for each. A dilemma for each results, however, from the inability to control or predict the other's behavior, together with the knowledge that cooperation will be disastrous if the counterpart defects.

The Prisoners' Game is not confined to prisoners, and it illustrates a dilemma that arises in many contexts in which cooperative behavior is the best course if uniformly followed but is disadvantageous for one player if the other defects. The terms "cooperate" and "defect" are used to describe the two strategies.

(2) *Lawyers and the Prisoners' Dilemma: From Civil Litigation to Environmental Law.* Because of the Prisoners' Dilemma, criminal lawyers sometimes execute formal, detailed joint defense agreements. The objective is to preserve privileged information and thus limit the downside risk of

	II	
	C (cooperate)	D (defect)
I C (cooperate)	3, 3	1, 4
D (defect)	4, 1	2, 2

Figure 4

The Prisoners' Dilemma: cooperate or defect?

cooperative strategies. We already have alluded to the civil litigation situation in which two defendants must decide whether to stick together or to blame each other. This too is the Prisoners' Game. And as we shall see, the Prisoners' Dilemma models environmental law, too.

(3) *Diagraming the Prisoners' Dilemma.* Figure 4 is a payoff matrix for this game. It is drawn, as is customary, in terms of positive payoffs; that is, a sentence of 4 years is less desirable and corresponds to a payoff of 1, while 3 years corresponds to a positive 2, 2 years to 3, and 1 year (the best outcome) to 4. Notice that the rows and columns are labeled "C" for cooperate and "D" for defect. If both cooperate, they obtain the best joint payoff (3, 3). If one defects and the other cooperates, the cooperating player suffers disastrous results while the defector wins big (4, 1) or (1, 4). If one defects, then the other is better off by having defected (2, 2) although neither does as well as if both had cooperated (3, 3).

EXAMPLES AND PROBLEMS

(1) *Laws, Treaties, and the Arms Race: Reframing the Prisoners' Dilemma.* The Prisoners' Dilemma can be reframed as "arms race," keeping the same payoffs. During the 1950's through 1980's, Russia (which then was part of the Soviet Union) and the United States each poured ever-increasing resources into strategic nuclear weapons. The United States feared unilateral limitation because the Russians would achieve dominance (1, 4), and the Russians feared the reverse (4, 1), and so they continued their arms race (2, 2, the both-defect outcome) until finally Strategic Arms Limitation Talks produced the "SALT" Treaty and the Soviet Union broke apart, ending the race (3, 3, the both-cooperate outcome).

		Soviet Union		**Figure 5**
		limit missiles, C	continue building, D	arms race: a variation of the Prisoners' Dilemma
United States	limit missiles, C	**3, 3** stop building	**1, 4** Soviet ahead	
	continue building, D	**4, 1** U.S. ahead	**2, 2** arms race	

Can you explain why this arms race game is the same as the Prisoners' Dilemma? This example shows one of its many applications.

(2)   *Reframing the Prisoners' Dilemma as "Golden Rule" and Deconstructing It.* One could refer to the Prisoners' Dilemma as the "golden rule" game: Do unto others as you would have them do unto you. The outcomes are (3, 3) if both players follow the golden rule, (4, 1) or (1, 4) if one follows the rule but the other takes advantage, and (2, 2) if neither follows the rule. How does this framing influence your perception?

(3) *Contract Law and Enforcement of Promises: What if the Parties Can Communicate?* Experiments comparing play with (a) no communication to (b) play with unenforced promises and to (c) play with promises enforced by penalties, demonstrate that cooperation is highest with enforced promises and lowest with no communication (not surprisingly). But the experiments with open communication (threats, promises or fraud) yield unexpected results.

In one experiment, subjects were given one of three sets of instructions, encouraging either competitive play, cooperation, or individual payoff maximization. It was only when subjects were encouraged to maximize their own individual interests that communication made a difference in increasing the level of cooperative moves. Can you explain this effect?

THE ITERATED PRISONERS' DILEMMA

(1)   *The Iterated Prisoners' Dilemma: Multiple Repetitions.*   What happens if the players play a finite series of Prisoners' Games, ten or a hundred in a row, against each other? Theoretically, each "iteration" of the

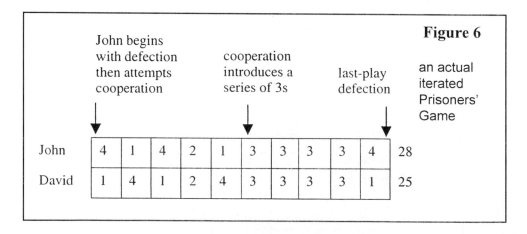

Figure 6

John begins with defection then attempts cooperation

cooperation introduces a series of 3s

last-play defection

an actual iterated Prisoners' Game

| John | 4 | 1 | 4 | 2 | 1 | 3 | 3 | 3 | 3 | 4 | 28 |
| David | 1 | 4 | 1 | 2 | 4 | 3 | 3 | 3 | 3 | 1 | 25 |

game remains the same as a single game; backward induction tells us so. But psychological effects tend to produce coordination.

Figure 6 is a scoreboard from an actual ten-game series between the author and the author's then-thirteen-year-old son John. I played a programmed strategy known as "Tit for Tat," which is discussed below. Initial defections prevented cooperation until the sixth move, which produced a series of four maximum-point payoffs. Had this strategy remained in place, both players would have earned 27 points each--a whopping seven more than purely defecting strategies would produce--except that, having correctly diagnosed my strategy, and having been asked to play a rational self-interested strategy, John defected on the last move. (This last-move defection, predicted by backward induction, reflects astute competitive play by a teenage video-combat veteran!) Even so, John won 28 points and I won 25, whereas the all-defect strategy would have produced only 20 for each. This sequence illustrates the mixed-motive nature of the game.

(2) *Robert Axelrod's Computer-Program Tournaments: The Tit-for-Tat Strategy.* One of the most fascinating developments in all of game theory came when Robert Axelrod invited submissions of programmed strategies to a Prisoners' Game tournament conducted by computer. Each entry played two hundred iterations against all other programs and against a clone of itself. The winner was a disarmingly simple program entered by game theorist Anatol Rappoport called "Tit for Tat," or "TFT."

TFT starts with a cooperative move, and thereafter its play simply echoes the opponent's last move, tit for tat. (See Figure 7 above (lower line) for scores resulting from TFT play.) Another program called "Random," which played C or D strategies at random, came in last, as you might guess. But the point is, TFT also beat more complex strategies.

Axelrod then conducted a second tournament, which attracted four times as many entries, and Tit for Tat again won. Notice that TFT can never best its opponent in a one-on-one contest--but it came out on top nevertheless!

EXAMPLES AND PROBLEMS:
UNDERSTANDING THE ITERATED PRISONERS' DILEMMA

(1) *The Four Qualities of a Winning Program in the Prisoners' Tournament: Nice, Retaliatory, Forgiving, and Clear.* Axelrod's conclusion

was that a "nice" program, one that never initiates a defection, generally beats a "nasty" one. In both tournaments, nice programs clustered in the top rankings, nasty ones in the bottom. But also, Axelrod saw that "niceness" wasn't enough. A winning program needed to be sufficiently "retaliatory": it needed to stand up for itself if the other player defected, by defecting itself.

Third, a winning program was "forgiving." It would resume cooperation even after an opponent's defection, under some conditions. And finally, a good program needed to be "clear," so that the other player could recognize both its cooperation and its retaliation. Given these conclusions, can you see why Tit for Tat was a winner?

(2) *Nastiness: Comparing the Double-Crossing Programs Called Joss or Nasty-Make-It-Up to TFT.* A program called "Joss" resembled TFT, but with ten percent random defections, followed by reversion to cooperative moves, built in. A related program is called "Nasty Make It Up."

Would this "touch of nastiness" improve Joss's score? No, because in playing against TFT, Joss's first double-cross would trigger a next-move defection by TFT at the same time that Joss tried to reestablish cooperation (DC), leading to a series of alternating CD, DC, CD moves. Then, the next time Joss mixed in a double-cross, it would occur when TFT was itself in defect mode, producing a DD pair. After that, all moves would be DD.

Axelrod concluded that, in real life, double-crossing people act in this way because they have not realized its consequence to their own self-interests. Double-crossers, in other words, arguably may not be so much dishonest as they are foolish: they don't understand how the world works. A corollary conclusion is that double-crosses are disproportionately costly. Do you agree? If so, consider the next note.

(3) *Last-Move Nastiness: Would It "Improve" Tit for Tat?* Perhaps we could improve TFT by altering it to "TFT-With-Last-Move-Defection." The resulting program would be identical to TFT except that it would double-cross the opponent on the last move--after which no retaliation is possible. The gain would be small, but would the difference of a few points make this last-move-nasty program the new winner? (Remember that it also has to play a clone of itself, although it plays more against others.)

(4) *Insufficient Retaliation: Comparing TFT to Tit for Two Tats.* One program, called "Tit for Two Tats" or "TFTT," was very forgiving. It did not retaliate until its opponent had defected twice. But in the tournament, TFTT placed far below TFT. Can you see why?

(5) *Axelrod's Natural Selection Simulation: TFT Again Prevails.* After his tournaments, Axelrod took the idea into the next dimension. He simulated natural selection or Darwinian survival by reproducing each of 63 programs according to its tournament performance, and then by adjusting its number of "offspring" in each successive round or "generation." After 1,000 generations of play, weak programs became extinct, and so did some "predator" programs that had survived by exploiting dwindling programs lower in the food chain. Once again, TFT won. It increased in each round, and grew to fourteen percent of the population.

Since that time, other experimenters have demonstrated that Tit for Tat can be beaten, although that outcome depends on the rest of the population. But the success of TFT, which literally cannot beat any other program in a head to head contest, shows why the key is survival in the environment, or natural selection, not survival of the abstractly "fittest."

(6) *Applications in the Law.* The iterated Prisoners' Dilemma furnishes models for so many kinds of legal issues, of such a variety, that we can only begin to cover them. That is what the next section is for.

EXAMPLES AND PROBLEMS: LEGAL IMPLICATIONS OF THE ITERATED PRISONERS' DILEMMA

(1) *Lawsuits, Discovery, and the Prisoners' Dilemma.* When two lawyers lock horns to do discovery in a civil lawsuit, the payoff matrix is that of the Prisoners' Dilemma. Here's why: by cooperating, the parties maximize their combined welfare (defined as the most information at lowest cost). But if one engages in Rambo tactics and the other does not, Rambo gets a high payoff and his opponent suffers the worst outcome. If two Rambos battle each other, they come out equally but neither with the best situation. Can you explain why these payoffs resemble the Prisoners' Dilemma?

(2) *Dispute Resolution and the Prisoners' Dilemma: Perlmutter's Theory of Lawsuit Cooperation.* In a book with the intriguing title "Why Lawyers

Lie and Engage in Other Repugnant Behavior," Mark Perlmutter describes Rambo-style litigation tactics ranging from verbal abuse to theft to perjury. But Perlmutter's polling of lawyers indicates that virtually all would prefer to operate in an environment free of these (and lesser) abuses.

Perlmutter's own solution to this dilemma is to send each opponent, at the beginning of each lawsuit, a letter agreement offering cooperative strategies for pretrial development of the case. Some lawyers sign Perlmutter's proposal, some verbally accept it, and some reject it vehemently. If an opponent deviates, Perlmutter remonstrates: "Do you think what you just did is in accordance with our agreement?"

First question: How does this (real-life) "game" correspond to the Prisoners' Dilemma? Second question: Would you think that Perlmutter's strategy would work, or does it contain deficiencies?

(3) *Environmental Law and the Prisoners' Dilemma.* Two farmers share a valley. If either pollutes, that farmer saves money but causes losses to the other. The best combined outcome is for both to avoid polluting, but each will be tempted. This fundamental scenario of environmental law mirrors the Prisoners' Dilemma. Why?

(4) *Oligopolists, Antitrust Laws, and the Prisoners' Dilemma.* We have seen in earlier chapters that oligopolists tend to follow a cooperative strategy, because defection in the form of price cuts or other competitive strategies causes retaliation. Can you see why this situation follows the Prisoners' Dilemma? The antitrust laws limit the cooperation by outlawing price fixing. This effort is analogous to the tactic of interrogating officers who separate the prisoners in the Prisoners' Dilemma. Can you explain?

(5) *Making It More Specific: Adapting the Iterated Prisoners' Dilemma to Competitor Analysis in an Oligopoly.* Specifically, the iterated Prisoners' Dilemma models the marketing strategies (offensive, defensive, and neutral) that we saw in the Management chapter. Each player attempts to maximize its own position, but to do so it cannot limit its strategy to its own moves but must take account of competitors. Indeed, usually it tacitly must cooperate with competitors. Remember the four elements that made Tit for Tat (TFT) such a formidable survivor in iterated games: it was "nice," "retaliatory," "forgiving," and "clear."

Figure 7 is a payoff matrix for a game that is strategically identical to the Prisoners' Dilemma, but its labels are adapted to a market with oligopolistic competition. An aggressive strategy such as expanded or comparative advertising, territorial expansion, or price discounts, if unmatched by the competitor, will produce a competitive advantage: a payoff of 4 to the competitor's 1. A cooperative strategy, avoiding aggressive moves, will produce the greatest net gain: 3 for each. But aggressive strategy by both produces the worst total outcome: 2, 2.

		Competitor 2		**Figure 7**
		price stability	discount	competitors' payoff matrix, resembling Prisoners' Dilemma
Competitor 1	price stability	3, 3	4, 1	
	discount	1, 4	2, 2	

Thus, if the competitor is capable of responsive increases in advertising, territorial expansion into the strategist's own territory, or reciprocal price discounts, the result will be a merchandising, product or price war that will hurt both competitors. Furthermore, in a market with five identifiable competitors, the strategist must think of these issues with respect to all five, and the strategy becomes like that of playing five simultaneous iterated Prisoners' Dilemma games, all with the same moves by the strategist but with different potential responses by other players.

(6) *Psychological Differences in Human Players (in Men and Women Lawyers): Gender and Cultural Variations in Cooperation.* A large number of experiments have demonstrated that cooperation in the Prisoners' Game, as well as in Chicken, varies with gender. Counterintuitively, men on average are more cooperative than women. This result seems particularly odd given the greater average tendency of women to seek compromise strategies when presented with ethical dilemmas, as we saw in the Ethics chapter. It also is surprising given the gender difference mentioned in the preceding chapter: Men are more prone to entrapment and escalation in dollar auctions. The gender effect sometimes, but not always, reduces when the game is administered by an experimenter who is a woman.

Is this gender difference, then, a result of a greater caution on the part of some women and a greater average recklessness in men? Perhaps. That answer is consistent with the gender differences in ethical-dilemma compromises and escalation entrapment. But it does not seem to square with women's average play in Chicken, where the apparently cautious move, cooperate (or "turn"), is played proportionally more by men! One game theorist, Andrew Colman, speculates that women tested by male experimenters experience a greater "evaluation apprehension" that makes them reluctant to "lose," even when the result is noncooperation that reduces the shares of both players.

Then there are the cultural studies, which have shown that Anglo subjects tend to be less cooperative than African-American, Hispanic or Asian subjects and that western-educated Liberians are less cooperative than less-western-educated Liberians. How would you explain these findings?

(7) *The Maximizing Difference Game and Civil Litigation: Perverse Outcomes.* We already have considered the "maximizing difference" game, which is of little interest to normative game theorists because there is only one rational strategy. If both players cooperate, they each get their highest possible payoff. (If one player defects, that player gets a lower payoff and the other gets zero; if both defect, both get zero.)

One would expect, then, to see monotonously repetitive games in experiments using the maximizing difference game, with all players adopting cooperative moves. But human psychology is complex. The experiments show high numbers of defections. In one, where subjects stood to earn large sums of money, they cooperated only about 50 percent of the time, meaning that both players gained less all the other times.

Speculation about the reasons includes the possibilities (1) that the subjects have misunderstood the game, (2) that they wish to "win" in relative terms by beating each other rather than to maximize mutual gain, or (3) that players' utility differs from recognized payoffs, e.g., that even reckless change is preferable to profitable boredom. See whether you can explain how this phenomenon might affect litigants in a lawsuit.

§ 15.04   Multi-Person Games and Coalition Formation

THE THEORY OF MULTI-PERSON COOPERATIVE GAMES

(1) *The Stockholders' Game: An Inquiry Into Coalition Formation.* Next, we go into the area of multi-person games. Here, the most interesting issues concern the formation of coalitions: when and how will two or more players join together and oppose other players? In an earlier chapter (on Politics), we encountered the Stockholders' Game as a method of inquiring into equality. Here, we consider game theory aspects.

Remember that the Stockholders' Game concerns an about-to-be-dissolved corporation with three stockholders: Abe, who controls 50% of the shares; Babe, with 30%; and Cabe, with 20%. All three also are employees, with roughly equal salaries. The corporation has received an offer of unexpected income in the form of 30 gold bars, which Abe, Babe and Cabe will be able to distribute among themselves just before dissolution of the corporation.

Abe, Babe and Cabe must decide two questions by a majority vote of the shares. First, they must decide whether to allow the corporation to receive the 30 gold bars as income. Second, they must decide how to distribute them. And let us make one more assumption: Abe, Babe and Cabe have no particular loyalty to each other, and their votes are motivated by self-interest.

(2) *The Grand Coalition, Coalitional Imputations, and the Characteristic Function.* A "grand coalition" includes all the players in the game. For obvious reasons, Abe, Babe and Cabe are likely to vote as a grand coalition to allow the corporation to receive the gold bars. An "imputation" is a payoff specification in which each coalition member receives at least as much as that player would if acting alone (and all together receive as much as the grand coalition would). The set of imputations, then, designates those coalitions that might turn out to be rational choices. The "characteristic function" of the game consists of laying out the values (signified as "v") that can be realized for each coalition contained within the grand coalition, thus:[4]

[one-person voting blocs] $v(A) = 0$, $v(B) = 0$, $v(C) = 0$
[two-person voting blocs] $V(AB) = 30$, $v(AC) = 30$, $v(BC) = 0$
[grand coalition] $V(ABC) = 30$

---

4   Strictly speaking, one of the imputations or sub-coalitions is the null set, which contains no one. Here, its value $v(\varnothing) = 0$. But since none of the illustrations here depends on $v(\varnothing)$, this coverage omits it from the characteristic function.

v(A), v(B) and v(C) are all zero because no shareholder can muster a majority alone. v(AB) is 30 because Abe and Babe can create a majority (80%) to vote to receive the 30 bars, v(AC) is 30 because Abe and Cabe can do the same (70%), but v(BC) is zero because Babe and Cabe produce only 50%. And v(ABC) is 30 because the grand coalition obviously can make a majority.

(3) *Dividing the Payoff: Absolutely Equal Shares Contrasted to Shapley Values (or Pivotal Values).*   The next, and harder, question is how the shareholders strategically might vote to divide the payoff. One way is to divide it with individually absolute equality: ten of the 30 bars to each, or 10 each to Abe, Babe and Cabe. Let us call this "individual" equality. It does not use voting strength as a basis for the division.

A second way is to divide according to numbers of shares: 15 to Abe (50%), 9 to Babe (30%), and 6 to Cabe (20%). Let us refer to this division as "share" or "by the shares" equality. It reflects the share ownership percentage, or the number of votes, as the determinant of the division.

But a very different method, described by game theorist Lloyd Shapley, depends upon what value each player brings to the voting coalition, or how often each player would be "pivotal" in completing a valuable coalition. In other words, what we have referred to as "share" equality is not the only model that reflects voting strength, and it may not be the most probable (or even the "fairest," depending on what is meant by fairness). Shapley's method depends on the importance of each player in forming a coalition. In a three-person game, there are 3x2x1 = 6 possible orders in which shareholders can vote to form a majority.[5] We refer to the player who completes the majority as "pivotal" or as "the pivot." Thus, a majority can form in the following orders: (1) A then B, in which case B is pivotal; A then C, with C pivotal; B then A, with A pivotal; B then C then A, with A pivotal; C then A, with A pivotal; and finally, C then B then A, with A pivotal.

Abe, then, is pivotal in four cases; Babe and Cabe each are pivotal in only one. The "Shapley numbers" for each, as they are called, are 2/3 (four pivots out of six) for Abe and 1/6 each for Babe and Cabe (each with one pivot out

---

5   Mathematically, the number of permutations, p, is given by p = (3!). The symbol (!) means "factorial," or the product of multiplying the total number by each lesser whole number. Here, 3! = 3x2x1. Generalizing, n! = n(n-1)(n-2) . . . (2)(1). But don't worry about the math, unless it interests you.

of six). Shapley's theory leads to the following division, then: 20 gold bars (or 2/3) to Abe, 5 (or 1/6) to Babe, and 5 (or 1/6) to Cabe.

Again, this seemingly lopsided division results because Abe brings more to the possible coalitions: Abe is pivotal (Abe completes the coalition) in two-thirds (four out of six) cases, for a Shapley number of 2/3, or 20 out of 30 gold bars, whereas Babe and Cabe each complete a meaningful coalition in only one out of six cases, for a Shapley number of 1/6 or 5 each.[6]

(4) *The Paradox of Shapley's Stable and Equitable Solution: It Corresponds Neither to Absolute Individual Equality Nor to Share Percentages.* The Shapley division of 20 bars to Abe (who has 50% of the stock), 5 to Babe (30%), and 5 to Cabe (20%) may seem paradoxical. It deviates sharply from individual equality, which would dictate 10 each. It also differs from share-vote proportionality, which would split the bars according to Abe's 50% (15 bars), Babe's 30% (9), and Cabe's 20% (6). In fact, the Shapley distribution arguably seems unfair, because Abe has only half the stock but gets 2/3 of the gold. Poor old Babe, in contrast, has 3/5 as much stock as Abe but gets only one-fourth as much gold (and Cabe gets as much gold as Babe, who has 1½ times as much stock)!

Still, game theorists tend to regard Shapley value distributions as "equitable." Why? Again, Shapley value corresponds to the contribution of each player to coalition formation, or to the coalitional "value" the player contributes toward creating a majority vote. The measure of "equity," in this view, lies in a precisely "equal" treatment of the different "values" of contributions toward resolving the question at hand by their votes. Also, Shapley's solution has the advantage of "stability." There are reasons, based on power relationships, for the grand coalition to accept it. Perhaps game theorists, more than other thinkers, see the equality of the division as driven by rational compromises of self-interest.

(5) *The "Shareholder Oppression Doctrine" in the Law: A Response to the Dark Side of This Game.* The "shareholder oppression" doctrine has been

---

6   For the mathematically inclined, the general equation for Shapley values for any player, I, is

$$\sum_{i=1}^{n} \frac{n!}{n!} \quad \frac{[(s_i -1)! \ (n\text{-}s_i)!]}{n!} \bullet D(S_i),$$

where n is the total number of players, s_i is the number of players in the ith coalition, and $D(S_i)$ stands for the difference in value of the ith coalition with, and without, player I (or if I is not in S_i, then $D(S_i) = O$). For the meaning of the exclamation point(!), see the preceding note. But again, don't worry about the math.

adopted in some states. It is simple to state: a majority cannot unfairly oppress a minority shareholder. But the doctrine is hard to apply, at least if we want uniformity and predictability. The reason should be obvious from the Stockholders' Game. There is a range of majority behaviors that can be labeled fair or unfair, depending on what we mean by those terms!

EXAMPLES AND PROBLEMS

(1) *In the Stockholders' Game, Don't A and C Have a Motivation to Form a Coalition That Excludes B?: The Rationale for Shareholder Oppression Laws.* If you are persuaded to consider Shapley values as "equitable," consider the following possibility. With A, B and C having contemplated a coalitional division of 20, 5, and 5, won't A and C act in their rational self-interests by declining this division, forming a coalition that excludes B, and dividing "B's" gold between them (so that Abe gets 22, Cabe gets 8, and Babe gets zero)?

(2) *An Alternative Divisional Theory to Shapley Values: Minimal Winning Coalition Theory and Shareholder Oppression.* In fact, "minimal winning coalition theory" states that the coalition that will emerge is either A-C or A-B, and not the grand coalition, A-B-C. Minimal winning coalition theory holds that a coalition must be large enough to win, but predictably will be the minimal coalition that fulfills this requirement. The coalition players, by this theory, will avoid adding unnecessary members, because they prefer not having to divide the payoff with those additional members. This is bad news. It means that shareholder oppression is likely to emerge, because it reflects rational self-interest for players in the majority.

(3) *Different Theories of Equality in the Law: Contrasting Individual, or Share-Determined, or Shapley Value, or Minimum Winning Coalition Theories.* Perhaps these discussions cast light on the shifting and varied meanings of the elusive word, "equality." A simple version of this concept, here, would split the gold bars according to absolute individual equality, 10 to each shareholder. This arguably is the Marxist solution (from each according to his ability, to each according to his needs)--or is it, perhaps, more closely akin to Rawls's distributive justice (see the Ethics chapter)?

But this individual-equality solution gives no weight to the stock percentages of the players, which presumably were obtained by different investments. Should the split instead be 15-9-6, in accordance with the 50-30-20 investment proportions? Perhaps.

But still, the more capitalistic solution of by-the-share equality is unequal in another respect. It gives no weight to negotiations and coalition formation, and perhaps it should. Presumably Abe was aware of voting strength in buying 50%, and so were Babe and Cabe in buying their percentages. Abe may have invested an extra amount--called a "control premium"--for the largest (50%) share. Since each stockholder knew the need for future coalitions, expected relative voting strengths to determine outcomes, and invested accordingly, perhaps it is "equal" for Shapley value to determine the split: 20 to A, 5 to B and 5 to C.

But by this reasoning, perhaps it also is "equal" for A and C to freeze out B and to divide the gold 22-to-8 between the two of them! Is this "equal"?

(4) *The Shareholder Oppression Doctrine and Game Theory.* The shareholder oppression doctrine, in corporate law, limits the ability of a majority to oppress the minority for the majority's advantage. But the doctrine usually is flexibly applied. It usually does not prohibit the majority from voting in a way that benefits itself at the minority's expense if all of the factors make this treatment equitable. For example, in the previous note, the Shapley value division would be more likely to be upheld if A had, indeed, paid a control premium, if B initially had the ability to foresee the effects of the share distribution, and if B in fact received a reasonable payment. The more severe inequality of freeze-out (zero to B) will be harder to defend. Does game theory help to understand the law?

(5) *The Legal Tradeoff Between Equality and Freedom, as Illustrated by the Stockholder Problem.* Politicians often refer to "equality" and "freedom" as if they were interchangeable. But perhaps this example, the Stockholders' Game, suggests that freedom and equality are not the same, and that in fact they are in conflict. Imagine that the outcome of free, private negotiations among Abe, Babe and Cabe would end in the adoption of a Shapley-value solution (A 20, B 5, C 5). But imagine that Babe is discontented by this distribution. Babe sues and obtains a court order directing an individually equal division (A 10, B 10, C 10).

First, notice that the court has chosen one political concept of equality over others that have arguably superior claims to being "equal." But isn't a political choice necessary, if law is to intervene? Second, consider whether the court has reduced the players' freedom to choose a private solution. Indeed, hasn't the court interfered with the freedom not only of these, but of all future stockholders who wish to structure their relations as Abe, Babe and Cabe attempted to do? But note that, even if it reduces freedom, the court's decision can be defended as arguably "correct." Can you see why?

(6) *Psychological Effects: Minimum Winning Coalition Theory and Coalitional-Power Payoff Division (or, "How Litigants Really Settle Business Lawsuits")*. Psychological experiments strongly demonstrate that subjects playing competitive games tend to adopt minimum winning coalition theory. In one experiment, a minimum coalition formed in almost 90% of trials.

But when it comes to payoff divisions, neither minimum winning coalition theory nor Shapley value completely predicts how experimental subjects react. The subjects appear to accept intuitively that coalitional power is relevant, because they do not exclusively use individually equal divisions either. Thus, while it is unlikely that they can compute such factors as Shapley values, subjects tend to be influenced by the underlying power concept.

The result: experiments consistently demonstrate a tendency to arrive at a division somewhere *between* individual equality and a coalitional-power (Shapley or minimum-winning) division. Can you explain these findings?

(7) *The Power Inversion Paradox: Minimal Resource Theory (or, the Chairman's Power under the Law Isn't Necessarily Powerful)*. Psychological experiments also demonstrate another surprising effect that deviates from game theory. If two weaker players have combined power to win against a stronger third one, they tend to form together in a "coalition of the weakest" rather than to split and coalesce, either one, with the strongest player.

Imagine, for example, that stockholders A, B and C hold 45, 30 and 25 percent of the shares, respectively. The experiments tend to show a preference for coalition formation by B and C (who have 55%) rather than A and B (75%) or A and C (70%). Minimum winning coalition theory predicts that each of the three possible combinations should be equally likely to occur, because each is an equally minimal winning coalition: 55% is exactly equivalent to 70 or 75%, since a simple majority governs. The observed psychological effect, however, is that A, who appears most powerful, is in fact least powerful, in that A disproportionately gets frozen out!

This is the "power inversion paradox." Its effect is, in fact, consistent with a separate hypothesis, different from minimum coalition theory, called "minimum resource theory," which predicts formation of not merely the smallest, but the *weakest* winning coalition. Question: Is it somehow rational for B and C to coalesce preferentially with each other rather than with the more powerful player, A?

Chapter 16
Rhetoric

Strategies for Questioning, Listening, Persuasion, and Negotiation

> *"Ethos, pathos and logos."--Aristotle's formula for persuasive argument, invoking values, sympathy, and logic*

> *"[N]egotiation is [one of] the most common and problematic involvement[s] of one person with another . . . ."--John Kenneth Galbraith, in endorsing Roger Fisher and William Ury's negotiation book, "Getting to Yes"*

§ 16.01   What This Chapter Is About

RHETORIC AND NEGOTIATION

(1) *Why Juxtapose Rhetoric With Game Theory?: Lawyers, Language, Falsehood, Negotiation, and Strategy.* This chapter is juxtaposed with coverage of game theory because rhetoric, like game theory, is strategic. In fact, some experiments have examined the effect of rhetoric in games (for example, the preceding chapter considered communication effects on players

of the prisoner's dilemma). Further, game strategy and rhetoric both influence methods of negotiation, which is considered in this chapter.

We begin the chapter by looking at methods of questioning, investigation, and listening. The chapter also covers resistance, fabrication, and persuasion. For lawyers, the significance of these activities is obvious. The quotation from Aristotle shows that rhetoric requires logic, but it must take account of strategic considerations too.

(2) *Negotiation.* Negotiation, as the quotation from John Kenneth Galbraith indicates, is one of the most pervasive activities in which humans engage, and it probably is the most highly developed competency that experienced lawyers share. Our coverage considers a variety of negotiation strategies, examines their effectiveness, and explores their ethical limits.

§ 16.02   Rhetoric: The Strategy of Communication

[A]   Questioning, Listening and Investigative Strategies

QUESTIONING FOR INVESTIGATION
OR FOR DEMONSTRATION

(1) *Investigative Questioning or Interviewing: How It Differs From Demonstrative Questioning, Such as In-Court Examinations.* Interview or discovery questioning differs sharply from the lawyer's techniques of direct examination or cross examination. Both of those in-court skills involve questioning that limits and guides the witness. This is especially true of cross, where the skillful examiner develops the testimony by rigorously guiding the witness through the testimony, using only leading questions. Most questioning in court is closed-ended, limited, and specific.

Investigative interviewing is very different. Interviewing is done not to prove facts, but to find them out: to discover the unknown. Unlike the direct or cross examiner, who may consciously attempt to avoid eliciting unfavorable information, the interviewer seeks to discover all relevant facts, favorable or not. The interviewer differs from the in-court examiner, also, in that the witness's version of the story is less known. The interviewer must use open-ended questioning.

(2) *The Funnel Sequence: Open-Ended Questions First.* Thus, psychologists advise use of what is called the "funnel" sequence. The interviewer begins with broad questions, such as, "What happened, from beginning to end?" or "Tell me what you saw."

These kinds of questions would almost always be inadvisable for a lawyer's cross examination, and even for direct examination they may not be skillful technique. But investigation is different. The effort is to induce the interviewee to narrate freely and fully. The metaphor is that of a funnel, whose entry is wide open. And therefore, the interviewer's beginning is wide open. The objective is to get the interviewee to narrate.

(3) *Exhausting the Narrative Potential of the Interviewee; "Squeezing."* In fact, when the interviewee stops narrating, the interviewer should not automatically assume that the story has been told fully. It might be wise to "squeeze," by asking, "Have you told me everything?" or, "Is there anything else that happened? Anything that you've left out?" The metaphor is that of obtaining the subject's full memory, like squeezing a sponge.

Why do this? The answer is, because the interviewer doesn't know everything yet. The interviewer doesn't even know what isn't known. Even if the interviewer has seen the very same event, in fact, the interviewer doesn't know how this particular interviewee would describe it. The only way to discover that is to invite the subject to narrate. As long as the interviewee continues to narrate about ostensibly relevant matters, it usually is wise for the interviewer's mouth to stay shut. This isn't always easy.

(4) *Specific Questions.* Specific, directed questions, even leading ones, may also be appropriate. The funnel sequence, however, uses specific questions only *after* the interviewee's memory has been probed through open-ended questions and the narrative ability of the interviewee has been exhausted. Again, the metaphor of the funnel fits. The beginning is done with broad, open questions, and narrow, specific questions come later. The funnel sequence requires patience.

EXAMPLES AND PROBLEMS

(1) *Depositions Taken by Lawyers in Lawsuits: Investigative Questioning.* A "deposition," in a lawsuit, is the questioning of a witness before trial. When done for investigative or discovery purposes, it is in

reality simply a peculiar kind of interview. The techniques that apply to interviewing apply to depositions, subject to the legal rules of procedure that govern. Can you see why the funnel sequence generally would be useful to a lawyer taking a pretrial deposition of a witness for discovery purposes?

(2) *The Funnel Sequence in a Deposition.* In a deposition, therefore, the skillful interrogator seeks to get the deponent to narrate. The beginning of the questioning about the relevant event is with open-ended questions: "Tell me what happened." Next, the examiner squeezes: "Is that all? Have you told me everything that happened?" The examiner uses narrow, specific questions too, but usually after inducing the witness to narrate.

There are other uses of depositions than discovery, such as the deposition of a friendly witness or expert who will be unavailable for trial. Those depositions are different. They more closely resemble in-court questioning. But most depositions are done for discovery purposes, and the funnel sequence is a useful technique for them. Can you explain how the proposed questions, here, conform to the funnel sequence?

(3) *Lawyers Aren't the Only Ones Who Should Use the Funnel Sequence: Managerial Investigations, Audits, Doctors, Architects, Etc.* A manager, let us say, receives a message that a floor worker is seeking to contact him, and the message says that "it has something to do with her claiming sexual harassment." When he meets with the worker, the manager might do well to adopt the funnel sequence in asking questions. Can you see why?

An architect meeting a client and an auditor interviewing financial personnel might also do well to use the funnel. Why? And can you critique the approach of a doctor greeting a patient with, "I see you've got a polyposis on your carborundum. How did it originate?" (You should immediately see the parallel. A lawyer greeting a client should ask an open-ended question first, such as, "How can I help?")

ACTIVE LISTENING

(1) *The Uses and Objectives of Active Listening: A Difficult but Important Tool for Lawyers.* The counterpart of investigative questioning, for the listener, is "active listening." Lawyers often have occasion to use this technique. The objectives of active listening are to: (a) fully understand what someone else is trying to say to you; (b) let other people know they

have been listened to; (c) overcome your own biases; (d) work toward the solution of a problem; and (e) possibly find agreement with another person. The basic situation in which active listening is used is when someone else has a problem with you, or a conflict with you, or someone has an opinion you disagree with.

(2) *The Beginning Steps in Active Listening.* Here is a simple outline of how active listening works. When someone raises a problem with you or seeks to tell you something, active listening means that you: (a) first, repeat back to them what they have said to you (Example: "So you think I don't listen to you. Is that what you're saying to me?"); and second, (b) ask whether you have correctly understood it and whether there's anything else that's a problem ("Have I understood it properly? Is there anything else that you need to add to it?")

Then, (c) if the person adds something else to it, repeat that back, too, and ask whether it's correct and whether there's anything else (Example: "Okay, so also, you feel insulted when I don't listen. Is that right? Is that everything?") Finally, (d) repeat these steps until the person says you have absorbed everything.

(3) *The Next Step: Inviting Solution.* After you have absorbed everything (and only after that), you are ready to go on to the next step. You now (a) ask the other person what that person thinks ought to be done about it (Example: "What do you say I should do about this problem?"); (b) listen to the person's proposed solution, repeat it, and ask whether you have understood it (Example: "So you think I ought to use active listening whenever you say something to me? Right?"); (c) tell the person what you agree to do about it and (if applicable) what you think you shouldn't agree to (Example: "I'm willing to use this method if you tell me something is a 'problem.' That is, if you want me to listen actively, say something like, 'I have a problem.' It would be too hard to use the method every time you said the least little thing to me."); and (d) negotiate the matter in this way until you either agree on how to proceed or agree to disagree about it.

EXAMPLES AND PROBLEMS

(1) *How a Lawyer in a Negligence Case can Use Active Listening Active Listening with a Difficult but Insecure Opponent.* "Okay, so you're saying you think there's some evidence your client was negligent, but he really

wasn't according to you; and you claim my client actually caused the accident by being contributorily negligent. Have I understood your position?" In at least some cases, this sort of statement may be effective in prying loose a reasonable offer of settlement. See whether you can explain why. Also, see whether you can predict the rest of the speaker's statements. Notice that the statement *does not* concede anything, and the speaker retains the ability to disagree with proposed solutions.

(2) *The Analogy to Psychotherapy.* Many psychotherapists use active listening in a modified form. Can you explain why?

(3) *When Not to Use Active Listening.* This technique is self-effacing and time-consuming. Obviously, you would not use it in speaking to a telephone solicitor who calls during dinner and wants to sell you something you don't want to buy. When else might you decline to use active listening?

(4) *Listening to Agitated, Abusive, Angry, Emotional or Exaggerating People (a Frequent Job for Lawyers).* There is a tendency to avoid active listening whenever the speaker is abusive. "You're a jerk, and you've just caused major problems for me!" yells the speaker. Should you respond with active listening? Every instinct is to defend oneself with reciprocal aggression. Except in extreme cases, however, it might be useful to active-listen even if the speaker is agitated, abusive, angry, emotional or exaggerating. This particularly is true for lawyers. How would you evaluate this suggestion?

(5) *Self-Denial and Discipline; the Urge to Defend.* Perhaps the biggest impediment to active listening is that it may require large amounts of discipline and self-denial. To put the matter another way, there is a tendency to defend one's self (or one's case) by blocking discussion of difficult or even painful issues. Though satisfying, this approach may be disadvantageous in the long run. Can you explain why?

(6) *"I" Statements: The Speaker's Role--Can a Lawyer Ask More Effectively for What Is Wanted?* What if you are the one who raises the issue, and you want the other person to active-listen? One technique suggested by psychologists is "I-statements": putting the issue in terms of the effects on you, the speaker, rather than attribution of wrongdoing to the listener.

For example, instead of, "You're an incredibly messy jerk and you keep this place a pig-pen," it might be better to say, "I have a problem because I don't like it when this place is disorganized and I can't find things." What is advantageous (and what might be disadvantageous) about this approach? Consider whether a lawyer usefully can employ the "I statement" (or "We statement") approach--whether it is more effective to say "We have a conflict on the date you have set for the deposition" instead of, "You've scheduled this deposition on the most inconvenient date possible!"

[B]   Barriers to Communication

SOURCES OF RESISTANCE

(1) *Social Factors That Create Resistance to Communication: How Lawyers Must Confront Status Incongruence, Etiquette, and Hostility.* When one person interviews another, what kinds of factors may cause the interviewee to withhold information? There are many of these inhibiting factors, and it is not easy to tell in a given case precisely which ones are at work. Obviously, these concerns are fundamental importance to lawyers.

First, (1) "status incongruence" refers to social or role differences between interviewer and interviewee. A female employee talking to a male manager about sexual harassment, or a juvenile gang member talking to a police officer, have differences in social roles that create resistance to communication even when there are reasons for cooperation. Second, (2) "etiquette"-based resistance is similar, but it focuses more on the content of the communication. Repeating a racist remark to an interviewer may be difficult, for example, even if its disclosure is relevant to an issue of discrimination in the workplace. Third, (3) hostility is an obvious barrier to communication. In addition to his social role, the juvenile gang member may have his own individual reasons for disliking police officers, which he transfers to the officer interviewing him.

(2) *Cognitive Barriers: Goal Inconsistency, Self-Esteem, Repression, Perception of Irrelevance, and Memory.* There also are "cognitive" barriers to communication, based on cognition (or knowledge of the content of the communication). First, (1) an interviewee may be reluctant because of "goal inconsistency," meaning a perception that the information is contrary to her goals. For example, a manager questioned about a pattern of thefts by another employee may give an incomplete account for fear of being penalized

for negligence. A second and closely related barrier is (2) "self-esteem": The manager may be reluctant to disclose all of the facts because she is unable to contemplate her own possible causal neglect. Third, in more serious cases, (3) "repression" may block cognition. Child abuse victims often exhibit denial and repression, hiding the secret to avoid the trauma that comes from remembering the experience.

A fourth and very different problem is (4) "perception of irrelevance." The interviewee fails to disclose an important fact because of ignorance, or failure to realize that it is related to the issues. For example, a mid-level manager may fail to disclose that a suspected embezzler's actions have been inconsistent with accounting controls because of ignorance about their connection with theft prevention, or because of unfamiliarity with the controls themselves. Finally, (5) "memory" issues sometimes block communication. Interviewees may be resistant to giving information about which they have incomplete or uncertain recall. Thus, the manager may be unwilling to volunteer even those facts that he does recall about suspicious conduct by the possible embezzler, because of a lack of complete memory about the matter.

(3) *The Manifestations of Resistance Do Not Always Correspond to the Actual Causes: Falsehood, Memory, Passive-Aggressive Behavior, Etc.* It is important to realize that the interviewee often does not explain the reason for resistance, may not know it, or may attempt to camouflage it. Feigned lack of memory is a frequent avoidance technique. "Passive-aggressive" behavior is another. The interviewee (or client) is hostile but expresses aggression by answering incompletely, so as to defeat communication and express contempt for the interviewer.

Finally, falsehood and resistance are closely related. Many of the above-listed barriers to communication can and do manifest themselves in falsehood. In fact, identifying reluctance to discuss a subject is one method of detecting falsehood, as we shall see in the next section.

FALSEHOOD AND ITS DETECTION

(1) *How a Lawyer Detects Falsehood Through Story Theory.* Probably the best method of detecting falsehood harks back to our discussion of "story theory" in Chapter 2, above. Imagine that your client, the defendant, is charged with forgery for having passed a check that had been stolen in a

burglary. He was arrested on the spot, and so the only likely defenses depend on his lack of knowledge of the forgery. When his lawyer asks where he got the check, the defendant's classic response is: "I found it in a poker game."[1]

The textual content of this message is inconsistent with all likely scenarios, or stories, that people in the real world would recognize as reasonable. The best single indicator of falsehood, then, is very simple: a story that does not make sense.

(2) *The Hazards of Relying on Story Theory Alone.* At the same time, it is important to realize that unlikely stories do happen to prove true in small numbers of cases. "I found it" is a highly suspicious defense to an accusation of theft, but not an impossible one. The issue, here, concerns the limits of logic and the fallibility of induction, which we discussed in Chapters 1 and 2 (remember the example of Bertrand Russell's chicken?). It is important, therefore, to distinguish between unrealistic stories ("I found it in a poker game") and unlikely ones ("So-and-so gave it to me to cash and I didn't know it was stolen and forged"), for which skepticism and further inquiry are warranted.

(3) *Resistance as Indicative of Falsehood.* Imagine that the defense lawyer says, "Okay, so you 'found it in a poker game.' Who were the other players, since we'll need them as witnesses?" The defendant responds with a claimed lack of memory (he "can't remember" any of them) or with passive-aggressive responses ("Just neighborhood guys, man. What's it to you?") Similarly, he won't tell where the "game" took place, what his "winning hand" was, or why he uses the anomalous term "found" to describe the acquisition. This kind of resistance to disclosure can be indicative of falsehood.

(4) *Presence of Reasons for Resistance.* In addition to an unreasonable story and resistance to disclosure, the interviewer should investigate falsehood by considering whether the social and cognitive causes for reluctance are present. For example, if the circumstances give rise to status incongruence (here, the interviewer is a lawyer, while the defendant may be unemployed or uneducated), or a goal inconsistency (here, truth means guilt),

---

1   This example is taken from the real experience of a lawyer who interviewed the defendant in question. It was the lawyer's first appointed criminal case, approximately six months after beginning to practice law.

or a threat to self-esteem (here, truth is a confession of theft), then, the case for inferring fabrication may be strengthened.

(5) *Internal or External Inconsistency.* Sometimes, an internal inconsistency in the story indicates fabrication. A contradiction unlikely to be produced by a mistake is different from contradictions in detail. Perhaps "I found it" exhibits this kind of inconsistency with "in a poker game." Furthermore, contradiction by a credible external source may indicate falsehood. A questioned document examiner's opinion that the signature on the check is the defendant's writing is an example.

(6) *Falsehood From Truthful Witnesses.* Even truthful interviewees sometimes give false information, unintentionally. There are at least three reasons. First, (1) they may be "suggestible"; that is, they may say what they believe the interviewer is signaling is appropriate. Second, (2) they may "confabulate," or unconsciously fill in facts from imagination to complete a coherent picture. And finally, (3) they may experience "memory hardening," which is enhanced confidence in both true and false memories, from repeated reconsideration of their stories. These effects have been observed particularly in subjects who have undergone hypnosis as a means of memory reconstruction, but they appear in other interviewees as well.

(7) *Arguably, the Law Emphasizes the Weakest Method of Detecting Falsehood: Demeanor.* One of the oldest methods of detecting falsehood, which actually appears to be a false method, is to observe the subject's demeanor by looking the person in the eye. The law invests especially high stock in this method, but psychological experiments uniformly indicate its weakness. Although people in general may be moderately skilled at detecting falsehood, the experiments show that they do it best by textual analysis, or in other words by evaluating the content, and in fact accuracy of detection decreases when they focus on demeanor. Story theory is better technique.

It seems that some human liars are better at feigning truthful demeanor than some human listeners are at sorting out the differences. Or, at the other end of the spectrum, listeners tend to mistake innocent nervousness as a sign of insincerity. The experiments also show that listeners detect falsehood more accurately from voice stress when the speaker is not observable than from demeanor, although this method too is inferior to content analysis.

OVERCOMING BARRIERS TO COMMUNICATION

(1) *How a Lawyer Overcomes the Reluctance of Ostensibly Cooperative Interviewees: Communication of Expectations.* Next, let us consider how an interviewer such as a lawyer can overcome all of these barriers. First, one of the most common manifestations of resistance is a claimed lack of memory. The examiner, through suggestion, may be able to reduce this tactic by communicating an expectation that the witness obviously *does* remember. Instead of, "Now I realize you may not recall this, but did the employee ever receive any cash that didn't appear in that day's journal?", the interviewer communicates a different expectation. "I know you can tell us this, and it's important to the investigation . . . ."

(2) *Appeals to Authority and Conformity.* Milgrim's and Asch's studies about authority and conformity, covered in a preceding chapter, suggest another set of techniques. Milgrim's official-looking "experimenter" overcame reluctance to a surprising degree with simple words such as, "the experiment requires that you go on," and Asch's stooges did the same by group effects. The lawyer might say, "Our investigation depends on your answering these questions fully and completely. Every one of your co-workers has done so."

(3) *Empathy and Dissonance Reduction.* In the alternative, the interviewer sometimes can overcome reluctance by recognizing the perceived cause of resistance and dealing with it. "Look, I can see how you're reluctant to talk about this, since you might think these embezzlements look bad for you as a manager. It's understandable and I'm sympathetic." To the extent possible, this gambit can be enhanced by offering a sympathetic explanation. "No manager can prevent thefts completely. Everybody knows that. Nobody thinks you're at all responsible for this." (An ethical question arises, of course, if the possibility of repercussions for the manager does exist.)

(4) *Motivational Statements.* "If we can find the source of these embezzlements, we can stop them before they become more serious. That will be better not only for your department, but for the suspect." In other words, the statement of a legitimate goal achievable by cooperation may help to secure cooperation.

(5) *Confidentiality: The Attorney-Client Privilege.* If confidentiality is an option, a promise to keep the matter confidential may be helpful. If the

interviewee is a client, invocation of the attorney-client privilege can be surprisingly useful (but beware of overpromising, because the privilege doesn't cover everything).

(6) *Timing, Different Approaches, and One-Step-at-a-Time.* Setting an issue aside and returning to it later sometimes works. So does varying the question pattern to use leading questions or suggestion (although this technique also can produce false information from suggestible subjects).

And sometimes, the one-step-at-a-time approach works. By leaving a subject and returning to it later, the interviewer may in the intervening questioning obtain information that can be used to open up the interviewee. "Okay: you told us a few minutes ago that the suspect seemed unusually nervous on that particular day. That's when one of the big losses occurred. Now, search your memory and tell us, again, whether you saw anything unusual about his journal entries that day."

(7) *Polite Confrontation: Coupling a Request for Clarification With Suggestion.* In a case of suspected falsehood, the same techniques for dealing with reluctant interviewees sometimes work. But sometimes more is required, and yet, an open confrontation may destroy whatever cooperation exists. A "polite" confrontation may be achieved by asking for "clarification" of an apparent contradiction, perhaps coupled with a suggestion or motivating statement.

This technique may be invoked by language like the following. "Look, here's what's got me confused. You've said that the suspect was 'unusually nervous' that day. We know that that's when the biggest loss occurred. Can you clarify for me how that could have happened without your observing anything else? You must have seen that his cash report was strange." This polite confrontation is more confrontational than other methods discussed earlier in this section, but it operates less offensively than more direct types of confrontation.

(8) *Role-Playing or Indirect Confrontation.* Sometimes the interviewer can confront the subject by presenting the real or hypothetical objections of a third person, either by playing the role of the third person or by giving the third person's actual version. "Mr. Manager, I've got to write a report to the CEO, and from experience, I know what she's going to say. 'This manager

can't have been unaware that the employee was taking cash; he must have seen something.' Now, what do I put in my report to answer that?"

Or, the interviewer sometimes can use a document. "Our outside accountants say the following in their audit: 'This kind of theft would have been accompanied by telltale signs such as employee substitution of checks for cash or forced balances.' How can I explain your claim that you saw none of these signs?" This technique escalates the confrontation above the level of mere implication, and it should be used carefully, but it has the advantage of challenging suspected fabrication while avoiding direct destruction of the cooperative relationship.

(9) *Direct Confrontation of Falsehood and the Mutt-and-Jeff Variation.* Sometimes direct confrontation of fabrication is called for, even by a lawyer talking to a client. "You're not telling me the truth." As a variation, sometimes it can be better to confront the story rather than the storyteller. "I'm sorry, but I refuse to go in front of a jury with the story that you 'found the check in a poker game.'" Another variation, used in police questioning of subjects, is the good-cop-bad-cop or Mutt-and-Jeff technique. One of two partners angrily confronts the subject, while the other empathizes. This technique presents ethical issues and is inappropriate in some circumstances.

EXAMPLES AND PROBLEMS

(1) *President Clinton's Impeachment: His Public Statements, Private Statements, Testimony in the Paula Jones Case, and Testimony before the Grand Jury.* President Clinton's testimony and public and private statements about Monica Lewinsky contained a number of falsehoods, for which he later apologized. He falsely explained to subordinates that Ms. Lewinsky had been "a stalker" and that she had threatened to lie about him. He testified and publicly stated that he couldn't recall ever being alone with Ms. Lewinsky. Can you explain how these misstatements possibly could have been produced by (a) social factors such as status incongruence or etiquette, (b) goal inconsistency, (c) self-esteem, or (d) perception of irrelevancy?

(2) *Detection of Falsehood in President Clinton's Public Statements and Testimony.* Before the grand jury, President Clinton refused to answer many questions by referring to a prepared statement and repeatedly claiming lack of recall, including whether he ever was alone with Ms. Lewinsky. What possible indicators of fabrication might be present in these statements?

A majority of the public, however, had credited the President's famous televised statement in which he wagged his finger and looked directly into the camera while explicitly denying any relationship with Ms. Lewinsky. His aides and cabinet members had been taken in by sincerely delivered private statements. Why were these people so successfully duped?

(3) *How Can an Interviewer Overcome These Kinds of Resistance and Fabrication?* Imagine, now, that you are the President's lawyer, and you are seeking to prepare him for a contempt of court proceeding involving the above-described behavior. (In fact, a federal district court did impose sanctions upon the President for his testimony in the Paula Jones case.) Describe how, as a lawyer interviewing a client, you might use (a) expectations, (b) appeals to authority and conformity, (c) empathy and dissonance reduction, (d) motivational statements, (e) confidentiality, (f) timing, (g) one step at a time, (h) polite confrontation, (i) indirect confrontation or (j) direct confrontation, in an effort to secure more complete responses (assuming you want them, in this particular case).

[C]   Persuasion

THE RHETORIC OF PERSUASION

(1) *Persuasion Psychology.* In the chapter on psychology, we examined persuasion. The reader should recall such concepts as attraction, framing, attribution, dissonance, conformity, and authority, all of which are related to persuasion. In this chapter we consider only a few concepts, related to the rhetorical aspects of persuasion.

(2) *Aristotle's Rhetoric: Ethos, Pathos and Logos.* Aristotle wrote that good argumentation should contain three important ingredients: "ethos," "pathos" and "logos." First, ethos is the appeal to values. "Ladies and gentlemen of the jury, Don Defendant was wrong when he plowed into Paul Payne's car in a commode-hugging, tub-thumping state of drunkenness." Second, pathos is the tragic or loss-related element, or the appeal to sympathy. "Now, as a result, Paul Payne is a quadriplegic who can't go to the bathroom by himself." Third, logos is the element of logical reasoning. "The law says that Don Defendant was negligent and that Paul Payne is entitled to compensation."

(3) *Simple, Clear, Expressive Words.* When doctors speak to their patients about "hematomas" or "pathogens," or even when they use decipherable but unfamiliar constructs such as "the conservative modality of treatment is indicated," they lose understanding and, therefore, persuasive force with their patients. Likewise, when a lawyer says to a jury, "The defendant's negligence was a proximate cause of the occurrence in question," the words are legally correct but hard to follow. If the legalisms are reworded as, "All I mean is, this driver's carelessness contributed to the accident," the concept is easier to swallow.

(4) *Symbolic Detail, or Rhetoric That Touches the Senses.* Saying that Don Defendant "was very drunk" may carry the message. But depending on the circumstances it might be more effective to say that he was in a "commode-hugging, tub-thumping state of drunkenness." Choosing the right detail to emphasize is important. Saying that Paul Payne is so impaired that he "can't even go to the bathroom by himself" carries a symbolic message that goes beyond the immediate image.

(5) *Connotations.* The connotations of the words are as important as their meaning. The plaintiff calls the defendant a "tub-thumping drunk." The defense lawyer calls him "a social drinker, just like many people you and I know."

(6) *Lowering or Raising the Standard With Rhetoric.* For related reasons, the plaintiff's lawyer refers to the defendant's alleged negligence as "carelessness." It is easier for the jury to apply an innocuous-sounding term such as carelessness to the defendant than the harsher-sounding word, negligence. For similar reasons, the defense lawyer says, "The plaintiff has to prove that my client was guilty of an unreasonable act." This formula is a translation of the negligence definition into lay language but makes it sound harsher (and implicitly, therefore, harder to infer).

(7) *Using Another Party's Rhetoric.* After hearing a prospective customer describe a teenage-owned car as "a dream," the used car seller shows him one--and says, "this one's a dream, too." During the Watergate hearings, one of President Nixon's aides made the mistake of referring to certain embarrassing evidence as "White House horrors." The committee chair, Senator Sam Ervin, adopted the phrase and repeatedly used it in his own questioning of that witness and others as well.

EXAMPLES AND PROBLEMS

(1) *Selling in the Restaurant.* Restaurant managers sometimes instruct wait-persons to sell by combining two adjectives, one general and one sensual. "Now, you'll probably want some nice, crispy french fries to go with that." Why use this two-adjective rhetoric?

(2) *The Doctor's Instructions.* The physician explains to the patient that immediate intervention is required; the patient needs to go to the hospital now and the procedure is indicated at seven tomorrow morning. But the physician does not rely on words like "intervention" or "procedure." The patient also is told, "It's like a bank robbery. If the policeman gets there right now, he can catch the robber, but if he waits for an hour he can't." Can you identify the techniques used here?

(3) *How Opposing Lawyers in an Intoxicated-Driving Case Refer to the Intoxylizer (and to the Case Itself).* In a drunk driving case, the assistant district attorney refers to the breath testing device (the intoxylizer) as "an instrument" and explains that "it relies on the same scientific principles as the space program and the tests your doctor orders." The defense lawyer, however, calls the intoxylizer a "machine" or a "gizmo" and expresses skepticism about "whether they change out the wheels and sprockets and rubber bands inside that thing as often as they're supposed to."

On another level, the defense lawyer refers to the charge against his client as "drunk driving," while the assistant district attorney calls it "driving under the influence." Can you explain the techniques used here?

§ 16.03   Negotiation

THE PREVALENCE OF NEGOTIATION

(1) *How Do People Settle Their Differences?: Lawyers's Negotiations in Litigation.* Next, we shift our focus sharply to a completely different kind of rhetoric: the techniques of negotiation and the language of dispute resolution. Just how do disputes get settled? We all are aware that most issues between people are negotiated, not resolved by combat, or trials, or other tests of strength. How does it happen?

In serious disputes involving lawsuits, it can happen at almost any stage of the proceedings, in almost any kind of case and in almost any way. The case can be settled before suit is filed, or it may be settled after the Supreme Court has denied review. Small claims cases are settled, and so are death penalty criminal cases. Settlement may be precipitated by a telephone call from defendant to plaintiff, culminating in the offhand question: "What will it take to settle this case?" Or it may be precipitated by the stern commands of an irascible federal judge to "sit down and settle this case," together with an implied (or explicit) threat to hold the failure to do so against any party appearing recalcitrant.

(2) *The Settings of Negotiation.* But it doesn't take a lawsuit for people to negotiate. Bosses negotiate with employees, parents with their children, real estate agents with buyers, salespeople with customers, and the President with congressional leaders. And husbands negotiate with wives--about big things, such as whether to buy a home, and about little things such as which movie to watch. In fact, an ability to negotiate effectively is essential to a marriage.

The description that follows attempts to catalog and explain certain negotiation techniques. It emphasizes lawsuit negotiations because the techniques are highly refined in that setting, but these methods work in many situations. Some of the listed techniques are ethically dubious. However, even an ethical negotiator needs to know *all* of the "tricks of the trade," so that she can deal with improper ones when they are used by others. Also, this catalog includes several techniques that can only be used in very limited situations. Finally, no claim is made of completeness, because the varieties of successful negotiating behaviors are infinite.

NEGOTIATION TACTICS[2]: THE BASIC ALTERNATIVES OF TAKE-IT-OR-LEAVE IT AND UNREASONABLE-FIRST-OFFER

(1) *Refusal to Bargain: The "Firm, Fair Offer," Take It or Leave It.* Conceptually, the simplest negotiating technique is to determine a satisfactory point of resolution, communicate it to one's adversary and refuse to bargain about it. There are situations in which this technique is the only reasonable approach. For example, the Charles Manson murder case was not

---

2 Adapted from Dorsaneo & Crump, How Does Litigation Get Settled? Copyright 1983 by Matthew Bender & Co., Inc. Reprinted with permission.

plea-bargained, and it could not have been unless the defendant had been willing to accept liability for the maximum sentence. Historically, the "firm, fair offer" is associated with a General Electric Company labor negotiator named Boulware, who customarily figured an acceptable settlement point and communicated it, along with his refusal to bargain, to the union. The technique was so successful at undermining the union's authority that the refusal to bargain has since become the archetypical unfair labor practice, illegal under the labor laws. It is sometimes known as "Boulwareism."

But the refusal to bargain is effective only if it is convincing enough so that rational negotiators will capitulate to it. Even then, one may have to resort often to a test of strength. And if one deals each time with a different adversary who has no reason to know or be convinced of one's track record, the firm, fair offer will not be an effective technique, because many will interpret it as an invitation to bargain further. An institutional litigator with a large volume of claims may successfully use the technique. The result will be that the litigant will have to try many cases that might more rationally be settled, but it may believe that its "tough" reputation among opponents has offsetting value.

Frequently, a prosecutor's office may be in a position to use a modified "firm, fair offer" approach. Interestingly, when given descriptions of such a system, law students generally appear to consider this technique ethically superior for a prosecutor's office, on the theory that variations in sentences owing to negotiating ability should be minimized. But there are situations, too, when the firm, fair offer can be ethically dubious, such as when an insurer engages in the unfair settlement practice of offering unrealistically low amounts upon pain of forcing economically impractical litigation.

(2) *Concealment of One's Own Settlement Point.* This is the opposite result from the firm, fair offer, and in a world of strangers negotiating for maximum advantage, it is generally the more successful approach. The technique works because an opponent who does not know the negotiator's true settlement point may have undervalued his or her own position, or overvalued the resistance of the negotiator, so that the opponent may make greater concessions than are really necessary to settle the dispute to the satisfaction of the negotiator.

Conversely, a negotiator who discloses her true settlement point has indicated to her opponent the maximum concession the opponent need make.

An opponent may not believe a statement of one's "true" settlement point and may require the negotiator to decide between further concessions and a test of strength.

(3) *Inducing the Opponent to Start the Bargaining: The Unreasonable-First-Offer Technique.* There is an advantage to having the opponent state a position first. By doing so, a negotiator not only can avoid giving away his or her own settlement point but can also begin to assemble data from which to infer the opponent's settlement point.

An inexperienced opponent may be induced to make the first offer by being asked the question, "What will it take to settle this case?" One with more experience is likely to respond differently. The experienced negotiator will make a first offer that is unrealistically high, concealing the realization that it is unrealistically high, and thus will avoid disclosing any information about her settlement point.

(4) *"The" Universal Negotiating Technique: (1) Making an Unreasonable First Offer While (2) Actively Defending It as Reasonable and (3) Thereby, Concealing One's Own Settlement Point (4) Without Refusing to Bargain.* This tactic--that of making an unreasonable offer as the first statement of position and communicating a belief that it is reasonable--is so common that it might be deemed *the* fundamental negotiating technique. The belief in reasonableness (which is frequently deceptive) may be stated explicitly, or it may be implied in non-verbal conduct, but it is an essential part of the technique.

Thus, the virtually universal negotiating technique is (1) to make an unreasonable first offer and (2) to actively communicate a belief that it is reasonable, as a means of (3) concealing one's own settlement point while (4) avoiding the trap of refusing to bargain. This technique sometimes is regarded as an alternative to the firm, fair offer or take-it-or-leave-it (arguably, it logically may be the only alternative). Successful invocation of the technique depends on concealment of one's true settlement point, which is to say, on posturing. Among lawyers, this is a highly developed skill.

Many people dislike negotiating because of the prevalence and undeniable success of this simple but seemingly dishonest technique. Several ethical theories have been advanced to justify the technique, including the argument that negotiation is a separate endeavor with rules different from that of other human activity and the argument that there may be an element of "self-fulfilling prophecy" in the mere statement of one's true position because it sets, instead, the perimeter of the opponent's maximum concession. But the fact remains: Real-world negotiation is a messy business with inherent ethical conflict. Meanwhile, it also is a necessary activity for peaceful, effective resolution of differences among people.

SUBSIDIARY TECHNIQUES: METHODS PEOPLE USE TO CARRY OUT THE BASIC TECHNIQUE OR TO PRODUCE MOVEMENT TOWARD RESOLUTION

(1) *The Multiple Varieties of Negotiating Behaviors: Games Lawyers Play.* But the description of this seemingly simple "universal" technique is not enough. There is an infinite variety of negotiating behaviors. They are used both (1) to implement the basic strategy of unreasonable first offer and (2) to produce movement away from initial offers toward resolution.

(2) *The Appearance of Irrationality.* Negotiation is a rational process. It depends upon the willingness of both parties to concede something to get something in return. If one of the parties is irrational, no negotiation can take place. A person negotiating with another perceived as "crazy" may understand that he will have to make greater concessions than he would against a rational opponent, or will have resort to a test of force. For example, Russian (then, Soviet) premier Nikita Khruschev took off his shoe and banged it on the table during another diplomat's speech at the United Nations. This incident, which was major worldwide news, was calculated to convey an impression of irrationality.

Anger, cantankerousness, indifference to consequences and even ignorance in some cases enhance a negotiator's bargaining strength. It follows that the *appearance* of anger, cantankerousness, indifference to consequences or ignorance may likewise create a bargaining advantage. Successful negotiators are often good actors.

(3) *Blaming the Client or Some Other Person Over Whom the Lawyer Has No Control.* This technique is really a different form of irrationality. It puts the opponent in the position of arguing with a rational person, but with the final result to be determined by another person impervious to rational arguments. "It's entirely up to my client, and he or she refuses your offer," is a typical way of invoking this technique. The "Mutt and Jeff Routine" (in

which one of a team of negotiators uses the feigned irrationality of another on the same team to induce concessions) is another example.

It should go without saying that blaming it on the client may be a statement of the true facts. But the point is that it may also be a pure negotiating technique. The client may have already given settlement authority to the negotiator or would accept the negotiator's advice, but the negotiator pretends that the client is independent.

(4) *Using a Mediator.* Sometimes, a person confronted with an ostensibly irrational opponent may call in a neutral third person to help dispose of the claim. Not infrequently in lawsuit litigation, the trial judge can be induced to occupy this role (assuming she does not naturally undertake it), or the judge may appoint a third person as mediator. A skillful mediator is a useful countervailing tool against most of the preceding techniques, undercutting the effort to avoid stating a realistic position as well as blaming the client.

(5) *Appeals to the Merits.* Inexperienced negotiators tend to place more stock in statements about the merits of the dispute than do experienced negotiators. However, there is an advantage to having one's opponent know the facts advantageous to one's position. Accordingly, even experienced negotiators often take great pains to ensure that the opposing side is aware of all facts that could possibly be helpful. The difference between the inexperienced and experienced negotiator is the former's belief that the latter will accept such information as dispositive.

Experienced negotiators do, however, do a fair amount of posturing over the merits of the suit. This posturing often takes the form of expressing unshakable conviction in the prediction that one will prevail. This approach is an effort to shore up the appearance of reasonableness that is essential to the unrealistically high offer technique. The experienced negotiator will also take a position more extreme than that of the inexperienced negotiator on the merits, and she will advance it with ironclad certainty. These approaches are part of the strategies of concealment of position.

(6) *Throwing Oneself on the Opponent's Mercy.* A negotiator may say, "We can't possibly dispute your claim. You've got us over a barrel. Please don't take advantage of your superior position and punish us." The technique is reserved to peculiar situations, specifically those in which one has little or

no bargaining strength and the opponent does not seem cold-blooded enough to take absolute advantage.

What must be borne in mind is that throwing one's self on the mercy of one's opponent is a bargaining technique. For example, it is not unheard of for a person using this gambit, and who is successful in inducing a "merciful" offer, to respond by saying, "Oh! That doesn't seem fair. What I had in mind was the following," and then to state an unreasonably high counteroffer, having thus induced the opponent to make the first step in the bargaining.

(7) *Inducing the Opponent to Bargain Against Himself or Herself.* Sometimes, an inexperienced opponent, having made the first offer, can be induced to make the first concession, too. The methodology is familiar: "Your offer is not even in the ballpark. Come up with something more realistic and then we'll talk." A pattern of concessions by one party not matched by the other tends to carry over into later stages of the process.

(8) *Forcing Two Opponents to Bargain Against Each Other.* This technique is often used by experienced negotiators in sales situations, sometimes with a "phantom" second bidder. In lawsuits, it requires the presence of multiple parties. The "Mary Carter" agreement, named after a case in which the Mary Carter Paint Company was one of the litigants, enables a plaintiff to settle with one of multiple defendants on the condition that the settling defendant will be repaid out of any recovery from others. Each of the defendants is exposed to the implied threat that such an agreement will be made with the others. Plaintiff may make the threat explicit, saying, "If you don't settle the case, I'll make an agreement with the other defendant and that will give me a war chest to go after you."

(9) *Ganging Up.* The Mary Carter agreement, or the multiple-party situation in general, carries another implied threat. A settling defendant may be retained in the lawsuit and may assist the plaintiff in pinning blame on the other defendant. A third party impleaded by a defendant may threaten, "If you don't release me, I'm going to cooperate with the plaintiff in pinning blame on you."

(10) *Flattery, Clubbiness, and Other Attitudes.* Experienced negotiators sometimes resort to flattery ("You're too good at what you do to be spending your time on this kind of dispute"). Or the negotiator may depict herself and the opponent as having more in common than the opponent and his client

("You have my sympathies in having to deal with a person as crazy as that. I know what you must be going through"). Behind these statements lies the psychological truth that it is easier for a person to make concessions if he or she can do so in an atmosphere of dignity.

(11) *Timing.* Time is usually on one side or the other in a negotiation. The person who can afford to wait, who can give the appearance of being able to afford to wait, or who forces himself or herself to wait, has an advantage. A litigant who has just been ordered to prepare a pretrial order that will require the assimilation and labeling of 100,000 documents may be more willing to settle at a reasonable figure than one who has done the work and is prepared for trial.

Bargaining terminated with all parties angry may be resumed at a later session with time having erased the rancor from the process. Experienced negotiators know that repeated statement of the same position, made in several separate sessions with intervening periods of waiting, is an effective negotiating technique.

(12) *Activity.* Vigorous, purposeful activity moving the issues toward a point of conclusion can have advantageous effects. In litigation, many cases settle on the courthouse steps. The initiation of sequential steps before trial, including discovery, motions and like steps, communicating to the opponent a determination to resolve the case and repeatedly inducing the opponent to confront and evaluate the situation, is an effective means of precipitating settlement.

At the same time, however, activity must be undertaken with the realization that it often costs money. A litigant who undertakes vigorous and purposeful activity, only to find that he has expended large amounts of money in discovery and in unsuccessful pretrial motions, may find his opponent's settlement position unaffected.

(13) *Collateral Consequences to the Opponent.* There are many litigants whose initial reaction is to "fight it all the way to the Supreme Court" until educated as to the cost of doing so. Some negotiators, taking this fact one step further, tend to increase expense to the opponent by causing collateral consequences to ensue. The drafting of questions that are expensive to answer, the taking of lengthy depositions that tie up the time of the opposing lawyer or make a client himself realize how much of his time is being wasted,

or the use of discovery to embarrass, threaten trade secrets and the like are all examples. Many of these tactics are ethically dubious, but they nevertheless occur.

(14) *Deadlines and "Locking In."* Some negotiators place deadlines upon the acceptance of a given offer in order to avoid the opponent's "riding" the case to get the benefit of future developments. Thus one may say, "If you wait until discovery is finished and I'm ready for trial, my settlement offer is going to go up by $10,000." The effectiveness of this technique is dependent upon its credibility. It is a variant of the "firm, fair offer," and, like that technique, it depends upon the opponent's belief that one is indeed "locked in" to the deadline.

(15) *Focal Point Solutions.* As differences narrow in the negotiation process, the likelihood of a "splitting of the difference" or adoption of some "standard" solution close to the bargaining position of the parties increases. Round numbers are more likely resolutions. The experienced negotiator attempts to make and elicit offers aiming for the elusive "point in the middle" that is advantageous. If the parties' latest positions are $5,000 and $12,000, respectively, the negotiator will try to keep his position a respectable increment over $10,000, so that this figure, rather than, say, $7,500, will be the natural focal point.

(16) *Drafting the Agreement.* In many situations, the drafting of the agreement may not be highly important. But in litigation involving a multiplicity of issues, such as a divorce or employment decision, it can be a significant advantage to be the drafter. There are frequently minor points that are incompletely negotiated. The drafter, naturally, drafts these so as to resolve them favorably. There is always the likelihood that the opponent will not notice the difference or may consider some objections too small to make.

(17) *Control of the Agenda.* In a matter with many issues to resolve, the person who sets the order of discussion may have an advantage. For some reason, concessions seem to come more easily at the beginning of a negotiation process (or at its end, when agreement is approached). Thus the experienced negotiator attempts to cause those matters that are most important to be considered early. The negotiator may even insist that the resolution of a particularly important point is a "precondition" to further negotiation. Conversely, she may suggest with reference to an important, but sticky, point, "Let's put that issue to the side and come back to it later,"

believing that her opponent will, in the meantime, acquire a stake in preserving agreement.

(18) *The "Bargaining Chip" or the False Demand.* One may ask for something one does not really want or expect so that one may appear to give it up in exchange for something else. If this happens, one has "given" a concession without really making one. Sometimes, for example, a party to a divorce case who really wants a reasonable property settlement and visitation schedule will demand custody as well. This technique (like the unrealistically high offer) is dependent upon the concealment of one's true position; *i.e.*, it is dependent upon the opponent's belief that the bargaining chip represents a real desire conceded.

(19) *"Reverse Psychology."* Against a perverse opponent, one expected to take a contrary position simply because it is contrary, one can occasionally get what one wants by appearing to be asking for the opposite. "The last thing we want is custody. My client wants to be free of the responsibility." Obviously, this technique [which sometimes is called the "Bre'r Rabbit"; can you see why?] is useful in its purest form only in very limited situations.

(20) *Physical Factors.* Negotiating on familiar ground, among familiar people and under familiar conditions gives one a psychological edge.

(21) *Direct Involvement of the Principal: The Four-Parties Meeting (Both Lawyers and Both Clients).* Occasionally, a negotiator may see some advantage in having her opponent and her principal communicate directly. The opponent may have undervalued the determination or persuasiveness of the principal (or vice versa). In some situations, *e.g.* criminal defense or personal injury plaintiff's litigation, exposure of the opponent to the human qualities of the principal may have a moderating influence. Sometimes direct communication facilitates balanced concessions that would be difficult to obtain through an intermediary. In a divorce case, the "four parties meeting" (with both attorneys and both clients present) may be a way of cutting through the posturing and animosity.

(22) *Giving the Opponent a Feeling of Having Negotiated Capably.* An experienced negotiator generally refrains from crowing about an attractive result. Knowing that one may have to meet any given opponent again, the negotiator instead makes the opponent feel that the result was advantageous to both parties and that the opponent handled the matter capably.

(23) *The Test of Strength, Total or Partial.* It is worth reemphasizing that not every dispute can be settled by negotiation. Some require a total--or partial--test of strength. The willingness to "go to the mat" is part of the arsenal of the skillful negotiator. However, the hallmark of the good negotiator is the settlement, without the delay or expense or trauma of combat, of that vast majority of disputes that can be settled.

EXAMPLES AND EXPLANATIONS

(1) *"What's This Lawyer Trying to Do to Me?": A Problem Requiring Identification of Negotiating Tactics.* Identify the technique that is used in each of the following negotiation statements and explain why the technique may "work," when it would be useful, how it might be defended against and whether it is ethical.

(a) "When we have a case that we don't think there's a good chance of liability on, we always take the position of offering out-of-pocket medical expenses, only."

(b) "This lawsuit's going to cost a lot just to try. Why don't you get with your client and tell me your best shot, and I'll see if I can get my people to take it."

(c) "My client is being totally unreasonable about this case. I'd almost be willing to recommend your last offer, but what it amounts to is that you're really dealing with him. I do think I can get him to take it if you up the offer another $5000, though."

(d) "Well, you keep telling me that we can't win on the merits of the case. Frankly, you're probably correct. But let's talk about what's right. The suit's incidental to the fact that your folks know they owe my client something. Why don't you approach it on that basis? I'm sure my client will take anything that is fair."

(e) "If you guys don't come up with at least a hundred thousand, I'm going to be forced to make a deal with the other defendants and have them testify at the trial."

(f) "My client really doesn't want the corporation to buy her stock back, even though that's what she's suing for, because then she'd miss out on what looks like a really good deal. The last thing she really wants is to be cashed out."

(2) *Negotiation Ethics.* Most of the preceding discussion has been done without consideration of the ethical aspects of each technique. Accordingly,

it seems appropriate to ask, which of the preceding techniques seem most vulnerable to ethical criticisms?

Actually, the preceding discussion omits some of the most dubious tactics. One team of writers posits the following technique: "After agreement has been reached, have your client reject it and raise his demands." Meltsner and Schrag, *Negotiating Techniques for Legal Services Lawyers*, 7 Clearinghouse Review 262 (1973). The authors acknowledge that "This is the most ethically dubious of the tactics listed, but there will be occasions where a lawyer will have to defend against it or even employ it."

(3) *How Important Are Negotiation Skills to Practicing Lawyers?* Decotiis and Steele observed a sample of skilled general practitioners and recorded how the practitioners spent their professional time. Decotiis and Steele, *The Skills of the Lawyering Process*, 41 Tex. B.J. 483 (1977). They conclude that negotiation is "the most highly developed skill" employed by the lawyers observed.

(4) *What (if Any) Importance Do Negotiating Lawyers Attach to the Underlying Merits (Are the Merits Irrelevant)?: Alexander, Do the Merits Matter? A Study of Settlements in Securities Class Actions*, 43 Stan. L. Rev. 497 (1991). Professor Alexander came to a curious insight from studying settlements of securities class actions. The stunning conclusion: Securities class actions settle for relatively consistent percentages of the projected damages, apparently without regard to the relative merits of the plaintiffs' liability cases!

In "big" disputes, apparently, both sides are risk-averse. The "bet the company" or "bet the plaintiffs' lawyers' entire investment" approach becomes unthinkable. In this atmosphere, the negotiators all know that the dispute will not be resolved by combat, and so settlement negotiations tend to be "based on non-merits factors." Question: Has our system reached a point where the merits of a dispute are irrelevant?

INDEX

[References are to pages.]

[References are to pages.]

[References are to pages.]

[References are to pages.]

[References are to pages.]

[References are to pages.]

[References are to pages.]

[References are to pages.]

[References are to pages.]

[References are to pages.]

[References are to pages.]

[References are to pages.]

[References are to pages.]

J

K

[References are to pages.]

[References are to pages.]

[References are to pages.]

[References are to pages.]

[References are to pages.]

[References are to pages.]

[References are to pages.]

[References are to pages.]

[References are to pages.]